Lecture Notes in Computer Science 2280

Edited by G. Goos, J. Hartmanis, and J. van Leeuwen

Springer
Berlin
Heidelberg
New York
Barcelona
Hong Kong
London
Milan
Paris
Tokyo

Joost-Pieter Katoen   Perdita Stevens (Eds.)

Tools and Algorithms for the Construction and Analysis of Systems

8th International Conference, TACAS 2002
Held as Part of the Joint European Conferences
on Theory and Practice of Software, ETAPS 2002
Grenoble, France, April 8-12, 2002
Proceedings

Springer

Series Editors

Gerhard Goos, Karlsruhe University, Germany
Juris Hartmanis, Cornell University, NY, USA
Jan van Leeuwen, Utrecht University, The Netherlands

Volume Editors

Joost-Pieter Katoen
University of Twente, Faculty of Computer Science, Formal Methods and Tools Group
P.O. Box 217, 7500 AE Enschede, The Netherlands
E-mail: katoen@cs.utwente.nl

Perdita Stevens
University of Edinburgh, Division of Informatics
JCMB, King's Buildings, Mayfield Road, Edinburgh EH9 3JZ, UK
E-mail: Perdita.Stevens@dcs.ed.ac.uk

Cataloging-in-Publication Data applied for

Die Deutsche Bibliothek - CIP-Einheitsaufnahme

Tools and algorithms for the construction and analysis of systems : 8th
international conference ; proceedings / TACAS 2002, held as part of the
Joint European Conferences on Theory and Practice of Software, ETAPS 2002,
Grenoble, France, April 8 - 12, 2002. Joost-Pieter Katoen ; Perdita Stevens
(ed.). - Berlin ; Heidelberg ; New York ; Barcelona ; Hong Kong ; London ;
Milan ; Paris ; Tokyo : Springer, 2002
    (Lecture notes in computer science ; Vol. 2280)
    ISBN 3-540-43419-4

CR Subject Classification (1998): F.3, D.2.4, D.2.2, C.2.4, F.2.2

ISSN 0302-9743
ISBN 3-540-43419-4 Springer-Verlag Berlin Heidelberg New York

Springer-Verlag Berlin Heidelberg New York
a member of BertelsmannSpringer Science+Business Media GmbH

http://www.springer.de

© Springer-Verlag Berlin Heidelberg 2002
Printed in Germany

Typesetting: Camera-ready by author, data conversion by PTP-Berlin, Stefan Sossna
Printed on acid-free paper   SPIN: 10846262   06/3142   5 4 3 2 1 0

Foreword

ETAPS 2002 was the fifth instance of the European Joint Conferences on Theory and Practice of Software. ETAPS is an annual federated conference that was established in 1998 by combining a number of existing and new conferences. This year it comprised 5 conferences (FOSSACS, FASE, ESOP, CC, TACAS), 13 satellite workshops (ACL2, AGT, CMCS, COCV, DCC, INT, LDTA, SC, SFEDL, SLAP, SPIN, TPTS, and VISS), 8 invited lectures (not including those specific to the satellite events), and several tutorials.

The events that comprise ETAPS address various aspects of the system development process, including specification, design, implementation, analysis, and improvement. The languages, methodologies, and tools which support these activities are all well within its scope. Different blends of theory and practice are represented, with an inclination towards theory with a practical motivation on one hand and soundly-based practice on the other. Many of the issues involved in software design apply to systems in general, including hardware systems, and the emphasis on software is not intended to be exclusive.

ETAPS is a loose confederation in which each event retains its own identity, with a separate program committee and independent proceedings. Its format is open-ended, allowing it to grow and evolve as time goes by. Contributed talks and system demonstrations are in synchronized parallel sessions, with invited lectures in plenary sessions. Two of the invited lectures are reserved for "unifying" talks on topics of interest to the whole range of ETAPS attendees. The aim of cramming all this activity into a single one-week meeting is to create a strong magnet for academic and industrial researchers working on topics within its scope, giving them the opportunity to learn about research in related areas, and thereby to foster new and existing links between work in areas that were formerly addressed in separate meetings.

ETAPS 2002 is organized by the Laboratoire Verimag in cooperation with

Centre National de la Recherche Scientifique (CNRS)
Institut de Mathématiques Appliquées de Grenoble (IMAG)
Institut National Polytechnique de Grenoble (INPG)
Université Joseph Fourier (UJF)
European Association for Theoretical Computer Science (EATCS)
European Association for Programming Languages and Systems (EAPLS)
European Association of Software Science and Technology (EASST)
ACM SIGACT, SIGSOFT, and SIGPLAN

The organizing team comprises

Susanne Graf - General Chair
Saddek Bensalem - Tutorials
Rachid Echahed - Workshop Chair
Jean-Claude Fernandez - Organization
Alain Girault - Publicity
Yassine Lakhnech - Industrial Relations

Florence Maraninchi - Budget
Laurent Mounier - Organization

Overall planning for ETAPS conferences is the responsibility of its Steering Committee, whose current membership is:

Egidio Astesiano (Genova), Ed Brinksma (Twente), Pierpaolo Degano (Pisa), Hartmut Ehrig (Berlin), José Fiadeiro (Lisbon), Marie-Claude Gaudel (Paris), Andy Gordon (Microsoft Research, Cambridge), Roberto Gorrieri (Bologna), Susanne Graf (Grenoble), John Hatcliff (Kansas), Görel Hedin (Lund), Furio Honsell (Udine), Nigel Horspool (Victoria), Heinrich Hußmann (Dresden), Joost-Pieter Katoen (Twente), Paul Klint (Amsterdam), Daniel Le Métayer (Trusted Logic, Versailles), Ugo Montanari (Pisa), Mogens Nielsen (Aarhus), Hanne Riis Nielson (Copenhagen), Mauro Pezzè (Milan), Andreas Podelski (Saarbrücken), Don Sannella (Edinburgh), Andrzej Tarlecki (Warsaw), Herbert Weber (Berlin), Reinhard Wilhelm (Saarbrücken)

I would like to express my sincere gratitude to all of these people and organizations, the program committee chairs and PC members of the ETAPS conferences, the organizers of the satellite events, the speakers themselves, and finally Springer-Verlag for agreeing to publish the ETAPS proceedings. As organizer of ETAPS'98, I know that there is one person that deserves a special applause: Susanne Graf. Her energy and organizational skills have more than compensated for my slow start in stepping into Don Sannella's enormous shoes as ETAPS Steering Committee chairman. Yes, it is now a year since I took over the role, and I would like my final words to transmit to Don all the gratitude and admiration that is felt by all of us who enjoy coming to ETAPS year after year knowing that we will meet old friends, make new ones, plan new projects and be challenged by a new culture! Thank you Don!

January 2002   José Luiz Fiadeiro

Preface

This volume contains the proceedings of the eighth International Conference on *Tools and Algorithms for Construction and Analysis of Systems* (TACAS 2002). TACAS 2002 took place in Grenoble, France, from April 8th to April 11th, as part of the fifth *European Joint Conference on Theory and Practice of Software* (ETAPS 2002), whose aims, organization, and history are detailed in the separate forward by José Luiz Fiadeiro.

TACAS is a forum for researchers, developers, and users interested in rigorously based tools for the construction and analysis of systems. The conference serves to bridge the gaps between different communities – including but not limited to those devoted to formal methods, real-time, software engineering, communications protocols, hardware, theorem proving, and programming languages – that have traditionally had little interaction but share common interests in, and techniques for, tool development. In particular, by providing a venue for the discussion of common problems, heuristics, algorithms, data structures, and methodologies, TACAS aims to support researchers in their quest to improve the utility, reliability, flexibility, and efficiency of tools for building systems.

Tool descriptions and case studies with a conceptual message and theoretical papers with a clear link to tool construction are particularly encouraged. As TACAS addresses a heterogeneous audience, potential authors are always strongly encouraged to write about their ideas in general and jargon-independent, rather than application- and domain-specific, terms.

TACAS 2002 comprises
- Invited Lectures by Dr Michael Lowry on Software Construction and Analysis Tools for Future Space Missions and by Daniel Jackson on Alloy: A New Technology for Software Modeling.
- Regular Sessions featuring 29 papers selected out of 95 submissions, ranging from foundational contributions to tool presentations including online demos, and
- ETAPS tool demonstrations, featuring four short contributions selected from nine submissions.

TACAS 2002 was organized by the Laboratoire Verimag; being part of ETAPS it shared the sponsoring and support described in José Luiz Fiadeiro's forward. With ETAPS, TACAS will take place in Warsaw next year.

As the program committee chairpeople we warmly thank the program committee and all the referees for their hard work in selecting the papers. All papers were reviewed by at least three reviewers, and many were further reviewed and discussed. We were helped in our organization of the reviewing process by the open-source conference management system Cyberchair (www.cyberchair.org). We thank Ric Klaren for his assistance in setting up and running the Cyberchair system.

Especially, we thank Hubert Garavel, who as Tools Chair managed the selection process for the ETAPS tool demonstrations that form part of TACAS 2002.

VIII   Preface

We also thank the ETAPS steering committee, the TACAS steering committee, and last but by no means least the local organizers, especially Susanne Graf, the General Chair of the Organizing Committee.

January 2002   Joost-Pieter Katoen & Perdita Stevens

Steering Committee

Ed Brinksma   University of Twente, The Netherlands
Rance Cleaveland   SUNY at Stony Brook, USA
Kim G. Larsen   BRICS Aalborg, Denmark
Bernhard Steffen   University of Dortmund, Germany

Program Committee

Thomas Ball   Microsoft Research, Redmond, USA
Ahmed Bouajjani   University of Paris 7, France
Paolo Ciancarini   University of Bologna, Italy
Rance Cleaveland   SUNY at Stony Brook, USA
Matthew Dwyer   Kansas State University, USA
Javier Esparza   University of Edinburgh, UK
Hubert Garavel (tool chair)   INRIA Rhône-Alpes, France
Patrice Godefroid   Bell Laboratories, USA
Daniel Jackson   MIT, USA
Claude Jard   IRISA Rennes, France
Joost-Pieter Katoen (co-chair)   University of Twente, The Netherlands
Yassine Lakhnech   VERIMAG Grenoble, France
Kim G. Larsen   BRICS Aalborg, Denmark
John Rushby   SRI International, Menlo Park, USA
Mary Sheeran   Chalmers University, Sweden
Bernhard Steffen   University of Dortmund, Germany
Perdita Stevens (co-chair)   University of Edinburgh, UK
Wang Yi   Uppsala University, Sweden

Referees

Parosh Abdulla

Yasmina Adbeddaïm

Rajeev Alur

Tobias Amnell

Christel Baier

Kai Baukus

Gerd Behrmann

Johan Bengtsson

Per Bjesse

Henrik Bohnenkamp

Marius Bozga

Volker Braun

Ed Brinksma

Søren Christensen

Byron Cook

Dennis Dams

Pedro R. D'Argenio

Alexandre David

Catalin Dima

Dino Distefano

Henrik Ejersbo Jensen

Steven Eker

Sandro Etalle

Kousha Etessami

Massimo Felici

Jean-Claude Fernandez

Emmanuel Fleury

Maarten Fokkinga

Stephen Gilmore

Peter Habermehl

Andreas Hagerer

John Hatcliff

Holger Hermanns

Gerard Holzmann

John Hughes

Marieke Huisman

Hardi Hungar

Radu Iosif

Paul Jackson

Roby Joehanes

Bengt Jonsson

Yan Jurski

Sriram K. Rajamani

Juliana Küster Filipe

Josva Kleist

Frédéric Lang

Martin Lange

Rom Langerak

Anders Möller

M. Oliver Möller

Markus Müller-Olm

Eric Madelaine

Angelika Mader

Monika Maidl

Oded Maler

Tiziana Margaria

Radu Mateescu

Marius Minea

Till Mossakowski

Peter Mosses

Laurent Mounier

Leonardo de Moura

Anca Muscholl

Kedar Namjoshi

Oliver Niese

Gordon Pace

Cyril Pachon

Corina Pasareanu

Paul Pettersson

Randy Pollack

Solofo Ramangalahy

Anders P. Ravn

Arend Rensink

R. A. Riemenschneider

Harald Ruess

Vlad Rusu

Joeri van Ruth

Theo C. Ruys

Andrei Sabelfeld

Claus Schröter

Michael Schwartzbach

Natarajan Shankar

Mihaela Sighireanu

Arne Skou

Maria Sorea

Colin Stirling

Aaron Stump

Ashish Tiwari

Tayssir Touili

Jan Tretmans

Stavros Tripakis

Frederic Tronel

Erik de Vink

Willem Visser

Sergei Vorobyov

Table of Contents

Partial-Order and Simulation Techniques

Debugging with Model Checking

Tool Papers

Software Construction and Analysis Tools for Future Space Missions

Michael R. Lowry

Computational Sciences Division
NASA Ames Research Center
Moffett Field, CA 94303 USA
mlowry@mail.arc.nasa.gov

Abstract. NASA and its international partners will increasingly depend on software-based systems to implement advanced functions for future space missions, such as Martian rovers that autonomously navigate long distances exploring geographic features formed by surface water early in the planet's history. The software-based functions for these missions will need to be robust and highly reliable, raising significant challenges in the context of recent Mars mission failures attributed to software faults. After reviewing these challenges, this paper describes tools that have been developed at NASA Ames that could contribute to meeting these challenges: 1) Program synthesis tools based on automated inference that generate documentation for manual review and annotations for automated certification. 2) Model-checking tools for concurrent object-oriented software that achieve scalability through synergy with program abstraction and static analysis tools.

This paper consists of five sections. The first section describes advanced capabilities needed by NASA for future missions that are expected to be implemented in software. The second section describes the risk factors associated with complex software in aerospace missions. To make these risk factors concrete, some of the recent software-related mission failures are summarized. There is a considerable gap between current technology for addressing the risk factors associated with complex software and the future needs of NASA. The third section develops a model of this gap, and suggests approaches to close this gap through software tool development. The fourth section summarizes research at NASA Ames towards program synthesis tools that generate certifiable code. The fifth section summarizes research at NASA Ames towards software model-checking tools.

1. Software: Enabling Technology for Future NASA Missions

NASA's strategic plan envisions ambitious missions in the next forty years that will project a major human presence into space. Missions being studied and planned include sample returns from comets, asteroids, and planets; detection of Earth-like planets around other stars; the search for the existence of life outside the Earth, intensive study of Earth ecosystems, and the human exploration of Mars. A major enabling factor for these missions is expected to be advanced software and computing systems. This section describes some of the requirements for these mission capabilities.

J.-P. Katoen and P. Stevens (Eds.): TACAS 2002, LNCS 2280, pp. 1–19, 2002.
© Springer-Verlag Berlin Heidelberg 2002

Autonomous Spacecraft and Rovers. NASA's mission of deep space exploration has provided the requirement for one of the most stressing applications facing the computer science research community — that of designing, building, and operating progressively more capable autonomous spacecraft, rovers, airplanes, and perhaps even submarines. NASA is planning to fill space with robotic craft to explore the universe beyond in ways never before possible. These surrogate explorers need to be adaptable and self-reliant in harsh and unpredictable environments. Uncertainty about hazardous terrain and the great distances from Earth will require that the rovers be able to navigate and maneuver autonomously over a wide variety of surfaces to independently perform science tasks. Robotic vehicles will need to become progressively smarter and independent as they continue to explore Mars and beyond.

In essence, robust autonomy software needs to be highly responsive to the environment of the robotic vehicle, without the constant intervention and guidance from Earth-based human controllers. In the case of Martian rovers, in the past Earth controllers would up-link commands each Martian day for limited maneuvers (e.g., roll ten meters forward northeast), which would be executed blindly by the rover. In the future, the commands will be for much more extensive maneuvers (e.g., navigate a kilometer towards a rock formation that is beyond the horizon) that require complex navigation skills to be executed autonomously by the rover, with constant adaptation to terrain and other factors. Such autonomy software, running in conjunction with an unknown environment, will have orders of magnitude more possible execution paths and behaviors than today's software.

In addition to autonomy for commanding and self- diagnosis, there is an increasing need for an autonomous or semi-autonomous on-board science capability. Deep space probes and rovers send data back to Earth at a very slow rate, limiting the ability of the space science community to fully exploit the presence of our machines on distant planets. There is a strong need for spacecraft to have the capacity to do some science processing on-board in an autonomous or semi-autonomous fashion.

Human Exploration of Space. A human mission to Mars will be qualitatively more complex than the Apollo missions to the moon. The orbital dynamics of the Mars-Earth combination means that low-energy (and hence reasonable cost) Mars missions will last two orders of magnitude longer than the Moon missions of the sixties and seventies - specifically, on the order of five hundred days. To achieve science returns commensurate with the cost of a human Mars mission, the scientist-astronauts will need to be freed from the usual role of handyman and lab technician. They will need to have robotic assistants that support both the scientific aspects of the mission and also maintain the equipment and habitat. A particularly interesting issue that arises is that as spacecraft systems become increasingly capable of independent initiative, then the problem of how the human crew and the autonomous systems will interact in these mixed-initiative environments becomes of central importance. The emerging area of Human-Centered Computing represents a significant shift in thinking about information technology in general, and about smart machines in particular. It embodies a systems view in which the interplay between human thought and action and technological systems are understood as inextricably linked and equally important aspects of analysis, design, and evaluation.

Developing and verifying software for mixed-initiative systems is very challenging, perhaps more so than for completely autonomous software. In contrast to the current human command/software executes blindly paradigm, mixed-initiative software has far more potential execution paths that depend on a continuous stream of human inputs. In this paradigm, the human becomes a complex aspect of the environment in which the software is executing, much more complex than the terrain encountered by a Martian rover. Furthermore, from the human viewpoint, mixed-initiative software needs to be understandable and predictable to the humans interacting with it. Today's methods for developing and verifying high-assurance mixed initiative software are woefully inadequate. For example, aviation autopilot and flight-management systems behave in ways that are often bewildering and unpredictable to human pilots. Even though they decrease the manual workload of human pilots, they increase the cognitive workload. *Automation surprises* have been implicated in a number of aviation fatalities. For a mixed human/robotic mission to Mars, the robotic assistants need to be both smart and well-behaved.

2. Aerospace Software Risk Factors

While advances in software technology could enable future mission capabilities at substantially reduced operational cost, there are concerns with being able to design and implement such complex software systems in a reliable and cost-effective matter. Traditional space missions even without advanced software technology are already inherently risky. Charles Perrow's book [1] identifies two risk dimensions for high-risk technologies: interactions and coupling. Complex interactions are those of unfamiliar or unexpected sequences, and are not immediately comprehensible. Systems that are tightly coupled have multiple time-dependent processes that cannot be delayed or extended. Perrow identifies space missions as having both characteristics; hence space missions are in the riskiest category.

The risks that software errors pose to space missions are considerable. Peter Neumann's book [2] catalogues computer-related problems that have occurred in both manned and unmanned space missions. Given the risks already inherent with today's software technology, flight project managers are understandably reluctant to risk a science mission on new unproved information technologies, even if they promise cost savings or enhanced mission capabilities. This creates a hurdle in deploying new technologies, since it is difficult to get them incorporated on their first flight for flight qualification. NASA is addressing this hurdle through flight qualification programs for new technology such as New Millennium. However, flight project managers also need to be convinced that any information technology can be verified and validated in the specific context of their mission. This poses a special challenge to advanced software technology, since traditional testing approaches to V&V do not scale by themselves.

This section next reviews several software errors that have had significant impact on recent space missions, in order to draw historical lessons on the difference between software failures and hardware failures.

Ariane 501. The first launch of Ariane 5 - Flight 501 - ended in a disaster that was caused by a chain of events originating in the inappropriate reuse of a component in Ariane 4's inertial reference frame software, and the lack of sufficient documentation describing the operating constraints of the software. Approximately 40 seconds after launch initiation, an error occurred when an unprotected conversion from a 64-bit floating point to a 16-bit signed integer value overflowed. This error occurred both in the active and backup system. The overflow of the value, related to horizontal velocity, was due to the much greater horizontal velocity of the Ariane 5 trajectory as compared to the Ariane 4 trajectory. This error was interpreted as flight data and led to swiveling to the extreme position of the nozzles, and shortly thereafter to self-destruction.

The full configuration of the flight control system was not analyzed or tested adequately during the Ariane 5 development program. The horizontal velocity value was actually critical only prior to launch, and hence the software was not considered flight critical after the rocket left the launch pad. However, in the case of a launch delayed near time zero, it could take a significant period for the measurements and calculations to converge if they needed to be restarted. To avoid the potential situation where a delayed launch was further delayed due to the need to recompute this value, the calculation of this value continued into the early stages of flight.

Like many accidents, what is of interest is not the particular chain of events but rather the failure to prevent this accident at the many levels the chain could have been intercepted: 1) The development organization did not perform adequate V&V. 2) Software reuse is often seen as a means of cutting costs and ensuring safety because the software has already been 'proven'. However, software which works adequately in one context can fail in another context. 3) As stated in the accident review report [3], there was a 'culture within the Ariane programme of only addressing random hardware failures', and thus duplicate back-up systems were seen as adequate failure-handling mechanisms. Software failures are due to design errors, hence failure of an active system is highly correlated with failure of a duplicate back-up system. 4) Real-time performance concerns, particularly for slower flight-qualified computers, can lead to removal of software protection mechanisms that are known to work; in this case the protection for the floating point conversion.

The board of inquiry concluded that: "software is an expression of a highly detailed design and does not fail in the same sense as a mechanical system. Software is flexible and expressive and thus encourages highly demanding requirements, which in turn lead to complex implementations which are difficult to access." The fact that this software worked without error on Ariane 4, and was not critical after the rocket left the launch pad, contributed to overlooking this problem.

Mars Pathfinder. Today's aerospace software is increasingly complex, with many processes active concurrently. The subtle interactions of concurrent software are particularly difficult to debug, and even extensive testing can fail to expose subtle timing bugs that arise later during the mission. In the July 1997 Mars Pathfinder mission, an anomaly was manifested by infrequent, mysterious, unexplained system resets experienced by the Rover, which caused loss of science data. The problem was ultimately determined to be a priority inversion bug in simultaneously executing processes. Specifically, an interrupt to wake up the communications process could occur while the high priority bus management process was waiting for the low priority meteorological process to complete. The communication process then blocked the high priority bus management process from running for a duration exceeding the period for a watchdog timer, leading to a system reset. It was judged after-the-fact that this anomaly would be impossible to detect with black box testing. It is noteworthy that a decision had been made not to perform the proper priority inheritance algorithm in the high-priority bus management process - because it executed frequently and was time critical, and hence the engineer wanted to optimize performance. It is in such situations where correctness is particularly essential, even at the cost of additional cycles.

Mars Climate Orbiter and Mars Polar Lander. In 1998 NASA launched two Mars missions. Unfortunately, both were lost, for software-related reasons. The Mars Climate Orbiter was lost due to a navigation problem following an error in physical units, most likely resulting in the spacecraft burning up in the Martian atmosphere rather than inserting itself into an orbit around Mars. An onboard calculation measured engine thrust in foot-pounds, as specified by the engine manufacturer. This thrust was interpreted by another program on the ground in Newton-meters, as specified by the requirements document. Similar to Ariane 501, the onboard software was not given sufficient scrutiny, in part because on a previous mission the particular onboard calculations were for informational purposes only. It was not appreciated that on this mission the calculations had become critical inputs to the navigation process. The ground-based navigation team was overloaded, and an unfortunate alignment of geometry hid the accumulating navigation error until it was too late.

The Mars Polar Lander was most probably lost due to premature shutdown of the descent engine, following an unanticipated premature signal from the touchdown sensors. The spacecraft has three different sequential control modes leading up to landing on the Martian surface: entry, descent and landing. The entry phase is driven by timing: rockets firings and other actions are performed at specific time intervals to get the spacecraft into the atmosphere. The descent phase is driven by a radar altimeter: the spacecraft descends under parachute and rocket control. At thirty meters above the surface the altimeter is no longer reliable, so the spacecraft transitions to the landing phase, in which the spacecraft awaits the jolt of the ground on one of its three legs; that jolt sets off a sensor which signals the engines to turn off. Unfortunately, the spacecraft designers did not realize that the legs bounce when they are unfolded at an altitude of 1.5km, and this jolt can set off the touchdown sensors which latch a software variable. When the spacecraft enters the landing phase at 30 m, and the software starts polling the flag, it will find it already set, and shut off the engines at that point. The resulting fall would be enough to fatally damage the spacecraft.

Lessons from Software Failures during Space Missions
1) Software failures are latent design errors, and hence are very different from hardware failures. Strategies for mitigating hardware failures, such as duplicative redundancy, are unlikely to work for software.

2) The complexity of aerospace software today precludes anything approaching 'complete' testing coverage of a software system. Especially difficult to test are the subtle interactions between multiple processes and different subsystems.

3) Performance optimizations resulting in removal of mechanisms for runtime protection from software faults (e.g., removal of Ariane 5 arithmetic overflow handler for horizontal velocity variable), even when done very carefully, have often led to failures when the fault arises in unanticipated ways.

4) Reuse of 'qualified' software components in slightly different contexts is not necessarily safe. The safe performance of mechanical components can be predicted based on a well-defined envelope encompassing the parameters in which the component successfully operated in previous space missions. Software components do not behave linearly, nor even as a convex function, so the notion of a safe operating envelope is fundamentally mistaken.

Although the missions beyond the next ten years are still conceptual, plans for the next ten years are reasonably well defined. Sometime in the next decade, most likely 2009, NASA plans to launch a robot mission that will capture a sample of Martian soil, rocks, and atmosphere and return it to Earth. The software for this mission could be 100 times more complex than for the Mars Climate Orbiter. The software for missions beyond this 2009 Mars sample return, requiring the capabilities described in the first section of this paper, will be even more complex. The next section of this paper presents a framework for assessing the likelihood of success for these missions if current trends continue, and the potential for software construction and analysis tools to reverse these trends.

3. A Model for Software Reliability versus Software Complexity

The aerospace industry, like most other industries, is seeing an increasing importance in the role played by software: the amount of software in a mission is steadily increasing over time. This has delivered substantial benefits in mission capabilities. Software is also comparatively easy to change to adapt to changing requirements, and software can even be changed after launch, making it an especially versatile means of achieving mission goals.

The following table provides historical data from a small number of space missions, and gives flight software in thousands of lines of source code. Note that while Cassini (a mission to Saturn that will be in orbit around Saturn in 2004) and Mars Pathfinder launched in the same year, development of Cassini started many years earlier. The data clearly indicates an exponential growth over time in the size of flight software. This exponential growth is consistent with other sectors of aerospace including civilian aviation and military aerospace. In a subsequent graph we will use a log scale for thousands of line of source code versus a log scale for expected number of mission-critical software errors to extrapolate a model for expected software reliability, and the potential impact of various kinds of tools.

Mission	Launch Year	Thousands SLOC
Voyager	1977	3
Galileo	1989	8
Cassini	1997	32
Mars Path Finder	1997	160
Shuttle	2000	430
ISS	2000	1700

Although qualitative data on software reliability, or lack thereof, is abundant, empirical quantitative data is difficult to find. Our graph will take advantage of 'iso-level' tradeoffs between reliability, cost, and schedule. Fortunately, the empirical data on software development cost and schedule has been well analyzed, providing a basis for extrapolating reliability from cost and schedule. At any stage of maturity of software engineering tools and process the multiple criteria of reliability, cost, and schedule can be traded off against each other (within limits). For example a software manager might choose to compress development schedule by increasing overall man-power; the empirical data indicates that this increases total man-years and hence cost. As another example a manager might limit the number of design and code reviews and incur greater risk of overlooking a mission-critical software error.

The empirical data on software development cost and schedule as it relates to increasing size and complexity has been extensively studied by Barry Boehm, who has developed mathematical models of cost and schedule drivers that have been statistically validated and calibrated. The models indicate a super-linear growth in cost and schedule with the increasing size of software, hence we should expect an accelerated exponential growth in cost and schedule for mission software in future years without changes in technology and methods. In Boehm's model [4], a primary factor contributing to this super-linear growth is the cost and time to fix unintended non-local interactions: that is, unintended interactions between separate software components and unintended interactions between software and systems.

Both the quantitative cost/schedule data and the qualitative record on software-induced failures are readily understandable: as the size of software systems increase (and the number of elements which interact increases proportionally) the number of potential interactions between elements grows quadratically. Tracking down these interactions is complex and difficult, fixing bad interactions without introducing new errors takes time and money, and the consequences of not fixing unintended interactions can be fatal. We thus extrapolate Barry Boehm's schedule/cost model to an analogous model for software reliability. The model is based on proportional factors of expected interactions between components as software size increases. If every one of S components interacted with every other one there would be S^2 interactions. Fortunately, the interactions are sparser; the best calibration over many projects gives an exponent of 1.2 as indicated by growth in cost and schedule. The data also indicates that improvements in software process not only reduce the total number of errors but also the growth in errors as software size increases. For software projects with high levels of process maturity, the exponent is 1.1. This makes sense: better engineering management gives a handle on unintended interactions through better communication and coordination across the development organization, as well as better documentation.

In the figure below we show the number of predicted mission-critical errors versus size of mission software (*LOC* - lines of source code), on a log-log scale. We assume that the number of errors is proportional to $(S/M)^N$, where S/M is the number of components (modules), computed as the number of source lines of code divided by the lines per module. For the baseline model, we take the number of lines of code per module, M, to be 100. For this baseline model the exponent N is assumed to be 1.2. The model is calibrated with an assumption of a 40% probability of a critical software error at 100K SLOC, based on recent deep space missions. (More specifically, the vertical axis is interpreted as the mean number of expected critical software errors.) This is a conservative estimate based on recent missions including Mars Polar Lander, Mars Climate Orbiter, and Mars PathFinder.

This model indicates that the probability of critical errors is small with systems under 10K SLOC, but grows super-linearly as the size grows towards what is expected of future missions incorporating advanced software technology. Without improvements in software tools and methods, this model predicts a low chance of a space mission being free of critical software errors beyond 200K SLOC level. Of course, there are many examples of *commercially viable* software systems that are much larger than 200K SLOC. However, commercial viability is a much lower standard of reliability, and in fact the first deployment of a commercial system seldom has fewer critical errors (that can crash the system) than predicted in this graph.

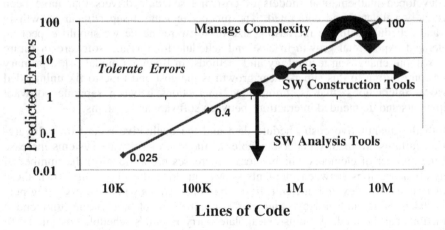

Although this graph is based on a model that has not been validated, it provides a conceptual basis for understanding past trends and making future predictions. It also enables us to visualize the potential impact of tools for software construction and analysis. This graph is annotated to indicate potential strategies for achieving complex yet highly reliable software. *Managing Complexity* means reducing the slope of the line by reducing the factor N. Scaling-up SE through *software construction tools* means shifting the line over to the right by enabling developers to produce more software than the mostly manual process prevalent today. Detecting Errors means shifting the line down through the use of *software analysis tools* that detect more errors than is possible through testing alone. *Tolerate errors* means being able to detect and recover from errors that occur at runtime, so that errors that would otherwise lead to mission failure are recognized and handled. A simple example of this is runtime overflow exception handling. Clearly all these strategies will need to be combined synergistically to achieve complex yet reliable software. Managing complexity is the focus of the software process community. Tolerate errors is the focus of the fault-tolerant computing community. The rest of this paper will describe work at NASA Ames towards the other two strategies that are the topics of TACAS: software construction tools and software analysis tools.

4. Software Construction Technology for Certifiable Software

Software construction technology such as autocoders (e.g., MatrixX) or rapid development environments (e.g., Matlab) have the potential for magnifying the effort of individual developers by raising the level of software development. Studies have shown that the number of lines of code generated by each individual per day remains roughly constant no matter at which level they program. For example, the same team of developers for the Cassini software, coding at the level of conventional programming languages, could in theory generate the software for the Mars Pathfinder mission in the same amount of time using autocoding technology. Thus the graphs for software cost and schedule versus size of software system are shifted to the right, by the log of the expansion factor from the size of the spec given to the autocoder to the size of the generated code. Furthermore, in theory, the organizational factors and non-local interactions that lead to the superlinear growth in software errors with increased software size are held constant no matter at which level the software coding is done. Thus the graph for software errors versus size of software system is also shifted to the right by the same factor.

This simple analysis breaks down for mission-critical or safety-critical software, particularly for software that needs to run efficiently on limited computational platforms (as is typical for space applications, where the computer needs to be radiation hardened). For mission-critical software, certification costs dominate development costs. Unless the certification can also be done at a higher level and then translated into a certification at a lower level, cost and schedule savings will not be realized. Similarly, for autocoders that produce efficient code, non-local interactions are introduced by the autocoder itself, just as optimizing compilers introduce non-local interactions at the object code level. The non-local interactions that are introduced must be guaranteed not to lead to software faults. Thus within the aerospace domain, the automated generation of code needs to be done with technology that ensures reliability and addresses certification issues to achieve the potential benefits of shifting the graph to the right.

The current generation of aerospace autocoding tools are based on traditional compiler technology, and are subject to the same limitations as compilers. A major limitation in today's aerospace autocoders is that they perform their process of code generation in a black-box manner. This leaves a major gap for certification, and means that with few exceptions any verification that is done at the source specification level for the autocoder does not count towards certification.

For the past several years, the Automated Software Engineering group at NASA Ames has been developing program synthesis technology that could address the certification problem. Specifically, the technology generates code through a process of *iterated, fine-grained refinement* – with each step justified through automated reasoning; we use a combination of deductive synthesis [5] and program transformations. Many sources of error are precluded through this method of generating software. The record of the justifications for each step provides documentation and other artifacts needed for certification. The code generation process is no longer opaque, in fact, the process can potentially be better documented than with manual code development. Part of the research at NASA Ames has been to realize the potential of this methodology with respect to certification, as described below.

Demonstrations of the automated construction of verifiably correct software in the 1980s focused on small examples relevant to computer science, such as programs that sorted lists. In the 1990s more ambitious demonstrations showed how more sophisticated programs could be generated. This involved representations of knowledge beyond low-level programming knowledge, including algorithm knowledge [6], design knowledge, and domain knowledge. These demonstrations included Amphion/NAIF [7], which demonstrated the generation of programs for calculating space observation geometries, and KIDS/Planware [8], which generated planning and scheduling programs for military logistics support as well as other applications.

Recently, the Automated Software Engineering group at NASA Ames has demonstrated scaling this technology to the avionics domain [9], and also demonstrated how this technology could be used to generate artifacts for certification. Guidance and navigation are primary control functions of the avionics in aerospace vehicles. Unfortunately, as documented in section 2, faulty geometric state estimation software within GN&C systems has been a factor in numerous aerospace disasters, including the Mars Polar lander, the Mars climate orbiter, and Ariane 501; as well as contributing to many near-misses. Thus in this domain verifiably correct software is critical.

Amphion/NAV [10] is a program synthesis system that generates geometric state estimation programs through iterative refinement. The generated programs iteratively estimate the values of *state variables* -such as position, velocity, and attitude- based on noisy data from multiple sensor sources. The standard technique for integrating multiple sensor data is to use a Kalman filter. A Kalman filter estimates the state of a linear dynamic system perturbed by Gaussian white noise using measurements linearly related to the state but also corrupted by Gaussian white noise. The Kalman filter algorithm is essentially a recursive version of linear least squares with incremental updates. More specifically, a Kalman filter is an iterative algorithm that returns a time sequence of estimates of the state vector, by fusing the measurements with estimates of the state variables based on the process model in an optimal fashion. The estimates minimize the mean-square estimation error.

Amphion/NAV takes as input a specification of the process model (a typical model is a description of the drift of an INS system over time), a specification of sensor characteristics, and a specification of the geometric constraints between an aerospace vehicle and any physical locations associated with the sensors - such as the position of radio navigation aids. The input specification also provides architectural constraints, such as whether the target program should have one integrated Kalman filter or a federation of separate Kalman filters. Amphion/NAV produces as output code that instantiates one or more Kalman filters. Like rapid prototyping environments, Amphion/NAV supports an iterative design cycle: the user can simulate this generated code, determine that it is lacking (e.g., that the simulated estimate for altitude is not sufficiently accurate), reiterate the design (e.g., by adding a radio altimeter sensor to the specification), and then rerun the simulation. However, Amphion/NAV also produces artifacts that support certification.

Within the Amphion/NAV system, the Snark theorem prover [11] is given the (negated) specification and the axioms of the domian theory and then generates a refutation proof and a vector of witness terms for the output variables, in our case these are applicative terms comprising the synthesized program. These terms are then subsequently transformed through a set of program transformations to produce code in the target programming language, which is C++ with subroutine calls to the Octave library (a Matlab clone).

Amphion/NAV produces extensive documentation both as a printed document and an HTML document indexed by links in the generated program. These are both derived from a common XML document that is generated through the algorithm described below. This documentation can be used by system developers for test and code review purposes, and also for system integration and maintenance. It supports code reviews in the certification process, as well as providing a trace from the code back to the specification. The process by which the code is generated is documented by mapping the derivation tree to English language text. The technology for generating this documentation consists of several components: an algorithm for generation of *explanation equalities* from the proof traces [12] together with instantiation of templates associated with axioms in the domain theory [10], and XLST translators. We focus here on the first two components.

Intuitively, an explanation of a statement in a generated program is a description of connections between the variables, functions and subroutines in that statement and the objects, relations, and functions in the problem specification or domain theory. In other words, an explanation traces back a statement in a program to the parts of the specification and domain theory from which it originated. The explanations are constructed out of templates and explanation equalities.

The algorithm for generating explanation equalities works on the proof derivation of the synthesized program. The proof derivation is a tree whose nodes are sets of formulas together with substitutions of the existentially quantified variables, and whose arcs are steps in the proof (i.e., they encode the derived-from relation). Thus, an abstract syntax tree (AST) of the synthesized program and the empty clause is the root of this derivation tree (recall that Amphion/NAV generates resolution refutation proofs). The leaves are domain theory axioms and the problem specification. Since the AST and all formulas are represented as tree-structured terms, the derivation tree is essentially a tree of trees.

For each position of the abstract syntax tree, the explanation equality generation procedure traces back through the derivation tree extracting explanation equalities along the way. These equalities record the links between positions of different terms in the derivation. Each explanation equality is a logical consequence of the semantics of the inference rule applied at that point in the derivation tree. For example, a resolution rule will induce a set of equalities from disjuncts in the parent clauses to disjuncts in the child clause. The transitive closure of these equalities, the *goal explanation equalities,* are derived which relate positions of the generated program with terms in the specification and formulas in the domain theory.

The second ingredient for constructing explanations that are understandable to engineers in the domain are explanation templates. Domain theory axioms are annotated with explanation templates, which consist of strings of words, and variables linked to the variables in the axiom. There can be multiple templates for each axiom, where each template is indexed to a particular position in the axiom.

For each position in the generated program, an explanation is constructed through instantiation of templates linked together through the explanation equalities. First, the chain of equalities is constructed linking each position in the generated program back through the derivation tree to the specification and domain theory. Second, the corresponding chain of templates is constructed by extracting the template (if any) associated with each node in this chain (that is, the template associated with the position in the axiom from which the term was derived). Third, the templates are instantiated by replacing the variables (corresponding to variables in the axioms) with the corresponding terms in the problem specification - this correspondence defined by the goal explanation equalities originating at the variable position. Finally, the templates are concatenated together in the order defined by the derivation tree. A more extensive mathematical description of this algorithm in terms of equivalence classes of terms can be found in [10].

Our current research on certifiable program synthesis focuses on generating other artifacts besides documentation that support the certification process. We have developed prototype algorithms that generate test cases which exercise the code. We are also developing the capability to generate formal annotations in the synthesized code that support independent certification algorithms based on extended static checking. These algorithms provide an independent check that the code conforms to safety properties, such as the consistent use of physical units and co-ordinate frames. Early results from this research can be found in [13].

5. Software Analysis Technology

Mathematical verification technology has had a profound effect on commercial digital hardware engineering, where finding errors prior to initial fabrication runs is orders of magnitude more cost-effective than discovering these errors afterwards. This technology includes equivalence checkers for combinatorial aspects of digital circuits and model checkers for sequential and concurrent aspects of digital hardware systems.

Software verification technology could have a similar effect on software systems, where finding an error prior to system deployment can be orders of magnitude more cost-effective than finding the error after it has caused a mission-critical failure. From the viewpoint of the graphical model of software errors versus software size presented in section 3, software analysis technology shifts the line downward by finding a substantial fraction of the software errors, which are then subsequently remedied. The downward shift on this log-log graph is the log of the fraction of errors that are not found by the analysis tools, e.g., if one percent of the errors are not found, then the graph is shifted down by a constant factor of negative two.

Software analysis technology faces greater technical challenges than digital hardware analysis technology: lack of regularity, non-local interactions, and scale. Digital hardware is highly regular and repetitive in its layout, a feature that is implicitly exploited by analysis technology such as BDD-based model checkers. The regularity of digital hardware appears to keep BDD representations of sets of states tractable in size for such model-checkers. In contrast, software compactly encapsulates regularity through constructs such as iteration and recursion. Hence on a line-by-line basis, software is denser than digital hardware circuits; it is a more compact representation of the state-space of a system. Partially because of this lack of regularity, digital hardware analysis techniques often hit combinatorial explosions rather quickly when applied to software. Similarly, physical constraints make non-local interactions in digital hardware costly in power and wiring layout. However, non-local interactions dominate software, from exception handling to interrupts to asynchronous interleaving of multiple threads. Finally, the reachable state space that needs to be analyzed for a software system is usually much larger than for even complex digital hardware systems such as a microprocessor. Even though the software executes on the hardware, its state space is an exponential function of not just a microprocessor, but also the memory in which the program and the data is stored.

This section will provide an overview of research at NASA Ames to develop model-checking technology suitable for software. Because model-checking thoroughly explores the graph of reachable states, it has the precision needed to find even subtle errors arising from concurrent software, and hence shift the graph downward substantially. The automated nature of model-checking makes it potentially attractive for use outside of the formal methods research community. However, because of the factors described in the paragraph above, the combinatorics for model-checking software is much worse than the combinatorics for similarly analyzing hardware. In addition, the semantics of object-oriented software fundamentally mismatches the assumptions of previous model-checking algorithms.

To meet these challenges and to increase the size of software systems that could be analyzed, our research has evolved from case studies using previous model-checking technology (e.g., SPIN [14]), to prototypes that translated from software artifacts to the modeling language for previously existing model checkers, (i.e. Promela), and finally to a new model-checking technology built from the ground-up for the semantics of object-oriented software. To meet the challenge of scale, we now use a synergy of technologies to cut down on the combinatorics of the reachable state space. In fact, our Java Pathfinder system incorporates static analysis algorithms [15], predicate abstraction algorithms [16] based on automated theorem proving, data abstraction algorithms based on abstract interpretation [17], and guided search techniques. The result over the last five years has been a steady increase in the number of source lines of code that can be analyzed, measured both by the size of the programs that can be analyzed before running out of main memory (the limiting factor in explicit state model-checking) and as measured by human productivity when using the technology. The source lines of code analyzed per person per day has gone up from 30 lines of code in 1997 to 1,000 lines of code in 2002.

Java PathFinder 2 (henceforth JPF) [18] is a Java model checker built on a custom-made Java virtual machine (JVM) that takes as input Java bytecode. The Java language was chosen as our initial research target because it is a streamlined modern object-oriented language without complicating factors such as arbitrary pointer arithmetic. Developing a custom JVM solved the problems of handling the semantics of an object-oriented language without ackward translations to a model-checker with mismatched semantics. JPF introduced a number of novel features for model checking:

- Support for dynamic object creation and class loading
- Support for garbage collection
- Support for floating point numbers

JPF is an explicit-state model checker : it enumerates each reachable system state from the initial state. In order to not redo work (and therefore be able to terminate) it is required to store each state reached in the graph of states. When analyzing a Java program each state can be very large and thus require significant memory to store, hence reducing the size of systems that can be checked. In JPF state-compression techniques [19] reduce the memory requirements of the model checker by an order of magnitude. Another novel feature of JPF is the use of symmetry reduction techniques to allow states that are the same modulo where an object is stored in memory to be considered equal [19]. Since object-oriented programs typically make use of many objects, this symmetry reduction often allows an order of magnitude less states to be analyzed in a typical program. JPF also supports distributed memory model checking, where the memory required for model checking is distributed over a number of workstations [19], hence enlarging the size of the state space that can be explored by the number of workstations. Experiments on partitioning the state space over different workstations showed that dynamic partitioning works best, where partitions change during a model checking run rather than be statically fixed at initialization.

When using JPF to analyze a program for adherence to properties, including properties specified in temporal logic, a user works with a collection of tools that analyze and manipulate the program in synergy with the core model-checking algorithm. Some of these tools, such as program slicing and abstraction, are invoked by the user prior to submitting the program to the model checker. Others, such as heuristics to guide the search of the model checker, are selected by the user as parameters to the model checker. Below a brief summary is presented of some of these tools and synergistic algorithms, the interested reader can find more detail in the cited papers.

Program Abstraction. Program abstraction supports the simplification and reduction of programs to enable more focused and tractable verification, often resulting in dramatic reductions of the state space. Although our tools support abstraction for both under- and over-approximations, in practice we mostly use over-approximations that preserve concrete errors under the abstraction mapping, but potentially introduce additional spurious errors. The abstractions are done through data type abstraction (abstract interpretation) and through predicate abstraction [16]. The data type abstractions are calculated offline with PVS [20]. The predicate abstraction technology invokes the Stanford Validity Checker (SVC) [21] to calculate abstract program statements given a predicate definition. Object-oriented programs are particularly challenging for predicate abstraction, since predicates can relate variables in different classes that have multiple dynamic instantiations at run-time.

Static Program Analysis. Static program analysis technology consists of several classes of algorithms that construct and analyze graphs that represent static dependencies within programs. Applications of this technology are in program slicing [22], control flow analysis, concurrency analysis, points-to and alias analysis. Static analysis information can be useful in optimizing and refining model checking and program abstraction techniques. All these applications of static analysis are incorporated in JPF and its associated tools.

Environment Modeling and Generation. One of the steps in behavioral verification is constructing a model of the environment to which the software reacts. Model checking applies to a closed system. In order to check a reactive system such as an autonomous controller, that system must be completed with a simulated *environment* with which it will interact — in much the same way as testing requires a test harness and suitable test cases. The environment must reproduce the different possible stimuli that the system will possibly meet when in operation, as alternative choices that the model checker can explore. Technology has been developed to support modeling of complex non-deterministic environments. Environment models are constructed using a combination of special object-oriented methods to support non-deterministic choice, generic reusable environment components, and environmental constraints specified in linear temporal logic [23].

During the course of the research leading to the JPF software model-checking technology, we have done a series of case studies that both demonstrate the increasing power of the technology to address NASA's needs for reliable software, and also provided us feedback to inform the direction of our research. Below we highlight some of these case studies related to the strategic NASA requirements described in the first section. The case studies address verification of autonomy software, verification of a next-generation aerospace operating systems, and verification of mixed-initiative human-machine systems.

Autonomy Software. Starting in 1997 the ASE group analyzed parts of the Remote Agent [24] that formed part of the Deep-Space 1 mission, the first New Millennium mission dedicated to flight validating new technology in space for future missions. The Remote Agent is an integrated set of AI-based autonomy software - planning/scheduling, robust execution, and model-based diagnosis - that is a prototype for future autonomy software that will control spacecraft and rovers with minimal ground intervention. The Remote Agent software was tested in space during the Deep-Space 1 mission. The Remote Agent team asked the ASE group to analyze portions of the Lisp code prior to going operational in May 1999. The analysis was performed through manual development of a model in PROMELA of parts of the code. The SPIN model checker [14], developed at Bell Labs, was used to analyze the model. The model checking was very successful in that it uncovered five previously undiscovered bugs in the source code [24]. The bugs were concurrency errors and data race conditions, many of which could have led to deadlock.

After launch, the Remote Agent was run as an experiment for a week in May 1999. Soon after the experiment began, the Remote Agent software deadlocked due to a missing critical section in a part of the code that was not analyzed prior to launch through model checking. After a dump of the program trace was downloaded to earth, the remote agent team was able to find the error. As a challenge to the ASE group, without telling us the specific nature of the error, they asked us to analyze the subsystem in which the deadlock occurred (10,000 lines of Lisp code), and gave us a weekend to find the error. We were able to find the error through a combination of inspection and model checking [25]; it turned out to be nearly identical to one that we previously found through model checking (on a different subsystem) prior to launch.

Next-Generation Aerospace Operating System. In 1998 Honeywell Technology Center approached the ASE group with a request to investigate techniques that would be able to uncover errors that testing is not well suited to find [26]. The next generation of avionics platforms will shift from federated system architectures to Integrated Modular Avionics (IMA) where the software runs on a single computer with an operating system ensuring time and space partitioning between the different processes. For certification of critical flight software the FAA requires that software testing achieve 100% coverage with a structural coverage measure called Modified Condition/Decision Coverage (MC/DC). Honeywell was concerned that even 100% structural coverage would not be able to ensure that behavioral properties like time-partitioning will be satisfied. In particular, Honeywell's real-time operating system, called DEOS, had an error in the time partitioning of the O/S that was not uncovered by testing.

Similar to the challenge from the Remote Agent team, Honeywell asked us to determine if model-checking could uncover the error without us knowing any specifics of the error. At this point we had developed a translator into SPIN, so the modeling was done directly in a programming language (Java). This considerably speeded up developing the abstracted model of DEOS. With this technology, we were able to find a subtle error in the algorithm DEOS used to manage time budgets of threads. The analysis of the DEOS system was well received by Honeywell and led to Honeywell creating their own model checking team to analyze future DEOS enhancements as well as the applications to run on top of DEOS.

Human-Computer Interactions. The environment generation technology is a critical part of our ongoing research in Human/Computer System Analysis. As described in section one, human/machine interactions are a common source of critical-software related errors. The technology for environment modeling has been extended for modeling the incorporation of human actors into system models containing actual software. This technology consists of specialized static analysis and program abstraction techniques. This was applied in the summer of 2001 by a summer student to model the interactions of an autopilot and a pilot, successfully uncovering automation surprise scenarios. In one scenario the autopilot fails to level out at the altitude specified by the pilot and continues to climb or descend, resulting in a potentially hazardous situation.

Summary

Complex software will be essential for enabling the mission capabilities required by NASA in the next forty years. Unfortunately, as NASA software systems evolved from the tens of thousands of source lines of code typical of the nineteen eighties deep-space missions to the hundreds of thousands of source lines of code typical of the nineteen nineties and beyond, software faults have led to a number of serious mission failures. A model of software errors versus size of software systems indicates that without new software development technology this trend will accelerate. This model is based on a reasonable extrapolation of models for software cost and schedule that have been calibrated, and an analysis of underlying causes.

Using this graphical model, we see that software engineering tools can mitigate this trend towards super-linear error growth through two orthogonal directions: shifting the graph to the right through software construction technology, and shifting the graph downwards through software analysis technology. Research at NASA Ames towards software construction tools for certifiable software and towards software model-checking tools was overviewed in this paper.

Acknowledgements. My colleagues in the Automated Software Engineering group at NASA Ames have compiled an enviable research track record while working to meet NASA's strategic goals and challenges described in the first two sections of this paper. The last two sections of this paper are essentially overviews of recent research within our group. More detailed descriptions can be found in the cited papers. The graphical model for software reliability found in section three was developed in conjunction with Cordell Green of the Kestrel Institute, with input and encouragement from Barry Boehm and Peter Norvig.

References

1.   Perrow, C.: <u>Normal Accidents: Living with High Risk Technologies</u>, Princton University Press (1999)

2. Neumann, P.: Computer Related Risks, Addison-Wesley Press, 1995
3. Lions, J. "Report of the Inquiry Board for Ariane 5 Flight 501 Failure", Joint Communication ESA-CNES (1996) Paris, France
4. Boehm, B. et al: Software Cost Estimation with COCOMO II, Prentice Hall PTR (2000)
5. Green, C.: Application of theorem proving to problem solving. Proceedings Intl. Joint Conf. on Artificial Intelligence (1969) 219-240
6. Smith, D., Lowry, M., Algorithm theories and design tactics. Lecture Notes in Computer Science, Vol. 375 (1989) 379-398, Springer-Verlag.
7. Stickel, M., Waldinger, R., Lowry, M., Pressburger, T., Underwood, I. : Deductive Composition of Astronomical Software from Subroutine Libraries. Lecture Notes in Computer Science, Vol. 814. Springer-Verlag (1994).
8. Smith, D.: Kids: A semiautomatic program development system. IEEE Trans. Software Engineering 16(9): 1024-1043 (1990).
9. Brat, G., Lowry, M., Oh, P., Penix, J., Pressburger, T., Robinson, P., Schumann, J., Subramaniam, M., Whittle, J.: Synthesis of Verifiably Correct Programs for Avionics. AIAA Space 2000 Conference & Exposition, (2000), Long Beach, CA
10. Brat, G., Lowry, M., Oh, P., Penix, J., Pressburger, T., Robinson, P., Schumann, J., Subramaniam, M., Van Baalen, J., Whittle, J.: Amphion/NAV: Deductive Synthesis of State Estimation Software. IEEE Automated Software Engineering Conference (2001), San Diego, CA
11. Stickel, M. The snark theorem prover, 2001. http://www.ai.sri.com/~stickel/snark.html.
12. Van Baalen, J., Robinson, P., Lowry, M., Pressburger, T.: Explaining synthesized software. IEEE Automated Software Engineering Conference (1998), Honolulu, Hawaii
13. Lowry, M., Pressburger, T., Rosu, G.: Certifying Domain-Specific Policies. IEEE Automated Software Engineering Conference (2001), San Diego, CA
14. Holzmann, G., Peled, D.: The State of SPIN. Lecture Notes in Computer Science, Vol. 1102 (1996), Springer-Verlag.
15. Corbett, J., Dwyer, M., Hatcliff, J., Pasareanu, C., Robby, Laubach, S., Zheng, H. : Bandera: Extracting Finite-state Models from Java Source Code. Proceedings of the 22nd International Conference on Software Engineering (2000), Limeric, Ireland.
16. Visser, W., Park, S., Penix, P.: Using Predicate Abstraction to Reduce Object-Oriented Programs for Model Checking. Proceedings of the 3rd ACM SIGSOFT Workshop on Formal Methods in Software Practice (2000).
17. Dwyer, M., Hatcliff, J., Joehanes, J., Laubach, S., Pasareanu, C., Robby, Visser, W., Zheng, H,: Tool-supported program abstraction for finite-state verification. Proceedings of the 23rd International Conference on Software Engineering (2001).
18. Visser, W., Havelund, K., Brat, G., Park, S.: Model checking programs. IEEE International Conference on Automated Software Engineering, (2000) Grenoble, France.
19. Lerda, F., Visser, W.: Addressing dynamic issues of program model checking. Lecture Notes Computer Science, Vol. 2057 (2001), Springer-Verlag.
20. Owre, S., Rushby, J., Shankar, N.,: PVS: A prototype verification system. Lecture Notes in Computer Science, Vol. 607 (1992), Springer-Verlag.
21. Barrett, C., Dill, D., Levitt, J.: Validity Checking for Combinations of Theories with Equality. Lecture Notes in Computer Science, Vol. 1166 (1996), Springer-Verlag.
22. Hatcliff, J., Corbett, J., Dwyer, M., Sokolowski, S., Zheng, H.: A Formal Study of Slicing for Multi-threaded Programs with JVM Concurrency Primitives. Proc. of the 1999 Int. Symposium on Static Analysis (1999).
23. Pasareanu, C.: DEOS kernel: Environment modeling using LTL assumptions. Technical Report NASA-ARC-IC-2000-196, NASA Ames, (2000).
24. Havelund, K., Lowry, M., Penix, P.: Formal Analysis of a SpaceCraft Controller using SPIN. Proceedings of the 4th SPIN workshop (1998), Paris, France.

25. Havelund, K., Lowry, M., Park, S., Pecheur, C., Penix, J., Visser, M., and White, J.:
     Formal Analysis of the Remote Agent Before and After Flight. Proceedings of the 5th
     NASA Langley Formal Methods Workshop (2000),
26. J. Penix, W. Visser, E. Engstrom, A. Larson, and N. Weininger. Verification of Time
     Partitioning in the DEOS Scheduler Kernel. In Proceedings of the 22nd International
     Conference on Software Engineering, (2000) Limeric, Ireland.

Alloy: A New Technology for Software Modelling

Daniel Jackson

Software Design Group, Laboratory for Computer Science
Department of Electrical Engineering & Computer Science, MIT
200 Technology Square, Cambridge, Mass 02139, USA

Abstract. Alloy is a lightweight language for software modelling. It's designed to be flexible and expressive, and yet amenable to fully automatic simulation and checking. At its core, Alloy is a simple first order logic extended with relational operators. A simple structuring mechanism allows Alloy to be used in a variety of idioms, and supports incremental construction of models. Alloy is analyzed by translation to SAT. The current version of the tool uses the Chaff and Berkmin solvers; these are powerful enough to handle a search space of 2^{100} or more. Alloy has been applied to problems from very different domains, from checking the conventions of Microsoft COM to debugging the design of a name server. Most recently, we have used it to check distributed algorithms that are designed for arbitrary topologies. We are also investigating the use of Alloy to analyze object-oriented code.

J.-P. Katoen and P. Stevens (Eds.): TACAS 2002, LNCS 2280, p. 20, 2002.

Improving the Verification of Timed Systems Using Influence Information

Víctor Braberman[1][*], Diego Garbervetsky[1], and Alfredo Olivero[2][**]

[1] Computer Science Department, FCEyN, Universidad de Buenos Aires, Argentina
vbraber@dc.uba.ar
dg2y@dc.uba.ar
[2] Department of Information Technology, FIyCE, Universidad Argentina de la
Empresa, Argentina
aolivero@uade.edu.ar

Abstract. The parallel composition with observers is a well-known approach to check or test properties over formal models of concurrent and real-time systems. We present a new technique to reduce the size of the resulting model. Our approach has been developed for a formalism based on Timed Automata. Firstly, it discovers relevant components and clocks at each location of the observer using influence information. Secondly, it outcomes an abstraction which is equivalent to the original model up to branching-time structure and can be treated by verification tools such as KRONOS [12] or OPENKRONOS [23]. Our experiments suggest that the approach may lead to significant time and space savings during verification phase due to state space reduction and the existence of shorter counterexamples in the optimized model.

1 Introduction

In formal models of concurrent systems, safety and liveness requirements are commonly expressed in terms of virtual components (Observers) which are composed in parallel with the set of components that constitutes the system under analysis (*SUA*) (e.g., [1]). It is also true that the *SUA* may comprise some irrelevant activities for the evolution of a given observer. In this work the *SUA* and the observer are specified basically in terms of sets of communicating Timed Automata (TAs) [3]. We present a syntactical technique that transforms the original model into an equivalent one up to TCTL formulas [2] over the observer.

Our technique statically calculates, for each location of the observer, a set of components and clocks whose activity may influence the observed evolution of the *SUA*. Then it obtains an optimized system that activates and deactivates components and clocks according to that information about relevance of clocks and components. Experiments show that model-checking tools like KRONOS [12] or OPENKRONOS [23] produce a noticeable smaller state space and shorter counterexamples when fed with the optimized model.

[*] Research supported by UBACyT grants X156 and TW72.
[**] Research supported by UADE grant ING6-01

J.-P. Katoen and P. Stevens (Eds.): TACAS 2002, LNCS 2280, pp. 21–36, 2002.

1.1 Related Work

The closest related work on automatic syntactic preprocessing of timed models is the clock reduction technique for TAs presented in [13]. Similarly to our approach, this technique examines timed-components at a syntactic level to derive reductions that preserve the branching-time structure. There is also a limited use of timing information (clocks are variables) to keep the preprocessing as light as possible. However, our technique includes an "activity calculus" that can be applied on a *SUA* given as a parallel composition (i.e., not-already composed) and the optimization also implies the deactivation of irrelevant components (not just clocks) during the possibly on-the fly verification step. It is also worth mentioning a method for the computation of delays on circuits [22], that uses topological structure of the circuit to make a partition of the network and a corresponding symbolic representation of the state space. The idea of ignoring some parts of the model while performing the verification also appears in [10], where dynamic transition relations are introduced in the setting of backward search for models used in the design of synchronous hardware. In essence, all these techniques are related to the cone of influence abstraction [11] and slicing techniques ([18, 5], etc.). Our technique can be understood as "slicing" the synchronized Cartesian product[1] without building it, instead of slicing each component, as previous works on slicing concurrent descriptions. By adapting static analysis ideas to the timed model setting, we developed a method for discovering a set of variables (standing for clocks and components) that can be safely eliminated at different locations of the final composed model. In particular, we need to know which variables may influence the future behavior of the observer at each location. Therefore, the granularity level of the static analysis over the Cartesian product is defined by the set of control locations of the observer. To obtain an optimized model that activates and deactivates those variables we perform a component-wise transformation. We do not resort to the concept of slicing criterion, instead the correctness of the procedure is stated in terms of the preservation of the branching structure of the transition system up to the propositional assignment given over the observer. This implies that our optimized model validates the same set of TCTL formula over the observer. Mentioned works on slicing concurrent models provide abstractions that either just preserve the linear-time structure of the system or are strongly bisimilar w.r.t. to the original one, a stronger condition than ours.

Our technique can also be understood as a way to perform a kind of selective search (avoiding transitions of deactivated components). Unlike partial order methods [16,21], etc., our notions are not based on independence but on influence. In fact, transitions eliminated in the optimized model, in general, are not independent to the remaining ones. Moreover, runs of our optimized model are subruns of the original one (i.e., irrelevant activity is not shown). Partial order methods could be applied in an orthogonal fashion.

---

[1] If synchronized Cartesian product is though as a non-deterministic guarded command program, traditional program slicing techniques seems to be of little help since all variables are likely to be classified as live.

In [7] we explain several differences between our technique and compositional reduction techniques that work over symbolic state space like [20] and [24].

Structure of the paper: In the next section we recall Timed Automata and some related notions. In Sect. 3 we present an extension of TAs that are the basis of our method: the I/O Timed Components. In this extension the labels are classified as input/output and that "uncontrollable/controllable" division of labels greatly helps to a better understanding of behavioral influence between automata. In Sect. 4 we show the rules that define the relevance of clocks and components, how to build the correct and complete abstraction, and finally some empirical results. The paper is summed up with conclusions.

2 Timed Automata

Timed Automata (TAs) has become one of the most widely used formalism to model and analyze timed systems and is supported by several tools (e.g., [12,4, 20,19], etc.). This presentation partially follows [27]. Given a finite set of clocks (non-negative real variables) $X = \{x_1, x_2, \ldots, x_n\}$ a *valuation* is a total function $v : X \xrightarrow{tot} I\!\!R_{\geq 0}$ where $v(x_i)$ is the value associated with clock x_i. We define V_X as the set $[X \xrightarrow{tot} I\!\!R_{\geq 0}]$ of total functions mapping X to $I\!\!R_{\geq 0}$ and $\mathbf{0} \in V_X$ denotes the function that evaluates to 0 all clocks. Given $v \in V_X$ and $t \in I\!\!R_{\geq 0}$, $v + t$ denotes the valuation that assigns to each clock $x \in X$ the value $v(x) + t$. Given a set of clocks $\alpha \subseteq X$ and a valuation v we define $Reset_\alpha(v)$ as a valuation that assigns zero to clocks in α and keeps the same value than v for the remaining clocks. Given a set of clocks X we define the sets of clock constraints Ψ_X according to the grammar: $\Psi_X \ni \psi ::= x \prec c | x - x' \prec c | \psi \wedge \psi | \neg \psi$, where $x, x' \in X$, $\prec \in \{<, \leq\}$ and $c \in I\!\!N$. A valuation $v \in V_X$ satisfies $\psi \in \Psi_X$ ($v \models \psi$) iff the expression evaluates **true** when each clock is replaced with its current value specified in v.

Definition 1 (Timed Automata (TAs)). *A timed automaton (TA) is a tuple* $A = \langle S, X, \Sigma, E, I, s_0 \rangle$ *where S is a finite set of locations, X is a finite set of clocks, Σ is a set of labels, E is a finite set of edges, (each edge $e \in E$ is a tuple $\langle s, a, \psi, \alpha, s' \rangle$ where: $s \in S$ is the source location, $s' \subset S$ is the target location, $a \in \Sigma$ is the label, $\psi \in \Psi_X$ is the guard, $\alpha \subseteq X$ is the set of clocks reset at the edge), $I : S \xrightarrow{tot} \Psi_X$ is a total function associating with each location a clock constraint called location's Invariant, and $s_0 \in S$ is the initial location.*

Given a TA $A = \langle S, X, \Sigma, E, I, s_0 \rangle$ we define $Locs(A) = S$, $Clocks(A) = X$, $Labels(A) = \Sigma$, $Edges(A) = E$, $Inv(A) = I$, $Init(A) = s_0$, and given an edge $e = \langle s, a, \psi, \alpha, s' \rangle \in E$ we define $src(e) = s$, $lab(e) = a$, $grd(e) = \psi$, $rst(e) = \alpha$, $tgt(e) = s'$. The *State Space* Q_A of A is the set of states $(s, v) \in S \times V_X$ for which $v \models I(s)$ and $q_0 = (Init(A), \mathbf{0})$ is its *initial state*. Given a state $q = (s, v)$ we denote; $q + t = (s, v + t)$, $q^@ = s$, and $q(x_i) = v(x_i)$. The semantics of A can be given in terms of the *Labeled Transition System* (LTS) of A, denoted $G_A = \langle Q_A, q_0, \mapsto_t^l, \Sigma \rangle$. The relation $\mapsto_t^l$ is the set of (time or discrete) transitions between states. Let $t \in I\!\!R_{\geq 0}$; the state (s, v) has a *time transition* to $(s, v + t)$ denoted $(s, v) \mapsto_t^\lambda (s, v + t)$ if for all $t' \leq t$, $v + t' \models I(s)$. Let $e \in E$ be an edge;

the state $(src(e), v)$ has a *discrete transition* to the state $(tgt(e), v')$ denoted $(src(e), v) \mapsto_0^{lab(e)} (tgt(e), v')$ if $v \models grd(e)$ and $v' = Reset_{rst(e)}(v)$; e is called the associated edge. We will say that $q \mapsto_t^l$ if there exists q' such that $q \mapsto_t^l q'$. A *run* r of A starting at q is an infinite sequence $q \mapsto_{t_0}^{a_o} q_1 \mapsto_{t_1}^{a_1} \dots$ of states and transitions in G_A. The set of runs starting at q is denoted as $R_A(q)$. The *time of occurrence* of the nth transition is equal to $\sum_{i=o}^{n-1} t_i$ and is denoted as $\tau_r(n)$. A *position* in r is a pair $(i, t) \in I\!N \times I\!R_{\geq 0}$ such that $t \leq t_i$. We call $L(r)$ the set of all labels in the run r and $\Pi(r)$ the set of all positions of run r. The time of the position $(i, t) \in \Pi(r)$, denoted $\tau_r((i, t))$ is defined as $\tau_r(i) + t$. Given $(i, t) \in \Pi(r)$ its associated state is $r((i, t)) = q_i + t$. A *divergent run* is a run such that $\sum_{i=o}^{\infty} t_i = \infty$. The set of divergent runs of a TA A starting at state q is denoted $R_A^{\infty}(q)$. A *finite run* starting at state q is simply a finite prefix of a run starting at q. A TA is *non-zeno* when any finite run starting at the initial state can be extended to a divergent run that is, the set of finite runs is equal to the set of finite prefixes of divergent runs. Since we will deal with non-zeno TAs, we say that the state q is *reachable* if there is a finite run starting at the initial state which ends at q; we denote the set of reachable states as $Reach(A)$. Usually, A has associated a mapping $\mathcal{P} : Locs(A) \mapsto 2^{Props}$ which assigns to each location a subset of the set of propositional variables $(Props)$. The parallel composition of TAs is defined over classical synchronous product of automata. Given a set $\mathcal{I} = \{0..n\}$, we denote $\|_{i \in \mathcal{I}} A_i$ the parallel composition of an indexed set of TA. If q is a state of that parallel composition $\Pi_i(q)$ will denote the local state of TA A_i (locations and local-clock values).

2.1   Continuous Observational Bisimulations

The theoretical notion that supports the correctness of our abstraction mechanisms is a bisimulation relation extending "branching bisimulation" (e.g., [14]) to timed systems[2]. This notion is weaker than strong timed bisimulation, however it still preserves branching structure (TCTL logic validity) unlike weaker versions of model bisimulations (e.g. the observational timed bisimulation of [25]).

Definition 2 (Observationally-τ transition). *Given a TA A, its associated LTS $G_A = \langle Q_A, q_0, \mapsto_t^l, \Sigma \rangle$, a relation $B \subseteq Q_A \times Q_A$ between states, two states p and q such that $(p, q) \in B$, and $t \in I\!R_{\geq 0}$ such that $p \mapsto_t^{\lambda}$, we say that the state q has an observationally-τ transition w.r.t. B and p, of duration t to q_n, denoted $q \xrightarrow{B, p}_t q_n$ iff there is a finite run $r = q \mapsto_{t_0}^{l_0} q_1 \mapsto_{t_1}^{l_1} \dots q_n$ such that $\tau_r(n) = t$, and for every position $k \in \Pi(r)$, $(p + \tau_r(k), r(k)) \in B$ holds (remember that $\mapsto_{t_i}^{l_i}$ could be $\mapsto_0^{\lambda}$ i.e., a stutter).*

Definition 3 (Continuous Observational Bisimulations). *Given a LTS $G_A = \langle Q_A, q_0, \mapsto_t^l, \Sigma \rangle$ and a propositional assignment $\mathcal{P} : Locs(A) \mapsto 2^{Props}$. We say that a symmetric binary relation $B \subseteq Q_A \times Q_A$ is a continuous observational bisimulation (CO-Bisimulation) of G_A w.r.t. $\mathcal{P}$ iff $(p, q) \in B$ implies*

---

[2] A more restrictive notion for timed systems is found in [26].

that $\mathcal{P}(p^@) = \mathcal{P}(q^@)$ *and for all* $a \in \Sigma$, $t \in \mathbb{R}_{\geq 0}$, *whenever* $p \mapsto_0^a p'$ *then, for some* $q', q'' \in Q, a' \in \Sigma \cup \{\lambda\}$, $q \xrightarrow{B,p}_0 q' \mapsto_0^{a'} q''$, *and* $(p', q'') \in B$, *and whenever* $p \mapsto_t^\lambda p'$ *then, for some* $q' \in Q$, $q \xrightarrow{B,p}_t q'$ *(which also means that* $(p', q') \in B$*)*.

Two TA A_1 and A_2 are *Continuous Observational Bisimilar* (CO-Bisimilar) w.r.t. the propositional assignments $\mathcal{P}_1$ and $\mathcal{P}_2$ $(A_1 \simeq^{\mathcal{P}_1, \mathcal{P}_2} A_2)$ iff there exists a CO-Bisimulation B of $G_{A_1} \cup G_{A_2}$ w.r.t. $\mathcal{P}_1 \cup \mathcal{P}_2$, such that $(q_{01}, q_{02}) \in B$. Two CO-Bisimilar TAs are equivalent up to TCTL logic (see [6,9]).

3   I/O Timed Components

I/O Timed Components (I/O TCs) [8] is a formalism built on top of TAs, developed for expressing non-zeno timed behavior (it is always possible to make time diverge) and to support "assume-guarantee" compositional reasoning without resorting to receptiveness games[17]. I/O TCs are immediately supported by several checking tools like KRONOS [12], UPPAAL [4], etc.[3]. As we discuss in Sect. 4, I/O interfaces make possible our static calculus of influence. Given a TA A, we divide $Labels(A)$ into three sets: (1) the set of input-labels (In_A), (2) the set of output-labels (Out_A) and (3) the set of internal-labels (ϵ_A), such that $\{In_A, Out_A, \epsilon_A\} \in Part(Labels(A))$, where $Part(Set)$ is the set of all partitions of the set Set. We define the set Exp_A of *exported* labels (or interface labels) of A as $Exp_A = In_A \cup Out_A$.

A set of *input selections* of A is a set $I^A = \{I_1^A, \ldots, I_k^A\} \in Part(In_A)$, a set of *output selections* of A is a set $O^A = \{O_1^A, \ldots, O_h^A\} \in Part(Out_A)$. Note that $I^A \cup O^A \cup \{\epsilon_A\} \in Part(Labels(A))$.

Definition 4 (I/O TCs). *An I/O Timed Component (or I/O TC) is a pair* $(A, (I^A, O^A))$ *where* A *is a non-zeno TA and* (I^A, O^A) *is an admissible I/O interface for* A: *the sets* I^A *and* O^A *are input and output selections (resp.) of* Λ, *and for any state* $q \in Reach(A)$ *the following conditions hold:*

1. *for any input selection* $I_n^A \in I^A$ *there exists a label* $i \in I_n^A$ *such that* $q \mapsto_0^i$. *That is, given any input selection* $I_n^A \in I^A$, *the TA can always synchronize using some of the labels of* I_n^A *(there is always at least one alternative of every input selection enabled at each state).*
2. *there exists a run* $r \in R_A^\infty(q)$ *such that* $L(r) \cap In_A = \emptyset$. *Input is not mandatory and thus non-zenoness must be guaranteed without them.*
3. *for any output selection* $O_m^A \in O^A$, *if there exists a label* $o \in O_m^A$ *such that* $q \mapsto_0^o$ *then* $q \mapsto_0^{o'}$ *for all* $o' \in O_m^A$. *All labels of an output selection are simultaneously enabled or disabled.*
4. *for any infinite run* $r \in R_A(q)$, *if a label* $o \in Out_A$ *appears an infinite number of times in* r, *then necessarily* $r \in R_A^\infty(q)$ *(non-transientness of outputs).*

---

[3] Liveness and I/O interfaces have been considered in a general setting for simulation proof methods "à la" Lynch-Vaandrager [17] geared towards theorem provers. A further discussion on related work can be found in [8].

An output selection of size greater than one models alternative behaviors of the component according to the state of the component exporting those labels as input. This is similar to an external non-deterministic choice in Process Algebra like notations.

Definition 5 (Compatible Components). *Given two I/O TCs* $\mathbf{A_1} = (A_1, (I^{A_1}, O^{A_1}))$ *and* $\mathbf{A_2} = (A_2, (I^{A_2}, O^{A_2}))$, *they are compatible components iff:*

1. *Labels*$(A_1) \cap$ *Labels*$(A_2) \subseteq Exp_{A_1} \cap Exp_{A_2}$ *(i.e., all common labels are exported by both* A_1 *and* A_2),
2. *for all* $I_n^{A_1} \in I^{A_1}$ *and* $I_m^{A_2} \in I^{A_2}$ *if* $\#I_n^{A_1} > 1$ *and* $\#I_m^{A_2} > 1$ *then* $I_n^{A_1} \cap I_m^{A_2} = \emptyset$ *(intersection of input selections of size greater than one must be empty).*
3. *Out*$_{A_1} \cap$ *Out*$_{A_2} = \emptyset$ *(there are not common output-labels).*
4. *for all* $O \in O^{A_1} \cup O^{A_2}$ *and* $I \in I^{A_1} \cup I^{A_2}$ *then either* $I \cap O = \emptyset$ *or* $I \subseteq O$.

We refer to a set of pair-wise compatible components as a *compatible set of components*. I/O compatibility is a syntactic condition that implies that underlying TAs can not block each other and, moreover, in [8] we show that the composition of compatible components is itself a component and therefore a non-zeno TA.

Example 1. Fig. 1 introduces the example of a pipe-line of sporadic tasks. The pipe-line is composed of tasks together with latches for buffering signals between them. The observer checks whether an end-to-end response-time requirement is guaranteed.

4   Optimizing the Composition of I/O Components

4.1   Influence

The core of our technique is a notion of potential "direct influence" of a component behavior over another component behavior. A naive solution is to consider that two components influence each other if they share a label. Unfortunately, this definition would lead to a rather large symmetric overestimation[4]. By using the I/O interface attached to TA (the I/O TCs), we can define a better asymmetric condition for behavioral influence. Besides, our notion of influence is relative to the locations considered for each automaton (i.e., assuming that A is at some location which belongs to the set $S_A \subseteq Locs(A)$ and B is at some location which belongs to the set $S_B \subseteq Locs(B)$). Using two compatible I/O Timed Component $\mathbf{A} = (A, (I^A, O^A))$ and $\mathbf{B} = (B, (I^B, O^B))$, $S_A \subseteq Locs(A)$, $S_B \subseteq Locs(B)$, $e_a \in Edges(A)$, $e_b, e_b' \in Edges(B)$, and $x \in Clocks(B)$, we define in Table 1 the following notions of influence:

1. $\mathbf{A}$ influences $\mathbf{B}$ while they are sojourning S_A and S_B resp., denoted $\mathbf{A}|_{S_A} \rightarrow \mathbf{B}|_{S_B}$.

---

[4] An asynchronous variable sharing mechanism of communication would make dependence checking easier using read-write operations.

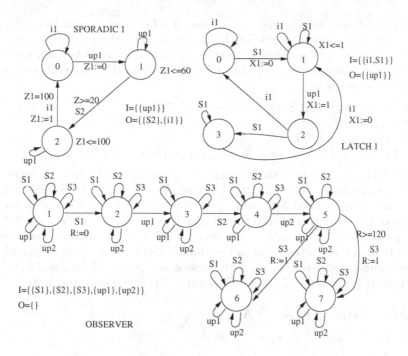

Fig. 1. Some components of Pipe-line System

Table 1. Influence rules

$$\frac{src(e_a){\in}S_A,lab(e_a){\in}Out_A,src(e_b){\in}S_B,lab(e_b){=}lab(e_a),tgt(e_b){\neq}src(e_b)}{\mathbf{A}|_{S_A}{\rightarrow}\mathbf{B}|_{S_B}}$$

$$\frac{I{\in}I^A,\#I{>}1,lab(e_b){\in}I,src(e_b){\in}S_B}{\mathbf{A}|_{S_A}{\rightarrow}\mathbf{B}|_{S_B}} \qquad \frac{src(e){\in}S_B,x{\in}grd(e)}{x{\rightarrow}\mathbf{B}|_{S_B}} \qquad \frac{l{\in}S_B,x{\in}Inv(l)}{x{\rightarrow}\mathbf{B}|_{S_B}}$$

$$\frac{I{\in}I^A,lab(e_b){\in}I,lab(e'_b){\in}I,lab(e_b){\neq}lab(e'_b),src(e_b){\in}S_B,src(e'_b){\in}S_B,x{\in}rst(e_b),x{\notin}rst(e'_b)}{\mathbf{A}|_{S_A}{\rightarrow}x|_{S_B}}$$

$$\frac{src(e_a){\in}S_A,lab(e_a){\in}Out_A,src(e_b){\in}S_B,lab(e_a){=}lab(e_b),x{\in}rst(e_b)}{\mathbf{A}|_{S_A}{\rightarrow}x|_{S_B}} \qquad \frac{src(e_b){\in}S_B,x{\in}rst(e_b)}{\mathbf{B}|_{S_B}{\rightarrow}x}$$

2. **A** influences clock x of **B** while they are sojourning S_A and S_B resp., denoted $\mathbf{A}|_{S_A} \rightarrow x|_{S_B}$.
3. **B** influences its clock x while it is sojourning S_B, denoted $\mathbf{B}|_{S_B} \rightarrow x$.
4. x influences its component **B** while it is sojourning S_B, denoted $x \rightarrow \mathbf{B}|_{S_B}$.

Note that if $\mathbf{A}|_{S_A} \rightarrow \mathbf{B}|_{S_B}$, $S_A \subseteq S'_A$, and $S_B \subseteq S'_B$ then $\mathbf{A}|_{S'_A} \rightarrow \mathbf{B}|_{S'_B}$. The same is also true for the rest of notions of influence.

In what follows, we consider the system of I/O timed components $\{A_i / i \in \{0..n\}\}$ where A_0 plays the role of the observer while the rest of components constitutes the *SUA*. We define a function S_l that associates to each observer location l and component A_i a *Sojourn Set*: a set of locations that A_i may visit while the observer is at l.

Definition 6 (Sojourn Set). *Given a set of TAs* $\{A_i / i \in \mathcal{I}\}$ *where* $\mathcal{I} = \{0..n\}$, $l \in Locs(A_0)$, *we define*
$S_l(0) = \{l\}$, *and for* $1 \leq i \leq n$,
$S_l(i) = \{\Pi_i(q)^@ \in Locs(A_i) / q \in Reach(\|_{i \in \mathcal{I}} A_i)$ *and* $\Pi_0(q)^@ = l\}$.

The exact calculation of the sojourn set is unpractical because it would require the computation we want to optimize: $Reach(\|_{i \in \mathcal{I}} A_i)$. However, these sets can be overestimated by several procedures [7]. Experience has shown us that one of the most cost-effective strategies is $S_l'(i) = \{l' \in Locs(A_i) / (l, l') \in Locs(A_0 \| A_i)\}$. Since in many cases, even timed systems with relatively small control structures are intractable (a few thousands of nodes), it is reasonable to use the untimed composition to get those sets, i.e., $S_l'(i) = \{l' \in Locs(A_i) / \exists s \in Locs(A_0 \| A_1 \| ... \| A_n) \wedge \Pi_0(s) = l \wedge \Pi_i(s) = l'\}$. Hereafter, we denote

- $\mathbf{A_i}|_{S_l(i)} \rightarrow \mathbf{A_j}|_{S_l(j)}$ as $\mathbf{A_i} \overset{S_l}{\rightarrow} \mathbf{A_j}$,
- $\mathbf{A_i}|_{S_l(i)} \rightarrow x|_{S_l(j)}$ or $\mathbf{A_i}|_{S_l(i)} \rightarrow x$ as $\mathbf{A_i} \overset{S_l}{\rightarrow} x$, and
- $x \rightarrow \mathbf{A_j}|_{S_l(j)}$ as $x \overset{S_l}{\rightarrow} \mathbf{A_j}$.

4.2   Relevance

Firstly, let us present a couple of definitions that are necessary to calculate activity of components and clocks to latter optimize the *SUA* w.r.t. the observer.

Definition 7 (Determination of Components). *Given an I/O Timed Component* $\mathbf{A} = (A, (I^A, O^A))$, $S \subseteq Locs(A)$, *and* $i \in \Sigma_A$, *we say that* i *determine* $\mathbf{A}$ *while it is sojourning* S *denoted* $Det_A(i, S)$ *iff* $\{i\} \in I^A$ *and* $\forall e, e' \in Edges(A)$: $src(e), src(e') \in S, lab(e) = lab(e') = i$ *implies* $tgt(e) = tgt(e')$ *and we denote* $tgt(e)$ *as* $tgt(S, i)$.

Definition 8 (Determination of Clocks). *Given a Timed Automata A,* $x \in Clocks(A)$, $S \subseteq Locs(A)$, *and* $a \in Labels(A)$, $Reset_A(a, S)$ *is the maximum set of clocks* $X' \subseteq Clocks(A)$ *such that for all* $e \in Edges(A)$, $src(e) \in S$ *and* $lab(e) = a$ *then* $X' \subseteq rst(e)$.

We are ready to show how to calculate a pair of functions, that we call *Active* and *RelClocks*, which defines the components and clocks whose activity may influence the behavior of the observer. Following the static analysis terminology *Active* and *RelClocks* are calculated as the solution of a data flow analysis problem over the control structure of the observer: a combination of a transitive closure of the direct influence relation plus a backwards transference function. For the sake of readability, we present them using a formal system notation in Table 2. We say that *Active* and *RelClocks* conform a correct activity pair of functions for A_0 if they are the minimal functions satisfying the Activity

Table 2. Activity rules

$$\frac{-}{0\in Active(l)} \quad \textbf{[ObsRel]} \qquad\qquad \frac{j\in Active(l),x \xrightarrow{S_l} \mathbf{A_j}}{x\in RelClocks(l)} \quad \textbf{[Transitivity I]}$$

$$\frac{x\in RelClocks(l),\mathbf{A_i} \xrightarrow{S_l} x}{i\in Active(l)} \quad \textbf{[Transit. II]} \qquad \frac{j\neq i,j\in Active(l),\mathbf{A_i} \xrightarrow{S_l} \mathbf{A_j}}{i\in Active(l)} \quad \textbf{[Transit. III]}$$

$$\frac{src(e)=l,i\in Active(tgt(e)),\neg Det_{A_i}(lab(e),S_l(i))}{i\in Active(l)} \quad \textbf{[Tranference I]}$$

$$\frac{src(e)=l,x\in Clocks(A_j),x\in RelClocks(tgt(e))-Reset_{A_j}(lab(e),S_l(j))}{x\in RelClocks(l)} \quad \textbf{[Tranference II]}$$

where $\mathcal{I} = \{0..n\}$, $\{A_i\}_{i\in\mathcal{I}}$ is a set of pair-wise compatible I/O Timed Components, $Active : Locs(A_0) \mapsto 2^{\mathcal{I}}$, $RelClocks : Locs(A_0) \mapsto 2^X$, X is the union of the set of clocks of all components, $l \in Locs(A_0)$, and $e \in Edges(A_0)$.

rules. When a clock is not marked as relevant at l that means that the values it acquires while the *SUA* is sojourning l has no effect on the future observed behavior till it becomes relevant again. The same is true for components that are not marked as active. The optimized system will only keep track of active components and relevant clocks. Table 3 shows a correct activity function *Active* for the example 1.

Table 3. Relevance Function for Sporadic Pipe-line

Obs loc.	Active(loc)
0	$Obs, source, latch_1, proc_1, latch_2, proc_2$
1	$Obs, latch_1, proc_1, latch_2, proc_2$
2	$Obs, proc_1, latch_2, proc_2$
3	$Obs, latch_2, proc_2$
4	$Obs, proc_2$
5	Obs
6	Obs

4.3 Transformation

In this section we define a procedure to build the optimization according to *RelClocks* and *Active* over A_0 (the observer) and the *SUA*. The transformation modifies each component of the *SUA* adding new transitions and an "idle" location named * to model deactivation of the component. The optimization process implies a total relabeling of transitions. Old labels are embedded and new ones are added to communicate the change of locations done by the observer (actually the projections of a new label tell which components should be enabled or disabled when the edge is traversed). We generate a new label for each edge of the observer. The idea is that, when the transformed observer jumps from l to l', disabled components (i.e., active components at l that are inactive at l') synchronize and jump to their idle locations. The effect is similar to the elimination of variables standing for the control location of disabled components. On the other hand, enabled components (active components at l' but non active at l) are forced to jump to their right location: the target location of Def. 7. Clocks are treated in a similar way. What follows formalizes the previous notions.

Given a set of I/O TCs $\mathbf{A_i} = (A_i, (I^{A_i}, O^{A_i}))$, where $A_i = (S_i, X_i, \Sigma_i, E_i, Inv_i, s0_i)$ with $i \in \mathcal{I} = \{0..n\}$, *Active* and *RelClocks* as defined in Table 2, first let us define the new set of labels $NL = \Sigma \times 2^{\mathcal{I}} \times 2^X \times (\mathcal{I} \mapsto S)$, with *Lab*, *Dis*, *Rst*, *Ena* as its projections respectively. The operators $Emb()$ and $Nl()$ build new labels from the original ones and the observer edges.

Given a label $a \in \Sigma$, and an edge $e \in E_0$, the new labels $b \overset{def}{=} Emb(a) \in NL$ and $b \overset{def}{=} Nl(e) \in NL$ are such that:

	$Emb(a)$	$Nl(e)$
$Lab(b)$	a	$lab(e)$
$Dis(b)$	$\emptyset$	$Active(src(e)) - Active(tgt(e))$
$Rst(b)$	$\emptyset$	$RelClocks(tgt(e)) - RelClocks(src(e))$
$Ena(b)$	$\emptyset$	$\{(i, tgt(lab(e), S_{src(e)}(i)))/i \in Active(tgt(e)) - Active(src(e))\}$

We define $NLabs = \{Emb(a) \in NL/a \in \Sigma\} \cup \{Nl(e)/e \in E_0\}$ and $NLabs_i = \{b \in NLabs/Lab(b) \in \Sigma_i \vee i \in Dis(b)\}$.

The optimization is defined as

$Opt_{Active}(A_0) = \langle S_0, X_0, NLabs_0, E'_0, Inv_0, s0_0 \rangle$,
where $E'_0 = \{\langle src(e), Nl(e), grd(e), rst(e), tgt(e) \rangle / e \in E_0\}$

For $1 \leq i \leq n$:

$Opt_{Active}(A_i) = \langle S_i \cup \{*\}, X_i, NLabs_i, E'_i, Inv_i \cup \{(*, true)\}, \quad s0_i$ if $i \in Active(s0_0)$ else $* \rangle$, where E'_i is defined by rules of Table 4.

The Fig. 2 shows the working example optimized respect to *Active*. Although the syntactic size of each component is enlarged, deactivation locations reduces the state space because unnecessary interleaving is avoided [7]. Some experimental results that back up this conjecture are shown in next section. Moreover, *RelClocks* could be used to deactivate and activate clocks in the very same spirit that [13]. More precisely, a clock x such that $x \notin RelClocks(l)$ could be deactivated whenever the observer performs a jump to l. Tools like OPENKRONOS [23] allows to explicitly specify deactivation of clocks and this information could also dramatically improve performance[5]. It is not difficult to see that this kind of

---

[5] In the figures the assignment $x := 1$ means that the clock x is deactivated.

Table 4. Edges rules

$$\frac{b\in NLabs_i,\langle s,Lab(b),g,r,s'\rangle\in E_i,i\notin Dis(b)}{\langle s,b,g,r,s'\rangle\in E'_i} \qquad \frac{b\in NLabs_i,\langle s,Lab(b),g,r,s'\rangle\in E_i,i\in Dis(b)}{\langle s,b,g,r,*\rangle\in E'_i}$$

$$\frac{b\in NLabs_i,Lab(b)\notin\Sigma_i,i\in Dis(b)}{\langle s,b,true,\{\},*\rangle\in E'_i} \qquad \frac{b\in NLabs_i,i\in Domain(Ena(b))}{\langle *,b,true,Rst(b)\cap Clocks(A_i),Ena(b)(i)\rangle\in E'_i}$$

$$\frac{b\in NLabs_i,Lab(b)\in In_{A_i},i\notin Domain(Ena(b))}{\langle *,b,true,Rst(b)\cap Clocks(A_i),*\rangle\in E'_i} \qquad \frac{b\in NLabs_i,Lab(b)\notin\Sigma_i,i\in Dis(b)}{\langle *,b,true,Rst(b)\cap Clocks(A_i),*\rangle\in E'_i}$$

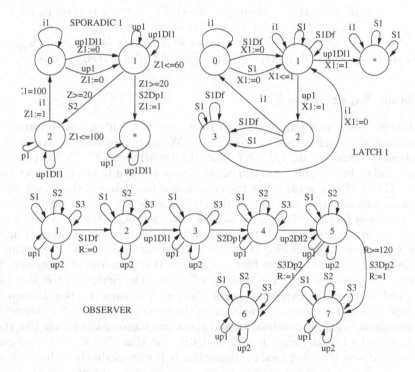

Fig. 2. Transformed components of Pipe-line System

abstraction could be directly built on-the-fly adapting verification engines like OPENKRONOS [23] or TREAT [19] to verify reachability.

The resulting model is CO-Bisimilar to the normal composition and therefore validates the same TCTL formula over the observer for instance reachability. Moreover, in the proof of Theorem 1 which is given in [7], it is noticeable that closed runs[6] of the optimized models are the projections of the runs of the

---

[6] A run is closed if all events are internal or output event of at least one component.

original model, exhibiting only relevant activity, i.e., lost labels are the events performed by the non relevant components.

Theorem 1. *Given an indexed set of compatible I/O Timed Components $\{A_i\}_{0 \leq i \leq n}$, and an assignment mapping $\mathcal{P} : Locs(A_0) \mapsto 2^{Props}$, if Active is a correct activity function then $(Opt_{Active}(A_0) \parallel Opt_{Active}(A_1) \parallel \ldots \parallel Opt_{Active}(A_n)) \simeq^{\mathcal{P}'^{*},\mathcal{P}^{*}} (A_0 \parallel A_1 \parallel \ldots \parallel A_n)$ where $\mathcal{P}^{*}$ and $\mathcal{P}'^{*}$ are the natural extensions of $\mathcal{P}$ on the locations of $A_0 \parallel A_1 \parallel \ldots \parallel A_n$ and $(Opt_{Active}(A_0) \parallel Opt_{Active}(A_1) \parallel \ldots \parallel Opt_{Active}(A_n))$ resp.*

As mentioned, from the TCTL preservation theorem in [6,9] we obtain:

Corollary 1. *Given an indexed set of compatible I/O Timed Components $\{A_i\}_{0 \leq i \leq n}$, and an assignment mapping $\mathcal{P} : Locs(A_0) \mapsto 2^{Props}$, If Active is a correct activity function. Then, for all TCTL formula ϕ $(Opt_{Active}(A_0) \parallel Opt_{Active}(A_1) \parallel \ldots \parallel Opt_{Active}(A_n)) \models_{\mathcal{P}'^{*}} \phi \iff A_0 \parallel A_1 \parallel \ldots \parallel A_n \models_{\mathcal{P}^{*}} \phi$ where $\mathcal{P}^{*}$ and $\mathcal{P}'^{*}$ are the natural extensions of $\mathcal{P}$ on the locations of $A_0 \parallel A_1 \parallel \ldots \parallel A_n$ and $(Opt_{Active}(A_0) \parallel Opt_{Active}(A_1) \parallel \ldots \parallel Opt_{Active}(A_n))$ resp.*

4.4   Some Experiments

OPENKRONOS [23] was our testbed to show how these ideas can improve the performance of a verification back-end tool. We have ran several experiments with OPENKRONOS on an AMD K7 1333Mhz 256Mbytes LINUX 7.2 platform. Tables 5 and 6 show verification times, the size of the symbolic state space built by OPENKRONOS in the case that the error is not reachable or the length of the shortest counterexample we could find[7]. O/M stands for "out of memory": the internal memory has been exhausted and the verifier process trashed. O/T stands for "out of time", meaning that the verification process over the original model has been stopped after waiting more than 100 times the verifier performance over the optimized model. The first example is the pipe-line of processes. We play with three parameters: the number of stages, the period of the incoming signal, and the deadline expressed in the observer (we take $n \times 60$). Remember that there are two automata for each stage (the process and the latch) therefore, n stages means $n \times 2 + 2$ automata and the same number of clocks. The state space is halved when the error is not reachable and this allows us to treat cases that trash without this proposed optimization. It is remarkable how dramatically the time and length of counterexamples are reduced using the optimized system. Again, some intractable cases has been treated in less than one second. It seems that the exploration tool works in much more guided fashion over the optimized system specially while sojourning observer locations where some components are discarded.

The second example is an extension of the FDDI token ring protocol [23] plus an observer that monitors the time the token takes to return to a given station. The model is composed by a ring and n stations which, in turn, are composed

---

[7] *time* is the time it takes to inform the existence of a counterexample, while *time** is the time it takes to build the shortest counterexample when we provide a maximum depth for the search.

by the station itself (containing 2 clocks) plus an automata that keeps track of the parity of the times the station received the token (this is needed to know how to manipulate clocks each time). In this case, stations perform some internal activity after releasing the token and before obtaining it again. This increases the state space with intuitively irrelevant activity for the observed behavior. Thanks to transference rules, our method discovers this phenomena. Just one station should be active at each locations of the observer. However, it safely keeps all clocks and parity automata active since they are needed whenever the station is interrupted by a new arrival of the token. Table 6 shows the important impact of this reduction. Other experiments using backward verification of full TCTL can be found in [15].

Table 5. Verification results for the Pipe-line example

Hit Error = false		Original			Optimized		
# stages	period	# st	# tr	time	# st	# tr	time
4	180	4,009	7,485	0.25	2,383	4,391	0.13
4	120	38,376	90,478	3.82	22,817	53,817	2.00
5	180	61,081	136,388	6.90	32,523	71,938	3.23
5	120	O/M	-	-	680,421	2,009,126	234.67
6	180	O/M	-	-	573,541	1,507,124	184.80
6	120	O/M	-	-	O/M	-	-
Hit Error = true							
# stages	period	depth	time	time *	depth	time	time *
4	99	35	O/M	2.90	22	0.15	0.02
4	40	33	3.38	1.56	22	0.01	0.11
5	99	O/M	O/M	O/M	27	0.01	0.01
5	40	50	241.19	241.19	27	0.01	0.01
6	99	O/M	O/M	O/M	299	0.45	65.70
6	40	O/M	O/M	O/M	75	0.02	41.40

5 Conclusions and Future Work

It is well known that in order to mitigate state explosion problem combinations of different techniques should be applied. We provide a correct and complete approach to optimize the analysis of timed systems. Our technique can be fed naively with the components of the timed system under analysis plus the observer. It statically discovers the underlying dependence among components and the observer and provides the set of elements (components and clocks) that can be safely ignored, from the observational point of view. This implies significant time savings during the verification step. The tool is also rather easy to use and integrate as a preprocessor for known tools: it just requires I/O (uncontrollable/controllable) declarations which, in general, are intuitively known

Table 6. Verification results for the FDDI example

Hit Error = false		Original			Optimized		
# stations	deadline	# st	# tr	time	# st	# tr	time
6	430	169,952	1,137,408	66.89	3,828	4,540	0.50
8	480	O/M	O/M	-	18,419	21,833	4.35
10	530	O/M	O/M	-	81,574	96,559	32.68
Hit Error = true							
# stations	deadline	depth	time	time *	depth	time	time *
6	420	447	66.13	0.63	14	0.48	0.01
8	470	2,045	O/T	9.23	18	4.36	0.03
10	520	12,305	O/T	224.61	22	32.62	0.07

by modelers or can be automatically provided by high-level front-end modeling
languages. It is worth remarking that in some cases we are able to treat cases
where the analysis of the original standard composition is unfeasible under the
same conditions. In all case studies, the verification tool run faster and obtains
shorter counterexamples over the optimized than over the original model. Two
main factors affecting the efficiency of the technique: the influence "coupling"
of components and the topology of the observer. For instance there are cases
where the more detailed the observer is (in the sense of the sequence of events)
the more reduction is obtained; particularly when the detailed observer shows
an expected sequence of events and thus irrelevance of components is more likely
to be detected at some locations of that observer. We believe that the ideas of
our approach can be migrated to several frameworks and are complementary to
many state space reduction techniques. Future work also includes less conservative definitions of influence, the extension of these techniques to automata with
variables and the integration with other popular tools like UPPAAL [4]. Our technique could also obtain the basic information to calculate the relevant events for
each component. Then, components could be abstracted to exhibit the same set
of runs up to those relevant events. Linear-time properties like reachability may
be checked using these simulation equivalent reductions. An ad hoc automatic
procedure for the aforementioned reduction is presented in [6].

References

1. B. Alpern and F. Schneider, "Verifying Temporal Properties without Temporal
   Logic," *ACM Trans. Programming Lang. and Systems*, Vol. 11, No. 1, 1989, pp.
   147-167.
2. R. Alur, C. Courcoubetis, and D. Dill, "Model-Checking for Real-Time Systems,"
   In *Information and Computation,*, Vol. 104, No. 1, pp.2-34, 1993.
3. R. Alur and D. Dill, "A Theory of Timed Automata," *Theoretical Computer
   Science*, Vol. 126, 1994, pp. 183-235.

4. J. Bengtsson, K.G. Larsen, F. Larsson, P. Pettersson, and W. Yi, "UPPAAL- A Tool Suite for the Automatic Verification of Real-Time Systems," *Proc. Hybrid Systems III*, LNCS 1066, 1996, pp. 232-243.
5. M. Bozga, J.-C. Fernandez, and L.Ghirvu, "Using Static Analysis to Improve Automatic Test Generation," *TACAS 2000*, LNCS 1785, March/April 2000.
6. V. Braberman, *Modeling and Checking Real-Time System Designs*, Ph.D Thesis, Universidad de Buenos Aires, 2000.
7. V. Braberman, D. Garbervetsky, and A. Olivero, "Influence Information to Improve the Verification of Timed Systems," *Tech. Report DC-UBA 2001-003*.
8. V. Braberman, and A. Olivero, "Extending Timed Automata for Compositional Modeling Healthy Timed Systems," *2nd Workshop on Models for Timed Critical Systems 2001*. To be published in Electronic Notes in Theoretical Computer Science.
9. V. Braberman, and A. Olivero, "Preserving Branching-Time Structure in Timed Systems," *Argentinian Workshop on Theoretical Computer Science 2001*. 30th JAIIO Proceedings.
10. S. Campos, O. Grumberg, K. Yorav, and C. Fady. "Test Sequence Generation and Model Checking Using Dynamic Transition Relations," *Submitted to : FMCAD 2000*.
11. E. Clarke, O. Grumberg and D. Peled, *Model Checking*, MIT Press, January 2000.
12. C. Daws, A. Olivero, S. Tripakis and S. Yovine, "The Tool KRONOS," *In Proc. of Hybrid Systems III*, LNCS 1066, 1996, pp. 208-219.
13. C. Daws and S.Yovine, "Reducing the Number of Clock Variables of Timed Automata," *Proc. IEEE RTSS '96*, IEEE Computer Soc. Press, 1996.
14. R. De Nicolla, U. Montanari, and F.Vaandrager, "Back and Forth Bisimulations," *Proc. CONCUR '90*, Amsterdam, LNCS 458, 1990, pp.152–165.
15. D. Garbervetsky, *Un Método de Reducción para la Composición de Sistemas Temporizados*, Master Thesis, Univ. de Buenos Aires, 2000.
16. P. Godefroid, "Partial-Order Methods for the Verification of Concurrent Systems", LNCS 1032, 1996.
17. R. Gawlick, R. Segala, J. Sogaard-Andersen, N. Lynch "Liveness in Timed and Untimed Systems," *Proceedings of ICALP* , LNCS 820, Springer Verlag, pp. 166-177, 1994. Also in, *Information and Computation*, March 1998.
18. J. Hatcliff, J. Cobett, M. Dwyer, S.Sokolowski, and H.Zheng "A Formal Study of Slicing for Multi-Threaded Programs with JVM Concurrency Primitives," *SAS*. LNCS 1694, 1999.
19. I. Kang, I. Lee, and Y.S. Kim, "An Efficient Space Generation for the Analysis of Real-Time Systems". *Trans. on Software Engineering*, Vol. 26, No. 5, pp. 453-477, May 2000.
20. K.G. Larsen, F. Laroussinie, "CMC: A Tool for Compositional Model-Checking of Real-Time Systems," *Proc. FORTE-PSTV'98*, 439-456, Kluwer Academic Publishers, 1998.
21. R Sloan, U. Buy, "Stubborn Sets for Real-Time Petri Nets," *Form. Methods in Syst. Design*, Vol. 11(1), pp.23-40, July 1997.
22. S. Tasiran, S. P. Khatri, S. Yovine, R. K. Brayton, and A. Sangiovanni-Vincentelli. "A Timed Automaton-Based Method for Accurate Computation of Circuit Delay in the Presence of Cross-Talk," *FMCAD'98*, 1998.
23. S. Tripakis *L'Analyse Formelle des Systemès Temporisés en Practique*, Phd. Thesis, Univesité Joseph Fourier, December 1998.

24. F. Wang, "Efficient and User-Friendly Verification," *Transaction in Computers,* Accepted for Publication, June 2001.
25. Wang Yi, "Real-Time Behavior of Asynchronous Agents," *Proc. CONCUR'90,* LNCS 458, 1990.
26. S. Yovine, *"Méthodes et Outiles pour la Vérification Symbolique de Systemès Temporisés,"* doctoral disertation, Insitut National Polytechnique de Grenoble, 1993.
27. S. Yovine, "Model-Checking Timed Automata," *Embedded Systems,* G. Rozemberg and F. Vaandrager eds., LNCS 1494, 1998.

Digitisation and Full Abstraction for Dense-Time Model Checking*

Joël Ouaknine

Department of Mathematics, Tulane University,
New Orleans LA 70118, USA
joelo@math.tulane.edu

Abstract. We study the digitisation of dense-time behaviours of timed processes, and show how this leads to exact verification methods for a large class of dense-time specifications. These specifications are all *closed under inverse digitisation*, a robustness property first introduced by Henzinger, Manna, and Pnueli (on timed traces), and extended here to timed failures, enabling us to consider liveness issues in addition to safety properties. We discuss a corresponding model checking algorithm and show that, in many cases, automated verification of such dense-time specifications can in fact be directly performed on the model checker FDR (a commercial product of Formal Systems (Europe) Ltd.). We illustrate this with a small case study (the railway level crossing problem). Finally, we show that integral—or digitised—behaviours are fully abstract with respect to specifications closed under inverse digitisation, and relate this to the efficiency of our model checking algorithm.

1 Introduction

Real-time systems appear in an increasingly large number of applications, from kitchen appliances to nuclear power, telecommunications, aeronautics, and so on. In many instances, it is crucial that such systems behave exactly as they were intended to, lest catastrophic consequences ensue. For this reason, real-time systems have elicited a large amount of research in recent years.

Timed systems can broadly be divided into two subclasses, depending on whether time is modelled in a *discrete* or *dense* fashion. Early research focussed mostly on the former, as the verification techniques already in circulation could readily be extended to this case. There are however a number of drawbacks associated with discrete modelling of time, and chief among them is the obvious limit on the accuracy of the analysis. Dense-time systems (typically modelled over the reals), on the other hand, have infinite (usually uncountable) state spaces, ruling out the direct application of techniques such as model checking.

One of the earliest attempts to circumvent this problem was the technique of *timewise refinement* [24,22,26]. The crux of this method consists in removing

---

* This research was supported in part by the U.S. Office of Naval Research under contract N00014-95-1-0520 and by the Fonds FCAR (Québec).

J.-P. Katoen and P. Stevens (Eds.): TACAS 2002, LNCS 2280, pp. 37–51, 2002.
© Springer-Verlag Berlin Heidelberg 2002

all timing information from a timed system, keeping only the relative order in which state changes occur. In this way one obtains an untimed (discrete) system, which can then be handled by standard model checking algorithms. The obvious disadvantage of this technique is that the class of specifications that can be soundly verified with it is rather restricted; on the other hand, timewise refinement is usually extremely efficient in those cases in which it can be applied.

At the other end of the spectrum we find the technique of *region graphs* [1, 2]. This consists in defining an equivalence relation on the state space of a timed system, giving rise to a finite number of partitions, or *regions*. Points within a given region are indistinguishable insofar as the verification of specifications (usually expressed as TCTL formulas) is concerned; this observation yields a model checking procedure. The advantage of this approach is the large class of specifications it is able to handle. On the other hand, it tends to be computationally very expensive, as regions partition the state space extremely finely.

Many intermediate and related techniques have since appeared, of which the following is only a partial list: [15,13,4,5,3,14,16,28,12,11,29,19]. Some are concerned with discretisation methods or symbolic analysis, while others offer various trade-offs (space economy vs. runtime efficiency, or runtime efficiency vs. wideness of applicability, etc.). There have also been a small number of model checking tools developed for timed systems, such as COSPAN [6], UPPAAL [7], KRONOS [8], and HYTECH [10].

Our interest lies in the connection between discrete-time and dense-time paradigms for modelling timed systems, and in particular the scope and limitations of applying discrete-time methods to dense-time verification problems. Henzinger, Manna, and Pnueli studied this question in [13], and concluded that one must restrict one's attention both to systems *closed under digitisation* and to specifications *closed under inverse digitisation*. Their analysis focussed on *timed transition systems* and considered a *timed trace* semantics. In this paper, we extend their results to *timed failures*, enabling us to address liveness issues in addition to safety properties.

The framework we have chosen is Reed and Roscoe's Timed CSP [20,21, 27,25]. Timed CSP is a well-known process algebra for timed systems and is a natural extension of CSP, which itself has been used to model timed systems discretely [23]. In addition, Timed CSP is endowed with both denotational and operational semantics, so that questions may be studied from both viewpoints. For reasons of space, however, the work we present here focusses on the denotational side; one may find an operational account of it in [18].

One of our main results is the *digitisation lemma*, which states that all Timed CSP processes are closed under digitisation. On the specification side, we find indeed that specifications closed under inverse digitisation are verifiable, and moreover that this is a hard restriction which essentially cannot be relaxed. Another very interesting result is that integral behaviours are in fact *fully abstract* with respect to the class of specifications under consideration; in other words, integral behaviours contain precisely the right amount of information required for our verification aims, without any junk.

These results lead us to a model checking algorithm, which can in fact be implemented on FDR [23], a CSP model checker. We illustrate this in a small case study.

2 Timed CSP Syntax and Conventions

Let Σ be a finite set of *events*. In the notation below, we have $a \in \Sigma$ and $A \subseteq \Sigma$. The parameter n ranges over the non-negative integers $\mathbb{N}$. f represents a function $f : \Sigma \longrightarrow \Sigma$. The variable X is drawn from a fixed infinite set of process variables $VAR \cong \{X, Y, Z, \dots\}$.

Timed CSP terms are constructed according to the following grammar:

$$P := STOP \mid a \longrightarrow P \mid a : A \longrightarrow P(a) \mid SKIP \mid WAIT\ n \mid P_1 \overset{n}{\rhd} P_2 \mid$$
$$P_1 \,\square\, P_2 \mid P_1 \,\sqcap\, P_2 \mid P_1 \underset{A}{\parallel} P_2 \mid P_1 \,|||\, P_2 \mid P_1 \,\fatsemi\, P_2 \mid P \setminus A \mid$$
$$f^{-1}(P) \mid f(P) \mid X \mid \mu X \cdot P\ .$$

These terms have the following intuitive interpretations:

- *STOP* is the deadlocked, stable process which is only capable of letting time pass.
- $a \longrightarrow P$ initially offers at any time to engage in the event a, and subsequently behaves like P. The general prefixed process $a : A \longrightarrow P(a)$ is initially prepared to engage in any of the events $a \in A$, at the choice of the environment, and thereafter behave like $P(a)$; this corresponds to *STOP* when $A = \emptyset$.
- *SKIP* intuitively corresponds to the process $\checkmark \longrightarrow STOP$, where the event $\checkmark$ represents successful termination.
- *WAIT* n is the process which idles for n time units, and then becomes *SKIP*.
- $P \overset{n}{\rhd} Q$ is a timeout process that initially offers to become P for n time units, after which it silently becomes Q if P has failed to communicate any visible event.
- $P \sqcap Q$ represents the nondeterministic (or internal) choice between P and Q. Which of these two processes $P \sqcap Q$ becomes is independent of the environment, and how the choice is resolved is considered to be outside the domain of discourse.
- $P \,\square\, Q$, on the other hand, denotes a process which is willing to behave either like P or like Q, at the choice of the environment. This decision is taken on the first visible event that is communicated, and is nondeterministic only if this initial event, when it occurs, is possible for both P and Q.
- The parallel composition $P_1 \underset{A}{\parallel} P_2$ of P_1 and P_2, over the interface set A, requires P_1 and P_2 to agree and synchronise on all events in A, and to behave independently of each other with respect to all other events. The interleaving $P_1 \,|||\, P_2$ corresponds to parallel composition over an empty interface.
- $P \,\fatsemi\, Q$ corresponds to the sequential composition of P and Q: it denotes a process which behaves like P until P successfully terminates (silently), at which point the process seamlessly starts to behave like Q.

- $P \setminus A$ is a process which behaves like P but with all communications in the set A hidden (made invisible to the environment); the assumption of *maximal progress*, or τ-*urgency*, dictates that no time can elapse while hidden events are on offer—in other words, hidden events happen as soon as they become available.
- The renamed processes $f^{-1}(P)$ and $f(P)$ derive their behaviours from those of P in that, whenever P can perform an event a, $f^{-1}(P)$ can engage in any event b such that $f(b) = a$, whereas $f(P)$ can perform $f(a)$.
- The process variable X has no intrinsic behaviour of its own, but can imitate any process P as part of a recursion—see below.
- The recursion $\mu X \cdot P$ represents a process which behaves like P but with every free occurrence of X in P (recursively) replaced by $\mu X \cdot P$. Semantically, this corresponds to the unique solution to the equation $X = P$. Note that the variable X here usually appears freely within P's body.

Let us write **TCSP** to denote the collection of closed terms of the language thus generated, i.e., terms in which every occurrence of a variable X is within the scope of a μX operator. We refer to these terms as *processes*.

Note our requirement that all *delays* (parameters n in the terms *WAIT* n and $P_1 \overset{n}{\triangleright} P_2$) be integral. This restriction is both necessary (since otherwise the main questions considered here become theoretically intractable) and essentially harmless, because of the freedom to scale time units. We could equivalently have required *rational* delays, as many authors do.

We occasionally use the following derived constructs: abbreviating $a \longrightarrow STOP$ as simply $\dot{a}$, and writing $a \overset{n}{\longrightarrow} P$ instead of $a \longrightarrow WAIT\ n\ \mathring{,}\ P$. We also tend to express recursions by means of the equational notation $X = P$, rather than the functional $\mu X \cdot P$ prescribed by the definition.

Lastly, some mild additional technical syntactic restrictions, which we omit here, are required to ensure that processes are *non-Zeno*, or in other words that they never force time to *converge*. The reader may find more detailed discussion of this point in [17,21,27].

3   Dense-Time Modelling, Specification, and Verification

The standard denotational semantics for Timed CSP is Reed and Roscoe's *timed failures model*, $\mathcal{M}_{\mathbb{R}}$, a brief synopsis of which we now present. It comes equipped with a compositional[1] evaluation map $\mathbb{R}[\![\cdot]\!] : \textbf{TCSP} \longrightarrow \mathcal{M}_{\mathbb{R}}$. This model allows one to assign dense-time (in fact, continuous-time) interpretations to Timed CSP processes. References include [20,21,27].

Timed failures are pairs $(s, \aleph)$, with s a *timed trace* and $\aleph$ a *timed refusal*. A *timed trace* is a finite sequence of *timed events* $(t, a) \in \mathbb{R}^+ \times \Sigma$, with the time values in non-decreasing order. Notationally, we enclose the elements of a timed trace in angled brackets, e.g., $\langle (0, a), (3.2, b), (3.2, a), (4.76, a) \rangle$, etc. A

---

[1] By *compositional*, we mean that the value of a compound expression can be calculated from the values of its constituting subexpressions.

timed refusal is a set of timed events consisting of a finite union of *refusal tokens* $[t, t') \times A$ (with $0 \leqslant t \leqslant t' < \infty$ and $A \subseteq \Sigma$). A timed failure $(s, \aleph)$ is interpreted as an observation of a process in which the events that the process has engaged in are recorded in s, whereas the intervals during which other events have been refused are recorded in $\aleph$. All recorded time values are absolute, i.e., measured relative to the process's 'start'. The set of timed failures is denoted by $TF_{\mathbb{R}}$.

The model $\mathcal{M}_{\mathbb{R}}$ consists of all subsets of $TF_{\mathbb{R}}$ that meet certain 'axioms', general properties that all processes are deemed to have. One then defines the semantic map $\mathbb{R}[\![\cdot]\!] : \mathbf{TCSP} \longrightarrow \mathcal{M}_{\mathbb{R}}$ by induction on the structure of Timed CSP syntax. This map simply assigns to each syntactic process its set of possible behaviours, or timed failures.

Two fundamental assumptions are that processes evolve over a *continuous*, ergo *dense*, time domain ($\mathbb{R}^+$); and that processes are subject to *maximal progress*, or τ-*urgency*, which requires silent events (internal transitions) to occur as soon as they become available. Technical details and more thorough presentations of the timed failures model can be found in any of the references quoted earlier.

A *dense-time specification* is an assertion concerning processes; more precisely, it is a predicate on the set of behaviours of processes. In this paper, the specifications we are interested in are *behavioural*; that is to say, a dense-time specification can always be identified with a set $S \subseteq TF_{\mathbb{R}}$ of timed failures, and a process $P \in \mathbf{TCSP}$ *satisfies* S if $\mathbb{R}[\![P]\!] \subseteq S$; we denote this by $P \vDash_{\mathbb{R}} S$.

As an example, the assertion: "P cannot perform the event *crash*" can be expressed as $P \vDash_{\mathbb{R}} S_1$, where $S_1 = \{(s, \aleph) \in TF_{\mathbb{R}} \mid crash \notin \sigma(s)\}$. (Here $\sigma(s)$ simply denotes the set of events occurring in the timed trace s.)

S_1 is an example of a *(timed) trace* specification: it restricts the set of allowable timed traces of a process, but places no constraints on refusals. Such specifications are often termed *safety* properties, in that they specify that 'nothing bad should happen'. By contrast, a specification restricting the allowable timed refusals of a process is often called a *liveness* property, since it requires that 'certain (presumably good) things not be prevented from happening'. Such a specification, for example, could be the requirement of constant availability of the 'eject' option on a combat aircraft, perhaps expressed as: "The event *eject* is never refused".

A specification S is said to be *syntactic* if it can be written as the set of behaviours of a process, in other words if there exists some $Q \in \mathbf{TCSP}$ such that $S = \mathbb{R}[\![Q]\!]$. In this case we write $P \vDash_{\mathbb{R}} Q$ (rather than $P \vDash_{\mathbb{R}} \mathbb{R}[\![Q]\!]$) to mean $P \vDash_{\mathbb{R}} S$, i.e., $\mathbb{R}[\![P]\!] \subseteq \mathbb{R}[\![Q]\!]$.

It turns out that S_1 above is not syntactic; however, a discrete-time version of S_1 *is* syntactic, as we shall see in the following section. This is an important observation since our model checking algorithm (as well as its implementation on FDR) requires specifications to be expressed syntactically.

As explained earlier, a sort of specification that we are particularly interested in consists in specifications that are *closed under inverse digitisation*, a generalisation of a notion of Henzinger, Manna, and Pnueli [13]. Closure under inverse digitisation can be viewed as a robustness property: if a specification contains all 'digitisations' of a particular behaviour, then it should contain the behaviour in question as well. If we understand specifications to be sets of 'allowable' behaviours, it would seem dangerous to ban a particular behaviour if many neighbouring behaviours were themselves deemed acceptable. We postpone the precise definition of closure under inverse digitisation until Sect. 5.

Given a process P and a specification S, the *dense-time verification* problem we are interested in is deciding whether $P \vDash_\mathbb{R} S$ holds. Since P and S are in most cases infinite (in fact uncountable), this is often a far from straightforward task. The remainder of this paper develops techniques to accomplish this goal under certain assumptions.

4   Discrete-Time Modelling, Specification, and Verification

We now present a discrete-time model to interpret Timed CSP processes. As discussed in the introduction, this model, $\mathcal{M}_\mathbb{Z}$, is in fact an integral submodel of the timed failures model presented in the previous section.

Processes' behaviours as recorded in $\mathcal{M}_\mathbb{Z}$ are precisely those 'integral' behaviours that are recorded in $\mathcal{M}_\mathbb{R}$. Moreover, the forthcoming *digitisation lemma* (Lemma 4) tells us that *any* dense-time behaviour of a process recorded in $\mathcal{M}_\mathbb{R}$ gives rise to several closely related integral behaviours, so that, modulo some 'timing fuzziness', all of the behaviours of a process that are recorded in $\mathcal{M}_\mathbb{R}$ are also accounted for in $\mathcal{M}_\mathbb{Z}$.

Integral timed failures are defined in the obvious way: all time values appearing in timed traces, and all time bounds of refusal tokens, are required to be integral. Thus events occur at integral times and are refused over integral intervals of time. We let $TF_\mathbb{Z}$ stand for the set of integral timed failures.

The model $\mathcal{M}_\mathbb{Z}$ then consists of all subsets of $TF_\mathbb{Z}$ that meet certain axioms, essentially integral versions of the axioms for $\mathcal{M}_\mathbb{R}$. The semantic map $\mathbb{Z}[\![\cdot]\!] : \mathbf{TCSP} \longrightarrow \mathcal{M}_\mathbb{Z}$ can then be defined compositionally in exactly the same way as the dense-time mapping $\mathbb{R}[\![\cdot]\!] : \mathbf{TCSP} \longrightarrow \mathcal{M}_\mathbb{R}$, with obvious 'integral' restrictions on the ranges of the various parameters.

For $T \subseteq TF_\mathbb{R}$ a set of dense-time timed failures, let $\mathbf{Z}(T) \cong T \cap TF_\mathbb{Z}$ denote the subset of integral timed failures of T. As expected, we have the following:

Lemma 1. *For any process $P \in \mathbf{TCSP}$, $\mathbb{Z}[\![P]\!] = \mathbf{Z}(\mathbb{R}[\![P]\!])$.*

Proposition 2. *The model $\mathcal{M}_\mathbb{Z}$ is strictly coarser than $\mathcal{M}_\mathbb{R}$. In other words, there are processes in $\mathbf{TCSP}$ which are identified in $\mathcal{M}_\mathbb{Z}$ yet distinguished in $\mathcal{M}_\mathbb{R}$ (but never vice-versa).*

Proof. The parenthesised assertion is immediate from Lemma 1. For the main statement, we let $R = \dot{a} \overset{0}{\triangleright} WAIT\ 1 \,\dot{\S}\, R$, and then define $P = R \,|\!|\!|\, \dot{b}$ and $Q = (R \,|\!|\!|\, b \longrightarrow R) \,\|_{\{a\}}\, \dot{a}$. We now show that $\mathbb{Z}[\![P]\!] = \mathbb{Z}[\![Q]\!]$ but $\mathbb{R}[\![P]\!] \neq \mathbb{R}[\![Q]\!]$.

To see that $\mathbb{Z}[\![P]\!] = \mathbb{Z}[\![Q]\!]$, note that either process may communicate, in any order and at any time, a single a and a single b. Moreover, both processes can refuse everything but b until such time as b occurs, at which point any set of events can be refused.

On the other hand, the timed trace $\langle (0.5, b), (1.5, a) \rangle$ is a valid trace of $\mathbb{R}[\![Q]\!]$ but not of $\mathbb{R}[\![P]\!]$, which concludes the proof. $\qquad\square$

Following our approach with $\mathcal{M}_{\mathbb{R}}$, behavioural *discrete-time specifications* on $\mathcal{M}_{\mathbb{Z}}$ processes are naturally (identified with) sets of integral timed failures. Thus given a specification $S \subseteq TF_{\mathbb{Z}}$, we say that a process $P \in \mathbf{TCSP}$ satisfies S, written $P \vDash_{\mathbb{Z}} S$, if $\mathbb{Z}[\![P]\!] \subseteq S$.

We note that dense-time specifications (subsets of $TF_{\mathbb{R}}$) naturally give rise to discrete-time specifications, simply by excluding non-integral behaviours. Thus for $S \subseteq TF_{\mathbb{R}}$, we also write $P \vDash_{\mathbb{Z}} S$ to express $\mathbb{Z}[\![P]\!] \subseteq \mathbf{Z}(S)$.

Let us now consider once again the example "P cannot perform the event *crash*". Understood as a discrete-time specification, it can be written as $P \vDash_{\mathbb{Z}} S_2$, where $S_2 = \{(s, \aleph) \in TF_{\mathbb{Z}} \mid crash \notin \sigma(s)\}$. We could also have expressed S_2 as the set of behaviours of the process $CHAOS_{\Sigma - \{crash\}}$, where we define, for any

$$A \subseteq \Sigma, \ CHAOS_A = (a : A \longrightarrow CHAOS_A) \overset{0}{\rhd} WAIT\ 1 \ \fatsemi \ CHAOS_A.$$

A discrete-time specification S is said to be *syntactic* if it can be written as $S = \mathbb{Z}[\![Q]\!]$ for some process Q. S_2 above is therefore syntactic. Note that, thanks to Lemma 1, a dense-time specification that is syntactic is automatically also syntactic when viewed as a discrete-time specification, although the converse need not be true.

Let S be a syntactic discrete-time specification, i.e., $S = \mathbb{Z}[\![Q]\!]$ for some $Q \in \mathbf{TCSP}$. Let $P \in \mathbf{TCSP}$. There is an algorithm to decide whether $P \vDash_{\mathbb{Z}} S$, which is guaranteed to terminate provided the discrete *labelled transition systems* associated with P and Q are finite.[2] In fact, depending on its implementation, the algorithm may also terminate in certain other cases.

The idea underlying the algorithm is to form the *power labelled transition system (PLTS)* of a process, which identifies certain states in such a way that the resulting graph is *deterministic*. One then introduces a notion of *power simulation*, which is subsequently shown to correspond to the satisfaction relation $\vDash_{\mathbb{Z}}$. Since the existence of a power simulation can always be decided in the case of finite PLTS's, this algorithm is a decision procedure for discrete-time specification satisfaction. In fact, the model checker FDR employs similar (if rather more sophisticated) methods for deciding refinement between CSP processes.

An assertion of the form $P \vDash_{\mathbb{Z}} S$ can also be decided directly on FDR, via simple coding techniques, provided S is a syntactic *trace* specification.[3] We illustrate this in a case study in the following section.

---

[2] A discrete operational semantics, derived from that presented by Schneider for Timed CSP in [25], can be given for **TCSP** processes. This semantics simply associates to each process a discrete labelled transition system, from which the integral timed failures of the process can be calculated—the operational and denotational semantics are said to be *congruent*.

[3] Certain other types of specifications can also be handled by FDR.

5   Relating Dense-Time and Discrete-Time Verification

We now consider the relationship between the dense-time and discrete-time behaviours $\mathbb{R}[\![P]\!]$ and $\mathbb{Z}[\![P]\!]$ of a given Timed CSP process P.

5.1   The Digitisation Lemma

We first present one of our main results, the *digitisation lemma*, which enables us to tightly relate the dense-time and discrete-time semantics for Timed CSP.

We begin with a small piece of notation. Let $t \in \mathbb{R}^+$, and let $0 \leqslant \varepsilon \leqslant 1$ be a real number. Decompose t into its integral and fractional parts, thus: $t = \lfloor t \rfloor + t'$. (Here $\lfloor t \rfloor$ represents the greatest integer less than or equal to t.) If $t' < \varepsilon$, let $[t]_\varepsilon \mathrel{\widehat{=}} \lfloor t \rfloor$, otherwise let $[t]_\varepsilon \mathrel{\widehat{=}} \lceil t \rceil$. (Naturally, $\lceil t \rceil$ denotes the least integer greater than or equal to t.) The $[\cdot]_\varepsilon$ operator therefore shifts the value of a real number t to the preceding or following integer, depending on whether the fractional part of t is less than the 'pivot' ε or not.

We can then extend $[\cdot]_\varepsilon$ to timed failures, by pointwise application to, respectively, the time component of the trace's events, and the time bounds of the refusal's tokens:

$$\left[\left(\langle (t_1, a_1), (t_2, a_2), \dots, (t_k, a_k) \rangle, \bigcup_{i=1}^{l} [u_i, v_i) \times A_i \right) \right]_\varepsilon \mathrel{\widehat{=}}$$
$$\left(\langle ([t_1]_\varepsilon, a_1), ([t_2]_\varepsilon, a_2), \dots, ([t_k]_\varepsilon, a_k) \rangle, \bigcup_{i=1}^{l} [[u_i]_\varepsilon, [v_i]_\varepsilon) \times A_i \right).$$

(The reader can verify that, in the case of timed refusals, this operation is independent of the particular representation of the refusal as a finite union of refusal tokens.) This definition extends to sets of timed failures in the obvious way.

Definition 3. *A set of timed failures $P \subseteq TF_\mathbb{R}$ is **closed under digitisation** if, for any $0 \leqslant \varepsilon \leqslant 1$, $[P]_\varepsilon \subseteq P$.*

We note that our version of 'digitisation' extends that presented in [13], which is only concerned with timed traces.

The digitisation lemma now reads:

Lemma 4. *For any $P \in \mathbf{TCSP}$, $\mathbb{R}[\![P]\!]$ is closed under digitisation.*

Proof. The proof proceeds by structural induction on Timed CSP terms. Note that the assumption that all delays are integral is crucial. Details of the proof can be found in [18]. □

5.2   Verification

Definition 5. *A set of timed failures $\phi \subseteq TF_\mathbb{R}$ is **closed under inverse digitisation** if, whenever a timed failure $(s, \aleph)$ is such that $[(s, \aleph)]_\varepsilon \in \phi$ for all $0 \leqslant \varepsilon \leqslant 1$, then $(s, \aleph) \in \phi$.*

As a convention, we use lowercase Greek letters to designate specifications that are closed under inverse digitisation.

The following lemma extends a result of [13]:

Lemma 6. *If $P \subseteq TF_{\mathbb{R}}$ is closed under digitisation and $\phi \subseteq TF_{\mathbb{R}}$ is closed under inverse digitisation, then $\mathbf{Z}(P) \subseteq \mathbf{Z}(\phi) \Leftrightarrow P \subseteq \phi$.*

*On the other hand, suppose $S \subseteq TF_{\mathbb{R}}$ is **not** closed under inverse digitisation. Then there exists $P \subseteq TF_{\mathbb{R}}$ closed under digitisation such that $\mathbf{Z}(P) \subseteq \mathbf{Z}(S)$ yet $P \not\subseteq S$.*

Proof. For the first part, we note that the right-to-left implication is immediate (and requires in fact no assumptions on ϕ).

Going in the other direction, assume that $\mathbf{Z}(P) \subseteq \mathbf{Z}(\phi)$, and let $(s, \aleph) \in P$. Since P is closed under digitisation, $[(s, \aleph)]_\varepsilon \in P$ for all $0 \leqslant \varepsilon \leqslant 1$. Of course, each such digitised behaviour also belongs to $\mathbf{Z}(P)$, and hence to $\mathbf{Z}(\phi)$ by assumption. Since ϕ is closed under inverse digitisation, it follows that $(s, \aleph) \in \phi$, as required.

The second part is straightforward and is left to the reader.   □

We now come to the main verification result:

Theorem 7. *Let $P \in \mathbf{TCSP}$, and let $S, \phi \subseteq TF_{\mathbb{R}}$ be specifications with ϕ being closed under inverse digitisation. Then*

1. *$P \not\models_{\mathbb{Z}} S \Rightarrow P \not\models_{\mathbb{R}} S$*
2. *$P \models_{\mathbb{Z}} \phi \Leftrightarrow P \models_{\mathbb{R}} \phi$.*

Proof. Follows directly from the digitisation lemma and Lemma 6.   □

As the above results indicate, the class of specifications that are closed under inverse digitisation is particularly important to us. As pointed out in [13], this class includes *qualitative properties*, as well as *bounded-response* and *bounded-invariance* properties. It is closed under arbitrary intersections (which corresponds to logical conjunction). Lastly, if $P \subseteq TF_{\mathbb{R}}$ is closed under digitisation, then its complement $TF_{\mathbb{R}} - P$ is closed under inverse digitisation. As the reader may easily verify, those facts remain true in the present context.

We also note that, as implied by Lemma 6, specifications that are *not* closed under inverse digitisation cannot directly be verified exactly via digitisation methods; see, however, our discussion on time granularity below.

Unfortunately, closure under inverse digitisation is an undecidable property in Timed CSP, as the next proposition indicates. An interesting problem is to find further straightforward criteria capturing large classes of processes that are closed under inverse digitisation. This task is however made difficult by the fact that closure under inverse digitisation is not preserved by either the parallel or sequential composition operators, nor by (nondeterministic) process refinement.

Proposition 8. *The problem of deciding, given a process $Q \in \mathbf{TCSP}$, whether $\mathbb{R}[\![Q]\!]$ is closed under inverse digitisation is undecidable.*

Proof. This follows immediately from the undecidability of the halting problem for two-counter machines. Counters can be implemented in Timed CSP as processes of the form $C = up \longrightarrow (C \parallel\mskip-2mu\parallel down \longrightarrow C)$. If H is a process closed under inverse digitisation and R isn't, deciding whether $Q = H \mathbin{\text{\textcircled{\tiny 9}}} R$ itself is closed under inverse digitisation is equivalent to deciding whether H fails to be able to terminate successfully.   □

5.3   Time Granularity

Let us define an integral multiplication operation on processes: for $P \in \mathbf{TCSP}$ and $k \in \mathbb{N}^{\geqslant 1}$, define $kP \in \mathbf{TCSP}$ to be identical to P except that every delay n in P has been replaced by a delay of kn in kP. This operation can be given a straightforward inductive definition, which we omit.

We can also define integral multiplication on timed failures, by pointwise application to traces' and refusals' events. This definition, which we also omit, extends to sets of times failures in the obvious way.

For $S \subseteq TF_\mathbb{R}$ a dense-time specification, an assertion of the form $P \vDash_\mathbb{Z} S$ is only concerned with the integral behaviours of P. One might like to strengthen this requirement to half-integral behaviours of P, i.e., those behaviours which are integral multiples of $1/2$. Indeed, one can strengthen the requirement to $1/k$-th integral behaviours of P for any $k \in \mathbb{N}^{\geqslant 1}$, by considering the assertion $kP \vDash_\mathbb{Z} kS$. This, of course, simply corresponds to refining the granularity of time by a factor of k.

In practice, it is often the case that, while S may not be closed under inverse digitisation, $2S$ or kS may be. For example, if $Q = \dot{a} \overset{0}{\rhd} WAIT\ 1 \mathbin{\text{\textcircled{\tiny 9}}} Q$ is a process that may communicate a single a at any integral time and then stop, we find that $\mathbb{R}[\![Q]\!]$ is not closed under inverse digitisation, whereas $k\mathbb{R}[\![Q]\!]$ is, for any $k \geqslant 2$.

We are led to the following theorem:

Theorem 9. *Let $P \in \mathbf{TCSP}$, and let $S \subseteq TF_\mathbb{R}$ be a dense-time specification. Then, for any $k \in \mathbb{N}^{\geqslant 1}$,*

1. *$kP \vDash_\mathbb{Z} kS \Rightarrow P \vDash_\mathbb{Z} S$*
2. *$kP \nvDash_\mathbb{Z} kS \Rightarrow P \nvDash_\mathbb{R} S$*
3. *If kS is closed under inverse digitisation, then $kP \vDash_\mathbb{Z} kS \Leftrightarrow P \vDash_\mathbb{R} S$.*

Proof. This rests on the facts that $\mathbb{Z}[\![kP]\!] \supseteq k\mathbb{Z}[\![P]\!]$ and $\mathbb{R}[\![kP]\!] = k\mathbb{R}[\![P]\!]$.   □

Unfortunately, given a specification $S \subseteq TF_\mathbb{R}$, it need not be the case that kS be closed under inverse digitisation for *any* value of k; in other words, there are specifications which seemingly cannot be handled (even theoretically) within the sort of discrete frameworks we are considering.

Proposition 10. *There exists a syntactic specification $S \subseteq TF_\mathbb{R}$ such that kS is not closed under inverse digitisation, for any $k \in \mathbb{N}^{\geqslant 1}$.*

Proof. Let $Q = \dot{a} \,\|\|\, a \xrightarrow{\;0\;} (\dot{a} \mathrel{\rhd} STOP)$, and set $S = \mathbb{R}[\![Q]\!]$. Note that $kS = S$ for any $k \in \mathbb{N}^{\geqslant 1}$. Let $s = \langle (0.1, a), (0.2, a), (0.3, a) \rangle$. Observe that $(s, \emptyset) \notin S$, even though every digitisation of $(s, \emptyset)$ clearly belongs to S. $\qquad\square$

However, we have the following result:

Theorem 11. *Let $S \subseteq TF_\mathbb{R}$ be a syntactic specification, and let $P \in \mathbf{TCSP}$ be a process. Suppose that $kP \vDash_\mathbb{Z} kS$ for arbitrarily large values of k. Then $P \vDash_\mathbb{R} S$.*

We remark that the hypothesis that S is syntactic is necessary.

Proof. The proof is somewhat intricate and requires careful analysis. Details can be found in [18]. $\qquad\square$

5.4 Full Abstraction

Definition 12. *Let $P, Q \in \mathbf{TCSP}$ be two processes. We say that P and Q are* **equivalent**, *written $P \simeq Q$, if for all specifications $\phi \subseteq TF_\mathbb{R}$ that are closed under inverse digitisation, $P \vDash_\mathbb{R} \phi \Leftrightarrow Q \vDash_\mathbb{R} \phi$.*

Our full abstraction result now reads:

Theorem 13. *For any processes $P, Q \in \mathbf{TCSP}$, $P \simeq Q \Leftrightarrow \mathbb{Z}[\![P]\!] = \mathbb{Z}[\![Q]\!]$.*

Proof. The right-to-left implication follows directly from Theorem 7.

For the other direction, assume without loss of generality that there exists an integral timed failure $(s, \aleph) \in \mathbb{Z}[\![P]\!]$ such that $(s, \aleph) \notin \mathbb{Z}[\![Q]\!]$. We must show that $P \not\simeq Q$.

Let $\phi \subseteq TF_\mathbb{R}$ be the least specification closed under inverse digitisation that contains $\mathbb{Z}[\![Q]\!]$. ϕ can be constructed by adding all the non-integral timed failures to $\mathbb{Z}[\![Q]\!]$ that are required by inverse digitisation. Note that $\mathbf{Z}(\phi) = \mathbb{Z}[\![Q]\!]$. Since $(s, \aleph)$ is an integral behaviour and $(s, \aleph) \notin \mathbb{Z}[\![Q]\!]$, we have $(s, \aleph) \notin \phi$.

Since ϕ is closed under inverse digitisation and $Q \vDash_\mathbb{Z} \phi$, Theorem 7 tells us that $Q \vDash_\mathbb{R} \phi$. However $P \not\vDash_\mathbb{R} \phi$, since $(s, \aleph) \in \mathbb{Z}[\![P]\!] \subseteq \mathbb{R}[\![P]\!]$, yet $(s, \aleph) \notin \phi$. Thus $P \not\simeq Q$, as required. $\qquad\square$

5.5 Example: Railway Level Crossing

We now present a small verification case study based on a simplified version of the well-known railway level crossing problem [9].[4]

We describe in Timed CSP a closed system made up of four distinct components: trains, travelling at bounded speeds on a stretch of rail incorporating a level crossing; cars, able to cross the tracks in a bounded amount of time; a traffic light, meant to signal cars not to attempt crossing the railway when a train is nearby; and a monitor, whose rôle is to signal that a collision has happened.

---

[4] See also [23] for an interesting alternative CSP-based discrete-time approach to this example.

For simplicity we assume that only at most one train and one car are present at any one time within the system.

Trains are modelled via the process $TRAIN$: in its initial state, this process assumes that there are no trains on the tracks, and offers the event $train.in$. This event represents a sensor signal which indicates that an incoming train is at least 60 s away from the crossing. When the train reaches the crossing, the event $train.on$ is triggered, and as soon as the train is a safe distance past the crossing, the event $train.out$ registers. We assume that the train takes at least 20 s to cross the crossing, and that the process $TRAIN$ returns to its initial state as soon as the event $train.out$ is received.

The process CAR models the cars: initially there are no cars on the crossing, and CAR offers the event $car.on$, subject to synchronisation with the traffic light, indicating that a car is just about to drive onto the crossing. The car stays in this vulnerable position for at most 10 s, sending out the event $car.out$ as soon as it is safely on the other side. For simplicity we will make the conservative assumption that the time taken to cross the tracks is actually exactly 10 s. In order to ensure that the car does step out immediately after this time, however, we will later on hide the event $car.out$, to enforce its urgency. A new car is allowed on the crossing as soon as the car ahead has left it.

The traffic light is green to start with, modelled by the process $GREEN$, and becomes red as soon as a train ($train.in$) is detected. While it is red, the event $car.on$ is disabled (modelling the assumption that any car not yet on the crossing obeys the red light), and is only re-enabled after $train.out$ has registered.

A collision will occur if the train enters the crossing while a car is already there, or vice-versa; in either case this will cause the monitoring process $WATCH$ to send out the catastrophic event $crash$.

The entire level crossing system $CROSSING$ is modelled as the parallel composition of these four components, with $car.out$ hidden.

Translating this description into Timed CSP, we get:

$$TRAIN = train.in \xrightarrow{60} train.on \xrightarrow{20} train.out \longrightarrow TRAIN$$

$$CAR = car.on \xrightarrow{10} car.out \longrightarrow CAR$$

$$GREEN = (train.in \longrightarrow RED) \,\square\, (car.on \longrightarrow GREEN)$$

$$RED = train.out \longrightarrow GREEN$$

$$WATCH = (train.on \longrightarrow WATCH_{train}) \,\square\, (car.on \longrightarrow WATCH_{car})$$

$$WATCH_{train} = (car.on \longrightarrow crash \longrightarrow STOP) \,\square\, (train.out \longrightarrow WATCH)$$

$$WATCH_{car} = (train.on \longrightarrow crash \longrightarrow STOP) \,\square\, (car.out \longrightarrow WATCH)$$

$$CROSSING = ((TRAIN \underset{A}{\parallel} (GREEN \underset{B}{\parallel} CAR)) \underset{C}{\parallel} WATCH) \setminus \{car.out\}$$

where $A = \{train.in, train.out\}$, $B = \{car.on\}$, and $C = \{train.on, car.on, train.out, car.out\}$.

We would now like to prove that this system is 'safe', i.e., that no collision can ever occur. To this end, let us define the specification $SAFE$ to be: 'The event *crash* is never witnessed'; in other words, $SAFE = \{(s, \aleph) \in TF_{\mathbb{R}} \mid crash \notin \sigma(s)\}$. We aim to establish that $CROSSING \vDash_{\mathbb{R}} SAFE$.

$SAFE$ is a qualitative behavioural timed trace specification, and is therefore closed under inverse digitisation (as can also be seen by inspection). It follows from Theorem 7 that $CROSSING \vDash_{\mathbb{Z}} SAFE \Leftrightarrow CROSSING \vDash_{\mathbb{R}} SAFE$.

For model checking purposes, recall that, as claimed in Sect. 4, $\mathbf{Z}(SAFE) = \mathbf{Z}[\![CHAOS_{\Sigma - \{crash\}}]\!]$, where $\Sigma = \{train.in, train.on, train.out, car.on, car.out, crash\}$ represents $CROSSING$'s alphabet. The question therefore reduces to deciding whether $CROSSING \vDash_{\mathbb{Z}} CHAOS_{\Sigma - \{crash\}}$ holds.

This can be encoded and checked as a trace refinement using the model checker FDR. A special event *tock* is introduced to represent the passage of one time unit. Most of the CSP operators must be modified to consistently handle the passage of time; this is achieved in most cases via simple coding tricks. The most significant difficulty is enforcing τ-urgency, the requirement that time cannot pass while hidden events are on offer. This is taken care of by invoking the *priority* operator of FDR which simply disables *tock*-transitions whenever τ-transitions are pending.

Since both $CROSSING$ and $CHAOS_{\Sigma - \{crash\}}$ are finite state (as they only comprise *tail recursions*), the FDR check is guaranteed to terminate. Indeed, it did confirm that $CROSSING \vDash_{\mathbb{R}} SAFE$, as surmised.

6   Conclusion

The main results of this paper are that Timed CSP processes are closed under digitisation, and as a consequence that specifications closed under inverse digitisation can be verified exactly using an integral behaviour model. This yields a model checking algorithm, implementable on FDR, which however requires that specifications be expressed as syntactic processes. As our case study suggests, this should not turn out to be a serious impediment in practice. Another important result is that integral behaviours are fully abstract with respect to specifications closed under inverse digitisation, and therefore that checks performed by our model checking algorithm are not only sufficient, but also necessary, in general, for verification purposes.

For reasons of space, we have presented our work exclusively within a denotational context. As explained in the introduction, our results apply equally well to the operational setting (cf. [18]). Our restriction to *behavioural* specifications, on the other hand, is arguably much more difficult to lift. We do note, however, that many important non-behavioural specifications, such as *reachability* requirements, can perfectly well be handled within our framework.

Our focus on Timed CSP was convenient, but not necessary: the results presented here are reasonably robust and should carry over without great difficulty to other settings, whether process algebraic or transition-systems-based. We refer the reader to [18] for a more detailed discussion on the matter.

The question of the efficiency of the algorithm presented here has only been briefly discussed. As with every other approach to the subject of automated verification, trade-offs are inevitable. We expect our algorithm to prove reasonably efficient in cases where all delays are relatively small, or at least of similar sizes. This is a topic for further research.

The question of full abstraction is interesting and does not seem to have been extensively studied, whether in relation to algorithmic efficiency or not. The matter resurfaces as soon as we vary the basic parameters under consideration (the process algebra, the verification framework, the class of allowable specifications). For instance, are region graphs fully abstract with respect to TCTL formulas? This, too, seems an interesting starting point for further work.

Acknowledgements. I am grateful to Mike Reed, Bill Roscoe, Steve Schneider, James Worrell, Mike Mislove, Michael Goldsmith, and Formal Systems for fruitful discussions and support with FDR. Thanks are also due to the anonymous referees for their careful review and insightful suggestions.

References

[1] R. Alur, C. Courcoubetis, and D. Dill. Model-checking for real-time systems. In *Proceedings of the Fifth Annual Symposium on Logic in Computer Science (LICS 90)*, pages 414–425. IEEE Computer Society Press, 1990.

[2] R. Alur, C. Courcoubetis, and D. Dill. Model-checking in dense real-time. *Information and Computation*, 104(1):2–34, 1993.

[3] R. Alur and D. Dill. A theory of timed automata. *Theoretical Computer Science*, 126:183–235, 1994.

[4] R. Alur and T. A. Henzinger. Real-time logics: Complexity and expressiveness. *Information and Computation*, 104(1):35–77, 1993.

[5] R. Alur and T. A. Henzinger. A really temporal logic. *Journal of the ACM*, 41(1):181–204, 1994.

[6] R. Alur and R. P. Kurshan. Timing analysis in COSPAN. In *Proceedings of Hybrid Systems III*, volume 1066, pages 220–231. Springer LNCS, 1996.

[7] J. Bengtsson, K. G. Larsen, F. Larsen, P. Pettersson, and W. Yi. UPPAAL: A tool-suite for automatic verification of real-time systems. In *Proceedings of Hybrid Systems III*, volume 1066, pages 232–243. Springer LNCS, 1996.

[8] C. Daws, A. Olivero, S. Tripakis, and S. Yovine. The tool KRONOS. In *Proceedings of Hybrid Systems III*, volume 1066, pages 208–219. Springer LNCS, 1996.

[9] C. L. Heitmeyer, R. D. Jeffords, and B. G. Labaw. A benchmark for comparing different approaches for specifying and verifying real-time systems. In *Proceedings of the Tenth International Workshop on Real-Time Operating Systems and Software*, 1993.

[10] T. A. Henzinger, P.-H. Ho, and H. Wong-Toi. HyTECH: A model checker for hybrid systems. In *Proceedings of the Ninth International Conference on Computer-Aided Verification (CAV 97)*, volume 1254, pages 460–463. Springer LNCS, 1997.

[11] T. A. Henzinger and O. Kupferman. From quantity to quality. In *Proceedings of the First International Workshop on Hybrid and Real-time Systems (HART 97)*, volume 1201, pages 48–62. Springer LNCS, 1997.

[12] T. A. Henzinger, O. Kupferman, and M. Y. Vardi. A space-efficient on-the-fly algorithm for real-time model checking. In *Proceedings of the Seventh International Conference on Concurrency Theory (CONCUR 96)*, volume 1119, pages 514–529. Springer LNCS, 1996.

[13] T. A. Henzinger, Z. Manna, and A. Pnueli. What good are digital clocks? In *Proceedings of the Nineteenth International Colloquium on Automata, Languages, and Programming (ICALP 92)*, volume 623, pages 545–558. Springer LNCS, 1992.

[14] T. A. Henzinger, X. Nicollin, J. Sifakis, and S. Yovine. Symbolic model checking for real-time systems. *Information and Computation*, 111(2):193–244, 1994.

[15] D. M. Jackson. *Logical Verification of Reactive Software Systems*. PhD thesis, Oxford University, 1992.

[16] F. Laroussinie and K. G. Larsen. Compositional model checking of real time systems. In *Proceedings of the Sixth International Conference on Concurrency Theory (CONCUR 95)*, volume 962, pages 27–41. Springer LNCS, 1995.

[17] J. Ouaknine. Specification as refinement in timed systems. In preparation.

[18] J. Ouaknine. *Discrete Analysis of Continuous Behaviour in Real-Time Concurrent Systems*. PhD thesis, Oxford University, 2001. Technical report PRG-RR-01-06.

[19] J. Ouaknine and G. M. Reed. Model-checking temporal behaviour in CSP. In *Proceedings of the 1999 International Conference on Parallel and Distributed Processing Techniques and Applications (PDPTA 99)*. CSREA Press, 1999.

[20] G. M. Reed. *A Mathematical Theory for Real-Time Distributed Computing*. PhD thesis, Oxford University, 1988.

[21] G. M. Reed and A. W. Roscoe. The timed failures-stability model for CSP. *Theoretical Computer Science*, 211:85–127, 1999.

[22] G. M. Reed, A. W. Roscoe, and S. A. Schneider. CSP and timewise refinement. In *Proceedings of the Fourth BCS-FACS Refinement Workshop*, Cambridge, 1991. Springer WIC.

[23] A. W. Roscoe. *The Theory and Practice of Concurrency*. Prentice-Hall International, London, 1997.

[24] S. A. Schneider. *Correctness and Communication in Real-Time Systems*. PhD thesis, Oxford University, 1989.

[25] S. A. Schneider. An operational semantics for Timed CSP. *Information and Computation*, 116:193–213, 1995.

[26] S. A. Schneider. Timewise refinement for communicating processes. *Science of Computer Programming*, 28:43–90, 1997.

[27] S. A. Schneider. *Concurrent and Real Time Systems: the CSP approach*. John Wiley, 2000.

[28] O. V. Sokolsky and S. A. Smolka. Local model checking for real time systems. In *Proceedings of the Seventh International Conference on Computer-Aided Verification (CAV 95)*, volume 939, pages 211–224. Springer LNCS, 1995.

[29] Y. Yu, P. Manolios, and L. Lamport. Model checking TLA$^+$ specifications. In *Proceedings of the Tenth Advanced Research Working Conference on Correct Hardware Design and Verification Methods (CHARME 99)*, volume 1703, pages 54–66. Springer LNCS, 1999.

Probabilistic Symbolic Model Checking with PRISM: A Hybrid Approach*

Marta Kwiatkowska, Gethin Norman, and David Parker

School of Computer Science, University of Birmingham,
Birmingham B15 2TT, United Kingdom
{mzk,gxn,dxp}@cs.bham.ac.uk

Abstract. In this paper we introduce PRISM, a probabilistic model checker, and describe the efficient symbolic techniques we have developed during its implementation. PRISM is a tool for analysing probabilistic systems. It supports three models: discrete-time Markov chains, continuous-time Markov chains and Markov decision processes. Analysis is performed through model checking specifications in the probabilistic temporal logics PCTL and CSL. Motivated by the success of model checkers such as SMV, which use BDDs (binary decision diagrams), we have developed an implementation of PCTL and CSL model checking based on MTBDDs (multi-terminal BDDs) and BDDs. Existing work in this direction has been hindered by the generally poor performance of MTBDD-based numerical computation, which is often substantially slower than explicit methods using sparse matrices. We present a novel hybrid technique which combines aspects of symbolic and explicit approaches to overcome these performance problems. For typical examples, we achieve orders of magnitude speed-up compared to MTBDDs and are able to almost match the speed of sparse matrices whilst maintaining considerable space savings.

1 Introduction

In the design and analysis of software and hardware systems it is often desirable or even necessary to include probabilistic aspects of a system's behaviour. Examples include representing unreliable or unpredictable behaviour in fault-tolerant systems; deriving efficient algorithms by using electronic coin flipping in decision making; and modelling the arrivals and departures of calls in a wireless cell.

Probabilistic model checking refers to a range of techniques for calculating the likelihood of the occurrence of certain events during the execution of systems which exhibit such behaviour. One first constructs a probabilistic model of the system. Properties such as "shutdown occurs with probability 0.01 or less" and "the video frame will be delivered within 5ms with probability 0.97 or greater" can be expressed in probabilistic temporal logics. Model checking algorithms

---

* Supported in part by EPSRC grant GR/M04617 and MathFIT studentship for David Parker.

J.-P. Katoen and P. Stevens (Eds.): TACAS 2002, LNCS 2280, pp. 52–66, 2002.

have been developed which then automatically verify whether the model satisfies these properties.

Motivated by the success of symbolic model checkers, such as SMV [28] which use BDDs (binary decision diagrams) [11], we have developed a symbolic *probabilistic* model checker. In the non-probabilistic setting, model checking involves analysing properties of state transition systems and the manipulation of sets of states. Both these entities can be represented naturally as BDDs, often very compactly [13]. In the probabilistic case, since probability transition matrices and probability vectors are required, BDDs alone are not sufficient, and hence we also use MTBDDs (multi-terminal binary decision diagrams) [17,3], a natural extension of BDDs for representing real-valued functions.

Symbolic probabilistic model checking has been considered by a number of people [5,21,4,26,19,23,7,25,27] and it has been shown that it is feasible to use MTBDDs to construct and compute the reachable state space of extremely large, structured, probabilistic models. In these cases, it is often also possible to verify *qualitative* properties, where model checking reduces to reachability-based analysis. For example, in [19], systems with over 10^{30} states have been verified.

Model checking *quantitative* properties, on the other hand, involves numerical computation. In some cases, such as in [27], MTBDDs have been very successful, being applied to systems with over 10^{10} states. Often, however, it turns out that such computation is slow or infeasible. By way of comparison, we have also implemented the equivalent numerical computation routines explicitly, using sparse matrices. In these cases, we find that sparse matrices are orders of magnitude faster. Here, we present a novel hybrid approach which uses extensions of the MTBDD data structure and borrows ideas from the sparse matrix techniques to overcome these performance problems. We include experimental data which demonstrates that, using this hybrid approach, we can achieve speeds which are orders of magnitude faster than MTBDDs, and in fact almost match the speed of sparse matrices, whilst maintaining considerable space savings.

The outline of this paper is as follows. Section 2 gives an overview of probabilistic model checking, introducing the probabilistic models and temporal logics we consider. In Section 3, we describe our tool, PRISM, which implements this model checking. We then move on to discuss the implementation. Section 4 introduces the MTBDD data structure and explains how it is used to represent and analyse probabilistic models. We identify a number of performance problems in this implementation and, in Section 5, describe how we overcome these limitations. In Section 6, we present experimental results and analyse the success of our technique. Section 7 concludes the paper.

2   Probabilistic Model Checking

In this section we briefly summarise the three probabilistic models and two temporal logics that PRISM supports. The simplest probabilistic model is the *discrete-time Markov chain* (DTMC), which specifies the probability $\mathbf{P}(s, s')$ of making a transition from state s to some target state s', where the probabilities of reaching the target states from a given state must sum up to 1, i.e.

$\sum_{s'} \mathbf{P}(s, s') = 1$. *Markov decision processes* (MDPs) extend DTMCs by allowing both probabilistic and non-deterministic behaviour. More formally, in any state there is a non-deterministic choice between a number of discrete probability distributions over states. Non-determinism enables the modelling of asynchronous parallel composition of probabilistic systems, and permits the under-specification of certain aspects of a system. A *continuous-time Markov chain* (CTMC), on the other hand, specifies the rates $\mathbf{R}(s, s')$ of making a transition from state s to s', with the interpretation that the probability of moving from s to s' within t time units (for positive real valued t) is $1 - e^{-\mathbf{R}(s,s')\cdot t}$.

Probabilistic specification formalisms include PCTL [20,10,8], a probabilistic extension of the temporal logic CTL applicable in the context of MDPs and DTMCs, and the logic CSL [7], a specification language for CTMCs based on CTL and PCTL.

PCTL allows us to express properties of the form "under any scheduling of processes, the probability that event A occurs is at least p (at most p)". By way of illustration, we consider the asynchronous randomized leader election protocol of Itai and Rodeh [24] which gives rise to an MDP. In this algorithm, the processors of an asynchronous ring make random choices based on coin tosses in an attempt to elect a leader. We use the atomic proposition *leader* to label states in which a leader has been elected. Examples of properties we would wish to verify can be expressed in PCTL as follows:

- $\mathcal{P}_{\geq 1}[\lozenge \, leader]$ - "under any fair scheduling, a leader is eventually elected with probability 1".
- $\mathcal{P}_{\leq 0.5}[\lozenge^{\leq k} \, leader]$ - "under any fair scheduling, the probability of electing a leader within k discrete time steps is at most 0.5".

The specification language CSL includes the means to express both transient and steady-state performance measures of CTMCs. Transient properties describe the system at a fixed real-valued time instant t, whereas steady-state properties refer to the behaviour of a system in the "long run". For example, consider a queueing system where the atomic proposition *full* labels states where the queue is full. CSL then allows us to express properties such as:

- $\mathcal{P}_{\leq 0.01}[\lozenge^{\leq t} \, full]$ - "the probability that the queue becomes full within t time units is at most 0.01"
- $\mathcal{S}_{\geq 0.98}[\neg full]$ - "in the long run, the chance that the queue is not full is at least 0.98".

Model checking algorithms for PCTL have been introduced in [20,10] and extended in [8,4] to include fairness. An algorithm for CSL was first proposed in [7] and has since been improved in [6,25]. The model checking algorithms for both logics reduce to a combination of reachability-based computation (manipulation of sets of states) and numerical computation. The former corresponds to finding all those states that satisfy the formula under study with probability exactly 0 or 1. The latter corresponds to calculating the probabilities for the remaining states. For DTMCs, this entails solution of a linear equation system, for MDPs, solving a linear optimisation problem, and for CTMCs, either solution of a linear equation system or a standard technique known as uniformisation.

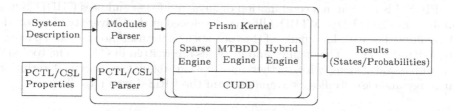

Fig. 1. PRISM System Architecture

These numerical problems are typically too large for the application of direct methods, and instead iterative techniques which approximate the solution up to some specified accuracy are used.

3   The Tool

PRISM is a tool developed at the University of Birmingham which supports the model checking described in the previous section. The tool takes as input a description of a system written in PRISM's system description language, a probabilistic variant of Reactive Modules [1]. It first constructs the model from this description and computes the set of reachable states. PRISM accepts specifications in either the logic PCTL or CSL depending on the model type. It then performs model checking to determine which states of the system satisfy each specification. All reachability-based computation is performed using BDDs. For numerical analysis, however, there is a choice of three engines: one using pure MTBDDs, one based on conventional sparse matrices, and a third using the hybrid approach we present in this paper. Figure 1 shows the structure of the tool and Figure 2 shows a screen-shot of the graphical user interface.

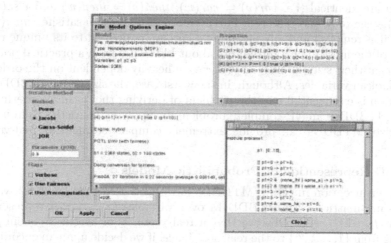

Fig. 2. The PRISM Graphical User Interface

PRISM is written in a combination of Java and C++ and uses CUDD [32], a publicly available BDD/MTBDD library developed at the University of Colorado at Boulder. The high-level parts of the tool, such as the user interface and parsers, are written in Java. The engines and libraries are written in C++. The tool and its source code, along with further information about the system description language and case studies, is available from the PRISM web page [31].

4 An MTBDD Implementation

We now describe the implementation of the tool. The fundamental data structures in PRISM are MTBDDs and BDDs. MTBDDs can be used to represent all three of the supported models: DTMCs, MDPs and CTMCs. Furthermore, all algorithms for the construction and analysis of these models can be implemented using these data structures. In this section, we summarise how this is done and discuss its performance.

Introduction to MTBDDs

Let $x_1 < \cdots < x_n$ be a set of distinct, totally ordered, Boolean variables. An MTBDD M over $(x_1, \ldots, x_n)$ is a rooted, directed acyclic graph with vertex set $V = V_n \cup V_t$ partitioned into *non-terminal* and *terminal* vertices. A non-terminal vertex $v \in V_n$ is labelled by a variable $var(v) \in \{x_1, \ldots, x_n\}$ and has two children $then(v), else(v) \in V$. A terminal vertex $v \in V_t$ is labelled by a real number $val(v)$.

We impose the Boolean variable ordering $<$ onto the graph by requiring that a child w of a non-terminal vertex v is either terminal or is non-terminal and satisfies $var(v) < var(w)$. The MTBDD represents a function $f_M(x_1, \ldots, x_n) : \mathbb{B}^n \to \mathbb{R}$. The value of $f_M(x_1, \ldots, x_n)$ is determined by traversing M from the root vertex, following the edge from vertex v to $then(v)$ or $else(v)$ if $var(v)$ is 1 or 0 respectively. Note that a BDD is merely an MTBDD with the restriction that the labels on terminal vertices can only be 1 or 0.

MTBDDs are efficient because they are stored in reduced form. If vertices v and w are identical (i.e. $var(v) = var(w)$, $then(v) = then(w)$ and $else(v) = else(w)$), then only one is stored. Furthermore, if a vertex v satisifes $then(v) = else(v)$, it is removed and any incoming edges are redirected to its unique child.

One of the most important factors about MTBDDs from a practical point of view is that their size (number of vertices) is heavily dependent on the ordering of the Boolean variables. Although, in the worst case, the size of an MTBDD representation is exponential and the problem of deriving the optimal ordering for a given MTBDD is an NP-complete problem, by applying heuristics to minimise graph size, MTBDDs can provide extremely compact storage for real-valued functions.

MTBDD Represention of Probabilistic Models

From their inception in [17,3], MTBDDs have been used to encode real-valued vectors and matrices. An MTBDD M over variables $(x_1, \ldots, x_n)$ represents a function $f_M : \mathbb{B}^n \to \mathbb{R}$. Observe that a real vector **v** of length 2^n is simply a mapping from $\{1, \ldots, 2^n\}$ to the reals $\mathbb{R}$. Hence, if we decide upon an encoding of

$\{1, \ldots, 2^n\}$ in terms of $\{x_1, \ldots, x_n\}$ (for example the standard binary encoding), then an MTBDD M can represent **v**.

In a similar fashion, we can consider a square matrix **M** of size 2^n by 2^n to be a mapping from $\{1, \ldots, 2^n\} \times \{1, \ldots, 2^n\}$ to $\mathbb{R}$. Taking Boolean variables $\{x_1, \ldots, x_n\}$ to range over row indices and $\{y_1, \ldots, y_n\}$ to range over column indices, we can represent **M** by an MTBDD over $\{x_1, \ldots, x_n, y_1, \ldots, y_n\}$. DTMCs and CTMCs are described by such matrices, and hence are also straightforward to represent as MTBDDs. The case for MDPs is more complex since we need to encode the non-deterministic choices. If the maximum number of non-deterministic choices in any state is bounded by 2^k for some integer k, we can view the MDP as a function from $\{1, \ldots, 2^k\} \times \{1, \ldots, 2^n\} \times \{1, \ldots, 2^n\}$ to $\mathbb{R}$. By adding k extra Boolean variables to encode this third index, we can represent the MDP as an MTBDD.

Figure 3 shows an example of a CTMC and its rate matrix. The CTMC includes one state which is unreachable. This is explained in Section 5. Figure 4 gives the MTBDD which represents this CTMC and a table explaining its construction. For clarity, in our notation for MTBDDs, we omit edges which lead directly to the zero terminal vertex.

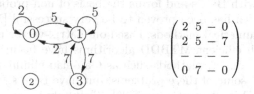

$$\begin{pmatrix} 2 & 5 & - & 0 \\ 2 & 5 & - & 7 \\ - & - & - & - \\ 0 & 7 & - & 0 \end{pmatrix}$$

Fig. 3. A CTMC and its rate matrix

Transition	x_1 x_2	y_1 y_2	x_1 y_1 x_2 y_2	R
$0 \xrightarrow{2} 0$	0 0	0 0	0 0 0 0	2
$0 \xrightarrow{5} 1$	0 0	0 1	0 0 0 1	5
$1 \xrightarrow{2} 0$	0 1	0 0	0 0 1 0	2
$1 \xrightarrow{5} 1$	0 1	0 1	0 0 1 1	5
$1 \xrightarrow{7} 3$	0 1	1 1	0 1 1 1	7
$3 \xrightarrow{7} 1$	1 1	0 1	1 0 1 1	7

Fig. 4. An MTBDD representing the CTMC in Figure 3

Observe that, in Figure 4, row and column variables are ordered alternately. This is one of the most common variable ordering heuristics to minimise MTBDD size. To achieve compact MTBDD representations of probabilistic systems, however, we must also consider the actual encoding of row and column indices to Boolean variables. A well known rule of thumb is to try and preserve structure in the entity being represented [23]. In practice, this can be accomplished by performing a direct translation from a high-level description of the model (in our case the PRISM system description language) to MTBDDs. We presented such a scheme in [19] which is not only fast but can lead to a very compact encoding of probabilistic systems. The resulting variable ordering encodes unreachable states, as well as reachable states, and hence reachability analysis (via a simple BDD fixpoint calculation) must be performed to identify them.

Our experimental data is presented in Section 6. For reasons of space we only include statistics for two typical examples: firstly, an MDP model of the coin protocol from Aspnes and Herlihy's randomized consensus algorithm [2], parameterised by N (the number of processes) and an additional parameter K fixed at 4; secondly, a CTMC model of a Kanban manufacturing system [16] parameterised by N (the number of pallets in the system). Figure 8 gives the memory requirements for storing these models. Compare the 'MTBDD' and 'Sparse' columns: significant savings in memory can be achieved using the symbolic scheme described above over an explicit storage method. For other examples which demonstrate this result, see the PRISM web page [31].

Probabilistic Model Checking with MTBDDs

We have implemented the entire model checking procedure for PCTL and CSL in MTBDDs and BDDs. As we saw in Section 2, essentially this reduces to a combination of reachability-based computation and numerical calculation. The former can be performed with BDDs and forms the basis of non-probabilistic symbolic model checking which has been proven to be very successful [13,28]. The latter involves iterative numerical methods, based on matrix-vector multiplication, an operation for which efficient MTBDD algorithms have been introduced [3,17]. In fact, alternative, direct, methods such as Gaussian elimination and Simplex could be applied to some of these problems, but have been shown to be unsuitable for an MTBDD implementation [3,26]. They rely on modifying the model representation through operations on individual rows, columns or elements. This is not only slow, but leads to a loss in regularity and a subsequent explosion in MTBDD size.

The results of this implementation in MTBDDs can be summarised as follows. There is a clear distinction between the two different aspects of model checking. Reachability-based computation, which is sufficient for model checking qualitative properties, can be implemented efficiently with BDDs, as is shown in [19,27]. Numerical computation, which is required for checking of quantitative properties, is more unpredictable. This is the problem we focus on here.

We have found a number of case studies for which MTBBDs outperform explicit techniques on numerical computation. One such example is the coin protocol, introduced previously. We include results for this model in the top half of Figure 9. Compare the columns for 'MTBDD' and 'Sparse': it would be impossible to even store the sparse matrix for the larger examples, assuming a reasonable amount of memory. We have found this pattern to hold for several of the other MDP case studies we have considered. Other examples which illustrate this can be found on the PRISM web site [31], and include a Byzantine agreement protocol and the IEEE 1394 FireWire root contention protocol.

For a second class of models, namely CTMCs, we find that the symbolic implementation of numerical iterative methods is far from efficient. Despite a compact MTBDD representation of the model, the process is generally very slow or infeasible. This inefficiency is caused by the MTBDD representation of the iteration vectors becoming too large. For vectors to be represented compactly by MTBDDs the main requirement is a limited number of distinct elements. However, in general, when performing numerical analysis, the iteration vector quickly acquires almost as many distinct values as there are states in the system under study. Figure 9 shows the contrast in performance of MTBDDs between the Kanban CTMC and the coin protocol MDP. The sparse matrix based implementation is much faster.

5   A Hybrid Approach

We now present a method to overcome the inefficiencies with MTBDDs outlined in the previous section. Recall that sparse matrix techniques can yield extremely fast numerical computation. Since the iteration vector is stored in a full array, it remains a constant size. A single matrix-vector multiplication is carried out by traversing the sparse matrix and extracting all the non-zero entries, each of which is needed exactly once to compute the new iteration vector. Unfortunately, since the probabilistic model is also stored explicitly, application to large examples is often limited by memory constraints.

The approach taken here is to a use a hybrid of the two techniques: MTBDDs and sparse matrices. We store the transition matrix in an MTBDD-like data structure but use a full array for the iteration vector. We can then perform matrix-vector multiplication, and hence iterative methods, using these two data structures. The key difference in this hybrid approach is that we need to extract the non-zero matrix entries from an MTBDD rather than a sparse matrix. For clarity, this presentation focuses on the case of CTMCs, where we solve a linear equation system by iterative methods to compute the steady-state probabilities. We have also applied these techniques to DTMC and MDP models.

If we restrict ourselves to certain iterative methods, namely Power, Jacobi and JOR, then the matrix entries can be extracted in any order to perform an iteration. This means that we can can proceed via a recursive traversal of the MTBDD: it does not that matter that this will enumerate the entries in an essentially random order, rather than row-by-row (or column-by-column) as with a sparse matrix.

Since the matrix indices are encoded with the standard binary representation of integers, it is trivial to keep track of the row and column index during traversal by noting whether a *then* or *else* edge is taken at each point and summing the appropriate powers of 2. Unfortunately, there are a number of problems with this naive approach. To resolve these, we make a number of modifications to the MTBDD data structure.

Modifying the MTBDD Data Structure

First, recall from Section 4, that to get an efficient MTBDD representation of our transition matrix, it must contain unreachable states. Performing matrix-vector multiplication as just described on such an MTBDD would require the vector array to store entries for all states, including those that are unreachable. The number of unreachable states is potentially very large, in some cases orders of magnitude larger than the reachable portion. This puts unacceptable limits on the size of problem which we can handle.

The solution we adopt is to augment the MTBDD with vertex labels: integer offsets which can be used to compute the actual indices of the matrix elements (in terms of reachable states only) during our recursive traversal. Figure 5 illustrates this idea on the example from Section 4, which included an unreachable state. On the left is the modified MTBDD representing the transition matrix $\mathbf{R}$ of the CTMC. The table on the right explains how the traversal process works. Each row corresponds to a single matrix entry (transition). The first five columns describe the path taken through the MTBDD. The next four columns give the vertex offsets along this path. The last column gives the resulting matrix entry. In Figure 6, we give the actual traversal algorithm. This would be called as follows: TRAVERSEREC($root$, 0, 0), where $root$ is the top-level vertex in the MTBDD.

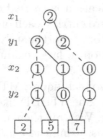

Path					Offsets				Transition
x_1	y_1	x_2	y_2	$\mathbf{R}$	x_1	y_1	x_2	y_2	
0	0	0	0	2	-	-	-	-	$0 \xrightarrow{2} 0$
0	0	0	1	5	-	-	-	1	$0 \xrightarrow{5} 1$
0	0	1	0	2	-	-	1	-	$1 \xrightarrow{2} 0$
0	0	1	1	5	-	-	1	1	$1 \xrightarrow{5} 1$
0	1	1	1	7	-	2	1	0	$1 \xrightarrow{7} 2$
1	0	1	1	7	2	-	0	1	$2 \xrightarrow{7} 1$

Fig. 5. The modified MTBDD representing the CTMC in Figure 5

The key idea is that indices are computed by summing offsets. A vertex's offset is only added when leaving the *then* edge of that vertex. Note that row and column indices are computed independently, rows from offsets on x_i vertices, and columns from offsets on y_i vertices. As an example, consider the last line of the table. We take the path $1, 0, 1, 1$ through the MTBDD which leads to the 7 terminal vertex. We only use the offsets at levels x_1, x_2 and y_2 where we exited via *then* edges. The row index is $2 + 0 = 2$, the column index is 1 and we obtain the matrix entry $(2, 1) = 7$. Note that references to state 3 in Figure 4 have changed to state 2 in Figure 5, since we only have three *reachable* states.

There are two further points to consider about the conversion of the MTBDD (Figure 4) to its new form (Figure 5). First, note that some vertices in an MTBDD can be reached along several different paths. These shared vertices correspond to repeated sub-matrices in the overall matrix. Consider the matrix in Figure 3 and its MTBDD representation in Figure 4. The bottom-left and top-right quadrants of the matrix are identical (since rows and columns of unreachable states are filled with zeros). This is reflected by the fact that the x_2 vertex in the MTBDD has two incoming edges. The two identical sub-matrices do not, however, share the same pattern of reachable states. This means that there is a potential clash as to which offset should label the vertex.

We resolve this by adding extra copies of the vertex where necessary, labelled with different offsets. Note the additional two vertices on the right hand side in

```
TRAVERSEREC(v, row, col)
    if (v is a non-zero terminal vertex) then
        found matrix element (row, col) = val(v)
    elseif (v is a row vertex) then
        TRAVERSEREC(else(v), row, col)
        TRAVERSEREC(then(v), row + offset(v), col)
    elseif (v is a row vertex) then
        TRAVERSEREC(else(v), row, col)
        TRAVERSEREC(then(v), row, col + offset(v))
    endif
end
```

Fig. 6. Hybrid Traversal Algorithm

Figure 5. Effectively, we have modified the condition under which two MTBDD vertices are merged, requiring not only that are they are on the same level and have identical children, but also that they have the same offset label. It should be noted here that we transform the MTBBD once, use it for as many iterations are required, and then discard it. Hence, we only need to be able to traverse the data structure, not manipulate it in any way.

The second point to make about the conversion involves skipped levels. In an MTBDD, if a vertex has identical children, it is omitted to save space. This causes potential problems, because we must be careful to detect this during traversal. In fact, the solution we adopt is to perform this check only once, during the initial conversion, and replace skips with extra vertices. This allows us to ignore the issue entirely during traversal and makes the process faster. There is an example of this in Figure 5 – note the extra x_2 vertex on the left hand side. The exception to this rule is that we do allow edges to skip from any vertex directly to the zero terminal vertex, since we are only interested in the non-zero entries.

Optimising the Approach

We can optimise our method considerably via a form of caching. MTBDDs exploit structure in the model being analysed giving a significant space saving. This is achieved by identical vertices (representing identical sub-matrices) being merged and stored only once. During traversal, however, each of these shared vertices will be visited several times (as many times as the sub-matrix occurs in the overall matrix) and the entries of the sub-matrix will be computed every time. By storing and reusing the results of this computation, we can achieve a significant speed-up in traversal time.

Rather than store these results in a cache, which would need to be searched through frequently, we simply attach the information directly to MTBDD vertices. We select some subset of the vertices, build explicit (sparse matrix) representations of their associated sub-matrices and attach them to the MTBDD. There is an obvious trade-off here between the additional space required to store the data and the resulting improvement in speed. The space required and time improvement both depend on how many vertices (and which ones) we attach matrices to. From our experiences, a good policy is to replace all the vertices in one (fairly low) level of the MTBDD. In Figure 7, we demonstrate this technique on the running example, replacing all vertices on the x_2 level with the matrices they represent.

In practice, we find that caching can improve traversal speed by an order of magnitude. In the next section, we give experimental results from our implementation which includes all the techniques described here.

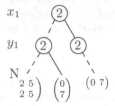

Fig. 7. The modified MTBDD labelled with explicit sub-matrices

6   Results

In this section, we present our experimental results, obtained from the PRISM tool. We compare the performance of the three implementations discussed in this paper: pure MTBDDs, sparse matrices, and our hybrid approach, focusing on the problem of iterative numerical computation.

In Figure 8, we give storage requirements for the coin protocol and Kanban models introduced earlier. We compare the size of the MTBDD, the sparse matrix and the modified MTBDD used in the hybrid approach, with and without optimisation. In Section 4, we observed the significant advantage of MTBDDs over sparse matrices. Note that, even when storing offset information, extra vertices and explicit sub-matrices, the hybrid approach remains memory efficient. Furthermore, the time for adding this information to the MTBDD was in all cases negligle compared to that for model checking.

In Figure 9, we present model checking times for the same two case studies. For the coin protocol, we verify a quantitative PCTL property which requires solution of a linear optimisation problem. For the Kanban system, we model check a quantitative CSL property which requires computation of the steady-state probabilities via the solution of a linear equation system. We use the JOR iterative method. All experiments were run on a 440 MHz Sun Ultra 10 workstation with 1 GB memory. The iterative methods were terminated when the relative error between subsequent iteration vectors was less than 10^{-6}.

As we remarked in Section 4, the coin protocol model, and many of our other MDP models, are efficient for MTBDDs. The problem we try to address with our hybrid approach is typified by the Kanban example, where MTBDDs alone are inefficient. By using the techniques presented in this paper, we were able to consider larger models than with sparse matrices. Furthermore, using the optimised version, we can almost match the speed of sparse matrices. Other CTMC case studies we have considered, such as queueing networks and workstation clusters, confirm these results. Details can be found on the PRISM web page [31].

Model	N	States	Memory (KB)			
			MTBDD	Sparse	Hybrid	Hybrid Opt.
	2	528	6.4	16.5	10.4	12.3
Coin	4	43,136	28.5	2,265	56.7	69.8
protocol	6	2,376,448	61.2	173,424	93.3	314
	8	114,757,632	109	10,673,340	171	1,669
	10	5,179,854,848	170	584,181,500	275	3,600
	3	58,400	48.3	5,459	86.0	99.9
Kanban	4	454,475	95.7	48,414	171	231
system	5	2,546,432	123	296,588	219	337
	6	11,261,376	154	1,399,955	272	486
	7	41,644,800	186	5,441,445	327	685

Fig. 8. Storage requirements for the coin protocol and Kanban examples

Model	N	States	Iter.s	Time per iteration (sec.)			
				MTBDD	Sparse	Hybrid	Hybrid Opt.
	2	528	1,740	0.008	0.0002	0.001	0.0006
Coin	4	43,136	6,133	0.173	0.034	0.07	0.039
protocol	6	2,376,448	12,679	1.01	1.741	5.58	3.02
	8	114,757,632	21,110	3.17	-	-	-
	10	5,179,854,848	31,255	8.38	-	-	-
	3	58,400	300	41.7	0.044	0.451	0.052
Kanban	4	454,475	466	-	0.436	6.09	0.502
system	5	2,546,432	663	-	2.76	33.4	3.150
	6	11,261,376	891	-	-	146	14.76
	7	41,644,800	1,148	-	-	558	58.87

Fig. 9. Model checking times for the coin protocol and Kanban examples

Related Work: We are aware of three other probabilistic model checking tools. ProbVerus [21] is an MTBDD-based model checker which only supports DTMCs and a subset of PCTL. The tool E⊢MC^2 [22] supports model checking of CTMCs against CSL specifications using sparse matrices. The tool described in [18] uses abstraction and refinement to perform model checking for a subset of PCTL over MDPs. There are a number of sparse-matrix based DTMC and CTMC tools, such as MARCA [33], which do not allow logic specifications but support steady-state and transient analysis.

An area of research which has close links with our work is the Kronecker approach [30], a technique for the analysis of very large, structured CTMCs and DTMCs. The basic idea is that the matrix of the full system is defined as a Kronecker algebraic expression of smaller matrices, which correspond to sub-components of the overall system. It is only necessary to store these small matrices and the structure of the Kronecker expression. Iterative solution methods can be applied to the matrix while in this form. As with our approach, storage requirements for the matrix are relatively small, but ingenious techniques must be developed to minimise the time overhead required for numerical solution. Tools which support Kronecker based methods include APNN [9] and SMART [14].

In particular, SMART incorporates matrix diagrams [15], a data structure developed as an efficient implementation of the Kronecker techniques. The matrix diagram approach has much in common with the hybrid method we present in this paper. In particular, both methods use a decision-diagram like data structure for storing matrices and full array to store vectors. The key difference is that matrix diagrams are tied to the Kronecker representation and as such require more work to extract the transition matrix entries. In addition to traversing the data structure, as we do, computation of matrix elements requires multiplication of entries from the smaller matrices.

Another important difference is that Kronecker and matrix diagram approaches permit the use of more efficient iterative methods, such as Gauss-Seidel. Our approach does not presently support these. Hence, although we have less work to do per iteration, we may require more iterations using our methods. In addition, Gauss-Seidel can be implemented with a single iteration vector, whereas methods such as Jacobi and JOR require two.

One issue that unites the Kronecker approach, matrix diagrams and our method is that their limiting factor is the space required to store the iteration vector. However compact the matrix representation is, memory proportional to the number of states is required for numerical solution. Buchholz and Kemper consider an interesting technique in [12] using PDGs (Probabilistic Decision Graphs). This attempts to store the iteration vector in a structured way, as is done with the matrix. More investigation is required to discover the potential of this approach.

7   Conclusion

We have introduced PRISM, a tool to build and analyse probabilistic systems which supports three types of models (DTMCs, MDPs and CTMCs) and two probabilistic logics (PCTL and CSL). As well as MTBDD and sparse matrix based model checking engines, PRISM includes a novel, hybrid engine which combines symbolic and explicit approaches. We have shown that very large probabilistic systems can be constructed and analysed using MTBDDs, but that, often, numerical computation is very inefficient. Our hybrid approach addresses these performance problems, allowing verification, at an acceptable speed, of much larger systems than would be feasible using sparse matrices. Further details of this will be available in [29].

One problem with our current techniques is that they presently only support the Power, Jacobi and JOR iterative methods. We plan to extend the work to allow more rapidly converging alternatives such as Gauss-Seidel or Krylov methods to be used.

The development of PRISM is an ongoing activity. In the near future we intend to consider extensions of PCTL for expressing expected time and long run average properties and of CSL to include rewards, expand the PRISM input language to allow process algebra terms, and develop model checking engines for PRISM which work in a parallel or distributed setting.

References

1. R. Alur and T. Henzinger. Reactive modules. In *Proc. LICS'96*, 1996.
2. J. Aspnes and M. Herlihy. Fast randomized consensus using shared memory. *Journal of Algorithms*, 15(1), 1990.
3. I. Bahar, E. Frohm, C. Gaona, G. Hachtel, E.Macii, A. Pardo, and F. Somenzi. Algebraic decision diagrams and their applications. In *Proc. ICCAD'93*, 1993.
4. C. Baier. On algorithmic verification methods for probabilistic systems. Habilitation thesis, Universität Mannheim, 1998.
5. C. Baier, E. Clarke, V. Hartonas-Garmhausen, M. Kwiatkowska, and M. Ryan. Symbolic model checking for probabilistic processes. In *Proc. ICALP'97*, 1997.
6. C. Baier, B. Haverkort, H. Hermanns, and J.-P. Katoen. Model checking continuous-time Markov chains by transient analysis. In *Proc. CAV'00*, 2000.
7. C. Baier, J.-P. Katoen, and H. Hermanns. Approximative symbolic model checking of continuous-time Markov chains. In *Proc. CONCUR'99*, 1999.
8. C. Baier and M. Kwiatkowska. Model checking for a probabilistic branching time logic with fairness. *Distributed Computing*, 11(3), 1998.
9. F. Bause, P. Buchholz, and P. Kemper. A toolbox for functional and quantitative analysis of DEDS. In *Computer Performance Evaluation (Tools)*, 1998.
10. A. Bianco and L. de Alfaro. Model checking of probabilistic and nondeterministic systems. In *Proc. FST & TCS*, 1995.
11. R. Bryant. Graph-based algorithms for boolean function manipulation. *IEEE Transactions on Computers*, C-35(8), 1986.
12. P. Buchholz and P. Kemper. Compact representations of probability distributions in the analysis of superposed GSPNs. In *Proc. PNPM'01*, 2001.
13. J. R. Burch, E. M. Clarke, K. L. McMillan, D. L. Dill, and J. Hwang. Symbolic model checking: 10^{20} states and beyond. In *Proc. LICS'90*, 1990.
14. G. Ciardo and A. Miner. SMART: Simulation and Markovian analyser for reliability and timing. In *Tool Descriptions from PNPM'97*, 1997.
15. G. Ciardo and A. Miner. A data structure for the efficient Kronecker solution of GSPNs. In *Proc. PNPM'99*, 1999.
16. G. Ciardo and M. Tilgner. On the use of Kronecker operators for the solution of generalized stocastic Petri nets. ICASE Report 96-35, Institute for Computer Applications in Science and Engineering, 1996.
17. E. Clarke, M. Fujita, P. McGeer, J. Yang, and X. Zhao. Multi-terminal binary decision diagrams: An efficient data structure for matrix representation. In *Proc. IWLS'93*, 1993.
18. P. D'Argenio, B. Jeannet, H. Jensen, and K. Larsen. Reachability analysis of probabilistic systems by successive refinements. In *Proc. PAPM/PROBMIV'01*, 2001.
19. L. de Alfaro, M. Kwiatkowska, G. Norman, D. Parker, and R. Segala. Symbolic model checking of concurrent probabilistic processes using MTBDDs and the Kronecker representation. In *Proc. TACAS'00*, 2000.
20. H. Hansson and B. Jonsson. A logic for reasoning about time and probability. *Formal Aspects of Computing*, 6, 1994.
21. V. Hartonas-Garmhausen, S. Campos, and E. Clarke. ProbVerus: Probabilistic symbolic model checking. In *Proc. ARTS'99*, 1999.
22. H. Hermanns, J.-P. Katoen, J. Meyer-Kayser, and M. Siegle. A Markov chain model checker. In *Proc. TACAS'00*, 2000.

23. H. Hermanns, J. Meyer-Kayser, and M. Siegle. Multi terminal binary decision diagrams to represent and analyse continuous time Markov chains. In *Proc. NSMC'99*, 1999.
24. A. Itai and M. Rodeh. Symmetry breaking in distributed networks. *Information and Computation*, 88(1), 1990.
25. J.-P. Katoen, M. Kwiatkowska, G. Norman, and D. Parker. Faster and symbolic CTMC model checking. In *Proc. PAPM-PROBMIV'01*, 2001.
26. M. Kwiatkowska, G. Norman, D. Parker, and R. Segala. Symbolic model checking of concurrent probabilistic systems using MTBDDs and Simplex. Technical Report CSR-99-1, School of Computer Science, University of Birmingham, 1999.
27. M. Kwiatkowska, G. Norman, and R. Segala. Automated verification of a randomized distributed consensus protocol using Cadence SMV and PRISM. In *Proc. CAV'01*, 2001.
28. K. McMillan. *Symbolic Model Checking*. Kluwer Academic Publishers, 1993.
29. D. Parker. *Implementation of symbolic model checking for probabilistic systems*. PhD thesis, University of Birmingham, 2002. To appear.
30. B. Plateau. On the stochastic structure of parallelism and synchronisation models for distributed algorithms. In *Proc. 1985 ACM SIGMETRICS Conference on Measurement and Modeling of Computer Systems*, 1985.
31. PRISM web page. http://www.cs.bham.ac.uk/~dxp/prism/.
32. F. Somenzi. CUDD: Colorado University decision diagram package. Public software, Colorado Univeristy, Boulder, 1997.
33. W. Stewart. MARCA: Markov chain analyser, a software package for Markov modelling. In *Proc. NSMC'91*, 1991.

Timed Automata with Asynchronous Processes: Schedulability and Decidability

Elena Fersman, Paul Pettersson, and Wang Yi*

Uppsala University, Sweden

Abstract. In this paper, we exend timed automata with asynchronous processes i.e. tasks triggered by events as a model for real-time systems. The model is expressive enough to describe concurrency and synchronization, and real time tasks which may be periodic, sporadic, preemptive or non-preemptive. We generalize the classic notion of schedulability to timed automata. An automaton is schedulable if there exists a scheduling strategy such that all possible sequences of events accepted by the automaton are schedulable in the sense that all associated tasks can be computed within their deadlines. We believe that the model may serve as a bridge between scheduling theory and automata-theoretic approaches to system modeling and analysis. Our main result is that the schedulability checking problem is decidable. To our knowledge, this is the first general decidability result on dense-time models for real time scheduling without assuming that preemptions occur only at integer time points. The proof is based on a decidable class of updatable automata: timed automata with subtraction in which clocks may be updated by subtractions within a bounded zone. The crucial observation is that the schedulability checking problem can be encoded as a reachability problem for such automata. Based on the proof, we have developed a symbolic technique and a prototype tool for schedulability analysis.

1 Introduction

One of the most important issues in developing real time systems is *schedulability analysis* prior to implementation. In the area of real time scheduling, there are well-studied methods [8] e.g. rate monotonic scheduling, that are widely applied in the analysis of periodic tasks with deterministic behaviours. For *non-periodic* tasks with non-deterministic behaviours, there are no satisfactory solutions. There are approximative methods with pessimistic analysis e.g. using periodic tasks to model sporadic tasks when control structures of tasks are not considered. The advantage with automata-theoretic approches e.g. using timed automata in modeling systems is that one may specify general timing constraints on events and model other behavioural aspects such as concurrency and synchronization. However, it is not clear how timed automata can be used

---

* Corresponding author: Wang Yi, Department of Information Technology, Uppsala University, Box 325, 751 05, Uppsala, Sweden. yi@docs.uu.se

J.-P. Katoen and P. Stevens (Eds.): TACAS 2002, LNCS 2280, pp. 67–82, 2002.

for schedulability analysis because there is no support for specifying resource requirements and hard time constraints on computations e.g. deadlines.

Following the work of [11], we study an extended version of timed automata with asynchronous processes i.e. tasks triggered by events. A task is an executable program characterized by its worst case execution time and deadline, and possibly other parameters such as priorities etc for scheduling. The main idea is to associate each location of an automaton with a task (or a set of tasks in the general case). Intuitively a transition leading to a location in the automaton denotes an event triggering the task and the guard (clock constraints) on the transition specifies the possible arrival times of the event. Semantically, an automaton may perform two types of transitions. Delay transitions correspond to the execution of running tasks (with highest priority) and idling for the other waiting tasks. Discrete transitions correspond to the arrival of new task instances. Whenever a task is triggered, it will be put in the scheduling queue for execution (i.e. the ready queue in operating systems). We assume that the tasks will be executed according to a given scheduling strategy e.g. FPS (fixed priority scheduling) or EDF (earliest deadline first). Thus during the execution of an automaton, there may be a number of processes (released tasks) running in parallel (logically).

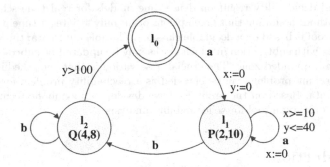

Fig. 1. Timed automaton with asynchronous processes.

For example, consider the automaton shown in Figure 1. It has three locations l_0, l_1, l_2, and two tasks P and Q (triggered by a and b) with computing time and relative deadline in brackets $(2, 10)$, and $(4, 8)$ respectively. The automaton models a system starting in l_0 may move to l_1 by event a at any time, which triggers the task P. In l_1, as long as the constraints $x \geq 10$ and $y \leq 40$ hold and event a occurs, a copy of task P will be created and put in the scheduling queue. However, in l_1, it can not create more than 5 instances of P because the constraint $y \leq 40$ will be violated after 40 time units. In fact, every copy will be computed before the next instance arrives and the scheduling queue may contain at most one task instance and no task instance will miss its deadline in l_1. In l_1, the system is also able to accept b, trigger Q and then switch to l_2. In l_2, because there is no constraints labelled on the b-transition, it may accept any number of b's, and create any number of Q's in 0 time. This is the so-called zeno-behavior. However, after more than two copies of Q, the queue will be non-schedulable. This means that the system is non-schedulable. Thus, zeno-behaviour will correspond to non-schedulability, which is a natural property of the model.

We shall formalize the notion of schedulability in terms of reachable states. A state of an extended automaton will be a triple (l, u, q) consisting of a location l, a clock assignment u and a task queue q. The task queue contains pairs of remaining computing times and relative deadlines for all released tasks. Naturally, a state (l, u, q) is schedulable if q is schedulable in the sense there exists a scheduling strategy with which all tasks in q can be computed within their deadlines. An automaton is schedulable if all reachable states of the automaton are schedulable. Note that the notion of schedulability here is relative to the scheduling strategy. A task queue which is not schedulable with one scheduling strategy, may be schedulable with another strategy. In [11], we have shown that under the assumption that the tasks are non-preemptive, the schedulability checking problem can be transformed to a reachability problem for ordinary timed automata and thus it is decidable. The result essentially means that given an automaton it is possible to check whether the automaton is schedulable with any *non-preemptive* scheduling strategy. For *preemptive scheduling* strategies, it has been suspected that the schedulability checking problem is undecidable because in *preemptive scheduling* we must use stop-watches to accumulate computing times for tasks. It appears that the computation model behind preemptive scheduling is stop-watch automata for which it is known that the reachability problem is undecidable. Surprisingly the above intuition is wrong. In this paper, we establish that the schedulability checking problem for extended timed automata is decidable for preemptive scheduling. In fact, our result applies to not only preemptive scheduling, but any scheduling strategy. That is, for a given extended timed automata, it is checkable if there exists a scheduling strategy (preemtive or non-preemtive) with which the automaton is schedulable. The crucial observation in the proof is that the schedulability checking problem can be translated to a reachability problem for a decidable class of updatable automata, that is, timed automata with subtraction where clocks may be updated with subtraction only in a bounded zone.

The rest of this paper is organized as follows: Section 2 presents the syntax and semantics of timed automata extended with tasks. Section 3 describes scheduling problems related to the model. Section 4 is devoted to the main proof that the schedulability checking problem for preemptive scheduling is decidable. Section 5 concludes the paper with summarized results and future work, as well as a brief summary and comparison with related work.

2 Timed Automata with Tasks

Let $\mathcal{P}$, ranged over by P, Q, R, denote a finite set of task types. A task type may have different instances that are copies of the same program with different inputs. We further assume that the *worst case execution times* and *hard deadlines* of tasks in $\mathcal{P}$ are known[1]. Thus, each task P is characterized as a pair of natural numbers denoted $P(C, D)$ with $C \leq D$, where C is the worst case execution time of P and D is the relative deadline for P. We shall use $C(P)$ and $D(P)$ to denote the worst case execution time and relative deadline of P respectively.

As in timed automata, assume a finite alphabet $\mathcal{A}ct$ ranged over by a, b etc and a finite set of real-valued clocks $\mathcal{C}$ ranged over by x_1, x_2 etc. We use $\mathcal{B}(\mathcal{C})$ ranged over by g to denote the set of conjunctive formulas of atomic constraints in the form: $x_i \sim C$ or $x_i - x_j \sim D$ where $x_i, x_j \in \mathcal{C}$ are clocks, $\sim \in \{\leq, <, \geq, >\}$, and C, D are natural numbers. The elements of $\mathcal{B}(\mathcal{C})$ are called *clock constraints*.

Definition 1. *A timed automaton extended with tasks, over actions $\mathcal{A}ct$, clocks $\mathcal{C}$ and tasks $\mathcal{P}$ is a tuple $\langle N, l_0, E, I, M \rangle$ where*

- $\langle N, l_0, E, I \rangle$ *is a timed automaton where*
  - N *is a finite set of locations ranged over by l, m, n,*
  - $l_0 \in N$ *is the initial location, and*
  - $E \subseteq N \times \mathcal{B}(\mathcal{C}) \times \mathcal{A}ct \times 2^{\mathcal{C}} \times N$ *is the set of edges.*
  - $I : N \mapsto \mathcal{B}(\mathcal{C})$ *is a function assigning each location with a clock constraint (a location invariant).*
- $M : N \hookrightarrow \mathcal{P}$ *is a partial function assigning locations with tasks[2].*

Intuitively, a discrete transition in an automaton denotes an event triggering a task annotated in the target location, and the guard on the transition specifies all the possible arrival times of the event (or the annotated task). Whenever a task is triggered, it will be put in the scheduling (or task) queue for execution (corresponding to the ready queue in operating systems).

Clearly extended timed automata are at least as expressive as timed automata; in particular, if M is the empty mapping, we will have ordinary timed automata. It is a rather general and expressive model. For example, it may model time-triggered periodic tasks as a simple automaton as shown in Figure 2(a) where P is a periodic task with computing time 2, deadline 8 and period 20. More generally it may model systems containing both periodic and sporadic tasks as shown in Figure 2(b) which is a system consisting of 4 tasks as annotation on locations, where P_1 and P_2 are periodic with periods 10 and 20 respectively (specified by the constraints: x=10 and x=20), and Q_1 and Q_2 are sporadic or event driven by event a and b respectively.

In general, there may be a number of released tasks running logically in parallel. For example, an instance of Q_2 may be released before the preceding instance of P_1 is finished because there is no constraint on the arrival time of b_2. This means that the queue may contains at least P_1 and Q_2. In fact, instances of all four task types may appear in the queue at the same time.

---

[1] Tasks may have other parameters such as fixed priority for scheduling and other resource requirements e.g. on memory consumption. For simplicity, in this paper, we only consider computing time and deadline.

[2] Note that M is a partial function meaning that some of the locations may have no task. Note also that we may also associate a location with a set of tasks instead of a single one. It will not introduce technical difficulties.

Shared Variables. To have a more general model, we may introduce data variables shared among automata and tasks. For example, shared variables can be used to model precedence relations and synchronization between tasks. Note that the sharing will not add technical difficulties as long as their domiains are finite. For simplicity, we will not consider sharing in this paper. The only requirement on the completion of a task is given by the deadline. The time when a task is finished does not effect the control behavior specified in the automaton.

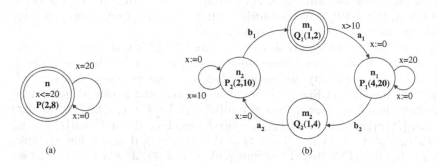

Fig. 2. Modeling Periodic and Sporadic Tasks.

Parallel Composition. To handle concurrency and synchronization, a parallel composition of extended timed automata may be defined as a product automaton in the same way as for ordinary timed automata (e.g. see [16]). Note that the parallel composition here is only an operator to construct models of systems based on their components. It has nothing to do with multi-processor scheduling. A product automaton may be scheduled to run on a one- or multi-processor system.

Semantically, an automaton may perform two types of transitions. Delay transitions correspond to the execution of running tasks with highest priority (or earliest deadline) and idling for the other tasks waiting to run. Discrete transitions corresponds to the arrivals of new task instances.

We represent the values of clocks as functions (i.e. clock assignments) from $\mathcal{C}$ to the non–negative reals $\mathcal{R}_{\geq 0}$. We denote by $\mathcal{V}$ the set of clock assignments for $\mathcal{C}$. Naturally, a semantic state of an automaton is a triple (l, u, q) where l is the current location, $u \in \mathcal{V}$ denotes the current values of clocks, and q is the current task queue. We assume that the task queue takes the form: $[P_1(c_0, d_0), P_2(c_1, d_1)...P_n(c_n, d_n)]$ where $P_i(c_i, d_i)$ denotes a released instance of task type P_i with remaining computing time c_i and relative deadline d_i.

Assume that there are a fixed number of processors running the released task instances according to a certain scheduling strategy Sch e.g. FPS (fixed priority scheduling) or EDF (earliest deadline first) which sorts the task queue whenever new tasks arrives according to task parameters e.g. deadlines. An action transition will result in a sorted queue including the newly released tasks by the transition. A delay transition with t time units is to execute the task in the first positon of the queue with t time units. Thus the delay transition will decrease the computing time of the first task with t. If its computation time becomes 0, the task should be removed from the queue. Moreover, all deadlines in the queue will be decreased by t (time has progressed by t). To summarize the above intuition, we introduce the following functions on task queues:

- Sch is a sorting function for task queues (or lists), that may change the ordering of the queue elements only. For example, $\mathsf{EDF}([P(3.1, 10), Q(4, 5.3)]) = [Q(4, 5.3), P(3.1, 10)])$. We call such sorting functions a scheduling strategy that may be preemptive or non-preemptive[3].
- Run is a function which given a real number t and a task queue q returns the resulted queue after t time units of execution according to available resources. For simplicity, we assume that only one processor is available[4]. Then the meaning of $\mathsf{Run}(q, t)$ should be obvious and it can be defined inductively as follows: $\mathsf{Run}(q, 0) = q$, $\mathsf{Run}([P_0(c_0, d_0), P_1(c_1, d_1)...P_n(c_n, d_n)], t) = \mathsf{Run}([P_1(c_1, d_1 - c_0) ... P_n(c_n, d_n - c_0)], t - c_0)$ if $c_0 \leq t$ and $\mathsf{Run}([P_1(c_0, d_0) ... P_n(c_n, d_n)], t) = [P_1(c_0 - t, d_0 - t) ... P_n(c_n, d_n - t)]$ if $c_0 > t$. For example, let $q = [Q(4, 5), P(3, 10)]$. Then $\mathsf{Run}(q, 6) = [P(1, 4)]$ in which the first task is finished and the second has been executed for 2 time units.

We use $u \models g$ to denote that the clock assignment u satisfies the constraint g. For $t \in \mathcal{R}_{\geq 0}$, we use $u + t$ to denote the clock assignment which maps each clock x to the value $u(x) + t$, and $u[r \mapsto 0]$ for $r \subseteq \mathcal{C}$, to denote the clock assignment which maps each clock in r to 0 and agrees with u for the other clocks (i.e. $\mathcal{C} \backslash r$). Now we are ready to present the operational semantics for extended timed automata by transition rules:

Definition 2. *Given a scheduling strategy* Sch, *the semantics of an automaton* $\langle N, l_0, E, I, M \rangle$ *with initial state* (l_0, u_0, q_0) *is a labelled transition system defined by the following rules:*

- $(l, u, q) \xrightarrow{a}_{\mathsf{Sch}} (m, u[r \mapsto 0], \mathsf{Sch}(M(m) :: q))$ *if* $l \xrightarrow{gar} m$ *and* $u \models g$
- $(l, u, q) \xrightarrow{t}_{\mathsf{Sch}} (l, u + t, \mathsf{Run}(q, t))$ *if* $(u + t) \models I(l)$

where $M(m) :: q$ *denotes the queue with* $M(m)$ *inserted in* q.

Note that the transition rules are parameterized by Sch (scheduling strategy). and Run (function representing the available computing resources). According to the transition rules, the task queue is growing with action transitions and shrinking with delay transitions. Multiple copies (instances) of the same task type may appear in the queue.

---

[3] A non-preemptive strategy will never change the position of the first element of a queue and a preemtive strategy may change the ordering of task types only, but never change the ordering of task instances of the same type.

[4] The semantics may be extended to multi-processor setting by modifying the function Run according the number of processors available.

Whenever it is understood from the context, we shall omit Sch from the transition relation. Consider the automaton in Figure 2(b). Assume that preemptive earliest deadline first (EDF) is used to schedule the task queue. Then the automaton with initial state $(m_1, [x = 0], [Q_1(1, 2)])$ may demonstrate the following sequence of typical transitions:

$$(m_1, [x = 0], [Q_1(1, 2)])$$
$$\xrightarrow{1} (m_1, [x = 1], [Q_1(0, 1)]) = (m_1, [x = 1], [])$$
$$\xrightarrow{9.5} (m_1, [x = 10.5], [])$$
$$\xrightarrow{a_1} (n_1, [x = 0], [P_1(4, 20)])$$
$$\xrightarrow{0.5} (n_1, [x = 0.5], [P_1(3.5, 19.5)])$$
$$\xrightarrow{b_2} (m_2, [x = 0.5], [Q_2(1, 4), P_1(3.5, 19.5)])$$
$$\xrightarrow{0.3} (m_2, [x = 0.8], [Q_2(0.7, 3.7), P_1(3.5, 19.2)])$$
$$\xrightarrow{a_2} (n_2, [x = 0], [Q_2(0.7, 3.7), P_2(2, 10), P_1(3.5, 19.2)])$$
$$\xrightarrow{b_1} (m_1, [x = 0], [Q_2(0.7, 3.7), Q_1(1, 2), P_2(2, 10), P_1(3.5, 19.2)])$$
$$\xrightarrow{10} (n_1, [x = 10], [])$$
$$\dots$$

This is only a partial behaviour of the automaton. A question of interest is whether it can perform a sequence of transitions leading to a state where the task queue is non-schedulable.

3 Schedulability Analysis

In this section we study verification problems related to the model presented in the previous section. First, we have the same notion of reachability as for timed automata.

Definition 3. *We shall write* $(l, u, q) \longrightarrow (l', u', q')$ *if* $(l, u, q) \xrightarrow{a} (l', u', q')$ *for an action a or* $(l, u, q) \xrightarrow{t} (l', u', q')$ *for a delay t. For an automaton with initial state* (l_0, u_0, q_0), (l, u, q) *is reachable iff* $(l_0, u_0, q_0) \longrightarrow^* (l, u, q)$.

In general, the task queue is unbounded though the constraints of a givn automaton may restrict the possibility of reaching states with infinitely many different task queues. This makes the analysis of automata more difficult. However, for certain analysis, e.g. verification of safety properties that are not related to the task queue, we may only be interested in the reachability of locations. A nice property of our extension is that the location reachability problem can be checked by the same technique as for timed automata [14,19]. So we may view the original timed automaton (without task assignment) as an abstraction of its extended version preserving location reachability. The existing model checking tools such as [20,17] can be applied directly to verify the abstract models.

But if properties related to the task queue are of interests, we need to develop new verification techniques. One of the most interesting properties of extended automata related to the task queue is schedulability.

Definition 4. *(Schedulability) A state (l, u, q) with $q = [P_1(c_1, d_1) \ldots P_n(c_n, d_n)]$ is a failure denoted (l, u, Error) if there exists i such that $c_i \geq 0$ and $d_i < 0$, that is, a task failed in meeting its deadline. Naturally an automaton A with initial state (l_0, u_0, q_0) is non-schedulable with Sch iff $(l_0, u_0, q_0)(\longrightarrow_{\mathsf{Sch}})^*(l, u, \mathsf{Error})$ for some l and u. Otherwise, we say that A is schedulable with Sch. More generally, we say that A is schedulable iff there exists a scheduling strategy Sch with which A is schedulable.*

The schedulability of a state may be checked by the standard test. We say that (l, u, q) is schedulable with Sch if $\mathsf{Sch}(q) = [P_1(c_1, d_1) \ldots P_n(c_n, d_n)]$ and $(\sum_{i \leq k} c_i) \leq d_k$ for all $k \leq n$. Alternatively, an automaton is schedulable with Sch if all its reachable states are schedulable with Sch.

Checking schedulability of a state is a trivial task according to the definition. But checking the relative schedulability of an automaton with respects to a given scheduling strategy is not easy, and checking the general schedulability (equivalent to finding a scheduling strategy to schedule the automaton) is even more difficult.

Fortunately the queues of all schedulable states of an automaton are bounded. First note that a task instance that has been started can not be preempted by another instance of the same task type. This means that there is only one instance of each task type in the queue whose computing time can be a real number and it can be arbitrarily small. Thus the number of instances of each task type $P \in \mathcal{P}$, in a schedulable queue is bounded by $\lceil D(P)/C(P) \rceil$ and the size of schedulable queues is bounded by $\sum_{P \in \mathcal{P}} \lceil D(P)/C(P) \rceil$.

We will code schedulability checking problems as reachability problems. First, we consider the case of non-preemptive scheduling to introduce the problems. We have the following positive result.

Theorem 1. *The problem of checking schedulability relative to non-preemptive scheduling strategy for extended timed automata is decidable.*

Proof. A detailed proof is given in [11]. We sketch the proof idea here. It is to code the given scheduling strategy as a timed automaton (called the scheduler) denoted $E(\mathsf{Sch})$ which uses clocks to remember computing times and relative deadlines for released tasks. The scheduler automaton is constructed as follows: Whenever a task instance P_i is released by an event $\mathsf{release}_i$, a clock d_i is reset to 0. Whenever a task is started to run, a clock c is reset to 0. Whenever the constraint $d_i = 0$ is satisfied, and P_i is not running, an error-state (non-schedulable) should be reached. We also need to transform the original automaton A to $E(A)$ to synchronize with the scheduler that P_i is released whenever a location, say l to which P_i is associated, is reached. This is done simply by replacing actions labeled on transitions leading to l with $\mathsf{release}_i$. Finally we construct the product automaton $E(\mathsf{Sch})\|E(A)$ in which both $E(\mathsf{Sch})$ and $E(A)$ can only synchronize on identical action symbols namely $\mathsf{release}_i$'s. It can be proved that if an error-state of the product automaton is reachable, the original extended timed automaton is non-schedulable.

For *preemptive scheduling* strategies, it has been conjectured that the schedulability checking problem is undecidable. The reason is that if we use the same ideas as for non-preemptive scheduling to encode a preemptive scheduling strategy, we must use stop-watches (or integrators) to add up computing times for suspended tasks. It appears that the computation model behind preemptive scheduling is stop-watch automata for which it is known that the reachability problem is undecidable. Surprisingly this conjecture is wrong.

Theorem 2. *The problem of checking schedulability relative to a preemptive scheduling strategy for extended timed automata is decidable.*

The rest of this paper will be devoted to the proof of this theorem. It follows from Lemma 3, 4, and 5 established in the following section. Before we go further, we state a more general result that follows from the above theorem.

Theorem 3. *The problem of checking schedulability for extended timed automata is decidable.*

From scheduling theory [8], we know that the preemptive version of Earliest Deadline First scheduling (EDF) is optimal in the sense that if a task queue is non-schedulable with EDF, it can not be schedulable with any other scheduling strategy (preemptive or non-preemptive). Thus, the general schedulability checking problem is equivalent to the relative schedulability checking with respects to EDF.

4   Decidability and Proofs

We shall encode the schedulability checking problem as a reachability problem. For the case of non-preemptive scheduling, the expressive power of timed automata is enough. For preemptive scheduling, we need a more expressive model.

4.1   Timed Automata with Subtraction

Definition 5. *A timed automaton with subtraction is a timed automaton in which clocks may be updated by subtraction in the form $x := x - C$ in addition to reset of the form $x := 0$, where C is a natural number.*

This is the so called updatable automata [7]. It is known that the reachability problem for this class of automata is undecidable. However, for the following class of suspension automata, location reachability is decidable.

Definition 6. *(Bounded Timed Automata with Subtraction) A timed automaton is bounded iff for all its reachable states (l, u, q), there is a maximal constant C_x for each clock x such that*

1. *$u(x) \geq 0$ for all clocks x, i.e. clock values should not be negative and*
2. *$u(x) \leq C_x$ if $l \xrightarrow{gar} l'$ for some l' and C such that $g(u)$ and $(x := x - C) \in r$.*

In general, it may be difficult to compute the maximal constants from the syntax of an automaton. But we shall see that we can compute the constants for our encoding of scheduling problems.

Because subtractions on clocks are performed only within a bounded area, the region equivalence is preserved by the operation. We adopt the standard definition due to Alur and Dill [5].

Definition 7. *(Region Equivalence denoted $\sim$) For a clock $x \in C$, let C_x be a constant (the ceiling of clock x). For a real number t, let $\{t\}$ denote the fractional part of t, and $\lfloor t \rfloor$ denote its integer part. For clock assignments $u, v \in V$, u, v are region-equivalent denote $u \sim v$ iff*

1. *for each clock x, either $\lfloor u(x) \rfloor = \lfloor v(x) \rfloor$ or $u(x) > C_x$ and $v(x) > C_x$), and*
2. *for all clocks x, y if $u(x) \leq C_x$ and $u(y) \leq C_y$ then*
   a) $(\{u(x)\} = 0$ iff $\{v(x)\} = 0$ and
   b) $\{u(x)\} \leq \{u(y)\}$ iff $\{v(x)\} \leq \{v(y)\}$

It is known that region equivalence is preserved by the delay (addition) and reset. In the following, we establish that region equivalence is also preserved by subtraction for clocks that are bounded as defined in Definition 6. For a clock assignment u, let $u(x - C)$ denote the assignment: $u(x - C)(x) = u(x) - C$ and $u(x - C)(y) = u(y)$ for $y \neq x$.

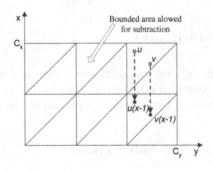

Fig. 3. Region equivalence preserved by subtraction when clocks are bounded.

Lemma 1. *Let $u, v \in V$. Then $u \sim v$ implies*

1. *$u + t \sim v + t$ for a positive real number t, and*
2. *$u[x \mapsto 0] \sim v[x \mapsto 0]$ for a clock x and*
3. *$u(x - C) \sim v(x - C)$ for all natural numbers C such that $C \leq u(x) \leq C_x$.*

Proof. It is given in the full version of this paper [13].

In fact, region equivalence over clock assignments induces a bisimulation over reachable states of automata, which can be used to partition the whole state space as a finite number of equivalence classes.

Lemma 2. *Assume a bounded timed automaton with subtraction, a location l and clock assignments u and v. Then $u{\sim}v$ implies that*

1. *whenever $(l, u) \longrightarrow (l', u')$ then $(l, v) \longrightarrow (l', v')$ for some v' s.t. $u'{\sim}v'$ and*
2. *whenever $(l, v) \longrightarrow (l', v')$ then $(l, u) \longrightarrow (l', u')$ for some u' s.t. $u'{\sim}v'$.*

Proof. It follows from Lemma 1.

The above lemma essentially states that if $u{\sim}v$ then (l, u) and (l, v) are bisimular, which implies the following result.

Lemma 3. *The location reachability problem for bounded timed automata with subtraction, whose clocks are bounded with known maximal constants is decidable.*

Proof. Because each clock of the automaton is bounded by a maximal constant, it follows from lemma 2 that for each location l, there is a finite number of equivalence classes of states which are equivalent in the sense that they will reach the same equivalence classes of states. Because the number of locations of an automaton is finite, the whole state space of an automaton can be partitioned into finite number of such equivalence classes.

4.2   Encoding of Schedulability as Reachability

Assume an automaton A extended with tasks, and a *preemptive scheduling* strategy Sch. The aim is to check if A is schedulable with Sch. As for the case of *non-preemptive scheduling* (Theorem 1), we construct $E(A)$ and $E(\mathsf{Sch})$, and check a pre-defined error-state in the product automaton of the two. The construction is illustrated in figure 4.

$E(A)$ is constructed as a timed automaton which is exactly the same as for the non-preemptive case (Theorem 1) and $E(\mathsf{Sch})$ will be constructed as a timed automaton with subtraction.

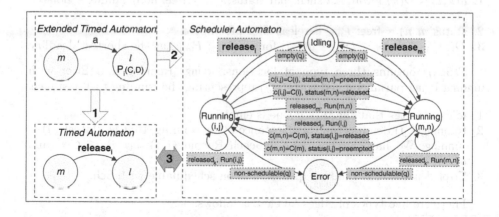

Fig. 4. Encoding of schelulability problem.

We introduce some notation. Let $C(i)$ and $D(i)$ stand for the worst case execution time and relative deadline respectively for each task type P_i. We use P_{ij} to denote the jth instance of task type P_i.

For each task instance P_{ij}, we have the following state variables: status(i, j) initialized to free. Let status(i, j) = running stand for that P_{ij} is executing on the processor, preempted for that P_{ij} is started but not running, and released for that P_{ij} is released, but not started yet. We use status(i, j) = free to denote that P_{ij} is not released yet or position (i, j) of the task queue is free.

According to the definition of scheduling strategy, for all i, there should be only one j such that status(i, j) = preempted (only one instance of the same task type is started), and for all i, j, there should be only one pair (k, l) such that status(k, l) = running (only one is running for a one-processor system).

We need two clocks for each task instance:

1. $c(i, j)$ (a computing clock) is used to remember the accumulated computing time since P_{ij} was started (when Run(i, j) became true)[5], and subtracted with $C(k)$ when the running task, say P_{kl}, is finished if it was preempted after it was started.
2. $d(i, j)$ (a deadline clock) is used to remember the deadline and reset to 0 when P_{ij} is released.

We use a triple $\langle c(i, j), d(i, j), \text{status}(i, j) \rangle$ to represent each task instance, and the task queue will contain such triples. We use q to denote the task queue. Note that the maximal number of instances of P_i appearing in a schedulable queue is $\lceil D(i)/C(i) \rceil$. We have a bound on the size of queue as claimed earlier, which is $\sum_{P_i \in \mathcal{P}} \lceil D(i)/C(i) \rceil$. We shall say that queue is empty denoted empty(q) if status(i, j) = free for all i, j.

For a given scheduling strategy Sch, we use the predicate Run(m, n) to denote that task instance P_{mn} is scheduled to run according to Sch. For a given Sch, it can be coded as a constraint over the state variables. For example, for EDF, Run(m, n) is the conjunction of the following constraints:

1. $d(k, l) \leq D(k)$ for all k, l such that status$(k, l) \neq$ free: no deadline is violated yet
2. status$(m, n) \neq$ free: P_{mn} is released or preempted
3. $D(m) - d(m, n) \leq D(i) - d(i, j)$ for all (i, j): P_{mn} has the shortest deadline

$E(\text{Sch})$ contains three type of locations: Idling, Running and Error with Running being parameterized with (i, j) representing the running task instance.

1. Idling denotes that the task queue is empty.
2. Running(i, j) denotes that task instance P_{ij} is running, that is, status(i, j) = running. We have an invariant for each Running(i, j): $c(i, j) \leq C(i)$ and $d(i, j) \leq D(i)$.
3. Error denotes that the task queues are non-schedulable with Sch.

There are five types of edges labeled as follows:

---

[5] In fact, for each task type, we need only one clock for computing time because only one instance of the same task type may be started.

1. Idling to Running(i, j): there is an edge labeled by
   - guard: none
   - action: release$_i$
   - reset: $c(i,j) := 0$, $d(i,j) := 0$, and status$(i,j) :=$ running
2. Running(i, j) to Idling: there is only one edge labeled with
   - guard: empty(q) that is, status$(i,j) =$ free for all i, j (all positions are free).
   - action: none
   - reset: none
3. Running(i, j) to Running(m, n): there are two types of edges.
   a) The running task P_{ij} is finished, and P_{mn} is scheduled to run by Run(m, n). There are two cases:
      i. P_{mn} was preempted earlier:
         - guard: $c(i,j) = C(i)$, status$(m, n) =$ preempted and Run(m, n)
         - action: none
         - reset: status$(i,j) :=$ free, $\{c(k,l) := c(k,l) - C(i)|$status$(k,l) =$ preempted$\}$, and status$(m, n) :=$ running
      ii. P_{mn} was released, but never preempted (not started yet):
         - guard: $c(i,j) = C(i)$, status$(m, n) =$ released and Run(m, n)
         - action: none
         - reset: status$(i,j) :=$ free, $\{c(k,l) := c(k,l) - C(i)|$status$(k,l) =$ preempted$\}$, $c(m,n) := 0, d(m,n) := 0$ and status$(m,n) :=$ running
   b) A new task P_{mn} is released, which preempts the running task P_{ij}:
      - guard: status$(m, n) =$ free, and Run(m, n)
      - action: released$_m$
      - reset: status$(m, n) :=$ running, $c(m, n) := 0$, $d(m, n) := 0$, and status$(i,j) :=$ preempted
4. Running(i, j) to Running(i, j). There is only one edge representing the case when a new task is released, and the running task P_{ij} will continue to run:
   - guard: status$(k, l) -$ free, and Run(i, j)
   - action: released$_k$
   - reset: status$(k, l) :=$ released and $d(k, l) := 0$
5. Running(i, j) to Error: for each pair (k, l), there is an edge labeled by $d(k, l) > D(k)$ and status$(k, l) \neq$ free meaning that the task P_{kl} which is released (or preempted) fails in meeting its deadline.

The third step of the encoding is to construct the product automaton $E(Sch) \parallel E(A)$ in which both $E(Sch)$ and $E(A)$ can only synchronize on identical action symbols. Now we show that the product automaton is bounded.

Lemma 4. *All clocks of $E(\mathsf{Sch})$ in $E(Sch) \parallel E(A)$ are bounded and non-negative.*

Proof. It is given in the full version of this paper [13].

Now we have the correctness lemma for our encoding. Assume, without losing generality, that the initial task queue of an automaton is empty.

Lemma 5. *Let A be an extended timed automaton and* Sch *a scheduling strategy. Assume that* (l_0, u_0, q_0) *and* $(\langle l_0, \mathsf{Idling}\rangle, u_0)$ *are the initial states of A and the product automaton* $E(A)\|E(\mathsf{Sch})$ *respectively where* l_0 *is the initial location of A,* u_0 *and* v_0 *are clock assignments assigning all clocks with* 0 *and* q_0 *is the empty task queue. Then for all* l *and* u:

$$(l_0, u_0, q_0) \longrightarrow^* (l, u, \mathsf{Error}) \; \textit{iff} \; (\langle l_0, \mathsf{Idling}\rangle, u_0 \cup v_0) \longrightarrow^* (\langle l, \mathsf{Error}\rangle, u \cup v) \textit{for some } v$$

Proof. It is by induction on the length of transition sequence.

The above lemma states that the schedulability analysis problem can be solved by reachability analysis for timed automata extended with subtraction. From Lemma 4, we know that $E(\mathsf{Sch})$ is bounded. Because the reachability problem is decidable due to Lemma 3, we complete the proof for our main result stated in Theorem 2.

5   Conclusions and Related Work

We have studied a model of timed systems, which unifies timed automata with the classic task models from scheduling theory. The model can be used to specify resource requirements and hard time constraints on computations, in addition to features offered by timed automata. It is general and expressive enough to describe concurrency and synchronization, and tasks which may be periodic, sporadic, preemptive and (or) non-preemptive. The classic notion of schedulability is naturally extended to automata model.

Our main technical contribution is the proof that the schedulability checking problem is decidable. The problem has been suspected to be undecidable due to the nature of preemptive scheduling. To our knowledge, this is the first decidability result for preemptive scheduling in dense-time models. Based the proof, we have developed a symbolic schedulability checking algorithm using the DBM techniques extended with a subtraction operation. It has been implemented in a prototype tool [6]. We believe that our work is one step forward to bridge scheduling theory and automata-theoretic approaches to system modeling and analysis. A challenge is to make the results an applicable technique combined with classic methods such as rate monotonic scheduling. We need new algorithms and data structures to represent and manipulate the dynamic task queue consisting of time and resource constraints. As another direction of future work, we shall study the schedule synthesis problem. More precisely given an automaton, it is desirable to characterize the set of schedulable traces accepted by the automaton.

Related work. Scheduling is a well-established area. Various analysis methods have been published in the literature. For systems restricted to periodic tasks, algorithms such as rate monotonic scheduling are widely used and efficient methods for schedulability checking exist, see e.g. [8]. These techniques can be used to handle non-periodic tasks. The standard way is to consider non-periodic tasks as periodic using the estimated *minimal* inter-arrival times as *task periods*. Clearly,

the analysis based on such a task model would be pessimistic in many cases, e.g.
a task set which is schedulable may be considered as non-schedulable as the inter-
arrival times of the tasks may vary over time, that are not necessary minimal.
Our work is more related to work on timed systems and scheduling.

A nice work on relating classic scheduling theory to timed systems is the
controller synthesis approach [2,3]. The idea is to achieve schedulability by
construction. A general framework to characterize scheduling contstraints as
invariants and synthesize scheduled systems by decomposition of constraints is
presented in [3]. However, algorithmic aspects are not discussed in these work.
Timed automata has been used to solve non-preemptive scheduling problems
mainly for job-shop scheduling[1,12,15]. These techniques specify pre-defined
locations of an automaton as goals to achieve by scheduling and use reachability
analysis to construct traces leading to the goal locations. The traces are used
as schedules. There have been several work e.g. [18,10,9] on using stop-watch
automata to model preemptive scheduling problems. As the reachability analysis
problem for stop-watch automata is undecidable in general [4], there is no
guarantee for termination for the analysis without the assumption that task
preemptions occur only at integer points. The idea of subtractions on timers
with integers, was first proposed by McManis and Varaiya in [18]. In general,
the class of timed automata with subtractions is undecidable, which is shown
in [7]. In this paper, we have identified a decidable class of updatable automata,
which is precisely what we need to solve scheduling problems without assuming
that preemptions occur only at integer points.

Acknowledgement. Thanks to the anonymous referees for their insights and
constructive comments.

References

1. Y. Abdeddaïm and O. Maler. Job-shop scheduling using timed automata. In
   *Proceedings of 13th Conference on Computer Aided Verification, July 18-23, 2001
   Paris, France*, 2001.
2. K. Altisen, G. Gößler, A. Pnueli, J. Sifakis, S. Tripakis, and S. Yovine. A framework
   for scheduler synthesis. In *Proceedings of the 20th IEEE Real-Time Systems Symposium, Phoenix, AZ, USA, 1-3 December, 1999*, pages 154–163. IEEE Computer
   Society Press, 1999.
3. K. Altisen, G. Gößler, and J. Sifakis. A methodology for the construction of
   scheduled systems. In *Proceedings of FTRTFT 2000, Pune, India, September 2000,
   LNCS 1926, pp.106-120*, 2000.
4. R. Alur, C. Courcoubetis, N. Halbwachs, T. A. Henzinger, P.-H. Ho, X. Nicollin,
   A. Olivero, J. Sifakis, and S. Yovine. The algorithmic analysis of hybrid systems.
   Theoretical Computer Science, 138(1):3–34, 1995.
5. R. Alur and D. L. Dill. A theory of timed automata. *Theoretical Computer Science*,
   126(2):183–235, 1994.
6. T. Amnell, E. Fersman, L. Mokrushin, P. Pettersson, and W. Yi. TIMES - a
   tool for modelling and implementation of embedded systems. In *Proceedings of
   TACAS02*. Springer–Verlag, 2002.

7. P. Bouyer, C. Dufourd, E. Fleury, and A. Petit. Are timed automata updatable? In *Proceedings of the 12th International Conference on Computer-Aided Verification*, Chicago, IL, USA, July 15-19, 2000, 2000. Springer-Verlag.

8. G. C. Buttazzo. *Hard Real-Time Computing Systems. Predictable Scheduling Algorithms and Applications*. Kulwer Academic Publishers, 1997.

9. F. Cassez and F. Laroussinie. Model-checking for hybrid systems by quotienting and constraints solving. In *Proceedings of the 12th International Conference on Computer-Aided Verification*, pages 373–388, Standford, California, USA, 2000. Springer-Verlag.

10. J. Corbett. Modeling and analysis of real-time ada tasking programs. In *Proceedings of 15th IEEE Real-Time Systems Symposium, San Juan, Puerto Rico, USA*, pages 132–141. IEEE Computer Society Press, 1994.

11. C. Ericsson, A. Wall, and W. Yi. Timed automata as task models for event-driven systems. In *Proceedings of the 6th International Conference on Real-Time Computing Systems and Applications (RTCSA'99)*. IEEE Computer Society Press, 1999.

12. A. Fehnker. Scheduling a steel plant with timed automata. In *Proceedings of the 6th International Conference on Real-Time Computing Systems and Applications (RTCSA'99)*. IEEE Computer Society Press, 1999.

13. E. Fersman, P. Pettersson, and W. Yi. Timed automata with asynchronous processes: Schedulability and decidability. Technical report, Department of Information Technology, Uppsala University, Sweden, 2002.

14. T. Henzinger, X. Nicollin, J. Sifakis, and S. Yovine. Symbolic model checking for real-time systems. *Information and Computation*, 111(2):193–244, 1994.

15. T. Hune, K. G. Larsen, and P. Pettersson. Guided Synthesis of Control Programs using UPPAAL. *Nordic Journal of Computing*, 8(1):43–64, 2001.

16. K. G. Larsen, P. P., and W. Yi. Compositional and symbolic model-checking of real-time systems. In *Proceedings of 16th IEEE Real-Time Systems Symposium, December 5-7, 1995 — Pisa, Italy*, pages 76–89. IEEE Computer Society Press, 1995.

17. K. G. Larsen, P. Pettersson, and W. Yi. UPPAAL in a Nutshell. *Journal on Software Tools for Technology Transfer*, 1(1–2):134–152, October 1997.

18. J. McManis and P. Varaiya. Suspension automata: a decidable class of hybrid automata. In *Proceedings of the 6th International Conference on Computer-Aided Verification*, pages 105–117, Standford, California, USA, 1994. Springer-Verlag.

19. W. Yi, P. Pettersson, and M. Daniels. Automatic verification of real-time communicating systems by constraint-solving. In *Proceedings of the 7th International Conference on Formal Description Techniques*, 1994.

20. Sergio Yovine. A Verification Tool for Real Time Systems. *Int. Journal on Software Tools for Technology Transfer*, 1(1–2):134–152, October 1997.

Validating Timing Constraints of Dependent Jobs with Variable Execution Times in Distributed Real-Time Systems

Hojung Cha[1] and Rhan Ha[2]

[1] Dept. of Computer Science, Yonsei University, Seoul 120-749, Korea
hjcha@cs.yonsei.ac.kr
[2] Dept. of Computer Engineering, Hongik University, Seoul 121-791, Korea
rhanha@cs.hongik.ac.kr

Abstract. In multiprocessor and distributed real-time systems, scheduling jobs dynamically on processors can be used to achieve better performance. However, analytical and efficient validation methods for determining whether all the timing constraints are met do not yet exist for systems using modern dynamic scheduling strategies, and exhaustive methods are often infeasible or unreliable since the execution time and release time of each job may vary. In this paper, we present several upper bounds and efficient algorithms for computing the worst-case completion times of dependent jobs in dynamic systems where jobs are dispatched and scheduled on available processors in a priority-driven manner. The bounds and algorithms consider arbitrary release times and variable execution times. We present conditions under which dependent jobs execute in a predictable manner.

1 Introduction

Many safety-critical real-time applications, (*e.g.*, air-traffic control and factory automation) have timing constraints that must be met for them to be correct. Their timing constraints are often specified in terms of the release times and deadlines of the jobs that make up the system. A *job* is a basic unit of work to be scheduled and executed. It can begin execution when its data and control dependencies are met only after its *release time*, and it must complete by its *deadline*. The failure of a job to complete by its deadline can lead to a performance degradation or complete failure.

We assume here that the scheduler never schedules any job before its release time and focus on the problem of how to validate that every job indeed completes by its deadline when executed according to a given priority-driven discipline used by the scheduler. A scheduling algorithm is *priority-driven* if it never leaves any processor idle intentionally. Such an algorithm can be implemented by assigning priorities to jobs, placing jobs ready for execution in one or more queues and scheduling the jobs with the highest priorities among all jobs in the queue(s) on the available processors. Specifically, we consider here only *dynamic systems*: in

J.-P. Katoen and P. Stevens (Eds.): TACAS 2002, LNCS 2280, pp. 83–97, 2002.

a dynamic system, ready jobs are placed in a common queue and are dispatched to available processors in a priority-driven manner.

Recently, many real-time load balancing and scheduling algorithms for dynamic systems have been developed. These algorithms are likely to make better use of the processors and achieve a higher responsiveness than the traditional approach to scheduling jobs in multiprocessor and distributed environments. According to the traditional approach, jobs are first statically assigned and bound to processors, and then a uniprocessor scheduling algorithm is used to schedule the jobs on each processor.

A system that uses a priority-driven scheduling algorithm can have unexpected timing behavior [1]. A job may complete later where it and other jobs execute for shorter amounts of time and when jobs are released sooner. Consequently, it is impractical and unreliable to validate that all jobs meet their deadlines using exhaustive testing and simulation when their execution times and release times may vary. Recently, several efficient and analytical methods for validating timing constraints of static multiprocessor and distributed systems have been developed, e.g., [2,3,4] (In a static system, jobs are assigned and bound to processors.). These methods are based on worst-case bounds and schedulability conditions for uniprocessor systems[5,6,7,8]. They allow us to bound the completion times of jobs that are scheduled in a priority-driven manner even when their release times and execution times may vary. Several efficient algorithms for computing the worst-case completion times of independent jobs in dynamic systems now exist[9]. This paper is concerned with the case where jobs have dependencies, the processors are identical, and the system is dynamic. The works in [10,11] are also related to the problem solved in this paper. In [10,11], they have studied the validation problem to bound the completion times of jobs on one processor. Our work provides the bounds of completion times of jobs in multiprocessor or distributed systems.

The rest of the paper is organized as follows. Section 2 presents the formal definition of the validation problem addressed by the paper. Sections 3 and 4 give conditions for predictable execution and present an efficient algorithm for bounding the completion times of dependent jobs. Conclusions are given in Section 5.

2 Problem

The general validation problem addressed here and in [9] can be stated as follows: given n jobs, m identical processors, and the priority-driven scheduling algorithm that dynamically schedules the jobs on the processors, determine whether all the jobs meet their deadlines analytically or by using an efficient algorithm. We let $J = \{J_1, J_2, \ldots, J_n\}$ denote the set of jobs. As in [3,4,5,6,7,8] each job J_i has the following parameters: release time r_i, deadline d_i and execution time e_i. These parameters are rational numbers. The actual execution time e_i of J_i is in the range $[e_i^-, e_i^+]$. We call e_i^- its *minimum execution time* and e_i^+ its *maximum execution time*. We assume that the scheduler knows the parameters r_i, d_i and

$[e_i^-, e_i^+]$ of every job J_i before any job begins execution, but the actual execution time e_i is unknown.

The jobs in $\boldsymbol{J}$ are dependent; data and control dependencies between them impose *precedence constraints* in the order of their execution. A job J_i is a *predecessor* of another job J_j (and J_j is a *successor* of J_i) if J_j cannot begin to execute until J_i completes. We denote this precedence relation by $J_i \prec J_j$. J_i is an *immediate predecessor* of J_j (and J_j is an *immediate successor* of J_i) if $J_i \prec J_j$ and there is no other job J_k such that $J_i \prec J_k \prec J_j$. Two jobs J_i and J_j are *independent* if neither $J_i \prec J_j$ nor $J_j \prec J_i$. Independent jobs can be executed in any order. We use a *precedence graph* $G = (\boldsymbol{J}, \boldsymbol{R})$ to represent the precedence relations between jobs. There is a node J_i in this graph for each job J_i in $\boldsymbol{J}$, and there is an edge from J_i to J_j in $\boldsymbol{R}$ whenever J_i is an immediate predecessor of J_j. We say that a job becomes *ready* when the time is at or after its release time and either it has no predecessor or all of its predecessors are completed, and it remains ready until it completes.

We confine our attention to scheduling algorithms that assign fixed priorities to jobs and do not choose priorities based on the actual execution times of the jobs. Therefore, the given scheduling algorithm is completely defined by the list of priorities it assigns to the jobs. Without loss of generality, we assume that the priorities of jobs are distinct. We will always index the job in decreasing priority order (*i.e.*, the priority list is $(J_1, J_2, \ldots, J_n)$) except where it is stated to be otherwise. $\boldsymbol{J_i} = \{J_1, J_2, \ldots, J_i\}$ denotes the subset of jobs with priorities equal to or higher than the priority of J_i.

The scheduler maintains a common priority queue and places all ready jobs in the queue. In this paper, we consider the case when jobs are preemptable and migratable. In this case, a ready job can be scheduled on any processor. It may be preempted when a higher priority job becomes ready. Its execution may resume on any processor. We refer the jobs as P/M/Z or P/M/F jobs depending on whether the jobs have identical (zero) release times or fixed arbitrary release times.

We will use $\boldsymbol{J_n^+} = \{J_1^+, J_2^+, \ldots, J_n^+\}$ as a shorthand notation to mean that every job has its maximum execution time. Similarly, $\boldsymbol{J_n^-} = \{J_1^-, J_2^-, \ldots, J_n^-\}$ means that every job has its minimum execution time. We refer to the schedule of $\boldsymbol{J_n}$ produced by the given algorithm as the *actual schedule* $\boldsymbol{A_n}$. To determine whether any job completes in time, we sometimes generate simulated schedules of $\boldsymbol{J_n}$ using the given scheduling algorithm and assuming every job has its maximum execution time or every job has its minimum execution time. In particular, we call the schedule of $\boldsymbol{J_n^+}$ (or $\boldsymbol{J_n^-}$) produced by the same algorithm the *maximal* (or the *minimal*) *schedule* $\boldsymbol{A_n^+}$ (or $\boldsymbol{A_n^-}$) of $\boldsymbol{J_n}$.

Let $S(J_i)$ be the (actual) *start time* of J_i, the instant of time at which the execution of J_i begins according to the actual schedule $\boldsymbol{A_n}$. Let $S^+(J_i)$ and $S^-(J_i)$ be the *start times* of J_i in the schedules $\boldsymbol{A_n^+}$ and $\boldsymbol{A_n^-}$, respectively. We say that the start time of J_i is *predictable* if $S^-(J_i) \leq S(J_i) \leq S^+(J_i)$. Similarly, let $F(J_i)$ be the (actual) *completion time* of J_i, the instant at which J_i completes execution according to the actual schedule $\boldsymbol{A_n}$. The *response time* of a job is the length of time between its release time and its completion time. Let $F^+(J_i)$ and $F^-(J_i)$ be the *completion times* of J_i according to the schedules A_n^+ and A_n^-, respectively. The completion times of J_i is said to be *predictable* if $F^-(J_i) \leq F(J_i) \leq F^+(J_i)$.

We say that *the execution of J_i is predictable* if both its start time and completion time are predictable. In this case, the completion time $F^+(J_i)$ in the schedule A_n^+ minus the release time r_i of J_i gives J_i's worst-case response time. J_i meets its deadline if $F^+(J_i) \leq d_i$.

To find the worst-case completion time of J_i when all the jobs are preemptable, we only need to consider the jobs which are the predecessors of J_i, jobs which have higher priorities than J_i and the predecessors of J_i, and jobs which are predecessors of these higher-priority jobs. To be more precise, we define a new precedence relation R_i^* as follows: Let Y_n^i be the subset of J_n which contains all the jobs that are not successors of J_i. Let R_i^* be the union of (1) the given precedence relation R restricted to the subset Y_n^i and (2) the relation over Y_n^i defined by a graph in which there is a node for each job in Y_n^i and there is an edge from J_i to J_j whenever J_i has a higher priority than J_j. Let X_n^i be the subset of Y_n^i which contains J_i and all the predecessors of J_i under the new relation R_i^*. When we try to find the worst-case completion time of J_i, we must consider the jobs in the subgraph of precedence graph G induced by X_n^i. We call the subset X_n^i the *interfering subset* of J_i.

3   Identical Release Time Case

Unlike independent P/M/Z jobs [9], the execution of P/M/Z jobs with precedence constraints is not predictable in general. This fact is illustrated by the example in Figure 1 where the precedence graph is an out-tree. According to the maximal and minimal schedules shown in parts (b) and (c), J_8's completion times are 8 and 6, respectively. (We omit the values of the execution times here because they are not relevant. It suffices that the execution time of every job in (b) is larger than the execution time of the corresponding job in (c).) Part (d) shows a possible actual schedule obtained when the execution time of every job is between the extreme values used in (b) and (c). According to this actual schedule, J_8 completes at 18. Hence the execution of J_8 is not predictable.

In the next section, we will present an algorithm that can be used to bound the completion times of P/M/Z jobs with arbitrary precedence graphs. Here, we examine a special case when all the jobs have identical release times and the precedence graph is a forest of in-trees. The execution of P/M/Z jobs with this type of precedence graph is predictable. Theorem 1 states this fact. To prove it, we need the following lemmas.

Lemma 1. *No job in a set of P/M/Z jobs is preempted in the actual schedule when every job has at most one immediate successor.*

Proof. A job preempts another job if when it becomes ready, all the processors are busy. At the time when the preempting job becomes ready, the number of

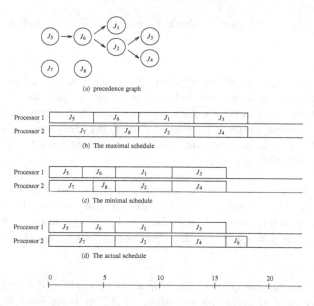

(a) precedence graph

| Processor 1 | J_5 | J_6 | J_1 | J_3 |
| Processor 2 | J_7 | J_8 | J_2 | J_4 |

(b) The maximal schedule

| Processor 1 | J_5 | J_6 | J_1 | J_3 |
| Processor 2 | J_7 | J_8 | J_2 | J_4 |

(c) The minimal schedule

| Processor 1 | J_5 | J_6 | J_1 | J_3 |
| Processor 2 | J_7 | J_2 | J_4 | J_8 |

(d) The actual schedule

```
0          5          10         15         20
├──────────┼──────────┼──────────┼──────────┤
```

Fig. 1. Unpredictable execution of P/M/Z jobs in out-trees

jobs that are ready increases by at least one. However, when the precedence graph is a forest of in-trees, every job has at most one immediate successor. Moreover, all jobs have the same release time. As each job J_i completes, at most one immediate successor of J_i becomes ready. Hence, as time increases, the number of jobs that are ready to execute cannot increase. The lemma follows.

□

Lemma 2. *Let $A_n(i, \epsilon)$ be the schedule of the set of n jobs whose parameters and precedence constraints are the same as those of jobs in J_n except that the execution time of J_i is $e_i - \epsilon$ for some $\epsilon > 0$. When every job is a P/M/Z job and the precedence graph is an in-tree forest, the start time of every job J_j according to $A_n(i, \epsilon)$ is no later than its actual start time $S(J_j)$ according to the actual schedule A_n of J_n.*

Proof. We need to consider only the jobs that start at or later than $F(J_i) - \epsilon$ in A_n. Let J_l be such a job. According to A_n, a processor is available to execute J_l at $S(J_l)$. From Lemma 1, no job is preempted in A_n. Hence at most $(m - 1)$ higher-priority jobs that become ready at or before $S(J_l)$ are not yet complete at $S(J_l)$ according to the schedule A_n. In the set of jobs scheduled according to $A_n(i, \epsilon)$, the execution time of every job is no larger than the execution time of the corresponding job in J_n, and as time increases, the number of ready jobs cannot increase. Moreover, from Lemma 1, no job is preempted according to $A_n(i, \epsilon)$. Consequently, we can conclude that according to $A_n(i, \epsilon)$, at most $(m-1)$ higher-priority jobs that become ready at or before $S(J_l)$ are not complete at $S(J_l)$. There is a processor available to execute J_l at or before $S(J_l)$. The lemma follows.   □

Corollary 1. *Let $A_n^+(i, \epsilon)$ be the schedule of the set of n jobs whose parameters and precedence constraints are the same as those of the jobs in J_n^+ except that the execution time of J_i is $e_i^+ - \epsilon$ for some $\epsilon > 0$. When every job is a $P/M/Z$ job and the precedence graph is an in-tree forest, the start time of every job J_j according to $A_n^+(i, \epsilon)$ is no later than its maximal start time $S^+(J_j)$ according to the maximal schedule A_n^+ of J_n^+.*

Let $A_n^+[k]$, for $1 \le k \le n$, be the schedule of the set of n jobs which is such that (1) the precedence constraints of all jobs are the same as those of the jobs in J_n, (2) the execution time of J_j is e_j for $j = 1, 2, \cdots, k$, and (3) the execution time of J_j is e_j^+ for $j = k+1, k+2, \cdots, n$. Let $A_n^+[0]$ be another notation for A_n^+.

Lemma 3. *When the precedence graph of a set of n $P/M/Z$ jobs is an in-tree forest, the start time of every job according to $A_n^+[k]$ is no later than the start time of the corresponding job according to the schedule $A_n^+[k-1]$ for $1 \le k \le n$.*

Proof. We note that $A_n^+[1]$ is just $A_n^+(1, e_1^+ - e_1)$ defined in Corollary 1. From this corollary, the start time of every job in $A_n^+[1]$ is no later than the maximal start time of the corresponding job in A_n^+.

To show that the lemma is true for $k > 1$, let J_l be a job which starts at or after $(e_k^+ - e_k)$ time units before the completion time of J_k^+ according to $A_n^+[k-1]$. Because no job is preempted, at the time t when J_l starts in $A_n^+[k-1]$, at most $(m - 1)$ higher-priority jobs that become ready at or before t are not complete. The number of higher-priority jobs that become ready at or before t but are not complete at t cannot increase when the execution time of J_k^+ is reduced from e_k^+ to e_k because every job has at most one immediate successor and the release times of all jobs are the same. Consequently, according to $A_n^+[k]$, there are at most $(m - 1)$ ready jobs with priorities higher than J_l at the time t. This means that J_l can start no later than t in $A_n^+[k]$.   □

Let $A_n[k]$, for $1 \le k \le n$, be the schedule of the set of n jobs whose precedence constraints are the same as those of jobs in J_n, the execution time of J_j is e_j^- for $j = 1, 2, \cdots, k$ and the execution time of J_j is e_j for $j = k+1, k+2, \cdots, n$. $A_n[0]$ is another notation of A_n. The proof of the following corollary is similar to that of Lemma 3.

Corollary 2. *When the precedence graph of a set of n $P/M/Z$ jobs is an in-tree forest, the start time of every job according to $A_n[k]$ is no later than the start time of the corresponding job according to the schedule $A_n[k-1]$ for $1 \le k \le n$.*

Theorem 1. *When the precedence graph of a set of n $P/M/Z$ jobs is an in-tree forest, the start time of every job is predictable, that is, $S^-(J_i) \leq S(J_i) \leq S^+(J_i)$.*

Proof. We note that $\boldsymbol{A}_n^+[n]$ is just the actual schedule $\boldsymbol{A}_n$. That the start time $S(J_i)$ of every job J_i in $\boldsymbol{A}_n$ is no later than $S^+(J_i)$ in $\boldsymbol{A}_n^+$ follows straight-forwardly from Lemma 3. Similarly, the fact that $S^-(J_i) \leq S(J_i)$ follows from Corollary 2.   □

Corollary 3. *When the precedence graph of a set of n $P/M/Z$ jobs is an in-tree forest, the completion time of every job is predictable, that is, $F^-(J_i) \leq F(J_i) \leq F^+(J_i)$.*

4 Arbitrary Release Time Case

In contrast to $P/M/Z$ jobs, the execution of jobs with arbitrary release times is not predictable even when the precedence graph of jobs is a set of chains. This fact is illustrated by the example in Figure 2. The simple system in this figure contains eight jobs and two identical processors. The release time of each job is indicated by a number on top of each node in the precedence graph. The execution times of all the jobs are known except for J_3. Its execution time can be any value in the range [2,8]. Parts (b), (c) and (d) of this figure show the maximal, minimal and actual schedules, respectively. The completion time of J_6 in the actual schedule is 13; it is later than its completion time of 11 in the maximal schedule. Similarly, the execution of $P/M/F$ jobs is not predictable when the precedence graph is a forest of in-trees. This is illustrated in Figure 3. In this example, all jobs are released at 0 except J_2 whose release time is marked by an arrow in the schedules. We note that the execution of J_4 and J_5 is not predictable. However, in the following special cases, we have predictable execution.

4.1 Predictable Execution Case

We consider here a set of $P/M/F$ jobs whose precedence graph is a forest of in-trees. The execution of every job is predictable when the assumption of the following theorem holds. The assumption is stated in terms of $S_z^-(J_i)$, which is the start time of J_i in the schedule of $\boldsymbol{J}_n^-$ constructed by assuming that all jobs are released at time 0.

Theorem 2. *When the precedence graph of a set $\boldsymbol{J}_n$ of $P/M/F$ jobs is a forest of in-trees, the execution of every job is predictable if every job J_k is released at or before $S_z^-(J_k)$.*

Proof. When all the jobs are released at time 0, their execution is predictable according to Theorem 1 and Corollary 3. Moreover, no job J_k can start execution before $S_z^-(J_k)$ in any schedule of the set $\boldsymbol{J}_n$. $S_z^-(J_k)$ gives the earliest time

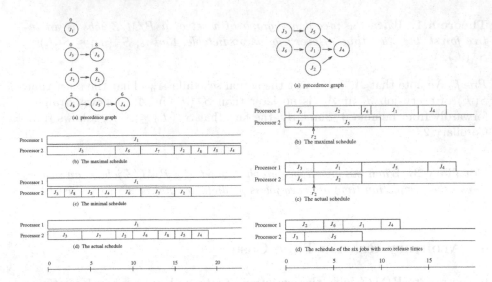

Fig. 2. Unpredictable execution of P/M/F jobs in chains

Fig. 3. Unpredictable execution of P/M/F jobs in in-trees

instant at which all the predecessors of J_k and all but at most $(m-1)$ jobs with higher priorities than J_k can complete. Hence, if every job J_k is released at or before $S_z^-(J_k)$, the schedule of the given P/M/F jobs is the same as their schedule constructed by assuming that all jobs are released at time 0. From Theorem 1 and Corollary 3, the theorem follows.   □

Theorem 2 gives us a way to check whether the execution of a set of jobs whose release times are arbitrary and precedence graph is an in-tree is predictable. For example, the assumption of Theorem 2 does not hold for the jobs in Figure 3. The schedule in Figure 3 (d) is constructed based on the assumptions of zero release times and minimum execution times. According to this schedule, $S_z^-(J_2)$ is 0, but J_2 is released after 0. In contrast, the assumption holds for the system in Figure 4; hence, the jobs in this system have predictable execution. This system has the same set of jobs, the same precedence graph and the same number of processors as the system in Figure 3, except for the release times of jobs. The release time of each job J_k in Figure 4 is equal to its start time $S_z^-(J_k)$ in the schedule in Figure 3 (d) and is indicated by the number on top of each node.

Theorem 3 stated below gives us another condition for predictable execution: the precedence graph consists of chains and every job has a higher priority than its successor. To prove it, we need the following lemma.

Lemma 4. *Let J_i be a job in a set of P/M/F jobs which is such that (1) its precedence graph is a set of chains and (2) every job in the set has a priority higher than its immediate successor. The completion time of J_i is predictable if its start time is predictable and the start times of all the jobs which start before its completion time $F^+(J_i)$ according to the maximal schedule A_n^+ are predictable.*

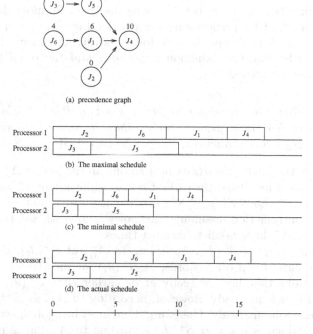

(a) precedence graph

(b) The maximal schedule

(c) The minimal schedule

(d) The actual schedule

Fig. 4. Predictable execution of P/M/F jobs in in-trees

Proof. We need to consider two cases, when J_i has no predecessors and when J_i has predecessors.

Suppose that J_i has no predecessors. To show that its completion time is predictable when the assumption of the lemma is true, we suppose for the moment that $F(J_i) > F^+(J_i)$. For this condition to be true, the total amount of processor time demanded in the interval $[S^+(J_i), F^+(J_i)]$ by all the jobs with higher priorities than J_i according to A_n must be larger than their total demand of time in this interval according to A_n^+; otherwise, since $S(J_i) < S^+(J_i)$, $e_k^+ \geq e_k$ for all k, and the scheduling algorithm is preemptable and migratable, J_i would be able to complete by $F^+(J_i)$. Therefore, there must be at least one job J_h with a higher priority than J_i which is ready in $[S^+(J_i), F^+(J_i)]$ according to A_n but is not ready in this interval according to A_n^+. (J_h is not in the subset of all chains each of which contains higher-priority jobs that are ready in $[S^+(J_i), F^+(J_i)]$ according to A_n^+.) This job J_h must have a predecessor that has a priority lower than J_i and is not completed before $F^+(J_i)$ in A_n^+ but is completed before $F^+(J_i)$ in A_n. However, J_h cannot have a priority higher than J_i because every job has a higher priority than its successors. We therefore have a contradiction. The supposition $F(J_i) > F^+(J_i)$ cannot be true. Similarly, we can prove that $F^-(J_i) \leq F(J_i)$.

We prove that the completion time of a job J_i that has predecessors is predictable by induction. The case above gives us the basis. Suppose that the completion times of all of its predecessors are predictable. The proof of that the completion time of J_i is also predictable follows straightforwardly from the assumption of the lemma, the induction hypothesis and the proof for the case where the job has no predecessor.   □

Theorem 3. *When the precedence graph of a set of P/M/F jobs is a set of chains and every job has a priority higher than its immediate successor, the start time of every job is predictable, that is, $S^-(J_i) \leq S(J_i) \leq S^+(J_i)$.*

Proof. Let J_k be the job that starts earliest among all the jobs in A_n^+. Clearly, J_k starts at its release time; it has the earliest release time among all jobs that have no predecessors. $S^-(J_k) \leq S(J_k) \leq S^+(J_k)$. We now prove that $S(J_i) \leq S^+(J_i)$ for any J_i by contradiction, assuming that all the jobs whose start times are before $S^+(J_i)$ in A_n^+ have predictable start times.

Suppose that $S(J_i) > S^+(J_i)$. According to A_n^+, at $S^+(J_i)$, a processor is available to execute J_i. In other words, at $S^+(J_i)$, at most $(m-1)$ of all the higher-priority jobs that become ready at or earlier than $S^+(J_i)$ are not yet completed and hence are ready. However, according to A_n, at $S^+(J_i)$, at least m higher-priority jobs are ready. Therefore, there must be a job J_h with a priority higher than J_i which is ready at $S^+(J_i)$ according to A_n but is not ready at $S^+(J_i)$ according to A_n^+. We need to consider two cases: J_h is not a predecessor of J_i and J_h is a predecessor of J_i.

Because the scheduling algorithm is preemptable and migratable, if J_h is not a predecessor of J_i, it must have a predecessor J_p that has a priority lower than J_i and is not completed before $S^+(J_i)$ in A_n^+ but is completed at or before $S^+(J_i)$ in A_n. Because every job has a priority higher than its successors, J_h, which is a successor of J_p, cannot have a priority higher than J_i. This fact contradicts that J_h has a priority higher than J_i.

It is possible that J_h is a predecessor of J_i. At $S^+(J_i)$, it is completed according to A_n^+ but is not completed according to A_n. However, this is not possible because of the induction hypothesis and Lemma 4.

Similarly, $S^-(J_i) \leq S(J_i)$ can be proved.   □

Corollary 4. *When the precedence graph of a set of P/M/F jobs is a set of chains and every job has a priority higher than its immediate successor, the completion time of every job is predictable, that is, $F^-(J_i) \leq F(J_i) \leq F^+(J_i)$.*

Proof. The proof of this corollary follows straightforwardly from Theorem 3 and the proof of Lemma 4.   □

Similarly, in the case where the precedence graph of jobs is a forest of intrees, when every job has a priority higher than its immediate successor, we have the following corollaries. Their proofs follow from those of Theorem 3 and Corollary 4 and hence are omitted.

Corollary 5. *When the precedence graph of a set of P/M/F jobs is an in-tree forest and every job has a priority higher than its immediate successor, the start time of every job is predictable, that is, $S^-(J_i) \leq S(J_i) \leq S^+(J_i)$.*

Corollary 6. *When the precedence graph of a set of P/M/F jobs is an in-tree forest and every job has a priority higher than its immediate successor, the completion time of every job is predictable, that is, $F^-(J_i) \leq F(J_i) \leq F^+(J_i)$.*

4.2   Arbitrary Precedence Case

As stated in Section 2, in general, when we want to bound the completion time of a job J_i, we need to consider all the jobs in its interfering subset X_n^i. Again, X_n^i is a subset of J_n containing jobs that are predecessors of J_i, jobs that have higher priorities than J_i and predecessors of J_i, and jobs that are predecessors of these higher-priority jobs. However, in the given interfering set X_n^i and for the given scheduling algorithm, there may be some lower-priority jobs that can never complete before the completion of J_i. We want to identify these jobs and their successors, because we do not need to consider them when computing an upper bound of $F(J_i)$. The following lemma allows us to do so. It is stated in terms of $bs(J_i)$, the start time of J_i according to the schedule of J_n^- on an infinite number of processors. $bs(J_i)$ is equal to $max(r_i, max\{bs(J_p) + e_p^-\})$ where J_p is an immediate predecessor of J_i. $bs(J_i)$ is the *best possible start time* of J_i, and no job J_i can start before $bs(J_i)$.

Lemma 5. *When J_i has no predecessor, J_i completes no later than any lower-priority job J_k according to the actual schedule A_n if $r_i \leq bs(J_k)$ and $e_i^+ \leq e_k^-$.*

Proof. If $r_i \leq bs(J_k)$, J_i starts no later than J_k in the actual schedule since the scheduling algorithm is priority-driven. Even when J_k can start before J_i completes in the actual schedule, J_i completes no later than J_k since $e_i^+ \leq e_k^-$ and J_k has a priority lower than J_i. □

The algorithm, called Algorithm $\mathcal{DPMF}$, described by the pseudo code in Figure 5, is based on this lemma. In this description, we use the notation $C_i^{(1)}$, which is the subset of the interfering set X_n^i containing every job J_k in X_n^i that has a lower priority than J_i and parameters $bs(J_k)$ and e_k^- larger than or equal to r_i and e_i^+, respectively. Because of Lemma 5, when J_i has no predecessor, we do not need to consider the jobs in $C_i^{(1)}$ and their successors for computing an upper bound of the completion time of J_i.

Algorithm $\mathcal{DPMF}$ computes upper bounds of the completion times of preemptable and migratable jobs by performing three steps. Its time complexity is $O(n^4)$. Its first step finds the jobs in X_n^i that cannot postpone the completion of J_i in the actual schedule. Specifically, when J_i has no predecessor, Step 1 finds the subset $C_i^{(1)}$ of X_n^i and eliminates them from further consideration.

Algorithm $\mathcal{DPMF}$:

Input: Parameters of the given job set J and the precedence graph G
Output: Upper bounds of completion times of J_i for $i = 1, 2, \cdots, n$

Begin
    Step 1. **for** $i = 1$ **to** n **do**
        $C_i = X_n^i$.
        if J_i has no predecessor in G,
          { find the subset $C_i^{(1)}$ of X_n^i in which every job J_k has a priority
          lower than J_i and parameters $bs(J_k)$ and e_k^- larger than or equal
          to r_i and e_i^+, respectively.
          $C_i = C_i - C_i^{(1)} - \{$successors of jobs in $C_i^{(1)}\}$. }
    endfor
    Step 2. Construct a new dependence graph G_i' for each J_i for $i = 1, 2, \cdots, n$:
        for $i = 1$ **to** n **do**
          $G_i' =$ subgraph of G induced by X_n^i
          for $l = 1$ **to** n **do**
            if J_l has no predecessor in G_i', flag$[l] = 1$
            else flag$[l] = 0$
          endfor
          for each job J_p in G_i' such that flag$[p]$ is 0 and flag$[l]$ is 1 for every
          predecessor J_l of J_p **do**
          Insert new dependencies into G_i' from each job J_k in C_p to J_p
          if J_k has a higher priority than J_p and there is no dependency
          from J_k to J_p or any predecessor of J_p in G_i'.
          flag$[p] = 1$
          endfor
          Prune the jobs not in $C_i \cup \{J_i\}$ from G_i'.
        endfor
    Step 3. **for** $i = 1$ **to** n **do**
        Schedule the remaining jobs in G_i' with their maximum execution
        times. An upper bound of $F(J_i) =$ the completion time of J_i
        in the generated schedule.
        endfor
End

Fig. 5. Pseudo code of Algorithm $\mathcal{DPMF}$

Let C_i be the set $X_n^i - C_i^{(1)} - \{$successors of jobs in $C_i^{(1)}\}$, if J_i has no predecessor, or X_n^i if J_i has a predecessor. When trying to bound the completion time of J_i, Step 2 of Algorithm $\mathcal{DPMF}$ inserts pseudo dependencies to the jobs in C_i and J_i as follows: we use G_i' to denote a new precedence graph after inserting pseudo dependencies. Initially, G_i' is the subgraph of G induced by X_n^i. In order to construct a new precedence graph G_i', for every job J_p in G_i', a new edge from each job J_k in C_p to J_p is inserted if J_k has a higher priority than J_p and G_i' does not yet contain an edge from J_k to J_p or to any predecessor of J_p. Then Step 2 prunes the jobs not in $C_i \cup \{J_i\}$ from G_i'. In Step 3, the completion time of the job J_i is bounded by J_i's completion time according to the schedule of the jobs that are in G_i' assuming every job has its maximum execution time, and their precedence relations are given by G_i'.

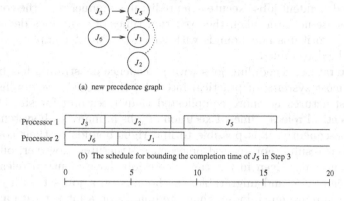

(a) new precedence graph

(b) The schedule for bounding the completion time of J_5 in Step 3

Fig. 6. An example illustrating Algorithm $\mathcal{DPMF}$ for P/M/F jobs

Theorem 4 allows us to conclude that if J_i can complete by the deadline d_i in the schedule of the jobs in G'_i generated by Algorithm $\mathcal{DPMF}$, then J_i always completes by d_i. Figure 6 illustrates how Algorithm $\mathcal{DPMF}$ bounds the completion time of J_5 in Figure 3. Figure 6 (a) is the new precedence graph G'_5 where the dashed edges are the edges added in Step 2. Figure 6 (b) is the schedule of the five jobs with their maximum execution times and precedence graph G'_5. According to this schedule, J_5 completes at time 16. Thus, 16 is the upper bound of the completion time of J_5. In this example, this bound is only one unit of time higher than the actual completion time of J_5, 15, given by Figure 3. In general, the bounds obtained by this algorithm are loose, and can be much looser than indicated by this example.

Theorem 4. *The completion time $F(J_i)$ of J_i is no later than the completion time of J_i according to the schedule generated by Algorithm $\mathcal{DPMF}$.*

Proof. From Lemma 5, when J_i has no predecessor, the lower-priority jobs in $C_i^{(1)}$ do not have a chance to complete before $F(J_i)$ in the actual schedule. Therefore, if J_i has no predecessor, we do not need to consider the jobs in $C_i^{(1)}$ and their successors when computing an upper bound of the completion time of J_i. This justifies Step 1. After pruning, C_i contains all the jobs that can possibly start before the completion of J_i in the actual schedule. Algorithm $\mathcal{DPMF}$ inserts new precedence relations into the precedence graph G'_i so that every job in C_i completes before J_i starts. Therefore the theorem follows.   □

5   Conclusion

This paper is concerned with validating timing constraints of dependent jobs that have arbitrary timing constraints and variable execution times and are scheduled on processors dynamically in a priority-driven manner. We present conditions under which dependent jobs execute in a predictable manner, *i.e.*, the completion times of jobs are no later when the execution times of some jobs decrease. We also present algorithms and bounds with which the latest completion times of all jobs can be determined.

In the literature, scheduling jobs with precedence constraints has been well studied. In most systems of practical interests, the precedence graphs are restricted to structures no more complicated than trees and forests. Often, all jobs have identical release times. Execution of jobs in many such systems is predictable. Consequently, it is possible to find tight bounds to their completion times with our results. For general precedence structures, however, our results are less encouraging. Even in the case where jobs have identical release times and are preemptable and migratable, the bounds on a job set with a general precedence graph are much looser than the bounds on a job set with a forest of in-tree precedence graph.

The results presented here, as well as the results on independent jobs in homogeneous systems and heterogeneous systems in [9,12], make up the theoretical basis for comprehensive validation methods in dynamic distributed real-time systems. Methods for bounding the worst-case completion times of jobs that share resources and have precedence constraints are not yet available. Furthermore, release time jitter is often unavoidable in real-life systems. The release time jitter problem needs to be further investigated.

Acknowledgement. This work is supported by the University Research Program of the Ministry of Information & Communication in republic of Korea (2001-076-3) and BK(Grant 991031001).

References

1. Graham, R.: Bounds on multiprocessing timing anomalies. SIAM Journal of Applied Mathematics. **17(2)** (1969) 416–429
2. Sha, L., Sathaye, S.: A systematic approach to designing distributed real-time systems. IEEE Computer. **26(9)** (1993) 68–78
3. Rajkumar, L. Sha, L, Lehoczky, J.: Real-time synchronization protocols for multiprocessors. Proc. of IEEE 9th Real-Time Systems Symposium. (1988) 259–269
4. Sun, J., Bettati, R., Liu, J.: An end-to-end approach to schedule tasks with shared resources in multiprocessor systems. Proc. of IEEE 11th Workshop on Real-Time Operating Systems and Software. (1994) 18–22
5. Liu, C., Layland, J.: Scheduling algorithms for multiprogramming in a hard-real-time environment. Journal of the Association for Computing Machinery. **20(1)** (1973) 46–61
6. Lehoczky, J., Sha, L., Ding, Y.: The rate monotone scheduling algorithm: Exact characterization and average case behavior. Proc. of IEEE 10th Real-Time Systems Symposium. (1989) 166–171
7. Han, C., Tyan, H.: A better polynomial-time schedulability test for teal-time fixed-priority scheduling algorithms. Proc. of IEEE 18th Real-Time Systems Symposium. (1997) 36–45

8. Palencia, J., Harbour, M.: Schedulability analysis for tasks with static and dynamic offsets. Proc. of IEEE 19th Real-Time Systems Symposium. (1998) 26–37
9. Liu, J., Ha, R.: Methods for validating real-time constraints. Journal of Systems and Software. **30** (1995) 85–98
10. Sun, J., Liu, J.: Bounding completion times of jobs with arbitrary release times and variable execution times. Proc. of IEEE 17th Real-Time Systems Symposium. (1996) 2–12
11. Meyer, M., Wong-Toi, H.: Schedulability analysis of acyclic processes. Proc. of IEEE 19th Real-Time Systems Symposium. (1998) 274–283
12. Ha, R., Cha, H., Liu, J.: Validating real-time constraints in heterogeneous multiprocessor and distributed systems. Journal of Systems Integration. **9(3)** (1999) 207–222

An Analysis of Zero-Clairvoyant Scheduling

K. Subramani

Lane Department of Computer Science and Electrical Engineering,
West Virginia University,
Morgantown, WV
ksmani@csee.wvu.edu

Abstract. In the design of real-time systems, it is often the case that certain process parameters, such as its execution time are not known precisely. The challenge in real-time system design is to develop techniques that efficiently meet the requirements of impreciseness. Traditional models tend to simplify the issue of impreciseness by assuming *worst-case* values. This assumption is unrealistic and at the same time, may cause certain constraints to be violated at run-time. In this paper, we study the problem of scheduling a set of ordered, non-preemptive jobs under non-constant execution times. Typical applications for variable execution time scheduling include process scheduling in Real-time Operating Systems such as Maruti, compiler scheduling, database transaction scheduling and automated machine control. An important feature of application areas such as robotics is the interaction between execution times of various processes. We explicitly model this interaction through the representation of execution time vectors as points in convex sets. Our algorithms do not assume any knowledge of the distributions of execution times, i.e. they are *zero-clairvoyant*. We present both sequential and parallel algorithms for determining the existence of a zero-clairvoyant schedule.

1 Introduction

Scheduling strategies for real-time systems confront two principal issues that are not addressed by traditional scheduling models viz. parameter variability and the existence of complex timing constraints between constituent jobs. Impreciseness in problem data is of both theoretical and practical significance. From an empirical perspective, system designers have used *worst-case* values in order to address non-determinism of execution time values [Pin95]. However, the assumption that every job will have an execution time equal to the maximum value in its allowable range is unrealistic and at the same time, may cause constraint violation at run-time. In this paper, we study the problem of scheduling a set of ordered, non-preemptive jobs with non-constant execution times, with the goal of obtaining a single, rational, start time vector, such that the constraints on the jobs are satisfied. We explicitly model execution time non-determinism through convex sets. To the best of our knowledge, our work represents the first effort in studying this generalization of execution time domains. Our algorithm

J.-P. Katoen and P. Stevens (Eds.): TACAS 2002, LNCS 2280, pp. 98–112, 2002.

is Zero-Clairvoyant in that it makes no assumptions about the distribution of execution times; we present both sequential and parallel algorithms for determining the existence of such a schedule. Zero-clairvoyant schedules are also called *Static schedules*, since the schedule in every single window is the same (with appropriate offsets)[1].

We shall be concerned with the following problems:

(a) Determining the static schedulability of a job set in a periodic real-time system (defined in Section §2),
(b) Determining the dispatch vector of the job set in a scheduling window.

The rest of this paper is organized as follows: In Section §2, we detail the static scheduling problem and pose the static schedulability query. The succeeding section, viz. Section §3, motivates the necessity for Static Scheduling, while Section §4 describes related approaches to this problem. Section §5 commences the process of answering the static schedulability query posed in Section §2 through the application of *convex minimization* algorithms. The algorithm we present is very general, in that it is applicable as long as the execution time vectors belong to a convex set and the constraints on the system are linear. A straightforward parallelization of the algorithm is provided, subsequent to the complexity analysis. Section §6 specializes the algorithm in Section §5 to a number of interesting restrictions. We conclude in Section §7 by tabulating the results discussed in this paper.

2   Statement of Problem

2.1   Job Model

Assume an infinite time-axis divided into windows of length L, starting at time $t = 0$. These windows are called *periods* or *scheduling windows*. There is a set of non-preemptive, ordered jobs, $\mathcal{J} = \{J_1, J_2, \ldots, J_n\}$ that execute in each scheduling window.

2.2   Constraint Model

The constraints on the jobs are described by System (1):

$$\mathbf{A}.[s\ e]^{\mathbf{T}} \leq b, \quad e \in \mathbf{E}, \tag{1}$$

where,

- $\mathbf{A}$ is an $m \times 2.n$ rational matrix, b is a rational $m-$vector; $(\mathbf{A}, b)$ is called the constraint matrix;
- $\mathbf{E}$ is an arbitrary convex set;

---

[1] We shall be using the terms Static and Zero-Clairvoyant interchangeably, for the rest of this paper

- $s = [s_1, s_2, \ldots, s_n]$ is the start time vector of the jobs, and
- $e = [e_1, e_2, \ldots, e_n] \in \mathbf{E}$ is the execution time vector of the jobs

In this work, we consider generalized linear constraints among jobs i.e. those that can be expressed in the form: $\sum_{i=1}^{n} a_i.s_i + b_i.e_i \leq k$, for arbitrary rationals a_i, b_i, k.

The convex set $\mathbf{E}$ serves to model the following situations:

1. Execution time variability - In real-time systems such as Maruti [MKAT92], a number of statistical runs are executed on jobs, to determine upper and lower bounds on their running time under various conditions. These intervals provide a stronger confidence factor than that provided by assuming constant values for execution times. Accordingly, the convex set $\mathbf{E}$ can be restricted to an axis-parallel hyper-rectangle (aph) represented by: $[l_1, u_1] \times [l_2, u_2] \ldots \times [l_n, u_n]$.

2. Execution time interaction - In power applications, the execution of processes are constrained through requirements such as: The total power consumed in a cycle is bounded by k. Note that the power consumed is proportional to the square of the execution time. Consequently, this situation can be modeled by restricting $\mathbf{E}$ to the sphere represented by: $e_1^2 + e_2^2 + \ldots + e_n^2 \leq r^2$, for suitably chosen r.

Remark: 21 *To the best of our knowledge, this work is the first attempt at modeling execution time interaction within a scheduling paradigm.*

2.3   Query Model

Before we state the schedulability query, a few definitions are in order.

Definition 1. *Static (Zero Clairvoyant) Schedule - A schedule for a set of jobs that assumes no knowledge of their execution times prior to the execution of the complete job set.*

Observe that a static schedule is perforce a rational vector, i.e. no online computation of schedules is permitted.

In this paper, we are concerned with the following problems:

1. Determining whether there exists a single rational vector $s \in \Re_{+}^{n}$, such that the set of constraints represented by System (1) is satisfied. This corresponds to deciding the static schedulability query, which is carried out by the offline schedulability analyzer,

2. Computing the dispatch vectors for the current scheduling window, which is carried out by the online dispatcher. In Static scheduling, the online dispatching is obviated by the fact that deciding the static schedulability query coincides with the generation of the dispatch schedule.

We are now ready to state the static schedulability query formally:

$$\exists s = [s_1, s_2 \ldots s_n] \quad \forall e = [e_1, e_2, \ldots e_n] \in \mathbf{E} \qquad \mathbf{A}.[s, e] \leq b, \quad ? \qquad (2)$$

The combination of the Job Model, the Constraint Model and the Query Model, together constitute an instance of a scheduling problem in the E-T-C scheduling framework [Sub01][2].

3 Motivation

One of the fundamental aspects of real-time scheduling is the recognition of interdependencies among jobs [DMP91,Sak94] and the conversion of event-based specifications into temporal distance constraints between jobs [Das85,JM86]. For instance, the event-based requirement: *Wait 50 ms after the first message has been dispatched before dispatching the next message* spawns the following temporal distance constraint: $s_i + 50 \leq s_j$, where s_i and s_j denote the dispatch times of successive invocations of the message generating job. Real-Time Operating Systems, such as Maruti [LTCA89,MAT90,MKAT92] and MARS [DRSK89], permit interaction of jobs through linear relationships between their start and execution times. The Real-Time specification Language MPL (Maruti Programming Language) [SdSA94] explicitly includes programmer constructs that specify temporal constraints between processes (jobs). These constructs are easily transformed into linear relationships between the start and execution times of the jobs. Real-time database applications involve the scheduling of transactions; the execution of these transactions is constrained through linear relationships [BFW97]. In database transactions, temporal constraints are used to specify when processes can access a particular data item or write out a particular data value; these constraints are also easily expressible as relationships between the start times of these processes. *Static Scheduling is the only refuge of real-time systems which do not permit the online computation of schedules.*

Traditional models use *worst-case* values for execution time variables. The following example establishes that using worst-case values for execution times will not necessarily provide a valid solution.

Example 1. Consider the following constraint system imposed on a job set with two jobs viz. $\{J_1, J_2\}$.

1. J_1 finishes before J_2 commences: $s_1 + e_1 \leq s_2$,
2. J_2 commences within 1 unit of J_1 finishing: $s_2 \leq s_1 + e_1 + 1$,
3. J_2 starts at or before time $t = 6$: $s_2 \leq 6$
4. $e_1 \in [4, 6]$.

---

[2] In the E-T-C real-time scheduling framework, a scheduling problem is completely described, by describing the execution time domain, the nature of the constraint set and the type of schedulability query as a triplet.

Substituting the worst-case time for e_1, i.e. 6 in the constraints, we obtain:

$$s_1 + 6 \leq s_2, \tag{3}$$
$$s_2 \leq s_1 + 7 \tag{4}$$
$$s_2 \leq 6 \tag{5}$$

It is not hard to see (graphically) that the only solution to the above system is:

$$\begin{bmatrix} s_1 \\ s_2 \end{bmatrix} = \begin{bmatrix} 0 \\ 6 \end{bmatrix}$$

However, during actual execution, suppose $e_1 = 4$. Then, we have,

$$s_2 > s_1 + e_1 + 1$$

thereby violating the second constraint. In Section §5.2, we will show that the above constraint system is infeasible, i.e. there do not exist start times that can guarantee the meeting of all constraints, for all execution times.

4   Related Work

Scheduling in real-time systems has received considerable attention in system design research [Sak94,SB94,HG93]. Variations of the problem that we are studying have been studied in [Sak94], [HL89], [HL92b] and [HL92a]. This problem is briefly mentioned in [Sak94] as part of *parametric scheduling*, however no algorithm is presented for the general case. In [HL89,HL92b], the problem of scheduling real-time tasks under distance and separation constraints is considered, but the execution times are regarded as constant. To the best of our knowledge, our work represents the first attempt at studying the Static Scheduling problem, in its generality. Here, we focus on the problem of scheduling a set of jobs, in which the ordering sequence is known (and supplied as part of the input), but there exist complex inter-job dependencies, captured through linear relationships between their start and execution times. Although we restrict ourselves to addressing the feasibility of the job system, the judicious use of objective functions can be used to improve the quality of our solutions. The determination of a feasible schedule coincides with the generation of a *static dispatch-calendar* that contains the dispatching information for each job: e.g. $s_1 = 2; s_2 = 15; s_3 = 24$, is a *dispatch-calendar* for a 3-job system.

5   The Static Scheduling Algorithm

We can interpret the static schedulability query (2) as asking whether there exists a rational start time vector s, without any dependencies on the execution times. The static approach is to work individually with each constraint and find the execution times that make the constraint tight (or *binding*). We then argue in Section §5.2 that the strategy is correct, inasmuch as the goal is to produce a single start time vector s that holds for all execution time vectors $e \in E$.

We formalize the ideas discussed above into Algorithm (5.1), which decides the static schedulability query for arbitrary, convex-constrained execution time vectors and arbitrary constraint sets between the start and execution times of the jobs.

Function STATIC-SCHEDULER $(\mathbf{E}, \mathbf{A}, b)$
1: $\{\mathbf{E}$ is the execution time domain and $\mathbf{A}[s, e] \leq b$ is the constraint system$\}$
2: Rewrite the constraint matrix as: $\mathbf{G}.s \leq b - \mathbf{H}.e$.
3: Set $r = [r_1, r_2, \ldots, r_m]^T = b - \mathbf{H}.e$
     $\{$ each r_i is an affine function of $e = [e_1, e_2, \ldots, e_n]\}$
4: **for** (i=1 **to** m) **do**
5:      Let $\rho_i = \min_{\mathbf{E}} r_i$ $\{$ ρ_i is a rational number$\}$
6: **end for**
7: **if** $(s : \mathbf{G}.s \leq \rho \neq \phi)$ **then**
8:      return(System has static schedule s)
         $\{$ $\mathbf{G}.s \leq \rho$ is the **Static Polytope**$\}$
9: **else**
10:     return(System has no static schedule)
11: **end if**

Algorithm 5.1: Static Scheduling Algorithm

The principal step in the algorithm is the reduction of execution time variables in the constraints to rational numbers, through convex minimization (Step 5). Once all constraints are so reduced, we get a simple linear system in the start time variables. This linear system is called the *Static Polytope*. We declare that System (1) is statically schedulable (i.e. query (2) is true) if and only if the Static Polytope is non-empty.

We note that Algorithm (5.1) is the offline schedulability analyzer. In case of Static Scheduling, online computation during dispatching is unnecessary, since the determination of feasibility coincides with the generation of the dispatch schedule.

5.1   Example

Before proceeding with proving the correctness of the STATIC-SCHEDULER() algorithm, we present an example to demonstrate our approach.

Example 2. Consider the two job set $\{J_1, J_2\}$, with execution times $[e_1, e_2]$, constrained through the following convex domain:

- $e_1 \in [0, 6], e_2 \in [0, 6]$
- $e_1 + e_2 \leq 4$

Figure (1) describes the domain.

Let the system have the following constraints:

1. J_1 finishes execution at or before job J_2 commences: $s_1 + e_1 \leq s_2$.
2. J_2 finishes at or before 12 units: $s_2 + e_2 \leq 12$.

Expressing the constraints in matrix form, we get :

$$\begin{bmatrix} 1 & -1 & 1 & 0 \\ 0 & 1 & 0 & 1 \end{bmatrix} \cdot \begin{bmatrix} s_1 \\ s_2 \\ e_1 \\ e_2 \end{bmatrix} \leq \begin{bmatrix} 0 \\ 12 \end{bmatrix}$$

We first rewrite this system to separate the s and the e vectors:

$$\begin{bmatrix} 1 & -1 \\ 0 & 1 \end{bmatrix} \begin{bmatrix} s_1 \\ s_2 \end{bmatrix} + \begin{bmatrix} 1 & 0 \\ 0 & 1 \end{bmatrix} \begin{bmatrix} e_1 \\ e_2 \end{bmatrix} \leq \begin{bmatrix} 0 \\ 12 \end{bmatrix}$$

Moving the e variables to the RHS, we get

$$\begin{bmatrix} 1 & -1 \\ 0 & 1 \end{bmatrix} \begin{bmatrix} s_1 \\ s_2 \end{bmatrix} \leq \begin{bmatrix} 0 \\ 12 \end{bmatrix} - \begin{bmatrix} 1 & 0 \\ 0 & 1 \end{bmatrix} \begin{bmatrix} e_1 \\ e_2 \end{bmatrix}$$

which is equivalent to:

$$\begin{bmatrix} 1 & -1 \\ 0 & 1 \end{bmatrix} \begin{bmatrix} s_1 \\ s_2 \end{bmatrix} \leq \begin{bmatrix} -e_1 \\ 12 - e_2 \end{bmatrix}$$

Minimizing $-e_1$ over the constraint domain in Figure (1), we get $\rho_1 = -4$. Likewise, minimizing $12 - e_2$ over the constraint domain, we get $\rho_2 = 8$. Thus, the static polytope is determined by:

$$\begin{pmatrix} 1 & -1 \\ 0 & 1 \end{pmatrix} \cdot \begin{bmatrix} s_1 \\ s_2 \end{bmatrix} \leq \begin{bmatrix} -4 \\ 8 \end{bmatrix}$$

as shown in Figure (2).

Using a Linear Programming solver [Ber95], we solve the above system, to get:

$$\begin{bmatrix} s_1 \\ s_2 \end{bmatrix} = \begin{bmatrix} 0 \\ 6 \end{bmatrix}$$

5.2   Correctness

Lemma 1. *If the final polytope[3] in algorithm (5.1) is non-empty, then any point on it serves as a suitable vector of start times* $s = [s_1, s_2, \ldots, s_n]$.

---

[3] The resultant polyhedron will always be bounded because the jobs are ordered, i.e. $s_1 < s_2 < \ldots s_n$ and the last job has a deadline, i.e. $s_n + e_n \leq L$, where L represents the time at which the current scheduling window expires.

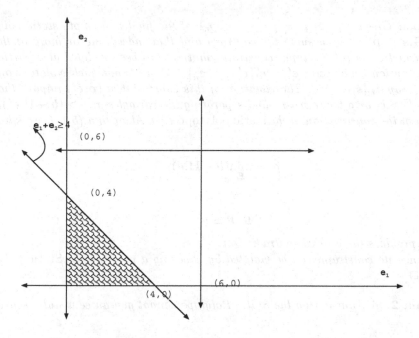

Fig. 1. Convex constrained execution times for Example (2)

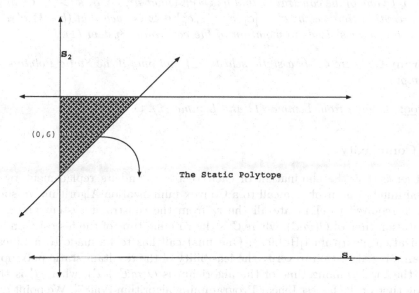

Fig. 2. The Static Polytope for Example (2)

We use a_i to denote the ith row of $\mathbf{A}$, g_i to denote the ith row of $\mathbf{G}$ and b_i to denote the ith element of $\boldsymbol{b}$.

Proof: *Given a point $p = [p_1, p_2, \ldots, p_n]$ of the final non-empty static polytope $\mathbf{G}.s \leq \rho$, let us assume the contrary and that indeed one or more of the input constraints (of the input constraint matrix) has been violated at a particular execution time vector $e' = [e'_1, e'_2, \ldots, e'_n] \in \mathbf{E}$. Pick one such violated constraint, say $a_i.[s, e] \leq b_i$. The violation of this constraint at (p, e') implies that $a_i.[p, e'] > b_i$ or after rewriting and separating the variables $g_i.p > (b - \mathbf{H}.e')_i$. But from the construction of the static polytope (See Algorithm (5.1)), we know that*

$$\rho_i = \min_{\mathbf{E}}(b - \mathbf{H}.e)_i$$

and

$$g_i.p \leq \rho_i$$

which provides the desired contradiction.

Hence no constraint can be violated by choosing a point on the Static polytope. □

Lemma 2. *A point not on the Static Polytope cannot guarantee a static schedule.*

Proof: *Consider a point $s' = [s'_1, s'_2, \ldots, s'_n]$ such that $s' \notin \{s : \mathbf{G}.s \leq \rho\}$. Let $g_i.s \leq \rho_i$ be one of the constraints that has been violated[4], i.e. $g_i.s' > \rho_i$. Clearly, if the execution time vector $e' = [e'_1, e'_2, \ldots, e'_n] \in \mathbf{E}$ is such that $(b - \mathbf{H}.e')_i = \rho_i$, then the point s' leads to violation of the constraint System (1).* □

Theorem 1. *There exists a static schedule if and only if the Static Polytope is non-empty.*

Proof: *Follows from Lemma (1) and Lemma (2).* □

5.3   Complexity

We observe that the elimination of each vector r_i and its replacement by a rational number ρ_i involves a call to a Convex minimization Algorithm. m such calls are required to eliminate all the r_i from the constraint system giving a computation time of $O(m.\mathcal{C})$, where $\mathcal{C}$ is the running time of the fastest Convex minimization algorithm ([HuL93]). One final call has to be made to a Linear Programming algorithm to verify the feasibility of the resultant static polytope. Thus, the total running time of the algorithm is $O(m.\mathcal{C} + \mathcal{L})$, where $\mathcal{L}$ is the running time of the fastest Linear Programming algorithm [Vai87]. We point out that we are using Linear Programming in the sense of determining feasibility of a linear system, as opposed to the standard optimization version. Since Linear Programming is a special case of convex minimization, we have $\mathcal{L} \leq \mathcal{C}$ and hence the complexity of our algorithm is $O(m.\mathcal{C})$.

---

[4] At least one such constraint exists; otherwise, s' belongs to the Static Polytope!

5.4 Parallelization

The ρ_i are created independently for each constraint; thus the steps involving the determination of the ρ_i can be carried out in parallel. This suggests the parallel[5] implementation of the **for** loop, described in Algorithm (5.2).

Function PARALLEL-STATIC-SCHEDULER($\mathbf{E}, \mathbf{A}, b$)
1: Carry out the initialization steps as in Sequential Algorithm
2: **for** ($i = 1$ **to** m) **pardo**
3:     Let $\rho_i = \min_\mathbf{E} r_i$
4: **end for**
5: Perform feasibility check as in Algorithm (5.1).

Algorithm 5.2: Parallel version of Static Scheduling Algorithm

Clearly the steps associated with creating the static polytope have a parallel running time of $O(\mathcal{C})$ with a total work of $O(m.\mathcal{C})$. An additional $O(\mathcal{L})$ sequential time is required for the final feasibility check.

Observation: 51 *The dispatch calendar obtained by Algorithm (5.1), can be used in every scheduling window with the appropriate offset.*

6 Special Case Analysis

We now analyze the complexity of a number of restrictions to the execution time domain $\mathbf{E}$ and the constraint matrix $\mathbf{A}$.

6.1 E Is an Axis-Parallel Hyper-Rectangle

In this case, the execution time domain can be represented by: $\Upsilon = [l_1, u_1] \times [l_2, u_2] \times \ldots \times [l_n, u_n]$ (say). The static schedulability query (2) becomes:

$$\exists s = [s_1, s_2 \ldots s_n] \forall e = [e_1, e_2, \ldots e_n] \in \Upsilon \quad \mathbf{A}.[s, e] \leq b \quad ? \qquad (6)$$

We can apply the same algorithm as in Section §5, in which case we solve $(m + 1)$ linear programs to give a total running time of $O(m.\mathcal{L})$.

However, we can do much better, as we shall show shortly.

Lemma 3. *The minimum of an affine function on an axis-parallel hyper-rectangle (aph) is reached at a vertex of the* **aph**.

Proof: *From [Sch87], we know that the lemma is true over all polyhedral domains and axis-parallel hyper-rectangles are restricted polyhedral domains.* $\square$

---

[5] We are using the PRAM Model, see [Ja'92]

Lemma 4. *When the domain is an* aph, *an affine function can be minimized by minimizing over each dimension individually.*

Proof: *See [Sch87].* □

Lemma (4) gives us the following strategy to minimize an affine function $f = a_1.e_1 + a_2.e_2 + \ldots + a_n.e_n + c$ over the aph $\Upsilon = [l_1, u_1] \times [l_2, u_2] \times \ldots \times [l_n, u_n]$:

- $\forall i$, if $a_i > 0$, set $e_i = l_i$
- $\forall i$, if $a_i < 0$, set $e_i = u_i$

A simple summation gives the minimum value of f over the aph.

Using this strategy it is clear that the STATIC-SCHEDULER algorithm runs in $O(m.n + \mathcal{L})$ sequential time.

6.2   At Most 2 Start-Time Variables per Constraints

We now consider the case, in which the relationships among the jobs can be expressed through *network constraints*, i.e. constraints in which there are at most 2 start-time variables and the execution time domain is an aph. Using the techniques from Section §6.1, we know that we can eliminate the execution time variables from the system in $O(m)$ time. The elimination results in a network linear system of constraints in the start time variables, i.e. in each constraint at most two variables have non-zero coefficients. [HN94] presents a fast implementation of the Fourier-Motzkin procedure to solve network linear systems in time $O(m.n^2.\log m)$. Thus, we have

Lemma 5. *Static Schedulability can be decided in time* $O(m.n^2.\log m)$, *if the execution time domain is an* aph *and the constraints are* network.

Proof: *From the above discussion.* □

Lemma 6. *If the constraints are strict relative timing constraints, statit schedulability can be decided in time* $O(m.n)$.

Proof: *When the constraint system consists of strict relative constraints only [GPS95, Cho00], we can represent it as a network graph (Single Source). Since the execution time domain is an* aph, *the execution time variables can be eliminated in* $O(m)$ *time. We can then use the Bellman-Ford algorithm, which takes* $O(m.n)$ *time, to check if the resultant network has a negative cost cycle. The existence of such a cycle coincides with the infeasibility of the input system [CLR92]. Likewise, non-existence of a negative cost cycle implies that the constraint system is feasible.*
□

7   Summary

In this paper, we analyzed the complexity of static schedulability specifications in the E-T-C scheduling model, which is described at depth in [Sub00]. The model finds applicability in a number of domains. We demonstrated the existence of polynomial time algorithms for the general case and presented faster algorithms for a number of special cases. Table (1) summarizes our contributions in this paper.

Table 1. Summary of Results for Static Scheduling

	`<arb|arb|stat>`	`<aph|stan|stat>`	`<aph|net|stat>`
Schedulability	$O(m.\mathcal{C})$	$O(m.n)$	$O(m.n^2.\log m)$
Online Dispatching		$O(1)$	

The principal advantages of Static Scheduling are:

1. *No online computation* - As mentioned in Section §5, static scheduling obviates the need for an online computing during the dispatching phase. The start time vector computed by Algorithm (5.1) is used in every scheduling window.
2. *Efficient decidability* - We demonstrated that the static schedulability query can be decided in polynomial time, irrespective of the execution time domain (as long as it is a convex set) or the constraint matrix. This feature is particularly useful, when the real-time system is constrained through power-equations which can be approximated through convex sets.

An interesting open project is the integration of our work within the kernel of existing real-time operating systems and studying its performance in a more complete setting.

Acknowledgements. We wish to thank Michael Bond of the WVU libraries for his contributions towards the implementation.

A   Implementation

We implemented our static scheduling algorithm on a Linux box, with Red Hat Linux. We used *lp-solve*[6] [Ber95] for all our algorithms. Table (2) details the machine characteristics, while table (3) tabulates our results[7]:

Most of the constraints were chosen from the boeing data-set, provided as part of [LTCA89], while some of them were randomly generated. The execution time domain **E** for most inputs was an axis-parallel hyper-rectangle, although we did use general polyhedra for some constraint sets.

---

[6] Version 2.1. This software is available free of cost at the URL in [Ber95].

[7] We have more detailed implementation statistics which are part of an extended version of this paper

Table 2. Machine Characteristics

Speed	500 Mhz
Processor	Pentium III
Memory	128 Mb RAM
Cache	L2
Operating System	Redhat Linux 6.0
Kernel	2.2.16
Language	Perl 5.005-03
Software	*lp-solve*

Table 3. Summary of Results for Static Scheduling

Number of jobs	Number of Constraints	Time (seconds)
5	10	0.27
10	20	0.42
15	30	0.54
20	40	1.14
25	50	1.82
30	60	2.74
35	70	4.49
40	80	6.45
45	90	7.45
50	100	10.91

A.1   Interpretation

Table (3) demonstrates that even for for fairly large job and constraint sets, static schedules can be computed quickly. Although we used an open-source software product viz. *lp-solve*, our performance did not degrade. We are confident that using a commercial product such as AMPL should decrease the computation time significantly.

References

[Ber95]   M. Berkelaar. Linear programming solver. *Software Library for Operations Research, University of Karlsruhe*, 1995.

[BFW97]   Azer Bestavros and Victor Fay-Wolfe, editors. *Real-Time Database and Information Systems, Research Advances.* Kluwer Academic Publishers, 1997.

[Cho00]   Seonho Choi. Dynamic time-based scheduling for hard real-time systems. *Journal of Real-Time Systems*, 2000.

[CLR92]   T. H. Cormen, C. E. Leiserson, and R. L. Rivest. *Introduction to Algorithms.* MIT Press and McGraw-Hill Book Company, 6th edition, 1992.

[Das85]   B. Dasarathy. Timing Constraints of Real-Time Systems: Constructs for
            Expressing Them, Methods of Validating Them. *IEEE Transactions on
            Software Engineering*, SE-11(1):80–86, January 1985.

[DMP91]   R. Dechter, I. Meiri, and J. Pearl. Temporal constraint networks. *Artificial
            Intelligence*, 49:61–95, 1991.

[DRSK89]   A. Damm, J. Reisinger, W. Schwabl, and H. Kopetz. The Real-Time
            Operating System of MARS. *ACM Special Interest Group on Operating
            Systems*, 23(3):141–157, July 1989.

[GPS95]   R. Gerber, W. Pugh, and M. Saksena. Parametric Dispatching of Hard
            Real-Time Tasks. *IEEE Transactions on Computers*, 1995.

[HG93]   S. Hong and R. Gerber. Compiling real-time programs into schedulable
            code. In *Proceedings of the ACM SIGPLAN '93 Conference on Program-
            ming Language Design and Implementation*. ACM Press, June 1993. *SIG-
            PLAN Notices, 28(6):166-176*.

[HL89]   C. C. Han and K. J. Lin. Job scheduling with temporal distance con-
            straints. Technical Report UIUCDCS-R-89-1560, University of Illinois at
            Urbana-Champaign, Department of Computer Science, 1989.

[HL92a]   C. C. Han and K. J. Lin. Scheduling Distance-Constrained Real-Time
            Tasks. In *Proceedings, IEEE Real-time Systems Symposium*, pages 300–
            308, Phoenix, Arizona, December 1992.

[HL92b]   C. C. Han and K. J. Lin. Scheduling real-time computations with separa-
            tion constraints. *Information Processing Letters*, 12:61–66, May 1992.

[HN94]   Dorit S. Hochbaum and Joseph (Seffi) Naor. Simple and fast algorithms
            for linear and integer programs with two variables per inequality. *SIAM
            Journal on Computing*, 23(6):1179–1192, December 1994.

[HuL93]   J. B. Hiriart-urruty and C. Lemarechal. *Convex Analysis and Minimiza-
            tion Algorithms*. Springer-Verlag, 1993.

[Ja'92]   Joseph Ja'Ja'.   An introduction to parallel algorithms (contents).
            *SIGACTN: SIGACT News (ACM Special Interest Group on Automata
            and Computability Theory)*, 23, 1992.

[JM86]   F. Jahanian and A.K. Mok. Safety analysis of timing properties in real-
            time systems. *IEEE Transactions on Software Engineering*, SE-12(9):890–
            904, September 1986.

[LTCΛ89]   S. T. Levi, S. K. Tripathi, S. D. Carson, and A. K. Agrawala. The Maruti
            Hard Real-Time Operating System. *ACM Special Interest Group on Op-
            erating Systems*, 23(3):90–106, July 1989.

[MAT90]   D. Mosse, Ashok K. Agrawala, and Satish K. Tripathi. Maruti a hard
            real-time operating system. In *Second IEEE Workshop on Experimental
            Distributed Systems*, pages 29–34. IEEE, 1990.

[MKAT92]   D. Mosse, Keng-Tai Ko, Ashok K. Agrawala, and Satish K. Tripathi.
            Maruti: An Environment for Hard Real-Time Applications. In Ashok K.
            Agrawala, Karen D. Gordon, and Phillip Hwang, editors, *Maruti OS*, pages
            75–85. IOS Press, 1992.

[Pin95]   M. Pinedo. *Scheduling: theory, algorithms, and systems*. Prentice-Hall,
            Englewood Cliffs, 1995.

[Sak94]   Manas Saksena. *Parametric Scheduling in Hard Real-Time Systems*. PhD
            thesis, University of Maryland, College Park, June 1994.

[SB94]   A. Stoyenko and T. P. Baker. Real-Time Schedulability Analyzable Mech-
            anisms in Ada9X. *Proceeding of the IEEE*, 82(1):95–106, January 1994.

[Sch87]   Alexander Schrijver. *Theory of Linear and Integer Programming*. John
            Wiley and Sons, New York, 1987.

[SdSA94]   M. Saksena, J. da Silva, and A. Agrawala. Design and Implementation of Maruti-II. In Sang Son, editor, *Principles of Real-Time Systems*. Prentice Hall, 1994. Also available as CS-TR-2845, University of Maryland.

[Sub00]   K. Subramani. *Duality in the Parametric Polytope and its Applications to a Scheduling Problem*. PhD thesis, University of Maryland, College Park, July 2000.

[Sub01]   K. Subramani. Modeling clairvoyance and constraints in real-time scheduling. In *Proceedings of the 6th European Conference on Planning*, September 2001.

[Vai87]   P. M. Vaidya. An algorithm for linear programming which requires $O(((m + n)n^2 + (m + n)^{1.5}n)L)$ arithmetic operations. In Alfred Aho, editor, *Proceedings of the 19th Annual ACM Symposium on Theory of Computing*, pages 29–38, New York City, NY, May 1987. ACM Press.

Preemptive Job-Shop Scheduling Using Stopwatch Automata*

Yasmina Abdeddaïm and Oded Maler

VERIMAG, Centre Equation, 2, av. de Vignate 38610 Gières, France
Yasmina.Abdeddaim@imag.fr Oded.Maler@imag.fr

Abstract. In this paper we show how the problem of job-shop scheduling where the jobs are preemptible can be modeled naturally as a shortest path problem defined on an extension of timed automata, namely stopwatch automata where some of the clocks might be freezed at certain states. Although general verification problems on stopwatch automata are known to be undecidable, we show that due to particular properties of optimal schedules, the shortest path in the automaton belongs to a finite subset of the set of acyclic paths and hence the problem is solvable. We present several algorithms and heuristics for finding the shortest paths in such automata and test their implementation on numerous benchmark examples.

1 Introduction

In [AM01] we have described a first step in a research programme intended to re-formulate scheduling problems using (timed) automata-based formalisms. Apart from the undeniable joy of re-inventing the wheel, this work is motivated by the belief that such automata provide timing problems with faithful state-based dynamic models on which a systematic study of semantic and computational problems can be done — the reader is referred to [AM01] for some of the motivation and background and to [AM99, AGP99,NTY00,NY01,BFH$^+$01] for other recent results in this spirit. In this framework the runs of the timed automaton correspond to feasible schedules and finding a time-optimal schedule amounts to finding the shortest path (in terms of elapsed time) in the automaton. In [AM01] we have shown how this works nicely for the job-shop scheduling problem which can be modeled by a certain class of *acyclic* timed automata, having finitely many qualitative[1] runs. Each such qualitative run is an equivalence class of a non-countable number of quantitative runs, but as we have shown, one of those (a "non-lazy" run which makes transitions as soon as possible) is sufficient to find the optimum over the whole class. These observations allowed us to apply efficient search algorithms over single configurations of clocks rather than work with zones.

In this work we extend these results to preemptible jobs, i.e. jobs that can use a machine for some time, stop for a while and then resume from where they stopped. Such

---

* This work was partially supported by the European Community Project IST-2001-35304 AME-TIST http://ametist.cs.utwente.nl

[1] By a qualitative run of a timed automaton we mean a sequence of states and transitions without metric timing information.

situations are common, for example, when the machines are computers. While extending the framework of [AM01] to treat this situation we encounter two problems:

1. The corresponding class of automata goes beyond timed automata because clocks are stopped but not reset to zero when a job is preempted. General reachability problems for such stopwatch automata (also known as *integration graphs*) are known to be undecidable [C92,KPSY99].
2. Due to preemption and resumption, which corresponds to a loop in the underlying transition graph, the obtained automata are cyclic (unlike the non-preemptive case) and they have an *infinite* number of qualitative runs.

We will show however that these problems can be overcome for the class of stopwatch automata that correspond to preemtible job shop problems, and that efficient algorithms can be constructed.

The rest of the paper is organized as follows. In section 2 we give a short introduction to the preemptive job-shop scheduling problem including a fundamental property of optimal schedules. In section 3 we recall the definition of stopwatch automata and show how to transform a job-shop specification into such an automaton whose runs correspond to feasible schedules. In section 4 we describe efficient algorithms for solving the shortest-path problem for these automata (either exactly or approximately) and report the performance results of their prototype implementation on numerous benchmark examples.

2   Preemptive Job-Shop Scheduling

The Job-shop scheduling problem is a generic resource allocation problem in which common resources ("machines") are required at various time points (and for given durations) by different tasks. The goal is to find a way to allocate the resources such that all the tasks terminate as soon as possible. We consider throughout the paper a fixed set M of resources. A *step* is a pair (m, d) where $m \in M$ and $d \in \mathbb{N}$, indicating the required utilization of resource m for time duration d. A *job specification* is a finite sequence

$$J = (m_1, d_1), (m_2, d_2), \ldots, (m_k, d_k) \tag{1}$$

of steps, stating that in order to accomplish job J, one needs to use machine m_1 for d_1 time, then use machine m_2 for d_2 time, etc.

Definition 1 (Job-Shop Specification). *Let M be a finite set of resources (machines). A job specification over M is a triple $J = (k, \mu, d)$ where $k \in \mathbb{N}$ is the number of steps in J, $\mu : \{1..k\} \to M$ indicates which resource is used at each step, and $d : \{1..k\} \to \mathbb{N}$ specifies the length of each step. A job-shop specification is a set $\mathcal{J} = \{J^1, \ldots, J^n\}$ of jobs with $J^i = (k^i, \mu^i, d^i)$.*

In order to simplify notations we assume that each machine is used exactly once by every job. We denote $\mathbb{R}_+$ by T, abuse $\mathcal{J}$ for $\{1, \ldots, n\}$ and let $K = \{1, \ldots, k\}$.

Definition 2 (Feasible Schedules). *Let $\mathcal{J} = \{J^1, \ldots, J^n\}$ be a job-shop specification. A feasible schedule for $\mathcal{J}$ is a relation $S \subseteq \mathcal{J} \times K \times T$ so that $(i, j, t) \in S$ indicates that job J^i is busy doing its jth step at time t and, hence, occupies machine $\mu^i(j)$. We let T^i_j be the set of time instants where job $i \in \mathcal{J}$ is executing its jth step, i.e. $T^i_j = \{t : (i, j, t) \in S\}$.[2] A feasible schedule should satisfy the following conditions:*

1. *Ordering: if $(i, j, t) \in S$ and $(i, j', t') \in S$ then $j < j'$ implies $t < t'$ (steps of the same job are executed in order).*
2. *Covering: For every $i \in \mathcal{J}$ and $j \in K$*

$$\int_{t \in T^i_j} dt \geq d^i(j)$$

   (every step is executed).
3. *Mutual Exclusion: For every $i \neq i' \in \mathcal{J}$, $j, j' \in K$ and $t \in T$, if $(i, j, t) \in S$ and $(i', j', t) \in S$ then $\mu^i(j) \neq \mu^{i'}(j')$ (two steps of different jobs which execute at the same time do not use the same machine).*

Note that we allow a job to occupy the machine *after* the step has terminated. The *length* $|S|$ of a schedule is the supremal t over all $(i, j, t) \in S$. We say that a step j of job i is *enabled* in time t if $t \in \mathcal{E}^i_j = (\max T^i_{j-1}, \max T^i_j]$. The *optimal job-shop scheduling problem* is to find a schedule of a minimal length. This problem is known to be NP-hard [GJ79]. From the relational definition of schedules one can derive the following commonly used definitions:

1. The *machine allocation function* $\alpha : M \times T \to \mathcal{J}$ stating which job occupies a machine at any time, defined as $\alpha(m, t) = i$ if $(i, j, t) \in S$ and $\mu^i(j) = m$.
2. The *task progress function* $\beta : \mathcal{J} \times T \to M$ stating what machine is used by a job is at a given time, defined as $\beta(i, t) = m$ if $(i, j, t) \in S$ and $\mu^i(j) = m$.

These functions are partial — a machine or a job might be idle at certain times.
Example 1: Consider $M = \{m_1, m_2, m_3\}$ and two jobs $J^1 = (m_1, 3), (m_2, 2), (m_3, 4)$ and $J^2 = (m_2, 5)$. Two schedules S_1 and S_2 appear in Figure 1. The length of S_1 is 9 and it is the optimal schedule. As one can see, at $t = 3$, J^1 preempts J^2 and takes machine m_2.

We conclude this section with a reformulation of a well-known result concerning optimal preemptive schedules which will be used later. In essence this result formalizes the following two intuitive observations: *1) When jobs can be preempted and resumed at no cost, there is no reason to delay a step not being in a conflict with another. 2) Two jobs that keep on preempting each other do not contribute to the general progress.*

Definition 3 (Conflicts and Priorities). *Let S be a feasible schedule. We say that job i is in conflict with job i' on machine m in S (denoted by $i \parallel_m i'$) when there are two respective steps j and j' such that $\mu^i(j) = \mu^{i'}(j') = m$ and $\mathcal{E}^i_j \cap \mathcal{E}^{i'}_{j'} \neq \emptyset$. We say that i has priority on m over a conflicting job i' (denoted by $i \prec_m i'$) if it finishes using m before i' does, i.e. $\sup T^i_j < \sup T^{i'}_{j'}$.*

---

[2] We may assume further that T^i_j is can be decomposed into a countable number of left-closed right-open intervals.

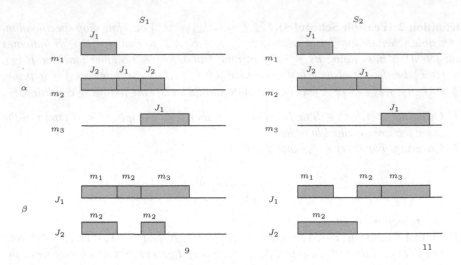

Fig. 1. Two schedule S_1 and S_2 visualized as the machine allocation function α and the task progress function β.

Note that conflicts and priorities are always induced by a schedule S although S is omitted from the notation.

Definition 4 (Efficient Schedules). *A schedule S is efficient if for every job i and a step j such that $\mu^i(j) = m$, job i uses m during all the time interval $\mathcal{E}^i_j$ except for times when another job i' such that $i' \prec_m i$ uses it.*

The following is a folk theorem, whose roots go back at least to [J55] with some reformulation and proofs in, for example, [CP90,PB96].

Theorem 1 (Efficiency is Good). *Every preemptive job-shop specification admits an efficient optimal schedule.*

Sketch of Proof: The proof is by showing that every inefficient schedule S can be transformed into an efficient schedule S' with $|S'| \leq |S|$. Let I be the first interval when inefficiency occurs for job i and machine m. We modify the schedule by shifting some of the later use of m by i into I. If m was occupied during I by another job i' such that $i \prec_m i'$, we give it the time slot liberated by i. The termination of the step by i' is not delayed by this modification because it happens anyway after i terminates its step. ◀

As an illustration consider the schedules appearing in Figure 2 with $J_1 \prec_m J_2 \prec_m J_3$ and where J_2 is enabled in the interval $[t_1, t_2]$. The first inefficiency in S_1 is eliminated in S_2 by letting J_2 use the free time slot before the arrival of J_1. The second inefficiency occurs when J_3 uses the machine while J_2 is waiting, and it is removed in S_3. The last inefficiency where J_3 is waiting while m is idle is removed in S_4.

This result reduces the set of candidates for optimality from the non-countable set of feasible schedules to the finite set of efficient schedules, each of which corresponds to

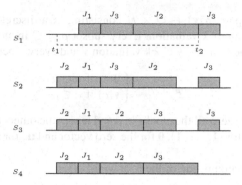

Fig. 2. Removal of inefficiency, $J_1 \prec J_2 \prec J_3$.

a fixed priority relation.[3] There are potentially $kn!$ priority relations but only a fraction of those needs to be considered because when i and i' are never in conflict concerning m, the priority $i \prec_m i'$ has no influence on the schedule.

3 Stopwatch Automata

Timed automata [AD94] are automata augmented with continuous clock variables whose values grow uniformly at every state. Clocks are reset to zero at certain transitions and tests on their values are used as pre-conditions for transitions. Hence they are ideal for describing concurrent time-dependent behaviors. There are however situations, preemptive scheduling being among those, in which we need to measure the overall accumulated time that a systems spends in some state. This motivated the extension of the model to have clocks with derivative zero at certain states. Unlike timed automata, the reachability problem for these automata is undecidable [C92]. Some sub-classes, *integration graphs*, were investigated in [KPSY99], where a decision procedure based on reducing the problem into linear constraint satisfaction was reported. Similar automata were studied in [MV94] and in [CL00] where an implementation of an approximate verification algorithm was described.

Definition 5 (Stopwatch Automaton).
A stopwatch automaton is a tuple $\mathcal{A} = (Q, C, s, f, \mathbf{u}, \Delta)$ where Q is a finite set of states, C is a finite set of n clocks, $\mathbf{u} : Q \rightarrow \{0, 1\}^n$ assigns a constant slope to every state and Δ is a transition relation consisting of elements of the form (q, ϕ, ρ, q') where q and q' are states, $\rho \subseteq C$ and ϕ (the transition guard) is a boolean combination of formulae of the form $(c \in I)$ for some clock c and some integer-bounded interval I. States s and f are the initial and final states, respectively.

A *clock valuation* is a function $\mathbf{v} : C \rightarrow \mathbb{R}_+ \cup \{0\}$, or equivalently a $|C|$-dimensional vector over $\mathbb{R}_+$. We denote the set of all clock valuations by $\mathcal{H}$. A configuration of the

---

[3] This might explain the popularity of priority-based approach in computer scheduling.

automaton is hence a pair $(q, \mathbf{v}) \in Q \times \mathcal{H}$ consisting of a discrete state (sometimes called "location") and a clock valuation. Every subset $\rho \subseteq C$ induces a reset function $\text{Reset}_\rho : \mathcal{H} \to \mathcal{H}$ defined for every clock valuation $\mathbf{v}$ and every clock variable $c \in C$ as

$$\text{Reset}_\rho \, \mathbf{v}(c) = \begin{cases} 0 & \text{if } c \in \rho \\ \mathbf{v}(c) & \text{if } c \notin \rho \end{cases}$$

That is, Reset_ρ resets to zero all the clocks in ρ and leaves the others unchanged. We use $\mathbf{1}$ to denote the unit vector $(1, \ldots, 1)$, $\mathbf{0}$ for the zero vector and $\mathbf{u}_q$ for $\mathbf{u}(q)$, the derivative of the clocks at q.

A *step* of the automaton is one of the following:

- A discrete step: $(q, \mathbf{v}) \xrightarrow{0} (q', \mathbf{v}')$, where there exists $\delta = (q, \phi, \rho, q') \in \Delta$, such that $\mathbf{v}$ satisfies ϕ and $\mathbf{v}' = \text{Reset}_\rho(\mathbf{v})$.
- A time step: $(q, \mathbf{v}) \xrightarrow{t} (q, \mathbf{v} + t\mathbf{u}_q), t \in \mathbb{R}_+$.

A *run* of the automaton starting from $(q_0, \mathbf{v}_0)$ is a finite sequence of steps

$$\xi : \quad (q_0, \mathbf{v}_0) \xrightarrow{t_1} (q_1, \mathbf{v}_1) \xrightarrow{t_2} \cdots \xrightarrow{t_l} (q_l, \mathbf{v}_l).$$

The *logical length* of such a run is l and its *metric length* is $|\xi| = t_1 + t_2 + \cdots + t_l$. Note that discrete transitions take no time.

Next we construct for every job $J = (k, \mu, d)$ a timed automaton with one clock such that for every step j with $\mu(j) = m$ there are three states: a state $\overline{m}$ which indicates that the job is waiting to start the step, a state m indicating that the job is executing the step and a state $\tilde{m}$ indicating that the job is preempted after having started. Upon entering m the clock is reset to zero, and measures the time spent in m. Preemption and resumption are modeled by transitions to and from state $\tilde{m}$ in which the clock does not progress. When the clock value reaches $d(j)$ the automaton can leave m to the next waiting state. Let $\overline{M} = \{\overline{m} : m \in M\}$, $\tilde{M} = \{\tilde{m} : m \in M\}$ and let $\overline{\mu} : K \to \overline{M}$ and $\tilde{\mu} : K \to \tilde{M}$ be auxiliary functions such that $\overline{\mu}(j) = \overline{m}$ and $\tilde{\mu}(j) = \tilde{m}$ whenever $\mu(j) = m$.

Definition 6 (Stopwatch Automaton for a Job). *Let $J = (k, \mu, d)$ be a job. Its associated automaton is $\mathcal{A} = (Q, \{c\}, u, \Delta, s, f)$ with $Q = P \cup \overline{P} \cup \tilde{P} \cup \{f\}$ where $P = \{\mu(1), \ldots \mu(k)\}, \overline{P} = \{\overline{\mu}(1), \ldots, \overline{\mu}(n)\}$ and $\tilde{P} = \{\tilde{\mu}(1), \ldots, \tilde{\mu}(n)\}$. The slope is defined as $u_q = 1$ when $q \in P$ and $u_q = 0$ otherwise.[4] The transition relation Δ consists of the following types of tuples*

type	q	ϕ	ρ	q'	
1) begin	$\overline{\mu}(j)$	true	$\{c\}$	$\mu(j)$	$j = 1..k$
2) pause	$\mu(j)$	true	$\emptyset$	$\tilde{\mu}(j)$	$j = 1..k$
3) resume	$\tilde{\mu}(j)$	true	$\emptyset$	$\mu(j)$	$j = 1..k$
4) end	$\mu(j)$	$c \geq d(j)$	$\emptyset$	$\overline{\mu}(j+1)$	$j = 1..k-1$
end	$\mu(k)$	$c \geq d(k)$	$\emptyset$	f	

The initial state is $\overline{\mu}(1)$.

---

[4] Note that the slope at state $\overline{m}$ can be arbitrary because clock c is *inactive* in this state: it is reset to zero without being tested upon leaving $\overline{m}$.

The automata for the two jobs in Example 1 are depicted in Figure 3.

For every automaton $\mathcal{A}$ we define a *ranking function* $g : Q \times \mathbb{R}_+ \to \mathbb{R}_+$ such that $g(q, v)$ is a lower-bound on the time remaining until f is reached from (q, v):

$$g(f, v) = 0$$
$$g(\overline{\mu}(j), v) = \sum_{l=j}^{k} d(l)$$
$$g(\mu(j), v) = g(\overline{\mu}(j), v) - \min\{v, d(j)\}$$
$$g(\tilde{\mu}(j), v) = g(\overline{\mu}(j), v) - \min\{v, d(j)\}$$

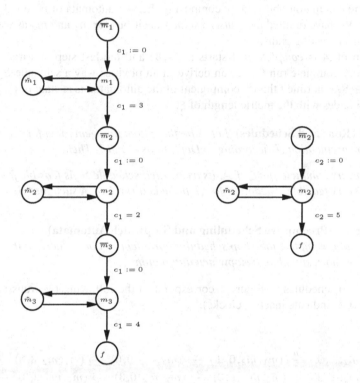

Fig. 3. The automata corresponding to the jobs $J^1 = (m_1, 3), (m_2, 2), (m_3, 4)$ and $J^2 = (m_2, 5)$.

In order to obtain the timed automaton representing the whole job-shop specification we need to compose the automata for the individual tasks. The composition is rather standard, the only particular feature is the enforcement of mutual exclusion constraints by forbidding global states in which two or more automata are in a state corresponding to the same resource m. An n-tuple $q = (q^1, \ldots, q^n) \in (M \cup \overline{M} \cup \tilde{M} \cup \{f\})^n$ is said to be *conflicting* if it contains two distinct components q^i and $q^{i'}$ such that $q^i = q^{i'} = m \in M$.

Definition 7 (Mutual Exclusion Composition). *Let $\mathcal{J} = \{J^1, \ldots, J^n\}$ be a job-shop specification and let $\mathcal{A}^i = (Q^i, C^i, u^i, \Delta^i, s^i, f^i)$ be the automaton corresponding to*

*each J^i. Their mutual exclusion composition is the automaton $\mathcal{A} = (Q, C, \mathbf{u}, \Delta, s, f)$
such that Q is the restriction of $Q^1 \times \ldots Q^n$ to non-conflicting states, $C = C^1 \cup \ldots \cup C^n$,
$s = (s^1, \ldots, s^n)$, $f = (f^1, \ldots, f^n)$. The slope $\mathbf{u}_q$ for a global state $q = (q^1, \ldots q^n)$ is
$(u_{q^1}, \ldots, u_{q^n})$ and the transition relation Δ contains all the tuples of the form*

$$((q^1, \ldots, q^i, \ldots, q^n), \phi, \rho, (q^1, \ldots, p^i, \ldots, q^n))$$

*such that $(q^i, \phi, \rho, p^i) \in \Delta^i$ for some i and the global states $(q^1, \ldots, q^i, \ldots, q^n)$ and
$(q^1, \ldots, p^i, \ldots, q^n)$ are non-conflicting.*

Part of the automaton obtained by composing the two automata of Figure 3 appears in
Figure 4. We have omitted the *pause/resume* transitions for m_1 and m_3 as well as some
other non-interesting paths.

A run of $\mathcal{A}$ is *complete* if it starts at $(s, \mathbf{0})$ and the last step is a transition to f.
From every complete run ξ one can derive in an obvious way a schedule S_ξ such that
$(i, j, t) \in S_\xi$ if at time t the ith component of the automaton is at state $\mu(j)$. The length
of S_ξ coincides with the metric length of ξ.

Claim 1 (Runs and Schedules) *Let $\mathcal{A}$ be the automaton generated for the preemptive
job-shop specification $\mathcal{J}$ according to Definitions 6 and 7. Then:*

1. *For every complete run ξ of $\mathcal{A}$, its associated schedule S_ξ is feasible for $\mathcal{J}$.*
2. *For every feasible schedule S for $\mathcal{J}$ there is a run ξ of $\mathcal{A}$ such that $S_\xi = S$.*

Corollary 1 (Preemptive Scheduling and Stopwatch Automata).
*The optimal preemptive job-shop scheduling problem can be reduced to the problem of
finding the shortest path in a stopwatch automaton.*

The two schedules of Figure 1 correspond to the following two runs (we use the
notation $\perp$ to indicate inactive clocks):

S_1 :
$$(\overline{m}_1, \overline{m}_2, \perp, \perp) \xrightarrow{0} (m_1, \overline{m}_2, 0, \perp) \xrightarrow{0} (m_1, m_2, 0, 0) \xrightarrow{3} (m_1, m_2, 3, 3) \xrightarrow{0}$$
$$(\overline{m}_2, m_2, \perp, 3) \xrightarrow{0} (\overline{m}_2, \tilde{m}_2, \perp, 3) \xrightarrow{0} (m_2, \tilde{m}_2, 0, 3) \xrightarrow{2} (m_2, \tilde{m}_2, 2, 3) \xrightarrow{0}$$
$$(\overline{m}_3, \tilde{m}_2, \perp, 3) \xrightarrow{0} (\overline{m}_3, m_2, \perp, 3) \xrightarrow{0} (m_3, m_2, 0, 3) \xrightarrow{2} (m_3, m_2, 2, 5) \xrightarrow{0}$$
$$(m_3, f, 2, \perp) \xrightarrow{2} (m_3, f, 4, \perp) \xrightarrow{0} (f, f, \perp, \perp)$$

S_2 :
$$(\overline{m}_1, \overline{m}_2, \perp, \perp) \xrightarrow{0} (m_1, \overline{m}_2, 0, \perp) \xrightarrow{0} (m_1, m_2, 0, 0) \xrightarrow{3} (m_1, m_2, 3, 3) \xrightarrow{0}$$
$$(\overline{m}_2, m_2, \perp, 3) \xrightarrow{2} (\overline{m}_2, m_2, \perp, 5) \xrightarrow{0} (\overline{m}_2, f, \perp, \perp) \xrightarrow{0} (m_2, f, 0, \perp) \xrightarrow{2}$$
$$(m_2, f, 2, \perp) \xrightarrow{0} (\overline{m}_3, f, \perp, \perp) \xrightarrow{0} (m_3, f, 0, \perp) \xrightarrow{4} (m_3, f, 4, \perp) \xrightarrow{0} (f, f, \perp, \perp)$$

The job-shop automaton admits a special structure: ignoring the *pause* and *resume*
transitions, the automaton is *acyclic* and its state-space admits a natural partial-order.
It can be partitioned into levels according to the number of *begin* and *end* transitions
from s to the state. There are no staying conditions (invariants) and the automaton can

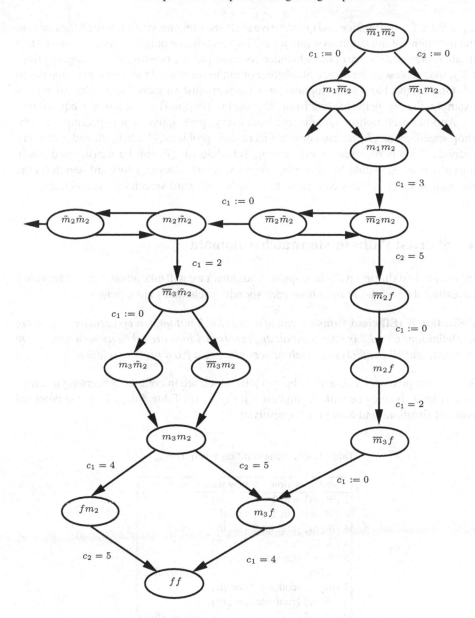

Fig. 4. The global stopwatch automaton for the two jobs.

stay forever in any given state. Recall that in any automaton extended with auxiliary variables the transition graph might be misleading, because two or more transitions entering *the same* discrete state, e.g. transitions to (m_3, f) in Figure 4, might enter it with different clock valuations, and hence lead to different continuations. Consequently, algorithms for verification and quantitative analysis might need to explore all the nodes in the unfolding of the automaton into a tree. Two transitions outgoing from the same state might represent a choice of the scheduler, for example, the two transitions outgoing from $(\overline{m}_2, m_2)$ represent the choice of whether or not to preempt J^2 and give machine m_2 to J^1. On the other hand some duplication of paths are just artifacts due to interleaving, for example, the two paths leading from $(\overline{m}_1, \overline{m}_2)$ to (m_1, m_2) are practically equivalent.

Another useful observation is that from every (preemptive or non-preemptive) job-shop specification $\mathcal{J}$ one can construct its reverse problem $\mathcal{J}'$ where the order of every individual job is reversed. Every feasible schedule for $\mathcal{J}'$ can be transformed easily into a feasible schedule for $\mathcal{J}$ having the same length. Doing a forward search on the automaton for $\mathcal{J}'$ is thus equivalent to doing a backward search on the automaton for $\mathcal{J}$.

4   Shortest Paths in Stopwatch Automata

In order to find shortest paths in stopwatch automata we will take advantage of Theorem 1 to restrict the search to runs whose corresponding schedules are efficient.

Definition 8 (Efficient Runs). *A run of a stopwatch automaton constructed according to Definitions 6 and 7 is efficient if all discrete transitions are taken as soon as they are enabled, and all conflicts are resolved according to a fixed priority relation.*

To be more precise, let J_1 and J_2 be two jobs which are in conflict concerning machine m and let J_1 be the one with the highest priority on m. Table 4 depicts all the potential conflict situations and how they are resolved.

Table 1. Resolving conflicts when $J_1 \preceq_m J_2$.

state	action	new state	remark
1 $(\overline{m}, \overline{m})$	start 1	$(m, \overline{m})$	
2 $(\overline{m}, \tilde{m})$	start 1	$(m, \tilde{m})$	
3 $(\overline{m}, m)$	preempt 2	$(\overline{m}, \tilde{m})$	
4 $(\tilde{m}, \overline{m})$	resume 1	$(m, \overline{m})$	
5 $(\tilde{m}, \tilde{m})$	resume 1	$(m, \tilde{m})$	
6 $(\tilde{m}, m)$			(impossible)
7 $(m, \overline{m})$	(continue)	$(m, \overline{m})$	
8 $(m, \tilde{m})$	(continue)	$(m, \tilde{m})$	
9 (m, m)			(impossible)

In situations 1, 2, 4, and 5 J_1 is waiting for the machine which is not occupied and so it takes it. Such situations could have been reached, for example, by a third job of higher priority releasing m or by J_1 finishing its prior step and entering $\overline{m}$. Situation 3 is similar but with J_2 occupying m and hence has to be preempted to reach situation 2. Situation 6, where J_1 is preempted and J_1 is executing, contradicts the priority and is not reachable. In situations 7 and 8, J_1 is executing and no preemption action is taken. Finally situation 9 violates mutual exclusion.

The restriction to efficient runs makes the problem decidable: we can just enumerate all priority relations, derive the schedules implied by each of them and compare their lengths. The search algorithm that we employ on the unfolding of the automaton generates priorities *on the fly* whenever two jobs come into conflict. In the example of Figure 3 the first conflict is encountered in state $(\overline{m}_2, m_2)$ and from there we may choose between two options, either to continue with time passage or preempt J_2. in the first case we fix the priority $J_2 \prec J_1$ and let J_2 finish without considering preemption anymore while in the second case the priority is $J_1 \prec J_2$, we move to $(\overline{m}_2, \tilde{m}_2)$ and the transition back to $(\overline{m}_2, m_2)$ becomes forbidden. From there we can only continue to $(m_2, \tilde{m}_2)$ and let the time pass until J_1 releases m_2.

To formalize this we define a *valid successors* relation over tuples of the form $(q, \mathbf{x}, \Pi, \theta)$ where $(q, \mathbf{x})$ is a global configuration of the automaton, Π is a (partial) priority relation and θ is the total elapsed time for reaching $(q, \mathbf{x})$ from the initial state. When there are no immediate transitions enabled in $(q, \mathbf{x})$ we have

$$Succ(q, \mathbf{x}, \Pi, \theta) = \{(q, \mathbf{x} + t \cdot \mathbf{u}_q, \Pi, \theta + t)\}$$

where t is the minimal time until a transition becomes enabled, that is, the least t such that a guard on a transition from q is satisfied at $\mathbf{x} + t \cdot \mathbf{u}_q$.

When there are immediate transition enabled in $(q, \mathbf{x})$ we have

$$Succ(q, \mathbf{x}, \Pi, \theta) = L_1 \cup L_2 \cup L_3$$

where

$$L_1 = \{(q', \mathbf{x}', \Pi, \theta) : (q, \mathbf{x}) \xrightarrow{\tau} (q', \mathbf{x}')\}$$

for every immediate transition τ such that τ is non-conflicting or belongs to the job whose priority on the respective machine is higher than those of all competing jobs. In addition, if there is a conflict on m involving a new job i whose priority compared to job i^*, having the highest priority so far, has not yet been determined, we have

$$L_2 = \{(q, \mathbf{x}, \Pi \cup \{i^* \prec i\}, \theta)\}$$

and

$$L_3 = \{(q, \mathbf{x}, \Pi \cup \bigcup_{\{i' : i' \#_m i\}} \{i \prec i'\}, \theta)\}.$$

The successor in L_2 represent the choice to prefer i^* over i (the priority of i relative to other waiting jobs will be determined only after i^* terminates), while S_3 represents the choice of preferring i over all other jobs.

Using this definition we can construct a search algorithm that explores all the efficient runs of $\mathcal{A}$.

Algorithm 1 (Forward Reachability for Stopwatch Automata)
Waiting: $= \{(s, \mathbf{0}, \emptyset, 0)\}$;
while *Waiting* $\neq \emptyset$; **do**
  Pick $(q, \mathbf{x}, \Pi, \theta) \in$ *Waiting;*
  For every $(q', \mathbf{x}', \Pi', \theta') \in Succ(q, \mathbf{x}, \Pi, \theta)$;
    Insert $(q', \mathbf{x}', \Pi', \theta')$ *into Waiting;*
  Remove $(q, \mathbf{x}, \Pi, \theta)$ *from Waiting*
end

The length of the shortest path is the least θ such that $(f, \mathbf{x}, \Pi, \theta)$ is explored by the algorithm.

This exhaustive search algorithm can be improved into a best-first search as follows (similar ideas were investigated in [BFH+01]). We define an evaluation function for estimating the quality of configurations.

$$E((q_1, \ldots, q_n), (v_1, \ldots, v_n), \Pi, \theta) = \theta + \max\{g^i(q_i, v_i)\}_{i=1}^n$$

where g^i is the previously-defined ranking function associated with each automaton $\mathcal{A}^i$. Note that $\max\{g^i\}$ gives the most optimistic estimation of the *remaining* time, assuming that no job will have to wait. It is not hard to see that $E(q, \mathbf{x}, \Pi, \theta)$ gives a lower bound on the length of every complete run which passes through $(q, \mathbf{x})$ at time θ.

The following algorithm orders the waiting list of configurations according to their evaluation. It is guaranteed to produce the optimal path because it stops the exploration only when it is clear that the unexplored states cannot lead to schedules better than those found so far.

Algorithm 2 (Best-first Forward Reachability)
Waiting: $= \{(s, \mathbf{0}, \emptyset, 0)\}$;
Best: $= \infty$
$(q, \mathbf{x}, F, \theta)$*:= first in Waiting;*
while *Best* $> E(q, \mathbf{x}, F, \theta)$
do
  $(q, \mathbf{x}, \Pi, \theta)$*:= first in Waiting;*
  For every $(q', \mathbf{x}', \Pi', \theta') \in Succ(q, \mathbf{x}, \Pi, \theta)$;
    if $q' = f$ **then**
      Best: $= \min\{Best, E((q', \mathbf{x}', \Pi', \theta'))\}$
    else
      Insert $(q', \mathbf{x}', \Pi', \theta')$ *into Waiting;*
  Remove $(q, \mathbf{x}, \Pi, \theta)$ *from Waiting*
end

Using this algorithm we were able the find optimal schedules of systems with up to 8 jobs and 4 machines (12^8 discrete states and 8 clocks). In order to treat larger problems we abandon optimality and use a heuristic algorithm which can quickly generate sub-optimal solutions. The algorithm is a mixture of breadth-first and best-first search with a fixed number w of explored nodes at any level of the automaton. For every level we take the w best (according to E) nodes, generate their successors but explore only the best w among them, and so on.

In order to test this heuristics we took 16 problems among the most notorious job-shop scheduling problems.[5] For each of these problems we have applied our algorithms for different choices of w, both forward and backward (it takes, on the average few minutes for each problem). In Table 5 we compare our best results on these problems to the most recent results reported by Le Pape and Baptiste [PB96,PB97] where the problem was solved using state-of-the-art constraint satisfaction techniques. As the table shows, the results our first prototype are very close to the optimum.

Table 2. The results of our implementation on the benchmarks. Columns #j and #m indicated the number of jobs and machines, followed by the best known results for non-preemptive scheduling, the known optimum for the preemptive case, the results of Le Pape and Baptiste, followed by our results and their deviation from the optimum.

problem			non preempt	preemptive			
name	#j	#m	optimum	optimum	[PB96,PB97]	stopwatch	deviation
LA02	10	5	655	655	655	655	0.00 %
FT10	10	10	930	900	900	911	1.21 %
ABZ5	10	10	1234	1203	1206	1250	3.76 %
ABZ6	10	10	943	924	924	936	1.28 %
ORB1	10	10	1059	1035	1035	1093	5.31 %
ORB2	10	10	888	864	864	884	2.26 %
ORB3	10	10	1005	973	994	1013	3.95 %
ORB4	10	10	1005	980	980	1004	2.39 %
ORB5	10	10	887	849	849	887	4.28 %
LA19	10	10	842	812	812	843	3.68 %
LA20	10	15	902	871	871	904	3.65 %
LA21	10	15	1046	1033	1033	1086	4.88 %
LA24	10	15	936	909	915	972	6.48 %
LA27	10	20	1235	1235	1235	1312	5.87 %
LA37	15	15	1397	1397	1397	1466	4.71 %
LA39	15	15	1233	1221	1221	1283	4.83 %

5   Conclusion

We have demonstrated that the automata-theoretic approach to scheduling can be extended to preemptive scheduling and can be applied successfully to very large systems. Future work will investigate the applicability of this approach to scheduling of periodic tasks in real-time systems. In retrospect, it looks as if the undecidability results for *arbitrary* stopwatch automata have been taken too seriously. Timed and stopwatch automata arising from specific application domains have additional structure and their analysis might turn out to be feasible (see also recent results in [FPY02]).

---

[5] The problems are taken from ftp://mscmga.ms.ic.ac.uk/pub/jobshop1.txt

Acknowledgment. We thank Eugene Asarin and Stavros Tripakis for numerous useful comments.

References

[AM01]   Y. Abdeddaïm and O. Maler, Job-Shop Scheduling using Timed Automata in
           G. Berry, H. Comon and A. Finkel (Eds.), *Proc. CAV'01*, 478-492, LNCS 2102,
           Springer 2001.

[AGP99]   K. Altisen, G. Goessler, A. Pnueli, J. Sifakis, S. Tripakis and S. Yovine, A Frame-
           work for Scheduler Synthesis, *Proc. RTSS'99*, 154-163, IEEE, 1999.

[AD94]   R. Alur and D.L. Dill, A Theory of Timed Automata, *Theoretical Computer Science*
           126, 183-235, 1994.

[AM99]   E. Asarin and O. Maler, As Soon as Possible: Time Optimal Control for Timed
           Automata, *Proc. HSCC'99*, 19-30, LNCS 1569, Springer, 1999.

[BFH⁺01]   G. Behrmann, A. Fehnker T.S. Hune, K.G. Larsen, P. Pettersson and J. Romijn,
           Efficient Guiding Towards Cost-Optimality in UPPAAL, *Proc. TACAS 2001*, 174-
           188, LNCS 2031, Springer, 2001.

[CP90]   J. Carlier and E. Pinson, A Practical Use of Jackson's Preemptive Schedule for
           Solving the Job-Shop Problem, *Annals of Operations Research* 26, 1990.

[CL00]   F. Cassez and K.G. Larsen, On the Impressive Power of Stopwatches, in
           C. Palamidessi (Ed.) *Proc. CONCUR'2000*, 138-152, LNCS 1877, Springer, 2000.

[C92]   K. Cerans, *Algorithmic Problems in Analysis of Real Time System Specifications*,
           Ph.D. thesis, University of Latvia, Riga, 1992.

[FPY02]   E. Fersman, P. Pettersson and W. Yi, Timed Automata with Asynchronous Pro-
           cesses: Schedulability and Decidability, *TACAS 2002*, this volume, 2002.

[GJ79]   M. R. Garey and D. S Johnson, *Computers and Intractability, A Guide to the Theory
           of NP-Completeness*, W. H. Freeman and Company, 1979.

[J55]   J. R. Jackson, Scheduling a Production Line to Minimize Maximum Tardiness,
           Research Report 43, *Management Sciences Research Project*, UCLA, 1955.

[JM99]   A.S. Jain and S. Meeran, Deterministic Job-Shop Scheduling: Past, Present and
           Future, *European Journal of Operational Research* 113, 390-434, 1999.

[KPSY99]   Y. Kesten, A. Pnueli, J. Sifakis and S. Yovine, Decidable Integration Graphs, *In-
           formation and Computation* 150, 209–243, 1999.

[MV94]   J. McManis and P. Varaiya, Suspension Automata: A Decidable Class of Hybrid
           Automata, in D.L Dill (Ed.), *Proc. CAV'94*, 105-117, LNCS 818, Springer, 1994.

[NTY00]   P. Niebert, S. Tripakis S. Yovine, Minimum-Time Reachability for Timed Au-
           tomata, *IEEE Mediteranean Control Conference*, 2000.

[NY01]   P. Niebert and S. Yovine, Computing Efficient Operation Schemes for Chemical
           Plants in Multi-batch Mode, *European Journal of Control* 7, 440-453, 2001.

[PB96]   C. Le Pape and P. Baptiste, A Constraint-Based Branch-and-Bound Algorithm for
           Preemptive Job-Shop Scheduling, *Proc. of Int. Workshop on Production Planning
           and Control*, Mons, Belgium, 1996.

[PB97]   C. Le Pape and P. Baptiste, An Experimental Comparaison of Constraint-Based
           Algorithms for the Preemptive Job-shop Sheduling Problem, *CP97 Workshop on
           Industrial Constraint-Directed Scheduling*, 1997.

Explicit Modeling of Influences, and of Their Absence, in Distributed Systems

Horst F. Wedde and Arnim Wedig

Informatik III, University of Dortmund
D-44221 Dortmund, Germany
{wedde,wedig}@ls3.cs.uni-dortmund.de

Abstract. Specific problems in practical distributed system design arise from *incomplete information* about the cooperation requirements, up to, or even beyond, the final design stage. Events in components *will* occur, or they *may* occur, depending on (local) user decisions. The latter *may* also *not* occur, as a result of yet unknown external influences or design faults. Adequate formal modeling tools should allow for distinguishing between such different event types. Our approach for this purpose to be introduced here is the *formal model of I–Systems*. As a particularly relevant and unique feature, the presence as well as the absence of interactional influences (as part of distributed cooperation requirements) can be *explicitly* modeled, with no side effects. A non-trivial synchronization problem is modeled *incrementally* in order to demonstrate both the modeling and analysis capabilities in I–Systems.

1 Introduction

In modeling distributed systems, specific problems arise from *incomplete information* up to, or even beyond, the final design stage, as much as from the *distribution of control*. While the structure or the behavior of components could be considered manageable this is different for distributed systems. Here conditions and constraints on the cooperation between components are local, i.e. they concern small subsystems of interacting components while typically imposing a global propagation effect that is often not known at the design phase, or even undesirable. Thus expected or needed events in a subsystem may never occur because some of its preconditions may never hold, due to unforeseen propagation effects from restrictions elsewhere. In such cases models turn inadequate during test or debugging phases unless appropriate formal tools were available to trace design or implementation failures back to their origin.

Another complication under distributed control is that the components' behavior, as observed from an interacting component, exhibits two different types of transitions: some *will* occur, some *may* (or may never) occur. The reasons for the latter behavior are not observable from the interacting components. Events that *will* occur will do so (unless prevented through external influences) for two reasons:

J.-P. Katoen and P. Stevens (Eds.): TACAS 2002, LNCS 2280, pp. 127–141, 2002.
© Springer-Verlag Berlin Heidelberg 2002

- according to the local operational semantics (e.g. for program execution) which are otherwise comparable to *organizational duties* imposed on the employees in a company;
- through implemented external influences that trigger the events.

Events that *may* occur come from two sources of influences:

- Local decisions, e.g. by a user in an interactive mode of operation;
- Incomplete information about unknown, or unpredictable, external influences (as discussed in the previous paragraph).

In order to cope with the problems mentioned and at the same time to develop a both reliable and incremental modeling methodology our approach is based on elementary binary relations between system components and their operational semantics (*action rules*). These specify the restrictive effect on the involved components.

Based on the observation that components in distributed systems may be *passive/ reactive* (like main memory management in a uniprocessor operating system) or *active* (like in an interactive user operating mode), we distinguish in our terminology between *inert* and *autonomous* components, respectively.

Previous and Related Work. In [12] W. Reisig has considered two classes of transitions in Petri Nets specifying *progressive* actions (that *will* occur in the terms of our discussion) and *quiescent* actions (that may occur), respectively. The firing of quiescent transitions depends on information that has not been available at the modeling stage. If a quiescent transition does not fire, however (e.g. because a precondition can never be satisfied, due to a synchronization condition which might be too restrictive), this cannot, by definition of quiescence, be traced back to the originating cause. For the novel trace semantics that we have defined for I-Systems (local) influences and their global propagation are specified in such a way that external influences can be traced back to the originating system component or the originating behavioral restriction (whatever applies). Even the absence of influences (restrictions) is clearly visible from the specification. Reisig's work is the only approach related to our work. While the absence of influences is particularly required in synchronization constraints I–Systems are the only formal structures, up to our knowledge, that allow for explicitly modeling and analyzing such constraints incrementally. Earlier results of our theoretical work were reported in [11] and [13]. Additional information about interactive systems can be found in [3,16,17].

Organization of the Paper. The next section gives a brief survey on I–Systems, their basic concepts, semantics, and those behavioral properties that are needed in the subsequent sections. The main feature in section 3 is a general theorem on representing and at the same time generating an arbitrary local behavior structure through an elementary interaction with a passive component. Section 4 is devoted to demonstrating the incremental potential of I–Systems by stepwise modeling a solution for a non-trivial synchronization problem that includes requirements about the absence of external influences. Conclusions are briefly summarized at the end.

2   I–Systems

In order to model events in a distributed system as well as the cooperation between its components we define I–Systems. System components are presented as *parts*. These are constituted through their local states that are relevant for the interaction. The local states are called *phases*. The only thing we assume about the components is that they are in exactly one state at any time. The interaction is specified through two binary relations, denoted as *coupling* and *excitement relations*, respectively.

Definition 1 (I–System). A structure $IS = (P, B, \underline{B}, K, E)$ is called *I–System*, iff:

(1) P is a finite set of *phases*
(2) B is a set of *parts* with:
   a) $\forall b \in B : b \subseteq P$
   b) $\bigcup_{b \in B} b = P$
   c) $\forall b_1, b_2 \in B, b_1 \neq b_2 : b_1 \cap b_2 = \emptyset$
(3) $\underline{B}$ is a distinguished set of so-called *inert parts* $(\underline{B} \subseteq B)$
(4) $K \subseteq P \times P$ is the *coupling relation of IS* with:
   a) $K = K^{-1}$
   b) $\forall b \in B \, \forall p, p' \in b, p \neq p' : (p, p') \in K$
(5) $E \subseteq P \times P$ is the *excitement relation of IS* with
   a) $E \cap (E^{-1} \cup K) = \emptyset$

For $p \in P$, $b(p)$ denotes the part of p with $b(p) = b'$ iff $p \in b' \in B$. $AB(IS) := B \setminus \underline{B}$ is called the *set of autonomous parts*.   □

Fig. 1 depicts an I–System IS_1. The small circles are the phases (e.g. p_1, v_2) grouped by ovals, the parts. The parts may have names (e.g. b_1, b_2). The inert parts (e.g. $\underline{b}_3$) have gray fillings or/and an underlined name. Arrows (e.g. from p_3 to q_2) depict the excitement relation and lines between phases (e.g. from p_1 to v_1) the symmetrical coupling relation.

Remark 1. *Inert parts* represent special components in distributed systems. They are found e.g. in reactive systems and reactive software components (see e.g. [2,5,9]). Events in inert parts are always triggered by environmental influences. In the absence of external stimuli nothing will happen in such components.   □

The symmetrical coupling relation K specifies the subset of pairs of *mutually exclusive* phases. Condition 4.b implies therefore that two different phases in a part exclude each other from holding at any given time. The coupling relations between phases in the same part are omitted in graphical representations.

Based on local states of components we define global system situations by making use of the causal relationships between parts given by K. We term the

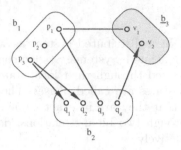

Fig. 1. I–System IS_1

new objects *cases*. A case is a subset c of phases such that $|c \cap b| = 1$ for all $b \in B$ and $(p_1, p_2) \notin K$ for all $p_1, p_2 \in c$. The phases of a case c may hold *concurrently.*

$\{p_1, q_4, v_2\}$ and $\{p_3, q_3, v_1\}$ are cases of the I–System in Fig. 1. $\{p_1, q_3, v_2\}$ is not a case because p_1 and q_3 are mutually exclusive phases.

Events are described by *phase transitions* which lead from one case to another. A phase transition $p \to q$ *may occur* in a case c iff $(c \setminus \{p\}) \cup \{q\}$ is a case. Two phase transitions $p_1 \to q_1$, $p_2 \to q_2$ are called *concurrent in a case* c iff each transition may occur in c and $(q_1, q_2) \notin K$. Two concurrent phase transitions may occur in arbitrary order or simultaneously. Thus they are causally independent, and according to the definition this global causal relationship can be checked by testing *local* static relations.

In the case $\{p_2, q_1, v_1\}$ the phase transition $p_2 \to p_1$ can never occur. In the case $\{p_2, q_1, v_2\}$ of IS_1, the phase transitions $p_2 \to p_1$ and $q_1 \to q_2$ may occur and they are concurrent.

While the coupling relation enables, in a given case, a phase transition to occur it is not guaranteed that it eventually *will* occur. In order explicitly to cover such kind of progress quality we introduce *forces* arising from external influences which enforce phase transitions to occur. Enforced phase transitions *will* occur unless prevented through different external influences. An element (p, q) in the *excitement relation* E expresses a potential excitation from phase p in part b to phase q in part b'. If p and q belong to a case c then b exerts a force on b' to leave p. The other idea behind is that the force is released only after the excited phase has been left. No force vanishes but by b' leaving the excited phase.

For the case $\{p_3, q_2, v_2\}$ of IS_1 in Fig. 1, b_1 influences b_2 to leave q_2. b_1 has to stay in p_3 as long as b_2 is in q_2. In $\{p_2, q_2, v_2\}$ no exciting influence is external.

In order to formalize the effects of influences and to distinguish between phase transitions that *may* and phase transitions that *will* occur, our idea is to assign certain qualities of activity (*phase qualities*) to every phase p, thus refining the concept of case to *global activity state* in which the phase qualities are reflected.

Definition 2 (Local / Global Activity State). Let $IS = (P, B, \underline{B}, K, E)$ be an I–System and $b \in B$. The mapping $z\langle b \rangle : b \longrightarrow b \cup \{0, 1, \mathsf{F}\}$ such that

(L1) $\forall p, p' \in b : (z\langle b \rangle(p) = p' \Rightarrow p' \notin \{p, 0, 1, \mathsf{F}\} \wedge b(p) \in AB(IS))$

(L2) $\exists! \, p \in b : z\langle b \rangle(p) \neq 0$

is called *local activity state* of b.

$LState(b)$ denotes the set of all local activity states of b. For a phase p in part b we interpret the *phase qualities* in the following way:

$$z\langle b \rangle(p) = \begin{cases} q : b \text{ is in } p, \, b \text{ has made the (control) decision to enter } q. \\ \mathsf{F} : b \text{ is in/ assumes } p, \, b \text{ is } unstable \text{ in } p \text{ (as an effect of an external} \\ \quad \text{influence), } b \text{ is to take action to leave } p. \\ 1 : b \text{ is in/ assumes } p, \, b \text{ is } stable \text{ in } p \text{ (no decision has been made,} \\ \quad \text{and there is no necessity to leave } p \text{ as a result of some external} \\ \quad \text{influence).} \\ 0 : b \text{ is not in/ does not assume } p. \end{cases}$$

If $B = \{b_1, \ldots, b_n\}, n \in \mathbb{N}$ and $z\langle b_i \rangle \in LState(b_i)$, $i = 1, \ldots, n$, then the mapping $z : P \longrightarrow P \cup \{0, 1, \mathsf{F}\}$ such that

(G1) $z|_{b_i} = z\langle b_i \rangle$

(G2) $\forall p, p' \in P : (z(p) \neq 0 \wedge z(p') \neq 0) \Rightarrow (p, p') \notin K$

is called *global activity state* of IS.

$z|_{b_i}$ is the restriction of z to the part b_i. $GState(IS)$ denotes the set of all global activity states. In this terminology, a global activity state z is a tuple of local activity states. □

According to Remark 1: In our terms, phase transitions in inert parts are always effects of external influences. Inert parts cannot make any decision.

Definition 3 (free / exciting). If a part b does not assume p in a global activity state z with $p \in b$ then we say p *is free in* z iff p is not coupled to any phase p', such that $z(p') \neq 0$ and $p' \notin b$: $(p, p') \notin K$.

If part b assumes p in z and another part b' assumes p' in z and $(p, p') \in E$ then we say that p *is exciting* p' *in* z. □

Action rules formulated as distributed algorithms (the syntax is similar to that in [10]) specify the interaction between the parts of an I–System and compute changes of phase qualities *in a single part*. From a *global view* the action rules specify how, starting from a global activity state z, the successor states z' would be derived, making use of Definition 3. Because of the strict page limitation we do not present the action rules. These can be found as an appendix in [15]. In the sequel we will present the basic ideas.

Two successive global activity states $z_1.z_2$ represent a specific activity (specified by the action rules) in the parts of an I–System IS. Let p, q be phases of a part b of IS.

AC1. If $z_1(p) = 1$ and $z_2(p) = q$ then we say that b *makes a decision* to enter q. b *may* make a decision or may not. b must be an autonomous part (def.1). b is bound to the decision, and a phase transition from p to q *will* occur unless q is not a free phase in z_1. If q is not free, b influences every part b' of IS with b' beeing in a phase v ($z(v) \neq 0$) and $(v,q) \in K$ to leave v. After every such b' has left v, b will enter q.

AC2. If $z_1(p) = 1$ and $z_2(p) = \mathsf{F}$ then we say that b *becomes unstable*. The cause for this unstability is either an excitation (it exists a phase v with $z_1(v) \neq 0$ and $(v,p) \in E$) or an influence from another part b' to leave p, because $(p,v) \in K$ and v is not free (AC1 or AC2). b *will* eventually leave p unless there exists no free successor phase. In the latter case, b influences every part b' of IS to leave a phase v if b' is in v and $(v,q) \in K$ for any $q \in b$.

AC3. If $z_1(p) = q$ and $z_2(p) = 1$ then we say that *the decision* of b to enter q *is cancelled*. In this case p is exciting a phase w assumed by a part b'.

AC4. If $z_1(p) = q$ and $z_2(q) = 1$ then we say that a *free phase transition* from p to q occurs in b. We call that transition free because it depends on a decision of b that *may* occur anytime (AC1).

AC5. If $z_1(p) = \mathsf{F}$ and $z_2(q) = 1$ then we say that an *enforced phase transition* from p to q occurs in b. We call that transition enforced because it originates from a condition of unstability that will occur inevitably (AC2).

A recursive application of AC2 represents a global propagation effect of local conditions. We call the influences in AC1 and AC2 (b influences b' to leave v because b takes action to enter a phase that is not free and coupled to v) *propagated influences*.

A sequence of global activity states as permitted by the action rules defines a *run* in the I–System. The set of all such sequences forms the *behavior* of the I–System.

Definition 4 (Behavior of an I–System). Let IS be an I–System. We define the *behavior* $\mathcal{V}[\![IS]\!]$ of IS as:
$\mathcal{V}[\![IS]\!] = \{z_0 z_1 z_2 \dots \mid z_0 z_1 z_2 \dots$ represents a run in IS with $z_i \in GState(IS)$ and $z_i \neq z_{i+1}$ for $i = 0, 1, 2, \dots \}$.   □

A complete and more formal definition can be found in [15]. Properties of the trace semantics 'behavior' (see [15]) can be used for proving that the action rules are complete and are not contradicting each other. As mentioned in section 1, Reisig [12] distinguishes between between two different kinds of actions: 'progressive' ones that will occur and 'quiescent' ones that may occur. Please remember that if a quiescent action does not occur the cause can not be traced back in general. If, for an I–System IS, two successive global activity states in a trace of the behavior $\mathcal{V}[\![IS]\!]$ represent a free or an enforced phase transition (AC4 or AC5, respectively) then we are able to trace back to the local causes (AC1 or AC2, respectively).

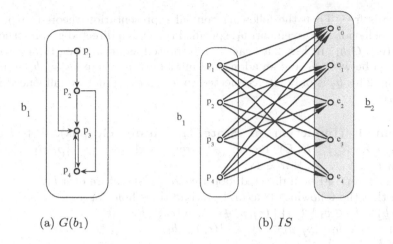

(a) $G(b_1)$ (b) IS

Fig. 2. Interaction inducing a state/transition graph

3   Example: Sequential Processes with Enforced and Free Phase Transitions

From the viewpoint of distributed, interacting system components each of them has a certain amount of *autonomy*. (In the extreme case of technical components, some may be passive, though.) Beyond the interaction with other components there may exist an *internal organizational scheme* specifying the component's process structure. On the human administration level such schemes are typically described as *role-based* state/event structures (e.g. in distributed security, see [4,14]). Part of a role is *decision making*. Other actions are the result of *organizational duties*. Each action belongs to one of these classes.

In I–Systems, actions occur in phases (local states). When a decision has been made then *all possible* actions in this phase are considered autonomous (*decision situations*). In every other situation *all* actions meant to be *organizationally enforced* (*procedural situations*). The formal approach discussed in section 2 follows exactly this organizational context. In the components (parts) there are two types of local situations (phases). Transitions from one type of phases are free (see AC4), the other phases allow for enforced transitions only (see AC5). In this way an organizational scheme for the phases of any part is defined. (External influences may superpose the local organizational scheme.)

Definition 5 (Organizational Scheme). A phase/transition structure in a part b of an I–System consisting of decision and procedural situations will be called an *organizational scheme for b*.   □

If one disregards the difference between decision and procedural situations an organizational scheme is just a state/transition graph (see Fig. 2.a). As a possible interpretation let us assume that every transition in a phase/transition structure is free. Then the following general representation theorem expresses that the behavior in a given part b_1, specified through a directed graph structure over b_1 (e.g. $G(b_1)$ in Fig. 2.a), can be interpreted as originating from a simple interaction between b_1 and an additional inert part $\underline{b}_2$ where $|\underline{b}_2| = |b_1| + 1$ (see IS in Fig. 2.b). $\underline{b}_2$ is only interconnected to b_1, so $\underline{b}_2$ cannot be influenced from elsewhere.

Theorem 1 (Induction of State/Transition Graphs).
Let $IS = (P, \{b_1, \underline{b}_2\}, \{\underline{b}_2\}, K, E)$ be an I–System with $b_1 = \{p_1, p_2, \ldots, p_m\}$, $\underline{b}_2 = \{e_0, e_1, e_2, \ldots, e_m\}$, $m \in I\!N$.
Let $G(b_1) = (b_1, \rightarrowtail)$ be a directed loop-free graph structure over b_1.
Assume that the following structural preconditions hold for $j = 1, 2, \ldots, m$ [1]:
$K(e_j) \setminus \underline{b}_2 = \{p \in b_1 \setminus \{p_j\} \mid (p_j, p) \not\rightarrowtail\}$, $K(e_0) \setminus \underline{b}_2 = \emptyset$,
$E^{-1}(e_j) = \{p \in b_1 \mid (p_j, p) \in \rightarrowtail\}$, $E^{-1}(e_0) = b_1$,
$E(e_j) = E(e_0) = \emptyset$.
Then the following holds for every $z_0 z_1 z_2 \ldots z_i \ldots \in \mathcal{V}[\![IS]\!]$, $i \in I\!N$, $p, q \in b_1$:
possible phase transitions
$((p, q) \in \rightarrowtail) \Leftrightarrow ((z_i(p) \neq \emptyset) \Rightarrow (\exists z_1', z_2', \ldots, z_k' \in GState(IS), k \in I\!N : z_0 z_1 z_2 \ldots z_i z_1' z_2' \ldots z_k' \ldots \in \mathcal{V}[\![IS]\!]$ with $z_1'(p) \neq 0, z_2'(p) \neq 0, \ldots, z_{k-1}'(p) \neq 0$ and $z_k'(q) \neq 0))$ □

The number of phases in $\underline{b}_2$ (equalling $b_1 + 1$) does not depend on the complexity of the process structure. In fact, through $\underline{b}_2$ there is a one-to-one correspondence between the graph structure $G(b_1)$ and a specific standard interaction between b_1 and $\underline{b}_2$. The proof of the theorem checks the action rules and utilizes semantic properties of $\mathcal{V}[\![IS]\!]$. (The properties can be found in [15].)

In organizational schemes as defined in Definition 5, we distinguish between decision and procedural situations. In the corresponding graphs (e.g. $G'(b_1)$ in Fig. 3.a) we depict these two types of situations by two different sets of edges. Arrows with a single head are representing transitions from decision situations, and arrows with a double head start from procedural situations.
Following this example we extend the idea behind Theorem 1 such that any organizational scheme for b can be generated, or imposed, by an additional inert part connected solely to b.

Corollary 1 (Induction of Organizational Schemes).
Let IS' be an I–System with parts and phases like IS from Theorem 1.
Let $G'(b_1) = (b_1, \rightarrowtail_1, \rightarrowtail_2)$ be a directed loop-free graph structure over b_1 with $\{p \in b_1 \mid \rightarrowtail_1(p) \neq \emptyset \wedge \rightarrowtail_2(p) \neq \emptyset\} = \emptyset$ [2]. Set $\rightarrowtail := \rightarrowtail_1 \cup \rightarrowtail_2$.
Assume that the structural preconditions from Theorem 1 hold, *but* with:

---

[1] For a binary relation $R \subseteq P \times P$ we define $R(p) := \{p' \mid (p, p') \in R\}$ and $R^{-1}(p) := \{p' \mid (p', p) \in R\}$.
[2] p represents either a decision situation or a procedural situation.

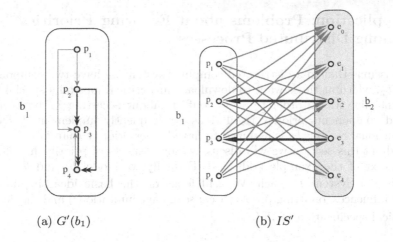

(a) $G'(b_1)$ (b) IS'

Fig. 3. Decision and procedural situations. A double arrow head depicts an enforced, a single arrow head depicts a free phase transition.

$$E(e_j) = \begin{cases} \{p_j\} \text{ iff } \rightarrowtail_2(p_j) \neq \emptyset \\ \emptyset \text{ else} \end{cases}.$$

Then the following holds for every $z_0 z_1 z_2 \ldots z_i \ldots \in \mathcal{V}[\![IS']\!]$, $i \in \mathbb{N}$, $p, q \in b_1$:

a) *possible phase transitions*
   Analogous to Theorem 1 with IS' instead of IS.
b) *free phase transition*
   $((p, q) \in \rightarrowtail_1) \Leftrightarrow ((z_i(p) \neq 0 \wedge z_{i+1}(q) \neq 0) \Rightarrow (z_i(p) = q \wedge z_{i+1}(q) = 1))$
c) *enforced phase transition*
   $((p, q) \in \rightarrowtail_2) \Leftrightarrow ((z_i(p) \neq 0 \wedge z_{i+1}(q) \neq 0) \Rightarrow (z_i(p) = \mathsf{F} \wedge z_{i+1}(q) = 1))$ $\square$

The idea behind this variation of the construction in Theorem 1 is that if b_1 is in a phase p_i representing a procedural situation then we need an additional influence that forces b_1 to leave p_i. We realize such an influence by simply adding an excitement edge $(e_i, p_i) \in E$. Now, if b_1 is in p_i then $\underline{b}_2$ eventually enters e_i which, in turn, will excite p_i. p_i becomes unstable and eventually enters a successor phase.

In Fig. 3.a p_2 and p_3 represent procedural situations. In order to model the behavior we extend the interaction IS from Fig. 2.b by two excitement edges (e_2, p_2) and (e_3, p_3). We get IS' in Fig. 3.b.

Remark 2. Since the inert parts are connected solely to those part where they induce the organizational scheme the specification of further external influences between parts is not changed (superposition of restrictive influences). $\square$

As a formal **convention** *for I–Systems, if no internal behavior is specified in b it is assumed that transitions between any 2 phases are possible.*

4   Application: Problems about Ensuring Priorities among Distributed Processes

Let us assume that in a distributed computer system we have two components, b_1 and b_2, which at times want to download time critical jobs on a special high-speed machine M. In order to avoid conflicts about accessing M between the involved components priority regulations are frequently implemented. Due to organizational reasons b_2 is assumed to have higher priority than b_1.

Throughout this section we will discuss various aspects of priority handling in the context of the example addressed. Formally we model b_1 and b_2 by one part of an I–System $\widetilde{IS}$ each. We will focus on the basic ideas in modeling mutual influences, omitting proofs (because of page limitations) and the detailed semantical specification of $\mathcal{V}[\![\widetilde{IS}]\!]$.

4.1   Local Behavior of b_1 and b_2

The local behavior of b_j, $j = 1, 2$, can be depicted by the organizational scheme

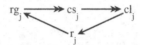

The procedure of accessing M is described by a 3-phase process structure: The registration phase rg_j is the only predecessor of the critical section phase cs_j in which b_j is allowed to access M. The clearing phase cl_j is the only successor of the critical section phase. The transitions $rg_j \to cs_j$ and $cs_j \to cl_j$ are enforced and will occur if no global influences impose further blocking restrictions. The other activities in b_j will be summarized into a remainder phase r_j, from which, and to which, phase transitions are assumed to be free. They depend on local control decisions e.g. resulting from interactions with users.

The local behavior in part b_j can be generated by an I–System according to Corollary 1.

4.2   Static Access Priority

If the access to a shared resource is to be arranged on the basis of mutual exclusion then the resulting priority requirement is that if two processes are both ready to access the resource then the one of higher priority is to go ahead while the other one has to wait. In the context of the example in 4.1 this condition can be phrased as follows.

Requirements 1.

PR0. If b_j is in rg_j, $j = 1, 2$, then only b_2 may enter cs_2 while b_1 has to wait.

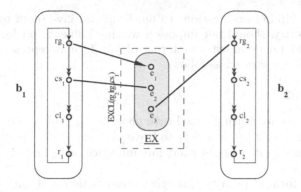

Fig. 4. Minimal realization of PR0

In order to realize the restriction PR0 we use the formal construction $EXCL(rg_2 \mid rg_1, cs_1)$. Here an inert part $\underline{EX}$ interacts with b_1 and b_2 as depicted in Fig. 4. For every global activity state of $\widetilde{IS}$, the interaction satisfies the following requirements:

E1. If b_2 is in rg_2 then no transition $rg_1 \to cs_1$ is possible in b_1.

E2. b_2 cannot be prevented from entering or leaving rg_2. b_1 has no influence on b_2 as to leaving rg_2.

E3. Once b_2 has left rg_2, b_1 cannot be prevented from performing the phase transition $rg_1 \to cs_1$ unless b_2 reenters rg_2.

E4. b_2 has no influence on b_1 as to leaving rg_1 or cs_1.

The interaction is *minimal* in the sense that through this connection no further restriction is imposed on b_1 or b_2. PR0 is an immediate consequence of E1, E2, and the local behavior of b_1. (Please remember from the end of section 3 that transitions between any 2 phases in $\underline{EX}$ are possible yet would occur only through external influence.) The proof of E1-E4 would be done by analyzing $\mathcal{V}[\![\widetilde{IS}]\!]$.

Remark 3. $EXCL(rg_2 \mid rg_1, cs_1)$ is an example for a *standard construction*. Through standard constructions we are able to model a large set of complex interaction and synchronization relationships, including the behavioral patterns unique for Interaction Systems. The correctness proofs are done by analyzing the trace semantics. Due to page limitations we refer to [15] for more details. □

4.3   Enforcing Access Priority

In the scenario described at the beginning of section 4 at most one of the components b_1, b_2 may have a job residing and executing on M (sensitive data). Also, if b_1 is executing a job on M and a job is waiting for execution at b_2, then because of b_2's higher priority some influence should be exerted on b_1

(e.g. through a kind of notification) to finish up and give room to b_2. (b_1, due to its lower priority, should not impose a waiting influence on b_2, i.e., *priority inversion* should be excluded.) In terms of our formal representation, these conditions can be rephrased as follows:

Requirements 2.

PR1. cs_1 and cs_2 are mutually exclusive phases.
PR2. If b_2 is in rg_2, it influences b_1 to leave cs_1.
PR3. If b_1 is in rg_1, it does not exert any influence on b_2 as to leaving cs_2.

We realize this form of priority through a construction with an inert part $\underline{PR}$ which is shown in Fig. 5.

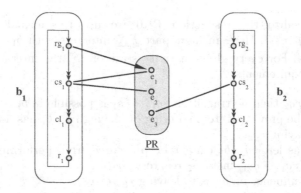

Fig. 5. Minimal realization of PR1, PR2, PR3

This construction is a variation of the standard construction in Fig. 4, with edge (cs_2, e_3) instead of (rg_2, e_3), and by adding a coupling edge (e_1, cs_1). This edge represents an additional interaction/influence that is necessary because property E4 satisfied by the previous standard construction contradicts requirement PR2 for enforcing access priority. PR1 is satisfied as well by this simple extension. E2 is still valid (with cs_2 instead of rg_2) and leads to PR3.

4.4   Reserved Access Right

In the context of our application example let us assume that b_1 has a series of time critical jobs to download onto M. They carry short deadlines. Each of them is supposed to be rather small in comparison to the jobs without deadlines coming from b_2. M's scheduler may therefore, in order to meet the deadlines, decide to start executing a job of b_1 instead of processing a job of b_2, despite of b_2's high priority. Obviously this problematic configuration (another example of *priority inversion*) may be repeated indefinitely often resulting in starvation of b_2. In order to avoid this undesirable effect we formulate the following conditions.

Requirements 3.

PR4. Through the interaction, b_j, $j = 1, 2$, cannot be prevented from entering rg_j anytime.

PR5. If b_2 is in rg_2 while b_1 is in cs_1 then b_1 can proceed only as far as rg_1 as long as b_2 has not entered cs_2.

PR6. After b_2 has left cs_2, b_1 has the chance to reenter cs_1.

The main idea is to establish the needed communication between b_1 and b_2 through a single inert part $\underline{CP}$ the behavior of which is to be restricted by another inert part $\underline{EX'}$. The formal construction including the necessary relations is to be found in Fig. 6. The second inert part is part of a parametrization of the standard construction introduced in section 4.2. Its known properties E1, E2, E3, E4 in conjunction with the interaction through $\underline{CP}$ are the basis for the proof of PR4, PR5, PR6.

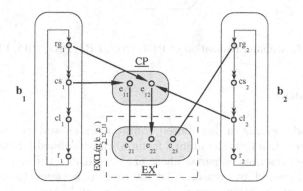

Fig. 6. Minimal realization of PR4, PR5, PR6

4.5   Guaranteed Access under Priority

If we assume, in the course of our developing example, that the critical sections in b_1 and b_2 underlie the restrictions PR1, PR2, PR3, PR4, PR5, PR6 then we would simply combine the constructions in Fig. 5 and Fig. 6 in order to overcome the shortcomings of the solution that is solely taking care of the priority restrictions. We can combine the effects of the two constructions since *they have no side-effects*. Graphically this is depicted in Fig. 7.

While the discussion in the context of our example scenario could easily continue by further elaborating on open priority problems our purpose here was simply to demonstrate, in the dimension of a large real system design, the *modularity* and *incrementality* of our formal tools. Recent research related to compositionality/ modularity within the design and analysis of distributed systems can be found in [1,6,8].

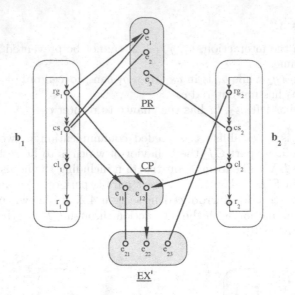

Fig. 7. Minimal realization of PR1, PR2, PR3, PR4, PR5, PR6

5 Conclusion

In order to model events in distributed components as well as cooperation between components in a formally unified framework we defined I–Systems. System
components are presented as *parts*. These are constituted through their relevant
(local) states, denoted by *phases*. The interaction between parts is specified
through two binary relations, denoted as *coupling* and *excitement* relations, respectively. Their (restrictive) influences on the involved parts is defined through
action rules for which novel trace semantics have been constructed thus formally
introducing the *global effect* of the local cooperation, in terms of propagating
local influences.

Modeling distributed behavior in large systems is done in two different ways.
Traditional approaches start with modeling behavior of components and next
interaction between components. The problem is to understand/ analyze the effect of the interaction on the component behavior. In our approach we model
interaction between components starting with elementary interaction relations
and by explicitly defining their influence on the behavior of the involved components. We have proven to cover the range of representations given by the
first approach but our tools are even more powerful. They allow for explicitly
distinguishing between *free* and *enforced* actions (transitions) which is crucial
for adequately modeling *organizational processes*. We have shown the additional
advantage through I–Systems to *incrementally* model complex distributed (software) systems and to guarantee their correctness at the same time.

We have done much research on finding a tool set of *standard constructions* for
the efficient formal representation of all forms of synchronization and cooperation between distributed components. Currently we are finalizing our efforts

to generate these formal constructions through a very small set of elementary restrictions, and through particular principles for their refinement and modification.

References

1. Rajeev Alur, Luca de Alfaro, Thomas A. Henzinger, and Freddy Y. C. Mang. Automating Modular Verification. In *CONCUR'99*, volume 1664 of *LNCS*, pages 82–97. Springer-Verlag, 1999.
2. Rajeev Alur and Thomas A. Henzinger. Reactive Modules. In *Formal Methods in System Design*, volume 15, pages 7–48. Kluwer Academic Publishers, 1999.
3. Ralph Back, Anna Mikhajlova, and Joakim von Wright. Reasoning About Interactive Systems. In *FM'99, Vol. II*, volume 1709 of *LNCS*, pages 1460–1476. Springer-Verlag, 1999.
4. Piero Bonatti, Sabrina de Capitani di, and Pierangela Samarati. A modular approach to composing access control policies. In *Proceedings of the 7th ACM Conference on Computer and Communications Security*, pages 164 – 173, Athens Greece, nov 2000.
5. Paul Caspi, Alain Girault, and Daniel Pilaud. Automatic Distribution of Reactive Systems for Asynchronous Networks of Processors. *IEEE Transactions on Software Engineering*, 25(3):416–427, 1999.
6. Michael Charpentier and K. Mani Chany. Towards a Compositional Approach to the Design and Verification of Distributed Systems. In *FM'99, Vol. I*, volume 1708 of *LNCS*, pages 570–589. Springer-Verlag, 1999.
7. V. Diekert and G. Rozenberg. *The Book of Traces*. World Scientific, 1995.
8. Valérie Issarny, Luc Bellissard, Michel Riveill, and Apostolos Zarras. Component-Based Programming of Distributed Applications. In *Distributed Systems*, volume 1752 of *LNCS*, pages 327–353. Springer-Verlag, 2000.
9. Man Lin, Jacek Malec, and Simin Nadjm-Tehrani. On Semantics and Correctness of Reactive Rule-Based Programs. In *PSI'99*, volume 1755 of *LNCS*, pages 235–246. Springer-Verlag, 2000.
10. Nancy A. Lynch. *Distributed Algorithms*. Morgan Kaufmann, 1996.
11. Andrea Maggiolo-Schettini, Horst F. Wedde, and Józef Winkowski. Modeling a Solution for a Control Problem in Distributed Systems by Restrictions. *Theoretical Computer Science*, 13:61–83, 1981.
12. W. Reisig. *Elements of Distributed Algorithms*. Springer-Verlag, 1998.
13. Horst F. Wedde. An Iterative and Starvation-free Solution for a General Class of Distributed Control Problems Based on Interaction Primitives. *Theoretical Computer Science*, 24, 1983.
14. Horst F. Wedde and Mario Lischka. Modular authorization. In *Proceedings of the 6th ACM Symposium on Access Control Models and Technologies (SACMAT)*, Chantilly, Virginia, May 3-4 2001.
15. Horst F. Wedde and Arnim Wedig. Explicit Modeling of Influences, and of Their Absence, in Distributed Systems (Extended version). Technical report, University of Dortmund, October 2001.
    http://ls3-www.cs.uni-dortmund.de/IS/P/techrep1001.ps.
16. Peter Wegner. Why interaction is more powerful than algorithms. *Communications of the ACM*, 40(5):81–91, May 1997.
17. Peter Wegner and Dina Goldin. Interaction as a Framework for Modeling. In *LNCS*, volume 1565. Springer-Verlag, 1999.

A Functional Semantics of Attribute Grammars

Kevin Backhouse

Oxford University Computing Laboratory

Abstract. A definition of the semantics of attribute grammars is given, using the lambda calculus. We show how this semantics allows us to prove results about attribute grammars in a calculational style. In particular, we give a new proof of Chirica and Martin's result [6], that the attribute values can be computed by a structural recursion over the tree. We also derive a new *definedness test*, which encompasses the traditional closure and circularity tests. The test is derived by abstract interpretation.

1 Introduction

This paper introduces a new definition of the semantics of attribute grammars (AGs), which we believe is easier to manipulate mathematically. The semantics is based on the lambda calculus, so a calculational proof style is possible. We illustrate the power of the semantics by proving Chirica and Martin's result [6]: that AGs can be evaluated by structural recursion. More importantly though, we show that the semantics is an excellent basis from which to derive tools and algorithms. We illustrate this by deriving a new *definedness test* for AGs. Our original goal was to derive Knuth's circularity test [12,13], but we were surprised to discover a new test that is actually slightly more powerful than Knuth's.

Notation and Semantic Framework. Our notation is based on the notation of the functional language Haskell [4]. Although the definitions given in Section 2 are valid Haskell, we do not restrict ourselves to Haskell's lazy semantics. Instead we merely assume that the computations are over a semantic domain in which the least fixed points exist. This is so as not to rule out work such as Farrow's [9], in which non-flat domains are used to great effect. For example, Farrow uses the set domain to do data flow analysis. Throughout the paper, we use a number of standard functions such as *fst* and *map*. These are defined in the appendix. Our definition of sequences, which is a little unusual, is also given in the appendix.

2 The Semantics of Attribute Grammars

In this section, we define the semantics of AGs as a least fixed point computation. Our approach is to represent abstract syntax trees as *rose trees* and then define the semantics using functions over rose trees. Throughout, we illustrate our definitions with Bird's *repmin* problem [3]. As noted by Kuiper and Swierstra [14], repmin can be easily written as an attribute grammar. The input to repmin is a binary tree of integers. Its output is a tree with identical structure, but with every leaf value replaced by the minimum leaf value of the input tree.

J.-P. Katoen and P. Stevens (Eds.): TACAS 2002, LNCS 2280, pp. 142–157, 2002.

2.1   Abstract Syntax Trees as Rose Trees

We use rose trees (see appendix) to represent abstract syntax trees.

type $AST = Rose\ ProdLabel$

The type *ProdLabel* is a sum type representing the different productions of the grammar. In repmin, The abstract syntax tree is a binary tree, so *ProdLabel* is:

data $ProdLabel = Root \mid Fork \mid Leaf\ Int$

A single *Root* production appears at the top of the tree. It has one child, which is the binary tree. *Fork* nodes have two children and *Leaf* nodes have zero. Note that the type *ProdLabel* can contain terminal information such as integer constants and strings, but it does not contain non-terminal information. The non-terminals of a production are represented as children in the rose tree.

2.2   Attributes

A drawback of our use of rose trees is that every node in the tree must have the same set of attributes. That is, if leaf nodes have a *code* attribute then root nodes have a *code* attribute too. However, attributes can be left undefined and our definedness test ensures that undefined attributes are not used. Repmin has one inherited attribute for the global minimum leaf value and two synthesised attributes: the minimum leaf value for the current subtree and the output tree for the current subtree. So we define the following datatypes:[1]

type $Inh = Int_\perp$
type $Syn = (Int_\perp,\ AST_\perp)$

In an AG with more attributes, we might use records or lookup tables, rather than tuples to store the attributes. Our definition of AGs below uses *polymorphism* to leave this choice open.

2.3   Attribute Grammars as Functions

In the following definition of an attribute grammar, the inherited and synthesised attributes are represented by the type parameters α and β, respectively. As explained above, this means that we are not bound to a particular implementation of attributes. (*Seq* is defined in the appendix.)

type $AG\ \alpha\ \beta \qquad = ProdLabel \rightarrow SemRule\ \alpha\ \beta$
type $SemRule\ \alpha\ \beta = (\alpha,\ Seq\ \beta) \rightarrow (\beta,\ Seq\ \alpha)$

---

[1] The $\perp$ subscript on the types indicates that we have lifted them to a flat domain by adding $\perp$ and $\top$ elements. We use a similar informal notation for lifting functions and values: if x has type A, then $x_\perp$ has type $A_\perp$ and if f has type $A \rightarrow B$, then $f_\perp$ has type $A_\perp \rightarrow B_\perp$.

This definition states that an AG is a set of semantic rules, indexed by the productions of the grammar. Our concept of a semantic rule deviates slightly from tradition. Traditionally, there is one semantic rule per attribute. In our model, a single semantic rule defines all the attribute values. It is a function from the "input" attributes to the "output" attributes. The input attributes are the inherited attributes of the parent node and the synthesised attributes of the children. The output attributes are the synthesised attributes of the parent and the inherited attributes of the children. The fact that we are using a single function does not mean that the attribute values have to be computed simultaneously. For example, in Haskell [4] attribute values would be evaluated on demand, due to the lazy semantics. In Farrow's model [9], attribute values are computed iteratively, so the function would be called several times.

Repmin. Repmin is encoded as a value of type AG as follows:

$$
\begin{aligned}
&repAG &&:: \ AG \ Inh \ Syn \\
&repAG \ Root \ (\_, \ syns) &&= (\, (\bot, \ Node_\bot \ Root \ [snd \ syns_1]), \ [fst \ syns_1] \,) \\
&repAG \ Fork \ (gmin, \ syns) &&= (\, (\ min_\bot \ (fst \ syns_1) \ (fst \ syns_2), \\
& && \qquad\quad Node_\bot \ Fork \ [snd \ syns_1, \ snd \ syns_2] \,), \\
& && \quad [gmin, \ gmin] \,) \\
&repAG \ (Leaf \ k) \ (gmin, \ syns) &&= (\, (k_\bot, \ Node_\bot \ (Leaf_\bot \ gmin) \ [\,]), \ [\,] \,)
\end{aligned}
$$

This should be read as follows. The local minimum of the root production is undefined, because it will remain unused. The output tree of the root production is equal to the output tree of its subtree. In the root production, the local minimum of the subtree becomes the inherited global minimum attribute. (The $gmin$ attribute of the root node is ignored.) In the fork production, the local minimum is the minimum of the two local minima of the subtrees. The output tree is built from the output trees of the two subtrees and the global minimum is passed unchanged to the subtrees. The local minimum in the leaf production equals the value at the leaf and the new tree is a leaf node with the global minimum as its value.

Semantic Trees. Given an AST and an AG, we can compute a *semantic tree*, which is a tree containing semantic functions. This is done by simply mapping the AG over the tree:

$$
\mathbf{type} \ SemTree \ \alpha \ \beta \ = \ Rose \ (SemRule \ \alpha \ \beta)
$$

$$
\begin{aligned}
&mkSemTree \ :: \ AG \ \alpha \ \beta \ \rightarrow \ AST \ \rightarrow \ SemTree \ \alpha \ \beta \\
&mkSemTree \ = \ mapRose
\end{aligned}
$$

We will often work with semantic trees rather than abstract syntax trees, because it makes some of our definitions and proofs more concise.

2.4   Shifting Attributes Up and Down the Tree

The goal of an attribute grammar evaluator is to produce a tree containing the attribute values. In other words we wish to produce a value of type $Rose\,(\alpha, \beta)$, where α and β are the types of the inherited and synthesised attributes. However, this format is not easily compatible with the semantic rules defined earlier. Instead we use the following two formats to represent annotated trees:

> **type** $InputTree\ \alpha\ \beta$ $= Rose\,(\alpha,\ Seq\ \beta)$
> **type** $OutputTree\ \alpha\ \beta = Rose\,(\beta,\ Seq\ \alpha)$

In the *input* format, the synthesised attributes of a node are stored by the node's parent. The parent uses a sequence to store the synthesised attributes of all its children. Similarly, in the *output* format, the inherited attributes of a node are stored by the node's parent. The output tree is the result of applying the semantic tree to the input tree. Note that in the input format, the synthesised attributes of the root node are not stored. Similarly, in the output format the inherited attributes are not stored. Therefore, this data needs to be stored separately.

The *shift* function is used to convert from the output to the input format. It encapsulates the idea that inherited attributes are passed down the tree and synthesised attributes are passed up. Note that *shift* merely moves attributes around; the calculation of the attribute values is done by the semantic tree.

> $shift$ $:: \alpha \rightarrow OutputTree\ \alpha\ \beta \rightarrow InputTree\ \alpha\ \beta$
> $shift\ a\ (Node\ (b, as)\ ts) = Node\ (a, bs)\ (zipWith\ shift\ as\ ts)$
>   **where** $bs = map\ (fst \circ root)\ ts$

Note that the inherited attributes of the root node are the first parameter of *shift*. The inherited attributes of the root node are always an external parameter to an attribute grammar.

2.5   The Semantics as a Least Fixed Point Computation

We explained above how we can produce a *semantic tree* by mapping an AG over an AST. Given a semantic tree *semtree* and the inherited attributes a of the root node, we expect the following equations to hold:

$$inputTree = shift\ a\ outputTree \qquad (1)$$

$$outputTree = appRose\ semtree\ inputTree \qquad (2)$$

As we discussed above, the attributes of the tree can be stored either in the input or the output format. Equation (1) states that the input tree can be computed from the output tree with the *shift* function. Equation (2) says that the output tree can be computed by applying the semantic tree to the input tree. Equations (1) and (2) form a pair of simultaneous equations that can be used to compute *inputTree* and *outputTree*. Following Chirica and Martin [6], we define the semantics of attribute grammars to be the *least* solution of the equations. This choice has no effect if the attributes are not circularly defined, because the solution to the equations is unique. If our domains are flat, then circularly defined attributes will evaluate to ⊥. Farrow [9] discusses some interesting applications of working with non-flat domains. The least solution can be computed with the following function:

$$eval \qquad :: SemTree\ \alpha\ \beta\ \rightarrow\ \alpha\ \rightarrow\ OutputTree\ \alpha\ \beta$$
$$eval\ semtree\ a\ =\mu\ (appRose\ semtree\ \circ\ shift\ a)$$

This function is our definition of the semantics of attribute grammars. Please note that we do not propose it as an efficient implementation though! In the following section, we define a more convenient version called *io* and demonstrate it on the repmin problem (Section 3.4).

3   AG Semantics as a Structural Recursion

The *eval* function given above computes attribute values for the entire tree. In practice, we often only want to know the values of the synthesised attributes of the root node of the tree. Therefore, it is convenient to define the function *io*:

$$io \qquad :: SemTree\ \alpha\ \beta\ \rightarrow\ \alpha\ \rightarrow\ \beta$$
$$io\ semtree\ a\ =fst\ (root\ (eval\ semtree\ a))$$

The name *io* stands for input-output. It converts the semantic tree into a function from inherited attributes to synthesised attributes.

Johnsson [11] showed that AGs can be viewed as an idiom of lazy functional programming. Using the idea that a semantic tree is simply a function from inherited to synthesised attributes, he recursively builds the input-output function for the entire AST. The idea that input-output functions can be computed by structural recursion was also stated much earlier by Chirica and Martin [6]. We state the idea formally with the following theorem:

Theorem 1. *The following definition of io is equivalent to the one given above:*

$$io = foldRose\ knit$$

where:

$$knit \qquad :: (SemRule\ \alpha\ \beta,\ Seq\ (\alpha\ \rightarrow\ \beta))\ \rightarrow\ (\alpha\ \rightarrow\ \beta)$$
$$knit\ (semrule, fs)\ a\ =fst\ (\mu\ \langle\ b, as\ \bullet\ semrule\ (a,\ appSeq\ fs\ as)\rangle)$$

The definition of *knit* is rather unintuitive, but it has appeared in different forms in many papers on AGs, including one of our own [8]. Other examples are Gondow & Katayama [10] and Rosendahl [18]. Very briefly, *as* and *appSeq fs as* are respectively the inherited and synthesised attributes of the subtrees. Their values are mutually dependent (using *semrule*), so they are computed by a least fixed point computation. For a better understanding of *knit*, see Johnsson [11].

Our proof is essentially the same as the proof given by Chirica and Martin [6], although our notation is rather different. The most important step is to use the mutual recursion rule and we will start by proving a lemma, that adapts the mutual recursion rule to rose trees. Another important step is to use the abstraction rule though. The use of the abstraction rule is the motivation for our use of sequences rather than lists throughout this document.

3.1   The Mutual Recursion Rule on Rose Trees

The most crucial step in our proof of Theorem 1 is to use the *mutual recursion rule* (see the appendix). This theorem allows us to factorise least fixed point computations. In this section, we shall show how it can be applied to rose trees. We do this by proving the following lemma:

Lemma 1. *If f is a monotonic function of type Rose $A \to$ Rose A, then:*

$$root\,(\mu\,f) \;=\; \mu\,\langle\,x\,\bullet\,g_1\,(x,\,\mu\,\langle\,xs\,\bullet\,g_2\,(x,xs)\rangle)\rangle$$

where:

$$
\begin{aligned}
g_1 &= fst \,\circ\, g\\
g_2 &= snd \,\circ\, g\\
g\; &= split \,\circ\, f \,\circ\, merge
\end{aligned}
$$

Proof:

$$
\begin{aligned}
&\quad root\,(\mu\,f)\\
=&\qquad \{\ merge \circ split = id\ \}\\
&\quad root\,(\mu\,(merge \circ split \circ f))\\
=&\qquad \{\ \text{rolling rule (see the appendix)}\ \}\\
&\quad root\,(merge\,(\mu\,(split \circ f \circ merge)))\\
=&\qquad \{\ root \circ merge = fst,\ \text{Definition } g\ \}\\
&\quad fst\,(\mu\,g)\\
=&\qquad \{\ \text{mutual recursion rule (see the appendix)}\ \}\\
&\quad \mu\,\langle x \bullet g_1\,(x,\,\mu\,\langle xs \bullet g_2\,(x,xs)\rangle)\rangle
\end{aligned}
$$

3.2   Proving Theorem 1

We now prove Theorem 1, deriving the definition of *knit* in the process. First we apply a general result about folds:

$$
\begin{aligned}
&\quad io = foldRose\ knit\\
\equiv&\qquad \{\ \text{Universal property of fold, Bird \& de Moor [5, page 46]}\ \}\\
&\quad \forall\langle s, ss, a \bullet io\,(Node\ s\ ss)\ a = knit\,(s,\,map\ io\ ss)\ a\,\rangle
\end{aligned}
$$

We continue by manipulating the expression *io* (*Node s ss*) *a* until we obtain an expression from which it is easy to derive the definition of *knit*:

$$
\begin{aligned}
&\quad io\,(Node\ s\ ss)\ a\\
=&\qquad \{\ \text{Definition } io\ \}\\
&\quad fst\,(root\,(\mu\,(appRose\,(Node\ s\ ss) \circ shift\ a)))
\end{aligned}
$$

We can apply the mutual recursion rule on rose trees (Lemma 1) to this expression. By simply expanding the definitions of g_1 and g_2, as specified in Lemma 1, we find that:

$$g_1 \, ((b, as), \, ts) \; = s \, (a, \; map \; (fst \circ root) \; ts)$$

$$g_2 \, ((b, as), \, ts) \; = zipWith \; appRose \; ss \; (zipWith \; shift \; as \; ts)$$

Therefore, Lemma 1 implies that $io \; (Node \; s \; ss) \; a$ is equal to:

$$fst \, (\mu \, \langle b, as \bullet \; g_1 \, ((b, as), \; \mu \, \langle ts \bullet \; g_2 \, ((b, as), ts) \rangle) \rangle)$$

(With g_1 and g_2 as defined above.) Consider the sub-expression containing g_2:

$$\mu \, \langle ts \bullet \; g_2 \, ((b, as), ts) \rangle$$
$$=\qquad \{ \text{ Definition } g_2 \, \}$$
$$\mu \, \langle ts \bullet \; zipWith \; appRose \; ss \; (zipWith \; shift \; as \; ts) \rangle$$
$$=\qquad \{ \text{ Claim (see the appendix) } \}$$
$$\mu \, \langle ts \bullet \; appSeq \; (zipWith \; (\circ) \; (map \; appRose \; ss) \; (map \; shift \; as)) \; ts \rangle$$
$$=\qquad \{ \text{ abstraction rule (see the appendix) } \}$$
$$\langle k \bullet \; \mu \, (zipWith \; (\circ) \; (map \; appRose \; ss) \; (map \; shift \; as) \; k) \rangle$$
$$=\qquad \{ \text{ Definitions } zipWith \text{ and } map \, \}$$
$$\langle k \bullet \; \mu \, (appRose \; (ss \; k) \; \circ \; shift \; (as \; k)) \rangle$$
$$=\qquad \{ \text{ Definition } eval \, \}$$
$$\langle k \bullet \; eval \; (ss \; k) \; (as \; k) \rangle$$

We continue with the main expression:

$$fst \, (\mu \, \langle b, as \bullet \; g_1 \, ((b, as), \; \mu \, \langle ts \bullet \; g_2 \, ((b, as), ts) \rangle) \rangle)$$
$$=\qquad \{ \text{ Substitute the new sub-expression } \}$$
$$fst \, (\mu \, \langle b, as \bullet \; g_1 \, ((b, as), \; \langle k \bullet \; eval \; (ss \; k) \; (as \; k) \rangle) \rangle)$$
$$=\qquad \{ \text{ Definition } g_1 \, \}$$
$$fst \, (\mu \, \langle b, as \bullet \; s \, (a, \; map \; (fst \circ root) \; \langle k \bullet \; eval \; (ss \; k) \; (as \; k) \rangle) \rangle)$$
$$=\qquad \{ \text{ Definitions } map \text{ and } io \, \}$$
$$fst \, (\mu \, \langle b, as \bullet \; s \, (a, \langle k \bullet \; io \; (ss \; k) \; (as \; k) \rangle) \rangle)$$
$$=\qquad \{ \text{ Definitions } appSeq \text{ and } map \, \}$$
$$fst \, (\mu \, \langle b, as \bullet \; s \, (a, \; appSeq \; (map \; io \; ss) \; as) \rangle)$$
$$=\qquad \{ \text{ Definition } knit \, \}$$
$$knit \; (s, map \; io \; ss) \; a$$

In the final step, we have derived the definition of $knit$.

3.3   A More Convenient Version of the *io* Function: *trans*

The *io* function operates on semantic trees. It is usually more convenient to operate on abstract syntax trees, so we define the *trans* function:

$$trans \quad :: AG \, \alpha \, \beta \rightarrow AST \rightarrow \alpha \rightarrow \beta$$
$$trans \; ag = io \circ mkSemTree \; ag$$

In the next section, it is important that *trans* can be written as a fold:

$$trans \; ag = foldRose \, (knit \circ (ag \times id))$$

The proof is a simple application of fold-map fusion [4, page 131].

3.4   Repmin as a Recursive Function

Let us expand *trans repAG* to demonstrate that it is equivalent to the functional program for repmin. Expanding the definitions of *trans* (above), *foldRose* (appendix), *knit* (page 146) and *repAG* (page 144), we obtain:

$$
\begin{aligned}
repmin &\qquad :: AST \rightarrow Inh \rightarrow Syn \\
repmin \,(Node \; Root \; [t]) \, _- &\quad = (\bot, \; Node_\bot \; Root \; [nt]) \\
&\qquad \textbf{where} \, (gm, nt) \; = \; repmin \; t \; gm \\
repmin \,(Node \; Fork \; [t_1, t_2]) \; gm &= (min_\bot \; lm_1 \; lm_2, \; Node_\bot \; Fork \; [nt_1, \; nt_2]) \\
&\qquad \textbf{where} \, (lm_1, nt_1) \; = \; repmin \; t_1 \; gm \\
&\qquad\qquad\qquad\;\; (lm_2, nt_2) \; = \; repmin \; t_2 \; gm \\
repmin \,(Node \,(Leaf \; k) \, _-) \; gm &= (k_\bot, \; Node_\bot \,(Leaf_\bot \; gm) \, [\,])
\end{aligned}
$$

This is indeed very similar to the program given by Bird [3]. Of course Bird's emphasis is on the recursive definition of *gm* at the root of the tree, which is valid in a language with lazy evaluation.

4   The Definedness Test

When Knuth [12] introduced attribute grammars, he also gave algorithms for testing them for closure and circularity. Closure is the property that there are no 'missing' semantic rules for attributes. An AG is circular if there exists an input tree on which the attributes are circularly defined. We present a new algorithm, which is very similar to the circularity test, but encompasses the roles of both the closure and the circularity tests. It computes equivalent results to the circularity test and improves upon the closure test (which is based on a very shallow analysis of the dependency structure) by reducing the number of false negatives. In other work on extending attribute grammars [19] we have found this improvement essential.

In our model, an undefined attribute is an attribute with the value $\bot$. Similarly, circularly defined attributes over a flat domain will evaluate to $\bot$, because our semantics is a least fixed point semantics.[2] So in our model, the goal of both the closure and the circularity tests is to detect attributes which will evaluate to $\bot$. Our *definedness test* accomplishes both of these goals by analysing *strictness*. This concept is very similar to the concept of "dependence" used in the circularity test. A function f is *strict* if $f \perp = \perp$. In our model, an undefined attribute is an attribute with the value $\bot$, so a strict function 'depends' on its parameter. However, the expression $f\ x$ is said to depend on x even if f is not strict, so the two concepts are not identical. Luckily, semantic rules in a traditional AG are always strict in the attributes that they depend on.

Our presentation of the circularity test consists of two parts. In the first part we explain how the strictness analysis is done as an abstract interpretation. In the second part we explain how the AG can be statically tested for circularity on *all* possible input trees.

4.1   Strictness Analysis and Abstract Interpretation

Strictness analysis is very important for the optimisation of lazy functional programs. Peyton Jones [16, pages 380-395] explains this and gives a good introduction to *abstract interpretation*, which is the technique used to perform the analysis. The use of strictness analysis in AGs has been studied before by Rosendahl [18]. However, Rosendahl's emphasis is on the optimisation of AGs, rather than definedness.

The prerequisite for abstract interpretation (first introduced by Cousot & Cousot [7]) is a *Galois Connection* between the "concrete" domain $(A, \leq)$ and the "abstract" domain $(A^{\#}, \preceq)$. For an introduction to Galois Connections, see Aarts [1]. Briefly, there should be an *abstraction* function abs of type $A \to A^{\#}$ and a *concretisation* function con of type $A^{\#} \to A$. The "connection" is:

$$\forall \langle x, y \bullet\ abs\ x \preceq y\ \equiv\ x \leq con\ y \rangle$$

The Galois Connection used in strictness analysis is between any domain $(A, \leq)$ and the boolean domain $(Bool, \Rightarrow)$:

$$abs_A\ ::\ A \to Bool \qquad\qquad con_A\ ::\ Bool \to A$$
$$abs_A\ x = (x \neq \perp) \qquad\qquad con_A\ b = \textbf{if}\ b\ \textbf{then}\ \top\ \textbf{else}\ \perp$$

The idea is that in the abstract domain, $\bot$ is represented by *False* and other values by *True*. Given a function f, we derive an abstract version $f^{\#}$ that models the strictness of f using booleans. Suppose for example that f has type $A \to B$. Then $f^{\#}$ will have type $Bool \to Bool$. The result of $f^{\#}$ is *False* if and only if the result of f is $\bot$. Mathematically, this relationship between f and $f^{\#}$ is:[3]

$$\forall \langle x \bullet\ abs_B\ (f\ x)\ =\ f^{\#}\ (abs_A\ x)\ \rangle \tag{3}$$

---

[2] If the domain is non-flat, then circular attributes may not evaluate to $\bot$, but in this situation circularity is usually intended rather than erroneous. Farrow [9] suggests some useful applications of circular attributes over non-flat domains.

[3] Abstract interpretations are often only able to give *conservative* results, so the equation is an inequality: $abs\ (f\ x) \leq f^{\#}\ (abs\ x)$. However, in most AGs such as repmin, an exact result can be given.

Often, if this equation has a solution, it is the function $f^\# = abs_B \circ f \circ con_A$. We will use this technique when we discuss repmin below.

Repmin. Let us apply strictness analysis to repmin. First we must define abstract versions of the types Inh and Syn, defined on page 143:

type $Inh^\# = Bool$
type $Syn^\# = (Bool,\ Bool)$

Inh and $Inh^\#$ are Galois Connected, as are Syn and $Syn^\#$:

$$absInh = abs_{Int} \qquad\qquad absSyn = abs_{Int} \times abs_{AST}$$
$$conInh = con_{Int} \qquad\qquad conSyn = con_{Int} \times con_{AST}$$

Now we need to derive an abstract version of $repAG$, the attribute grammar for repmin, defined on page 144. The type of $repAG$ is $AG\ Inh\ Syn$, so $repAG^\#$ should have type $AG\ Inh^\#\ Syn^\#$. Following the suggestion above, we define:

$$repAG^\#\ p = (absSyn \times map\ absInh) \circ repAG\ p \circ (conInh \times map\ conSyn)$$

A simple calculation reveals that $repAG$ and $repAG^\#$ satisfy an equation similar to (3), which is required by Theorem 2. An equivalent definition of $repAG^\#$ is:

$$
\begin{aligned}
repAG^\# &:: AG\ Inh^\#\ Syn^\# \\
repAG^\#\ Root\ (\_,\ syns) &= ((False,\ snd\ syns_1),\ [fst\ syns_1]) \\
repAG^\#\ Fork\ (gmin,\ syns) &= ((\ fst\ syns_1 \wedge fst\ syns_2, \\
&\qquad\qquad snd\ syns_1 \wedge snd\ syns_2),\ [gmin,\ gmin]) \\
repAG^\#\ (Leaf\ k)\ (gmin,\ \_) &= ((True,\ gmin),\ [\,])
\end{aligned}
$$

The reader should compare this definition with the definition of $repAG$, given on page 144. Where $repAG$ computes the value $\bot$, this function computes $False$.

Using the Abstract Interpretation. Now that we have $ag^\#$, the abstract interpretation of ag, what happens when we evaluate an abstract syntax tree using it? Our hope is that the result of evaluating the tree with $ag^\#$ can be used to predict something about the result of evaluating the tree with ag. The following theorem is what we need:

Theorem 2. *Suppose we are given an attribute grammar* ag *and its abstract interpretation* $ag^\#$. *By definition, they are related as follows, for all* p:

$$(absSyn \times map\ absInh) \circ ag\ p = ag^\#\ p \circ (absInh \times map\ absSyn)$$

Then, for all t:

$$absSyn \circ trans\ ag\ t = trans\ ag^\#\ t \circ absInh$$

This theorem could be worded as: if $ag^\#$ is the abstract interpretation of ag, then *trans* $ag^\#$ is the abstract interpretation of *trans* ag. The theorem can be proved manually using fixpoint fusion or fixpoint induction, but we have discovered that it follows immediately from the polymorphic type of *trans*. This is the topic of a forthcoming paper [2], which presents a result based on Reynold's parametricity theorem [17], similar to Wadler's "Theorems for free" [20].

4.2   Computing the Strictness for All Possible Trees

In general an attribute grammar will have n inherited attributes and m synthesised attributes. Therefore, the types $Inh^{\#}$ and $Syn^{\#}$ will be:

type $Inh^{\#}$ $= (Bool, \ldots, Bool)$
type $Syn^{\#}$ $= (Bool, \ldots, Bool)$

This means that there are 2^n different values of type $Inh^{\#}$ and 2^m of type $Syn^{\#}$. Consequently, there are only a finite number of functions of type $Inh^{\#} \rightarrow Syn^{\#}$. So even though there are an infinite number of input trees, *trans ag*$^{\#}$ can only have a finite number of values. In this section we derive an algorithm, very similar to the traditional circularity test algorithm, for computing those values in a finite amount of time.

The Grammar. Until this point we have ignored the fact that abstract syntax trees are constrained by a *grammar*. We are using rose trees to represent ASTs, which means that we are not prevented from building grammatically incorrect trees. The definedness test depends crucially on the grammar, so let us define it.

A grammar consists of a set of *symbols* and an associated set of *productions*. Just like productions, we represent the symbols with a simple enumeration datatype. In repmin, there are just two symbols:

data $Symbol$ $=$ $Start$ | $Tree$

Every symbol in the grammar is associated with zero or more productions. Every production has a sequence of symbols on its right hand side. We represent this as a *partial function* with the following type:

$grammar$ $::$ $(ProdLabel, Seq\ Symbol) \nrightarrow Symbol$

This function is partial, because it only accepts inputs where the sequence of symbols matches the production. For example, the grammar for repmin is:

$grammar\ (Root, [Tree])$ $= Start$
$grammar\ (Fork, [Tree, Tree])$ $= Tree$
$grammar\ (Leaf\ \_, [\,])$ $= Tree$

The following function checks whether a tree is grammatically correct:

$foldRose\ grammar$ $::$ $AST \nrightarrow Symbol$

This function is also partial. It is only defined on grammatically correct trees.

Generating Grammatically Correct Trees. We can generate the set of all grammatically correct trees by *inverting* the grammar:

$trees$ $::$ $Symbol \leftrightarrow AST$
$trees$ $= (foldRose\ grammar)^{\circ}$

As indicated by the type signature, *trees* is a relation. Relations can be thought of as set-valued functions, so given a symbol, *trees* produces the set of all grammatically correct trees with that symbol-type.

The above definition is known as an *unfold*. See Bird and de Moor [5] for a proper discussion of folds and unfolds over relations.

Testing all Grammatically Correct Trees. We now have the two necessary ingredients for the definedness test. We can test an individual tree for definedness and we can generate the set of all grammatically correct trees. We can put them together as follows:

$$circ :: Symbol \leftrightarrow (Inh^{\#} \rightarrow Syn^{\#})$$
$$circ = trans \, ag^{\#} \circ trees$$

Given a symbol, *circ* produces the test results for all trees of that type. As we explained earlier, these results form a set of finite size, despite the fact that the number of trees involved might be infinite. So the question is: how do we compute the results in a finite amount of time? The answer is provided by the hylomorphism theorem (see the appendix). Recalling that *trans* can be written as a fold and *trees* as an unfold, we see that an equivalent definition for *circ* is:

$$circ = \mu \, \langle c \bullet knit \circ (ag^{\#} \times map \, c) \circ grammar^{\circ} \rangle \qquad (4)$$

The result of this fixpoint computation can be computed by *iteration*. Iteration is a technique for computing the value of μf in finite sized domains. The technique is to compute the sequence $\bot, f(\bot), f(f(\bot)), \ldots$, which is guaranteed to stabilise at μf within a finite number of steps. In the context of computing *circ*, c is a relation over a finite domain, so we represent it as a set of pairs. We start with the empty set and iterate until c ceases to change.

Testing repmin. Let us evaluate *circ* for repmin. We start with c equal to the empty relation. After one iteration, c' equals:

$$c' = knit \circ (repAG^{\#} \times map \, c) \circ grammar^{\circ}$$
$$= \langle \, Tree \mapsto \langle a \bullet (True, a) \rangle \, \rangle$$

After the second iteration:

$$c'' = \langle \, Start \mapsto \langle a \bullet (False, True) \rangle, \, Tree \mapsto \langle a \bullet (True, a) \rangle \, \rangle$$

On the third iteration, we find that $c''' = c''$, so the iteration has stabilised and $circ = c''$. What does this value of *circ* tell us about repmin? On the root node, the *lmin* attribute will never be defined, regardless of whether the inherited *gmin* attribute is defined, but the *ntree* attribute is always defined. On internal nodes of the tree, *lmin* is always defined and *ntree* is defined if *gmin* is defined.

5 Conclusion

We have defined a semantics for attribute grammars based on the lambda calculus and given a new proof of Chirica and Martin's important result [6]. We also derived a definedness test, which is very similar to the traditional circularity test. However, our test also encompasses the closure test. The use of the hylomorphism theorem is very important in our derivation of the definedness test and it results in an algorithm based on iteration. We think this may also help to explain why the algorithm for the circularity test is based on iteration.

Our decision to use rose trees comes with one major drawback: loss of type safety. If we had used algebraic datatypes to define the abstract syntax, then they would automatically be grammatically correct. We would not have needed to discuss "The Grammar" in Section 4.2. It is also common for different grammar symbols to have different attributes. For example, in *repmin* the *Start* symbol does not need a *locmin* or a *gmin* attribute. In our model, it is not possible to distinguish between the symbols in this way. It would be interesting to explore the use of category theory to extend our results to an arbitrary recursive datatype.

Acknowledgements. I am supported by a grant from Microsoft Research. I would like to thank Eric Van Wyk, Ganesh Sittampalam and Oege de Moor for all their help with this paper. I would also like to thank my father for his help with the paper and for teaching me about fixpoints.

References

1. C. J. Aarts. Galois connections presented calculationally. Graduating Dissertation, Department of Computing Science, Eindhoven University of Technology. Available from: http://www.cs.nott.ac.uk/\char'176rcb/MPC/galois.ps.gz, 1992.
2. R. C. Backhouse and K. S. Backhouse. Abstract interpretations for free. Available from: http://www.cs.nott.ac.uk/\char'176rcb/papers/papers.html.
3. R. S. Bird. Using circular programs to eliminate multiple traversals of data. *Acta Informatica*, 21:239–250, 1984.
4. R. S. Bird. *Introduction to Functional Programming using Haskell*. Prentice Hall, 2 edition, 1998.
5. R. S. Bird and O. de Moor. *Algebra of Programming*, volume 100 of *International Series in Computer Science*. Prentice Hall, 1997.
6. L. M. Chirica and D. F. Martin. An order-algebraic definition of Knuthian semantics. *Mathematical Systems Theory*, 13(1):1–27, 1979.
7. P. Cousot and R. Cousot. Abstract interpretation: a unified lattice model for static analysis of programs by construction or approximation of fixpoints. In *Conference Record of the Fourth Annual ACM SIGPLAN-SIGACT Symposium on Principles of Programming Languages*, pages 238–252, Los Angeles, California, 1977. ACM Press, New York, NY.
8. O. de Moor, K. Backhouse, and S. D. Swierstra. First-class attribute grammars. *Informatica*, 24(3):329–341, 2000.

9. R. Farrow. Automatic generation of fixed-point-finding evaluators for circular, but well-defined, attribute grammars. In *SIGPlan '86 Symposium on Compiler Construction*, pages 85–98, Palo Alto, CA, June 1986. Association for Computing Machinery, SIGPlan.

10. K. Gondow and T. Katayama. Attribute grammars as record calculus — a structure-oriented denotational semantics of attribute grammars by using cardelli's record calculus. *Informatica*, 24(3):287–299, 2000.

11. T. Johnsson. Attribute grammars as a functional programming paradigm. In Gilles Kahn, editor, *Proceedings of the Conference on Functional Programming Languages and Computer Architecture*, volume 274 of *LNCS*, pages 154–173, Portland, OR, September 1987. Springer-Verlag.

12. D. E. Knuth. Semantics of context-free languages. *Mathematical Systems Theory*, 2:127–146, 1968.

13. D. E. Knuth. Semantics of context-free languages: Correction. *Mathematical Systems Theory*, 5:95–96, 1971.

14. M. Kuiper and S. D. Swierstra. Using attribute grammars to derive efficient functional programs. In *Computing Science in the Netherlands CSN '87*, 1987.

15. Mathematics of Program Construction Group, Eindhoven University of Technology. Fixed-point calculus. *Information Processing Letters Special Issue on The Calculational Method*, 53:131–136, 1995.

16. S. L. Peyton Jones. *The Implementation of Functional Programming Languages*. Series in Computer Science. Prentice Hall, 1987.

17. J. C. Reynolds. Types, abstraction and parametric polymorphism. In R. E. A. Mason, editor, *Proceedings 9th IFIP World Computer Congress, Information Processing '83, Paris, France, 19–23 Sept 1983*, pages 513–523. North-Holland, Amsterdam, 1983.

18. M. Rosendahl. Strictness analysis for attribute grammars. In *PLILP'92*, volume 631 of *LNCS*, pages 145–157. Springer-Verlag, 1992.

19. E. Van Wyk, O. de Moor, K. Backhouse, and P. Kwiatkowski. Forwarding in attribute grammars for modular language design. Compiler Construction 2002.

20. P. Wadler. Theorems for free! In *FPCA'89, London, England*, pages 347–359. ACM Press, September 1989.

A Definitions and Theorems

Pairs $fst\ (x,y) = x$ $snd\ (x,y) = y$ $(f \times g)\ (x,y) = (f\ x,\ g\ y)$

Sequences. Throughout this paper, we use sequences rather than lists. Our motivation is that this simplifies the use of the abstraction rule (see below). The type of sequences is:

type $Seq\ \alpha\ =\ Nat^+ \rightarrow \alpha$

Every sequence xs in this document has a finite length n, which means that $\forall \langle k > n \bullet xs_k = \bot \rangle$. (Hence, sequences should be over a domain with a $\bot$ element.) We sometimes use the notation $[a, b, c]$ to denote a finite length sequence and xs_k is equivalent to $xs\ k$. Some useful operations on sequences are:

$$
\begin{aligned}
map &\quad :: (\alpha \rightarrow \beta) \rightarrow Seq\ \alpha \rightarrow Seq\ \beta \\
map\ f\ xs &\quad = f \circ xs \\[6pt]
appSeq &\quad :: Seq\ (\alpha \rightarrow \beta) \rightarrow Seq\ \alpha \rightarrow Seq\ \beta \\
appSeq\ fs\ xs\ k &\quad = fs\ k\ (xs\ k) \\[6pt]
zipWith &\quad :: (\alpha \rightarrow \beta \rightarrow \gamma) \rightarrow Seq\ \alpha \rightarrow Seq\ \beta \rightarrow Seq\ \gamma \\
zipWith\ f\ xs\ ys\ k &\quad = f\ (xs\ k)\ (ys\ k)
\end{aligned}
$$

Note that *appSeq* and *zipWith* are equivalent to the S and S' combinators, respectively (see Peyton Jones [16, pages 260 and 270]). Therefore, the claim on page 148 can be stated as, for all c_1, c_2, xs, ys and k:

$$
S'\ c_1\ xs\ (S'\ c_2\ ys\ zs)\ k\ =\ S\ (S'\ (\circ)\ (c_1 \circ xs)\ (c_2 \circ ys))\ zs\ k
$$

The proof is a simple manipulation of the definitions of S and S'.

Rose Trees. Our rose trees differ from Bird's [4, page 195], because we use sequences, rather than lists:

data *Rose* $\alpha\ =\ Node\ \alpha\ (Seq\ (Rose\ \alpha))$

All our rose trees are finite in size. Some useful functions are:

$$
\begin{aligned}
split &:: Rose\ \alpha \rightarrow (\alpha, Forest\ \alpha) \qquad & merge &:: (\alpha, Forest\ \alpha) \rightarrow Rose\ \alpha \\
split\ (Node\ x\ xs) &= (x, xs) & merge\ (x, xs) &= Node\ x\ xs
\end{aligned}
$$

$$
\begin{aligned}
mapRose &:: (\alpha \rightarrow \beta) \rightarrow Rose\ \alpha \rightarrow Rose\ \beta \qquad & root &:: Rose\ \alpha \rightarrow \alpha \\
mapRose\ f\ (Node\ x\ xs) &= & root &= fst \circ split \\
\multicolumn{2}{l}{\quad Node\ (f\ x)\ (map\ (mapRose\ f)\ xs)}
\end{aligned}
$$

$$
\begin{aligned}
appRose &:: Rose\ (\alpha \rightarrow \beta) \rightarrow Rose\ \alpha \rightarrow Rose\ \beta \\
appRose\ (Node\ f\ fs)\ (Node\ x\ xs) &= Node\ (f\ x)\ (zipWith\ appRose\ fs\ xs)
\end{aligned}
$$

$$
\begin{aligned}
foldRose &:: ((\alpha, Seq\ \beta) \rightarrow \beta) \rightarrow Rose\ \alpha \rightarrow \beta \\
foldRose\ r\ (Node\ x\ xs) &= r\ (x, map\ (foldRose\ r)\ xs)
\end{aligned}
$$

The hylomorphism theorem [5, page 142] on rose trees states that, for all r, s:

$$
(foldrose\ r) \circ (foldrose\ s)^\circ\ =\ \mu\ \langle h \bullet r \circ (id \times map\ h) \circ s^\circ \rangle
$$

Fixpoint Theorems. A proper introduction to these theorems is given by the Eindhoven MPC group [15]. The theorems assume that the fixpoints exist.

1. Rolling Rule. *If f is a monotonic function of type $A \rightarrow B$ and g is a monotonic function of type $B \rightarrow A$ then: $\mu\ (f \circ g) = f\ (\mu\ (g \circ f))$.*

2. Abstraction Rule. *Suppose f is a function of type $A \rightarrow B \rightarrow B$. If f is monotonic in both its arguments then: $\mu\ (S\ f) = \langle x \bullet \mu\ (f\ x) \rangle$. In the context of sequences, this means that for all xs: $\mu\ (appSeq\ xs) = map\ \mu\ xs$.*

3. Mutual Recursion Rule. *Suppose f is a monotonic function of type $(A, B) \rightarrow (A, B)$. If we define $f_1 = fst \circ f$ and $f_2 = snd \circ f$, then:*

$$\mu f \;=\; (\; \mu \langle x \bullet f_1 (x, p\,x)\rangle, \;\; \mu \langle y \bullet f_2 (q\,y, y)\rangle \;)$$

$$\textbf{where } p\,x \;=\; \mu \langle v \bullet f_2 (x, v)\rangle$$
$$q\,y \;=\; \mu \langle u \bullet f_1 (u, y)\rangle$$

Relative Completeness of Abstraction Refinement for Software Model Checking

Thomas Ball[1], Andreas Podelski[2], and Sriram K. Rajamani[1]

[1] Microsoft Research
[2] Max-Planck-Institut für Informatik

Abstract. Automated methods for an undecidable class of verification problems cannot be complete (terminate for every correct program). We therefore consider a new kind of quality measure for such methods, which is completeness relative to a (powerful but unrealistic) oracle-based method. More precisely, we ask whether an often implemented method known as "software model checking with abstraction refinement" is complete relative to fixpoint iteration with "oracle-guided" widening. We show that whenever *backward* fixpoint iteration with oracle-guided widening succeeds in proving a property φ (for some sequence of widenings determined by the oracle) then software model checking with a particular form of *backward* refinement will succeed in proving φ. Intuitively, this means that the use of fixpoint iteration over abstractions and a particular backwards refinement of the abstractions has the effect of exploring the entire state space of all possible sequences of widenings.

1 Introduction

Automatic abstraction is a fundamental problem in model checking software. A promising approach to construct abstractions automatically, called *predicate abstraction*, is to map the concrete states of a system to abstract states according to their evaluation under a finite set of predicates. Many efforts have been made to construct predicate abstractions of systems [1,2,7,9,14,16,17,25,26,27, 28,29]. Where do the predicates for predicate abstraction come from? A popular scheme for generating predicates is to guess a set of initial predicates, and use (spurious) counterexamples from a model checker to generate more predicates as necessary [4,7,23,25]. Such schemes go by the name of *abstraction refinement*.

Property checking for software is undecidable, even for properties such as invariants (assertion violations). Thus it is impossible to come up with an abstraction refinement procedure that always generates a set of predicates that is guaranteed to (in)validate a program against a property. As a result, the process of abstraction refinement is largely a black-art, and little attention has been paid to even understand what the goal of predicate generation should be. This paper makes two contributions in this regard:

- We formalize a goodness criterion for abstraction refinement, namely relative completeness with respect to a comparable "oracle-guided" widening

J.-P. Katoen and P. Stevens (Eds.): TACAS 2002, LNCS 2280, pp. 158–172, 2002.

method. Since the termination argument of most fixpoint analyses that operate on infinite state spaces and lose precision can be explained using widening, this criterion is appropriate. Without such a criterion, any abstraction refinement procedure would seem like "just another" simple and practical heuristic.

- We give an abstraction refinement procedure which satisfies the above criterion, using the pre operator. Our definition of abstraction refinement captures the essence of the many implementation strategies based on counterexamples but avoids their technicalities.

If a set of states is represented by a formula φ (in disjunctive-normal form) then a *widening* of φ is obtained by dropping some conjuncts from some disjuncts in φ. Widenings are used to accelerate the termination of fixpoint analyses [10, 12]. For example, suppose $x \geq 0 \wedge x \leq n$ represents the set of states before an increment of variable x in a loop. The formula $x \geq 0$ obtained by a widening (dropping the conjunct $x \leq n$) represents the limit of an iterative reachability analysis. The precision of the analysis then depends on the *widening schedule*: which conjuncts are dropped and when in the fixpoint analysis they are dropped. *Oracle-guided* widening uses an oracle to guess the best possible widening schedule.

We use such an oracle-guided widening as a quality measurement for reasoning about the "relative completeness" of abstraction refinement. We design an abstraction refinement procedure using the pre operator, and show that if the oracle-guided widening terminates with success then the abstraction refinement (which does not use an oracle) will terminate with success. The basic idea of the procedure is to iteratively apply pre "syntactically" without performing a satisfiability check on the formula constructed at intermediate stages. The resulting procedure has the ability to "skip" over (potentially non-terminating) loops.

The term "relative completeness" of program verification methods has previously been used to refer to the existence of an oracle in the form of a theorem prover for an undecidable logic, e.g. integer arithmetic (the method succeeds whenever the oracle does) [8]. In contrast, our use of "relative completeness" refers to the existence of an oracle guiding the widening in another verification method (that method serves as a point of reference). Furthermore, our results hold for incomplete theorem provers—we do not assume that theorem provers are complete. Instead, we give the minimal requirements on a theorem prover (such as the provability of certain implications) in order to construct sound approximations.

Our formal setting accounts for the situation where a finite-state model checker is used. There, a Boolean variable is introduced for each predicate. The model checker no longer keeps track of the logical meaning of the predicate that a Boolean variable stands for. As a consequence, the fixpoint termination test becomes strictly weaker.

This paper is organized as follows. Section 2 provides the abstract formal setting for our work. Section 3 defines Method I, an algorithm for abstract fixpoint analysis and our abstract refinement procedure. Section 4 defines Method II, an algorithm for concrete fixpoint analysis with oracle-guided widening. Section 5 shows that a particular version of Method I (based on "backward refinement") is relatively complete with respect to Method II. Section 6 illustrates the difference between forward and backward refinement with a small example. Section 7 discusses some other technical issues and Section 8 concludes the paper.

2   The Formal Setting

In this section, everything but the "syntactic" definition of the operator pre and an "implementation-biased" (computable) definition of implication is standard.

Programs. We express programs in the standard format of 'guarded' *commands* to which other programming languages (also concurrent ones) can be easily translated. A program is a set C of guarded commands, which are logical formulas c of the form

$$c \equiv g(X) \wedge x'_1 = e_1(X) \wedge \ldots \wedge x'_m = e_m(X) \tag{1}$$

where $x_1, x_2, \ldots, x_m$ are all the program variables (including one or several program counters, here pc); the variable x'_i stands for the value of x after executing the guarded command c. We write X for the tuple of program variables, i.e. $X = \langle x_1, x_2, \ldots, x_m \rangle$. The formula g is written $g(X)$ in order to stress that its only free variables are among $x_1, \ldots, x_m$; it is called the *guard* of c. A program state is a valuation of X. We have a transition of one state into another one if the corresponding valuation of primed and unprimed variables satisfies one of the guarded commands $c \in C$. While each guarded command is deterministic, we note that program itself can be nondeterministic since multiple guards can hold at a given program state.

Symbolic representation. A 'symbolic' method uses formulas φ (also referred to as constraints or Boolean expressions) of a fixed formalism to effectively represent infinite sets of states. The exact nature of the formalism does not matter here, although we have in mind that it is some restricted class of first-order formulas over the algebraic structure on which the program computes (e.g. linear arithmetic). Reflecting existing implementations (see e.g. [18,12,22,20,15]), we assume a fixed *infinite* set of atomic formulas and represent an infinite set of states by a formula of the form

$$\varphi \equiv \bigvee_{i \in I} \bigwedge_{j \in J_i} \varphi_{ij} \tag{2}$$

where the φ_{ij}'s are atomic formulas. We define a partial order on formulas $\varphi' \leq \varphi$ as the provability of the implication $\varphi' \Rightarrow \varphi$ by a given theorem prover. Note that this ordering need not correspond to the entailment ordering; in many cases (e.g. integer arithmetic), the validity of implication is undecidable.

We purposefully do not require that theorem provers implement the test of the (in general, undecidable) validity of implication. As we will see, in order for our results to hold, a theorem prover only must be able prove that $\varphi \wedge \varphi' \Rightarrow \varphi$, as well as that $\varphi \Rightarrow \varphi \vee \varphi'$, for all formulas φ and φ'.

Pre and Post. For a guarded command c of the form (1), we define the application of the operator pre_c on a formula φ by the simultaneous substitution of the variables $x_1, x_2, \ldots, x_k$ in φ by the expressions $e_1, \ldots, e_k$. The operator pre for a program (a set of guarded commands) is simply the disjunction of the pre_c.

$$\mathsf{pre}_c(\varphi) \equiv g(X) \wedge \varphi[e_1(X), \ldots, e_m(X)/x_1, \ldots, x_m]$$
$$\mathsf{pre}(\varphi) \equiv \bigvee_{c \in C} \mathsf{pre}_c(\varphi)$$

In deviation from more familiar definitions, we do not perform a satisfiability check in the computation of pre_c. This is crucial in the definition of the backward refinement procedure in Section 3, but not for the fixpoint procedure in Section 4. In our formulation, we use a theorem prover only to check the ordering $\varphi \leq \varphi'$; we thus do not model the standard optimization of eliminating unsatisfiable disjuncts in a formula φ.

The application of the operator post_c on a formula φ is defined as usual; its computation requires a quantifier elimination procedure.

$$\mathsf{post}_c(\varphi) \equiv (\exists X.\ \varphi \wedge g(X) \wedge x_1' = e_1(X) \wedge \ldots \wedge x_m' = e_m(X))[X/X']$$
$$\mathsf{post}(\varphi) \equiv \bigvee_{c \in C} \mathsf{post}_c(\varphi)$$

Invariants. In order to specify correctness, we fix formulas init and safe denoting the set of *initial* and *safe* states, respectively, as well as formulas nonInit and unsafe denoting their complements. These formulas are in the form given for φ in (2). We define the given program to be *correct* if no unsafe state is reachable from an initial state.

The correctness can be proven by showing one of the two conditions below. Here, $\mathsf{lfp}(\mathsf{F}, \varphi)$ stands for the least fixpoint of the operator F above φ.

$$\mathsf{lfp}(\mathsf{post}, \mathsf{init}) \leq \mathsf{safe}$$
$$\mathsf{lfp}(\mathsf{pre}, \mathsf{unsafe}) \leq \mathsf{nonInit}$$

The least fixpoint implicitly refers to the quotient lattice of formulas wrt. the pre-order "$\leq$".

A *safe invariant* is an *inductive* invariant that implies safe, i.e. a formula ψ such that

- init $\leq \psi$,
- post$(\psi) \leq \psi$,
- $\psi \leq$ safe.

We will call a safe invariant a *forward invariant* in order to distinguish it from what we call a *backward invariant*, namely a formula ψ such that

- unsafe $\leq \psi$,
- $\mathsf{pre}(\psi) \leq \psi$,
- $\psi \leq \mathsf{nonInit}$.

We can establish correctness by computing either a forward invariant or a backward invariant. In order to have a generic notation that allows us to cover both cases, we introduce meta symbols F, start and bound such that $\langle \mathsf{F}, \mathsf{start}, \mathsf{bound} \rangle$ will be instantiated to $\langle \mathsf{post}, \mathsf{init}, \mathsf{safe} \rangle$ and to $\langle \mathsf{pre}, \mathsf{unsafe}, \mathsf{nonInit} \rangle$; an $\langle \mathsf{F}, \mathsf{start}, \mathsf{bound} \rangle$-invariant is then either a forward invariant or a backward invariant. Therefore we can express either of the two correctness conditions above as the existence of an $\langle \mathsf{F}, \mathsf{start}, \mathsf{bound} \rangle$-invariant, which is a formula ψ such that

- start $\leq \psi$,
- $\mathsf{F}(\psi) \leq \psi$,
- $\psi \leq$ bound.

The domain of formulas is closed under the application of F; the domain need not, however, contain $\mathsf{lfp}(\mathsf{F}, \mathsf{start})$. Even if it does not, it may still contain a formula denoting an $\langle \mathsf{F}, \mathsf{start}, \mathsf{bound} \rangle$-invariant. We note that we do not need the completeness of the domain for our results since we only consider fixpoints obtained by finite iteration sequences.

Using the generic notation, a possible approach to establish correctness is to find an upper abstraction F' of the operator F (i.e. where $\mathsf{F}(\varphi) \leq \mathsf{F}'(\varphi)$ holds for all formulas φ) such that $\mathsf{lfp}(\mathsf{F}', \mathsf{start})$, the least fixpoint of F' above start, can be computed and is contained in bound. Then, $\mathsf{lfp}(\mathsf{F}', \mathsf{start})$ is an $\langle \mathsf{F}, \mathsf{start}, \mathsf{bound} \rangle$-invariant because of the simple fact that $\mathsf{F}'(\varphi) \leq \varphi$ entails $\mathsf{F}(\varphi) \leq \varphi$.

In the following two sections, we will use two methods that use predicate abstraction and widening, respectively, to find such an upper abstraction F'. The two possible instantiations of $\langle \mathsf{F}, \mathsf{start}, \mathsf{bound} \rangle$ to $\langle \mathsf{post}, \mathsf{init}, \mathsf{safe} \rangle$ and to $\langle \mathsf{pre}, \mathsf{unsafe}, \mathsf{nonInit} \rangle$ yield the two basic variations of each of the two methods.

3   Method I: Predicate Abstraction with Refinement

We first describe the abstract fixpoint iteration method parameterized by a *refinement procedure* that generates a (generally infinite) sequence of finite sets $\mathcal{P}_n$ of predicates over states (for $n = 0, 1, \dots$). We then instantiate it with a particular refinement procedure (introduced below). We identify a predicate with the atomic formula φ defining it. Thus, each set $\mathcal{P}_n$ is a *finite* subset of the infinite set of atomic formulas.

We write $\mathcal{L}(\mathcal{P}_n)$ for the (finite!) free distributive lattice generated by the set of predicates $\mathcal{P}_n$, with bottom element false and top element true and the operators $\wedge$ and $\vee$. The notation $\mathcal{L}(\mathcal{P}_n)^{\sqsubseteq}$ is used to stress the partial order "$\sqsubseteq$" that comes with the lattice. We note that a constant-time fixpoint check in the free lattice can be implemented using Binary Decision Diagrams (BDD's) [5]. Each lattice element can be written in its disjunctive normal form (sometimes viewed as a

```
φ₀ := start
n := 0
loop
    𝒫ₙ := atoms(φₙ)
    construct abstract operator Fₙ# defined by 𝒫ₙ
    ψ := lfp(Fₙ#, start)
    if (ψ ≤ bound) then
        STOP with "Success"
    φₙ₊₁ := φₙ ∨ F(φₙ)
    n := n+1
endloop
```

Fig. 1. Method I: abstract fixpoint iteration with iterative abstraction refinement, where $\langle F, \text{start}, \text{bound}\rangle$ is either $\langle \text{post}, \text{init}, \text{safe}\rangle$ ("forward") or $\langle \text{pre}, \text{unsafe}, \text{nonInit}\rangle$ ("backward").

set of bitvectors). In the partial order "⊑" of the free lattice, predicates are pairwise incomparable. Therefore, elements written in disjunctive normal form are compared as follows.

$$\bigvee_{i \in I} \bigwedge_{j \in J_i} \varphi_{ij} \sqsubseteq \bigvee_{k \in K} \bigwedge_{j \in J'_k} \varphi'_{ij} \quad \text{if} \quad \forall i \in I \ \exists k \in K \ \{\varphi_{ij} \mid j \in J_i\} \supseteq \{\varphi'_{kj} \mid j \in J'_k\}$$

We will always have that $\mathcal{L}(\mathcal{P}_n)$ contains start, but generally $\mathcal{L}(\mathcal{P}_n)$ is not closed with respect to the operator F (we recall that the triple of meta symbols $\langle F, \text{start}, \text{bound}\rangle$ stands for either $\langle \text{post}, \text{init}, \text{safe}\rangle$ or $\langle \text{pre}, \text{unsafe}, \text{nonInit}\rangle$).

We use the framework of abstract interpretation [10] to construct the 'best' abstraction $F_n^\#$ of F with respect to $\mathcal{P}_n$. This operator is defined in terms of a Galois connection,

$$F_n^\# \equiv \alpha_n \circ F \circ \gamma$$

where the composition $f \circ g$ of two functions f and g is defined from right to left: $f \circ g(x) = f(g(x))$. The abstraction function α_n maps a formula φ to the smallest (wrt. "⊑") formula φ' in $\mathcal{L}(\mathcal{P}_n)$ that is larger (wrt. "≤") than φ, formally

$$\alpha_n(\varphi) \equiv \mu\varphi' \in \mathcal{L}(\mathcal{P}_n)^{\sqsubseteq}. \ \varphi \leq \varphi'.$$

The meaning function γ is the identity. As before, we omit the extension of the definitions to the quotient lattice.

The requirement that the mappings α_n and γ form a Galois connection (which guarantees the soundness of the approximation and hence the correctness of Method I) translates to the minimal requirement for the theorem prover: it must be able to prove the validity of the implications $\varphi \Rightarrow \varphi \vee \varphi'$ and $\varphi \wedge \varphi' \Rightarrow \varphi$

for all formulas φ and φ'. This is because the requirement of the Galois connection entails that γ is monotonic (i.e. $\varphi \sqsubseteq \varphi'$ entails $\gamma(\varphi) \leq \gamma(\varphi')$). In the free lattice, we also have that $\varphi \wedge \varphi' \sqsubseteq \varphi$ and $\varphi \sqsubseteq \varphi \vee \varphi'$. Hence, by the monotonicity of γ, $\varphi \wedge \varphi' \leq \varphi$ and $\varphi \leq \varphi \vee \varphi'$, which translates to the requirement on the theorem prover.

We will have that $\mathcal{P}_0 \subset \mathcal{P}_1 \subset \dots$ and hence $\mathcal{L}(\mathcal{P}_0) \subset \mathcal{L}(\mathcal{P}_1) \subset \dots$ which means an increasing precision of the abstraction α_n for increasing n.

Method I. The parametrized method starts with $n = 0$ and repeatedly

- constructs the abstract operator $\mathsf{F}_n^\#$ defined by $\mathcal{P}_n$,
- iterates $\mathsf{F}_n^\#$ to compute $\mathsf{lfp}(\mathsf{F}_n^\#, \mathsf{start})$,
- refines the set of predicates to get predicates $\mathcal{P}_{n+1}$,
- increases n by one

until $\mathsf{lfp}(\mathsf{F}_n^\#, \mathsf{start}) \leq \mathsf{bound}$.

If Method I terminates for some n, then $\mathsf{lfp}(\mathsf{F}_n^\#, \mathsf{start})$ is a (forward or backward) invariant (depending on whether F is instantiated by post or by pre). We note that $\mathsf{lfp}(\mathsf{F}_n^\#, \mathsf{start})$ is computed over a free lattice ordered by $\sqsubseteq$, and that its computation is guaranteed to terminate.

If we take the method with the forward or backward refinement procedure defined below, we obtain the automated verification method given in Figure 1. The algorithm uses the operator atoms to map a formula φ (in disjunctive-normal form) to its (finite) set of atomic constituent formulas:

$$\mathsf{atoms}(\bigvee_{i \in I} \bigwedge_{j \in J_i} \varphi_{ij}) = \{\varphi_{ij} \mid i \in I, j \in J_i\}.$$

Refinement. Our refinement procedure is to simply apply F to the current formula φ_n and disjoin the result with φ_n, to result in φ_{n+1}. The sequence of formulas produced by the algorithm is thus:

- $\varphi_0 = \mathsf{atoms}(\mathsf{start})$
- $\varphi_{n+1} = \varphi_n \vee \mathsf{F}(\varphi_n)$

We call the procedure 'backward refinement' if $\langle \mathsf{F}, \mathsf{start} \rangle$ is $\langle \mathsf{pre}, \mathsf{unsafe} \rangle$ and 'forward refinement' if $\langle \mathsf{F}, \mathsf{start} \rangle$ is $\langle \mathsf{post}, \mathsf{init} \rangle$.

4   Method II: Oracle-Guided Widening

Method II iteratively applies the 'concrete' operator F over formulas and afterwards calls an oracle which determines a widening operator and applies the widening operator to the result of the application of F (the chosen widening operator may be the identity function). The precise definition of the method is given in Figure 2. Again, the instantiations of $\langle \mathsf{F}, \mathsf{start}, \mathsf{bound} \rangle$ to $\langle \mathsf{post}, \mathsf{init}, \mathsf{safe} \rangle$ and to $\langle \mathsf{pre}, \mathsf{unsafe}, \mathsf{nonInit} \rangle$ yield the forward (resp. backward) variations of the method.

```
φ'_0, old, n := start, false, 0
loop
    if (φ'_n ≤ old) then
        if (φ'_n ≤ bound) then
            STOP with "Success"
        else
            STOP with "Don't know"
    else
        old := φ'_n
        i := guess provided by oracle
        φ'_{n+1} := widen(i, (φ'_n ∨ F(φ'_{n+1})))
        n := n + 1
endloop
```

Fig. 2. Method II: fixpoint iteration with abstraction by oracle-guided widening. Here, $\langle \mathsf{F}, \mathsf{start}, \mathsf{bound} \rangle$ is either $\langle \mathsf{post}, \mathsf{init}, \mathsf{safe} \rangle$ ("forward") or $\langle \mathsf{pre}, \mathsf{unsafe}, \mathsf{nonInit} \rangle$ ("backward").

The only requirement that we impose on each operator widen chosen by the oracle is that the application of widen on a formula φ yields a weaker formula φ' (denoting a larger set of states) in which some conjuncts in some disjuncts have been dropped (possibly none), i.e.

$$\mathsf{widen}(\bigvee_{i \in I} \bigwedge_{j \in J_i} \varphi_{ij}) = \bigvee_{i \in I} \bigwedge_{j \in J_i'} \varphi_{ij} \quad \text{where} \quad J_i' \subseteq J_i \text{ for all } i. \tag{3}$$

We suppose that we have an enumeration of widening operators $\mathsf{widen}(0)$, $\mathsf{widen}(1)$, ... and that the oracle determines a particular one, $\mathsf{widen}(i)$, by returning a natural number i at each iteration step. We write $\mathsf{widen}(i, x)$ short for $\mathsf{widen}(x)$ where $\mathsf{widen} = \mathsf{widen}(i)$. Thus, each sequence of natural numbers produced by the oracle uniquely determines a fixpoint iteration sequence.

5   Relative Completeness for Backward Refinement

For the following theorem, we consider Method I and Method II with $\mathsf{F}, \mathsf{start}$ and bound instantiated to $\mathsf{pre}, \mathsf{unsafe}$ and $\mathsf{nonInit}$, respectively. The theorem says that for every program, Method I is guaranteed to terminate with success (i.e. proving the correctness of the program) if there exists an oracle such that Method II terminates with success.

Theorem 1 (Relative Completeness of Abstract Backward Iteration with Backward Refinement). *Method I with* $\langle \mathsf{F}, \mathsf{start}, \mathsf{bound} \rangle$ *instantiated to* $\langle \mathsf{pre}, \mathsf{unsafe}, \mathsf{nonInit} \rangle$ *will terminate with success if Method II with* $\langle \mathsf{F}, \mathsf{start}, \mathsf{bound} \rangle$ *instantiated to* $\langle \mathsf{pre}, \mathsf{unsafe}, \mathsf{nonInit} \rangle$ *terminates with success.*

$\varphi_0 := \mathsf{safe}$
$n := 0$
loop
  $\mathcal{P}_n := \mathsf{atoms}(\varphi_n)$
  construct abstract operator $\mathsf{post}_n^{\#}$ defined by $\mathcal{P}_n$
  $\psi := \mathsf{lfp}(\mathsf{post}_n^{\#}, \mathsf{start})$
  if $(\psi \leq \mathsf{safe})$ **then**
    STOP with "Success"
  $\varphi_{n+1} := \varphi_n \vee \widetilde{\mathsf{pre}}(\varphi_n)$
  n := n+1
endloop

Fig. 3. Method III: forward abstract fixpoint iteration with backwards iterative abstraction refinement.

The theorem means that the (possibly infinite) sequence of finite abstract fixpoint iteration sequences

$$(\mathsf{start}, \mathsf{pre}_n^{\#}(\mathsf{start}), \dots, \mathsf{lfp}(\mathsf{pre}_n^{\#}, \mathsf{start}))_{n=1,2,\dots}$$

'simulates' the tree consisting of all the infinitely many, possibly infinite branches

$$(\mathsf{start}, \mathsf{widen}(i_1) \circ \mathsf{pre}(\mathsf{start}), \dots)_{(i_1, i_2, \dots) \in \mathbb{N}^{\mathbb{N}}}$$

that arise from the different choices for the operator $\mathsf{widen}(i_k)$ at each level k (corresponding to the different sequences $(i_1, i_2, \dots)$ of natural numbers that can be returned by the oracle). 'Simulates' here informally refers to the search of a backward invariant.

Forward fixpoint iteration with backward refinement. Can we use abstract *forward* fixpoint iteration with backward refinement and still have relative completeness? The answer is yes if we use the dual $\widetilde{\mathsf{pre}}$ of pre for the backward refinement. The operator $\widetilde{\mathsf{pre}}$ (sometimes called the weakest liberal precondition operator) is defined by $\widetilde{\mathsf{pre}}(\varphi) = \neg\mathsf{pre}(\neg\varphi)$.

    We define *dual* backward refinement as the procedure that iterates $\widetilde{\mathsf{pre}}$ starting from safe; i.e., it generates the sequence of sets of predicates $\mathcal{P}_i = \mathsf{atoms}(\varphi_i)$ $(n \geq 0)$ where

$-\ \varphi_0 = \mathsf{safe}$
$-\ \varphi_{n+1} = \varphi_n \vee \widetilde{\mathsf{pre}}(\varphi_n)$

This new method (Method III) is made precise in Figure 3. One possible interpretation of the following theorem is that the crucial item in the statement of Theorem 1 is the *backward* direction of the refinement (and not the direction of the abstract fixpoint iteration).

```
init  ≡  pc = ℓ₁                              L1:   x = 0;
unsafe  ≡  pc = error                         L2:   while (x >= 0) {
variables X = {x, y, z}                                  x = x + 1;
                                                    }
guarded commands:                             L3:   if (y == 25) {
   c₁ :   pc = ℓ₁ → pc := ℓ₂, x := 0          L4:     if (y != 25) {
   c₂ :   pc = ℓ₂ ∧ x ≥ 0 → x := x + 1        L5:       z = -1;
   c₃ :   pc = ℓ₂ ∧ x < 0 → pc := ℓ₃          L6:       while (z != 0) {
   c₄ :   pc = ℓ₃ ∧ y = 25 → pc := ℓ₄                     z = z - 1;
   c₅ :   pc = ℓ₄ ∧ y ≠ 25 → pc := ℓ₅                   }
   c₆ :   pc = ℓ₅ → pc := ℓ₆; z := −1                   error: ;
   c₇ :   pc = ℓ₆ ∧ z ≠ 0 → z := z − 1                }
   c₈ :   pc = ℓ₆ ∧ z = 0 → pc := error            }
```

Fig. 4. Example program: Method I, forward abstract fixpoint iteration with forward refinement, does not terminate; Method II (iterative application of **post** and oracle-guided widening) terminates with success. We here use 'syntactic sugar' for guarded commands and list only the 'true' updates; for example, c_2 stands for the formula $pc = \ell_2 \wedge x \geq 0 \wedge x' = x + 1 \wedge pc' = pc \wedge y' = y \wedge z' = z$. The right hand side shows the program in C-like notation

Theorem 2 (Relative Completeness of Abstract Forward Iteration with Dual Backward Refinement). *For every program, Method III is guaranteed to terminate with success if Method II terminates with success.*

Proofs of both Theorem 1 and Theorem 2 can be found in [3].

6   Example: Forward vs. Backward Refinement

The example program in Figure 4 shows that the completeness of Method I relative to Method II does not hold for the forward case, i.e. when F, start and bound are instantiated to post, init and safe, respectively. The values ℓ_1 through ℓ_6 for pc in the left hand side of Figure 4 correspond to labels L1 through L6 in the right hand side. In this example, for Method I to terminate, it is crucial to find the (contradictory) predicates $x = 25$ and $x \neq 25$. What is difficult is that the code path through these predicates is "bracketed" above and below by non-terminating **while** loops.

We observe the following facts about this example:

- Method II forward (iterative application of post and oracle-guided widening) terminates with success (the widening operator just drops all conjuncts containing the variable x).
- Method I with forward abstraction refinement does not terminate. Forward refinement will get "stuck" at the first **while** loop, generating an infinite sequence of predicates about x, namely $x = 0$, $x = 1$, $x = 2$, ...

This means that the analog of Theorem 1 does not hold for the forward case. Continuing the example, we also have that

- Method II (iterative application of pre and oracle-guided widening) terminates with success (the widening operator just drops all conjuncts containing the variable z).
- Method I backward terminates with success, which will follow by Theorem 1, but can also be checked directly by executing the method which terminates in four iterations. The first three iterations of pre are shown below. For readability, conjuncts of the form $(c = c)$ for some constant c have been dropped.

$$
\begin{aligned}
\text{unsafe} = \quad & (pc = error) \\
\text{pre}(\text{unsafe}) = \quad & (pc = \ell_6 \wedge z = 0) \\
\text{pre}^2(\text{unsafe}) = \quad & (pc = \ell_6 \wedge z \neq 0 \wedge z = 1) \vee \\
& (pc = \ell_5 \wedge -1 = 0) \\
\text{pre}^3(\text{unsafe}) = \quad & (pc = \ell_6 \wedge z \neq 0 \wedge z = 2) \vee \\
& (pc = \ell_5 \wedge -1 \neq 0 \wedge -2 = 0) \vee \\
& (pc = \ell_4 \wedge y \neq 25 \wedge -1 = 0)
\end{aligned}
$$

Note that it is crucial that we do not do a satisfiability test during the computation of pre; therefore, the backward refinement procedure retains disjuncts that have unsatisfiable conjuncts such as $-1 = 0$. Thus, the predicates $y = 25$, $y \neq 25$, $pc = error$, $pc = \ell_6$, $pc = \ell_5$, $pc = \ell_4$ are present in $\mathcal{P}_4$. These predicates are sufficient to ensure that $\mathsf{lfp}(\text{pre}_4^{\#}, \text{unsafe}) \leq \text{nonInit}$.

As a secondary point, neither the iteration of the concrete post operator post nor the iteration of the concrete predecessor operator pre terminates (without using widening). We leave open the problem of designing a forward refinement procedure with relative completeness.

7   Discussion

Boolean expressions. Our setting of the lattice $\mathcal{L}(\mathcal{P})$ generalizes the setting of Boolean expressions that has been used so far in work on abstract model checking [1,2,7,9,14,16,17,25,26,27,28,29]. Our more general setting allows us to determine a sense in which the negated versions of predicates generated by the abstraction refinement procedure are useless. This is important because the time for constructing the abstract fixpoint operator is exponential in the number of predicates.

Refinement Based on Error Traces. The definition of the abstraction refinement procedure in Section 3 is modeled after the standard refinement procedure as implemented e.g. by Clarke et al. [6], Ball and Rajamani [4] (who took forward refinement) and Lakhnech et al. [25], Henzinger et al. [21], and Das et al. [13] (who took backward refinement). The definition abstracts away the technicalities of the particular implementation strategy where a 'spurious'-error execution trace is used to selectively add predicates that can express a specific set of reachable states (with the effect of eliminating that error trace); the definition amounts to consider all traces of the same length as the 'spurious' execution trace. Theorems 1 and 2 also hold if we take that implementation strategy (which still generates all 'necessary' predicates under the assumption of the theorems).

More Powerful Refinement. The backward refinement procedure enhances the standard one in that it adds also predicates that occur in unsatisfiable conjuncts. For example, if c is the guarded command $pc = \ell_5 \wedge z' = -1 \wedge pc' = \ell_6$, then $\mathsf{atoms}(\mathsf{pre}_c(pc = \ell_6 \wedge z = 0))$ is $\mathsf{atoms}(pc = \ell_5 \wedge -1 = 0)$, which consists of the two predicates $pc = \ell_5$ and $-1 = 0$ (see Section 6); the predicate $-1 = 0$ will not appear in $\alpha_n(\varphi)$ for any φ. In terms of a practical, error trace-based strategy, this means that one adds predicates to eliminate more spurious transitions of the error trace than just the first one.

Forward vs. Backward Refinement. It is perhaps intriguing as to why Method I is as powerful as Method II with backward refinement, but not with forward refinement. We first try to give some intuition for the difference between the two cases and then give a more technical explanation.

In the forward direction, the 'concrete' execution of each guarded command $c \in \mathcal{C}$ is deterministic (even though the entire system defined by a set $\mathcal{C}$ of guarded commands may be non-deterministic). An 'abstract' execution (where abstraction is induced e.g. by widening) is in general non-deterministic and can reach more program points (and other program expressions) than the concrete execution. Note that abstraction refinement must be based on the concrete execution (otherwise, the spuriousness of an abstract error trace can not be detected). The deterministic execution follows only one branch and hence it may get "stuck in a loop" (for example the loop in line L2 of Figure 4).

In the backward direction, the concrete execution already is (in general) non-deterministic and can follow several branches; hence it does not get stuck in a loop (for example the loop in line L6 of Figure 4) and can reach as many program points (expressions) as an abstract execution; in order to make this always true, pre must produce also disjuncts with unsatisfiable conjuncts; we added Line L5 in the program in Figure 4 to demonstrate this point.

Widening. We use the notion of a widening operator essentially in the sense of [10,12]. In the standard setting, a widening operator is a binary operator that assigns two elements x and x' another element $x \nabla x'$ that is larger than both. In this paper, each widening operator widen is unary. This makes a difference in the context of a fixed widening operator (the second argument is used to determine the 'direction' of the extrapolation of the first by $x \nabla x'$); it does not restrict the power of the extrapolation in our setting (for each application $x \nabla x'$ of the binary operator the oracle can guess a unary one which, applied to x, yields the same result).

The restriction on the form of $\mathsf{widen}(x)$ is motivated by the goal to model widening operators such that each application can realistically be implemented (although, of course, the oracle can not). The intuition is that boundaries that need to be moved in each fixpoint iteration are getting weaker and weaker and will be dropped in the limit. Many widening operators that have been implemented by Cousot, Halbwachs, Jeannet and others (see e.g. [12,15,18,22]) seem to follow that intuition.

Widening vs. Predicate Abstraction. Our intent is not a comparison between the respective power of model checking based on predicate abstraction with refinement and of widening-based model checking. Such a comparison would be futile since the latter lacks the outer loop that performs a refinement of the abstraction. (What would such a loop look like in order to obtain relative completeness?)

It is illuminating, however, to see that predicate abstraction and widening can be formally related with each other as two abstraction methods for verification. Previously, this was thought to be impossible [24]. For static program analysis, widening was shown to be superior to predicate abstraction or any other 'static' abstraction [11]. As a consequence of our result, predicate abstraction with refinement can be understood as widening with 'optimal' guidance.

The converse of the theorems, i.e. the relative completeness of Method II wrt. Method I, does not hold.[1] Intuitively, this is because the widening in Method II (dropping a conjunct) is generally less precise than the extrapolation in Method II (which amounts to replacing a conjunct with a formula over already generated predicates). The converse would hold if we extended the widening accordingly. However, we consider that direction of relative completeness not interesting as long as we do not know of a realistic way to mimic the oracle for guessing a widening.

The power of either, Method I or II, depends on the given formalism which fixes the set of atomic formulas. For example, the methods are more powerful if equalities $x = y + c$ must be expressed by the conjunction of inequalities (e.g. if atoms($\{x = 0\}$) is not $\{x = 0\}$ but $\{x \leq 0, \ x \geq 0\}$, then Method I will succeed on the example in Section 6 also with forward refinement; similarly, Method I with backward refinement will succeed on the example program in [25]).

Termination for Incorrect Programs. Each verification method that we consider here can be modified in a straightforward way so that it will always detect (and will always terminate) in the case where the program is incorrect. The termination of a verification method is an issue only in the case of correct programs. Therefore we concentrate on that case, and gloss over the case of incorrect programs.

Finite quotients. If we assume that the program has a finite simulation or bisimulation quotient, termination of fixpoint computations can be guaranteed (both forward and backward) [26,19]. Our work does not make any such assumptions. We focus on the uniform evaluation of a method on *all* instances of

---

[1] To obtain a counterexample, consider a program with two independent branches, one that causes the generation of the predicates $x = y$ and $x = y + 1$, and another corresponding to the program fragment x=0; y=0; while(*){x++; y++}; while(x!=0){y--; x--}; if(y!=0){error:}.

the undecidable verification problem (and not on the instances of a decidable subproblem).

Optimization. Generating a small set of predicates is always a desirable feature in designing a refinement procedure. This was not our focus in this paper. Instead, we defined what the goal of the refinement procedure should be, and designed a refinement procedure to meet this goal. Once this goal is established, and only after such a goal is formulated as an algorithmic problem, it is possible to propose and evaluate optimizations. Our work enables this to happen.

8   Conclusion

Automated refinement is presently the least understood part of automated program verification methods known under the term 'software model checking'. Up to now, different refinement procedures could be evaluated only practically, by comparing their implementations in various existing tools. The work presented here is the first that tries to evaluate them on a principled basis. We think that this is a starting point to arrive at a systematic way to design and analyze refinement procedures.

References

1. P. A. Abdulla, A. Annichini, S. Bensalem, A. Bouajjani, P. Habermehl, and Y. Lakhnech. Verification of infinite-state systems by combining abstraction and reachability analysis. In *CAV 99: Computer-aided Verification*, LNCS 1633, pages 146–159. Springer-Verlag, 1999.
2. T. Ball, R. Majumdar, T. Millstein, and S. K. Rajamani. Automatic predicate abstraction of C programs. In *PLDI 01: Programming Language Design and Implementation*, pages 203–213. ACM, 2001.
3. T. Ball, A. Podelski, and S. K. Rajamani. On the relative completeness of abstraction refinement. Technical Report MSR-TR-2001-106, Microsoft Research, 2001.
4. T. Ball and S. K. Rajamani. Automatically validating temporal safety properties of interfaces. In *SPIN 01: SPIN Workshop*, LNCS 2057, pages 103–122. Springer-Verlag, 2001.
5. R. Bryant. Graph-based algorithms for boolean function manipulation. *IEEE Transactions on Computers*, C-35(8):677–691, 1986.
6. E. Clarke, O. Grumberg, S. Jha, Y. Lu, and H. Veith. Counterexample-guided abstraction refinement. In *CAV 00: Computer Aided Verification*, LNCS 1855, pages 154–169. Springer-Verlag, 2000.
7. E. M. Clarke, O. Grumberg, S. Jha, Y. Lu, and H. Veith. Counterexample-guided abstraction refinement. In *CAV 00: Computer-Aided Verification*, LNCS 1855, pages 154–169. Springer-Verlag, 2000.
8. S. A. Cook. Soundness and completeness of an axiom system for program verification. *SIAM Journal of Computing*, 7(1):70–91, February 1978.
9. J. Corbett, M. Dwyer, J. Hatcliff, C. Pasareanu, Robby, S. Laubach, and H. Zheng. Bandera: Extracting finite-state models from Java source code. In *ICSE 2000: International Conference on Software Engineering*, pages 439–448. ACM, 2000.

10. P. Cousot and R. Cousot. Systematic design of program analysis frameworks. In *POPL 79: Principles of Programming Languages*, pages 269–282. ACM, 1979.
11. P. Cousot and R. Cousot. Comparing the Galois connection and widening/narrowing approaches to abstract interpretation. In *Proceedings of PLILP 92: Programming Language Implementation and Logic Programming*, LNCS 631, pages 269–295. Springer-Verlag, 1992.
12. P. Cousot and N. Halbwachs. Automatic discovery of linear restraints among variables of a program. In *POPL 78: Principles of Programming Languages*, pages 84–96. ACM, 1978.
13. S. Das and D. L. Dill. Successive approximation of abstract transition relations. In *LICS 01: Symposium on Logic in Computer Science*, 2001.
14. S. Das, D. L. Dill, and S. Park. Experience with predicate abstraction. In *CAV 00: Computer-Aided Verification*, LNCS 1633, pages 160–171. Springer-Verlag, 1999.
15. G. Delzanno and A. Podelski. Model checking in CLP. In *TACAS 99: Tools and Algorithms for Construction and Analysis of Systems*, LNCS 1579, pages 223–239. Springer-Verlag, 1999.
16. R. Giacobazzi and E. Quintarelli. Incompleteness, counterexamples and refinements in abstract model checking. In *SAS 01: Static Analysis*, LNCS 2126, pages 356–373. Springer-Verlag, 2001.
17. S. Graf and H. Saïdi. Construction of abstract state graphs with PVS. In *CAV 97: Computer-aided Verification*, LNCS 1254, pages 72–83. Springer-Verlag, 1997.
18. N. Halbwachs, Y.-E. Proy, and P. Raymond. Verification of linear hybrid systems by means of convex approximations. In *SAS 94: Static Analysis*, LNCS 864, pages 223–237. Springer-Verlag, 1994.
19. T. Henzinger and R. Majumdar. A classification of symbolic transition systems. In *STACS 00: Theoretical Aspects of Computer Science*, LNCS 1770, pages 13–34. Springer-Verlag, 2000.
20. T. A. Henzinger, P. Ho, and H. Wong-Toi. Hytech: a model checker for hybrid systems. *Software Tools for Technology Transfer*, 1:110–122, 1997.
21. T. A. Henzinger, R. Jhala, R. Majumdar, and G. Sutre. personal communication, May 2001.
22. B. Jeannet. *Dynamic partitionning in linear relation analysis and application to the verification of synchronous programs*. PhD thesis, Institut National Polytechnique de Grenoble, September 2000.
23. R. Kurshan. *Computer-aided Verification of Coordinating Processes*. Princeton University Press, 1994.
24. Y. Lakhnech. Personal communication, April 2001.
25. Y. Lakhnech, S. Bensalem, S. Berezin, and S. Owre. Incremental verification by abstraction. In *TACAS 01: Tools and Algorithms for Construction and Analysis of Systems*, LNCS 2031, pages 98–112. Springer-Verlag, 2001.
26. K. S. Namjoshi and R. P. Kurshan. Syntactic program transformations for automatic abstraction. In *CAV 00: Computer-Aided Verification*, LNCS 1855, pages 435–449. Springer-Verlag, 2000.
27. V. Rusu and E. Singerman. On proving safety properties by integrating static analysis, theorem proving and abstraction. In *TACAS 99: Tools and Algorithms for Construction and Analysis of Systems*, LNCS 1579, pages 178–192. Springer-Verlag, 1999.
28. M. Sagiv, T. Reps, and R. Wilhelm. Parametric shape analysis via 3-valued logic. In *POPL 99: Principles of Programming Languages*, pages 105–118. ACM, 1999.
29. H. Saïdi and N. Shankar. Abstract and model check while you prove. In *CAV 99: Computer-aided Verification*, LNCS 1633, pages 443–454. Springer-Verlag, 1999.

Towards the Automated Verification of Multithreaded Java Programs

Giorgio Delzanno[1], Jean-François Raskin[2*], and Laurent Van Begin[2**]

[1] Dipartimento di Informatica e Scienze dell'Informazione
Università di Genova, via Dodecaneso 35, 16146 Genova, Italy
[2] Département d'Informatique, Université Libre de Bruxelles,
Blvd Du Triomphe, 1050 Bruxelles, Belgium

Abstract. In this paper we investigate the possible application of *parameterized verification* techniques to synchronization skeletons of *multithreaded Java programs*. As conceptual contribution, we identify a class of *infinite-state* abstract models, called Multi-Transfer Nets (MTNs), that preserve the main features of the semantics of concurrent Java. We achieve this goal by exploiting an interesting connection with the Broadcast Protocols of [7], and by introducing the notion of *asynchronous rendez-vous*. As technical contribution, we extend the symbolic verification techniques of [6] based on Covering Sharing Trees and structural invariants to MTNs. As practical contribution, we report on experimental results for verification of examples of multithreaded Java programs.

1 Introduction

In the last years there has been an increasing interest in automated verification techniques for parameterized systems. Contrary to approaches based on finite-state abstractions, in parameterized verification it is possible to handle infinite-state abstract models, with a potential gain of precision in the analysis of the underlying systems. Recently, this idea has been applied to the verification of safety properties of *multithreaded C programs* [2], a natural field of application for techniques related to Petri Nets. Concurrent Java, however, is going to become the standard language for multithreaded programming. Its success is due to technology like Applets and Servlets, widely used in the context of client-server applications for the World Wide Web. For this reason, we consider the specialization of parameterized verification techniques to concurrent Java programs an important (and challenging) research goal.

In this paper we will focus on problems that we think are propedeutic to further research in this direction. Specifically, we will first address the problem of finding adequate *infinite-state abstract models* for synchronization skeletons

* This author was partially supported by a "Crédit aux chercheurs", Belgian National Fund for Scientific Research.
** Supported by a "First Europe" grant, Walloon Region, Belgium. This work was partially done when this author was visiting Università di Genova.

J.-P. Katoen and P. Stevens (Eds.): TACAS 2002, LNCS 2280, pp. 173–187, 2002.
© Springer-Verlag Berlin Heidelberg 2002

of concurrent Java programs. The Petri Net model adopted for C programs in [2] is no more adequate here. The problem here is due to the presence of special Java built-in methods, namely `wait`, `notify` and `notifyAll`, whose semantics cannot be given via rendez-vous communication. We will solve this problem by resorting to the following connections: the semantics of `notifyAll` (a primitive that awakens all processes waiting on a lock) can be expressed in terms of the *broadcast* primitive introduced by Emerson and Namjoshi in [7]; the semantics of `notify` (a primitive that awakens only one of the waiting processes) can be expressed via *asynchronous rendez-vous*, i.e., a rendez-vous that is *non-blocking* for the sender. We will formalize these intuitions by introducing the new model of Multi-Transfer Nets (MTNs), a formalism that incorporates and extends the main feature of Petri Nets and Broadcast Protocols.

As a second step, we will study the problem of finding an adequate technology to *efficiently* model check this new class of infinite-state systems. We will first show that the backward reachability algorithm of Esparza, Finkel and Mayr used for Broadcast Protocols in [8] can be naturally extended to MTNs. Decidability still holds for the *control state reachability* problem that consists of deciding if a state taken from a given *upward closed* set of unsafe states is reachable from the initial states. In [5], we have define a graph-based data structure called Covering Sharing Trees (CSTs) to compactly represent upward closed sets of markings of Petri Nets. In this paper we will show that the CST-based verification techniques defined in [6] can be extended to MTNs. Specifically, we will define a CST-based symbolic algorithm to compute the pre-image operator associated to an MTN, and we will apply it to build a symbolic backward reachability algorithm to check parameterized safety properties. In [5,6] we proposed several heuristics for the analysis of Petri Nets. Most of them are based on the Structural Theory of Petri Nets, a theory that allows to statically compute over-approximations of the reachability set. Interestingly, MTNs can be viewed as a subclass of *Petri Nets with marking dependent cardinality arcs*, a class of models for which Ciardo [3] an extension of the Structural Theory of Petri Nets. As a nice consequence of this connection, we can still use the pruning techniques based on structural invariants proposed in [6] to efficiently cut the search space of an MTN during backward reachability.

As practical experiments, we have applied the extended CST-library to several parameterized safety problems taken from the literature, see e.g., [7, 8]. In this paper we will report on bechmarks performed over abstractions of multithreaded programs and we will compare the results with HyTech [11], a polyhedra-based model checker that provides backward reachability and that can handle the same class of parameterized systems.

2   Abstract Models for Multithreaded Java Programs

A Java thread is an object of the predefined Java classes `Thread` and `Runnable`. The code of a thread must be specified in the method `run` that is invoked to start its execution. Threads are executed in parallel and can share variables and

```
public class Inc extends Thread      public class Point
{private Point p;                    {private int x = 0;
 public Inc(Point p)                  private int y = 0;
   { this.p = p; }                    public synchronized void incx()
 private void incpoint()                { x = x + 1;
   { p.incx();                            notifyAll(); }
     p.incy(); }                      public synchronized void decx()
 public void run()                      { while (x == 0) wait();
   { while (true) incpoint(); }         x = x - 1; }
}                                      ...
 ....                                }
```

Fig. 1. An example of declaration of threads and synchronized methods.

objects. Every object comes with a *lock* that can be used to control concurrent accesses to its methods in a multithreaded program. Methods declared as **synchronized** compete for the lock on the corresponding instance object. Via the *synchronized* instruction, it is also possible to associate a lock to a given object. To avoid starvation and deadlocks, threads can suspend their activity and relinquish the lock on a given object while being inside a synchronized method using the **wait** primitive. Waiting processes can be awakened using the **notifyAll** primitive. Awakened processes compete for the locks they relinquish using **wait**. The primitive **notify** can be used to awake a thread arbitrarily chosen between the ones that are waiting. Both **notify** and **notifyAll** are *non-blocking*, i.e., the thread that invokes one of them does not wait for an acknowledgment.

As an example, consider the thread declarations of Fig. 1. The class **Point** provides methods to increment and decrement the coordinates of a **Point** object (the code of the methods **incy** and **decy** are omitted for brevity). The method **decx** enforces a thread to **wait** for the value of coordinate x to be *non zero*. Every time a coordinate is incremented a notification is broadcast to awake all suspended threads. Suspended threads will compete for the lock on the **Point** object. The thread **Inc** repeatedly invokes the method **incpoint** based on **incx** and **incy**. Symmetrically, the thread **Dec** (whose definition is omitted for brevity) repeatedly invokes the method **decpoint** based on **decx** and **decy**.

A possible way to use these definitions would be to declare a **main** method in which we create a **Point** object, n **Inc** threads, m **Dec** threads (all working on the same object), and then to let them run all threads in parallel. Note that, in order to ensure the consistency of the data of the shared object, increments and decrements should be performed atomically. This property should hold for *any possible number* of **Inc** and **Dec** threads, i.e. for any value of n and m. Our goal is to attack this kind of problems using *parameterized verification*. However, we first need to study adequate *infinite-state* abstract models for multithreaded Java programs.

2.1 Global Machines

Let us focus on our example and forget for a moment all synchronization primitives. Following [2], in order to extract the control skeleton of the classes Inc and Dec, we can apply the technique of *predicate abstraction*. We first unfold the methods of the Point class into the thread declarations. Then, we associate a boolean variable to each guard in the program (e.g. $x == 0$ will be represented via a boolean variable $zeroX$), and extrapolate the effect of the instructions on the resulting boolean program. This way, we obtain two finite-state automata. Each state of the automata corresponds to a control point in the flattened code of the methods of our threads. Method invocations can be represented using synchronization labels. Global boolean variables can be used to model the monitor that controls a shared object.

Let us now consider the synchronization skeleton of threads. Unfortunately, communication via rendez-vous cannot be used to model the operational semantics of the interplay between the built-in methods wait, notify and notifyAll. The type of synchronization we need here involves, in fact, a number of processes that depends on the *current global state* of the system (all processes that are *currently* waiting to be awakened). To solve this problem, we will resort to a new model, called global machines, obtained by merging concepts coming from the broadcast protocols of [7] and from the global/local machines of [2] with the new notion of *asynchronous rendez-vous*.

We start the description of global machines from the operations needed to handle global boolean variables.

Definition 1. Let $\mathbf{B} = \{b_1, \ldots, b_n\}$ be a finite set of *global boolean variables*, and let $\mathbf{B}'$ be their primed version. A *boolean guard* φ_g is either the formula *true* or the conjunction of literals $L_1 \wedge \ldots \wedge L_p$, $p \leq n$, such that L_i is either b or $\neg b$ for some $b \in \mathbf{B}$. A *boolean action* φ_a is a formula $b_1' = v_1 \wedge \ldots \wedge b_n' = v_n$, where $v_i \in \{true, false, b_i\}$ for $i : 1, \ldots, n$.

Boolean guards and actions are used to express pre-and post-conditions on the variables in $\mathbf{B}$. The behaviour of a thread will be modeled via the notion of local machine introduced below.

Definition 2. A *local machine* is a tuple $\langle Q, \Sigma, \delta \rangle$, where: Q is a finite set of states; Σ is the set of synchronization labels used to build the set of possible actions $\mathcal{A}$ of a process (defined later); and $\delta \subseteq (Q \times \mathcal{A} \times Q)$ is the local transition relation. In the following, we will use $s \xrightarrow{\alpha} s'$ to indicate that $\langle s, \alpha, s' \rangle \in \delta$.

The *actions* of a local machines are defined as follows (in the following φ represent the conjunction of a boolean guard with an action (Def. 1), and $\ell \in \Sigma$):

- *Internal action:* $\ell : \varphi$;
- *Rendez-vous:* $\ell! : \varphi$ (sending), and $\ell?$ (reception);
- *Asynchronous Rendez-vous:* $\ell\uparrow: \varphi$ (sending), and $\ell\downarrow$ (reception);
- *Broadcast.* $\ell!! : \varphi$ (sending), and $\ell??$ (reception).

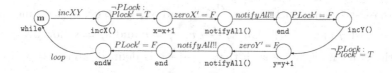

Fig. 2. The Global Machine for the `Inc` thread of Fig. 1.

Having in mind the translation from Java programs, we will also apply the following restrictions: the set of source and target states of a broadcast (asynchronous rendez-vous) reception must be distinct; broadcasts receptions associated to the same sending can be partitioned so that each partition is defined over a distinct set of states. Note, in fact, tha we will use asynchronous rendez-vous and broadcast to model the semantics of `notify` and `notifyAll`. Our restriction avoids cyclic rules like $sloc_1 \xrightarrow{n!!} sloc_2$, $rloc_1 \xrightarrow{n??} rloc_2$, and $rloc_2 \xrightarrow{n??} rloc_1$ that have no meaning if $sloc$ and $rloc$ are control points in the code of the sender and of the receiver, respectively, and n corresponds to a `notifyAll`. Furthermore, all the interesting examples of Broadcast Protocols we are aware of satisfy these conditions.

As an example, the abstract model that we extracted from thread `Inc` applying the technique of predicate abstraction can be represented via the local machine of Fig. 2.

Definition 3. A *global machine* is a tuple $\mathcal{G} = \langle \mathbf{B}, \langle \mathcal{L}_1, k_1 \rangle, \ldots, \langle \mathcal{L}_m, k_m \rangle \rangle$, where: $\mathbf{B} = \{b_1, \ldots, b_n\}$ is the set of *global boolean variables* for $i : 1, \ldots, m$; $\mathcal{L}_i = \langle Q_i, \Sigma_i, \delta_i \rangle$ is the i-th local machine; and k_i the number of its copies. Futhermore, we have that $Q_i \cap Q_j = \emptyset$ for any $i, j : 1, \ldots, m$ with $i \neq j$.

Definition 4. A *global state* of $\mathcal{G} = \langle \mathbf{B}, \langle \mathcal{L}_1, k_1 \rangle, \ldots, \langle \mathcal{L}_m, k_m \rangle \rangle$ is a tuple $G = \langle \rho, \mathbf{s} \rangle$ where $\rho : \mathbf{B} \to \{true, false\}$ is a valuation for the global boolean variables, and the tuple $\mathbf{s} = \langle s_{11}, \ldots, s_{1k_1}, \ldots, s_{m1}, \ldots, s_{mk_m} \rangle$ of dimension $k = k_1 + \ldots + k_m$ is such that $s_{ij} \in Q_i$ denotes the current local state of the j-th copy of the local machine $\mathcal{L}_i$.

The runs of a global machine are defined via the relation $\Rightarrow$ defined below.

Definition 5. Let $\mathcal{G} = \langle \mathbf{B}, \langle \mathcal{L}_1, k_1 \rangle, \ldots, \langle \mathcal{L}_m, k_m \rangle \rangle$ be a global machine, $G = \langle \rho, \langle s_1 \ldots, s_k \rangle \rangle$ and $G = \langle \rho', \langle s'_1 \ldots, s'_k \rangle \rangle$ be two global states, and $\gamma = \rho \cup \rho'$. Then, $G \Rightarrow_{\mathcal{G}} G'$ iff one of the following conditions holds:

- there exist i and u such that $s_i \xrightarrow{\ell . \varphi} u$, and $\gamma(\varphi) = true$, $s'_i = u$, and $s'_j = s_j$ for all $j \neq i$.
- there exist i, j, u and v such that $s_i \xrightarrow{\ell! : \varphi} u$, $s_j \xrightarrow{\ell?} v$, $\gamma(\varphi) = true$, $s'_i = u$, $s'_j = v$, and $s'_r = s_r$ for all $r \neq i, j$.

- there exist i and u such that $s_i \xrightarrow{\ell\uparrow:\varphi} u$, and $\gamma(\varphi) = true$, $s'_i = u$, and: either there exist j and v such that $s_j \xrightarrow{\ell\downarrow} v$, $s'_j = v$ and $s'_r = s_r$ for any $r \neq i, j$, or there are no j and v such that $s_j \xrightarrow{\ell\downarrow} v$ is defined, and $s'_r = s_r$ for any $r \neq i$.
- there exist i and u such that $s_i \xrightarrow{\ell!!:\varphi} u$, $\gamma(\varphi) = true$, $s'_i = u$, and for all j such that there exist v and $s_j \xrightarrow{\ell??} v$, we have $s'_j = v$; finally, $s'_r = s_r$ for all $r \neq i$ such that $\ell??$ is not defined in s_r.

A *run* of a global machine is a sequence of global states $G_0 G_1 \ldots G_n$ such that $G_i \Rightarrow_\mathcal{G} G_{i+1}$ for $0 \leq i < n$. G_0 is the *initial* global state of the run and G_n is the *target* global state of the run. A global state G' is reachable from G, written $G \stackrel{*}{\Rightarrow}_\mathcal{G} G'$, if and only if there exists a run with initial global state G and target global state G'. The set of reachable global states from a set of initial global states $\mathbf{G}$, noted $\mathsf{Reach}_\mathcal{G}(\mathbf{G})$, is equal to $\{G' \mid \exists G \in \mathbf{G} : G \stackrel{*}{\Rightarrow}_\mathcal{G} G'\}$.

3   Multi-transfer Nets

Following [8,10], in order to study safety properties of global machines, we will apply a *counting* abstraction that maps global states into markings (of a Petri Net model) that keep track of the number of processes in each one of the local states of the local machines. To be able to model the communication mechanisms of Def. 2, we need however an extended Petri Net-like model, we will call Multi-Transfer Nets (MTNs). MTNs have all the features of Petri Nets. In addition, MTNs allow us to capture the semantics of rendez-vous, asynchronous rendez-vous and of broadcast as an instance of a general notion of *transfer of at most c tokens*. Formally, this model is defined as follows.

Definition 6 (Multi-Transfer Net). A *Multi-Transfer Net* is a pair $\langle \mathcal{P}, \mathcal{B} \rangle$ where: $\mathcal{P} = \{p_1, \ldots, p_n\}$ is a set of places, and $\mathcal{B} = \{M_1, \ldots, M_m\}$ is a set of *multi-transfers*.

A *multi-transfer* M is a tuple $\langle T, \{S_1, \ldots, S_u\} \rangle$ such that

- $T = \langle \mathcal{I}, \mathcal{O} \rangle$ is the Petri Net *transition* of the *multi-transfer*, i.e. $\mathcal{I}, \mathcal{O} : \mathcal{P} \to \mathbb{N}$;
- each $S_k = \langle \{B_{k1}, \ldots, B_{kr_k}\}, c_k \rangle$ is a *transfer block*, where $c_k \in \mathbb{N} \cup \{+\infty\}$ is the *bound*, and each $B_{kj} = \langle P_{kj}, p_{kj} \rangle$ with $P_{kj} \subseteq \mathcal{P}$ and $p_{kj} \in \mathcal{P}$ is a *transfer*.

In order to avoid cyclic transfers, a multi-transfer M with set of transfer blocks $\{S_1, \ldots, S_u\}$ must satisfy the following conditions:

1. for any *transfer block* S_k with set of *transfers* $\{B_{k1}, \ldots, B_{kr_k}\}$, and for any such B_{kj}, we require that $p_{kj} \notin P_{kj}$;
2. for any *transfer* B_{ki} in the transfer block S_k and B_{lj} in the transfer block S_l with $B_{ki} \neq B_{lj}$, we require that $(P_{ki} \cup \{p_{ki}\}) \cap (P_{lj} \cup \{p_{lj}\}) = \emptyset$.

A *marking* is a mapping $\mathbf{m} : \mathcal{P} \to \mathbb{N}$ (a vector of natural numbers). Given $\mathcal{I} : \mathcal{P} \to \mathbb{N}$, we use $\mathcal{I} \geq \mathbf{m}$ to indicate that $\mathcal{I}(p) \geq \mathbf{m}(p)$ for all $p \in \mathcal{P}$. Furthermore, given $S \subseteq \mathcal{P}$ we define $\mathbf{m}(S) = \Sigma_{p \in S} \mathbf{m}(p)$.

Definition 7 (Enabling a Multi-Transfer). Let M be a multi-transfer with *transition* $\langle \mathcal{I}, \mathcal{O} \rangle$. We say that M is *enabled* in **m** if $\mathcal{I} \geq$ **m**.

Definition 8 (Firing a Multi-Transfer). Let $M = \langle T, \{S_1, \ldots, S_u\} \rangle$ be a multi-transfer enabled in **m**. *Firing M in* **m** leads to any marking **m'** (written **m** $\rightarrowtail_M$ **m'**) computed in accord to the following *sequence* of steps (in which we use the two intermediate markings $\mathbf{m}_1$ and $\mathbf{m}_2$):

1. let $T = \langle \mathcal{I}, \mathcal{O} \rangle$, $\mathbf{m}_1(p) = \mathbf{m}(p) - \mathcal{I}(p)$ for all $p \in \mathcal{P}$;
2. $\mathbf{m}_2$ can be any marking such that the following constraints are satisfied:
   - for each transfer block $S_k = \langle \{B_{k1}, \ldots, B_{kr_k}\}, c_k \rangle$:
     - if $r_k > 0$ and $\mathbf{m}_1(P_{k1} \cup \ldots \cup P_{kr_k}) > c_k$, then for all $d_1, \ldots, d_{r_k} \in \mathbb{N}$ be such that $d_1 + \ldots + d_{r_k} = c_k$ and for all j, $1 \leq j \leq r_k$:
       - $\mathbf{m}_2(p_{kj}) = \mathbf{m}_1(p_{kj}) + d_j$,
       - and $\mathbf{m}_2(P_{kj}) = \mathbf{m}_1(P_{kj}) - d_j$,
       - with the additional constraint that $\mathbf{m}_1(p) \geq \mathbf{m}_2(p)$ for any $p \in P_{kj}$.
     - if $r_k > 0$ and $\mathbf{m}_1(P_{k1} \cup \ldots \cup P_{kr_k}) \leq c_k$, then for all j, $1 \leq j \leq r_k$:
       - $\mathbf{m}_2(p_{kj}) = \mathbf{m}_1(p_{kj}) + \mathbf{m}_1(P_{kj})$ and
       - $\mathbf{m}_2(P_{kj}) = 0$;
   - $\mathbf{m}_2(p) = \mathbf{m}_1(p)$ for all $p \in \mathcal{P}$ not involved in transfer blocks;
3. $\mathbf{m}'(p) = \mathbf{m}_2(p) + \mathcal{O}(p)$ for all $p \in \mathcal{P}$.

Note that a *Petri Net transition* is obtained by considering multi-transfers with an empty set of transfer blocks. A *transfer arc* (all tokens in the sources are transferred to the target) is obtained instead by a multi-transfer with a single set of transfers with bound $c = +\infty$. A transfer block has a *non-deterministic* effect if the total number of tokens is strictly greater than c with $c \in \mathbb{N}$. The non-determinism is due to the numbers $d_1, \ldots, d_{r_k}$ of tokens that are transferred by each transfer, and from their distribution within the set P_{kj} of sources for $j : 1, \ldots, r_k$.

Definition 9 (Operational Semantics). Let $\mathcal{M} = \langle \mathcal{P}, \mathcal{B} \rangle$ be an MTN. A *run* of $\mathcal{M}$ is a sequence of markings $\mathbf{m}_0 \mathbf{m}_1 \ldots \mathbf{m}_n$ such that for any i, $0 \leq i < n$, there exists $M \in \mathcal{B}$ such that $\mathbf{m}_i \rightarrowtail_M \mathbf{m}_{i+1}$, $\mathbf{m}_0$ is the *initial* marking of the run and $\mathbf{m}_n$ the *target* marking of the run. A marking $\mathbf{m}'$ is *reachable* from a marking $\mathbf{m}$, written $\mathbf{m} \rightarrowtail^* \mathbf{m}'$, if and only if there exists a run with initial marking $\mathbf{m}_0$ and target marking $\mathbf{m}'$. The *set of reachable markings* of $\mathcal{M}$ from a set of markings I, written $\mathsf{Reach}_{\mathcal{M}}(I)$, is defined as the set $\{\mathbf{m}' \mid \exists \mathbf{m} \in I : \mathbf{m} \rightarrowtail^* \mathbf{m}'\}$.

3.1   From Global Machines to MTNs

Global machines can be naturally translated into MTNs, as we will informally explain in this section. In the following we will often refer to Fig. 3 to illustrate the intuition behind the translation. First of all, each *global boolean variable* b is modeled in the MTN by the two places T_b and F_b. Each local state s_{ij} appearing in the *local machine* $\mathcal{L}_i$ is modelled with a place with the same name

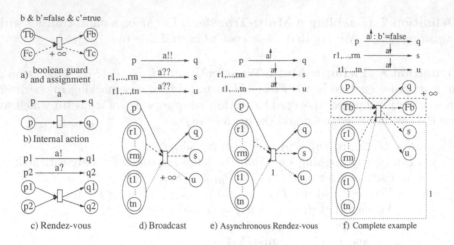

Fig. 3. From global machines rules to MTNs. $r_1, \ldots, r_n \xrightarrow{\ell??} s$ is an abbreviation for the set of transitions $r_1 \xrightarrow{\ell??} s$, ..., $r_n \xrightarrow{\ell??} s$, all of them having the same destination state s, similarly for $r_1, \ldots, r_n \xrightarrow{\ell\downarrow} s$.

s_{ij}. A global state $G = \langle \rho, \mathbf{s} \rangle$ is translated into the marking $\mathbf{m}_G$ such that: (1) for each $b \in B$, if $\rho(b) = true$ then $\mathbf{m}_G(T_b) = 1$ and $\mathbf{m}_G(F_b) = 0$, if $\rho(b) = false$ then $\mathbf{m}_G(T_b) = 0$ and $\mathbf{m}_G(F_b) = 1$; (2) for each local state s_{ij}, $\mathbf{m}_G(s_{ij}) = v_{ij}$, where v_{ij} is the number of occurrences of state s_{ij} in $\mathbf{s}$. In other words, the place s_{ij} contains as many tokens as the number of copies of the local machine $\mathcal{L}_i$ whose current state is s_{ij}. Let us now briefly explain how an action is translated into a *multi-transfer*. We first focus our attention on the boolean part of actions. Consider the boolean formula $\varphi = b \wedge b' = false \wedge c' = true$ with $d' = d$ for all other variables. Let M_φ be the multi-transfer that results from the translation of φ. Intuitively, M_φ has to check the presence of one token in place T_b, and ensure that, when the transition is taken, the token is removed from T_b and added to F_b. Furthermore, the only token shared by T_c and F_c must be in F_c after the firing. This can be achieved as shown in Fig. 3(a). Using the Petri Net transition of M_φ (thick lines in in Fig. 3), we ensure the presence of the token in T_b before the firing and in F_b after. To ensure the presence of a token in T_c after firing, we use an unbounded transfer block with a single transfer from the singleton $\{F_c\}$ to the place T_c (dashed lines in Fig. 3). If the token was already in T_c before the firing, the transfer block has no effect, on the other hand if the token was in F_c then it is transfered to T_c.

Starting from the previous idea, we incrementally add new components to M_φ so as to completely action of a global machine. An *internal action* a from state p to state q is simply modeled by adding an input arc from place p and an output arc to place q to the transition of the transfer (see Fig. 3(b)). A *rendez-vous* is treated similarly but with pairs of places (see Fig. 3(c)). A *broadcast* sending is modelled as an internal action. *Broadcast* receptions are modeled via an unbounded transfer block that contains a transfer for each possible destination state (see Fig. 3(d)).

Finally, an *asynchronous rendez-vous* sending is modeled as an internal action, whereas the corresponding receptions are modeled via a transfer block with bound 1 that contains a transfer for each possible destination state (see Fig. 3(e)). A complete example treating a boolean formula and asynchronous rendez-vous is given in Fig. 3(f). The asynchronous rendez-vous update the boolean formula b to false. The boolean part is modeled by an unbounded transfer block with one single transfer, the sender part by the petri net transition and the receivers part by a 1-bounded transfer block with two transfers. The following proposition formally relates global machines and MTNs.

Proposition 1. For any global machine $\mathcal{G}$ and any set of global states $\mathbf{G}$, we can construct automatically a MTN $\mathcal{M}_{\mathcal{G}}$ with only unbounded and 1-bounded multi-transfers such that $\alpha(\mathsf{Reach}_{\mathcal{G}}(\mathbf{G})) = \mathsf{Reach}_{\mathcal{M}_{\mathcal{G}}}(\alpha(\mathbf{G}))$.

4 Verification of MTN-Based Abstract Models

It is well-known that the class of safety properties of Petri Nets whose negation can be expressed in terms of upward closed sets of markings can be decided using backward reachability [1,9]. In this setting the goal is to prove that none of the markings in a given infinite set $\mathbf{U}$ of *unsafe configurations* can be reached from the set of initial markings $\mathbf{M}_0$. To achieve this goal, we can first compute the transitive closure of the *pre-image* operator, and then check that no elements of $\mathbf{M}_0$ is in the resulting set of markings. As shown in [1,8,9], this algorithm is guaranteed to terminate for Petri Nets and Broadcast Protocols whenever $\mathbf{U}$ is upward closed w.r.t. the componentwise ordering of tuples. Formally, let $cones(\mathbf{S}) = \{\mathbf{m}' \mid \mathbf{m} \preccurlyeq \mathbf{m}', \mathbf{m} \in \mathbf{S}\}$. Then, a set of markings $\mathbf{S}$ is upward closed if $cones(\mathbf{S}) = \mathbf{S}$. An upward closed set of markings $\mathbf{U}$ is always finitely generated by a set of minimal tuples, we will denote it as $gen(\mathbf{U})$. The termination of the algorithm is ensured by the following properties. The application of the pre-image operator (associated to Petri Nets and Broadcast Protocols) to an upward closed set of markings returns a set that is still upward closed. The containment relation between upward closed sets of markings is a *well-quasi ordering*. It is important to note that Karp-Miller's construction may fail to terminate for extensions of Petri Nets with broadcast communication [8].

In order to extend the algorithm of [8], we first need to study the properties of the pre-image operator of MTNs.

Definition 10 (Pre-image of an MTN). Let $\mathcal{M} = \langle \mathcal{P}, \mathcal{B} \rangle$ be an MTN, and let $M \in \mathcal{B}$, then $\mathsf{Pre}_M(\mathbf{S}) = \{\mathbf{m}' \mid \mathbf{m}' \rightarrowtail_M \mathbf{m}, \mathbf{m} \in \mathbf{S}\}$.

We can easily prove that MTNs are monotonic with respect to the pointwise ordering on markings, i.e., if $\mathbf{m}_1 \rightarrowtail \mathbf{m}_2$, then for any $\mathbf{m}'_1 \geq \mathbf{m}_1$ there exists $\mathbf{m}'_2 \geq \mathbf{m}_2$ such that $\mathbf{m}'_1 \rightarrowtail \mathbf{m}'_2$.

Proposition 2. Let $\mathcal{M} = \langle \mathcal{P}, \mathcal{B} \rangle$ be an MTN, and $M \in \mathcal{B}$. If $\mathbf{S}$ is an upward closed set of markings, then $\mathsf{Pre}_M(\mathbf{S})$ is still upward closed.

As a consequence, backward reachability for MTNs is guaranteed to terminate when taking an upward closed sets of markings as input. In the next section we will exploit the previous property to define a CST-based symbolic backward reachability for MTNs.

5   The Assertional Language of Covering Sharing Trees

Covering Sharing Trees (CSTs) are an extension of the sharing tree data structure introduced in [13] to efficiently store tuples of integers. A sharing tree S is a rooted acyclic graph with nodes partitioned in k-*layers* such that: all nodes of layer i have successors in the layer $i + 1$; a node cannot have two successors with the same label; finally, two nodes with the same label in the same layer do not have the same set of successors. Formally, S is a tuple $(N, V, root, end, val, succ)$, where $N = \{root\} \cup N_1 \cup \ldots \cup N_k \cup \{end\}$ is the finite set of *nodes* (N_i is the set of nodes of *layer* i and, by convention, $N_0 = \{root\}$ and $N_{k+1} = \{end\}$), $V = \{x_1, x_2, \ldots, x_k\}$ is a set of variables. Intuitively, N_i is associated to x_i. $val : N \rightsquigarrow \mathbb{Z} \cup \{\top, \bot\}$ is a labeling function for the nodes, and $succ : N \rightsquigarrow 2^N$ defines the successors of a node. Furthermore, (1) $val(n) = \top$ iff $n = root$, $val(n) = \bot$ iff $n = end$, $succ(end) = \emptyset$; (2) for $i : 0, \ldots, k$, $\forall n \in N_i$, $succ(n) \subseteq N_{i+1}$ and $succ(n) \neq \emptyset$; (3) $\forall n \in N$, $\forall n_1, n_2 \in succ(n)$, if $n_1 \neq n_2$ then $val(n_1) \neq val(n_2)$. (4) $\forall i, 0 \leq i \leq k$, $\forall n_1, n_2 \in N_i$, $n_1 \neq n_2$, if $val(n_1) = val(n_2)$ then $succ(n_1) \neq succ(n_2)$. A path of a k-sharing tree is a sequence of nodes $\langle n_1, \ldots, n_m \rangle$ such that $n_{i+1} \in succ(n_i)$ for $i = 1, \ldots, m$-1. Paths represent *tuples of size* k of natural numbers. We use $elem(S)$ to denote the *flat denotation* of a k-sharing tree S:

$$elem(S) = \{ \ \langle val(n_1), \ldots, val(n_k) \rangle \mid \langle \top, n_1, \ldots, n_k, \bot \rangle \text{ is a path of } S \ \}.$$

Conditions (3) and (4) ensure the maximal sharing of prefixes and suffixes among the tuples of the flat denotation of a sharing tree. The *size* of a sharing tree is the number of its *nodes* and *edges*. The number of tuples in $elem(S)$ can be exponentially larger than the size of S. As shown in [13], given a set of tuples A of size k, there exists a unique sharing tree such that $elem(S_A) = A$ (modulo isomorphisms of graphs). A CST is obtained by lifting the denotation of a sharing tree S as follows

$$cones(S) = \{\mathbf{m} \mid \mathbf{n} \preccurlyeq \mathbf{m}, \ \mathbf{n} \in elem(S)\}.$$

($cone(\mathbf{m})$ is defined in a similar way on a single marking $\mathbf{m}$). Given an upward closed set of markings $\mathbf{U}$, we define the CST $S_{\mathbf{U}}$ as the k-sharing tree such that $elem(S_{\mathbf{U}}) = gen(\mathbf{U})$. Thus, $S_{\mathbf{U}}$ can be used to *compactly* represent $gen(\mathbf{U})$ (in the best case the size of $S_{\mathbf{U}}$ is *logarithmic* in the size of $gen(\mathbf{U})$) and to *finitely* represent $\mathbf{U}$. A CST can also be viewed as a compact representation of the formula $\bigvee_{\mathbf{m} \in gen(\mathbf{U})} (x_1 \geq m_1 \wedge \ldots \wedge x_n \geq m_n)$. An examples of CST is given in the of Fig. 5(a).

```
 1:    function Step2 (S : CST after step (1), P : source, p_k : target) return R
 2:        R ⟵ Empty_CST
 3:        forall value v in the layer associated to place p_k do
 4:            S_v ⟵ S such that elem(S) = elem(S_v) \ {⟨c_1, c_2, ..., c_n⟩|c_k ≠ v}
 5:            forall layers of S_v corresponding to places P ∪ {p_k} do
 6:                replace all the nodes n of the current layer by the set of nodes
 7:                {n_0, n_1, ..., n_v} having the same successors and predecessors
 8:                than n and such that val(n_i) = i
 9:            Apply algorithm of [13] on S_v to ensure conditions (3)-(4)
10:            Compute Q_v such that m ∈ cones(Q_v) iff ∑_{p∈P∪{p_k}} m(p) ≥ v
11:            T_v ⟵ S_v ∩_CST Q_v
12:            R ⟵ R ∪_CST T_v
```

Fig. 4. Algorithm for Step (2).

6 CST-Based Symbolic *Pre* Operator for MTNs

In the context of Petri Nets, in [5], we presented an algorithm to symbolically compute the pre-image of a set of markings represented via a CST. In this section we will restrict ourselves to consider *transfer blocks* having bound $+\infty$. The algorithm can be extended however to any bound $c \in \mathbb{N}$, and in particular to $c = 1$. Let us first note that the Pre operator enjoys the following properties.

Remark 1. Consider the multi-transfer $M = \langle T, \{S_1, \ldots, S_k\}\rangle$ where $T = \langle \mathcal{I}, \mathcal{O}\rangle$. We define $\mathsf{Pre}_\mathcal{I}$, $\mathsf{Pre}_\mathcal{O}$, and Pre_{S_i} as the pre-image operator associated to the multi-transfers $M_\mathcal{I} = \langle\langle\mathcal{I},\emptyset\rangle,\emptyset\rangle$, $M_\mathcal{O} = \langle\langle\emptyset,\mathcal{O}\rangle,\emptyset\rangle$, and $M_i = \langle\langle\emptyset,\emptyset\rangle,\{S_i\}\rangle$, respectively. From Def. 6, we have that $\mathsf{Pre}_M = \mathsf{Pre}_\mathcal{I} \circ \mathsf{Pre}_{S_1} \circ \ldots \circ \mathsf{Pre}_{S_k} \circ \mathsf{Pre}_\mathcal{O}$. Furthermore, let S be the transfer block $\langle\{B_1,\ldots,B_r\},+\infty\rangle$, then $\mathsf{Pre}_S = \mathsf{Pre}_{B_1}\circ\ldots\circ\mathsf{Pre}_{B_r}$, where Pre_{B_i} is associated to the multi-transfer $N_i = \langle T', \{S_i'\}\rangle$ such that $T' = \langle\emptyset,\emptyset\rangle$ and $S_i' = \langle B_i, c\rangle$. The previous properties hold because transfers are defined on distinct set of places each other.

Based on the previous remark, let us consider then a *transfer block* M_B with bound $+\infty$ and with the single *transfer* $B = \langle P, p_k\rangle$, $P \subseteq \mathcal{P}$, and $p_k \in \mathcal{P}$. Furthermore, let $I_P = \{\, i \mid p_i \in P \,\}$ be the set of indexes of places in P. Given a CST S, our aim is to build an algorithm to construct a CST S' such that $cones(S') = \mathsf{Pre}_{M_B}(cones(S))$. We proceed in two steps.

The first step consists in removing all paths of S that do not satisfy the the post-condition induced by the semantics of transfer blocks with bound $+\infty$: *all source places in P must contain zero tokens after firing M_B.* Specifically, we compute the CST S_1 such that

$$elem(S_1) = \{\langle c_1, c_2, \ldots, c_n\rangle \in elem(S) \mid c_i = 0, \text{ for any } i \subset I_P\}.$$

By construction, it follows that $\mathsf{Pre}_{M_B}(cones(S_1)) = \mathsf{Pre}_{M_B}(cones(S))$. This step can be performed in *polynomial time* in the size of S: we simply have to remove all nodes n of the layers associated to places in P such that $val(n) \neq 0$.

This will give us what is called a *pre*-Sharing Tree in [13], a graph in which condition (4) of the definition of sharing tree might be violated. By applying the algorithm described in [13], the *pre*-Sharing Tree can be re-arranged into a Sharing Tree in polynomial time.

As a second step, we compute the predecessors of the elements of S_1, w.r.t. M_B (recall that M_B has only the *transfer* $B = \langle P, p_k \rangle$). Suppose $\mathbf{c} = \langle c_1, \ldots, c_n \rangle \in elem(S_1)$. Then, we know that the tuple $\mathbf{c}$ represents the upward-closed set of markings $\mathbf{S} = \{\mathbf{m} \mid \mathbf{m}(p_i) \geq c_i, \ i : 1, \ldots, n\}$. Applying Pre_{M_B} to $\mathbf{c}$, we should obtain a representation of the upward-closed set $\mathbf{S'}$ whose markings present one possible distribution of tokens *before* the transfer from P to p_k took place. Note that the relation between the number of tokens in P (say $\sum_{i \in I_P} x_i$) and in p_k (say x_k) before and after firing M_B is as follows: $x'_k = x_k + \sum_{i \in I_P} x_i$ and $x'_i = 0$ for any $i \in I_P$. Thus, $\mathbf{S'}$ will be generated by the set $gen(\mathbf{S'})$ consisting of the markings $\mathbf{d} = \langle d_1, d_2, \ldots, d_n \rangle$ having the following properties: $d_k + \sum_{i \in I_P} d_i = c_k$; whereas $d_j = c_j$ for any $j \notin (I_P \cup \{k\})$. Intuitively, all we need here is to forget about the labels of the nodes of S_1 associated to the places in $P \cup \{p_k\}$, and replace them with nodes so that the sum of the values (associated to $P \cup \{p_k\}$) along a path always gives c_k.

For instance, consider a transfer $\langle \{p_1\}, p_2 \rangle$, and let $c_2 = 2$ be the constant in the constraint associated to p_2 in S_1. Furthermore, suppose that p_1 and p_2 are associated to adjacent layers in our CST. Then, we simply have to add the labels $0, 1, 2$ in both layers, and then connect the resulting nodes so that the sum of the connected values is always equal to 2.

In the general case, we also have to take into account places stored in non-adjacent layers, consider more than one value for c_k, etc. To attack these problems, we split the algorithm in two sub-steps. For each possible value of c_k in S_1, we first compute an over-approximation (see the example below), and then, we select the exact paths by intersecting the resulting CST with a CST whose generators are the markings $\mathbf{m} = \langle m_1, \ldots, m_n \rangle$ in which $m_k + \sum_{i \in I_P} m_i = c_k$ and $m_j = 0$ for $j \notin I_P \cup \{k\}$. The complete algorithm is given in Fig. 4. The following example will help in understanding this technique.

As an example, consider the CST S in Fig. 5(a) consisting of the three elements $\langle 0, 2, 0, 1, 0, 0 \rangle$, $\langle 0, 1, 0, 2, 0, 0 \rangle$ and $\langle 0, 0, 0, 2, 2, 0 \rangle$ representing the formula $\Phi = (c_2 \geq 2 \wedge c_4 \geq 1) \vee (c_2 \geq 1 \wedge c_4 \geq 2) \vee (c_4 \geq 2 \wedge c_5 \geq 2)$. Now consider the transfer that moves the tokens from place p_5 into place p_2, defined through the equation $c'_2 = c_2 + c_5, c'_5 = 0$. When applied to the CST (a) the algorithm of Fig. 4 performs the steps shown in (b-g). Specifically, it first computes (b) by removing the tuple $\langle 0, 0, 0, 2, 2, 0 \rangle$ that do not satisfy $c'_5 = 0$. At the second iteration of the loop (line 3, Fig.4), it computes (c). By adding new nodes in the second and fifth layers, we obtain (d), an over-approximation of the backward reachable markings starting from (c). The CST Q_2 representing all the tuples satisfying $c_2 + c_5 \geq 2$ is shown in (e). The CST resulting from the intersection of (d) and Q_2 corresponding to the exact set of backward reachable markings starting from (c) is shown in (f). Finally, the result of the algorithm is the CST (g).

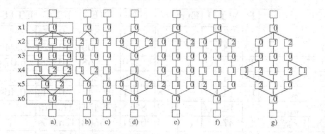

Fig. 5. Set of CST generated during the computation of the transfer $c_2' = c_2 + c_5, c_5' = 0$

Structural Heuristics. The MTNs that results from the translations from global machines enjoy the following interesting property. They can be viewed as *Petri Nets with arc dependent cardinality arcs* [3], an extension of Petri Nets in which edges are labeled with functions linear in the current marking. Ciardo has shown that *place invariants* for *Petri Nets with arc dependent cardinality arcs* can be computed by first reducing them to Petri Nets (Theorem 1 of [3]). When specialized to a given initial marking, place invariants can be used to infer structural invariants that must hold in all reachable markings (i.e. they represent an over-approximation of the reachability set). Structural invariants can then be used to prune the search space explored during backward reachability. On the basis of the previous observation, we can enhance the MTN-backward reachability algorithm with the efficient pruning techniques working on CSTs we proposed in [6]. In this technique we use the information coming from the *statically computed* invariants as follows. At each step during the search we remove paths of the CST representing the partial search space that do not satisfy the invariant. This operations can be efficiently performed by working directly on the structure of a CST. In the next section we will report on practical experiments we obtained with the resulting method.

7 Experimental Results

The table in Fig. 6 describes some of the results we obtained by applying the extended CSTs-library to examples of MTNs modeling multithreaded programs. As an example, we have tested the MTN corresponding to the global machine partially described in Fig. 2. We considered the following unsafe set of states: at least two threads have modified only one of the two coordinates of the Point object. This *upward closed set* of states can be represented by CSTs in which either at least two tokens are in the place corresponding to the incY() state of Fig. 2, or at least one token is in state incX() and at least one token is in state decY(), or at least two tokens are in state decY(). For this example, we have automatically computed *place invariants*, and we have applied them to prune the search as shown in Fig. 6 (I/D). Here m and n represent the number of Inc and Dec threads in the initial marking. We considered both *parametric initial markings* (e.g. $m \geq 1, n \geq 1$) as well as fixed initial markings (e.g. $m = 1, n = 1$).

MTN	m_0	P	MT	I	Err	S	NN	NE	ETC	ETH	R
I/D	$m,n \geq 1$	32	28		√	10	1542	1823	9.77s	↑	–
I/D	$m,n \geq 1$	32	28	√	√	10	538	209	0.82s	40.24s	49
I/D	$m,n=1$	32	28	√	√	10	279	68	0.22s	5.07s	23
P/C	$m,n=2$	18	14			25	860	12264	44.49s	↑	–
P/C	$m,n=2$	18	14	√		8	111	43	0.04s	0.46s	11.5
P/C	$m,n=50$	18	14	√		152	8511	179451	1h36m	↑	–
P/C_1	$k,l,m,n \geq 1$	44	37		√	14	20421	15543	37m55s	↑	–
P/C_1	$k,l,m,n \geq 1$	44	37	√	√	14	1710	1384	2.86s	↑	–
P/C_1	$k,l,m,n=1$	44	37	√	√	14	1231	736	1.88s	↑	–
P/C_2	$k,l,m,n \geq 1$	44	37			29	12479	8396	55m50s	↑	–
P/C_2	$k,l,m,n \geq 1$	44	37	√		1	46	1	0.02s	1.73s	86.5
P/C_2	$k,l,m,n=1$	44	37	√		1	46	1	0.00s	0.48s	> 48

Fig. 6. Benchmarks on an AMD Athlon 900Mhz 500Mbytes: m_0=initial marking, **P**=n. places, **MT**=n. multi-transfers; **I**=pruning via invariants; **Err**=bug found; **S**=n. iterations before reaching the fixpoint/finding a bug; **NN**=nodes of the CST-fixpoint; **NE**=paths in the CST-fixpoint; **ETC**=ex. time using CSTs; **ETH**=ex. time using HyTech (↑ indicates that HyTech ran out of memory); **R**=**ETH**/**ETC**.

In the second case the idea of pruning the search space via structural invariants is much more effective (see [6]). In all cases our tool found a *potential bug* (see Fig.6), that (after looking at the abstract trace) turns out to be a mistake in the Java program. In fact, though the primitive methods incx, incy, decx, and decy are protected by a monitor (they are declared as *synchronized*), the derived methods incpoint and decpoint are not. Thus, increments(decrements) on pair of coordinates are not executed atomically. To correct the error, we can declare the derived methods *synchronized*, too. This way mutual exclusion is automatically guaranteed by the semantics of Java.

We have also analyzed the Producer-Consumer example of [4] (P/C in Fig. 6) and a modified version of it (P/C$_1$ in Fig. 6) built as follows: We introduced new class declarations for *malicious* producers and consumers, and we artifically inserted the possibility of violating mutual exclusion. In this example the presence of violations depends on the values of boolean variables. Our tool finds the bug after 14 iterations (see Fig. 6). We also managed to verify the corrected version in less than one second (P/C$_2$ in Fig. 6). As shown in Fig. 6, we ran the same examples (using the same invariants) on HyTech [11]. Our execution times are always better. Furthermore, in some case HyTech ran out of memory before reaching a fixpoint or detecting the presence of the initial state.

8 Conclusions and Related Works

In this work we focused on the following points. Via a connection with previous works on parameterized verification [7,8], we have shown that there exists an extension of Petri Nets that captures the essential features of the concurrent model of Java. For this class, we can use *decision* procedures to automatically verify safety properties for arbitrary number of threads. This goal is achieved by extending the CST-based symbolic model checking algorithm previously defined for Petri Nets.

The use of parameterized verification via backward reachability is the main novelty of this approach over other approaches to software verification via *finite models* (see e.g. [4]) or with Petri Nets like model [2]. The verification approach of [2] is based on the Karp-Miller's coverability tree that amount to forward reachability with accelerations (see also [7]). Contrary to backward reachability, the automated construction of Karp-Miller coverability tree is not guaranteed to terminate for extensions of Petri Nets with transfer arcs as shown by the counterexample of Esparza, Finkel, and Mayr [8].

Our preliminary analysis of the problem, tune of the techniques, and experimental results indicate the potential interest of a second research phase aimed at producing automatically *infinite-state* skeletons of Java programs, a task that is in an advanced stage in the *finite*-case verification approach. This will be one of our main future directions of research. As we explain in the paper, our techniques find other interesting applications for the automated verification of Broadcast Protocols. Concerning this point, we are not aware of other tools designed to attack *symbolic state explosion* for this class of extended Petri Nets.

References

1. P. A. Abdulla, K. Cerāns, B. Jonsson and Y.-K. Tsay. General Decidability Theorems for Infinite-State Systems. In *Proc. LICS'96*, pages 313–321, 1996.
2. T. Ball, S. Chaki, S. K. Rajamani. Parameterized Verification of Multithreaded Software Libraries. In *Proc. TACAS'01*, LNCS 2031, pages 158-173, 2001.
3. G. Ciardo. Petri Nets with marking-dependent arc multiplicity: properties and analysis. In *Proc. ICATPN'94*, LNCS 815, pages 179-198, 1994.
4. J. C. Corbett. Constructing Compact Models of Concurrent Java Programs. In *Proc. ISSTA'98*, pages 1-10, 1998.
5. G. Delzanno, and J.-F. Raskin. Symbolic Representation of Upward Closed Sets. In *Proc. TACAS 2000*, LNCS 1785, pages 426-440, 2000.
6. G. Delzanno, J.-F. Raskin, and L. Van Begin. Attacking Symbolic State Explosion. In *Proc. CAV'01*, LNCS 2102, pages 298-310, 2001.
7. E. A. Emerson and K. S. Namjoshi. On Model Checking for Non-deterministic Infinite-state Systems. In *Proc. of LICS '98)*, pages 70-80, 1998.
8. J. Esparza, A. Finkel, and R. Mayr. On the Verification of Broadcast Protocols. In *Proc. LICS'99*, pages 352–359, 1999.
9. A. Finkel and P. Schnoebelen. Well-structured transition systems everywhere! TCS 256 (1-2):63–92, 2001.
10. S. M. German, A. P. Sistla. Reasoning about Systems with Many Processes. *JACM* 39(3): 675–735 (1992)
11. T. A. Henzinger, P.-H. Ho, and H. Wong-Toi. HyTech: a Model Checker for Hybrid Systems. In *Proc. CAV'97*, LNCS 1254, pages 460-463, 1997.
12. D. Lea. Concurrent Programming in Java. Design Principle and Patterns. Second Edition. The Java Series. Addison Wesley, 2000.
13. D. Zampuniéris, and B. Le Charlier. Efficient Handling of Large Sets of Tuples with Sharing Trees. In *Proc. DCC'95*, 1995.

CLPS-B – A Constraint Solver for B

Fabrice Bouquet, Bruno Legeard, and Fabien Peureux

Laboratoire d'Informatique
Université de Franche-Comté
16, route de Gray - 25030 Besançon cedex, France
Tel.: (33) 381 666 664
{bouquet, legeard, peureux}@lifc.univ-fcomte.fr

Abstract. This paper proposes an approach to the evaluation of B formal specifications using Constraint Logic Programming with sets. This approach is used to animate and generate test sequences from B formal specifications. The solver, called CLPS-B, is described in terms of constraint domains, consistency verification and constraint propagation. It is more powerful than most constraint systems, because it allows the domain of variable to contain other variables, which increase the level of abstraction. The constrained state propagates the non-determinism of the B specifications and reduces the number of states in a reachability graph. We illustrate this approach by comparing the constrained states graph exploration with the concrete one in a simple example: Process scheduler.

Keywords: B Method, CLP, CSP, Set constraints, Evaluation of specifications, Animation.

1 Introduction

This article presents a constraint solver to evaluate B formal models. The B method, developed by Jean–Raymond Abrial [Abr96] forms part of a formal specification model based on first order logic extended to set constructors and relations. The operations are described in the language of generalized substitutions, which is an extension of the language of guarded commands.Fig. 1 sets out the B specification of a simplified process scheduler. The B specification describes the system in terms of an abstract machine defined by a data model (sets and constants, state variables), invariant properties expressed on the variables and the operations described in terms of preconditions and substitutions. The objective of the constrained evaluation of B specifications, as proposed in this article, is to look into the graph of reachable states of the system described by the specification. More precisely, it is a question of being able to initialize the machine, evaluate substitutions and check properties of the new calculated state. This mechanism is used as a basis for the animation of B specifications [BLP00] and to generate functional tests from a B abstract model [LP01,LPU02].

This approach with constraints manipulates a store of constraints, called constrained states, instead of concrete states, classically handled in the animation

J.-P. Katoen and P. Stevens (Eds.): TACAS 2002, LNCS 2280, pp. 188–204, 2002.
© Springer-Verlag Berlin Heidelberg 2002

of specifications [Dic90,WE92]. The evaluator maintains the non-determinism of the specifications and reduces the number of generated states. For example, non-determinism expressed by the B expression:

$$\texttt{ANY xx WHERE xx} \in \texttt{Y THEN} \quad \texttt{substitution}$$

is maintained by the set constraint $xx \in Y$. Substitution is no longer calculated for a particular value, but for a variable xx whose domain is Y. The process scheduler example shows that for n processes, the number of constrained states in the entire reachability graph is at most $(n^2 + 3n + 2)/2$ against more than 3^n concrete states. This is a dramatic reduction, which makes it possible to model check or animate much larger state spaces than would be possible otherwise.

MACHINE
  SCHEDULER
SETS
  $PID = \{p1, p2, p3, p4, p5, p6\}$
VARIABLES
  active, ready, waiting
INVARIANT
  active $\subseteq$ *PID* $\wedge$ *ready* $\subseteq$ *PID* $\wedge$
  waiting $\subseteq$ *PID* $\wedge$ *ready* $\cap$ *waiting* $= \emptyset \wedge$
  ready $\cap$ *active* $= \emptyset \wedge$ *waiting* $\cap$ *active* $= \emptyset \wedge$
  active $\cap$ (*ready* $\cup$ *waiting*) $= \emptyset \wedge$
  card(*active*) $\leq 1 \wedge$
  (*active* $= \emptyset$) $\Rightarrow$ (*ready* $= \emptyset$)
INITIALIZATION
  active $:= \emptyset \|$
  ready $:= \emptyset \|$
  waiting $:= \emptyset$
OPERATIONS
  NEW(*pp*)
    PRE
      pp $\in$ *PID* $\wedge$
      pp $\nsubseteq$ (*active* cup*ready* $\cup$ *waiting*)
    THEN
      waiting $:=$ (*waiting* $\cup \{pp\}$)
    END;
  DEL(*pp*)
    PRE
      pp $\in$ *waiting*
    THEN

      waiting $:=$ *waiting* $- \{pp\}$
    END;
  READY(*rr*)
    PRE
      rr $\in$ *waiting*
    THEN
      waiting $:=$ (*waiting* $- \{rr\}$)$\|$
      IF (*active* $= \emptyset$) **THEN**
        active $:= \{rr\}$
      ELSE
        ready $:=$ *ready* $\cup \{rr\}$
      END
    END;
  SWAP
    PRE
      active $\neq \emptyset$
    THEN
      waiting $:=$ *waiting* $\cup$ *active*$\|$
      IF (*ready* $= \emptyset$)
      THEN
        active $:= \emptyset$
      ELSE
        ANY *pp* **WHERE** *pp* $\in$ *ready*
        THEN
          active $:= \{pp\}\|$
          ready $:=$ *ready* $- \{pp\}$
        END
      END
    END;

Fig. 1. B Specification of process scheduler

The constrained evaluation of B specifications requires a hypothesis of finite domains. For example, we must limit given sets. The CLPS-B solver is more general than traditional animation because one evaluation sequence captures the properties of a set of concrete animation sequences. It is less powerful than proof because it requires finiteness assumptions, but it is fully automatic. Thus, each state managed by the evaluator is a store of constraints which represents a set of concrete states of the B abstract machine.

We use the B abstract machine of process scheduler to illustrate the use of CLPS-B. Fig. 1 gives the B specification with a set *PID* composed of six processes {p1, p2, p3, p4, p5, p6}. The three state variables of the machine are *waiting, ready, active* which represent respectively the waiting, ready to be activated and active processes. In the initial state, the three sets are empty.

The four operations of the specification (Fig. 1) are:

- NEW: to create a new process and add it to *waiting*.
- DEL: to kill a process and delete it from *waiting*.
- READY: to activate a process of *waiting* and put it in *active* if this set is empty, add it to *ready* otherwise.
- SWAP: to disable the process of *active* and put it in *waiting*, and activate a process from *ready* if there is one (using the non-deterministic approach).

The evaluation of B expressions and the construction of the reachable states constitute a new problem area for set constraint resolution. The constrained states are built incrementally by substitutions from the initial state. So, if we consider the state of the process scheduler just after the creation of a process xx: $waiting = \{xx\} \wedge ready = \{\} \wedge active = \{\} \wedge xx \in \{p1, \ldots p6\}$, the evaluation of the operation *new(yy)* is translated by:

1. the addition of the constraints resulting from the preconditions:
$$yy \in \{p1, \ldots, p6\} \wedge yy \notin waiting \wedge yy \notin active \wedge yy \notin ready$$
2. the evaluation of substitutions: $waiting := waiting \cup \{yy\}$
3. the verification of the invariant properties on the new state.

The sets handled in the computation of substitutions are explicit sets of known cardinality whose elements are either constants or variables. In this context, the approaches of set constraint resolution based on a reduction of set intervals as in CLPS [ALL94] or CONJUNTO [Ger97] do not provide a sufficiently effective propagation of constraints. It is the same for the approaches using set constraints on regular sets [AW93,Koz94] used to analyze programs. This led us to develop a new solver, CLPS–B, based on an explicit representation of variable domains by the intersection of sets of variables and constants.

The remainder of the paper is structured as follows:

- section 2 characterizes the domain of constraints $S_{\mathcal{V}CO} \cup \mathcal{T}$, then sets out the rules of consistency and the reduction rules implemented in the solver CLPS–B, and finally defines the coverage of the operators in the treatment of the B notation,
- section 3 applies CLPS-B to animate B specifications,
- section 4 shows the application of CLPS-B to the animation on the example of the process scheduler.

2   B and Constraint Resolution with CLPS–B

This section presents the domain of the CLPS-B evaluator and shows the part of the B notation which is covered. We present the CLPS-B mechanism with the specific resolution of the Constraint Satisfaction Problem and the rules.

2.1 Computation Domain

The B method is based on set theory, with four set definitions:

1. Cartesian product: Set × Set
2. Power-set: $\mathbb{P}(\text{Set})$
3. Set comprehension: { Variable | Predicate}
4. Given set: let $\mathcal{T}$ be the set of all deferred sets.

The next definitions introduce the universe of computation of the CLPS-B variables.

Definition 1 (Set). *Let $\mathcal{V}$ be the set of all the variables, $\mathcal{C}$ the set of all the constants, and $\mathcal{O}$ the set of all the pairs over $\mathcal{C} \cup \mathcal{V}$ (including nested pairs). The set $S_{\mathcal{VCO}}$ is defined as fallows: $S_{\mathcal{VCO}} = \mathbb{P}(\mathcal{V} \cup \mathcal{C} \cup \mathcal{O})$*

Definition 2 (Computation domain). *The computation domain of constraints processed in CLPS-B is defined on the set $S_{\mathcal{VCO}} \cup \mathcal{T}$.*

The complete list of B operators supported by CLPS-B is given in Tables 2 and 3. These have some limitations for infinite sets because the resolution purpose to bound some set as the given set or infinite set.

Example 1 (Definition of CLPS-B variables).
List of CLPS-B expressions:

- explicit set: $X \in \{1, 2, 3\}$,
- type: $X \in \mathbb{N}$, because $(\mathbb{N} \in \mathcal{T})$,
- type: $X \subset \mathbb{N}$, because $(\mathbb{N} \in \mathcal{T})$,
- Cartesian product (pairs): $X \in \{1, 2, 3\} \times \{4, 5, 6\}$,
- Set of pairs: $X \in \{(1, 4), (1, 5) \ldots (3, 5), (3, 6)\}$,
- Set defined by comprehension (explicit domain): $\{X \in \mathbb{N} \mid X \leq 3 \land X \geq 0\}$.

List of non CLPS-B expressions:

- Set of sets: $X \in \{\{1, 2, 3\}, \{4, 5, 6\}\}$,
- Infinite set: $\{X \in \mathbb{N} \mid X \geq 3\}$.

2.2 Translating B Expressions into Constraints System

In CLPS-B, all the set relations are rewritten into an equivalent system with constraints $\in$, $=$, and $\neq$ as show in table 1. The rewriting uses rules or axioms of logic and the semantics of B operators [Abr96]. A, B are sets of $S_{\mathcal{VCO}}$, x and y are elements of $\mathcal{V} \cup \mathcal{C} \cup \mathcal{O}$, and s and r are relations.

Example 2. Set constraint transformation: $\{x_1, x_2\} \mapsto \{y_1, y_2\}$ is rewritten into $x_1 \in \{y_1, y_2\} \land x_2 \in \{y_1, y_2\} \land y_1 \in \{x_1, x_2\} \land y_2 \in \{x_1, x_2\}$

The constraints are rewritten into normal disjunctive form and each disjunction is explored by a separate prolog choice point.

Definition 3 (Domain of constraints). *We call Ω the **Domain of constraints**. It is the set of all the constraints over $S_{\mathcal{VCO}} \cup \mathcal{T}$. Also, the set constraints over $\mathcal{VCO}$ is called $\Omega_{\mathcal{VCO}}$ and the set of constraints over $\mathcal{T}$ called $\Omega_{\mathcal{T}}$.*

Remark 1. we do not translate all the system at once, but each predicate separately. So, the transformation is very fast, because we do not have to calculate the disjunction normal form of the whole specification.

Table 1. B set operators and their CLPS-B definitions

Terminology	Operator	Definition
membership	$x \in A$	CLPS-B primitive
not member	$x \notin A$	$\{y \mid y \in A \land x \neq y\}$
equality	$x = y$	CLPS-B primitive
not equality	$x \neq y$	CLPS-B primitive
subset	$A \subseteq B$	$A \in \mathbb{P}(B)$
set equal	$A =_s B$	$A \subseteq B \land B \subseteq A$
set not equal	$A \neq_s B$	$card(A) \neq card(B) \lor \exists x(x \in A \land x \notin B) \lor \exists x(x \notin A \land x \in B)$
cup	$A \cup B$	$\{x \mid x \in A \lor x \in B\}$
cap	$A \cap B$	$\{x \mid x \in A \land x \in B\}$
set minus	$A \setminus B$	$\{x \mid x \in A \land x \notin B\}$
cardinality	$card(A)$	CLPS-B primitive
identity	$id(A)$	$\{(x,x) \mid x \in A)\}$
reverse	r^{-1}	$\{(y,x) \mid (x,y) \in r\}$
domain	$dom(r)$	$\{x \mid \exists y((x,y) \in r)\}$
range	$ran(r)$	$\{y \mid \exists x((x,y) \in r)\}$

Terminology	Expression	Definition
restriction of:		
domain	$A \lhd r$	$\{(x,y) \mid (x,y) \in r \land x \in A\}$
range	$s \rhd B$	$\{(x,y) \mid (x,y) \in s \land y \in B\}$
subtraction of:		
domain	$A \lhd\!\!\!- r$	$\{(x,y) \mid (x,y) \in r \land x \notin A\}$
range	$s \rhd\!\!\!- B$	$\{(x,y) \mid (x,y) \in s \land y \notin B\}$
overriding	$s \Leftarrow\!\!\!+ r$	$\{(x,y) \mid (x,y) \in s \land x \notin dom(r) \lor (x,y) \in r\}$
relation	$s \leftrightarrow r$	$\mathbb{P}(s \times r)$
set of partial:		
function	$s \nrightarrow r$	$\{f \mid f \in s \leftrightarrow r \land (f^{-1}, f) \subseteq id(r)\}$
injection	$s \rightarrowtail\!\!\!\!\!\!\cdot\, r$	$\{f \mid f \in s \nrightarrow r \land f^{-1} \in s \nrightarrow r\}$
surjection	$s \twoheadrightarrow\!\!\!\!\cdot\, r$	$\{f \mid f \in s \nrightarrow r \land ran(f) = r\}$
bijection	$s \rightarrowtail\!\!\!\!\!\!\twoheadrightarrow\, r$	$s \rightarrowtail\!\!\!\!\!\!\cdot\, r \cap s \twoheadrightarrow\!\!\!\!\cdot\, r$
set of total:		
function	$s \rightarrow r$	$\{f \mid f \in s \nrightarrow r \land dom(f) = s\}$
injection	$s \rightarrowtail r$	$s \rightarrowtail\!\!\!\!\!\!\cdot\, r \cap s \rightarrow r$
surjection	$s \twoheadrightarrow r$	$s \twoheadrightarrow\!\!\!\!\cdot\, r \cap s \rightarrow r$
bijection	$s \rightarrowtail\!\!\!\!\!\!\twoheadrightarrow r$	$s \rightarrowtail r \cap s \twoheadrightarrow r$

Theorem 1 (Validity). *The set of constraints given by rewriting is semantically equal to the system given by the B specification.*

Proof. All logic identities used (table 1) are the definitions given and proved in the B-Book [Abr96]. The rewriting process always terminates because there is no recursion in the definitions. The consistency of operator definitions gives the soundness of the method and the termination property gives the completeness of the method.

Example 3. Rewritten predicates of the process scheduler invariant:

B Invariant	CLPS-B Form
$active \subseteq PID \land$	$active \in \mathbb{P}(PID) \land$
$ready \subseteq PID \land$	$ready \in \mathbb{P}(PID) \land$
$waiting \subseteq PID \land$	$waiting \in \mathbb{P}(PID) \land$
$ready \cap waiting = \emptyset \land$	$\{x \mid x \in ready \land x \in waiting\} = \emptyset \land$
$active \cap (ready \cup waiting) = \emptyset \land$	$\{x \mid x \in active \land x \in \{z \mid z \in ready \lor z \in waiting\}\} = \emptyset \land$
$card(active) \leq 1 \land$	$card(active) \leq 1 \land$
$(active = \emptyset) \Rightarrow (ready = \emptyset)$	$card(active) = 0 \Rightarrow card(ready) = 0$

2.3   Substitution

The B language describes actions in the operations or events by substitution of the state variables. Here, only the definition of a simple substitution is given, the reader can find all other substitution definitions in B-Book [Abr96].

Definition 4 (Substitution). *Let x be a variable, E an expression and F a formula,* $[x := E]F$ *is the* **substitution** *of all free occurrences of x in F by E.*

Example 4. The result of transformation by substitution of the swap operation of the process scheduler is:

(active $\neq \emptyset$) $\wedge$
   (waiting' := waiting $\cup$ active) $\wedge$ (waiting' $\subseteq$ *PID*) $\wedge$
   (((ready = $\emptyset$) $\wedge$ (active = $\emptyset$)) $\vee$
      ($\neg$ (ready = $\emptyset$) $\wedge$ (@pp.(pp$\in$ready) $\Rightarrow$
         (active' := {pp}) $\wedge$ (active' $\subseteq$ *PID*) $\wedge$
         (ready' := ready $-$ {pp}) $\wedge$ (ready'$\subseteq$ *PID*))))

Table 2. *List of operators in B notation and CLPS-B constrained solver. The symbol* ★ *means that the operator is not implemented.*

B Language Operator	Notation	Constrained solver	B langage Operator	Notation	Constrained solver
conjunction	$\wedge$	&	range of relation	*ran*	ran
disjunction	$\vee$	or	composition of two relations	;	;
negation	$\neg$	not		*o*	*circ*
implication	$\Rightarrow$	=>	identity relation	*id*	id
equivalence	$\Leftrightarrow$	<=>	domain restriction	$\triangleleft$	<|
universal quantification	$\forall$	!	range restriction	$\triangleright$	|>
existential quantification	$\exists$	#	domain subtraction	$\triangleleft\!\!\!-$	<<|
			range subtraction	$\triangleright\!\!\!-$	|>>
comprehension set	{|}	{x,y,z} extension set	range of a set under a relation	[]	[]
			overriding relation by another	$\Leftarrow$	<+
extension set	{x,y,z}	{x,y,z}	direct product of two relations	$\otimes$	><
empty set	$\emptyset$	{}	parallel product of two relations	||	||
set of relation	$\leftrightarrow$	<->	first projection	*prj*₁	prj1
inverse of a relation	$^{-1}$	~	second projection	*prj*₂	prj2
domain of a relation	*dom*	dom	application of a function	( )	()
less than or equal	$\leq$	<=	functional abstraction	$\lambda.(\|)$	★
less than	$<$	<	set of partial functions	$\rightarrow\!\!\!+$	+->
greater than or equal	$\geq$	>=	set of total functions	$\rightarrow$	-->
greater than	$>$	>	set of partial injections	$\rightarrowtail\!\!\!+$	>+>
adder	$+$	+	set of total injections	$\rightarrowtail$	>->
subtractor	$-$	-	set of partial surjections	$\twoheadrightarrow\!\!\!+$	+->>
multiplier	*	*	set of total surjections	$\twoheadrightarrow$	-->>
divisor	/	/	set of partial bijections	$\rightarrowtail\!\!\!\!+\!\!\!\rightarrow$	>+>>
			set of total bijections	$\rightarrowtail\!\!\!\!\rightarrow$	>->>

2.4   Coverage of the B Notation

The coverage of B set operators is high. More than 80% of set operators are achieved (Tables 2 and 3). The main integer primitives are implemented using

integer finite domain propagation rules [Tsa93] in order to express properties
of set cardinality and basic arithmetic operation. The finite tree structures and
finite sequences are not treated. One area of future work will include extending
the operator coverage.

Table 3. *In CLPS-B solver, the set operators are different on explicit $S_{\mathcal{VCO}}$ sets and
$\mathcal{T}$ universe sets. Note that only the operators on sets of sets are not implemented(★).*

B language		Constrained solver	
Operator	Notation	$S_{\mathcal{VCO}}$	$\mathcal{T}$
membership	$\in$	ins	ins
Cartesian product	$\times$	x	★
set of subsets of a set	$\mathbb{P}$	p_partie	★
set of non-empty subsets of a set	$\mathbb{P}_1$	p1_partie	★
set of finite subsets of a set	$\mathbb{F}$	f_partie	★
set of finite non-empty subsets of a set	$\mathbb{F}_1$	f1_partie	★
inclusion of one set in another	$\subseteq$	sub	sub
union of two sets	$\cup$	union	★
intersection of two sets	$\cap$	inter	★
difference of two sets	$-$	differ	★
non membership	$\notin$	nin	nin
equality	$=$	=	=
inequality	$\neq$	neq	neq
set equality	$=_S$	eqS	eqS
set inequality	$\neq_S$	neqS	neqS
cardinality of a set	$\#$	card	card

2.5   Constraint Management

The constraint system $\Omega_{\mathcal{VCO}}$ presents some characteristics of the Constraint Satisfaction Problem (CSP). In the CSP, each variable is associated with a domain
defined in the constant set $\mathcal{C}$. A domain D_x of a variable x is a finite set of
possible values which can be assigned to x. Formally, a CSP is denoted by a
triplet (V, D, C) where:

- V is a finite set of variables $\{V_1, \ldots, V_n\}$,
- D is a set of domains, D_x for each $x \in V$,
- C is a finite set of constraints on V.

Unlike ordinary CSP, the variables of $\Omega_{\mathcal{VCO}}$ can have several domains D_i^x
containing elements of $\mathcal{C} \cup \mathcal{V} \cup \mathcal{O}$ and defined by the constraints $x \in D_i^x$. The
resulting domain of x is the intersection of the domain $D^x = \bigcap_i D_i^x$. The ma-
jor difference to CSP is that each D_i^x may contain variables as well as values,
whereas in CSP each D_i^x only contains values. Note that $\bigcap_i D_i^x$ cannot always
be calculated deterministically when the domains D_i^x contain variables. This
problem is called V-CSP by analogy with CSP. In the case where all the V-CSP
domains only contains values, it reduces to a CSP.

Definition 5 (V-domain). *A **V-domain** $D_x = \bigcap_i D_i^x$ of a variable x is a
finite set of possible elements (variables or constants) which can be assigned to
x. Thus, D_x is included in $\mathcal{C} \cup \mathcal{V} \cup \mathcal{O}$.*

Initially, a V-domain D_x is defined by the constraint $x \in D_i^x$. Then, it is modified by the propagation rules. The V-Domain number, n_x, is the number of subdomains D_i^x. It increases when new constraints $x \in D_i^x$ are added, and decreases when simplification rules are applied.

Definition 6 (V-label). *A **V-label** is a pair $< x, v >$ that represents the assignment of the variable x.*

The V-label $< x, v >$ is meaningful if v is in a V-domain of x. Note that v can be either a constant or a variable. The concept of V-CSP can also be introduced and used to resolve the constraints on $S_{\mathcal{VCO}}$ by:

Definition 7 (V-CSP). *A **V-CSP** is a triplet (V, D, C) where:*

- *V is a finite set of variables $\{V_1, \ldots, V_n\}$,*
- *D is a set of V-domains, $\{D_1, \ldots, D_n\}$,*
- *C is a finite set of constraints of the form $V_i \neq V_j$, where $V_i, V_j \in V$.*

Remark 2. In CSP, D can be seen as a function which links a variable of V with a domain. In V-CSP, it is a relation because each variable x can have several domains D_i^x . Moreover, in contrast to CSP, the variables V of a V-CSP can appear in the domains.

2.6   Consistency and Satisfiability

Finally, the definitions of satisfiability and consistency of the constraint system $\Omega_{\mathcal{VCO}}$ have to be extended.

Definition 8 (Satisfiability). *A V-CSP $(V = \{V_1, \ldots, V_n\}, D, C)$ is **satisfiable** if and only if there is a subset $\mathcal{B} \subseteq D$, called the V-base of V-CSP, and a set of V-label $\mathcal{L} = (< V_1, B_1 >, \ldots, < V_n, B_n >)$ with $B_i \in \mathcal{B}$ such that all the constraints of C can be rewritten with:*

1. *$B_i \in \{B_1, \ldots, B_i, \ldots, B_k\}$ with $B_i \in \mathcal{B} \wedge B_1 \in \mathcal{B} \wedge \ldots \wedge B_k \in \mathcal{B}$*
2. *$B_i \neq B_j$ with $i \neq j \wedge B_i \in \mathcal{B} \wedge B_j \in \mathcal{B}$.*

Remark 3. constraints like (1) are trivially satisfied.

Example 5. Given the constraint systems on variables:

- $x_1 \in \{y_1, y_2\} \wedge x_2 \in \{y_1, y_2\} \wedge x_3 \in \{y_1, y_2\} \wedge y_1 \neq y_2 \wedge x_1 \neq x_2 \wedge x_1 \neq x_3 \wedge x_2 \neq x_3$
  It is not satisfiable because there is no V-base or a V-label to make constraints like (1) or (2). If we take $\mathcal{B} = \{y_1, y_2\}$ and $\mathcal{L} = (< x_1, y_1 >, < x_2, y_2 >, < x_3, y_1 >)$, we obtain $y_1 \neq y_1$.

$-\ x_1 \in \{y_1, y_2\} \wedge x_2 \in \{y_1, y_2\} \wedge y_1 \neq y_2 \wedge x_1 \neq x_2$

It is satisfiable. If $\mathcal{B} = \{y_1, y_2\}$ and $\mathcal{L} = (< x_1, y_1 >, < x_2, y_2 >)$, the resulting system only has constraints (1) and (2): $y_1 \in \{y_1, y_2\} \wedge y_2 \in \{y_1, y_2\} \wedge y_1 \neq y_2$.

Definition 9 (Consistency). *A V-CSP* $(\{V_1, \ldots, V_n\}, D, C)$ *is* **consistent** *if and only if the two following conditions are verified:*

1. $\forall i((V_i, D_{V_i}) \in D \Rightarrow \exists j(V_j \in D_{V_i} \wedge (V_j \neq V_i) \notin C))$
2. $\forall i(V_i \neq V_i) \notin C$

In other words, the domain D_V of a variable V is consistent if and only if there is an element e in this domain and $e \neq V$ is not a constraint of the specification. Arc-consistency is also performed in the constraint graph where the nodes represent variables and the edges represent the constraints $\neq$ (Example 7).

Example 6. An inconsistent constraints system:
$x_1 \in \{y_1, y_2\} \wedge y_1 \neq y_2 \wedge x_1 \neq y_1 \wedge x_1 \neq y_2$

Theorem 2. *A satisfiable constraint system on $S_{\mathcal{VCO}}$ is consistent.*

Proof. by negation,
Let S be an inconsistent V-CSP $(\{V_1, \ldots, V_n\}, D, C)$, $\mathcal{B} = \{B_1, \ldots, B_m\}$ a V-Base and $\{< V_1, B_{j_1} >, \ldots, < V_n, B_{j_n} >\}$ the V-label with $j_1, \ldots, j_n \in \{1, \ldots, m\}$, two cases are possible according to definition 9:

1. S inconsistent $\Rightarrow \exists i((V_i, D_{V_i}) \in D \wedge \forall j(V_j \notin D_{V_i} \vee (V_j \neq V_i) \in C)) \Rightarrow \exists i((B_{j_i}, D_{B_{j_i}}) \in D \wedge \forall k(B_{j_k} \notin D_{B_{j_i}} \vee (B_{j_k} \neq B_{j_i}) \in C)) \Rightarrow$ S non satisfiable. There is a pair $(B_{j_i}, D_{B_{j_i}})$ of D with an element B_{j_i} of the base B which does not appear in its domain $D_{B_{j_i}}$.
2. S inconsistent $\Rightarrow \exists i(V_i \neq V_i) \in C \Rightarrow \exists i(B_{j_i} \neq B_{j_i}) \in C \Rightarrow$ S non satisfiable

Thus, in both cases, S inconsistent $\Rightarrow$ S non satisfiable.

Remark 4. The reciprocal is not true, for example the following constraint system is consistent but not satisfiable:

$x_1 \in \{y_1, y_2\} \wedge x_2 \in \{y_1, y_2\} \wedge x_3 \in \{y_1, y_2\} \wedge y_1 \neq y_2 \wedge x_1 \neq x_2 \wedge x_1 \neq x_3 \wedge x_2 \neq x_3$

The inconsistency of a system can also be detected by the constraints $x \in \{\}$ and $x \neq x$. These concepts define the formal framework to resolve the $\Omega_{\mathcal{VCO}}$ system.

The correctness of the reduction procedure is ensured by two points: deleted values in the domains are inconsistent values (see rule P_1 below), and deleted constraints are trivially satisfied (see rule P_2 and P_3 below).

The reduction procedure does not ensure the assignment of the variables to an element of the domain, and is thus not complete. The completion can also be performed by a generation procedure, which is a variation of the *forward − checking* algorithm [Nad89].

2.7   Inferred Rules

The notion of consistency establishes the conditions which the elements of a domain must satisfy. If the consistency is not verified, the domain is reduced, i.e. elements are deleted in order to make it consistent. In the following, the element e_i belongs to $\mathcal{V} \cup \mathcal{C} \cup \mathcal{O}$ and τ belongs to $\mathcal{T}$. The notation $\Omega \cup \{C_1, C_2, \dots, C_n\}$ describes the conjunction of the current constraint system Ω and the constraints $C_1, C_2, \dots, C_n$. Ω is divided into two subsets $\Omega_{\mathcal{VCO}}$ and $\Omega_{\mathcal{T}}$ which correspond respectively to the constraints on the elements of $\mathcal{V} \cup \mathcal{C} \cup \mathcal{O}$ and $\mathcal{T}$.

Rule P_1 ensures the consistency on $\Omega_{\mathcal{VCO}}$:

$$P_1 : \quad \frac{\Omega \cup \{e \in \{e_1, \dots, e_{i-1}, e_i, e_{i+1}, \dots, e_n\}, e \neq e_i\}}{\Omega \cup \{e \in \{e_1, \dots, e_{i-1}, e_{i+1}, \dots, e_n\}, e \neq e_i\}}$$

The following two rules are simplification rules:

$$P_2 : \quad \frac{\Omega \cup \{e_i \in \{e_1, \dots, e_i, \dots, e_n\}\}}{\Omega}$$

$$P_3 : \quad \frac{\Omega \cup \{e \in \{e_1, \dots, e_n\}, e \in \{e_1, \dots, e_n, \dots, e_{n+m}\}\}}{\Omega \cup \{e \in \{e_1, \dots, e_n\}\}}$$

When a domain is reduced to one variable, unification is carried out:

$$P_4 : \quad \frac{\Omega \cup \{e_i \in \{e_j\}\}}{\Omega \cup \{e_i = e_j\}}$$

Two additional inference rules describe the cases where the constraint system $\Omega_{\mathcal{VCO}}$ is inconsistent:

$$P_5 : \quad \frac{\Omega \cup \{e \in \{\}\}}{fail} \qquad\qquad P_6 : \quad \frac{\Omega \cup \{e \neq e\}}{fail}$$

The following inference rule describes the case where the constraint system $\Omega_{\mathcal{T}}$ is inconsistent:

$$T_1 : \quad \frac{\Omega \cup \{e \in \tau, e \notin \tau\}}{fail}$$

Rule T_2 infers a new constraint on $\Omega_{\mathcal{VCO}}$ from the system $\Omega_{\mathcal{T}}$:

$$T_2 : \quad \frac{\Omega \cup \{e_i \in \tau, e_j \notin \tau\}}{\Omega \cup \{e_i \in \tau, e_j \notin \tau, e_i \neq e_j\}}$$

These inference rules are used until a fixed point is obtained, i.e. until no rules can be applied.

Example 7. Given the following system:

$x_0 \in \{x_1, x_2, x_3\} \land x_0 \in \{x_1, x_2, x_4\} \land x_5 \in \{x_3, x_4\} \land x_0 \neq x_5.$

When the constraint $x_3 \neq x_5$ is added to the system, the rules infer the following reductions:

$- \ x_0 \in \{x_1, x_2, x_3\} \wedge x_0 \in \{x_1, x_2, x_4\} \wedge \underline{x_5 \in \{x_3, x_4\}} \wedge x_0 \neq x_5 \wedge x_3 \neq x_5 \overset{P_1}{\Longrightarrow}$

$- \ x_0 \in \{x_1, x_2, x_3\} \wedge x_0 \in \{x_1, x_2, x_4\} \wedge \underline{x_5 \in \{x_4\}} \wedge x_0 \neq x_5 \wedge x_3 \neq x_5 \overset{P_4}{\Longrightarrow}$

$- \ x_0 \in \{x_1, x_2, x_3\} \wedge \underline{x_0 \in \{x_1, x_2, x_4\}} \wedge x_0 \neq x_4 \wedge x_3 \neq x_4 \overset{P_1}{\Longrightarrow}$

$- \ x_0 \in \{x_1, x_2, x_3\} \wedge \underline{x_0 \in \{x_1, x_2\}} \wedge x_0 \neq x_4 \wedge x_3 \neq x_4 \overset{P_3}{\Longrightarrow}$

$- \ x_0 \in \{x_1, x_2\} \wedge x_0 \neq x_4 \wedge x_3 \neq x_4$

the reduced system is consistent and satisfied, and offers two solutions:

1) $\mathcal{L} = (< x_0, x_1 >)$ 2) $\mathcal{L} = (< x_0, x_2 >)$
   $\mathcal{B} = \{x_1, x_2, x_3, x_4\}$ $\mathcal{B} = \{x_1, x_2, x_3, x_4\}$
   $\mathcal{C} = (x_1 \neq x_4 \wedge x_3 \neq x_4)$ $\mathcal{C} = (x_2 \neq x_4 \wedge x_3 \neq x_4)$

3   Simulation of B Machines in CLPS-B

This part describes the constrained evaluation process. It consists in resolving set logical B formulas with CLPS-B solver. This process can manage the evolution of the constrained state from the initial state of the B machine (given by the specifications) by executing operations.

Definition 10 (Constrained state). *A **constrained state** is a pair (V, C_V) where V is a set of state variables of the specification, and C_V is a set of constraints based on the state variables of the specification.*

The constrained evaluation models the evolution of the B machine state. It changes one constrained state to another by executing operations.

Definition 11 (Constrained evaluation). *Given a constrained state (V, C_V) and φ constraints of the specification. The **constrained evaluation** is a relation called $\mathcal{EVAL}$, which associates a constrained state to the next constrained state:*

$$\mathcal{EVAL} : (V, C_V) \mapsto (V', C_V \wedge \varphi)$$

where V' represents state variables V after substitution calculation φ.

More accurately, three procedures, based on the calculus of logical set B formula, have been defined to make this evaluation. These procedures can establish preconditions, compute substitutions and verify the invariant properties. This set solver is called CLPS-B. It ensures the reduction and propagation of constraints given by the B specifications.

3.1   Activating an Operation

From the initial state, any operation can be activated. An activation consists in verifying the preconditions of the operation, computing substitutions and verifying the invariant properties for the different computed states. CLPS-B evaluates each substitution, with eventual choice points, which give one or more new generated states.

Precondition Processing. The operation preconditions are a constraint set based on specification variables and local operation variables. Given the constrained state of the specification $\theta = (V, C_V)$ and φ_{pre} precondition constraints, the processing of preconditions adds the constraints φ_{pre} to C_V. The result is a system of constraints reduced by the CLPS-B solver to a system disjunction, where Red^i represents the ith rewritten constraints:

$$\bigcup_i Red^i(C_V \cup \varphi_{pre})$$

Finally, processing of preconditions can change the constrained state θ to the constrained states $\theta_i^{pre} = (V, Red^i(C_V \cup \varphi_{pre}))$.

The operation is activated in θ_i^{pre} if the constraint system $Red^i(C_V \cup \varphi_{pre})$ is satisfiable. To test satisfiability, a solution can be generated. Only the satisfiable states θ_i^{pre} are retained to activate operations. These are called activation states.

Substitution Calculus. φ_{sub} are the constraints induced by the substitutions. φ_{sub} incrementally builds a constraint model over the state variables. Thus, each state variable is always represented by a CLPS-B variable introduced by the last constrained substitution.

Substitution calculation is made by the reduction of the constraint system $C_V \cup \varphi_{sub}$. As in the precondition processing of φ_{sub}, the reduction can introduce choice points. Thus, substitution calculation φ_{sub} can change from a constrained state $\theta = (V, C_V)$ to the constrained states $\theta_i^{sub} = (V', Red^i(C_V \cup \varphi_{sub}))$ as: $\forall X' \in V', (X' \in V \vee (X' = exp \wedge X \in V))$, a solution can be generated to verify satisfiability of each resulting state. Only the satisfiable states θ_i^{sub} are retained.

Invariant Verification. This stage of evaluation is used to validate the constrained state $\theta = (V, C_V)$ given by the invariant $\varphi_I(V)$. The verification is made by an inclusion test in the constraint graph.

The procedure $\mathcal{P}_{NP}$ gives a disjunction of the system of constraints given by φ_I. It is called $\bigvee_i \varphi_I^i$. The invariant is verified if:

$$\exists i.(C_V \Rightarrow \varphi_I^i(V))) \Leftrightarrow \exists i.(\varphi_I^i(V) \subseteq C_V))$$

Assuming the inclusion test does not allow isomorphism of the sub-graph, the variables of the constrained state V verify the invariant. In this case, there is no advantage in using the constrained state for the concrete state. Efficiency of constrained evaluation is based on the minimization of the number of enumerated constrained states. The different processed applications gave good results [BLP00,LP01].

Synthesis. An operation can make a model from a pair $(\varphi_{pre}^i, \varphi_{sub}^i)$ where φ_{pre}^i are the constraints from preconditions and φ_{sub}^i are the substitution constraints. Evaluation of the operation $(\varphi_{pre}, \varphi_{sub})$ changes the system from a constrained state $\theta_i = (V, C_V)$ to a constrained state $\theta_{i+1} = (V', C_V \cup \varphi_{pre} \cup \varphi_{sub})$. Initially, state $\theta_i^{pre} = (V, C_V \cup \varphi_{pre})$ is computed from the preconditions. In the second stage, state $\theta_{i+1} = (V', C_V \cup \varphi_{pre} \cup \varphi_{sub})$ is computed from the addition of substitution constraints. In the last stage, verification of the invariant $\varphi_I(V')$ is made with state θ_{i+1}.

3.2   Complexity

In CLPS-B, the constraint satisfaction is based on the fact that:

- an element can possess domains,
- a domain can possess variables,
- adding a constraint can generate new constraints $\in, \notin, \neq$.

The S_{VCO} Constraints:
Adding a new constraint ($\in$ or $\neq$) implies, by propagation, the creation of other constraints ($\in$ and $\neq$). In the worst case, propagation generates **n.(n-1)/2** new difference constraints if all the variables are different from each other. This complexity is theoretical and, in practice, the number of system variables are linear.

Property 1 (Number of membership constraints) *Given a V-CSP composed of n variables, d is the size of the largest domain and n_d is the highest number of variable domains. The maximum number of membership constraints inferred is* **n² × n_d × d**

Proof. The membership constraints are inferred by propagation given by the P_1 and P_7 rules:

P_7 adds an element e to the common domain of the other elements. This rule does not create a new domain in the system.

P_1 substitutes a new domain exp' to exp with the relation: $exp' \subset exp \land (\#exp' = \#exp - 1)$. Thus, for each domain, d new membership constraints can be generated.

For a variable, the number of inferred membership constraints is, in the worst case, the $number\_of\_maximum\_domain * size\_of\_domain$, i.e. $(n * n_d) * d$. Finally, the number of inferred membership constraints for all variables is limited by $n^2 \times n_d \times d$.

The T constraints:
Given a number of set variables n_v and a number of elements n_e, the worst case is **n_e × n_v** membership constraints and no membership constraints are generated by propagation.

4   Application to the Process Scheduler

The B machine is a process scheduler. The first part presents constrained evaluation process with an execution sequence: NEW(PP1), NEW(PP2), READY(RR1), where PP1, PP2 and RR1 are variables. The second part deals with comparison between concrete and constrained graphs of the process scheduler.

4.1   Constrained Evaluation

This part explains the evolution of the constrained state in CLPS-B operation evaluation process. The evolution of the constrained state is described in Table 4. Only CLPS-B reduced constraints are added to the store.

All the invariant constraints are satisfied or are entailed by the constrained state. Thus, no generation phase is needed. The role of the rules, which infers new constraints and gives the powerful inclusion test procedure, should be noted.

Table 4. Constrained evaluation

		Operation	CLPS-B constraint store	
			B Variables	**Other constraints**
INIT	SUB	$waiting = \emptyset$ $ready = \emptyset$ $active = \emptyset$	$waiting = \emptyset$ $ready = \emptyset$ $active = \emptyset$	
NEW(PP1)	PRE	$PP1 \in PID$ $PP1 \notin \emptyset$ $PP1 \notin \emptyset$	$waiting' = \{PP1\}$ $ready = \emptyset$ $active = \emptyset$	$PP1 \in PID$
	SUB	$waiting' = \emptyset \cup \{PP1\}$		
NEW(PP2)	PRE	$PP2 \in PID$ $PP2 \notin \emptyset$ $PP2 \notin \{PP1\}$	$waiting'' = \{PP1, PP2\}$ $ready = \emptyset$ $active = \emptyset$	$PP1 \in PID$ $PP2 \in PID$ $PP1 \neq PP2$
	SUB	$waiting'' = \{PP1\} \cup \{PP2\}$		
READY(RR1)	PRE	$RR1 \in \{PP1, PP2\}$	$waiting^{(3)} = \{PP3\}$ $ready = \emptyset$ $active' = \{RR1\}$	$PP1 \in PID$ $PP2 \in PID$ $PP1 \neq PP2$ $RR1 \in \{PP1, PP2\}$ $PP3 \in \{PP1, PP2\}$ $RR1 \neq PP3$
	SUB	$waiting^{(3)} = \{PP1, PP2\} \setminus \{RR1\}$ $active' = \{RR1\}$		

The table of Fig. 3 presents the evolution of the number of state according to the *max* number of parameters for the reachable graph of the process scheduler.

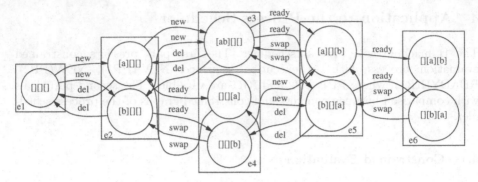

Fig. 2. Reachability concrete graph with $max = 2$

4.2   Experimental Results

The entire reachability graph for the process scheduler B machine was built. The number of processes was limited to max by adding the following precondition in the *NEW* operation: $card(waiting \cup ready \cup active) \leq max$. Figures 2 and 3present respectively the constrained and concrete graphs for $max = 2$ and $PID = \{a, b\}$.

Fig. 3shows the advantage of constrained evaluation to build an reachable graph. The number of states is reduced because one constrained state represents several concrete states.

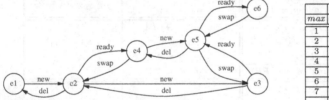

Fig. 3. Constrained reachability graph with $max = 2$

	number of states	
max	constrained	concrete
1	3	3
2	6	10
3	10	35
4	15	124
5	21	437
6	28	1522
7	36	5231
n	$\frac{n^2+3n+2}{2}$	$> 3^n$

5   Conclusion and Prospects

Classic Logic Programming is often used for animation of formal specifications but it is mostly a valued animation [SCT96,B-C01]. The CLPS-B constraint solver allows a constraint animation [BLP00] as ZETA used a concurrent constraint resolution [Gri00]. Test generation on the ground of CLP is known to be a flexible and efficient framework [OJP99], in structural testing [GBR00,Meu01] and in specification-based test generation [LP00,MA00]. Our proposal is a specific solver for the B notation.

This article introduced a constraint resolution system adapted to the evaluation of B formal specifications. The objective was to enable the traversal of the graph to reach states defined by the specifications, in particular to animate and check the model. The traversal of constrained states, rather than concrete ones, propagates the non-determinism of the specifications and reduced the number of states.

The key point of this approach is the expression of domains of constraints by explicit sets where the elements of the domains can be variables (constrained) as well as constants. Rules of propagation and consistency reduce the need for enumeration in entailment and consistency tests during the computation of substitution, the treatment of the preconditions and the checking of the invariant properties.

The constrained evaluator based on the solver CLPS-B is being used as a basis for several applications:

– an animator of B specifications [BLP00] for validation purposes,
– generation of test patterns from B specifications [LP01].

Animation of specifications and model checking complement the tools offered by environments dedicated to the B method - i.e. Atelier B [Cle01], B ToolKit [B-C01] - which essentially concern the syntactic verification of B notation, invariant proofs, code generation by refinement, and project management.

We have consolidated this technology using real-life size industrial applications, including the study of GSM 11-11 standard [Eur99] which gave very good results in term of coverage and saving of time [LP01]. Today, we are studying the transaction mechanism of Java Card Virtual Machine 2.1.1, in the framework of an industrial partnership. In parallel with this study, we are improving the solver CLPS-B, by:

– taking into account numerical constraints on continuous domains,
– consolidation of the inference rules to improve propagation.

References

[Abr96]   J-R Abrial. *The B Book*. Cambridge University Press, 1996.
[ALL94]   F. Ambert, B. Legeard, and E. Legros. Constraint Logic Programming on Sets and Multisets. In *Proceedings of ICLP'94*, pages 151–165, 1994.
[AW93]   A. Aiken and E.L. Wilmmers. Type Inclusion Constraints and Type Inference. In *Conference on FPL Computer Architecture*, pages 31–41, 1993.
[B-C01]   B-Core(UK) Ltd, http://www.b-core.com/btoolkit.html. *B-Toolkit*, 10/2001.
[BLP00]   F. Bouquet, B. Legeard, and F. Peureux. Constraint logic programming with sets for animation of B formal specifications. In *CL'2k Workshop LPSE*, 2000.
[Cle01]   Clearsy, http://www.atelierb.societe.com. *Atelier B V3*, 10/2001.
[Dic90]   J. Dick. Using Prolog to animate Z specifications. In *Z User Meeting 1989. Workshops in Computing*. Springer-Verlag, 1990.
[Eur99]   European Telecoms Std Institute. *GSM 11.11 v7*. http://www.etsi.org, 1999.
[GBR00]   A. Gotlieb, B. Botella, and M. Rueher. A CLP framework for computing structural test data. In Springer-Verlag, editor, *CL'2000*, pages 399–413, 2000.

[Ger97]   C. Gervet. Interval Propagation to Reason about Sets: Definition and Implementation of a practical language. *Constraints*, 1(2), 1997.

[Gri00]   Wolgang Grieskamp. A computation model for Z based on concurrent constraint resolution. In LNCS, editor, *ZB'00*, volume 1878, pages 414–432, 2000.

[Koz94]   D. Kozen. Set Constraints and logic Programming (abstract). In *Proceedings of the 1st International Conference Constraints in Computational Logics*, LNCS 845. Springer-Verlag, 1994.

[LP00]   H. Lotzbeyer and A. Pretschner. AutoFocus on constraint logic programming. In *CL'2000 Workshop LPSE*, London, UK, 2000.

[LP01]   B. Legeard and F. Peureux. Generation of functional test sequences from B formal specifications - presentation and industrial case-study. In 16th *IEEE International conference on ASE'2001*, pages 377–381, 2001.

[LPU02]   B. Legeard, F. Peureux, and M. Utting. A comparison of the LIFC/B and TTF/Z test-generation methods. In *The 2nd International Z and B Conference (ZB'02)*, page to appear, Grenoble, France, January 2002.

[MA00]   B. Marre and A. Arnould. Test Sequence generation from Lustre descriptions: GATEL. In *Proceedings of the 15th IEEE International Conference on Automated Software Engineering (ASE'00)*, Grenoble, France, 2000.

[Meu01]   C. Meudec. ATGEN: Automatic test data generation using constraint logic programming and symbolic execution. *The Journal of Software Testing, Verification and Reliability*, 11(2):81–96, 2001.

[Nad89]   B. A. Nadel. Constraint Satisfaction Algorithms. *Computer Intelligence*, 5:188–224, 1989.

[OJP99]   A.J. Offutt, Z. Jin, and J. Pan. The dynamic domain reduction procedure for test data generation. *The Journal of SPE*, 29(2):167–193, 1999.

[SCT96]   L. Sterling, P. Ciancarini, and T. Turnidge. On the animation of "not executable" specification by prolog. *in Journal of Software Engineering and Knowledge Engineering*, 6(1):63–87, 1996.

[Tsa93]   E. Tsang. *Foundation of constraint satisfaction*. Academic Press, 1993.

[WE92]   M.M. West and B.M. Eaglestone. Software Development: Two approaches to animation of Z specifications using Prolog. *Software Engineering Journal*, 7(4):264–276, 1992.

Formal Verification of Functional Properties of an SCR-Style Software Requirements Specification Using PVS*

Taeho Kim[1,2], David Stringer-Calvert[2], and Sungdeok Cha[1]

[1] Department of Electrical Engineering and Computer Science and
Advanced Information Technology Research Center (AITrc),
Korea Advanced Institute of Science and Technology (KAIST)
Taejon 305-701, Korea
{thkim, cha}@salmosa.kaist.ac.kr
[2] Computer Science Laboratory, SRI International
Menlo Park CA 94025, USA
dave_sc@csl.sri.com

Abstract. Industrial software companies developing safety-critical systems are required to use rigorous safety analysis techniques to demonstrate compliance to regulatory bodies. While analysis techniques based on manual inspection have been successfully applied to many industrial applications, we demonstrate that inspection has limitations in locating complex errors in software requirements.

In this paper, we describe the formal verification of a shutdown system for a nuclear power plant that is currently operational in Korea. The shutdown system is an embedded real-time safety-critical software, and has a description in a Software Cost Reduction (SCR) style specification language. The key component of the work described here is an automatic method for translating SCR-style Software Requirements Specifications (SRS) into the language of the PVS specification and verification system. A further component is the use of property templates to translate natural language Program Functional Specifications (PFS) into PVS, allowing for high-assurance consistency checking between the translated SRS and PFS, thereby verifying the required functional properties.

1 Introduction

Various approaches have been suggested for developing high-quality requirements specifications and conducting cost-effective analysis. Although inspection [1] can, in principle, detect all types of errors in requirements, experience in conducting inspections on the Software Requirements Specification (SRS) for

---

* This work was supported by the Korea Science and Engineering Foundation through the Advanced Information Technology Research Center and by the National Science Foundation under grants CCR-00-82560 and CCR-00-86096.

J.-P. Katoen and P. Stevens (Eds.): TACAS 2002, LNCS 2280, pp. 205–220, 2002.

the Wolsung[1] shutdown system number 2 (SDS2) revealed that inspection has potentially lethal limitations in demonstrating safety.

The Wolsung SDS2 is designed to continuously monitor the reactor state (e.g., temperature, pressure, and power) and to generate a trip signal (e.g., shutdown command, and display) if the monitored variables exceed predetermined safety parameters. The SDS2 SRS specifies 30 monitored variables (inputs from the environment), 59 controlled variables (outputs to the environment), and 129 computational functions relating them. The SRS is 374 pages in length and was subject to four relatively minor releases in less than a year. Inspection of the initial release of the SRS, conducted by four staff members, to validate consistency between the SRS and the natural language Program Functional Specification (PFS) took about 80 staff hours of formal inspection meetings, during which only 17 trivial notational errors and incomplete definitions in the PFS and SRS were discovered.

This experience with manual inspection motivated research to explore more robust and rigorous methods of analysis. To this end, (1) we provide an automatic method for translating SRS into the language of the PVS specification and verification system [2], and we implemented a tool for editing and translating, and (2) we translate from PFS into PVS using property templates and cross reference. Last, (3) we verify the consistency between translated SRS and PFS. In this case study, we concentrate on one trip condition (PDL trip), among three trip conditions, for which SRS is 22 pages, and PFS is 4 pages. The whole SRS for SDS2 is 374 pages, and the whole PFS is 21 pages.

Even though our example case study is in the nuclear domain, we believe the verification procedures we propose are general and applicable to wide range of safety-critical systems.

The rest of our paper is organized as follows. In Section 2, we review how an SCR-style software requirements specification, which is used in Wolsung SDS2, is organized. Section 3 describes the verification procedure developed, detailing the case study of the Wolsung SDS2, and Section 4 discusses results and comparisons with other approaches. Finally, Section 5 concludes this paper.

2   Background

2.1   SCR-Style SRS

An SCR-style formal specification [3] has four key attributes:

- Variable definitions
- Functional overview diagrams (FODs)
- Structured decision tables (SDTs)
- Timing functions

---

[1] The Wolsung nuclear power plant in Korea, used as a case study in this paper, is equipped with a software-implement emergency shutdown system.

It is slightly different from the SCR specification language developed by researchers at the Naval Research Laboratory and supported by the SCR* toolset [4]. The difference lies in how primitive functions are described - where SCR style uses a time-triggered AND-OR table, the SCR* uses an event-action table format. A system written in SCR-style requirements is designed to read monitor variables for an external environment (e.g., temperature, pressure, and power) and to generate control values (e.g., a shutdown command).

The detailed description of the attributes of an SCR-style SRS as follows:

Variable definitions : The interface between the computer system and its environment is described in terms of monitored and controlled variables. Monitored variables, whose names start with the m_ prefix, refer to the inputs to the computer system, and controlled variables, whose names start with the c_ prefix, refer to the outputs from the computer system. A variable may be analog or digital.

Functional Overview Diagrams (FODs) : An FOD illustrates, in a notation similar to data flow diagrams, a hierarchical organization of functions. A group, denoted by the g_ prefix, consists of subgroups or basic functions. Each basic function name starts with the f_ prefix. For example, the group g_Overview, illustrated in figure 1.(a), is refined into g_ProcessInputs, g_PDL, g_PZL, g_SLL groups as shown in figure 1.(b). The g_ProcessInputs is a preprocessor for the system. g_PDL, g_PZL, and g_SLL are trip signals for returning the system to a safe state.

Similarly, the group g_PDL is composed of six basic functions and two timing functions as shown in figure 1.(c). A basic function is a mathematical function with zero delay and are specified in a structured decision table. Outputs are synchronous with inputs in a basic function. The s_ prefix denotes a state name, used to store the previous value of a function, that is, with one clock delay. Timing functions are drawn as a bar (|), for example, t_Pending and t_Trip in figure 1.(c).

In addition to the hierarchical relations, the FOD specifies inputs, outputs, and internal data dependencies among various components. Such data dependencies implicitly dictate the proper order of carrying out a set of functions. For example, in figure 1.(c), the output of the f_PDLSnrI function is used as an input to the f_PDLTrip function, and the latter function therefore may be invoked only when the former is completed. This is the same concept used in dataflow languages such as LUSTRE [5].

Structured Decision Table (SDT) : The required behavior of each basic function is expressed in a tabular notation, called SDT, as shown in figure 2. The function f_PDLCond produces an output, whose value is either k_CondOut or k_CondIn. The k_ prefix indicates a constant value.

Condition macros are a substitution for specific conditions. For example, lines 2-5 of the condition macros in figure 2 define the macro w_FlogPDLCondLo [f_Flog]. If f_Flog<k_FlogPDLLo-k_CondHys, w_FlogPDLCondLo[f_Flog] is denoted "a" according to line 3.

As shown in the second column in the SDT, this function returns the value k_CondOut when the value m_PDLCond is equal to k_CondSwLo and

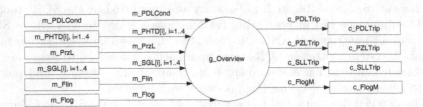

(a) A part of the FOD for SDS2

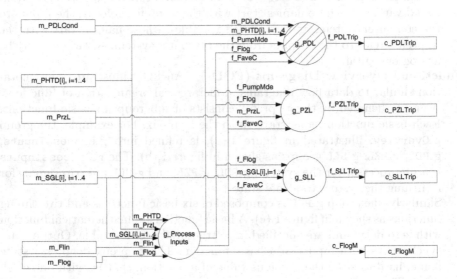

(b) A lower-level FOD of g_Overview

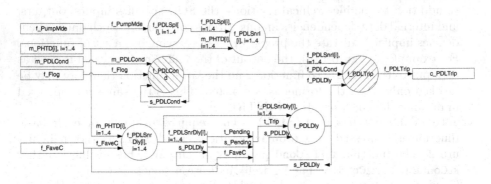

(c) A lower-level FOD of g_PDL

Fig. 1. Examples of the function overview diagram

1: **Condition Macros:**
2: w_FlogPDLCondLo[f_Flog]
3:         a   f_Flog < k_FlogPDLLo - k_CondHys
4:         b   f_FlogPDLLo - k_CondHys <= f_Flog < k_FlogPDLLo
5:         c   f_Flog >= k_FlogPDLLo
6: w_FlogPDLCondHi[f_Flog]
7:         a   f_Flog < k_FlogPDLHi - k_CondHys
8:         b   f_FlogPDLHi - k_CondHys <= f_Flog < k_FlogPDLHi
9:         c   f_Flog >= k_FlogPDLHi

Structured Decision Table:

CONDITION STATEMENTS								
m_PDLCond = k_CondSwLo	T	T	T	T	F	F	F	F
w_FlogPDLCondLo[f_Flog]	a	b	b	c	-	-	-	-
w_FlogPDLCondHi[f_Flog]	-	-	-	-	a	b	b	c
s_PDLCond = k_CondOut	-	T	F	-	-	T	F	-
ACTION STATEMENTS								
f_PDLCond = k_CondOut	X	X			X	X		
f_PDLCond = k_CondIn			X	X			X	X

Fig. 2. The SDT for f_PDLCond

w_FlogPDLCondLo[f_Flog] is equal to a. The '-' entries denote the 'don't care' condition.

Timing function : Timing functions are used for specifying timing constraints and real-time behavior. A prototype of a timing function is t_Wait is t_Wait(C(t), *Time_value, tol*), where C(t) is a logical condition at time t, the *Time_value* is a time interval, and *tol* is an acceptable time deviation. Intuitively speaking, the function stays true during *Time_value* when the immediately previous value of the function is false and C(t) is true at time t. The t_Wait at time 0 is FALSE. The formal semantic definition of a timing function is

$\quad$ t_Wait(C(t), Time_value, tol)

$$= \begin{cases} \text{true} & \text{if there exists an instant in time, } t\_s \in [t - \text{Timer\_value}, t] \\ & \text{such that } C(t\_s) \text{ AND } \neg t\_\text{Wait}(C(t\_s-\epsilon), \text{Time\_value}, \text{tol}) \\ \text{false} & \text{otherwise, including at } t = 0 \end{cases}$$

For example, t_Trip in figure 1.(c) is defined such that

$\quad$ t_Trip = t_Wait(C, k_PDLTrip, k_PDLTripTol)

$\qquad$ where C = (f_FaveC >= k_FaveCPDL AND

$\qquad\qquad\qquad$ t_Pending = false AND s_Pending = true)

This means that t_Trip is true between time t and time t + k_PDLTrip when t_Trip is false at time t-ε, and f_FaveC >= k_FaveCPDL AND t_Pending = false AND s_Pending = true. The k_PDLTripTol is the tolerance of k_PDLTrip.

2.2 Program Functional Specification (PFS)

A program functional specification (PFS) is a system specification written in natural language (English for Wolsung SDS2), as prepared by domain experts. The structure is highly intuitive, and an example is shown in figure 3. The PFS for SDS2 is 21 pages, and PDL trip in this case study accounts for 4 pages.

PHT Low Core Differential Pressure (PDL)

1: The PHT Low Core Differential Pressure (ΔP) trip parameter includes both
2: an immediate and a delayed trip setpoint. Unlike other parameters, the ΔP
3: parameter immediate trip low power conditioning level can be selected by the
4: operator. A handswitch is connected to a D/I, and the operator can choose
5: between two predetermined low power conditioning levels.
6: The PHT Low Core Differential Pressure trip requirements are:
7: $\cdots\cdots$
8: e. Determine the immediate trip conditioning status from the conditioning level
9:    D/I as follows:
10:    1. If the D/I is open, select the $0.3\%FP$ (Full Power) conditioning level.
11:       If $\phi_{LOG} < 0.3\%FP - 50mV$, condition out the immediate trip.
12:       If $\phi_{LOG} >= 0.3\%FP$, enable the trip.
13:    $\cdots\cdots$
14: g. If no PHT ΔP delayed trip is pending or active then execute a delayed
15:    trip as follows:
16:    1. Continue normal operation without opening the parameter trip D/O for
17:       nominally three seconds.
18:    2. After the delay period has expired, open the parameter trip D/O
19:          if f_{AVEC} equals or exceeds $80\%FP$.
20:          Do not open the parameter trip D/O if f_{AVEC} is below $80\%FP$.
21:    3. Once the delayed parameter trip has occurred,
22:       keep the parameter trip D/O open for one second.
23:    $\cdots\cdots$
24: h. Immediate trips and delayed trips (pending and active) can occur simultaneously.
25: $\cdots\cdots$

Fig. 3. Example of program functional specification

3 Verification of SCR-Style SRS

3.1 Translation from SCR-Style SRS to PVS

We describe a translation procedure of SCR-style SRS as embodied in our tool, and its application to the specific case study of the Wolsung SDS2 SRS. The translation procedure consists of five steps:

1. Definition of time (tick) model elements
2. Definition of types and constants
3. Definitions of types for monitored and controlled variables
4. Translation of SDTs
5. Definition and translation of timing functions

Step 1. Definition of Time Model Elements:

Time increases by a fixed period, so time can be specified using a `tick`, a positive number. A time is represented by the set of successive multiples of that period, starting from 0. This part is common through different specifications and is denoted in figure 4.[2] Time is described in the type `tick` definition in line 1, being declared as a `nat` (natural number). Line 2 defines `t`, representing a variable of type `tick`. In line 3, a constant `init` is defined to be 0, for use as the initial value of `tick`.

```
1: tick : TYPE+ = nat CONTAINING 0
2: t    : VAR tick
3: init : tick = 0
```

Fig. 4. Step 1. Definition of model elements

Step 2. Definition of Types and Constants:

The type of a variable in SCR-style SRS is different for analog variables and digital variables. The type for an analog variable is declared to be a real number (or subtypes of real), and the type for a digital variable is a given enumeration. Trajectories of the value of variables with time are declared as functions from `tick` to the variable type.

Figure 5 shows the types and constant definitions used in the Wolsung SDS2. Line 1 shows the definition of `millivolt`, defined in the SCR style as an analog variable, so it is translated to the `real` type. Line 2 is a definition of `t_Millivolt` as a function from `tick` to `millivolt`. Line 4 is a definition of the `zero_one` type for a digital variable, defined as set type whose membership includes 0 and 1. In line 5, `undef` will be used for constants whose values are undefined. An undefined value will be assigned a value during later phases of the software development process. `k_Trip` and `k_NotTrip` in lines 6 and 7 are constants of the digital variable type. Line 11 defines `to_TripNotTrip` as an enumeration of `k_Trip` and `k_NotTrip`. Lines 12 and 13 define a function `t_TripNotTrip` from `tick` to `to_TripNotTrip`. This type includes the trivial function mapping from any `tick` value t to the constant `k_Trip`. `to_CondInOut` is a enumeration type whose members are `k_CondIn` and `k_CondOut`. Line 15 is a function `t_CondInOut` from `tick` to `to_CondInOut`. Line 17 defines `enumabc` used within SDT. `enumabc` is an enumerative type for a, b, and c.

---

[2] The numbering on the left is merely a line number for reference in this paper, and is not part of the translation procedure or translated specification.

```
 1: millivolt : TYPE = real                        % analog variable
 2: t_Millivolt : TYPE = [tick -> millivolt]
 3:
 4: zero_one : TYPE+ = {x:int | x=0 OR x=1} CONTAINING 0  % digital var.
 5: undef : TYPE+                              % undefined-value constant
 6: k_Trip : zero_one = 0
 7: k_NotTrip : zero_one = 1
 8: k_CondIn : undef
 9: k_CondOut : undef
10:
11: to_TripNotTrip : TYPE = {x:zero_one | x = k_Trip OR x = k_NotTrip}
12: t_TripNotTrip : TYPE+ = [tick -> to_TripNotTrip]% function type from
13:     CONTAINING lambda (t:tick) : k_Trip      % tick to_TripNotTrip
14: to_CondInOut : TYPE = {k_CondIn, k_CondOut}    % incl. t->k_Trip
15: t_CondInOut : TYPE = [tick -> to_CondInOut]
16:
17: enumabc : TYPE = {a,b,c}
```

Fig. 5. Step 2. Definition of types and constants

Step 3. Definition of Types for Monitored and Controlled Variables:

This step defines the types of the monitored and controlled variables using the definitions from step 2. The variables are defined in the form `variable : type`. Figure 6 is an example for monitored variable m_Flog and controlled variable c_PDLTrip. m_Flog is a type t_Milivolt in line 1 and c_PDLTrip is a type t_TripNotTrip.

```
1: m_Flog : t_Milivolt       % Type definition for monitored variable
2: c_PDLTrip : t_TripNotTrip  % Type definition for controlled variable
```

Fig. 6. Step 3. Definition of types for monitored and controlled variables

Step 4. Translation of SDTs:

Functions in an SCR-style SRS are structured in a hierarchy. The lowest level of the hierarchy is an internal computation function expressed as an SDT or a timing function. The hierarchical information is not needed in the translation for checking functional correctness; hence, this step translates only the SDT and timing functions.

There are two kinds of function. One is a function that reads values at tick t and writes values at tick t. The other is a function which reads both values at tick t and at t-1 and writes values at tick t. SCR-style SRS assumes that it takes zero time to execute a function.

Let *f_output*, *f_input1*, *f_input2*, and *s_output* be function names or variable names. The first kind of function is

   f_output(t) = compute(*f_input1*(t), *f_input2*(t))

To compute *f_output*, it reads the values of the *f_input1* and *f_input2* at tick t and then compute *f_output* at tick t. For this function, the translation template is

```
1: f_output (t:tick):value_type = compute(f_input1(t),f_input2(t))
```

If the condition macro is defined within `compute`, the macro should be locally defined by the `LET` ··· `IN` construct. In this case, the translation template is[3]

```
1: f_output (t:tick) : value_type =
2:     LET
3:        w_condition_macro : enumeration_type = condition_macro
4:     IN
5:        compute(f_input1(t), f_input2(t))
```

The second kind of function is

   f_output(t) = compute(*f_input1*(t), *s_output*(t))

$$s\_output(t) - \begin{cases} initial\_value & \text{when } t = 0 \\ f\_output(t-1) & \text{when } t \neq 0 \end{cases}$$

In the second kind of a function, there is a circular dependency among the *f_output* and the *s_output*. The type checking of PVS does not admit circular dependencies in an explicit manner, so we use a definitional style with local definitions embedded within a recursive function, in this paper. The translation template for this kind of function introduces a local copy of the mutually dependent function.

```
 1: f_output (t:tick) : RECURSIVE value_type =
 2:             LET
 3:                 s_output : [tick->value_type]=LAMBDA (tt:tick):
 4:                     IF tt = 0 THEN initial_value
 5:                     ELSE f_output (tt-1)
 6:                     ENDIF
 7:             IN
 8:                 output(f_input1(t), s_output(t))
 9:             MEASURE t
10: s_output (t:tick) : value_type = IF t = 0 THEN initial_value
11:                     ELSE f_output (t-1)
12:                     ENDIF
```

The definition of *f_output* is given in lines 1–9. Line 8 refers to *s_output*, but as *s_output* is not defined until lines 10–12, so a local definition of *s_output*

---

[3] In SCR-style SRS, functions and condition macros are defined as tabular notation, so `condition_macro` and `computes` in translated PVS specification are expressed as a `TABLE` ··· `ENDTABLE` construct.

is given within the function *f_output* at lines 3–6. The keyword RECURSIVE is used to indicate a recursive function, and a MEASURE function provided to allow the type checker to generate proof obligations to show termination.

The translation of f_PDLCond in figure 2 is shown in figure 7. f_PDLCond at line 4 is recursively defined, so we define f_PDLCond as a recursive function using RECURSIVE. And we define condition macro w_FlogPDLCond and w_FlogPDLCondHi in lines 6–11.

We also explored an approach using AXIOMs to introduce mutually recursive functions. The approach separates the definition part and declaration part in a way similar to high-level languages, so it does not need local definition. However, a step-by-step proof may be required for safety auditing, so there is a tradeoff between automation and auditability. We chose to prefer automation, as an aid to finding errors quickly, rather than fully auditable verification.

The translated specification in this paper is more complex than the declarative style because of the local definition and recursive definition for circular dependent functions. The major advantage of the definitional style is that it enables greater automation of proofs. However, the step-by-step proof that may be required for safety auditing is sometimes difficult. The declarative style supports less automation for proving, but allows for auditing the proof. We recommend the declarative style for early prototyping and the definitional style for full specifications.

Step 5. Definition and Translation of Timing Functions:
The semantics of timing functions in SCR-style SRS is given in figure 8. The function twf at lines 1–7 defines the output as FALSE when tick t = 0 and TRUE for a specified time interval tv after triggering a condition to TRUE (*i.e.*, that ts is a current tick, the output at ts-1 is FALSE, and the condition at ts is TRUE). The function twfs at lines 9–10 specifies a function from tick to an output(bool) to specify a sequence of the function twf

An example of translating a specific timing function is given in figure 9. Lines 1–2 define the condition used in timing function t_Trip. cycletime in line 3 is an interval between two consecutive executions.

3.2   Translation from PFS to PVS

The Program Functional Specification (PFS) is translated into PVS to check consistency between the PFS and the SRS. In this paper, we extract properties to be checked from the PFS, but generally they are not limited to those from the PFS. FMEA (Failure Mode and Effects Analysis) results and domain experts' knowledge also could be used to generate putative theorems that may be proven of the system under analysis.

The PFS is written in unconstrained natural language, so the translation cannot be easily automated. However, we propose a systematic two-phase process— the first phase is to define a cross-reference between terms in PFS and SRS. The second phase is to translate sentences in PFS into PVS. During the first phase, we can often find inconsistent terms, that must be resolved by the original specification authors. The second phase also cannot be automated, but there

```
 1:   f_PDLCond(t:tick) : RECURSIVE to_CondInOut =
 2:     LET
 3:     s_PDLCond : t_CondInOut =  LAMBDA (tt:tick):IF tt=0 THEN k_CondIn
 4:                                ELSE f_PDLCond(tt-1)
 5:                                ENDIF,
 6:     w_FlogPDLCondLo : enumabc  =  TABLE
 7:         ...                          % similar to if-then-else
 8:        ENDTABLE,
 9:     w_FlogPDLCondHi :enumabc =  TABLE
10:         ...                          % similar to if-then-else
11:        ENDTABLE,
12:      X = (LAMBDA (x1: pred[bool]),
13:                  (x2: pred[enumabc]),
14:                  (x3: pred[enumabc]),
15:                  (x4: pred[bool]) :
16:          x1(m_PDLCond(t) = k_CondSwLo) &
17:          x2(     w_FlogPDLCondLo) &
18:          x3(          w_FlogPDLCondHi) &
19:          x4(               s_PDLCond(t) = k_CondOut))  IN TABLE
20:      %    |    |    |    |
21:      %    v    v    v    v
22:      %-------|----|----|----|------------%
23:      | X( T  , a? , dc , ~ )| k_CondOut ||
24:      %-------|----|----|----|------------%
25:      | X( T  , b? , dc , T )| k_CondOut ||
26:      %-------|----|----|----|------------%
27:      | X( T  , b? , dc , F )| k_CondIn  ||
28:      %-------|----|----|----|------------%
29:      | X( T  , c? , dc , ~ )| k_CondIn  ||
30:      %-------|----|----|----|------------%
31:      | X( F  , dc , a? , ~ )| k_CondOut ||
32:      %-------|----|----|----|------------%
33:      | X( F  , dc , b? , T )| k_CondOut ||
34:      %-------|----|----|----|------------%
35:      | X( F  , dc , b? , F )| k_CondIn  ||
36:      %-------|----|----|----|------------%
37:      | X( F  , dc , c? , ~ )| k_CondIn  ||
38:      %-------|----|----|----|------------%
39:        ENDTABLE
40:   MEASURE t
41:
42:   s_PDLCond(t:tick):to_CondInOut =  IF t = 0 THEN k_CondIn
43:                                     ELSE f_PDLCond(t-1)
44:                                     ENDIF
```

Fig. 7. Example of definitional style of SRS (f_PDLCond and s_PDLCond)

```
1: twf(C:pred[tick], t:tick, tv:tick): RECURSIVE bool =
2:     IF t = 0 THEN FALSE                    % initial value is FALSE
3:     ELSE EXISTS (ts: {t:tick | 0 < t}):
4:         (t-tv+1) <= ts AND ts <= t AND     % During a time interval
5:         (C(ts) AND NOT twf(ts-1))          % if it starts TRUE
6:     ENDIF                                  %  with just before FALSE,
7:   MEASURE t                                % output is  TRUE
8:
9: twfs(C:pred[tick], tv:tick) : pred[tick] =
10:       (LAMBDA (t:tick):twf(C,t,tv))
```

Fig. 8. Step 5 (1). The semantics of timing functions

```
1: C_Trip(t:tick) : bool = f_FaveC(t) >= k_FaveCPDL AND
2:                          (NOT t_Pending(t)) AND  s_Pending(t)
3: t_Trip(t:tick) : bool = twfs(C_Trip,k_trip/cycletime)(t)
```

Fig. 9. Step 5 (2). Translation of timing function

are three distinct classes, or 'patterns,' in the text of the PFS. Because of the real-time constraints involved, these patterns cannot be described in temporal logic classes such as LTL (Linear Temporal Logic) or CTL (Computational Tree Logic), so we directly encode in a classical logic. Many researches have proposed real-time extension of temporal logics, but there is no standard notation for this.

(Pattern 1) Input-Output specifications are requirements relating the input and output of functions. If $f\_condition(t) = k\_condition$ at tick t, the output f_output is k_output. They can be described as an implication (with implicit universal quantification over tick t) as a relation:

```
theorem_input_output : THEOREM
    (f_condition(t) = k_condition) => f_output(t) = k_output
```

(Pattern 2) Time-Duration specifications are real-time requirements such that if certain inputs are satisfied, the certain outputs should be maintained for a specified duration. If $f\_condition(t) = k\_condition$ at tick t, the output of the f_output is k_output between tick t and $t + duration$.

```
theorem_duration : THEOREM FORALL (t:{ts:tick|ts>0}) :
    (f_condition(t) = k_condition) =>
        (FORALL (ti: tick): (t <= ti and ti <= t+duration) =>
        f_output(ti) = k_output)
```

(Pattern 3) Time-Expiration specifications are real-time requirements such that if certain inputs are satisfied and a specified duration has elapsed, then a certain output should be generated. If $f\_condition(t) = k\_condition$ at tick t and tick *duration* has elapsed, the output of the f_output is changed to k_output.

```
theorem_expiration : THEOREM FORALL (t:{ts:tick|ts>0}) :
   (f_condition(t) = k_condition) =>
      (( 0 <= duration) => f_output(t+duration+1) = k_output)
```

The translation from PFS to PVS THEOREMs follows the example in figure 10, which shows the translation of the items from figure 3. Item e.1 in figure 3 is 'If the D/I is open, select the $0.3\%FP$ (Full Power) conditioning level. If $\phi_{LOG} < 0.3\%FP-50mV$, condition out the immediate trip. If $\phi_{LOG} >= 0.3\%FP$, enable the trip.' This sentence matches (Pattern 1), input-output specifications. 'The D/I' is described as 'hand switch' and 'low power conditioning level' in lines 3 and 4 in figure 3. So 'the D/I' is mapped to 'm_PDLCond.' And 'the D/I is open' means that m_PDLCond(t) = k_CondSwLo. In this state, 'immediate trip' is 'condition out' when $\phi_{LOG} < 0.3\%FP - 50mV$. ϕ_{LOG} is mapped f_Flog and $0.3\%FP$ is 2739 mv, that is, k_FlogPDLLo. This information is described in an appendix of PFS and SRS. In this state, immediate trip should not operate (condition out). It can be written as f_PDLCond = k_CondOut. In a similar way, 'enable trip' when $\phi_{LOG} >= 0.3\%FP$ translates THEOREM th_e_1_2.

```
th_e_1_1 : THEOREM (m_PDLCond(t) = k_CondSwLo AND f_Flog(t) < 2739-50)=>
               f_PDLCond(t) = k_CondOut
th_e_1_2 : THEOREM (m_PDLCond(t) = k_CondSwLo AND f_Flog(t) >= 2739) =>
               f_PDLCond(t) = k_CondIn
```

Fig. 10. Example of translation from PFS to PVS THEOREMs

3.3   Verification

The translated specification is stored in a file for verification by PVS. The verification in PVS cannot be entirely automated, but we found that there is a pattern when we prove similar properties. A proof template is (expand* "...")(grind :exclude ("...")) or (grind :exclude ("...")). The ... is related to the functions or definitions on the paths of dataflows. The PVS proof strategy grind tries to rewrite the definitions in all possible cases, and for circular definition it rewrites infinitely. So ... in exclude are definitions are circular dependency relations. expand is used for rewriting only one expansion of a definition. When we prove THEOREM th_e_1_1 and THEOREM th_e_1_2 in figure 3.2, f_PDLCond is a recursive definition. So we can prove them by (expand "f_PDLCond") (grind :exclude ("f_PDLCond")).

4   Discussion

During our verification experience, we discovered notational errors, different terms for the same concepts, and hidden assumptions.

First, we found that different terms were used in PFS during the construction of the cross-references. For example, the m_PDLCond is used as hand switch, low power conditioning level, and conditioning level. The m_PHTD is used as Core Differential Pressure measurement, ΔP_i, and DP signal. The f_PDLTrip, is used as the state of PHT low core differential pressure parameter trip, ΔP_{trip}, and parameter trip(D/O). Our method can be therefore valuable in encouraging that the PFS use terms in the same way that the SRS does.

Second, other different terms in the PFS are 'condition out the immediate trip' and 'enable trip.' The 'condition out' is actually the opposite of 'enable', but this is far from clear. Our analysis highlights such obfuscated wording, in figure 11. We present a modified PFS term, e.'the low power conditioning level' from 'the conditioning level' in figure 3. The 'condition in - enable' is also modified to 'disable - enable'.

---

e. Determine the immediate trip conditioning status from *the low power conditioning level* D/I as follows:

1. If the D/I is open, select the $0.3\%FP$ conditioning level. If $\phi_{LOG} < 0.3\%FP -$ $50mV$, *disable the immediate trip*. If $\phi_{LOG} >= 0.3\%FP$, *enable the immediate trip*.

Fig. 11. Unambiguous PFS

Third, there are hidden assumptions, such as in the following PFS. The g.2 and g.3 in figure 3 are translated into figure 12 in PVS. But we could not prove the THEOREM th_inappropriate_g_3.

```
th_appropriate_g_2_1 : THEOREM FORALL (t:{ts:tick|ts>0}) :
        f_FaveC(t)>= 80 AND t_Pending(t) = false AND
        s_Pending(t) = true AND t_Trip(t-1) = false
        => t_Trip(t)
th_appropriate_g_2_2 : THEOREM FORALL (t:{ts:tick|ts>0}) :
        f_FaveC(t)< 80 AND t_Pending(t) = false AND
        s_Pending(t) = true AND t_Trip(t-1) = false
        => t_Trip(t)
th_inappropriate_g_3 : THEOREM FORALL (t:{ts:tick|ts>0}):
        t_Trip(t-1) = false AND t_Trip(t) = true =>
        FORALL(t1 : tick): ((t <= t1 and t1 <= 1000/cycletime +t) =>
            t_Trip(t1) = true)
```

Fig. 12. Example of inappropriate translation of PFS

We investigated the reason and we concluded that there were hidden assumptions. Items g.2 and g.3 in figure 3 are not independent. In other words, the item g.3 can be true only if the item g.2 is true. 'Once the delayed parameter trip has occurred' does not mean 'the delayed parameter trip has occurred' directly, but it means 'f_{AVEC} equals or exceeds $80\%FP$ and then the delayed parameter trip has occurred'. So the assumption the delayed parameter trip has occurred in item g.3 should be strengthened with items g.2.1 and g.2.2. As a result of this investigation, we translated the above PFS into PVS specifications again, such as in figure 13. Then we succeeded in the proof of THEOREM th_appropriate_g_3. This error was not found through inspection, and is the kind of error that is difficult to find without formal analysis.

```
th_appropriate_g_3 : THEOREM FORALL (t:{ts:time|ts>0}):
    t_Trip(t-1) = false AND t_Trip(t) = true AND
    %% strengthen assumption from th_appropriate_g_2_1~g_2_2
    f_FaveC(t) >= 80 AND t_Pending(t)=false AND s_Pending(t)=true =>
    FORALL(t1 : time): ( (t <= t1 and t1 <= 1000/cycletime + t) =>
        t_Trip(t1) = true)
```

Fig. 13. Example of appropriate translation

Related Work

The work presented here is complemented by ongoing work at McMaster University by Lawford et al. [6]. Using a similar case study, their work concentrates on verification of the refinement of the requirements in the SRS into design elements, also expressed in SCR, in the software design description (SDD). They use an extension of the 4-variable model of Parnas [7] into a relational setting, and claim that their approach is more intuitive for system engineers. Our goal in the present work is essentially the same - to develop easier-to-use verification approaches - for application to the earlier part of the software development process.

Another approach for formal validation of requirements from PFS is done by Gervasi and Nuseibeh [8]. It provides a systematic and automated method to construct a model from a PFS, and then checking some structural properties (for example, function's domain is correct) of the constructed model. We think that their extraction technique can help in extracting functional properties; however, they do not check functional properties.

5   Conclusion

Based on our experience of inspecting the Wolsung SDS2 SRS, we have demonstrated that inspection has limitations. To verify functional properties, we developed a software tool with a graphical user interface that converts SCR-style requirements specifications into the PVS language. In addition, we provide a method for verifying functional properties in PFS using PVS. We believe that the procedure helps to construct high-quality safety-critical software.

Users of our approach need not be experts on formal methods or power users of PVS. Our graphical editor provides a user-friendly interface to allow editing of SCR-style specifications and automates the translation process. However, the proof process can be completed with a limited study of the proof pattern. The specifier translates PFS into PVS theorems manually, even though we can translate systematically using a cross-reference table.

Although we strongly believe that our approach delivers significant benefits to practitioners, the following further enhancements seem to be desirable:

- Development of translation rules so that a formal specification written in statecharts or modecharts can be verified using the same approach
- More systematic method of translating from PFS to PVS theorems, to enhance completeness of the current cross-reference methods
- Additional study of proof patterns, to the verification
- Enhancements to the SRS-style editor, such as XML translation, to increase its practical utility

References

1. M. Fagan, "Advances in Software Inspections," *IEEE Transactions on Software Engineering*, 12(7), pp. 133-144, 1986.
2. S. Owre, N. Shankar, J. Rushby, and D. Stringer-Calvert, *PVS System Guide, PVS Language Reference, and PVS Prover Guide Version 2.4* , Computer Science Laboratory, SRI International, 2001.
3. AECL CANDU, *Software Work Practice, Procedure for the Specification of Software Requirements for Safety Critical Systems*, Wolsung NPP, 00-68000-SWP-002, 1991.
4. C. Heitmeyer, J. Kirby, and B. Labaw, "The SCR Method for Formally Specifying, Verifying and Validating Software Requirements: Tool Support," *Proceedings of the 19th International Conference on Software Engineering (ICSE '97)*, pp. 610-611, 1997.
5. N. Halbwachs, P. Caspi, P. Raymond, and D. Pilaud, "The Synchronous Data Flow Programming Language LUSTRE," *Proceedings of the IEEE*, 79(9), pp. 1305-1320, 1991.
6. M. Lawford, J. McDougall, P. Froebel, and G. Moum, "Practical application of functional and relational methods for the specification and verification of safety critical software," *Proceedings of Algebraic Methodology and Software Technology, 8th International Conference (AMAST 2000)*, LNCS 1816, pp. 73-88, 2000.
7. D. Parnas and J. Madey, "Functional documentation for computer systems engineering," Technical Report CRL No. 273, Telecommunications Research Institute of Ontario, McMaster University, 1991.
8. V. Gervasi and B. Nuseibeh, "Lightweight Validation of Natural Language Requirements: a case study," *Proceedings of 4th IEEE International Conference on Requirements Engineering (ICRE 2000)*, 2000.

Beyond Parameterized Verification

Marco Bozzano and Giorgio Delzanno

Dipartimento di Informatica e Scienze dell'Informazione
Università di Genova, Via Dodecaneso 35, 16146 Genova, Italy
{bozzano,giorgio}@disi.unige.it

Abstract. We present a sound and fully automated method for the verification of safety properties of parameterized systems with unbounded local data variables, a new class of infinite-state systems parametric in several dimensions. The method builds upon a specification and an assertional language based on the combination of *multiset rewriting* and *constraints*. We introduce new classes of parameterized systems for which verification of safety properties is decidable, and we introduce abstractions, defined at the level of constraints, to handle examples outside these classes. As case-study, we apply the method to verify fully automatically mutual exclusion properties for formulations of the *ticket mutual exclusion algorithm* parametric in the number of clients, servers, and in which both clients and servers have unbounded local data.

1 Introduction

In recent years several attempts have been made in order to develop tools for the automated verification of *infinite state systems*. Interesting results have been specifically obtained for the class of *parameterized systems*. A typical parameterized system consists of a collection of an *arbitrary* but *finite* number of *finite-state* components interacting via synchronous or asynchronous communication [5,7, 20]. In many practical cases verification problems for this kind of systems can be reduced to problems related to Petri Nets by applying a *counting* abstraction that simply forgets local data while keeping track of the number of processes in a given state. Reachability procedures can then be used to verify the original property on the resulting Petri Net like model [10,14,15,19]. New results have also been obtained for the verification of another class of infinite-state systems, i.e., concurrent systems with a fixed number of components but *unbounded data*. As an example, in [8,12,18], *constraints* are used to symbolically represent and manipulate infinite collections of states for these systems.

In this paper we address the definition of techniques for the automatic verification of systems and protocols parametric in *several dimensions*. As an example, we mention *mutual exclusion protocols* for *multi-client systems* that make use of global and local variables, like, e.g., the *ticket* and *bakery* protocols [8]. In these case studies the *counting abstraction* turns out to be too rough to prove correctness. Inspired by the seminal paper [2] of Abdulla and Jonsson, in [11], we introduced a specification language and a corresponding assertional language for

J.-P. Katoen and P. Stevens (Eds.): TACAS 2002, LNCS 2280, pp. 221–235, 2002.
© Springer-Verlag Berlin Heidelberg 2002

systems parametric in several dimensions. The specification language is based on *multiset rewriting over first order formulas* as proposed by Cervesato et al. in [9] enriched, however, with *constraints*. This way, we keep separate the structure of processes from the relations over their local data. The assertional language combines symbolic reasoning (unification and subsumption of multisets of first order atomic formulas) and constraint programming (satisfiability, entailment, and variable elimination). Symbolic operations like predecessor operators and comparison tests exploit the operations of the underlying *constraint system*.

In this paper we extend the approach presented in [11] as follows.

We have isolated classes of multiset rewriting rules with constraints for which the verification of *safety properties* of practical interest is decidable. We consider a subclass of linear integer constraints, called NC, which allows us to handle an infinite collection of discrete values (e.g. integers) and to compare them using relations like $>$, $\geq$, and $=$. This domain can be used to represent local variables, process identifiers, priorities, and so on. The safety properties we can handle are such that the corresponding *unsafe states* consists of *upward closed sets* of configurations. Our algorithm follows the general approach of backward reachability proposed in [1] and exploits the theory of well and better quasi orderings for proving termination [1,4,17]. To attack verification problems for systems defined over *linear integer constraints* that lay outside the class for which termination is guaranteed, we use an *automated abstraction* that maps linear integer constraints into NC-constraints. This abstraction always returns a *conservative approximation* of the original property. Furthermore, it can be viewed as the counterpart of the *counting abstraction* used in [10] for systems properties that are data-sensitive. This way, we obtain a *fully-automatic* and *sound* algorithm for checking *safety properties* for a wide class of systems parametric in several dimensions.

We have implemented our automated verification method and applied it to analyze *mutual exclusion* for different formulations of the *ticket protocol*. As shown in [8], this protocol has an infinite-state space even for system configurations with only 2 processes. In this paper we extend the results of [8], where safety properties were proved for this special case, as follows. We have considered both a *multi-client, single-server* formulation, i.e., with an arbitrary but finite number of *dynamically* generated clients but a single shared resource, and a *multi-client, multi-server* system in which both clients and servers are created *dynamically*. Both examples have been modeled using *multiset rewriting rules* with *difference constraints*, that support arithmetic operations like *increment and decrement* of data variables. Our models are faithful to the original formulation of the algorithm, in that we do not abstract away global and local integer variables attached to individual clients, that in fact can still grow unboundedly. Using our symbolic backward reachability procedure combined with the dynamic use of abstractions, we have automatically verified that both models are safe for *any number of clients and servers* and for *any values of local and global variables*. To our knowledge both the techniques and the practical results are original.

THE SYSTEM WITH n PROCESSES

Program
  global var $s, t : integer$;
  begin
    $t := 0$;
    $s := 0$;
    $P_1 \mid \ldots \mid P_n$;
  end.

THE i-th COMPONENT

Process P_i ::=
  local var $a : integer$;
  repeat forever
  $\Big[$ *think* : $\langle\, a := t$;
  $\qquad\qquad t := t + 1;\, \rangle$
  $\quad$ *wait* : **when** $\langle\, a = s\, \rangle$ **do**
  $\quad$ *use* : $\Big[$ CRITICAL SECTION
  $\qquad\qquad \langle\, s := s + 1;\, \rangle$
end.

Fig. 1. The Ticket Protocol: n is a parameter of the protocol.

Plan of the Paper. In Section 2, we present the case-study. In Section 3, we introduce our specification language. In Section 4, we introduce the assertional language used to reason about safety properties. In Section 5, we describe the verification algorithm. In Section 6, we discuss decidability issues. In Section 7, we discuss experimental results. In Section 8 and 9, we discuss related works and address future works.

We leave the proofs of all results for a long version of the paper.

2   The Case-Study: The Ticket Protocol

The ticket protocol is a *mutual exclusion* protocol designed for multi-client systems operating on a shared memory. The protocol is based on a first-in first-served access policy. The algorithm is given in Fig. 1 (where we use $P \mid Q$ to denote the *interleaving parallel execution* of P and Q, and $\langle\cdot\rangle$ to denote atomic fragments of code). The protocol works as follows. Initially, all clients are thinking, while t and s store the same initial value. When requesting the access to the critical section, a client stores the value of the current ticket t in its local variable a. A new ticket is then emitted by incrementing t. Clients wait for their turn until the value of their local variable a equals the value of s. After the elaboration inside the critical section, a process releases it and the current turn is updated by incrementing s. During the execution, the *global state* of the protocol consists of the current values of s, t, and of the local variables of n processes. As remarked in [8], even for $n = 2$ (only 2 clients), the values of the local variables of individual processes as well as s and t may get *unbounded*. This implies that *any instance* of the scheme of Fig. 1 gives rise to an infinite-state system. The algorithm is supposed to work for any value of n, and it should also work if new clients enter the system at running time.

3   MSR($\mathcal{C}$): Multiset Rewriting with Constraints

The ticket protocol presented in the previous section is a practical example of protocol parametric in *several dimensions*: the *number* of processes and the *value* of their local variables (denoted by a in Fig. 1). In this paper we will adopt the specification language proposed in [11] that combines aspects peculiar of High Level and Colored Petri Nets and of Constraint Programming. The framework called MSR is based on *multiset rewriting systems* defined over first-order atomic formulas and it has been introduced by Cervesato et al. [9] for the formal specification of *cryptographic protocols*. In [11], the basic formalism (without existential quantification) has been extended to allow for the specification of relations over data variable using *constraints*, i.e., a logic language interpreted over a fixed domain. Multiset rewriting rules allow one to *locally* model *rendez-vous* and *internal* actions of processes, and constraints to symbolically represent the *relation between the data of different processes*, thus achieving a clear separation between process structure and data paths. This formalism can be viewed as a first-order extension of Petri Nets in which tokens carry along structured data. In this section we will review the definitions of [11] and call the resulting formalism MSR($\mathcal{C}$). Lets us start from the formal definition of constraint system.

Definition 1 (Constraint System). A constraint system is a tuple $\mathcal{C} = \langle \mathcal{V}, \mathcal{L}, \mathcal{D}, Sol, \sqsubseteq^c \rangle$ where: $\mathcal{V}$ is a denumerable set of variables; $\mathcal{L}$ is a *first-order* language with *equality* and closed with respect to $\exists$ and $\wedge$; we call an open formula $\varphi \in \mathcal{L}$ with free variables in $\mathcal{V}$ a *constraint*; $\mathcal{D}$ is the *domain* of interpretation of the variables in $\mathcal{V}$; $Sol(\varphi)$ is the set of solutions (mappings $\mathcal{V} \rightsquigarrow \mathcal{D}$) for φ; $\sqsubseteq^c$ is a relation such that $\varphi \sqsubseteq^c \psi$ implies $Sol(\psi) \subseteq Sol(\varphi)$.

We say that a *constraint* $\varphi \in \mathcal{L}$ is *satisfiable* whenever $Sol(\varphi) \neq \emptyset$. An example of constraint systems is given below.

Definition 2 (DC-constraints). We call *difference constraints* the subclass of *linear arithmetic constraints* having the form
$$\psi ::= \psi \wedge \psi \mid x = y + c \mid x > y + c \mid x \geq y + c \mid true, \quad c \in \mathbb{Z}.$$
Given $\mathcal{D} = \mathbb{Z}$, Sol maps constraints into sets of variable evaluations from $\mathcal{V}$ to $\mathbb{Z}$; by definition *true* is always satisfiable.

For instance, let φ be $x \geq y \wedge x \geq z$, then $\sigma = \langle x \mapsto 2, y \mapsto 1, z \mapsto 0, \ldots \rangle \in Sol(\varphi)$. Furthermore, φ is satisfiable and entails $x \geq y$, and $\exists y.\varphi$ is equivalent to the constraint $x \geq z$.

Let $\mathcal{C} = \langle \mathcal{V}, \mathcal{L}, \mathcal{D}, Sol, \sqsubseteq^c \rangle$ be a constraint system, and $\mathcal{P}$ be a set of predicate symbols. An *atomic formula* $p(x_1, \ldots, x_n)$ is such that $p \in \mathcal{P}$, and $x_1, \ldots, x_n$ are *distinct* variables in $\mathcal{V}$. A *multiset* of atomic formulas is indicated as $A_1 \mid \ldots \mid A_k$, where A_i and A_j have distinct variables, and $\mid$ is the multiset constructor. The *empty* multiset is represented as ϵ. In the rest of the paper will use $\mathcal{M}, \mathcal{N}, \ldots$ to denote *multisets* of atomic formulas.

Definition 3 (MSR($\mathcal{C}$) Rules). Let $\mathcal{C} = \langle \mathcal{V}, \mathcal{L}, \mathcal{D}, Sol, \sqsubseteq^c \rangle$ be a constraint system. An MSR($\mathcal{C}$) rule has the form $\mathcal{M} \longrightarrow \mathcal{M}' : \varphi$, where $\mathcal{M}$ and $\mathcal{M}'$ are two multisets of atomic formulas with *distinct* variables and built on predicates in $\mathcal{P}$, and $\varphi \in \mathcal{L}$.

Note that $\mathcal{M} \to \epsilon : \varphi$ and $\epsilon \to \mathcal{M} : \varphi$ are possible MSR($\mathcal{C}$) rules. An example of MSR(DC) rule R is $p(x,y) \mid r(u,v) \longrightarrow t(w) : x \geq y, w = v$. Let us call *ground* an atomic formula having the form $p(d_1, \ldots, d_n)$ where $d_i \in \mathcal{D}$ for $i : 1, \ldots, n$. A *configuration* is a multiset of *ground atomic formulas*. The ground instances of a multiset rewriting rule are defined as follows: $Inst(\mathcal{M} \longrightarrow \mathcal{M}' : \varphi) = \{\sigma(\mathcal{M}) \longrightarrow \sigma(\mathcal{M}') \mid \sigma \in Sol(\varphi)\}$, where $\sigma(\mathcal{M})$ denotes the straightforward extension of the mapping σ from variables to multisets. In the previous example we have that $p(1,0) \mid r(0,5) \longrightarrow t(5) \in Inst(R)$.

We are now in the position to define formally an MSR($\mathcal{C}$) specification. In the following we will use $\oplus$ and $\ominus$ to denote *multiset union* and *multiset difference*.

Definition 4 (MSR($\mathcal{C}$) Specification). An MSR($\mathcal{C}$) specification $\mathcal{S}$ is a tuple $\langle \mathcal{P}, \mathcal{C}, \mathcal{I}, \mathcal{R} \rangle$, where $\mathcal{P}$ is a set of predicate symbols, $\mathcal{C}$ is a constraint system, $\mathcal{I}$ is a set of *initial* configurations, and $\mathcal{R}$ is a set of MSR($\mathcal{C}$) rules over $\mathcal{P}$.

The operational semantics of a specification $\mathcal{S} = \langle \mathcal{P}, \mathcal{C}, \mathcal{I}, \mathcal{R} \rangle$ is defined as follows.

Definition 5 (One-step Rewriting). Given two configurations $\mathcal{M}_1$ and $\mathcal{M}_2$, $\mathcal{M}_1 \Rightarrow \mathcal{M}_2$ if and only if there exists a multiset of ground atomic formulas $\mathcal{Q}$ s.t. $\mathcal{M}_1 = \mathcal{N}_1 \oplus \mathcal{Q}$, $\mathcal{M}_2 = \mathcal{N}_2 \oplus \mathcal{Q}$, and $\mathcal{N}_1 \longrightarrow \mathcal{N}_2 \in Inst(\mathcal{R})$.

Definition 6 (Images and Reachable States). Given a set of configurations S, the *successor* operator is defined as $Post(S) = \{\mathcal{M}' \mid \mathcal{M} \Rightarrow \mathcal{M}', \mathcal{M} \in S\}$, the *predecessor* operator as $Pre(S) = \{\mathcal{M} \mid \mathcal{M} \Rightarrow \mathcal{M}', \mathcal{M}' \in S\}$, and the *reachability* set as $Post^*(\mathcal{I})$.

3.1   The MSR(DC) Encoding of the Ticket Protocol

In this section we exemplify the notions introduced in Section 3. Multiset rewriting allows us to give an accurate and flexible encoding of the ticket protocol. We will first consider a *multi-client, single resource* system.

One Server, Many Clients. Let us first consider a *single* shared resource controlled via the counters t and s as described in Section 2. The infinite collection of admissible initial states consists of all configurations with an *arbitrary* but finite number of thinking processes and *two* counters having the same initial value ($t = s$). The specification is shown in Fig. 2. The initial configuration is the predicate *init*, the seed of all possible runs of the protocol. The counters are represented here via the atoms $count(t)$ and $turn(s)$. Thinking clients are represented via the propositional symbol *think*, and can be generated *dynamically* via the second rule. The behaviour of an individual client is described via the third block of rules of Fig. 2, in which the relation between the local variable and the global counters are represented via DC-constraints. Finally, we allow thinking processes to terminate their execution as specified via the last rule of Fig. 2. The previous rules are independent of the current number of clients in the system. Note that in our specification we keep an explicit representation of the data variables; furthermore, we do not out any restrictions on their values. As a consequence, there are runs of our model in which s and t grow unboundedly as in the original protocol. A sample run of a system with 2 clients (as in [8]) is shown in Fig. 3.

Initial States

$$init \; \longrightarrow \; count(t) \mid turn(s) \; : \; t = s$$

Dynamic Generation

$$\epsilon \; \longrightarrow \; think \; : \; true$$

Individual Behaviour

$$think \mid count(t) \; \longrightarrow \; wait(a) \mid count(t') \; : \; a = t \; \wedge \; t' = t + 1$$
$$wait(a) \mid turn(s) \; \longrightarrow \; use \mid turn(s') \quad\;\; : \; a = s \; \wedge \; s' = s$$
$$use \mid turn(s) \; \longrightarrow \; think \mid turn(s') \quad : \; s' = s + 1$$

Termination

$$think \; \longrightarrow \; \epsilon \; : \; true$$

Fig. 2. Ticket protocol for *multi-client, single-server* system, with an example of run.

$$init \Rightarrow \ldots \Rightarrow think \mid count(8) \mid turn(8) \Rightarrow think \mid think \mid count(8) \mid turn(8)$$
$$\Rightarrow wait(8) \mid think \mid count(9) \mid turn(8) \Rightarrow wait(8) \mid wait(9) \mid count(10) \mid turn(8)$$
$$\Rightarrow use \mid wait(9) \mid count(10) \mid turn(8) \Rightarrow use \mid wait(9) \mid count(10) \mid turn(8) \mid think$$
$$\Rightarrow think \mid wait(9) \mid count(10) \mid turn(9) \mid think$$

Fig. 3. Example of run.

Many Servers, Many Clients. Let us consider now an *open* system with an *arbitrary* but *finite* number of *shared resources*, each one controlled by two local counters s and t. We specify this scenario by associating a *unique identifier* to each resource and to use it to stamp the corresponding pair of counters. Furthermore, we exploit non-determinism in order to simulate the capability of each client to choose which resource to use. The resulting specification is shown in Fig 4. We have considered an *open* system in which new clients can be generated *dynamically* via a *demon* process. The process $demon(n)$ maintains a local counter n used to generate a new identifier, say id, and to associate it to a newly created resource represented via the pair $count(id, t)$ and $turn(id, s)$. A thinking process non-deterministically chooses which resource to wait for by synchronizing with one of the counters in the system (the first rule of the third block in Fig. 4). After this choice, the algorithm behaves as usual w.r.t. to the chosen resource id. The termination rules can be specified as natural extensions of the single-server case. Note that in this specification the sources of infiniteness are the number of clients, the number of shared resources, the values of resource identifiers, and the values of tickets. An example of run is shown in Fig. 5.

4 Specification of Properties via an Assertional Language

Let us focus for a moment on the single-server ticket protocol. It should ensure mutual exclusion for any number of clients, and for any value of the global and local variables. In our specification mutual exclusion holds if every *reachable configuration* $\mathcal{M} \in Post^*(init)$ contains *at most* one occurrence of the predicate

Initial States

$$init \longrightarrow demon(n) : true$$

Dynamic Process and Server Generation

$$\epsilon \longrightarrow think : true$$

$$demon(n) \rightarrow demon(n') \mid count(id, t) \mid turn(id', s) :$$
$$n' = n+1 \wedge t = s \wedge id = n \wedge id' = id$$

Individual Behaviour

$$think \mid count(id, t) \longrightarrow think(r) \mid count(id', t') : r = id \wedge id' = id \wedge t' = t$$

$$think(r) \mid count(id, t) \longrightarrow wait(r', a) \mid count(id', t') :$$
$$r = id \wedge a = t \wedge t' = t+1 \wedge r' = r \wedge id' = id$$

$$wait(r, a) \mid turn(id, s) \longrightarrow use(r', a') \mid turn(id', s') :$$
$$r = id \wedge a = s \wedge a' = a \wedge s' = s \wedge r' = r \wedge id' = id$$

$$use(r, a) \mid turn(id, s) \longrightarrow think \mid turn(id', s') : r = id \wedge s' = s+1 \wedge id' = id$$

Termination

$$think(r) \longrightarrow \epsilon : true$$
$$think \longrightarrow \epsilon : true$$

Fig. 4. Ticket protocol for *multi-server, multi-client* systems.

$$init \Rightarrow demon(3) \Rightarrow count(3, 0) \mid turn(3, 0) \mid demon(4) \Rightarrow \ldots$$
$$\ldots \Rightarrow count(3, 0) \mid turn(3, 0) \mid think \mid think \mid demon(4)$$
$$\Rightarrow count(3, 0) \mid turn(3, 0) \mid count(4, 8) \mid turn(4, 8) \mid think \mid think \mid demon(5) \Rightarrow \ldots$$
$$\Rightarrow count(3, 0) \mid turn(3, 0) \mid count(4, 8) \mid turn(4, 8) \mid think(4) \mid think(3) \mid demon(5)$$
$$\Rightarrow count(3, 0) \mid turn(3, 0) \mid count(4, 9) \mid turn(4, 8) \mid wait(4, 8) \mid think(3) \mid demon(5).$$

Fig. 5. Example of run.

use. The state-space we have to generate to check the previous condition is infinite both in the size of the generated multisets and in the number of multisets of the same size (the latter due to the unboundedness of ticket variables). The only way to algorithmically check this property is using an adequate *assertional language* to finitely represent infinite collections of configurations. In [11], we proposed to use a special assertional language based on *constrained multisets*. To explain this idea, let us first note that an alternative way of formulating the validity of mutual exclusion is as follows: $init \notin Pre^*(U)$, where U is the infinite collection of *unsafe* states. U consists of all the configurations in which there are *at least* two occurrences of the predicate *use*. This set can be finitely represented using the following idea. Let us introduce the following ordering between configurations:

$$\mathcal{M} \preccurlyeq \mathcal{N} \text{ if and only if } Occ_A(\mathcal{M}) \leq Occ_A(\mathcal{N}) \text{ for any } ground \text{ atom } A,$$

where $Occ_A(\mathcal{M})$ is the number of occurrences of A in $\mathcal{M}$. A set of configurations S *generates* its *upward closure* $Up(S)$ defined as $Up(S) = \{\mathcal{N} \mid \mathcal{M} \preccurlyeq \mathcal{N}, \mathcal{M} \in S\}$. A set S is *upward-closed* whenever $Up(S) = S$. Let us go back to our case-study. It is easy to verify that the set of unsafe states U of the ticket protocol is indeed *upward closed*. Furthermore, U can be represented as the upward closure of the set S of configurations having the form $use(c_1) \mid use(c_2)$ where c_1 and c_2 are arbitrary integer values. Though S is still an infinite set, we can finitely represent it by re-introducing *constraints* as annotations of a multiset of atomic formulas. Specifically, if we define $M = use(x) \mid use(y) : true$, S corresponds to the set of instances of M w.r.t. the solutions of the constraint $true$ (all possible values for x and y). Similarly, the unsafe states for the multi-server ticket protocol can be expressed via the *constrained configuration* $use(id, x) \mid use(id', y) : id = id'$ meaning that at least two clients are in the critical section associated to the same resource with identifier id. This observation is at the basis of our verification method. Fixed $\mathcal{S} = \langle \mathcal{P}, \mathcal{C}, \mathcal{I}, \mathcal{R} \rangle$ and $\mathcal{C} = \langle \mathcal{V}, \mathcal{L}, \mathcal{D}, Sol, \sqsubseteq^c \rangle$, we generalize the previous ideas as follows.

Definition 7 (Constrained Configuration). A *constrained configuration* is a multiset of atomic formulas with distinct variables, annotated with a *satisfiable* constraint, i.e., $p_1(x_{11}, \ldots, x_{1k_1}) \mid \ldots \mid p_n(x_{n1}, \ldots, x_{nk_n}) : \varphi$ where $p_1, \ldots, p_n \in \mathcal{P}$, $x_{i1}, \ldots, x_{ik_i} \in \mathcal{V}$ for any $i : 1, \ldots n$ and constraint $\varphi \in \mathcal{L}$.

Given a constrained configuration $\mathcal{M} : \varphi$, the *set* of its *ground instances* is defined as $Inst(\mathcal{M} : \varphi) = \{\sigma(\mathcal{M}) \mid \sigma \in Sol(\varphi)\}$. This definition can be extended to sets of constrained configurations with *disjoint variables* (indicated as $\mathbf{S}, \mathbf{S}', \ldots$) in the natural way. However, instead of taking the set of instances as 'flat' denotation of a set of constrained configuration $\mathbf{S}$, we will choose the following rich denotation.

Definition 8 (Rich Denotation). The denotation of a set $\mathbf{S}$ of constrained configurations is the upward closed set of its ground instances $[\![\mathbf{S}]\!] = Up(Inst(\mathbf{S}))$.

We conclude this section by introducing a comparison test between (sets of) constrained configurations whose definition relies on the operations of the underlying constraints system $\mathcal{C}$. Given the atoms $A = p(x_1, \ldots, x_k)$ and $B = q(y_1, \ldots, y_l)$, we will use $A = B$ as an abbreviation for the constraint $x_1 = y_1 \wedge \ldots \wedge x_k = y_k$, provided $p = q$ and $k = l$.

Definition 9. The entailment relation $\sqsubseteq^m$ between constrained configurations is defined as follows: $(A_1 \mid \ldots \mid A_n : \varphi) \sqsubseteq^m (B_1 \mid \ldots \mid B_k : \psi)$ provided $n \leq k$, and there exist $j_1, \ldots, j_n$ *distinct* indices in $\{1, \ldots, k\}$, such that $\gamma \equiv \exists x_1 \ldots \exists x_r. \psi \wedge A_1 = B_{j_1} \wedge \ldots \wedge A_n = B_{j_n}$ and γ is satisfiable, where $x_1, \ldots, x_r$ are the variables in $B_1, \ldots, B_k$, and, finally, $\varphi \sqsubseteq^c \gamma$.

Definition 10. The entailment relation $\sqsubseteq^p$ (p stands for *pointwise* extension of the $\sqsubseteq^m$ relation) between sets of constrained configurations is defined as follows: $\mathbf{S} \sqsubseteq^p \mathbf{S}'$ iff for every $M \in \mathbf{S}'$ there exists $N \in \mathbf{S}$ such that $N \sqsubseteq^m M$.

The entailment relation $\sqsubseteq^p$ provides *sufficient* conditions (that are fully parametric w.r.t. $\mathcal{C}$) for testing containment and equivalence of the denotations of sets of constrained configurations. Let $\mathbf{S}, \mathbf{S}'$ be two sets of constrained configurations.

Proposition 1. If $\mathbf{S} \sqsubseteq^p \mathbf{S}'$ then $[\![\mathbf{S}']\!] \subseteq [\![\mathbf{S}]\!]$.

Procedure Pre^*(**U** : Set of DC-constrained config., Use_α : Bool, $UseInv$: Bool)
  begin
    S := **U**;
    R := $\emptyset$;
    while S $\neq \emptyset$ **do**
      remove M from **S**;
      if $UseInv$ **and** $Inv(M) = false$ **then** $skip$
      else
        $\left\lceil\right.$ **if** Use_α **then** $M' = \alpha(M)$
        $\left|\right.$ **else** $M' = M$;
        $\left|\right.$ **if** $\nexists\, N \in$ **R** s.t. $N \sqsubseteq^m M'$ **then**
        $\left|\right.$ $\left\lceil\right.$ **R** := **R** $\cup \{M'\}$;
        $\left\lfloor\right.$ $\left\lfloor\right.$ **S** := **S** $\cup$ **Pre**($\{M'\}$)
  end

Fig. 6. Symbolic backward reachability ($Inv(\mathcal{M} : \alpha) = true$ iff the statically computed place invariants hold in $\mathcal{M}$).

5   A Sound Verification Procedure

In order to lift to the symbolic level an ideal verification algorithm based on the computation of Pre^* (*backward reachability*), we need a *symbolic Pre* operator working on *sets* of constrained configurations. We first introduce the notion of *unification* between constrained configurations (with disjoint variables) as follows: $(A_1 \mid \dots \mid A_n : \varphi) =_\theta (B_1 \mid \dots \mid B_m : \psi)$ provided $m = n$ and the constraint $\theta = \varphi \wedge \psi \wedge \bigwedge_{i=1}^{n} A_i = B_{j_i}$ is *satisfiable*, $j_1, \dots, j_n$ being a permutation of $1, \dots, n$. The symbolic operator **Pre** is defined as follows:

Definition 11 (Symbolic Predecessor Operator). Given a set **S** of constrained configurations, $(\mathcal{A} \oplus \mathcal{N} : \gamma) \in$ **Pre**(**S**) if and only if there exist a renamed rule $\mathcal{A} \longrightarrow \mathcal{B} : \psi$ in $\mathcal{R}$, and a renamed constrained configuration $\mathcal{M} : \varphi$ in **S** such that $\mathcal{M}' \preccurlyeq \mathcal{M}$, $\mathcal{B}' \preccurlyeq \mathcal{B}$, $(\mathcal{M}' : \varphi) =_\theta (\mathcal{B}' : \psi)$, $\mathcal{N} = \mathcal{M} \ominus \mathcal{M}'$, and $\gamma \equiv \exists x_1 \dots \exists x_k.\theta$ where $x_1, \dots, x_k$ are the variables of θ not in $\mathcal{A} \oplus \mathcal{N}$.

The symbolic operator **Pre** returns a set of constrained configurations and it is correct and complete with respect to Pre, i.e., $[\![\mathbf{Pre}(\mathbf{S})]\!] = Pre([\![\mathbf{S}]\!])$ for any **S**.

    Based on this definition, we define a *symbolic backward reachability* procedure (see Fig. 6) we can use to check safety properties whose negation can be expressed via an upward closed set of configurations. The algorithm is not complete since it is possible to encode undecidable reachability problems (e.g. for two counter machines) as verification problems of generic MSR($\mathcal{C}$) specifications.

    As shown in Fig. 6, the theory of structural invariants for Petri nets can be used to optimize the backward search computation. Namely, we can use the so-called *counting abstraction* [10] to transform any MSR($\mathcal{C}$) specification S into a Petri Net N_S, which can then be used to automatically discover *invariants* that must hold for all reachable configurations of the original specification. For instance, in our case-study we can automatically infer that the number of tokens in place *turn* and *count* are always bounded by one. Since this analysis is conservative w.r.t. the abstraction, it follows that in all reachable configurations for the ticket specification, $Occ_{count(v)}(\mathcal{M}) \leq 1$ and $Occ_{turn(v)}(\mathcal{M}) \leq 1$ for any $v \in \mathbb{Z}$. A similar reasoning can be applied to the multi-server protocol concerning the counters associated to a given identifier (at most one copy of each counter) and the demon process (at most one copy). The invariants can be used during the fixpoint computation to *prune* the *search space*, by discharging every constrained multiset which violates the invariants, without any loss of precision.

6   Sufficient Conditions for Termination

We will now introduce a subclass of DC-constraints, called NC (*name constraints*), and corresponding MSRs for which computation of Pre^* (starting from an upward closed set of configurations) is effective.

Definition 12 (The Constraint System NC). The class NC consists of the constraints $\varphi ::= \varphi \wedge \varphi \mid x > y \mid x = y \mid x \geq y \mid true$, interpreted over the *integers* and ordered with respect to the entailment $\sqsubseteq^c$ of linear constraints.

Being a subclass of linear constraints and closed with respect to existential quantification, any constraint solver for linear constraints can still be used to handle NC-constraints. The class of *monadic* MSR over NC is defined as follows.

Definition 13 (The class $\mathrm{MSR}_1(\mathrm{NC})$). An $\mathrm{MSR}_1(\mathrm{NC})$ specification $\mathcal{S} = \langle \mathcal{P}, \mathrm{NC}, \mathcal{I}, \mathcal{R} \rangle$ is such that all predicates in $\mathcal{P}$ have arity *less or equal than one*, i.e., atomic formulas have the form p or $p(x)$ for $p \in \mathcal{P}$ and some variable x.

Let $\mathcal{A}_1$ be the set of constrained configurations with the same restrictions of the class $\mathrm{MSR}_1(\mathrm{NC})$. As an example, the rule $a \mid p(x) \mid q(y) \rightarrow q(z) : x > y \wedge y = z$ is in $\mathrm{MSR}_1(\mathrm{NC})$, and $p(x) \mid q(y) : x > y$ is an element of $\mathcal{A}_1$. Then, the following properties hold.

Lemma 1. (i) The class $\mathcal{A}_1$ is closed under applications of **Pre** for an $\mathrm{MSR}_1(\mathrm{NC})$ specification; (ii) the *entailment relation* $\sqsubseteq^p$ (see Def. 10) between sets of constrained configurations in $\mathcal{A}_1$ is a *well quasi ordering*.

Point (ii) is based on the notion of well and better quasi orderings [1,4] (the proof is available in the extended version of the paper). As a consequence, we obtain the following result.

Theorem 1. The backward reachability algorithm of Section 5 is guaranteed to terminate when taking as input an $\mathrm{MSR}_1(\mathrm{NC})$ specification and a set $\mathbf{U} \subseteq \mathcal{A}_1$.

The formulation of the ticket protocol for the multi-server system requires predicates with at least two arguments. Therefore, it seems natural to ask whether it is possible to extend Theorem 1 to the general case of arbitrary arity. However, the entailment relation $\sqsubseteq^m$ (see Def. 9) between NC-constrained multisets in which atoms have arbitrary arity is not a *well quasi ordering*. The counterexample to the well quasi ordering of $\sqsubseteq^m$ is as follows. Consider the sequence of constrained configurations $M_2, \ldots, M_i, \ldots$ such that M_i is defined as $p(x_1, x_2) \mid \ldots \mid p(x_{2*i-1}, x_{2*i}) : x_2 = x_3, \ldots, x_{2*i-2} = x_{2*i-1}, x_{2*i} = x_1$. Every constrained configuration in the sequence implicitly defines a *simple cyclic* relation with i edges. The well quasi ordering would imply for a subgraph of a simple cycle of order i to be isomorphic to a simple cycle of order $j < i$. The key point here is the possibility of using predicates in combination with NC-constraints to form cyclic relations. One possible way of avoiding potential circularities consists in restricting the form of constraints as follows.

Definition 14 (The Class $MSR_n(NC_n)$). It consists of predicates with at most arity n, and rules annotated with special NC-constraints having the following form: $\varphi \in NC_n$ iff φ can be partitioned in the subconstraints $\varphi_1 \ldots \varphi_n$, where φ_i contains only variables that occur in position i (arguments are ordered from left-to-right).

We will call $\mathcal{A}_n$ the class of NC_n-constrained configurations. As an example, the constrained configuration $p(\mathbf{y_1}) \mid p(\mathbf{x_1}, x_2) \mid q(\mathbf{w_1}, w_2) : \mathbf{y_1} > \mathbf{x_1} \wedge \mathbf{x_1} > \mathbf{w_1} \wedge x_2 > w_2$ is in $\mathcal{A}_2$, whereas $p(\mathbf{x_1}, x_2) \mid q(\mathbf{w_1}, w_2) : \mathbf{x_1} > w_2$ is not. Then, the following properties hold.

Lemma 2. (i) The class $\mathcal{A}_n$ is closed under applications of **Pre** for an $MSR_n(NC_n)$ specification; (ii) the *entailment relation* $\sqsubseteq^p$ (see Def. 10) between sets of constrained configurations in $\mathcal{A}_n$ is a *well quasi ordering*.

Point (ii) is based again on the notion of well and better quasi orderings [1,4]. As a consequence, we obtain the following result.

Theorem 2. The backward reachability algorithm of Section 5 is guaranteed to terminate when taking as input an $MSR_n(NC_n)$ specification and a set $\mathbf{U} \subseteq \mathcal{A}_n$.

6.1   Automated Abstraction Procedures

By exploiting the property that NC-constraints are a subclass of DC-constraints, we can enforce *termination* via the following abstraction.

Let $\# \in \{>, =, \geq\}$. The abstraction α from DC- to NC-constraints is defined on a *satisfiable* DC-constraint as follows: $\alpha(true) = true$; $\alpha(\varphi_1 \wedge \varphi_2) = \alpha(\varphi_1) \wedge \alpha(\varphi_2)$; $\alpha(x \# y + c) = x \# y$ if $c = 0$; $\alpha(x \# y + c) = x > y$ if $c > 0$; $\alpha(x \# y+c) = y > x$ if $c < 0$ and $\#$ is $=$; $\alpha(\varphi) = true$ otherwise. Furthermore, we define $\alpha(\mathcal{M} : \varphi) = \mathcal{M} : \alpha(\varphi)$ and we extend this definition to sets of constrained configurations in the natural way.

Since $Sol(\varphi) \subseteq Sol(\alpha(\varphi))$ holds, it follows that $[\![\mathcal{M} : \varphi]\!] \subseteq [\![\alpha(\mathcal{M} : \varphi)]\!]$, and $[\![\mathbf{S}]\!] \subseteq [\![\alpha(\mathbf{S})]\!]$. If we define $\mathbf{Pre}_\alpha = \alpha \circ \mathbf{Pre}$, we have that $\mathbf{Pre}_\alpha$ gives us a conservative approximation of **Pre** when applied to an abstraction (via α) of a set of DC-constrained configurations, i.e. $[\![\mathbf{Pre}(\mathbf{S})]\!] \subseteq [\![\mathbf{Pre}_\alpha(\alpha(\mathbf{S}))]\!]$. As a consequence, we have the following property.

Proposition 2. *Let* $\mathbf{U}$ *be a set of* DC-*constrained configurations and* $\mathcal{I}$ *be the initial configurations, then* $\mathcal{I} \cap [\![\mathbf{Pre}_\alpha^*(\alpha(\mathbf{U}))]\!] = \emptyset$ *implies* $\mathcal{I} \cap [\![\mathbf{Pre}^*(\mathbf{U})]\!] = \emptyset$.

This observation leads us to a new backward reachability algorithm obtained by *interleaving* every application of **Pre** with the application of the abstraction α. Termination is guaranteed by Theorems 1 and 2.

7   Verification of the Parameterized Ticket Protocol

We have verified *mutual exclusion* for both models of the ticket protocol presented in Section 2. According to Section 4, the set of violations can be represented through the constrained configurations $use(x)|use(y) : true$ for the single-server formulation, and $use(id, x)|use(id', y) : id = id'$ for the multi-server one. Thanks to the results of Section 6 and using the abstraction α of Section 6.1, our procedure is guaranteed to terminate (*symbolic state explosion* permitting). In Fig. 7, we describe the experimental results obtained using both the concrete (based on **Pre**) and abstract (based on $\mathbf{Pre}_\alpha$) backward reachability, on the specifications given in Section 3.1. In Fig. 7, $\sqrt{}$ indicates that the abstraction α or the pruning technique based on static analysis has been applied after each application of the symbolic predecessor operator; $\uparrow$ indicates that the procedure was still computing after several hours. Furthermore, **Steps** denotes the number of iterations needed to reach a fixpoint (before stopping the program); **Size** the number of constrained configurations contained in the fixpoint (when the program was stopped); and **Time** the execution time (in seconds). The backward search engine with DC-solver described in Fig. 6 has been implemented in ML and tested on the interpreter for Standard ML of New Jersey, version 110.0.7. All experiments have been executed on a Pentium III 450 Mhz, Linux 2.2.13-0.9. As shown in Fig. 7, using the abstract (theoretically always terminating) backward reachability algorithm we managed to prove all safety properties we were interested in (we prune the search space using the invariants discussed in Section 5). Furthermore, we managed to prove mutual exclusion without pruning the search for the first model, whereas it was necessary to cut the search space using structural invariants in the second example in order to avoid the state explosion problem. Note that pruning techniques do not introduce any kind of approximations, in fact, when used without α the fixpoint computation does not terminate as when executed on the pure symbolic algorithm. In an additional series of experiments, we verified again both models adding the structural invariants to the unsafe states. This technique is perfectly sound and, basically, it has the same effect as dynamic pruning.

8   Related Works

This work is inspired to the approach of [2,4]. In [2], Abdulla and Jonsson proposed an assertional language for Timed Petri Nets in which they use dedicated data structures to symbolically represent markings parametric in the number of tokens and in the *age* (a real number) associated to tokens. In [4], Abdulla and Nylén formulate a symbolic algorithm using *existential regions* to represent the state-space of Timed Petri Nets. Our approach generalizes the ideas of [2,4] to problems and constraint systems that do not depend on the notion of *time*. Following [4], we use the technique of better quasi orderings to build new classes of well quasi ordered symbolic representations. In [3], the authors apply similar ideas to (unbounded) channel systems in which messages can vary over an infinite *name* domain and can be stored in a finite (and fixed a priori) number of data variables; however, individual processes have finite-state control structures.

Ticket Specification	Seed	α	Prune	Steps	Size	Time	Verified?
Multi-client, Single-server (Fig. 2, Section 3.1)	U_s			$\uparrow$	--	--	--
	U_s		$\sqrt{}$	$\uparrow$	--	--	--
	U_s	$\sqrt{}$		17	222	$150s$	yes
	U_s	$\sqrt{}$	$\sqrt{}$	10	32	$< 1s$	yes
	$U_s \oplus I_s$	$\sqrt{}$		10	34	$< 1s$	yes
Multi-client, Multi-server (Fig. 4, Section 3.1)	U_m			$\uparrow$	--	--	--
	U_m		$\sqrt{}$	$\uparrow$	--	--	--
	U_m	$\sqrt{}$		> 18	> 3500	$> 4h$	--
	U_m	$\sqrt{}$	$\sqrt{}$	19	141	$15s$	yes
	$U_m \oplus I_m$	$\sqrt{}$		19	147	$19s$	yes

Unsafe states
$U_s \equiv \{ use(x) \mid use(y) : true \}$
$U_m \equiv \{ use(id,x) \mid use(id',y) : id = id' \}$

Structural invariants
$I_s \equiv \{ count(x) \mid count(y) : true, \quad turn(x) \mid turn(y) : true \}$
$I_m \equiv \{ count(id,x) \mid count(id',y) : id = id', \quad turn(id,x) \mid turn(id',y) : id = id',$
$\quad demon(id) \mid demon(id') : true \}$

Fig. 7. Analysis of the ticket protocol.

For networks of *finite-state* processes, it is important to mention the automata theoretic approach to parameterized verification followed, e.g., in [7,6, 20,21,22,23]. In this setting the set of possible *local states* of individual processes are abstracted into a *finite alphabet*. Sets of global states are represented then as *regular languages*, and transitions as relations on languages. Symbolic exploration can then be performed using operations over automata with ad hoc accelerations (see e.g. [7,20,23]), or with automated abstractions techniques (see e.g. [6]). Differently from the automata theoretic approach, in our setting we handle parameterized systems in which individual components have local variables that range over *unbounded* values. As an example, in our model of the ticket algorithm local variables and tickets range over unbounded integers. Furthermore, note that the abstraction with NC-constraints as target does not make the resulting symbolic representation finite. Nevertheless, termination can be guaranteed by applying the theory of well quasi ordering. This way, we do not have to apply *manual abstractions* to describe individual processes. This is an important aspect to take into account when comparing our results for the single-server model with those obtained in [20,22], in which an *idealized* version of the *ticket algorithm* has been verified using the regular model checking method (actually, a real comparison is difficult here because the verified model is not described in [20,22]). The previous features also distinguish our approach from the *verification with invisible invariants* method of [5]. Invisible invariants have been applied to automatically verify a *restricted* version of the parameterized *bakery* algorithm in which a special *reducing process* is needed to force the value of the tickets to stay within a given range. Our ideas are related to previous works connecting Constraint Logic Programming and verification, see e.g. [12,

18]. In this setting transition systems are encoded via CLP programs used to encode the *global* state of a system and its updates. We refine this idea by using multiset rewriting and constraints to *locally* specify updates to the *global* state. The notion of *constrained multiset* extends that of *constrained atom* of [12]. The *locality* of rules allows us to consider *rich* denotations (upward-closures) instead of *flat* ones (instances) like, e.g., in [12]. This way, we can lift the approach to the parameterized case. In [16] a combination of transformation of logic programs and of weak monadic second order logic has been applied to verify a parameterized formulation of the bakery algorithm. The proof however is done manually, furthermore, even if implemented, the method is not guaranteed to terminate. Finally, the use of *constraints, backward reachability, structural invariants* and *better quasi orderings* seem all ingredients that distinguish our *hybrid* method from classical approaches based on multiset and AC rewriting techniques (see e.g. [9,24]).

9   Conclusions

In this paper we have presented a sound and fully automated method to attack verification of parameterized systems with unbounded local data. Sufficient conditions for termination are given for new classes of infinite-state systems. The method is powered by using static analysis techniques coming from the structural theory of Petri Nets and by automatic abstractions working on constraints. As a practical application, we have automatically verified (as far as we know for the first time) a very general formulation of the *ticket* mutual exclusion protocol in which we allow many clients, many servers, and unbounded local variables. A formulation of the *single-server* ticket algorithm with 2 processes, but unbounded global and local variables, has been automatically verified using constraint-based model checkers equipped with a Presburger constraint solver [8], and a *real arithmetic* one [12]. However, we are not aware of other methods that can *automatically* handle the *parameterized* models of Section 3.1 in their generality.

Acknowledgment. We would like to thank Moshe Vardi, Parosh A. Abdulla, Bengt Jonsson, the people at VEPAS 2001, and James Larus and Microsoft Research for having supported our research in the last two years.

References

1. P. A. Abdulla, K. Cerāns, B. Jonsson, and Y.-K. Tsay. General Decidability Theorems for Infinite-State Systems. In *Proc. LICS'96*, pp. 313–321, 1996.
2. P. A. Abdulla and B. Jonsson. Verifying Networks of Timed Processes. In *Proc. TACAS'98, LNCS 1384*, pp. 298–312, 1998.
3. P. A. Abdulla and B. Jonsson. Channel Representations in Protocol Verification. In *Proc. CONCUR'2001, LNCS 2154*, p. 1–15, 2001.
4. P. A. Abdulla and A. Nylén. Better is Better than Well: On Efficient Verification of Infinite-State Systems. In *Proc. LICS'00*, pp. 132–140, 2000.

5. T. Arons, A. Pnueli, S. Ruah, Y. Xu, and L. D. Zuck. Parameterized Verification with Automatically Computed Inductive Assertions. In *Proc. CAV'01, LNCS* 2102, pp. 221–234, 2001.

6. K. Baukus, S. Bensalem, Y. Lakhnech, and K. Stahl. Abstracting WS1S Systems to Verify Parameterized Networks. In *Proc. TACAS'00, LNCS* 1785, pp. 188–203, 2000.

7. A. Bouajjani, B. Jonsson, M. Nilsson, and T. Touili. Regular Model Checking. In *Proc. CAV'00, LNCS* 1855, pp. 403–418, 2000.

8. T. Bultan, R. Gerber, and W. Pugh. Symbolic Model Checking of Infinite State Systems Using Presburger Arithmetics. In *Proc. CAV'97, LNCS* 1254, pp. 400–411, 1997.

9. I. Cervesato, N.A. Durgin, P.D. Lincoln, J.C. Mitchell, and A. Scedrov. A Meta-notation for Protocol Analysis. In *Proc. CSFW'99*, p. 55–69, 1999.

10. G. Delzanno. Automatic Verification of Parameterized Cache Coherence Protocols. In *Proc. CAV'00, LNCS* 1855, pp. 53–68, 2000.

11. G. Delzanno. An Assertional Language for Systems Parametric in Several Dimensions. In *Proc. VEPAS '01, ENTCS* volume 50, issue 4, 2001.

12. G. Delzanno and A. Podelski. Model checking in CLP. In *Proc. TACAS'99, LNCS* 1579, pp. 223–239, 1999.

13. G. Delzanno, J.-F. Raskin, and L. Van Begin. Attacking Symbolic State Explosion. In *Proc. CAV'01, LNCS* 2102, pp. 298–310, 2001.

14. E.A. Emerson and K.S. Namjoshi. On Model Checking for Non-Deterministic Infinite-State Systems. In *Proc. LICS'98*, pp. 70–80, 1998.

15. J. Esparza, A. Finkel, and R. Mayr. On the Verification of Broadcast Protocols. In *Proc. LICS'99*, pp. 352–359, 1999.

16. F. Fioravanti, A. Pettorossi, M. Proietti. Verifcation of Sets of Infinite State Systems Using Program Transformation. In *Proc. LOPSTR'01*, pp. 55-66, 2001.

17. A. Finkel and P. Schnoebelen. Well-Structured Transition Systems Everywhere! *Theoretical Computer Science*, 256(1-2):63–92, 2001.

18. L. Fribourg. Constraint Logic Programming Applied to Model Checking. In *Proc. LOPSTR'99, LNCS* 1817, pp. 30–41, 1999.

19. S. M. German and A. P. Sistla. Reasoning about Systems with Many Processes. *Journal of the ACM*, 39(3):675–735, 1992.

20. B. Jonsson and M. Nilsson. Transitive Closures of Regular Relations for Verifying Infinite-State Systems. In *Proc. TACAS'00, LNCS* 1785, pp. 220–234, 2000.

21. Y. Kesten, O. Maler, M. Marcus, A. Pnueli, and E. Shahar. Symbolic model checking with rich assertional languages. In *Proc. CAV'97, LNCS* 1254, pp. 424–435, 1997.

22. M. Nilsson. *Regular Model Checking*. PhD thesis, Department of Information Technology, Uppsala University, 2000.

23. A. Pnueli and E. Shahar. Liveness and Acceleration in Parameterized Verification. In *Proc. CAV'00, LNCS* 1855, pp. 328–343, 2000.

24. M. Rusinowitch and L. Vigneron. Automated Deduction with Associative and Commutative Operators. *Applicable Algebra in Engineering, Communication and Computing*, 6:23–56, 1995.

Resource-Constrained Model Checking of Recursive Programs*

Samik Basu[1], K. Narayan Kumar[1,2], L. Robert Pokorny[1], and
C.R. Ramakrishnan[1]

[1] Department of Computer Science,
State University of New York at Stony Brook
Stony Brook, New York, U.S.A.
{bsamik,kumar,pokorny,cram}@cs.sunysb.edu
[2] Chennai Mathematical Institute, Chennai, India.
kumar@smi.ernet.in

Abstract. A number of recent papers present efficient algorithms for LTL model checking for recursive programs with finite data structures. A common feature in all these works is that they consider infinitely long runs of the program without regard to the size of the program stack. Runs requiring unbounded stack are often a result of abstractions done to obtain a finite-data recursive program. In this paper, we introduce the notion of resource-constrained model checking where we distinguish between stack-diverging runs and finite-stack runs. It should be noted that finiteness of stack-like resources cannot be expressed in LTL. We develop resource-constrained model checking in terms of good cycle detection in a finite graph called R-graph, which is constructed from a given push-down system (PDS) and a Büchi automaton. We make the formulation of the model checker "executable" by encoding it directly as Horn clauses. We present a local algorithm to detect a good cycle in an R-graph. Furthermore, by describing the construction of R-graph as a logic program and evaluating it using tabled resolution, we do model checking without materializing the push-down system or the induced R-graph. Preliminary experiments indicate that the local model checker is at least as efficient as existing model checkers for push-down systems.

1 Introduction

Model checking is a widely used technique for verifying whether a system specification possesses a property expressed as a temporal logic formula [7,8,14]. Most early works on model checking have restricted system specifications to be finite state. A number of recent works have addressed the problem of model checking push-down processes with finite alphabets, which are natural models for recursive programs operating on finite data structures (e.g. [12,4,10,5,3]).

* This work was supported in part by NSF grants EIA-9705998, CCR-9876242, EIA-9805735, N000140110967, and IIS-0072927.

J.-P. Katoen and P. Stevens (Eds.): TACAS 2002, LNCS 2280, pp. 236–250, 2002.
© Springer-Verlag Berlin Heidelberg 2002

```
bool g;                     procedure flip() {      void flip(N) {
procedure main() {            if (g) {                int (0..7) i;
  g = false;                   if (*) {               if (g) {
  while (true) {                 flip();                i = 0;
    flip();                      flip();                while (i < 7) i++;
    flip();                    }}                     } else if (N > 0) {
    if (!g)                    g = !g;                  flip(N - 1);
reach:  skip                   return;                  flip(N - 1);
  }                          }                        }
}                                                     g = !g;
                                                      return;
                                                    }

     (a)                         (b)                         (c)
```

Fig. 1. Recursive programs with finite-domain variables

In this paper, we consider the problem of LTL model checking of recursive programs. Models of LTL formulas are usually described in terms of infinite runs of a system. For push-down systems, the stacks may diverge on some infinite runs, indicating runs not realizable in any implementation of the system. In fact, stack-diverging runs may be an artifact of abstractions performed to obtain finite-data recursive programs. Such abstractions are often performed to obtain a single program that represents the behaviors of an infinite family of programs. For instance, consider the finite-domain program shown in Fig. 1(a) and (b). The example was derived from ones used in [2] and [11]. The procedure flip() in Fig. 1(b) is an abstraction of procedure flip(N) in Fig. 1(c) (from [11]). In the program, the statement if (*)... indicates a non-deterministic choice, the result of abstracting away the conditional expression.

The need for resource-constrained model checking.   For the program in Fig. 1(a,b) consider the verification of the LTL property AGF reach starting from a state representing the first statement in procedure main. This property does not hold since the program has a run where it keeps recursively invoking flip. However, such a run is clearly unfeasible in any concrete implementation of the program, since the program stack grows without bound.

It is hence natural to restrict our attention to runs where the stacks remain finite. However, traditional mechanisms to restrict the runs under consideration such as adding fairness constraints cannot be used to capture stack-finiteness: separating a run that involves infinite number of unmatched pushes from the rest cannot be done using a regular language.

Returning to the example in Fig. 1(a,b), observe that the property AGF reach holds for every run that consumes only a finite stack. It is easy to see that flip, whenever it terminates, negates the global variable g. Hence two consecutive calls to flip leave g unchanged, making reach true in every iteration of the loop in main. Since flip terminates if and only if the program stack remains finite, AGF reach holds on all finite-stack runs.

Our approach.   In this paper, we describe a model checker, called *resource-constrained model checker*, that separates the finite-stack runs from stack-diverging runs. Our technique can determine that AGF **reach** holds for all finite-stack runs of the program in Fig. 1(a,b), while there are stack-diverging runs that violate the property. We give a brief overview of our technique below. For simplicity we assume in the following that the push-down system has a single control state: i.e., a context-free process. Our formal development in the later sections considers general push-down systems.

Given a push-down system $\mathcal{P}$ and a Büchi automaton $\mathcal{B}$ (corresponding to the given LTL property), we develop a model checker as follows. We first build a *finite* graph $\mathcal{R}$, called the *R-graph*, that abstracts the product of $\mathcal{P}$ and $\mathcal{B}$. The nodes of $\mathcal{R}$ are labeled with pairs (b, γ), where γ is a stack alphabet of $\mathcal{P}$ and b is a state in $\mathcal{B}$. Edges in $\mathcal{R}$ are labeled with a *goodness* label (*true* or *false*) and a *resource* label (0 or 1).

Intuitively, an edge in $\mathcal{R}$, say from (b, γ) to (b', γ') corresponds to a finite sequence of moves that take $\mathcal{P}$ from a configuration with γ on top of stack to one with γ' on top of stack, and correspondingly moves $\mathcal{B}$ from state b to state b'. The edge is *good* (i.e. its goodness label is *true*) if and only if there is some good state in $\mathcal{B}$ that is visited in that corresponding run in $\mathcal{B}$ from b to b'. The resource label on the edge is 0 if the corresponding run in $\mathcal{P}$ leaves the size of the stack unchanged; the resource label is 1 if the stack size increases by 1.

An accepting path in $\mathcal{R}$ is an infinite path where good edges appear infinitely often and only finitely many edges have resource label 1. We show that there is an accepting path in $\mathcal{R}$ if, and only if, there is a finite-stack run of $\mathcal{P}$ accepted by $\mathcal{B}$. The R-graph is analogous to the automaton A_{br} described in [12]. However, the resource labels of $\mathcal{R}$ distinguish between finite-stack and stack-diverging runs of $\mathcal{P}$. Thus, ignoring the resource labels in the acceptance criterion of $\mathcal{R}$, we obtain a model checker that is, in concept, equivalent to the ones previously defined in the literature [4,10,12,11]. Although R-graph has much in common with techniques described in these works in terms of formulation, our implementation strategy is substantially different, as described below.

Contributions.

- We introduce the notion of resource-constrained model checking of push-down systems. We formulate this problem in terms of good cycle detection in R-graph, a finite graph.
- We develop the R-graph $\mathcal{R}$ so that the equations defining the edge relation can be readily specified as a Horn-clause logic program (Section 3). The transition relation of $\mathcal{R}$ can be computed on the fly based on the transition relations of $\mathcal{P}$ and $\mathcal{B}$, which may themselves be derived from more basic procedures (such as LTL tableaus for Büchi automata construction).
- We present a local good-cycle detection algorithm based on Tarjan's algorithm [18] along the lines of [9], to handle the unique acceptance criteria of R-graph. The local algorithm detects good cycles as early as possible, ensuring that we explore only those transitions in $\mathcal{P}$ and $\mathcal{B}$ needed to complete the proof (Section 4). By evaluating these programs using the XSB logic programming system [19], we get a local, on-the-fly model checker.

– We show that, using tabled resolution, the model checker runs in $O(c \times b^3 \times 2^{g+l})$ time (where c is the size of program's control flow graph, b the size of Büchi automaton and g and l are the maximum number of global and local variables) and $O(c \times b^2 \times 2^{g+l})$ space. Our experiments show that our model checker is at least as efficient in practice as described in earlier literature, including the symbolic model checkers (Section 4).

We begin with a review of LTL model checking for push-down systems ignoring resource constraints.

2   Model Checking Push-Down Systems

In this section we give an overview of model checking push-down systems (PDS). PDSs can be used to model programs with procedures and can be extracted from the control flow graphs of programs. For details refer to [11].

Preliminaries.   A PDS is a triple $\mathcal{P} = (P, \Gamma, \Delta)$ where P is a finite set of *control locations*, Γ is a finite set of *stack alphabets* and $\Delta \subseteq (P \times \Gamma) \times (P \times \Gamma^*)$ is a finite set of *transition rules*. We shall use γ, γ' etc. to denote elements of Γ and use u, v, w etc. to denote elements of Γ^*. We write $\langle p, \gamma \rangle \hookrightarrow \langle p', w \rangle$ to mean that $((p, \gamma), (p', w)) \in \Delta$.

We restrict ourselves to PDSs such that for every rule $\langle p, \gamma \rangle \hookrightarrow \langle p', w \rangle$, $|w| \leq 2$; any PDS can be put into such a form with linear size increase.

A *configuration* or *state* of $\mathcal{P}$ is a pair $\langle p, w \rangle$ where $p \in P$ is a control location and $w \in \Gamma^*$ is a stack content. If $\langle p, \gamma \rangle \hookrightarrow \langle p', w \rangle$, then $\forall v \in \Gamma^*$ the configuration $\langle p', wv \rangle$ is an immediate successor of $\langle p, \gamma v \rangle$. Then we say $\langle p, \gamma v \rangle$ has a transition to $\langle p', wv \rangle$ and denote it by $\langle p, \gamma v \rangle \rightarrow \langle p', wv \rangle$. A *run* of $\mathcal{P}$ is a sequence of the form $\langle p_0, w_0 \rangle, \langle p_1, w_1 \rangle, \ldots, \langle p_n, w_n \rangle, \ldots$ where $\langle p_i, w_i \rangle \rightarrow \langle p_{i+1}, w_{i+1} \rangle$ for all $i \geq 0$. A run denotes a finite or an infinite run.

A *Büchi automaton* is defined as $(Q, \longrightarrow, \Sigma, Q_0, F)$ where Q is the finite set of states, $\longrightarrow \subseteq (Q \times \Sigma \times Q)$, Σ is the set of edge labels, $Q_0 \subseteq Q$ is the set of start states and $F \subseteq Q$ is the set of final states. An accepting run in the automaton is defined to be a sequence $q_0 \xrightarrow{\sigma_0} q_1 \xrightarrow{\sigma_1} \ldots \xrightarrow{\sigma_{k-1}} q_k \ldots$ with $q_0 \in Q_0$ where $q_k \in F$ appears infinitely many times.

A *Büchi PDS* is defined as $(P_{bp}, P_0, \Gamma_{bp}, \Delta_{bp}, G_{bp})$ where P_{bp} is the finite set of control locations, $P_0 \in P_{bp}$ is the set of starting control location, Γ_{bp} is the set of stack alphabets, $\Delta_{bp} \subseteq (P_{bp} \times \Gamma_{bp}) \times (P_{bp} \times \Gamma_{bp}^*)$ and $G_{bp} \subseteq P_{bp}$ is the set of good control locations. The subscript bp may be dropped whenever it is obvious from the context. An accepting run in the Büchi PDS is defined to be an infinite sequence where configurations with control locations $\in G_{bp}$ appear infinitely many times.

Let *Prop* be a finite set of propositions. Given a linear time temporal logic (LTL) formula ϕ over *Prop*, as is well known, one can construct a Büchi automaton with $\Sigma = 2^{Prop}$ that accepts the models of the formula ϕ.

Our aim is to verify PDSs against properties expressed as LTL formulas. Let $\mathcal{P} = (P, \Gamma, \Delta)$ be a PDS, and let $\lambda : (P \times \Gamma) \rightarrow \Sigma$ be a labeling function. The truth of a proposition at a configuration is determined by the control location and the symbol at the top of the stack in that configuration. Thus, any (infinite) run of $\mathcal{P}$ defines a model for LTL over *Prop*.

In order to solve the model checking problem for PDSs, i.e. determine whether (the model defined by) every run of $\mathcal{P}$ satisfies ϕ, it is sufficient to construct the Büchi automaton $\mathcal{B}$ corresponding to $\neg\phi$ and verify that no run of $\mathcal{P}$ is accepted by that Büchi automaton. This is done by constructing the product of $\mathcal{P}$ and $\mathcal{B}$ resulting in a Büchi PDS $\mathcal{BP}$ and verifying that it accepts the empty language. The definition of the system $\mathcal{BP}$ is as follows:

1. $P_{bp} = (P \times Q)$
2. $P_0 = \{(p,q) \in P_{bp} \mid q \in Q_0\}$
3. $\Gamma_{bp} = \Gamma$
4. $\Delta_{bp} = \{\langle(p,q),\gamma\rangle, \langle(p',q'),w\rangle \mid \langle p,\gamma\rangle \hookrightarrow \langle p,w\rangle, q \xrightarrow{\alpha} q', \text{ and } \alpha \subseteq \lambda(p,\gamma)\}$
5. $G_{bp} = \{(p,q) \mid q \in F\}$

In what follows we use $\hookrightarrow$ to denote a transition rule in Δ_{bp} of $\mathcal{BP}$.

Definition 1 *Given a Büchi PDS $\mathcal{BP}$, we say that p_1 can weakly erase γ and get to p_2 (written $(p_1,\gamma,p_2) \in$ Werase) if there is a run starting at the configuration $\langle p_1,\gamma\rangle$ and ending at $\langle p_2,\epsilon\rangle$. We say that p_1 can strongly erase γ and get to p_2 (written $(p_1,\gamma,p_2) \in$ Serase) if there is a run starting at the configuration $\langle p_1,\gamma\rangle$ and ending at $\langle p_2,\epsilon\rangle$ in which at least one of the intermediate control states belongs to G.*

Proposition 1. *Let* Erase *be the least relation satisfying:*

1. $(p_1,\gamma_1,g,p') \in$ Erase *if* $\langle p_1,\gamma_1\rangle \hookrightarrow \langle p',\epsilon\rangle, g \equiv p_1 \in G$
2. $(p_1,\gamma_1,(g \vee g'),p') \in$ Erase *if* $\langle p_1,\gamma_1\rangle \hookrightarrow \langle p,\gamma\rangle$ *and* $(p,\gamma,g',p') \in$ Erase*,* $g \equiv p_1 \in G$
3. $(p_1,\gamma_1,(g \vee g' \vee g''),p'') \in$ Erase *if* $\langle p_1,\gamma_1\rangle \hookrightarrow \langle p,\gamma\gamma_2\rangle$, $(p,\gamma,g',p') \in$ Erase *and* $(p',\gamma_2,g'',p'') \in$ Erase*,* $g \equiv p_1 \in G$

Then, $(p,\gamma,p') \in$ Werase *iff* $(p,\gamma,g,p') \in$ Erase *for some g and* $(p,\gamma,p') \in$ Serase *iff* $(p,\gamma,true,p') \in$ Erase*. Thus,* Serase *and* Werase *are computable.*

In what follows, we shall often write Erase(x,y,z) instead of $(x,y,z) \in$ Erase.

Erase corresponds to $pre^*(P)$ in [10]. Since Erase is the least fixed point of its defining equations, the following corollary is immediate.

Corollary 1. *There is an integer k such that, for any pair of control locations p,p' and any stack symbol γ whenever $(p,\gamma,p') \in$ Werase(Serase)*, *there is witnessing run from (p,γ) to (p',ϵ) in which the size of the stack is bounded by k.*

The Erase relation for the Büchi PDS in Fig. 2(a) is given in Fig. 2(b).

Definition 2 *Given a Büchi PDS $\mathcal{BP}$, we associate with it two binary relations $\xrightarrow{W}$ and $\xrightarrow{S}$, over the set $P \times \Gamma$, as follows: $(p, \gamma) \xrightarrow{W} (p', \gamma')$ iff there is a run from $\langle p, \gamma \rangle$ to $\langle p', \gamma'w \rangle$ for some $w \in \Gamma^*$. $(p, \gamma) \xrightarrow{S} (p', \gamma')$ iff there is a run from $\langle p, \gamma \rangle$ to $\langle p', \gamma'w \rangle$, for some $w \in \Gamma^*$, that visits at least one configuration whose control location belongs to G.*

Proposition 2. *Let the relation $\Longrightarrow \subseteq P \times \Gamma \times \{false, true\} \times P \times \Gamma$ be the least relation satisfying:*

1. $(p_1, \gamma_1) \overset{p_1 \in G}{\Longrightarrow} (p', \gamma')$ if $\langle p_1, \gamma_1 \rangle \hookrightarrow \langle p', \gamma \rangle$
2. $(p_1, \gamma_1) \overset{p_1 \in G}{\Longrightarrow} (p', \gamma')$ if $\langle p_1, \gamma_1 \rangle \hookrightarrow \langle p', \gamma'\gamma'' \rangle$
3. $(p_1, \gamma_1) \overset{p_1 \in G \vee g}{\Longrightarrow} (p', \gamma')$ if $\langle p_1, \gamma_1 \rangle \hookrightarrow \langle p, \gamma\gamma' \rangle$ and $\mathsf{Erase}(p, \gamma, g, p')$

Then, $(p, \gamma) \xrightarrow{W} (p', \gamma')$ iff $(p, \gamma) \Longrightarrow^* (p', \gamma')$ and $(p, \gamma) \xrightarrow{S} (p', \gamma')$ iff $(p, \gamma) \Longrightarrow^* \overset{true}{\Longrightarrow} \Longrightarrow^* (p', \gamma')$ where $\Longrightarrow = \overset{false}{\Longrightarrow} \cup \overset{true}{\Longrightarrow}$.
Thus the relations $\xrightarrow{S}$ and $\xrightarrow{W}$ are computable.

The following theorem, [12], shows that, given the above proposition, the emptiness problem for any Büchi push-down system is decidable. We present the proof here since its details inspire the definition of resource constrained model checking (Section 3).

Theorem 1 *A Büchi PDS $\mathcal{BP}$ accepts some word iff there are p, γ, p', γ' such that $p \in P_0, (p, \gamma) \xrightarrow{W} (p', \gamma')$ and $(p', \gamma') \xrightarrow{S} (p', \gamma')$.*

Proof : The following observation is useful.

Observation: If $\langle p_0, \gamma_0 w_0 \rangle \xrightarrow{*} \langle p_n, \gamma_n w_n \rangle$ is a run where for each i with $0 \leq i \leq n$, $|\gamma_i w_i| \geq |\gamma_0 w_0|$, then $(p_0, \gamma_0) \xrightarrow{W} (p_n, \gamma_n)$ and further if this run involves a configuration with $p_i \in G$ then $(p_0, \gamma_0) \xrightarrow{S} (p_n, \gamma_n)$. (In either case given run itself serves as a witness to this membership.)

Let the accepting run of $\mathcal{BP}$ be $S = \langle p_0, \gamma_0 \rangle, \langle p_1, \gamma_1 w_1 \rangle, \ldots \langle p_n, \gamma_n w_n \rangle \ldots$. The proof proceeds by considering two cases.

Case 1: For any integer d the set $\{w_i \mid |w_i| = d\}$ is finite(i.e. the stack size grows "monotonically").

Let i_d be the largest integer such that $|w_{i_d}| = d$. Clearly, i_d is monotonic on d. Let $\langle q_i, \gamma_i v_i \rangle = \langle p_{d_i}, w_{d_i} \rangle$, $\forall i \geq 1$. Then, $\langle q_i, \gamma_i \rangle \xrightarrow{*} \langle q_j, \gamma_j w_j \rangle$ $\forall j > i$ via the subrun of the given run and further at every point in this run the size of the stack is at least $|\gamma_i v_i|$. Thus, by the above observation, $(q_i, \gamma_i) \xrightarrow{W} (q_j, \gamma_j)$ $\forall i < j$. Further since the set of control locations and the stack alphabet are finite, there must be an infinite sequence $j_1, j_2, \ldots$ with $q' = q_{j_1} = q_{j_2} = \ldots$ and $\gamma' = \gamma_{j_1} = \gamma_{j_2} = \ldots$ and clearly there is a k such that in the subrun from $\langle q_{j_1}, \gamma_{j_1} v_{j_1} \rangle$ to $\langle q_{j_k}, \gamma_{j_k} v_{j_k} \rangle$ at least one of the intermediate configurations involves a control location from G. Thus, from the above observation $(q', \gamma') \xrightarrow{S} (q', \gamma')$. Once again using the above observation, $(p, \gamma) \overset{W}{\longmapsto} (q_i, \gamma_i)$ for each $i \geq 0$ and hence $(p, \gamma) \overset{W}{\longmapsto} (q', \gamma')$ and this completes the proof of this case.

Case 2: Otherwise, there is a least d such that there are infinitely many i with $|w_i| = d$. Then, clearly there is an N such that $\forall j \geq N \; |w_j| \geq d$. Therefore, there is an infinite sequence $j_1 < j_2 < \ldots$, with $d < j_1$ with $|w_{j_i}| = d$. Let $w_{j_i} = \gamma_{j_i} v_{j_i}$. Further, there is a sequence $j_1 < j_2 < \ldots$ such that $q' = q_{j_1} = q_{j_2} = \ldots$ and $\gamma' = \gamma_{j_1} = \gamma_{j_2} = \ldots$. Once again, using the above observation (since the size of the stack at any configuration beginning at $\langle q_{j_1}, \gamma_{j_1} \rangle \geq d$) we conclude that $(q', \gamma') \overset{S}{\longmapsto} (q', \gamma')$ and the proof follows as above.

For the converse, $(p, \gamma) \overset{W}{\longmapsto} (p', \gamma')$ and $(p', \gamma') \overset{S}{\longmapsto} (p', \gamma')$, then it is easy to see that there is an accepting run of the form $\langle p = p_1, \gamma = \gamma_1 \rangle \overset{*}{\to} \langle p', \gamma' v_0 \rangle \overset{*}{\to} \langle p', \gamma' v_1 v_0 \rangle \overset{*}{\to} \langle p', \gamma' v_1 v_1 v_0 \rangle \ldots$. $\qquad \square$

3   Resource-Constrained Model Checking

In Section 2, an accepting sequence in $\mathcal{BP}$ is defined without regard to the size of the stack in that sequence. This allows accepting sequences where the stack may diverge denoting an unfeasible run in any implementation of the program modeled by a PDS $\mathcal{P}$. We now focus only on runs where the stack size remains finite. We call the problem of determining whether a Büchi PDS has a finite-stack accepting run as the resource constrained model checking problem. Note that we do not bound the stack size *a priori* but consider all runs that have finite stack size.

We define two relations $\overset{W}{\circ\!\!\longrightarrow}_0$ and $\overset{S}{\circ\!\!\longrightarrow}_0$ similar to those in Definition 2.

Definition 3 *Given a Büchi PDS $\mathcal{BP}$, we associate with it a binary relation $\overset{S}{\circ\!\!\longrightarrow}_0$, over the set $P \times \Gamma$, as follows: $(p, \gamma) \overset{S}{\circ\!\!\longrightarrow}_0 (p', \gamma')$ iff there is a run from $\langle p, \gamma \rangle$ to $\langle p', \gamma' \rangle$, that visits at least one configuration whose control location belongs to G. Further $\overset{S}{\circ\!\!\longrightarrow}_0$ corresponds to finite runs without net change in the stack size.*

Hence we have the following theorem.

Theorem 2 *A given Büchi PDS $\mathcal{BP}$ has a finite stack accepting run iff there is p, γ, p', γ' such that $p \in P_0, (p, \gamma) \overset{W}{\circ\!\!\longrightarrow} (p', \gamma')$ and $(p', \gamma') \overset{S}{\circ\!\!\longrightarrow}_0 (p', \gamma')$.*

In order to show that the resource constrained model checking problem is decidable we need to show that the $\overset{S}{\circ\!\!\longrightarrow}_0$ relation is computable.

Proposition 3. *Given a Büchi PDS $\mathcal{BP}$ we define a relation $\Longrightarrow_0 \subseteq P \times \Gamma \times \{false, true\} \times \{0, 1\} \times P \times \Gamma$ as the least relation satisfying:*

1. $(p_1, \gamma_1) \overset{p_1 \in G}{\Longrightarrow}_0 (p', \gamma')$ *if* $\langle p_1, \gamma_1 \rangle \hookrightarrow \langle p', \gamma' \rangle$
2. $(p_1, \gamma_1) \overset{p_1 \in G \vee g}{\Longrightarrow}_0 (p', \gamma')$ *if* $\langle p_1, \gamma_1 \rangle \hookrightarrow \langle p, \gamma\gamma' \rangle$ *and* $\mathsf{Erase}(p, \gamma, g, \; p')$

Then, $(p, \gamma) \xrightarrow{S}_0 (p', \gamma')$ iff $(p, \gamma) \Longrightarrow_0^* \overset{true}{\Longrightarrow}_0 \Longrightarrow_0^* (p', \gamma')$. Hence, $\xrightarrow{S}_0$ is computable.

Proof : Let $(p, \gamma) \xrightarrow{S}_0 (p', \gamma')$ and let $\langle p = p_1, \gamma = \gamma_1 \rangle \to \langle p_2, \gamma_2 w_2 \rangle \ldots \to \langle p' = p_n, \gamma' = \gamma_n \rangle$ be the derivation witnessing this. Thus, there is an i such that $p_i \in G$.

We show that $(p, \gamma) \Longrightarrow_0^* \overset{true}{\Longrightarrow}_0 \Longrightarrow_0^* (p', \gamma')$ by induction on n. For $n = 0$, it must be the case that $p = p'$, $\gamma = \gamma'$ and $p \in G$ and thus there is nothing to prove.

Suppose the result holds for all computations of length less than n. Now, there are two cases, if $w_2 = \epsilon$, then, by induction hypothesis, either $p \in G$ and $(p_2, \gamma_2) \Longrightarrow_0^* (p_n, \gamma_n)$ or $(p_2, \gamma_2) \Longrightarrow_0^* \overset{true}{\Longrightarrow}_0 \Longrightarrow_0^* (p_n, \gamma_n)$. In either case we have the desired result.

Now, suppose $w_2 \neq \epsilon$. Then $w_2 = \hat{\gamma}$ for some $\hat{\gamma} \in \Gamma$. By the definition of a run for a PDS, it then follows that there is a least $j > 2$ such that $\gamma_j = \hat{\gamma}$ and $w_j = \epsilon$. Thus, p_2 erases γ_2 and reaches p_j. Hence, depending on whether $1 \leq i < j$ or not, we either have $(p_1, \gamma_1) \overset{true}{\Longrightarrow}_0 (p_j, \gamma_j) \Longrightarrow_0^* (p_n, \gamma_n)$ or $(p_1, \gamma_1) \Longrightarrow_0 (p_j \gamma_j) \Longrightarrow_0^* \overset{true}{\Longrightarrow}_0 \Longrightarrow_0^* (p_n, \gamma_n)$. In either case we have the desired result.

The converse is an easy induction on the iterative definition of $\overset{g}{\Longrightarrow}_0$ and the details are omitted.   □

Theorem 2 shows that resource constrained model checking of a Büchi PDS can be reduced to checking for cycles in a graph induced by finite relations $\xrightarrow{W}$ and $\xrightarrow{S}_0$. Such a graph called an R-graph is defined as follows.

Definition 4 *An R-graph of $\mathcal{BP}$ is defined as $\mathcal{R} = ((P \times \Gamma), \Longrightarrow)$ where nodes are labeled by pair of control location and stack alphabet and set of edges are labeled by a pair (goodness label, resource label) with goodness label $\in \{true, false\}$, resource label $\in \{0, 1\}$.*

The edge relation is such that there is an edge between nodes s_1 and s_2 iff $s_1 \overset{g}{\Longrightarrow} s_2$, where $\Longrightarrow$ is as defined in Proposition 2. g is called the goodness label of the edge.

The resource label of the edge is 0 if $s_1 \overset{g}{\Longrightarrow}_0 s_2$ where $\Longrightarrow_0$ is as defined in Proposition 3, and 1 otherwise.

A cycle in R-graph is said to be good if there is at least one edge in the cycle with goodness label *true* and resource labels of all edges in the cycle are 0. A path in R-graph starting at (p, γ) is said to be good if it reaches a good cycle.

Proposition 4. *A given Büchi PDS $\mathcal{BP}$ has a finite stack accepting run iff there is a good path in the corresponding R-graph.*

The R-graph corresponding to the Büchi PDS in Fig. 2(a) is shown in Fig. 2(c).

$$\stackrel{g}{\Longrightarrow}_r \text{ relation}$$

$$
\begin{aligned}
P &= \{p, q\} \\
P_0 &= \{p\} \\
\Gamma &= \{m_0, m_1, s_0, s_1, s_2\} \\
G &= \{q\} \\
\Delta &= \langle p, m_0 \rangle \hookrightarrow \langle p, s_0 m_1 \rangle \\
& \langle p, m_1 \rangle \hookrightarrow \langle p, m_1 \rangle \\
& \langle q, m_1 \rangle \hookrightarrow \langle q, m_1 \rangle \\
& \langle p, s_0 \rangle \hookrightarrow \langle p, s_1 \rangle \\
& \langle p, s_1 \rangle \hookrightarrow \langle p, s_0 s_2 \rangle \\
& \langle p, s_2 \rangle \hookrightarrow \langle q, \epsilon \rangle
\end{aligned}
$$

Erase relation

$(p, s_0, false, p)$
$(p, s_2, false, q)$
$(p, s_1, false, q)$
$(p, s_0, false, q)$

$(p, m_0) \stackrel{false}{\Longrightarrow}_1 (p, s_0)$
$(p, m_1) \stackrel{false}{\Longrightarrow}_0 (p, m_1)$
$(q, m_1) \stackrel{true}{\Longrightarrow}_0 (q, m_1)$
$(p, s_0) \stackrel{false}{\Longrightarrow}_0 (p, s_1)$
$(p, s_1) \stackrel{false}{\Longrightarrow}_1 (p, s_0)$
$(p, m_0) \stackrel{false}{\Longrightarrow}_0 (p, m_1)$
$(p, m_0) \stackrel{false}{\Longrightarrow}_0 (q, m_1)$
$(p, s_1) \stackrel{false}{\Longrightarrow}_0 (p, s_2)$
$(p, s_1) \stackrel{false}{\Longrightarrow}_0 (q, s_2)$

(a)   (b)   (c)

Fig. 2. (a) Büchi PDS, (b) corresponding Erase relation and (c) its R-graph

4   Implementation

We now describe the salient aspects of an implementation of the model checker developed in the previous sections using logic programming. Encoding the various relations such as Erase as a logic program, and evaluating the program in a goal-directed fashion, we get a local (*exploring* only the needed states) and on-the-fly (*constructing* states on demand) model checker.

From program to R-graph.   Given a control flow graph representation of a program, it is straightforward to construct the equivalent PDS. Following [11], the valuation of global variables form the control states while the current node label and the valuation of local variables form the stack alphabet. We illustrate the construction for a *call* statement below. A transition $\langle p, \gamma \rangle \hookrightarrow \langle p_1, \gamma_1 \gamma_2 \rangle$ is represented below as $\texttt{pds\_trans}(p, \gamma, p_1, [\gamma_1, \gamma_2])$.

```
pds_trans(G1, f(S1, L1), G2, [f(S,FL), f(S2,L1)]) :-
        cfg_node(S1, call(Proc, Params)),
        entry(Proc, S, Params, FL),
        cfg_edge(S1, _, S2).
```

In the fragment above, `cfg_edge` denotes the edge relation of a CFG (the 2-nd argument is a guard on the edge) and `cfg_node` denotes the mapping between node labels and the statements. The relation `entry` associates with each procedure `Proc` its entry point, formal parameters and local variables (which include the formals). Values are transformed at a basic level by *transfer functions* describing the behavior of statements such as assignments; the other statements propagate these changes.

A Büchi automaton can also be encoded with rules similar to those encoding a PDS. In fact, Horn clauses can be used to describe the construction of an automaton from the negation of an LTL formula [13]. Product construction to

```
erase(B1, Gamma, Good, B2) :-
      bpds_trans(B1, Gamma, B2, []),
      good_beuchi_state(B1, Good).
erase(B1, Gamma, Good, B2) :-
      bpds_trans(B1, Gamma, B3, [Gamma1]),
      erase(B3, Gamma1, G1, B2),
      good_beuchi_state(B1, G2), or(G1, G2, Good).
erase(B1, Gamma, Good, B2) :-
      bpds_trans(B1, Gamma, B3, [Gamma1, Gamma2]),
      erase(B3, Gamma1, G1, B4),
      erase(B4, Gamma2, G2, B2),
      good_beuchi_state(B1, G3), or(G1, G2, Gt), or(Gt, G3, Good).

edge(s(B1, Gamma1), l(Good, 0), s(B2, Gamma2)) :-
      bpds_trans(B1, Gamma1, B2, [Gamma2]),
      good_beuchi_state(B1, Good).
edge(s(B1, Gamma1), l(Good, 1), s(B2, Gamma2)) :-
      bpds_trans(B2, Gamma1, B2, [Gamma2, _]),
      good_beuchi_state(B1, Good).
edge(s(B1, Gamma1), l(Good, 0), s(B2, Gamma2)) :-
      bpds_trans(B1, Gamma1, B3, [Gamma, Gamma2]),
      erase(B3, Gamma, G1, B2),
      good_beuchi_state(B1, G2), or(G1, G2, Good).
```

Fig. 3. Generation of R-graphs from PDS models

derive Büchi PDS is also straightforward and omitted. We assume that the transitions of a Büchi PDS are given by a relation bpds_trans(P1,Gamma1,P2,Dest) where Dest is a list of up to two elements with nil representing ϵ transitions.

Finally, the Erase relation (Definition 1) as well as the edge relation of the R-graph(Definition 4) are directly encoded as logic programs, as shown in Fig. 3. We use the relation good_beuchi_state(B,G) to determine if B is an accepting state of $\mathcal{B}$.

Complexity. The crucial predicate in the encoding is erase. When evaluated with tabled resolution [17,6], erase can be computed in $O(|\Delta_{bp}| \times |P_{bp}|^2)$, where Δ_{bp} and P_{bp} are the number of transitions and control states, respectively, in the Büchi PDS. To derive the space and time complexity in terms of the input program's size, let c be the size of the control flow graph, b the size of the Büchi automaton, and g and l be the (maximum) number of global and local variables. Then the time complexity of computing erase is $O(c \times b^3 \times 2^{g+l})$. The cubic factor comes from the last rule of erase which performs a join and hence effectively iterates once over all states in the Büchi automaton (note that B4 is drawn only from the states of $\mathcal{B}$) for each tuple in the relation. The size of erase relation is $O(c \times b^2 \times 2^{g+l})$.

It can also be readily seen that the time taken to completely evaluate edge is $O(c \times b \times 2^{g+l})$ once erase has been computed. The size of the R-graph is also $O(c \times b \times 2^{g+l})$. Good cycles in the R-graph can be detected in time proportional to the size of the graph and hence the overall time to model check is $O(c \times b^3 \times 2^{g+l})$, matching the best-known algorithms. The time complexities assume unit-time table lookups. Organizing the tuples of the relations as binary trees would increase the complexity by a factor of $O((\log(c) + \log(b))(g + l))$. In an implementation platform, such as the XSB logic programming system [19], the tuples are a factor of $O((\log(c)+\log(b))(g+l))$. In a realistic implementation platform, such as the XSB logic programming system, the tuples are organized using trie data structures, giving close to unit-time lookups in practice. The tries sometimes induce parts of tuple representations to be shared, reducing the space complexity.

The analysis does not take into account the locality due to the goal-directedness of tabled evaluation, since it does not appear to reduce the worst case complexity. However, if the transfer functions were monotonic (as in data-flow analyses), the factor of 2^{g+l} will be brought to $g(g+l)^2$ with goal-directed evaluation. We now present a local cycle detection algorithm that exploits the locality, by invoking edge and, in turn, erase only until a good cycle is found.

Local detection of good cycles.   The final step in model checking is determining if there is a reachable good cycle in the R-graph. Recall that a good cycle is defined as one which has at least one edge with goodness label being true while all edges in the cycle have resource labels 0. The first condition is a disjunctive property: a cycle has a good edge if and only if an SCC has a good edge. Tarjan's SCC algorithm [18] can be adapted to perform local good-cycle detection when the acceptance condition is a disjunctive property: e.g., Couvreur's algorithm in [9]. The second condition, however, cannot be cast as a property of SCC. We present a local algorithm that incorporates both conditions. The algorithm, presented in Fig. 4, uses a modification of Couvreur's algorithm as a subroutine.

We handle the "all 0-edges" condition by partitioning the depth first search where we explore all edges with a 0 resource label before looking at any with a 1 resource label. Given a graph with nodes in set S and a starting node v_0, this partitions the nodes into sets S_0 and S_0', where S_0 consists of all (and only) those nodes that are reachable from v_0 using edges with 0 resource labels, and $S_0' = S - S_0$. We do this partitioning while looking for good cycles in the subgraph induced by S_0 using a modification of the algorithm in [9]. If no good cycles are found, we pick a node, say v_1 from S_0' that is reachable from some node in S_0 via a edge with resource label 1. We use v_1 to partition S_0' into S_1 and S_1', and so on. This procedure will partition the graph into subgraphs containing only 0-edges where the subgraphs are connected by 1-edges. If a good "all 0-edge" cycle exists it will be within one subgraph since there are no 0-edges from a node S_i to a node in S_j if $j > i$.

In the algorithm in Fig. 4, we use two global stacks: *Sstack*, the stack of DFS numbers of current SCC roots, and *Lstack* that summarizes the labels on edges in/between each of the components rooted in *Sstack*. These stacks guide the local detection of good cycles within a single subgraph. While exploring a subgraph, when a previously visited node in an incomplete SCC is seen via a 0-edge, say from v to w, then we combine the SCC roots of v and w. While doing so we update the status of labels in the combined SCC and return immediately if the summary indicates a *true* label (lines 15–23 in *good_cycle()*). We use a set *pending* to record nodes reachable via a 1-edge from the current subgraph. Thus, at the end of exploring a subgraph S_i, *pending* contains exactly the set of nodes in S_{i+1}. The algorithm also maintains various marks on each node: *visited* and *complete*, both initially *false* and *dfsnum* that records the node's DFS number.

```
                                1. Boolean good_cycle(v)
                                2. begin
                                3.    v.visited := true;
1. Boolean good_path(v0)        4.    v.dfsnum := DFSnum++;
2. begin                        5.    push(Sstack, v.dfsnum);
3.    pending := { v0 };        6.    forall (G,w such that there is an edge
4.    while ( v ∈ pending )     7.       from v to w with goodness label G
5.       pending := pending −{v}; 8.       and resource label 0)
6.       DFSnum := 1;            9.       if (not w.visited) then
7.       Sstack := empty;        11.         push(Lstack, G);
8.       Lstack := empty;        12.         if good_cycle(w) then
9.       push(Lstack, false);    13.            return true;
10.      if (good_cycle(v)) then 14.      else if not w.complete then
11.         return true;         15.         if (G) then
12.   end while                  16.            return true;
13.   return false;              17.         else
14. end                          18.            while (top(Sstack) > w.dfsnum)
                                 19.               if (top(Lstack)) then
                                 20.                  return true
                                 21.               else
                                 22.                  pop(Lstack); pop(Sstack);
                                 23.            end while
1. procedure mark(v)             24.   end forall
2. begin                         25.   if (top(Sstack) = v.dfsnum) then
3. if not v.complete then        26.      pop(Sstack); pop(LStack);
4.    v.complete := true;        27.      mark(v);
5.    forall (w such that there is 28.   forall (w such that there is an edge
6.       an edge from v to w)    29.      from v to w with resource label 1
7.       mark(w);                30.      and not w.visited)
8.    end forall                 31.      pending := pending + {w};
9. end                           32.   end forall
                                 33.   return false;
                                 34. end
```

Fig. 4. Local Good-cycle detection algorithm

It is easy to show that the local algorithm is linear. Although the algorithm only determines whether or not a good path exists, it can be readily modified to output such a path. Finally, by organizing *pending* as a queue, we can ensure that we will find a path with the smallest amount of stack consumed in the initial segment leading up to the good cycle.

Performance.   We tested the performance of our model checker on an example program, shown in Fig. 1(a,c) with one modification: main (Fig 1(a)) calls flip(N) instead of flip. The procedure in Fig. 1(c) is a concrete version of the one shown in Fig. 1(b) with the recursion control parameter left unabstracted. Note that in the concrete version calls to the procedure flip from main is done with the recursion depth parameter N. We verified the property AGF **reach** for different values of the recursion depth parameter N. Fig. 5(a) shows the running time and space statistics for model checking when the global variable g initialized to *false*. With this initial value the property is true, and there are no good cycles in the corresponding R-graph(recall that we check for negation of the property). Fig. 5(b) shows the performance of our model checker with g left uninitialized (thus exploring both *true* and *false* valuations). In this case, which is identical to the one reported in [2] and [11], the property is false, and we exit the model checker as soon as we see the first good cycle in the R-graph.

(g initially *false*: no good cycle)			
N	CPU Time	Space Total	Table
1K	0.5s	10M	5M
2K	1.1s	19M	10M
4K	2.1s	37M	20M
8K	4.4s	74M	40M
16K	8.9s	148M	81M
32K	17.2s	295M	161M

(a)

(g initially *undefined*: ∃ good cycle)			
N	CPU Time	Space Total	Table
8K	0.6s	19M	13M
16K	1.2s	37M	27M
32K	2.2s	74M	54M
64K	4.8s	147M	108M
128K	9.6s	294M	216M
256K	19.0s	587M	431M

(b)

Fig. 5. Performance of our model checker on AGF `reach` for program in Fig. 1(a,c) for g initialized to *false* (a) and left uninitialized (b). Measurements taken using XSB2.4 & Mandrake Linux 8.1 running on a 1.7GHz Xeon with 2GB memory.

The performance numbers are preliminary and only serve to highlight the unique aspects of our model checker. First of all, the figures show the impact of local model checking on this problem, with more than 7-fold difference in running time. Secondly, even though the performance reported here and in [11] were collected on different hardware platforms, the raw times in Fig. 5(a) are about 5 times smaller than those given in [11], indicating that a local explicit state checker can offer performance comparable to a symbolic one even when the entire state space is explored. Thirdly, the time and space performance for both cases is linear in the size of the input program, indicating no hidden costs in computing over a logic programming engine.

Finally, we ran our model checker on the abstract program shown in Fig. 1(a,b): the time and space consumption was too small to measure. That experiment shows the utility of resource-constrained checking: we have in effect shown the validity of the AGF `reach` for all values of the recursion parameter N in negligible time. It should be noted that program in Fig. 1(a,b) is natural abstraction of the case whose verification results are shown in Fig. 5(a).

5   Discussion

As mentioned earlier, our formulation of resource-constrained model checking is closely related to the works of [12,4,10,11], where efficient algorithms have been described for model checking PDSs. Apart from the annotation of resource consumption on the edges of the R-graph, we provide a considerably different implementation strategy. For instance, [10] presents a model checking technique where Pre^* relation (analogous to our Erase) is used in two phases: one to identify good cycles (repeating heads) and another to check if such cycles are reachable. The subsequent paper [11] presents a symbolic algorithm for model checking PDSs. In contrast, we encode our model checker so as to derive a local (explicit-state) algorithm, and avoid the second use of Erase.

Recent works in [1,3] show that (*recursive* or *hierarchical*) state machines can be used to model control flow of sequential programs consisting of recursive calls.

Both works give model checking algorithms that, when used for model checking push-down systems, run in time cubic in the size of the Büchi automaton and linear in the size of the push-down system. Furthermore, [3] describes special classes of state machines for which the model checking algorithms have better complexity. The main essence of both these works is to compute *summary* edges that reveal the relationship between the entry and exit points of each state machine. In addition, [1] points out that identifying edges that lead to increase in stack size, model checking can be restricted to finite-stack paths. The important similarities between [1,3] and our work are as follows:

- Summary edges are analogous to $\Longrightarrow_0$ relation as computed in Proposition 3.
- Edges F_a and F_u as computed in [1], revealing finite- and infinite-stack paths respectively, are identical to $\circ \stackrel{S}{\longrightarrow}_0$ and $\Longrightarrow_1$.
- Optimization techniques involving forward and backward analysis of summary edges as discussed in these papers can be directly incorporated in our work.

The distinguishing aspect of our work is that we concretely describe a high-level yet efficient implementation of a local, on-the-fly model checker that can distinguish finite-stack runs from arbitrary runs of a push-down system.

The idea behind of **Erase** and R-graph appears to be more universal than model checking of PDSs. For instance, inter-procedural data flow analysis techniques define summaries of calls, which are simply variants of **Erase**. Closer inspection of data flow techniques reveal striking (although not surprising) similarities. These similarities are best exhibited by [15] and related works, where data flow analysis is formulated in terms of graph-reachability. Some of the analogies are listed below:

- Same Level Inter-procedurally valid paths (SLIVP): All the calls in the path is matched by the corresponding return. This is analogous to $\circ \longrightarrow_0$ that we use to define a good cycle in R-graph.
- Inter-procedurally valid path (realizable path IVP) : All returns are matched but not all calls. This is similar to $\circ \longrightarrow_1$.
- Path Edge $\subset$ SLIVP: This is $\Longrightarrow_0{}^*$ and $\circ \longrightarrow_0$
- Summary Edge $\subset$ SLIVP: This is $\Longrightarrow_0$ restricted to call nodes.

Although the interplay between data flow analysis and model checking has been widely recognized (e.g. [16]), the closeness in the details of algorithms used indicates a potential for furthering the practice in both areas through a better understanding of the interactions. Finally, although model checking of recursive programs using mu-calculus has been explored [5], the techniques appear to have an exponential blowup to handle recursion. It will be interesting to explore the relationship between these techniques and the ones presented in this paper, and is a topic of current research.

References

1. R. Alur, K. Etessami, and M. Yannakakis. Analysis of recursive state machines. In *Computer-Aided Verification (CAV 2001)*. Springer-Verlag, 2001.

2. T. Ball and S. Rajamani. Bebop: A symbolic model checker for boolean programs. In *SPIN00: SPIN Workshop*, volume 1885 of *Lecture Notes in Computer Science*, pages 113–130, 2000.

3. M. Benedikt, P. Godefroid, and T. Reps. Model checking unrestricted hierarchical state machines. In *Twenty-Eighth Int. Colloq. on Automata, Languages, and Programming(ICALP 2001)*. Springer-Verlag, 2001.

4. A. Bouajjani, J. Esparza, and O. Maler. Reachability analysis of pushdown automata: Application to model checking. In *Concurrency Theory (CONCURR 1997)*, 1997.

5. O. Burkart and B. Steffen. Model checking the full-modal mu-calculus for infinite sequential processes. In *Proceedings of ICALP'97*, volume 1256 of *Lecture Notes in Computer Science*, pages 419–429, 1997.

6. W. Chen and D. S. Warren. Tabled evaluation with delaying for general logic programs. *Journal of the ACM*, 43(1):20–74, January 1996.

7. E. M. Clarke and E. A. Emerson. Design and synthesis of synchronization skeletons using branching-time temporal logic. In D. Kozen, editor, *Proceedings of the Workshop on Logic of Programs,* Yorktown Heights, volume 131 of *Lecture Notes in Computer Science*, pages 52–71. Springer Verlag, 1981.

8. E. M. Clarke, E. A. Emerson, and A. P. Sistla. Automatic verification of finite-state concurrent systems using temporal logic specifications. *ACM TOPLAS*, 8(2), 1986.

9. J.-M. Couvreur. On-the-fly verification of linear temporal logic. In *Proceedings of FM'99*, volume 1708 of *Lecture Notes in Computer Science*, pages 253–271, 1999.

10. J. Esparza, D. Hansel, P. Rossmanith, and S. Schwoon. Efficient algorithms for model checking pushdown systems. In *Computer-Aided Verification (CAV 2000)*, pages 232–247. Springer-Verlag, 2000.

11. J. Esparza and S. Schwoon. A bdd-based model checker for recursive programs. In *Computer-Aided Verification (CAV 2001)*, pages 324–336. Springer-Verlag, 2001.

12. A. Finkel, B. Willems, and P. Wolper. A direct symbolic approach to model checking pushdown systems. In *Second International Workshop on Verification of Infinite State Systems(INFINITY 1997)*, volume 9. Elsevier Science, 1997.

13. L.R. Pokorny and C.R. Ramakrishnan. LTL model checking using tabled logic programming. In *Workshop on Tabling in Parsing and Deduction*, 2000. Available from http://www.cs.sunysb.edu/~cram/papers.

14. J. P. Queille and J. Sifakis. Specification and verification of concurrent systems in Cesar. In *Proceedings of the International Symposium in Programming*, volume 137 of *Lecture Notes in Computer Science*, Berlin, 1982. Springer-Verlag.

15. T. Reps, S. Horwitz, and M. Sagiv. Precise interprocedural dataflow analysis via graph reachability. In *Twenty-Second ACM Symposium on Principles of Programming Languages*, pages 49–61, 1995.

16. D. A. Schmidt and B. Steffen. Program analysis as model checking of abstract interpretations. In *Static Analysis Symposium*, pages 351–380, 1998.

17. H. Tamaki and T. Sato. OLDT resolution with tabulation. In *International Conference on Logic Programming*, pages 84–98. MIT Press, 1986.

18. R. E. Tarjan. Depth first search and linear graph algorithms. *SIAM Journal of Computing*, 1(2):146–160, 1972.

19. XSB. The XSB logic programming system. Available from http://xsb.sourceforge.net.

Model Checking Large-Scale and Parameterized Resource Allocation Systems

E. Allen Emerson and Vineet Kahlon

Department of Computer Sciences*
The University of Texas at Austin, Austin TX-78712, USA

Abstract. In this paper, techniques are proposed for limiting state explosion in the context of resource allocation problems. It is shown that given any system organized into a — possibly irregular — network of n — possibly heterogeneous — processes, model checking over that system can be reduced by an efficient, fully automatic and exact method to model checking over a certain small system. These results are established for correctness properties expressed in LTL\X. The precise size and topology of the small system are dependent on the large system, as well as the correctness specification. When the network is symmetric and the processes homogeneous, this new method provides an efficient solution to the Parameterized Model Checking Problem. As an application, it is shown how to efficiently verify a variety of solutions to the parameterized Dining Philosophers Problem.

1 Introduction

Model checking has become a widely used method of verification. A key limitation to its use is the state explosion problem. A variety of techniques to limit state explosion have been investigated. Among these are techniques such as symmetry reduction (cf. e.g., [7], [16]) which typically focuses on large but constant size systems of homogeneous processes configured in a regular or symmetric interconnection topology. Other techniques include partial order methods ([20], [24]) and Binary Decision Diagrams ([4],[5]), which attempt to exploit regular organization embedded in the designs of systems.

In this paper, we first propose new methods for limiting state explosion when reasoning about potentially irregular systems, i.e., systems with an irregular network topology comprised of many heterogeneous processes. We go on to show how our methods can be specialized to reason about regular systems: systems comprised of many homogeneous processes arranged in a regular network. A benefit is a new approach to reasoning about parameterized systems, as described below.

We work in the context of resource allocation problems which are designed for the purpose of resolving conflicts in concurrent systems, a problem of considerable practical importance. We consider resource allocation systems organized into a (possibly irregular) network of (possibly heterogeneous) processes. The processes interact by

* This work was supported in part by NSF grant CCR-009-8141, SRC contract 99-1J-685, and TARP-003685-0650-1999. The authors can be reached at
{emerson,kahlon}@cs.utexas.edu

J.-P. Katoen and P. Stevens (Eds.): TACAS 2002, LNCS 2280, pp. 251–265, 2002.
© Springer-Verlag Berlin Heidelberg 2002

sharing resources, which are represented by *tokens*. Each edge connecting a pair of processes P_i and P_j is labeled by a token t which is shared between the two processes. Our results easily generalize to the case where a resource could be shared by more than two processes, but for the sake of simplicity, we restrict ourselves to the case where each resource is shared by exactly two processes. A process can perform certain independent actions internally, without possession of its tokens. But certain other actions require that the process acquire all of its neighboring tokens. Once it has them, it can perform token-guarded actions. Eventually a process releases all its tokens, returning them to their associated edges.

We show that model checking over any such large system can be reduced to model checking over an equivalent small system. The precise size and topology of the small system are dependent on the large system, as well as the number of indices (i.e., processes tracked) in the correctness specification. The reduction method is efficient, fully automatic and exact. We establish our results for correctness properties expressed in LTL\X.

All of the above techniques deal with reducing the cost of model checking a single large system, e.g., a system with k processes for some large constant k. In contrast, we might want to verify that a uniform infinite family of such systems is correct for all sizes n. The special case of such parameterized systems regularly organized with arbitrary number of homogeneous processes in a symmetric network is an important one with many applications. And our results specialize to apply to the associated *Parameterized Model Checking Problem (PMCP)*, which is the following: to decide whether a temporal property is true for every size system in a uniform family of systems. A key advantage is that one application of the PMCP settles the scalability and the state explosion problem in one fell swoop. We illustrate our techniques by applying them to the verification of a variety of parameterized Dining Philosophers solutions. To our knowledge, this is the first such fully automated verification for the parameterized formulation of this problem. We are able to reduce reasoning about the correctness for Dining Philosophers protocols of all sizes n to reasoning about at most 5 philosophers.

The rest of this paper is organized as follows: The model of computation is given in section 2. In section 3, we show how to reduce model checking over large resource allocation systems to small ones for correctness specifications involving finite behavior. Results involving unconditionally fair behaviour are considered in section 4. Deadlock issues are considered in section 5, while example applications are given in section 6. Some concluding remarks are given in section 7.

2   Preliminaries

2.1   Model of Computation

We consider *systems* $\mathcal{U} = (\mathcal{P}, \mathcal{T})$, where $\mathcal{P}$ is a set of a finite number n of possibly heterogeneous *processes* $P_1, ..., P_n$ and $\mathcal{T}$ is a set of *tokens* $t_1, ..., t_m$ representing resources shared between pairs of processes. The system $\mathcal{U}$ may be viewed as an undirected graph or network with node set $\mathcal{P}$ and edge set $\mathcal{T}$. In any global state of $\mathcal{U}$, each token of $\mathcal{T}$ can be in the possession of at most one process of $\mathcal{U}$. A token not in the possession of any process is said to be *free* in that global state. The set of tokens adjacent to and used by P_i is denoted by $Tok(P_i)$. We assume that the processes in $\mathcal{P}$ execute concurrently with interleaving semantics, competing for shared token resources, permitting access to guarded regions of code. The syntax of each process P_i ensures that each of its executions is of the form:

((internal transition)* *acquire* (internal transition)* *release*)$^+$.

An *internal* transition of P_i only changes its local state, and not the status of its adjacent tokens. The *external* transitions of P_i are the *acquire* and *release* transitions, which respectively grab free adjacent tokens and release them. We also classify transitions into two types: *token free* transitions of process P_i can always be executed irrespective of the current global state of the system; *token dependent* transitions of process P_i can can be executed only if P_i currently possesses all tokens in the set $Tok(P_i)$. Transitions bracketed within an *acquire-release* pair, including *release* but excluding *acquire* are *token depedent*. Note that a process P_i is not pre-emptible for tokens it is presently using. Once a token in $Tok(P_i)$ is obtained by an *acquire* transition of P_i, it cannot be released until all tokens in $Tok(P_i)$ have been obtained and the corresponding token *release* transition executed.

Each set $Tok(P_i)$ is partitioned into subsets $Tok(P_i, 1), ..., Tok(P_i, k(P_i))$. We assume that a partial order $\prec_{P_i}$, or $\prec_i$, for short, is imposed on these subsets. Process P_i when executing an *acquire* transition, accumulates its tokens in a manner consistent with this partial order and partitioning of $Tok(P_i)$, as described below.

A process P_i is described by its *synchronization skeleton* [8], formally given by the tuple $(S_i, \Sigma_i, R_i, i_i)$, where S_i is the set of local states of P_i, R_i is the transition relation of P_i, i_i is the initial state of P_i and $\Sigma_i = \Sigma_i^D \cup \Sigma_i^F \cup \{release_i, acquire_i\}$, where Σ_i^D and Σ_i^F represent the labels of the *token dependent* and the *token free* transitions, respectively. Permitted transitions in R_i are:

- $l_i \xrightarrow{a} m_i$: an internal local transition from local state l_i to local state m_i of process P_i labeled by $a \in \Sigma_i^D \cup \Sigma_i^F$.
- $l_i \xrightarrow{acquire_i} m_i$: a token acquire transition. When process P_i is at location l_i, it can fire this "molecular" transition. In each atomic step, P_i can acquire all tokens in $Tok(P_i, j)$, for some $j \in [1..k(P_i)]$, in case all tokens in the subset $Tok(P_i, j)$ are free; acquisition of these token sets must respect the partial order $\prec_i$ so that if for $p, q \in [1 : k(P_i)]$, $Tok(P_i, p) \prec_i Tok(P_i, q)$, then the set $Tok(P_i, p)$ must be acquired before the set $Tok(P_i, q)$. Once P_i possesses all tokens in $Tok(P_i)$, it transits to local state m_i. For multiple token sets, if process P_i has acquired *some* but not all of its token sets in $Tok(P_i)$, then execution appears to stutter in local state l_i. In other words, once P_i has acquired a token in state l_i it waits in l_i until all tokens in $Tok(P_i)$ have been acquired; and
- $l_i \xrightarrow{release_i} m_i$: a token release transition, which frees all tokens in $Tok(P_i)$.

We now define the semantics of the system $\mathcal{U} = (\mathcal{P}, \mathcal{T})$, where $\mathcal{P} = \{P_1, \ldots, P_n\}$ and $\mathcal{T} = \{t_1, \ldots, t_m\}$. The possession status of token t_l shared by the two processes P_i and P_j is an element of the status set $T_l = \{i, j, \text{free}\}$ corresponding to the token being possessed by process P_i or process P_j or being possessed by no process at all. It is convenient to denote the status of token t_l in global state s, by $status(s, t_l)$. We denote the set of tokens possessed by process P_i in global state s by $Pos(P_i, s)$. For process P_i and set $T \subseteq Tok(P_i)$, we use the phrase "T not grabbed at s" to mean that there exists $t \in T$, such that $status(s, t) \neq i$ and the phrase "T grabbed by process P_i at s" to mean that for each token $t \in T$, we have that $status(s, t) = i$.

Formally, we define the labeled transition system $\mathcal{M}_\mathcal{U}$ for $\mathcal{U}$ to be the tuple (S, Σ, R, i), where

- $S = S_1 \times \dots \times S_n \times T_1 \times \dots \times T_m$. A global state s is a tuple of the form $(s(1), \dots, s(n), s(n+1), \dots, s(n+m))$ where components $s(1), \dots, s(n)$ indicate respectively the local states of processes $P_1, \dots, P_n$ while components $s(n+1), \dots, s(n+m)$ describe respectively, the possession status of tokens $t_1, \dots, t_m$; note that $status(s, t_j) = s(n+j)$.

- $\Sigma = \bigcup_i \Sigma_i$.

- $R = \{s \xrightarrow{a} t \mid \exists i : \exists a \in \Sigma_i^D \cup \Sigma_i^F : \exists l_i \xrightarrow{a} m_i \in R_i : s(i) = l_i$ and $t(i) = m_i$ and $\forall j \neq i : s(j) = t(j)\}$

  $\cup \{s \xrightarrow{acquire_i} t \mid i \in [1:n]$ and $\exists l_i \xrightarrow{acquire_i} m_i \in R_i : s(i) = l_i$ and $Tok(P_i, j)$ not grabbed at s implies

  $\forall p : Tok(P_i, j) \prec_i Tok(P_i, p) :$

$Tok(P_i, p)$ not grabbed at s

  and $Tok(P_i)$ grabbed at s implies $t(i) = m_i$

  and $Tok(P_i)$ not grabbed at s implies $t(i) = l_i\}$

  $\cup \{s \xrightarrow{release_i} t \mid i \in [1:n]$ and $\exists l_i \xrightarrow{release_i} m_i \in R_i : s(i) = l_i$ and $t(i) = m_i$ and $\forall u \in Tok(P_i) : status(s, u) = i$, $status(t, u) = $ free and $\forall v \notin Tok(P_i) : status(s, v) = status(t, v)\}$

- $i = (i_1, \dots, i_{n+m})$, where for all $j \in [1..m]$, $i_{n+j} = $ free.

Process P' of system $\mathcal{V}$ is called a *replica* of process P of another system $\mathcal{U}$ iff the LTS corresponding to P is the same as the LTS corresponding to P'; however, the context, i.e., tokens sets $Tok(P)$ and $Tok(P')$ may be different.

2.2 Computation Paths and Stuttering

A *path* x of $\mathcal{U}$ is a sequence $s_0, s_1, \dots$ of global states of $\mathcal{U}$ such that for every i, (s_i, s_{i+1}) corresponds to a transition of a process of $\mathcal{U}$. A *fullpath* x of $\mathcal{U}$ is a maximal path, viz., either it is infinite or the last state s_k, say, has no successor in $\mathcal{U}$ as no process is enabled in s_k. In this case the system is said to be *globally deadlocked* in s_k. A *computation* is a path that starts at the initial state i of $\mathcal{U}$. We say that the sequence of global states $y = t_0, t_1, \dots$ is a *stuttering* of a path x iff y is of the form $z_0 z_1 \dots$ such that for each j there is an $r > 0$ with $z_j = (x_j)^r$ (cf. [3]). Sequences u and v of global states of $\mathcal{U}$ are said to be *stuttering equivalent* iff there exists a path w of $\mathcal{U}$ such that each of u and v is a stuttering of w.

2.3 Temporal Logic

We assume that our correctness specifications are formulated using LTL\X (Linear Temporal Logic minus Next-time). Formulae h are built up from the usual linear operators F (sometime), G (always), and U (weak until) combined with propositional connectives. If h is a LTL$\backslash$X formula then, for purposes of model checking, we have a very flat temporal logic that can express both Ah (for all futures h) and Eh (for some future h). As is usual for linear time, there is an implicit universal quantification over all possible futures. We write $\mathcal{U} \models h$ to mean that $\mathcal{U} \models$ Ah which is defined by $\mathcal{M}_{\mathcal{U}}, i \models$ Ah. Dually, $\mathcal{U} \models$ Eh is defined as $\mathcal{M}_{\mathcal{U}}, i \models$ Eh. The atomic propositions allowed in h are typically indexed; e.g., l_i means that process i is in local state l.

3   Reduction Results for Finite Behavior

In this section, we consider behavior along finite paths, with correctness formulated using a formula h of the logic LTL$\backslash$X. We use E_{fin} to denote existential quantification over finite paths, and A_{fin} to denote universal quantification over finite paths. Specifically, we focus on double index properties f of the form $E_{fin}h(i,j)$ or its dual $A_{fin}h(i,j)$, where $h(i,j)$ is a LTL$\backslash$X formula with atomic propositions over the local states of processes P_i and P_j. Our results will permit us to reason about safety properties.

Theorem 3.1 *Let $\mathcal{U}$ be a system with processes P_1, P_2, and $\mathcal{V}$ be a system with respective replica processes P_1', P_2' such that $Tok(P_1) \cap Tok(P_2) = \emptyset$ in $\mathcal{U}$ iff $Tok(P_1') \cap Tok(P_2') = \emptyset$ in $\mathcal{V}$. Then $\mathcal{U} \models E_{fin}h(1,2)$ iff $\mathcal{V} \models E_{fin}h(1,2)$.*

Proof Sketch ($\Rightarrow$) Given a finite path x of $\mathcal{U}$, we will construct a finite path y of $\mathcal{V}$ such that x projected onto coordinates 1 and 2, viz., processes P_1 and P_2, is stuttering equivalent to y projected onto 1 and 2. We present an informal description first. Along y all processes of $\mathcal{V}$ other than P_1' and P_2' idle in their initial states. To establish stuttering equivalence of x and y on 1 and 2, we ensure that P_1' and P_2' execute along y all the same visible local transitions in the same order as do respectively P_1 and P_2 along x, i.e. transitions causing a change in the local states along coordinates 1 and 2. With this in mind, we define an *event* of x to be a local transition along x that causes a change in the local states of process P_1 or P_2. We construct y in an inductive fashion by "scanning" for events of x starting from the initial state and mimicking them in the same order to get y.

In more detail, the construction is as follows. To start with y is initialized to $i_{\mathcal{V}}$, the initial state of $\mathcal{V}$. All subsequent invisible non-event transitions along x are skipped over. For the inductive step, assume that the next event e encountered along x is a transition fired by, say, process P_1. A similar argument applies if it is fired by P_2. First, if event e is a token free or token dependent transition, then we let replica P_1' execute the same transition. Next, if the event e is a release transition then we let P_1' execute the corresponding release transition. The only subtlety occurs when event e corresponds to a token acquisition transition of P_1. That transition may fire several times along x; only the last such firing causes a visible change in the local state upon grabbing the last tree block of tokens. (There may be a "race" between P_1 and P_2 to grab all their respective tokens, and the intervals during which they are trying may overlap. But along x, P_1 wins by getting all of its tokens first.) Hence, starting at the last global state of y constructed so far, we let P_1' execute a series of token acquisition transitions to acquire

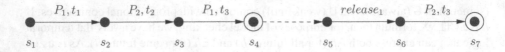

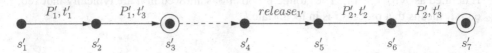

Fig. 1. Process P_1, with the token set $\{t_1, t_3\}$, completes acquisition of all of its tokens in state s_4 before P_2, which has the token set $\{t_2, t_3\}$, completes its in state s_7. We mimic this by letting P_1' acquire all of its tokens ﬁrst and only when P_1' has released them in state s_5' do we schedule P_2' to acquire all of its tokens.

all the tokens in $Tok(P_1')$. (If, having lost the race, P_2 eventually acquires all its tokens along x, then that defines a subsequent event, which will be mimicked then along y by P_2'.) This completes the construction of y. The idea is illustrated using figure 1.

($\Leftarrow$) Analogous to the above argument. $\square$

Given processes P_1 and P_2 of $\mathcal{U}$, we now define two small systems $\mathcal{V}_c(P_1, P_2)$ and $\mathcal{V}_{nc}(P_1, P_2)$ with P_1' and P_2', that are replicas of P_1 and P_2, respectively, sharing a common token t in $\mathcal{V}_c(P_1, P_2)$ but sharing no token in $\mathcal{V}_{nc}(P_1, P_2)$. Furthermore, in both systems we have, $\prec_{P_1'} = \emptyset = \prec_{P_2'}$. See figure 2.

Then the above result has important practical consequences. It shows that for reasoning about safety properties $h(1, 2)$ over two indices, we may reduce the model checking problem for an arbitrarily large system $\mathcal{U}$ involving processes P_1 and P_2 to model checking over one of the two systems $\mathcal{V}_c(P_1, P_2)$ or $\mathcal{V}_{nc}(P_1, P_2)$. Specifically, we have the following

Theorem 3.2 *Given system* $\mathcal{U}$ *containing* P_1 *and* P_2, *define*

$$\mathcal{V} = \begin{cases} \mathcal{V}_c(P_1, P_2) & \text{if } P_1 \text{ and } P_2 \text{ share a common token in } \mathcal{U} \\ \mathcal{V}_{nc}(P_1, P_2) & \text{if } P_1 \text{ and } P_2 \text{ do not share any common token in } \mathcal{U} \end{cases}$$

Then $\mathcal{U} \models \mathsf{E}_{\mathsf{fin}} h(1, 2)$ *iff* $\mathcal{V} \models \mathsf{E}_{\mathsf{fin}} h(1, 2)$.

Note that which of the two alternatives is used for $\mathcal{V}$ can be determined *efficiently* as all we need to do is decide whether in the given system, P_1 and P_2 share a common token or not. This can be done in time $O(|Tok(P_1)| + |Tok(P_2)|) = O(|\mathcal{U}|)$, where $|\mathcal{U}|$ denotes the sum of the sizes of the program texts of all the processes of $\mathcal{U}$.

4   Reduction Results for Fair Infinite Behavior

Given any system $\mathcal{U}$ containing the set $\mathcal{S}$ of processes, define the set of neighbours of $\mathcal{S}$, denoted by $\mathsf{N}(\mathcal{U}, \mathcal{S})$, to be the set of processes $\{X \mid X \notin \mathcal{S} \wedge (\forall S \in \mathcal{S} :$

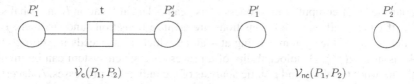

$$\mathcal{V}_c(P_1, P_2) \qquad\qquad\qquad\qquad \mathcal{V}_{nc}(P_1, P_2)$$

Fig. 2. Two Small Systems

$Tok(X) \cap Tok(S) \neq \emptyset)\}$. An infinite path x of $\mathcal{U}$ is said to be unconditionally fair provided that each of the processes $P_1, ..., P_n$ executes infinitely often in x. We write E_{uf} and A_{uf} to quantify purely over unconditionally fair paths of the system.

Theorem 4.1 *Given system $\mathcal{U}$ containing processes P_1 and P_2, let $\mathcal{V}$ be any system containing respectively replica processes P_1' and P_2' such that*

- $Tok(P_1) \cap Tok(P_2) = \emptyset$ *iff* $Tok(P_1') \cap Tok(P_2') = \emptyset$.
- $\mathsf{N}(\mathcal{U}, \{P_1, P_2\}) = \emptyset$ *iff* $\mathsf{N}(\mathcal{V}, \{P_1', P_2'\}) = \emptyset$.

Then $\mathcal{U} \models \mathsf{E}_{uf}h(1, 2)$ iff $\mathcal{V} \models \mathsf{E}_{uf}h(1, 2)$.

Proof Idea ($\Rightarrow$) Given an unconditionally fair path x of $\mathcal{U}$, we will construct an unconditionally fair path y of $\mathcal{V}$ such that x projected onto coordinates 1 and 2 is stuttering equivalent to y projected onto 1 and 2. The construction is similar to the one used in the proof of theorem 3.1, except that whenever process P_1' or process P_2' executes a release transition, we let processes of $\mathcal{V}$ other than P_1' and P_2' that are enabled, execute a transition each in round robin fashion. It is shown in the full paper([13]) that this modification ensures that if x is unconditionally fair, then along the resulting computation path y, all processes of $\mathcal{V}$ execute infinitely often.

($\Leftarrow$) Analogous to the above proof.   □

It can be shown that the above result allows us to *efficiently* reduce reasoning for behaviour along unconditionally fair paths from any given system to a systems with at most 3 processes.

5   Potential for Deadlock

We say that process P_i is *individually deadlocked* at location l_i in global state s of system $\mathcal{U}$ provided that there is no future behavior of the system along which P_i succeeds in executing a transition. In our framework, this can be captured in CTL\X as AGl_i or in LTL\X as just Gl_i. However, the important concept is whether P_i is *deadlockable*, i.e., whether it is *possible* for the system $\mathcal{U}$ to reach from its initial state some such deadlock state for process P_i. This is expressible in CTL\X straightforwardly by the truth of $EF \vee_l (AGl_i)$ at the initial state i of $\mathcal{U}$. However, the logic LTL\X cannot specify such potential for deadlock. We therefore develop separate methods for analysis of deadlockability.

In our model of computation, process P_i is deadlocked at location l_i in global state s of $\mathcal{U}$, iff (i) at l_i all outgoing transitions are acquire transitions and (ii) there is no future behaviour of the system starting at s along which P_i succeeds in getting all of the tokens in $Tok(P_i)$. Deadlockability of a process in a given system can be inferred from the network topology and a static analysis of the individual processes. A necessary condition for a process P_i to be deadlockable is that it lies on a "lollipop" in the graph of $\mathcal{U}$. A *lollipop* in $\mathcal{U}$ is a cycle or a finite path leading to a cycle. A necessary and sufficient condition for deadlock to occur in a global state is the existence of a "waiting chain" in that state, which may be viewed as an annotated lollipop. Formally, a *waiting chain* for process P_i in reachable global state s is a sequence of processes and tokens of the form $Q_0, t_1, Q_1, t_2, Q_2, ..., Q_j, t_{j+1}, ..., t_k, Q_k$ where $k \geq 2$, $P_i = Q_0$, for some $j \in [1 : k - 1]$: $Q_j = Q_k$ and for each $i \in [1 : k]$ token t_i is shared by both Q_{i-1} and Q_i, but possessed by Q_i.

For our general model, which permits arbitrary network topologies and heterogeneous processes, the cost of statically analyzing for deadlockability — as a function of the size of the system, which is the size of the network plus the sum of the size of the program texts for individual processes — is potentially high. In fact it can be shown that given system $\mathcal{U}$ and process P_i of $\mathcal{U}$, the problem of deciding whether P_i is deadlockable is NP-complete in the size of the program text of the given system.[1] Thus, in general, there can no efficient reduction from a big system to a small, constant sized system that preserves deadlockability characteristics of processes and their replicas. However for a wide range of potentially useful systems it is possible to give heuristics that reduce the size of a system while preserving the deadlockability characteristics of a given process (or a pair thereof), the discussion of which is deferred to the full paper [13].

In section 6, we give a provably efficient and systematic method of deadlockability analysis for ring structured systems that directly applies to our examples.

6   Applications and Examples

As examples, we consider parameterized formulations of a number of variants of the Dining Philosophers Problem. To our knowledge, our method provides the first fully automatic exact method for verifying parameterized versions of all these variants.

Traditionally, the Dining Philosophers problem is defined in terms of the following informal scenario. There are $n + 1$ philosophers $P_0, ..., P_n$, seated around a table in a counterclockwise fashion, *thinking*. Between each pair of philosophers P_i, P_{i+1} is a single fork (token) f_i. From time to time, any philosopher might become *hungry* and attempt to *eat*. In order to eat, the philosopher needs exclusive use of the two adjacent forks. After eating, the philosopher relinquishes the two forks and resumes thinking. Let the resulting system be denoted by $R(P_0, ..., P_n)$. We will consider solutions to the following variants of the Dining Philosophers problem:

Classic Dining Philosophers - which is the basic, naive solution comprised of deterministic, homogeneous philosophers.

---

[1] This could still be advantageous from the point of view of parameterized reasoning which is, in general, undecidable.

Nondeterministic Dining Philosophers - which is similar to the Classic, but imposes no restrictions on the order in which forks are acquired.

Asymmetric Dining Philosophers - which introduces a distinguished, dis-similar philosopher to ensure freedom from deadlock.

Right-Left Philosophers - which again involves heterogeneous philosophers. Assuming a ring of even size, the odd indexed philosophers give priority to grabbing their left fork while the even indexed philosophers favor their right.

6.1   Ring Topologies and Cutoffs for Deadlockability

In this section, we first give a systematic, general and efficient test for deadlockability of ring structured systems. We will then use it to provide a uniform treatment of all of the above mentioned Dining Philosophers solutions.

For each process P_i, in the system $R(P_0, ..., P_n)$, we define its *acquisition type*, denoted by *acquisition-type*(P_i), as a tuple of the form $(k(P_i), o(P_i))$, where

- $k(P_i)$ is the number of blocks into which $Tok(P_i)$ is partitioned, i.e., either 1 or 2, and
- $o(P_i)$ indicates the orderings in which tokens can be acquired and is defined as follows: if $k(P_i) = 1$ then $o(P_i)$ equals $\emptyset$ else if $k(P_i) = 2$ then $o(P_i)$ equals $<$, $>$ or $\emptyset$ respectively if P_i must acquire its left token before its right token, P_i must acquire its right token before its left token and, P_i's left and right tokens could be acquired in any order.

Then *acquisition-type*$(R(P_0, ..., P_n))$ is defined as the set $\{$*acquisition-type*$(P_i) \mid i \in [0 : n]\}$. We say that processes P_i and P_j each belonging to (possibly different) systems having ring topologies are *acquisition-equivalent* iff they have the same acquisition type. It is easy to see that acquisition-equivalence is an equivalence relation on the set of all processes belonging to systems having ring topologies. Note that if $k(P_j) = 1$, then P_j must have the acquisition type $(1, \emptyset)$; if $k(P_j) = 2$, then it has acquisition type $(2, <)$, $(2, >)$ or $(2, \emptyset)$. Thus the acquisition-equivalence relation partitions the set of all processes belonging to systems with a ring topology into 4 equivalence classes. The following important result establishes a cutoff exactly preserving deadlockability from a large ring to a small ring.

Theorem 6.1 *Given system* $R(P_0, ..., P_n)$ *where* $n \geq 1$, *let system* $R(P'_0, ..., P'_m)$ *be such that* $m \geq 1$, P'_0 *is a replica of* P_0 *and acquisition-type*$(R(P_0, ..., P_n)) = $ *acquisition-type*$(R(P'_0, ..., P'_m))$. *Then process* P_0 *is deadlockable in* $R(P_0, ..., P_n)$ *iff* P'_0 *is deadlockable in* $R(P'_0, ..., P'_m)$.

Proof $(\Rightarrow)$ Let process P_0 in $R(P_0, ..., P_n)$ be deadlockable. Then there is a reachable global state s of $R(P_0, ..., P_n)$ such that in s either the sequence $P_0, t_0, ..., P_n, t_n$ or the sequence $P_0, t_n, P_n, ..., P_1, t_0$ forms a waiting chain. Assume for definiteness that it is the former. Then since in global state s, each process P_i possesses its left token but not its right token it follows that $k(P_i) = 1$ and $o(P_i)$ equals $<$ or $\emptyset$. But since *acquisition-type*$(R(P_0, ..., P_n)) = $ *acquisition-type*$(R(P'_0, ..., P'_m))$, each process in the set $\{P'_0, ..., P'_m\}$ is acquisition-equivalent to a process in $\{P_0, ..., P_n\}$, and so we have that for each process P'_j in $\mathsf{R}(P'_0, ..., P'_m)$, $k(P'_j) = 1$ and $o(P'_j)$ equals $<$ or $\emptyset$. Recall that for each $i \in [0 : m]$, processes P'_i and P'_{i+1} share token t'_i in $\mathsf{R}(P'_0, ..., P'_m)$. Therefore, there is a reachable global state s' of $\mathsf{R}(P'_0, ..., P'_m)$ such that the sequence $P'_0, t'_0, ..., P'_m, t'_m$ forms a waiting chain in s' and so P'_0 is deadlockable in $\mathsf{R}(P'_0, ..., P'_m)$.

($\Leftarrow$) Analogous to the above direction. $\qquad\qquad\square$

When model checking for safety properties, we have

Corollary 6.2 $\mathsf{R}(P_0, P_1, ..., P_n) \models \mathsf{E_{fin}}h(0, 1)$ iff $\mathsf{R}(P'_0, P'_1, ..., P'_m) \models \mathsf{E_{fin}}h(0, 1)$, where P'_0 and P'_1 are replicas of P_0 and P_1, respectively.

Proof The result follows immediately from theorem 3.1, by noting that both the sets $Tok(P_0) \cap Tok(P_1) = \{t_0\}$ and $Tok(P'_0) \cap Tok(P'_1) = \{t'_0\}$ are non-empty. $\qquad\square$

When model checking while restricting ourselves to unconditionally fair paths, we have

Corollary 6.3 $\mathsf{R}(P_0, P_1, ..., P_n) \models \mathsf{E_{uf}}h(0, 1)$ iff $\mathsf{R}(P'_0, P'_1, ..., P'_m) \models \mathsf{E_{uf}}h(0, 1)$, where $m = n$ if $n \leq 2$ and $m \geq 3$ otherwise, and P'_0 and P'_1 are replicas of P_0 and P_1, respectively.

Proof The result follows immediately from theorem 4.1, by noting that both the sets $Tok(P_0) \cap Tok(P_1) = \{t_0\}$ and $Tok(P'_0) \cap Tok(P'_1) = \{t'_0\}$ are non-empty and $\mathsf{N}(\mathsf{R}(P_0, P_1, ..., P_n), \{P_0, P_1\})$ and $\mathsf{N}(\mathsf{R}(P'_0, P'_1, ..., P'_m), \{P'_0, P'_1\})$ are both equal to $\emptyset$ if $n = 1 = m$ or $n, m \geq 3$, and equal to $\{P_2\}$ and $\{P'_2\}$, respectively, if $n = 2 = m$. $\quad\square$

Then combining the results in 6.1, 6.2 and 6.3, we have the following

Theorem 6.4 *Given* $\mathcal{U} = \mathsf{R}(P_0, ..., P_n)$ *where* $n \geq 1$, *define* $\mathcal{V} = \mathsf{R}(P'_0, ..., P'_m)$, *where* $m = n$ *if* $n \leq 2$ *and* $m \geq 3$ *otherwise,* P'_0 *and* P'_1 *are replicas of* P_0 *and* P_1 *respectively, no two processes in* $\mathcal{V}$ *except possibly* P'_0 *and* P'_1 *are acquisition-equivalent and acquisition-type*$(\mathsf{R}(P_0, ..., P_n)) = $ *acquisition-type*$(\mathsf{R}(P'_0, ..., P'_m))$. *Then*

- P_0 *and* P_1 *are deadlockable in* $\mathcal{U}$ *iff* P'_0 *and* P'_1 *are deadlockable in* $\mathcal{V}$, *respectively*
- $\mathcal{U} \models \mathsf{E_{fin}}h(0, 1)$ *iff* $\mathcal{V} \models \mathsf{E_{fin}}h(0, 1)$ *and*
- $\mathcal{U} \models \mathsf{E_{uf}}h(0, 1)$ *iff* $\mathcal{V} \models \mathsf{E_{uf}}h(0, 1)$.

Since no two processes among $P'_0, P'_1, ..., P'_m$ in the statement of the above theorem except possibly P'_0 and P'_1 are acquisition-equivalent and *acquisition-type*$(\mathsf{R}(P_0, ..., P_n)) = $ *acquisition-type*$(\mathsf{R}(P'_0, ..., P'_m))$, we have that if $n \geq 3$ then m less than or equal to the maximum of 3 and the cardinality of *acquisition-type*$(\mathsf{R}(P_0, ..., P_n))$. Thus we have the following result.

Theorem 6.5 *We can reduce reasoning about the deadlock characteristics, safety properties and liveness properties under the assumption of unconditional fairness for* *a pair of adjacent processes for the ring* $R(P_0, ..., P_n)$ *where* $n \geq 3$ *to the ring* $V = R(P_0', ..., P_m')$, *where* m *less than or equal to the maximum of 3 and the cardinality of acquisition-type* $(R(P_0, ..., P_n))$.

Since the number of equivalence classes under the acquisition-equivalence relation is 4, therefore the cardinality of the set *acquisition-type* $(R(P_0, ..., P_n))$ is at most 4, we have

Corollary 6.6 *We can reduce reasoning about the deadlock characteristics, safety properties and liveness properties under assumptions of unconditional fairness for a pair of adjacent processes for an arbitrary ring to a ring of size at most 5.*

6.2   Classical Dining Philosophers

In the classical, "symmetric" solution, the philosophers are homogeneous (run the same program up to renaming), and each philosopher P_i tries first to pick up its left fork and only if it is able to get hold of that does it attempt to pick up its right fork. Thus for each i, we have $\prec_i = \{(f_{i-1}, f_i)\}$. We need to verify that for all adjacent pairs of philosophers P_i and P_{i+1}, the mutual exclusion requirement is met, viz., $\bigwedge_i A_{\mathsf{fin}} G \neg (eat_i \wedge eat_{i+1})$, and also test whether each of the processes is deadlockable or not. Using a simple symmetry argument (dubbed "state symmetry" in [17]), we see that it is necessary and sufficient to check whether the property $A_{\mathsf{fin}} G \neg (eat_0 \wedge eat_1)$ is satisfied and whether P_0 is deadlockable. (In short, if $\mathcal{U} \models A_{\mathsf{fin}} G \neg (eat_0 \wedge eat_1)$, and π is the rotation permutation driving 0 to i, then since $\mathcal{U}$ is symmetric under rotations, $\mathcal{U} \models A_{\mathsf{fin}} G \neg (eat_i \wedge eat_{i+1})$; and conversely. Similarly to check liveness for philosopher P_i under assumptions of unconditional fairness, viz., whether the property $A_{\mathsf{uf}} G(hungry_i \Rightarrow Feat_i)$ is satisfied in suffices to check whether $A_{\mathsf{uf}} G(hungry_0 \Rightarrow Feat_0)$ is satisfied. Using theorem 6.5, we have that it is both necessary and sufficient to model check the system comprised of up to 4 philosophers for $A_{\mathsf{fin}} G \neg (eat_0 \wedge eat_1)$, $A_{\mathsf{uf}} G(hungry_0 \Rightarrow Feat_0)$ and for deadlockability of process P_0. We emphasize that this establishes mutual exclusion correctness for philosopher rings of all sizes.

6.3   Non-deterministic Dining Philosophers

In the Non-deterministic Dining Philosophers variant the philosophers are homogeneous, and each philosopher P_i could potentially pick up forks f_{i-1} or f_i in any order. We need to verify that for all adjacent pairs of philosophers P_i and P_{i+1}, the mutual exclusion requirement is met, viz., $\bigwedge_i A_{\mathsf{fin}} G \neg (eat_i \wedge eat_{i+1})$ and test for the deadlockability of each individual philosopher in the system. Using a simple symmetry argument as before, we see that it is necessary and sufficient to check whether the property $A_{\mathsf{fin}} G \neg (eat_0 \wedge eat_1)$ is satisfied and that process P_0 is deadlockable. Again, since all philosophers are acquisition-equivalent, we see that it is both necessary and sufficient to model check the system composed of up to 4 philosophers for $A_{\mathsf{fin}} G \neg (eat_0 \wedge eat_1)$, $A_{\mathsf{uf}} G(hungry_0 \Rightarrow Feat_0)$ and deadlockability of P_0.

6.4   Asymmetric Dining Philosophers Problem

To ensure a deadlock free solution the symmetry is broken by making one process, P_0 say, different from the rest of the processes in that P_0 can either acquire both t_0 and t_n if they are free or none at all. The other philosophers could pick up any of the forks, if free, in a non-deterministic fashion. Thus all philosophers P_i, where $i \in [1..n]$ are acquisition-equivalent to each other, with P_0 belonging to a different equivalence class. To check that the mutual exclusion requirement is satisfied it is both necessary to sufficient to check whether the properties $\mathsf{AG}\neg(eat_0 \wedge eat_1)$ and $\mathsf{AG}\neg(eat_1 \wedge eat_2)$ are satisfied. Similarly to test for liveness and deadlockability it suffices to check for the liveness and deadlockability of P_0 and P_1. Then from theorem 6.5, it is necessary and sufficient to check that the systems $\mathsf{R}(P_0, P_1, ..., P_m)$, where $m \leq 3$, satisfies the desired properties.

6.5   Right-Left Dining Philosophers Algorithm

Although the asymmetric nature of the previous problem guarantees a deadlock free solution, there still exists the problem of long waiting chains with each process waiting for a token in possession of the next process in the chain. In the Right-Left Dining Philosophers problem the number of philosophers, n, is even. Each odd philosopher tries first to pick up its left token and only if it is able to acquire it does to proceed to acquire the right token. Each even numbered philosopher, on the other hand, tries first to pick up its right token and only when it is able to acquire it does it proceed to acquire the left token. Therefore $\prec_i$ equals $\{(t_i, t_{i-1})\}$ if i is even and $\{(t_{i-1}, t_i)\}$ if i is odd. Thus any two even philosophers or any two odd philosophers are acquisition equivalent and any odd philosopher and an even philosopher are not acquisition equivalent. Again, using state symmetry, we see that to check that the mutual exclusion requirement is satisfied, it is both necessary and sufficient to check whether the property $\mathsf{AG}\neg(eat_0 \wedge eat_1)$ is satisfied. Furthermore, it suffices to check for the liveness and deadlockability of processes P_0 and P_1 only. Using theorem 6.5, we see that this can be established by checking that a system with up to 4 philosophers, satisfies the requisite properties.

7   Concluding Remarks

In this paper, we have given techniques for limiting state explosion in the context of resource allocation problems. We considered resource allocation systems where processes share tokens representing resources that are needed to proceed. We show that given any such large system organized into a possibly irregular network of n possibly heterogeneous processes, model checking over that system can be efficiently reduced to model checking over a small system. We establish our results for correctness properties expressed in LTL\X, the choice of which was governed by the fact that it is simpler and technically easier to reason about than branching time logics. Furthermore, incorporating the next-time operator X in the temporal logic could enable us to count the number of processes in a given system, thus making it difficult to reduce reasoning of a system with a large number of processes to one with a small number. This justifies exclusion of the next-time operator from our logic. The precise size and topology of the small system is dependent on the large system, as well as the number of indices (processes tracked/observed) in the correctness specification When the network is symmetric and the processes homogeneous our method specializes to provide an efficient solution to the Parameterized Model Checking Problem. As an application we show how to efficiently verify the parameterized Dining Philosophers Problem.

There has been little work on reduction of state explosion for large irregular or heterogeneous systems. Perhaps the works that come closest in spirit to this paper are ([11], [18]) where various notions of approximate symmetry are considered to permit symmetry-like reductions for certain asymmetric systems. However, those methods do not seem to be as broadly applicable to flatly irregular networks of processes as the one proposed here. Most of the work in the literature seems to require highly regular systems with, e.g., homogeneous processes and symmetric or repetitive network topologies. This often makes it possible to directly exploit symmetry (cf. [7], [14], [15], [17], [21]).

PMCP is, in general, undecidable [2]. However, due to the importance of the problem, much effort has been devoted to obtaining (partial) solutions. Under restrictions positive results have been obtained ([9], [21], [22], [27]). Unfortunately most of these methods suffer, first, from the drawback of being only partially automated and hence requiring human ingenuity, and, second, from being sound but not guaranteed complete (i.e., a path "upstairs" maps to a path "downstairs", but paths downstairs do not necessarily lift). Other potentially useful methods can be fully automated but regrettably do not appear to have a clearly defined class of protocols on which they are guaranteed to terminate successfully ([10], [26]). More recently, a proof tree based decision procedure has been proposed in [23] that dealt solely with the parameterized verification for safety properties and handles a wide range of systems in a unified manner, but no complexity bounds were shown. In ([1],[25]), it is shown how to reduce the PMCP for safety for a certain class of systems to systems with a cutoff number of processes. While the results deal effectively with safety properties for a broad range of applications, extensions to properties other than safety were not given. The problem of reasoning about systems comprised of finite but arbitrarily large number indistinguishable processes communicating by rendezvous (two processes exchange a message) was considered by German and Sistla in [19]. They obtain a fully automated and efficient solution to PMCP for single index properties, modulo deadlock. Emerson and Namjoshi [15] show that in a single class (or client-server) synchronous framework PMCP is decidable but with PSPACE-complete complexity. However the closest results are those of Emerson and Namjoshi [14] who for the token ring model show how to reduce reasoning for multi-indexed temporal logic formulae, for rings of arbitrary size to rings of small cutoff size. Their results were formulated for a single process class, a single token and a restricted topology. In [12], Emerson and Kahlon show for systems with conjunctive and disjunctive guards how to reduce reasoning for systems of any size to a small cutoff size with efficient results being obtained for a broad class of properties including safety.

We believe that our results are significant for several reasons. They are applicable to arbitrarily large, heterogeneous, irregular systems; reducing such a system to an equivalent small system. Our methods specialize in the case of regular networks of homogeneous systems to permit efficient parameterized reasoning. Moreover, our methods are fully automated (algorithmic), returning a yes/no answer, are sound and complete, i.e., exact and efficient for many important properties including safety. Our techniques can be extended to the branching time logic CTL*\X, albeit at the cost of greater technical intricacy and computational complexity. Also the model of computation can be generalized in many ways. First we can allow each token to be shared by more than two processes giving us a bipartite graph over processes and tokens as a formal model. Furthermore, we can allow multiple acquire transitions that require different sets of tokens to be grabbed for execution thus allowing us to model, for instance, solutions to the Drinking Philosophers Problem [6].

References

1. T. Arons, A. Pnueli, S. Ruah, J. Xu, and L. Zuck. Parameterized Verification with Automatically Computed Inductive Assertions. CAV 2001, LNCS, 2001.
2. K. Apt and D. Kozen. Limits for automatic verification of finite-state concurrent systems. *Information Processing Letters*, 15, pages 307-309, 1986.
3. M.C. Browne, E.M. Clarke and O. Grumberg. Reasoning about Networks with Many Identical Finite State Processes. *Information and Control*, 81(1), pages 13-31, April 1989.
4. R.E. Bryant. Graph-based algorithms for boolean function manipulation. *IEEE Trans. on Computers*. C-35(8). pp 677-691, August 1986.
5. J.R. Burch, E.M. Clarke, K. L. McMillan, D.L. Dill and L.J. Hwang. Symbolic model checking: 10^{20} states and beyond. LICS 1990.
6. K.M. Chandy and J. Misra. The Drinking Philosophers Problem. *ACM Transactions on Programming Languages and Systems*, Vol. 6, No. 4, pp 632-646, 1 984.
7. E.M. Clarke, T. Filkorn and S. Jha. Exploiting Symmetry in Temporal Model Checking. In *Computer Aided Verification, Proceedings of the 5th International Conference*. LNCS 697, Springer-Verlag, 1993.
8. E.M. Clarke and E.A. Emerson. Design and synthesis of synchronization skeletons using branching time temporal logics. In *Proceedings of the IBM Workshop on Logics of Programs*, LNCS 131, 1981.
9. E.M. Clarke and O. Grumberg. Avoiding the State Explosion Problem in Temporal Logic Model Checking Algorithms. In *Proceedings of the Sixth Annual ACM Symposium on Principles of Distributed Computing*, pages 294-303, 1987.
10. E.M. Clarke, O. Grumberg and S. Jha. Verifying Parameterized Networks using Abstraction and Regular Languages. In *CONCUR '95: Concurrency Theory, Proceedings of the 6th International Conference*, LNCS 962, pages 395-407, Springer-Verlag, 1995.
11. E. A. Emerson, J. Havlicek and R. Trefler. Virtual Symmetry. LICS 2000.
12. E.A. Emerson and V. Kahlon. Reducing Model Checking of the Many to the Few. In *Automated Deduction - CADE-17*, LNAI 1831, Springer, pages 236-254, 2000.
13. E.A. Emerson and V. Kahlon. Model Checking Large-scale and Parameterized Resource Allocation Systems. Tech. Report, The Univ. of Texas at Austin, 2001.
14. E.A. Emerson and K.S. Namjoshi. Reasoning about Rings. In *Conference Record of POPL '95: 22nd ACM SIGPLAN-SIGACT Symposium on Principles of Programming Languages*, pages 85-94, 1995.
15. E.A. Emerson and K.S. Namjoshi. Automatic Verification of Parameterized Synchronous Systems. In *Computer Aided Verification, Proceedings of the 8th International Conference*. LNCS , Springer-Verlag, 1996.
16. E.A. Emerson and A.P. Sistla. Symmetry and Model Checking. In *Computer Aided Verification, Proceedings of the 5th International Conference*. LNCS 697, Springer-Verlag, 1993.

17. E.A. Emerson and A.P. Sistla. Utilizing Symmetry when Model-Checking under Fairness Assumptions: An Automata-Theoretic Approach. ACM Trans. on Prog. Lang. and Systems (TOPLAS), pp. 617–638, vol. 19, no. 4, July 1997.
18. E. Emerson and R. Trefler. From Asymmetry to Full Symmetry. CHARME99, LNCS, 1999.
19. S.M. German and A.P. Sistla. Reasoning about Systems with Many Processes. *J. ACM*,39(3), July 1992.
20. P. Godefroid and P. Wolper. Using Partial orders for the efficient verification of deadlock-freedom and safety properties. *Formal Methods in Systems Design*. 2(2), pp 149-164, 1993.
21. C. N. Ip and D. Dill, Verifying Systems with Replicated Components in Murphi, pp. 147-158 CAV 1996.
22. R. P. Kurshan and K. L. McMillan. A Structural Induction Theorem for Processes. In *Proceedings of the Eight Annual ACM Symposium on Principles of Distributed Computing*, pages 239-247, 1989.
23. M. Maidl. A Unifying Model Checking Approach for Safety Properties of Parameterized Systems. CAV 2001, LNCS, 2001.
24. D. Peled. Combining partial order reductions with on-the-fly model checking. *Formal Aspects of Computing*, 8, pp 39-64, 1996.
25. A. Pnueli, S. Ruah, and L. Zuck. Automatic Deductive Verification with Invisible Invariants. TACAS 2001, LNCS, 2001.
26. A. P. Sistla. Parameterized Verification of Linear Networks Using Automata as Invariants, CAV, 1997, 412-423.
27. P. Wolper and V. Lovinfosse. Verifying Properties of Large Sets of Processes with Network Invariants. In J. Sifakis(ed) *Automatic Verification Methods for Finite State Systems*, Springer-Verlag, LNCS 407, 1989.

Exploring Very Large State Spaces Using Genetic Algorithms

Patrice Godefroid[1] and Sarfraz Khurshid[2]

[1] Bell Laboratories, Lucent Technologies, god@bell-labs.com
[2] Laboratory for Computer Science, Massachusetts Institute of Technology,
khurshid@lcs.mit.edu

Abstract. We present a novel framework for exploring very large state spaces of concurrent reactive systems. Our framework exploits application-independent heuristics using genetic algorithms to guide a state-space search towards error states. We have implemented this framework in conjunction with VeriSoft, a tool for exploring the state spaces of software applications composed of several concurrent processes executing arbitrary code. We present experimental results obtained with several examples of programs, including a C implementation of a public-key authentication protocol. We discuss heuristics and properties of state spaces that help a genetic search detect deadlocks and assertion violations. For finding errors in very large state spaces, our experiments show that a genetic search using simple heuristics can significantly outperform random and systematic searches.

1 Introduction

Model checking [4] is an automatic technique for verifying finite-state concurrent systems. The *state space* of a concurrent system is a directed graph that represents the combined behavior of all the concurrent components in the system. Model checking typically involves exhaustively searching the state space of a system to determine whether some property of the system is satisfied or not. State-space exploration techniques have been used successfully to detect subtle yet important errors in the design and implementation of several complex hardware and software concurrent reactive systems (e.g., see [19, 3, 1, 9]). It is worth noting that the main practical interest of systematic state-space exploration (and of "verification" in general) is to find errors that would be hard to detect and reproduce otherwise.

The main practical limitation when model checking real systems is dealing with the so-called *state-explosion* problem: the number of states contained in the state space of large complex systems can be huge, even infinite, thereby making exhaustive state-space exploration intractable. Several approaches have been proposed to address the state-explosion problem, including symbolic verification, partial-order methods and symmetry methods. Although these approaches have increased the scope of model checking to state spaces that are several orders of

J.-P. Katoen and P. Stevens (Eds.): TACAS 2002, LNCS 2280, pp. 266–280, 2002.

magnitude larger, many realistic state spaces are still too large to be handled, and state explosion remains a fundamental problem in model checking.

When a problem is computationally too hard to solve using an exact and complete algorithm, it is common in computer science to explore the use of heuristics in order to find approximate solutions to the problem, or to converge faster towards some solutions. Maybe surprisingly, the idea of exploiting heuristics for model checking has received very little attention so far. This may be due to two reasons. First, model checking is not an optimization problem: the primary goal is not to find a best solution (e.g., the shortest path leading to some state), it is to find any solution (e.g., any reachable error state). Second, the historic emphasis in model checking has been on completeness: the primary goal is to exhaustively check every reachable state of the system.

In this paper, we explore the use of *genetic algorithms* [11] for exploring very large state spaces in search for error states. Genetic algorithms are search algorithms inspired by the mechanics of genetics and natural selection. These search algorithms combine survival of the fittest among chromosome-like string structures with a structured yet randomized information exchange. Genetic algorithms are often viewed as function optimizers, although the range of problems they have been applied to is quite broad [18].

We present a framework that uses genetic algorithms to exploit heuristics for guiding a search in the state space of a concurrent reactive system towards errors like deadlocks and assertion violations. At each visited state during a state-space exploration, the genetic algorithm decides which transition to explore next when there are more than one enabled outgoing transitions. We have implemented this framework in conjunction with VeriSoft [8], an existing tool for exploring the state spaces of systems composed of several concurrent software processes executing arbitrary code. We present experimental results obtained with several examples of programs, including a C implementation of a public-key authentication protocol. From these experiments, we discuss general properties of state spaces that seem to help a genetic search find errors quickly. When the state space to be explored is very large, our experiments show that a genetic search using simple application-independent heuristics can significantly outperform random and systematic searches.

The rest of the paper is organized as follows. In Section 2, we recall the basic principles of genetic algorithms. Section 3 describes our framework and the genetic algorithms we use. We discuss how to modify a model checker to let its search be guided by a genetic algorithm. In Section 4, we describe several programs and properties we have analyzed using our implementation. We then discuss results of experiments, and study the influence of various parameters on the effectiveness of a genetic search. In Section 5 we present concluding remarks and discuss related work.

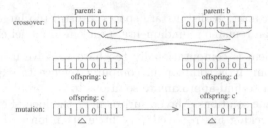

Fig. 1. Illustration of crossover and mutation operators. Candidate solutions are encoded as strings of bits. Parents a and b are recombined to produce offsprings c and d: a crossover is performed at the 4th bit, i.e., the tails of both parents are swapped starting from the 4th bit. Offspring c is then mutated to produce c': a mutation is performed at the 3rd bit, i.e., the value of the 3rd bit is flipped.

2   Genetic Algorithms

A *genetic algorithm* provides an algorithmic framework for exploiting heuristics that simulates natural-evolution processes like selection and mutation. It evolves candidate solutions to problems that have large solution spaces and are not amenable to exhaustive search or traditional optimization techniques. Genetic algorithms have been applied to a broad range of learning and optimization problems [18] since their inception by Holland [11].

Typically, a genetic algorithm starts with a random population of encoded candidate solutions, called *chromosomes*. Through a *recombination* process and *mutation* operators, it evolves the population towards an optimal solution. Generating an optimal solution is not guaranteed and the challenge is thus to design a "genetic" process that maximizes the likelihood of generating such a solution. The first step is typically to evaluate the *fitness* of each candidate solution in the current population, and to select the fittest candidate solutions to act as parents of the next generation of candidate solutions. After being selected for reproduction, parents are recombined (using a *crossover* operator) and mutated (using a *mutation* operator) to generate offsprings (see Figure 1 for a description of these operators). The fittest parents and the new offsprings form a new population, from which the process is repeated to create new populations. Figure 2 gives a standard genetic algorithm in pseudocode.

To illustrate an iteration of a genetic algorithm, consider the boolean satisfiability problem. Assume that we want to find a satisfying assignment to the following boolean formula: $(x_1 \vee x_2 \vee \neg x_3) \wedge (x_2 \vee x_3 \vee x_4) \wedge (\neg x_2 \vee x_5 \vee \neg x_6) \wedge (\neg x_4 \vee \neg x_5 \vee \neg x_6) \wedge (x_3 \vee \neg x_5 \vee \neg x_6) \wedge (x_3 \vee x_4 \vee x_5)$. Let's say we have two (randomly generated) candidate solutions, $a : \{x_1 = 1, x_2 = 1, x_3 = 0, x_4 = 0, x_5 = 0, x_6 = 1\}$ and $b : \{x_1 = 0, x_2 = 0, x_3 = 0, x_4 = 0, x_5 = 1, x_6 = 1\}$. If we evaluate the formula on a, we see that clauses 3 and 6 are false, whereas evaluating the formula on b makes clauses 2 and 5 false. Both a and b are not satisfying assignments. We now recombine a and b to produce an offspring $c : \{x_1 = 1, x_2 = 1, x_3 = 0, x_4 = 0, x_5 = 1, x_6 = 1\}$, which takes the first three variable assignments from a and the last three from b. Offspring c does not define a satisfying assignment

```
gen := 0;
P[gen] := random population;
fitness[gen] := evaluate(P[gen]);
while (fitness[gen] < T) {        // fitness has not reached desired level
  gen++;
  S[gen] := select(P[gen-1]);     // select fittest chromosomes
  CM[gen] := crossover(S[gen]);   // perform crossover on pairs
  CM[gen] := mutate(CM[gen]);     // mutate resulting chromosomes
  P[gen] := S[gen] + CM[gen];     // produce next generation
  fitness[gen] := evaluate(P[gen]); }
```

Fig. 2. Pseudocode for a standard genetic algorithm

either since it makes clause 5 false. However, if we mutate the value c assigns to x_3 to produce d : $\{x_1 = 1, x_2 = 1, x_3 = 1, x_4 = 0, x_5 = 1, x_6 = 1\}$, we see that d does provide a satisfying assignment to our boolean formula.

The operations of evaluation, selection, recombination and mutation are usually performed many times in a genetic algorithm. Selection, recombination, and mutation are generic operations in any genetic algorithm and have been thoroughly investigated in the literature. On the other hand, evaluation is problem specific and relates directly to the structure of the solutions (i.e., how candidate solutions are encoded as chromosomes and relate to each other). Therefore, in a genetic algorithm, a major issue is the choice of the structure of solutions and of the method of evaluation (fitness function). Other parameters include the size of the population, the portion of the population taking part in recombination, and the mutation rate. The mutation rate defines the probability with which a bit is flipped in a chromosome that is produced by a crossover.

3   Genetic Algorithms for State-Space Exploration

In this section, we discuss how genetic algorithms can be used to guide a search in the state space of a concurrent reactive system.

3.1   Combining Genetic Algorithms and Model Checking

In our context, the search space to be explored is the (possibly inifinite) state space of the system. For simplicity and without loss of generality, we assume that the state space has a unique initial state. Candidate solutions are finite sequences of transitions in the state space starting from the initial state. Each candidate solution is encoded by a chromosome, i.e., a finite string of bits. Figure 3 shows a simple example of encoding. How to encode finite paths in a graph using chromosomes is discussed in details below.

To evaluate the fitness of a chromosome, the genetic algorithm *executes* the path encoded by the chromosome. This is done by combining the genetic algorithm with a model checker. Given a representation of a system, the model

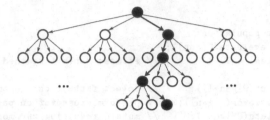

Fig. 3. Example encoding. Assume a state space with fixed branching (of 4) and fixed depth (of 4); 8 bits are used to represent a chromosome. The chromosome '10 01 00 11' encodes the path that visits the filled states (following the bold edges) in state space.

checker determines the state space to explore. The execution of a path starts in the initial state. If there are more than one possible transitions from the current state, the model checker informs the genetic algorithm about the number of possibilities. The genetic algorithm decodes a part of the chromosome it is currently processing and informs the model checker of which transition to take. The model checker then checks whether the state following that transition is an error state. If so, the current path is saved and the user is notified. Otherwise, the model checker repeats this process from the new state.

Since a chromosome can only encode a finite number of transitions, the state space is explored up to a fixed depth. Whenever the model checker has explored a path up to this maximum depth, it prompts the genetic algorithm to evaluate the fitness of the current chromosome. This operation is discussed further below. Once the fitness of the current chromosome has been computed, another chromosome of the current population is evaluated using the same process.

3.2   Genetic Encoding

We now discuss a novel chromosome-encoding scheme that can be applied to arbitrary state spaces. Indeed, the simple encoding technique described in Figure 3 is not satisfactory for several reasons.

First, the number of enabled transitions in a state is typically not constant. Moreover, an upper bound on the number of enabled transitions in a state may not be known a priori[1]. Therefore, a practical encoding cannot use a fixed number of bits to encode a single transition. We resolve this issue by *dynamically* interpreting a chromosome: if there are n enabled transitions from the current state being processed during the state-space search, we read the next $log(n)$ bits from the current chromosome to decide which next transition to explore.

Second, the number of enabled transitions in a state is not necessarily a power of 2. This means that we may have to deal with *spurious* encodings: encodings that fall outside the desired interval of values. The traditional approach [10] to deal with this issue is to map the decoded integer linearly into the desired interval. This approach, however, typically introduces bias toward some values

---

[1] We assume that the number of enabled transitions in any given state is finite, and hence that such a bound exists.

in the desired interval. Therefore, we deal with spurious encodings by *updating* such chromosomes instead: if there are n enabled transitions from the current state and the next $log(n)$ bits of the current chromosome decode to a value greater than or equal to n, we randomly generate a number between 0 and $n-1$ and replace the last $log(n)$ bits read of the chromosome by the binary encoding of this number. Note that our procedure for updating chromosome bits in this case is necessary to avoid multiple fitness evaluations of the same chromosome to evaluate to different values.

Third, a suitable length (i.e., number of bits) for chromosomes cannot be determined in advance. Since a chromosome can only encode a finite number of transitions, the model checker only explores paths up to a fixed depth. For a maximum depth d, we use sufficiently long chromosomes so that they can encode any path of length up to d, and we track the *effective* length of chromosomes. The effective length at any point during a genetic evolution is the maximum number of bits that have been read from any single chromosome up to that point in the search. Mutations and crossovers are performed only on initial segments of chromosomes up to the (current) effective length.

3.3   Fitness Function

An important parameter of a genetic algorithm is the fitness function that defines the fitness of each chromosome. We consider in this work two classes of errors that we wish to detect in state spaces: deadlocks and assertion violations. Deadlocks are states with no outgoing transitions (all the processes in the system are blocked). Assertions are boolean expressions involving program variables that are said to be violated when the corresponding boolean expression evaluates to false. We now discuss heuristics for guiding a genetic search towards both classes of error states.

For deadlock detection, a simple heuristic to measure the fitness of a chromosome is to sum the number of enabled transitions at each state along the execution path represented by the chromosome. The intuition behind this heuristic is that chromosomes with a smaller sum seem more likely to lead to deadlocks, and should therefore be considered fitter.

For detecting assertion violations, a possible heuristic is to attempt maximizing assertion evaluations. To achieve this, one can award *bonus* scores for chromosomes that lead to as many as possible assertion evaluations. One can also award bonuses to chromosomes that make choices leading towards assertion statements at control points in the control flow graph of the program; this can be done by instrumenting the execution of tests (such as "if-then-else" statements) in the program using a static analysis of the program text.

When analyzing protocols with message exchanges, a sensible heuristic is to attempt maximizing the number of messages being exchanged. We use this simple heuristic in the analysis of Needham-Schroeder public key authentication protocol [15] and identify a (previously known [14]) attack on the protocol (see Section 4 for details).

Note that our framework can be used to discover multiple (independent) errors of a same type in a system without requiring to fix previously detected errors. This can be done by awarding *penalty* scores to chromosomes that lead to states where a previously discovered error is detected. Application-specific heuristics can also be used in our framework to fine tune the performance of the genetic algorithm if needed.

3.4   Dynamically Adapting Parameters

The genetic algorithm we use in this work is a slight variation of the pseudocode in Figure 2 where the value of some parameters are adapted as the genetic evolution progresses. In particular, we keep track of the best and worst chromosome fitness in each generation, and, if both fitness values become equal, we increase the mutation rate, in order to help the genetic evolution get out of local maximas. Once there is an improvement in the overall fitness, we restore the original mutation rate to continue evolution as normal.

As mentioned in Section 3.2, we also update the effective length of chromosomes during evolution.

If evolution stabilizes (i.e., the fitness does not seem to improve for several generations) and the search does not find any error, we re-start the genetic algorithm with the initial default parameter values and a new randomly generated seed to generate a new random initial population. This reduces any bias that may have been introduced in a previous run that used a "bad" seed.

4   Experimental Evaluation

We have implemented the framework presented in the previous section in conjunction with VeriSoft [8], a tool that implements model-checking algorithms for exploring the state spaces of systems composed of several concurrent software processes executing arbitrary code written in full-fledged programming languages such as C or C++. We report in this section results of experiments comparing the performances of four state-space search algorithms:

- GA is the genetic algorithm described in the previous section;
- GA_M is GA with no crossovers (only mutations);
- $RAND$ is a "random search" that explores random paths in a state space; and
- EXH is a search algorithm that systematically explores the state space up to some fixed depth[2], and attempts to explore it exhaustively.

The purpose of these experiments is also to identify heuristics and properties of state spaces that help a genetic search detect deadlocks and assertion violations.

---

[2] Note that, in general, the depth of the state space of a software system composed of processes executing arbitrary C or C++ code may not be bounded, making the state space infinite and a fully exhaustive search impossible.

4.1   Examples of Programs and Properties

We report experiments performed with two sample C programs.

Dining philosophers. Consider the following variant of the well-known dining-philosophers problem:

```
while (true) {
  think;
  nondeterministically
    pick left-fork; pick right-fork;
    OR
    pick right-fork; pick left-fork;
  eat;
  drop left-fork; drop right-fork; }
```

The above pseudocode describes a philosopher process. A philosopher starts by thinking, which then makes him hungry at which point he nondeterministically decides to either pick his left fork followed by his right fork, or to pick his right fork followed by his left fork. Once a philosopher has both forks adjacent to him in his hands, he eats. Finally, he drops first the left fork and then the right fork back onto the table, and repeats this process indefinitely. Since several philosophers are sitting around the same table and hence sharing one fork with each of their two adjacent neighbors, they compete for forks with each other. For instance, if all philosophers around the table have picked their left fork, the entire system is then in a deadlock.

We denote by $PHIL$ a C implementation of the above system with 17 philosophers. We arbitrarily choose this large number of processes so that it is not possible to explore the state space of the system exhaustively within a reasonable amount of time. Nondeterminism is simulated using the system call VS_toss supported by VeriSoft (see [8]). In what follows, we compare the effectiveness of various search algorithms to find deadlocks in this system.

Needham-Schroeder protocol. The Needham-Schroeder public-key authentication protocol [15] aims at providing mutual authentication, so that two parties can verify each other's identity before engaging in a transaction. The protocol involves a sequence of message exchanges between an *initiator*, a *responder*, and a mutually-trusted key server. The exact details of the protocol are not necessary for the discussion that follows and we omit these here. An attack against the original protocol involving six message exchanges was reported in [14]: an intruder *Carol* is able to impersonate an initiator *Alice* to set up a false session with responder *Bob*, while *Bob* thinks he is talking to *Alice*.

We denote by $AUTH$ a C implementation[3] of the Needham-Schroeder protocol. This implementation is described by about 500 lines of C code and is much more detailed than the protocol description analyzed in [14]. The C code also contains an assertion that is violated whenever an attack to the protocol

---

[3] John Havlicek provided us this implementation.

Table 1. Genetic search versus random and exhaustive search

		error found?	#errors #runs	runtime (hrs)	average time to find error	depth searched
	GA	yes	26/50	1:16:21	2 min 57 sec	65
PHIL	RAND	no	0/1	8:00:00	-	65
	EXH	no	0/1	8:00:00	-	34
	GA	yes	3/100	2:33:24	51 min 8 sec	110
AUTH	RAND	no	0/1	8:00:00	-	110
	EXH	no	0/1	8:00:00	-	45

occurs. We compare below the effectiveness of various search algorithms to find assertion violations representing attacks to this implementation of the protocol.

4.2 Experimental Results

In the experiments that follow, whenever a genetic search is applied to $PHIL$ to detect deadlocks, the heuristic (fitness function) used is to minimize the sum of enabled transitions along a single execution path. In contrast, whenever a genetic search is applied to $AUTH$ to detect protocol attacks, the heuristic used in the experiments below is to maximize the number of messages exchanged among parties involved in the protocol along a single execution path. All experiments were performed on a Pentium III 700 MHz processor with 256 MB of RAM.

The genetic parameters we use are as follows. The population size is set to 200 chromosomes. The best 100 chromosomes in a generation reproduce. The default mutation rate is 200, i.e., each bit of a chromosome that is produced by a crossover is flipped with probability 1/200. The effective length of chromosomes varies between 70 and 320 bits.

Genetic Search versus Random and Exhaustive Searches. We compare the performance of the search algorithms GA, $RAND$ and EXH for analyzing $PHIL$ and $AUTH$. For GA and $RAND$, we limit the depth of the search to paths of length about twice the length of the shortest path that leads to an error. (We discuss this choice later in this section.) For EXH, we limit the search depth to about the length of the shortest path that leads to an error (with the hope of helping EXH as much as possible).

Table 1 summarizes our results. For $PHIL$, we run GA 50 times (each run starts with a randomly-generated seed), and let it evolve for 50 generations in each run. More than 50% of the runs identify a deadlock. In contrast, both $RAND$ and EXH are unable to find a deadlock in 8 hours of search. For $AUTH$, we run GA 100 times (each run uses a randomly-generated seed), and let it evolve for 100 generations in each run. Only 3 runs identify an attack on the C implementation of the Needham-Schroeder protocol. Again, both $RAND$ and EXH are unable to find an attack in 8 hours.

Despite that GA is able to find an attack in $AUTH$, its performance is worse than when analyzing $PHIL$. This may be due to our choices of fitness functions:

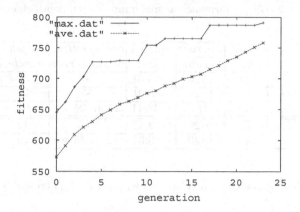

Fig. 4. *GA* deadlock-detection performance. The maximum and average fitness among the parent chromosomes in a generation is plotted against the generation number.

the heuristic for finding deadlocks may be a better measure of fitness, than the simple heuristic of maximizing message exchanges used when exploring the state space of *AUTH*. We chose to use and evaluate these particular heuristics in our experiments because they are application-independent and hence can be used to analyze other applications.

Figure 4 illustrates a run of *GA* on *PHIL*. Typically, a genetic algorithm makes quick progress in the beginning stages of evolution. Then, there are phases when it hits local maximas before mutations further improve its performance. Notice how the average fitness of the parents steadily increases. This indicates that the genetic operators are effective in maximizing fitness while exploring the state space. It should not come as a surprise that the maximum (average) fitness among parents never decreases since we are using the so-called *elitist* model, in which the best chromosomes always survive to the next generation.

Search Deeper. We now investigate how the effectiveness of a genetic search varies as we increase the maximum depth of the search. In these experiments, we consider a simplified version of *AUTH* where the first two message exchanges from a known attack (involving a path of 42 steps in the state space) are hardwired into the search algorithm and the algorithm needs only to find the last 4 message exchanges necessary to complete the attack. We call this simpler problem $AUTH_2$, and use it in the experiments below in order to amplify differences between results we observe.

Table 2 tabulates our results. We run *GA* on *PHIL* for 50 generations. We compare the results of 20 runs using each of the depths 34, 51 and 68, where 34 is the minimum depth required to find a deadlock in *PHIL*. When using depths 34 and 51, *GA* is unable to detect a deadlock, whereas when we increase the depth to 68, 14 out of 20 runs detect a deadlock. When exploring the state space of $AUTH_2$ using a depth of 42, *GA* is unable to find an attack in 20 tries, whereas when we increase the depth to 60, *GA* finds an attack 6 times.

Table 2. *GA* performance as maximum search depth changes

	error found?	#errors / #runs	runtime (hrs)	average time to find error	depth searched
PHIL	no	0/20	0:25:33	-	34
	no	0/20	0:30:01	-	51
	yes	14/20	0:33:44	2 min 24 sec	68
$AUTH_2$	no	0/20	0:33:47	-	42
	yes	6/20	0:28:31	4 min 45 sec	60

Table 3. Genetic search with (GA) and without (GA_M) crossover operator

		error found?	#errors / #runs	runtime (hrs)	average time to find error	depth searched
PHIL	*GA*	yes	26/50	1:16:21	2 min 57 sec	65
	GA_M	yes	26/50	0:59:16	2 min 16 sec	65
$AUTH_2$	*GA*	yes	16/50	1:11:18	4 min 27 sec	60
	GA_M	yes	3/50	1:27:07	29 min 2 sec	60

The reason why a deeper maximum search depth can actually help a genetic search may be the following. From most reachable states in the state spaces of *PHIL* and *AUTH*, there exists a path that leads to an error state. Chromosomes that encode "bad" initial segments are therefore not necessarily penalized since their tails may contain a path that leads to an error state and are sufficient to detect the error. If the exploration was limited to the minimum depth necessary to find an error, chromosomes that encoded the "wrong" first moves would have a very low probability of producing an offspring that corrects these first moves.

On the other hand, increasing the depth of the search should be done with caution since it obviously increases the search space and hence the length of chromosomes, which in turn leads to slower genetic operations and convergence of the algorithm.

Mutation Alone. Here, we investigate the effectiveness of the crossover operator by comparing the performance of GA and GA_M, i.e., GA without crossover operations, when exploring the state spaces of *PHIL* and $AUTH_2$. The same parameter values are used for both GA and GA_M.

Table 3 summarizes our results. The performances of GA and GA_M are comparable on *PHIL*: both algorithms find the deadlock 26 times out of 50 runs. This may be explained as follows. A deadlock in *PHIL* results from a *set* of choices made by the philosophers, namely that they all choose to pick their left forks or they all choose to pick their right forks. In particular, it does not matter in which order the philosophers pick their forks; what matters is which fork they pick. Mutations alone seem effective in finding a deadlock since each

Table 4. GA performance with and without partial-order reduction

	error found?	#errors / #runs	runtime (hrs)	average time to find error	depth searched
$PHIL$	yes	26/50	1:16:21	2 min 57 sec	65
$PHIL^{PO}$	yes	5/50	1:07:32	13 min 30 sec	65
$AUTH_2$	yes	16/50	1:11:18	4 min 27 sec	60
$AUTH_2^{PO}$	yes	1/50	1:24:34	1 hr 24 min 34 sec	60

mutation alters some philosopher's choice and once the right set of choices is attained, a deadlock is reached.

In contrast, GA is more effective than GA_M in finding an attack on $AUTH_2$. An attack on the protocol is formed by a specific *sequence* of message exchanges that allows intrusion: the messages have to be exchanged in a precise order, simply finding the exact set of messages involved in the attack is not sufficient. Since crossovers combine and preserve sub-sequences (of messages in this case), their effect in converging quickly toward a solution becomes more important.

Therefore, it seems preferable to use GA over GA_M when exploring arbitrary state spaces, since GA is effective irrespective of the search being for a set or a sequence of transitions.

Partial-Order Reduction. Finally, we investigate how the use of partial-order reduction techniques (e.g., see [7]) affects the performance of a genetic search. Roughly speaking, partial-order reduction algorithms can dynamically prune the state space of a concurrent system in a completely reliable way (i.e., without missing any errors) by taking advantage of independent (i.e., commutative) actions executed by concurrent processes, hence avoiding to consider all their interleavings during a state-space exploration. The pruned state space defined with partial-order algorithms is thus a subset of the full state space. In the following experiments, we consider a partial-order reduction algorithm using a combination of the persistent-set and sleep-set techniques as implemented in VeriSoft (see [8]). Let $PHIL^{PO}$ and $AUTH_2^{PO}$ denote the reduced state spaces of $PHIL$ and $AUTH_2$, respectively, that are explored when partial-order reduction is used.

Results of experiments are tabulated in Table 4. When exploring $PHIL^{PO}$, GA detects a deadlock only 5 times out of 50 runs. Recall that GA detected a deadlock 26 times during a same number of runs when exploring $PHIL$. A similar decrease in performance is observed when GA explores $AUTH_2^{PO}$.

A possible explanation for this phenomenon is the following. In the reduced state space resulting from partial-order reduction, most reachable states have few outgoing transitions that can be selected to be explored next (thanks to the pruning). Hence, the set of actions corresponding to a set of possible next transitions can vary a lot from state to state. This means that selecting transition number i in a state s may result in executing a program action totally different from the action executed when selecting transition i in another state

s'. In other words, same transition choices made in different context may yield totally different program actions, especially when using partial-order reduction. After a crossover or mutation operation, the tail of each resulting chromosome may be interpreted in an entirely different context, which harms the beneficial effect of these operators.

5 Conclusion and Related Work

We have shown in this paper that, when exploring very large state spaces of concurrent reactive systems, genetic algorithms using simple application-independent heuristics can significantly outperform traditional random and systematic state-space searches used in current model checkers. We have discussed in detail the engineering challenges faced when extending a model checker with a genetic search algorithm. We believe the use of heuristics in model checking could contribute to broadening its applicability by several additional orders of magnitude. Further experiments and studies are needed to validate this claim.

As mentioned in the introduction, genetic algorithms have already been used for a broad range of applications. In particular, genetic algorithms have been used to perform structural and functional testing of sequential programs. For instance, Pargas et al. [16] present a goal-oriented technique for automatic test-data generation using a genetic algorithm guided by program control dependencies; their implementation aims at achieving statement and branch coverage. Jones et al. [12] use genetic algorithms to generate test sets that satisfy the requirements for test-data-set adequacy of structural testing. More recently, Bueno et al. [2] build upon [12] and present a tool for the automation of both test-data generation and infeasible-path identification. In [13], a framework using genetic algorithms is developed for testing methods manipulating complicated data structures; this framework was successfully applied to identify several flaws in a naming architecture for dynamic networks of devices and computers.

In contrast with all this previous work, the problem addressed in this paper is the exploration of (very large) state spaces of concurrent reactive systems as defined with a model checker. This requires the use of original chromosome encodings and fitness functions suitable for the application domain considered here. We are not aware of any other work where genetic algorithms have been used for state-space exploration.

Heuristics for choosing a search order that favor visiting first successor states that are most likely to lead to an error ("best-first search") are discussed in [21] in the context of symbolic model checking and in [5] in the context of explicit model checking. It is worth noting that a best-first search (BFS) can be viewed as a particular case of genetic search (GS). Indeed, the latter can simulate the former as follows: GS uses the same fitness function as that of BFS; crossover and mutation rates are set to 0; the effective length of chromosomes is set to n where n is the current generation; only a single best chromosome in a generation produces the next generation; the number of offsprings produced by this unique parent is the number of outgoing transitions at the last state visited by the parent and each offspring contains the entire parent path plus one more (unique) transition. Backtracking strategies (breadth-first, depth-first, etc.) that can be used in conjunction with BFS can also be simulated by dynamically adapting parameters of GS and appropriately defining the creation of next generation. In contrast, a best-first search cannot simulate a genetic search in general since its "fitness function" is restricted to local heuristics based on the current state and next possible transitions, and hence lacks the ability to simulate the global evaluation of an entire chromosome. Intuitively, a best-first search is also more "deterministic" than a genetic search since it is less general and does not include randomized operations like crossovers and mutations, which improve robustness with respect to sub-optimal fitness functions by helping the search avoid being trapped in local maxima. Further studies are needed to determine which parameter values of a genetic search (including BFS) are best suited for analyzing specific classes of programs and properties.

Heuristics for over and under approximating BDD representations when these become too large or for finding pseudo-optimal BDD-variable orderings are also commonly used in symbolic verification. Such heuristics tackle different problems related to model checking and are of different nature than the ones used here.

The issue of changing parameter values during the run of a genetic algorithm is an active area of research in genetic algorithms. A recent survey is given in [6]. The "1/5 rule" of Rechenberg [17] constitutes a classical adaptive method for setting the mutation rate. This rule states that the ratio of mutations in which the offspring is fitter than the parent, to all mutations should be 1/5, hence if the ratio is greater than 1/5, the mutation rate is increased, and if the ratio is less than 1/5, the mutation rate is decreased.

The "Dynamic Parameter Encoding" [20] (DPE) algorithm provides the ability to encode real-valued parameters of arbitrary precision. DPE first searches for optimal values of more significant digits of the parameters. Next it fixes the values discovered and progressively searches for lesser significant digits. This way the same fixed length chromosome encodes different digits of parameters at different points during the algorithm execution. Notice that DPE requires a priori knowledge of an upper bound on parameter values.

Our dynamic encoding of paths in a state space is novel to the best of our knowledge; it does not require a priori knowledge of the maximum number of enabled transitions in any given state of a state space.

Acknowledgments. We thank John Havlicek for sharing with us his implementation of the Needham-Schroeder protocol. We also thank Darko Marinov and Audris Mockus for helpful comments on this paper, and Enoch Peserico for inspiring discussions on genetic algorithms. The work of the second author was done partly while visiting Bell Laboratories and was also funded in part by ITR grant #0086154 from the National Science Foundation.

References

1. B. Boigelot and P. Godefroid. Model checking in practice: An analysis of the ACCESS.bus protocol using SPIN. In *Proceedings of Formal Methods Europe'96*, volume 1051 of *Lecture Notes in Computer Science*, pages 465–478, Oxford, March 1996. Springer-Verlag.

2. Paul Marcos Siqueira Bueno and Mario Jino. Identification of potentially infeasible program paths by monitoring the search for test data. In *Proceedings of the 15th IEEE International Conference on Automated Software Engineering (ASE)*, Grenoble, France, September 2000.

3. E. M. Clarke, O. Grumberg, H. Hiraishi, S. Jha, D. E. Long, K. L. McMillan, and L. A. Ness. Verification of the Futurebus+ cache coherence protocol. In *Proceedings of the Eleventh International Symposium on Computer Hardware Description Languages and Their Apllications*. North-Holland, 1993.

4. Edmund M. Clarke, Orna Grumberg, and Doron A. Peled. *Model Checking*. The MIT Press, Cambridge, MA, 1999.

5. S. Edelkamp, A. L. Lafuente, and S. Leue. Directed explicit model checking with hsf-spin. In *Proceedings of the 2001 SPIN Workshop*, volume 2057 of *Lecture Notes in Computer Science*, pages 57–79. Springer-Verlag, 2001.

6. A. E. Eiben, R. Hinterding, and Z. Michalewicz. Parameter control in evolutionary algorithms. *IEEE Transactions on Evolutionary Computation*, 3(2):124–141, 1999.

7. Patrice Godefroid. *Partial-Order Methods for the Verification of Concurrent Systems – An Approach to the State-Explosion Problem*, volume 1032 of *Lecture Notes in Computer Science*. Springer-Verlag, January 1996.

8. Patrice Godefroid. Model checking for programming languages using VeriSoft. In *Proceedings of the 24th Annual ACM Symposium on the Principles of Programming Languages (POPL)*, pages 174–186, Paris, France, January 1997.

9. Patrice Godefroid, Robert Hanmer, and Lalita Jagadeesan. Model Checking Without a Model: An Analysis of the Heart-Beat Monitor of a Telephone Switch using VeriSoft. In *Proceedings of ACM SIGSOFT ISSTA'98 (International Symposium on Software Testing and Analysis)*, pages 124–133, Clearwater Beach, March 1998.

10. David E. Goldberg. *Genetic Algorithms in Search, Optimization, and Machine Learning*. Addison-Wesley Publishing Company, Inc., Reading, MA, 1989.

11. John Holland. *Adaptation in Natural and Artificial Systems*. The University of Michigan Press, Ann Arbor, MI, 1975.

12. B. F. Jones, H. H. Sthamer, and D. E. Eyres. Automatic structural testing using genetic algorithms. *Software Engineering Journal*, pages 299–306, Sep 1996.

13. Sarfraz Khurshid. Testing an intentional naming system using genetic algorithms. In *Proceedings of the 7th International Conference on Tools and Algorithms for Construction and Analysis of Systems (TACAS)*, Genova, Italy, April 2001.

14. Gavin Lowe. An attack on the Needham-Schroeder public-key authentication protocol. *Information Processing Letters*, 1995.

15. Roger Needham and Michael Schroeder. Using encryption for authentication in large networks of computers. *Communications of the ACM*, 21(12):993–999, 1978.

16. Roy P. Pargas, Mary Jean Harrold, and Robert Peck. Test-data generation using genetic algorithms. *Journal of Software Testing, Verification, and Reliability*, 9(4):263–282, 1999.

17. Ingo Rechenberg. *Evolutionsstrategie: Optimierung technischer Systeme nach Prinzipien der biologischen Evolution*. Frommann-Holzbog, Stuttgart, 1973.

18. Peter Ross and Dave Corne. Applications of genetic algorithms. *AISB Quaterly on Evolutionary Computation*, pages 23–30, Autumn 1994.

19. H. Rudin. Protocol development success stories: Part I. In *Proc. 12th IFIP WG 6.1 International Symposium on Protocol Specification, Testing, and Verification*, Lake Buena Vista, Florida, June 1992. North-Holland.

20. Nicol N. Schraudolph and Richard K. Belew. Dynamic parameter encoding for genetic algorithms. *Machine Learning*, 9(1):9–21, 1992.

21. C. H. Yang. *Prioritized Model Checking*. PhD thesis, Stanford University, 1998.

Local Model-Checking of Modal Mu-Calculus on Acyclic Labeled Transition Systems

Radu Mateescu

INRIA Rhône-Alpes / VASY, 655, avenue de l'Europe
F-38330 Montbonnot Saint Martin, France
Radu.Mateescu@inria.fr

Abstract. Model-checking is a popular technique for verifying finite-state concurrent systems, whose behaviour can be modeled using Labeled Transition Systems (LTSs). In this paper, we study the model-checking problem for the modal μ-calculus on acyclic LTSs. This has various applications of practical interest such as trace analysis, log information auditing, run-time monitoring, etc. We show that on acyclic LTSs, the full μ-calculus has the same expressive power as its alternation-free fragment. We also present two new local model-checking algorithms based upon a translation to boolean equation systems. The first algorithm handles μ-calculus formulas φ with alternation depth $ad(\varphi) \geq 2$ and has time complexity $O(|\varphi|^2 \cdot (|S| + |T|))$ and space complexity $O(|\varphi|^2 \cdot |S|)$, where $|S|$ and $|T|$ are the number of states and transitions of the acyclic LTS and $|\varphi|$ is the number of operators in φ. The second algorithm handles formulas φ with alternation depth $ad(\varphi) = 1$ and has time complexity $O(|\varphi| \cdot (|S| + |T|))$ and space complexity $O(|\varphi| \cdot |S|)$.

1 Introduction

Model-checking [3] is a popular approach for efficiently verifying the correctness of concurrent finite-state systems. This approach proceeds by translating the system into a finite *model*, represented as a state transition graph or a Labeled Transition System (LTS), on which the desired correctness properties, expressed in temporal logic, are verified using specific model-checking algorithms. According to the way in which they handle the construction of the LTS, model-checking algorithms can be divided in two classes: *global* algorithms, which require to construct the LTS completely before starting the verification, and *local* algorithms, which allow to construct the LTS in a demand-driven way during verification. The latter algorithms are able to detect errors even if the LTS cannot be entirely constructed (e.g., because of insufficient computing resources).

Although model-checking has been mainly used for verifying concurrent systems (communication protocols, distributed applications, hardware architectures), the underlying techniques and algorithms are useful in other contexts as well. In particular, several problems related to the analysis of sequential systems can be formulated as model-checking problems on single trace LTSs: *intrusion detection* by auditing of log file information, as in the USTAT rule-based expert

J.-P. Katoen and P. Stevens (Eds.): TACAS 2002, LNCS 2280, pp. 281–295, 2002.

system [13], in which security properties of log files are encoded as state transition diagrams; *trace analysis* for program debugging, as in the OPIUM trace analyzer for Prolog [8], which uses a dedicated language for describing trace queries; and *run-time monitoring* by observation of event traces in real-time, as in the MOTEL monitoring system [6], which uses LTL [19] for expressing test requirements and for synthesizing observers. It appears that, when analyzing sequential systems, existing modal-checking algorithms can be optimized significantly, especially by reducing their memory consumption, which is crucial for scaling up to larger systems. Therefore, optimizing the performance of model-checking algorithms on sequential systems becomes an interesting issue, with applications in all aforementioned domains.

In this paper, we consider the problem of model-checking temporal properties on acyclic LTSs (ALTSs), of which traces are a particular case. As regards the property specification language, we adopt the modal μ-calculus [15], a powerful fixed point-based temporal logic that subsumes virtually all temporal logics defined in the literature (in-depth presentations of modal μ-calculus can be found in [18,2,22]). Various global algorithms [9,4,5] and local algorithms [16, 1,24,17,21] have been proposed for model-checking μ-calculus formulas on arbitrary LTSs. However, as far as we know, no attempt has been made to optimize these algorithms in the case of ALTSs.

Our results concern both the expressiveness of μ-calculus interpreted on ALTSs, and the underlying model-checking algorithms. We first show that the full modal μ-calculus interpreted on ALTSs has the same expressive power as its alternation-free fragment [9]. Our result is based upon a succinct translation (quadratic blow-up of the formula size) from full μ-calculus to guarded μ-calculus [15], followed by a reduction to alternation-free μ-calculus. Together with the linear-time complexity results for alternation-free μ-calculus [5], this yields a model-checking procedure for the full μ-calculus on ALTSs which is quadratic in the size of the formula (number of operators) and linear in the size of the ALTS (number of states and transitions).

We also propose two local model-checking algorithms for μ-calculus on ALTSs based upon a translation to boolean equation systems (BESs) [18]. The first algorithm handles full μ-calculus formulas and has a time complexity $O(|\varphi|^2 \cdot (|S|+|T|))$ and a space complexity $O(|\varphi|^2 \cdot |S|)$, where $|\varphi|$ is the size of the formula and $|S|$, $|T|$ are the number of states and transitions in the ALTS. The second algorithm handles only alternation-free formulas and has a time complexity $O(|\varphi| \cdot (|S|+|T|))$ and a space complexity $O(|\varphi| \cdot |S|)$. Both algorithms exploit the particular structure of the underlying BES to avoid storing ALTS transitions and thus to achieve a lower space complexity than existing local model-checking algorithms [1,24,17,7] executed on ALTSs.

The paper is organized as follows. Section 2 defines the modal μ-calculus and its guarded fragment, and presents the simplification results for μ-calculus formulas on ALTSs. Section 3 describes the local model-checking algorithms for full μ-calculus and alternation-free μ-calculus on ALTSs. Section 4 gives some concluding remarks and directions for future work.

2   Modal Mu-Calculus and Acyclic LTSs

In this section we study the expressiveness of μ-calculus formulas interpreted on acyclic LTSs, our goal being to simplify formulas as much as possible in order to increase the efficiency of model-checking algorithms. We first define the syntax and semantics of the modal μ-calculus, then we propose a succinct translation of the μ-calculus to its guarded fragment, and finally we present the simplification results obtained.

2.1   Syntax and Semantics

As interpretation models, we consider labeled transition systems (LTSs), which are suitable for action-based description languages such as process algebras. An LTS is a tuple $M = (S, A, T, s_0)$, where: S is a (finite) set of *states*; A is a (finite) set of *actions*; $T \subseteq S \times A \times S$ is the *transition relation*; and $s_0 \in S$ is the *initial state*. A transition $(s_1, a, s_2) \in T$ (also noted $s_1 \xrightarrow{a} s_2$) means that the system can move from state s_1 to state s_2 by performing action a. The notation $s_1 \xrightarrow{*} s_2$ means that there exists a sequence of (0 or more) transitions leading from s_1 to s_2. All states in S are reachable from s_0 via sequences of transitions in T ($s_0 \xrightarrow{*} s$ for all $s \in S$). If T does not contain cycles, M is called an *acyclic* LTS (ALTS). In the sequel, we assume the existence of an LTS $M = (S, A, T, s_0)$ on which all temporal logic formulas will be interpreted.

The μ-calculus variant we consider here (see Table 1) is slightly extended w.r.t. the original one [15]: instead of simple actions $a \in A$, the modalities contain action formulas α built from actions and standard boolean operators (derived connectives are $\mathsf{F} = a \wedge \neg a$ for some $a \in A$, $\mathsf{T} = \neg \mathsf{F}$, $\alpha_1 \vee \alpha_2 = \neg(\neg\alpha_1 \wedge \neg\alpha_2)$, etc.). State formulas φ are built from propositional variables $X \in \mathcal{X}$, standard boolean operators, possibility and necessity modal operators $\langle \alpha \rangle \varphi$ and $[\alpha] \varphi$, minimal and maximal fixed point operators $\mu X.\varphi$ and $\nu X.\varphi$. The μ and ν operators act as binders for variables in a way similar to quantifiers in first-order logic. A formula φ without free occurrences of variables is *closed*. In the sequel, we assume that state formulas are in *normal form*, i.e., all propositional variables bound by fixed point operators have distinct names. We use the symbol σ to denote μ or ν.

The interpretation $[\![\alpha]\!] \subseteq A$ of an action formula α yields the set of LTS actions satisfying α. The interpretation $[\![\varphi]\!] \rho \subseteq S$ of a state formula φ, where $\rho : \mathcal{X} \to 2^S$ is a propositional context assigning state sets to variables, yields the set of LTS states satisfying φ in the context ρ ($\rho[U/X]$ denotes a context identical to ρ except for variable X, which is assigned state set U). The $\langle \alpha \rangle \varphi$ and $[\alpha] \varphi$ modalities characterize the states for which some, respectively all outgoing transitions whose actions satisfy α lead to states satisfying φ. The $\mu X.\varphi$ and $\nu X.\varphi$ formulas characterize the states satisfying the minimal, respectively maximal solution (over 2^S) of the equation $X = \varphi$. For closed state formulas φ, we simply write $[\![\varphi]\!]$, since the interpretation of these formulas does not depend upon any propositional context. An LTS $M = (S, A, T, s_0)$ satisfies a closed state formula φ (notation $M \models \varphi$) iff $[\![\varphi]\!] = S$.

Table 1. Syntax and semantics of the modal μ-calculus

Syntax ($X \in \mathcal{X}$ are propositional variables):
$$\alpha ::= a \mid \neg\alpha \mid \alpha_1 \wedge \alpha_2$$
$$\varphi ::= \mathsf{F} \mid \mathsf{T} \mid \varphi_1 \vee \varphi_2 \mid \varphi_1 \wedge \varphi_2 \mid \langle\alpha\rangle\,\varphi \mid [\alpha]\,\varphi \mid X \mid \mu X.\varphi \mid \nu X.\varphi$$

Semantics ($\rho : \mathcal{X} \to 2^S$ are propositional contexts):
$$[\![a]\!] = \{a\}$$
$$[\![\neg\alpha]\!] = A \setminus [\![\alpha]\!]$$
$$[\![\alpha_1 \wedge \alpha_2]\!] = [\![\alpha_1]\!] \cap [\![\alpha_2]\!]$$

$$[\![\mathsf{F}]\!]\,\rho = \emptyset$$
$$[\![\mathsf{T}]\!]\,\rho = S$$
$$[\![\varphi_1 \vee \varphi_2]\!]\,\rho = [\![\varphi_1]\!]\,\rho \cup [\![\varphi_2]\!]\,\rho$$
$$[\![\varphi_1 \wedge \varphi_2]\!]\,\rho = [\![\varphi_1]\!]\,\rho \cap [\![\varphi_2]\!]\,\rho$$
$$[\![\langle\alpha\rangle\,\varphi]\!]\,\rho = \{s \in S \mid \exists s \xrightarrow{a} s' \in T.a \in [\![\alpha]\!] \wedge s' \in [\![\varphi]\!]\,\rho\}$$
$$[\![[\alpha]\,\varphi]\!]\,\rho = \{s \in S \mid \forall s \xrightarrow{a} s' \in T.a \in [\![\alpha]\!] \Rightarrow s' \in [\![\varphi]\!]\,\rho\}$$
$$[\![X]\!]\,\rho = \rho(X)$$
$$[\![\mu X.\varphi]\!]\,\rho = \bigcap\{U \subseteq S \mid [\![\varphi]\!]\,\rho[U/X] \subseteq U\}$$
$$[\![\nu X.\varphi]\!]\,\rho = \bigcup\{U \subseteq S \mid U \subseteq [\![\varphi]\!]\,\rho[U/X]\}$$

2.2 Reduction of Full Mu-Calculus to Guarded Mu-Calculus

In order to simplify the interpretation of modal μ-calculus on ALTSs, we must first translate all fixed point formulas $\sigma X.\varphi$ in *guarded form* [15,23]: all free occurrences of X in φ must be guarded, i.e., in the scope of a $\langle\,\rangle$ or $[\,]$ modality. The translations proposed in [15,23] require repeated transformations of subformulas in conjunctive normal form, leading to an exponential blow-up of the formula. We present below a more succinct translation in guarded form, which (by using factorization of common subformulas) yields only a quadratic blow-up. This translation is purely syntactic, i.e., it does not depend upon the structure of the LTS $M = (S, A, T, s_0)$ on which formulas are interpreted.

Definition 1 (guarded and weakly guarded formulas). *Let φ be a state formula and $\mathcal{X}$ be a set of variables. φ is called* guarded, *resp.* weakly guarded *w.r.t. $\mathcal{X}$ iff it satisfies the predicate $g(\varphi, \mathcal{X})$, resp. $wg(\varphi, \mathcal{X})$, defined inductively below. φ is called* guarded *iff it satisfies $g(\varphi, \emptyset)$.*

φ	$g(\varphi, \mathcal{X})$	$wg(\varphi, \mathcal{X})$
F, T	T	T
$\varphi_1 \vee \varphi_2$, $\varphi_1 \wedge \varphi_2$	$g(\varphi_1, \mathcal{X}) \wedge g(\varphi_2, \mathcal{X})$	$wg(\varphi_1, \mathcal{X}) \wedge wg(\varphi_2, \mathcal{X})$
$\langle\alpha\rangle\,\varphi$, $[\alpha]\,\varphi$	$g(\varphi, \emptyset)$	$g(\varphi, \emptyset)$
X	$X \notin \mathcal{X}$	T
$\mu X.\varphi$, $\nu X.\varphi$	$g(\varphi, \mathcal{X} \cup \{X\})$	$g(\varphi, \mathcal{X} \cup \{X\})$

Intuitively, a formula φ weakly guarded w.r.t. $\{X\}$ allows unguarded occurrences of X only at top-level, i.e., outside any fixed point subformula of φ. The formula below, obtained by translating in μ-calculus the PDL [11] regular modality $\langle (a|b^*)^*.c \rangle$ T, is unguarded w.r.t. $\{X\}$:

$$\varphi_1 = \mu X.(\langle c \rangle \text{ T} \vee \langle a \rangle X \vee \mu Y.(X \vee \langle b \rangle Y))$$

To make this formula guarded, we must eliminate the unguarded occurrence of X contained in the μY-subformula. The first step is to bring this occurrence at the top-level of the body of φ_1. This is done by unfolding the μY-subformula, resulting in the formula below, whose body is weakly guarded w.r.t. $\{X\}$:

$$\varphi_2 = \mu X.(\langle c \rangle \text{ T} \vee \langle a \rangle X \vee (X \vee \langle b \rangle \mu Y.(X \vee \langle b \rangle Y)))$$

The second step is to eliminate the top-level unguarded occurrence of X. This is done using the transformation below, which replaces, in a formula $\mu X.\varphi$ (resp. $\nu X.\varphi$), all unguarded occurrences of X at the top-level of φ by F (resp. T).

Definition 2 (flattening). *Let φ be a state formula, X be a variable, and $\sigma \in \{\mu, \nu\}$. The formula $f(\varphi, X, \sigma)$ defined inductively below is called the* flattening *of φ w.r.t. X.*

φ	$f(\varphi, X, \sigma)$	φ	$f(\varphi, X, \sigma)$
F	F	T	T
$\varphi_1 \vee \varphi_2$	$f(\varphi_1, X, \sigma) \vee f(\varphi_2, X, \sigma)$	$\varphi_1 \wedge \varphi_2$	$f(\varphi_1, X, \sigma) \wedge f(\varphi_2, X, \sigma)$
$\langle \alpha \rangle \varphi$	$\langle \alpha \rangle \varphi$	$[\alpha] \varphi$	$[\alpha] \varphi$
Y	Y *(if $Y \neq X$)*	X	if $\sigma = \mu$ then F else T
$\mu Y.\varphi$	$\mu Y.\varphi$	$\nu Y.\varphi$	$\nu Y.\varphi$

By flattening the formula φ_2, we obtain the guarded formula below:

$$\varphi_3 = \mu X.(\langle c \rangle \text{ T} \vee \langle a \rangle X \vee (\text{F} \vee \langle b \rangle \mu Y.(X \vee \langle b \rangle Y)))$$

This formula can be translated back into the PDL modality $\langle (a|(b.b^*))^*.c \rangle$ T, which is equivalent to the initial formula $\langle (a|b^*)^*.c \rangle$ T.

The following results state that flattening of fixed point formulas does not change their interpretation.

Lemma 1. *Let φ be a state formula, X be a variable, and $U \subseteq S$. Then:*

$$[\![f(\varphi, X, \nu)]\!] \, \rho[U/X] \cap U \subseteq [\![\varphi]\!] \, \rho[U/X] \subseteq [\![f(\varphi, X, \mu)]\!] \, \rho[U/X] \cup U$$

for any propositional context ρ.

Proposition 1. *Let $\sigma X.\varphi$ be a state formula. Then:*

$$[\![\sigma X.\varphi]\!] \, \rho = [\![\sigma X.f(\varphi, X, \sigma)]\!] \, \rho$$

for any propositional context ρ.

Proof. We show only the case $\sigma = \mu$, the other case being similar. Since some occurrences of X in φ have been replaced by F in $f(\varphi, X, \mu)$, it follows by monotonicity that $[\![\mu X.f(\varphi, X, \mu)]\!]\,\rho \subseteq [\![\mu X.\varphi]\!]\,\rho$. To show the converse, let $U \subseteq S$ such that $[\![f(\varphi, X, \mu)]\!]\,\rho[U/X] \subseteq U$. Using Lemma 1, this implies $[\![\varphi]\!]\,\rho[U/X] \subseteq [\![f(\varphi, X, \mu)]\!]\,\rho[U/X] \cup U = U$. This further implies $\{U \subseteq S \mid [\![f(\varphi, X, \mu)]\!]\,\rho[U/X] \subseteq U\} \subseteq \{U \subseteq S \mid [\![\varphi]\!]\,\rho[U/X] \subseteq U\}$, which by interpretation of formulas (Table 1) yields $[\![\mu X.\varphi]\!]\,\rho = \bigcap\{U \subseteq S \mid [\![\varphi]\!]\,\rho[U/X] \subseteq U\} \subseteq \bigcap\{U \subseteq S \mid [\![f(\varphi, X, \mu)]\!]\,\rho[U/X] \subseteq U\} = [\![\mu X.f(\varphi, X, \mu)]\!]\,\rho.$ □

The transformation defined below, consisting of two mutually recursive functions t and t', reduces state formulas to guarded form. These functions implement the transformation outlined in the previous example when φ_1 was translated to φ_3: for every fixed point formula $\sigma X.\varphi$, the unguarded occurrences of X are brought to the top-level of φ using $t'(\varphi)$ and then they are eliminated by flattening using $f(t'(\varphi), X, \sigma)$. By applying $t'(\varphi)$, the fixed point subformulas of φ that are not in the scope of a modality are unfolded ($\varphi'[\varphi''/X]$ denotes the syntactic substitution of the free occurrences of X in φ' by φ'').

Definition 3 (translation to guarded μ-calculus). *Let φ be a state formula. The functions t, t' defined inductively below translate φ in guarded form.*

φ	$t(\varphi)$	$t'(\varphi)$
F	F	F
T	T	T
$\varphi_1 \vee \varphi_2$	$t(\varphi_1) \vee t(\varphi_2)$	$t'(\varphi_1) \vee t'(\varphi_2)$
$\varphi_1 \wedge \varphi_2$	$t(\varphi_1) \wedge t(\varphi_2)$	$t'(\varphi_1) \wedge t'(\varphi_2)$
$\langle \alpha \rangle\, \varphi$	$\langle \alpha \rangle\, t(\varphi)$	$\langle \alpha \rangle\, t(\varphi)$
$[\alpha]\, \varphi$	$[\alpha]\, t(\varphi)$	$[\alpha]\, t(\varphi)$
X	X	X
$\sigma X.\varphi$	$\sigma X.f(t'(\varphi), X, \sigma)$	$f(t'(\varphi), X, \sigma)[\sigma X.f(t'(\varphi), X, \sigma)/X]$

The interested reader can easily check that $t(\varphi_1) = \varphi_3$. The syntactic and semantic properties below state that this transformation indeed reduces formulas to guarded form while preserving their interpretation.

Proposition 2. *Let φ be a state formula. Then:*

$$g(t(\varphi), \emptyset) \wedge wg(t'(\varphi), fv(\varphi))$$

where $fv(\varphi)$ is the set of free variables of φ.

Proposition 3. *Let φ be a state formula. Then:*

$$[\![t(\varphi)]\!]\,\rho = [\![t'(\varphi)]\!]\,\rho = [\![\varphi]\!]\,\rho$$

for any propositional context ρ.

Proof. By structural induction on φ. We show only the case $\varphi = \sigma X.\varphi_1$, the other cases being straightforward. By definition of t' and unfolding of fixed points, we have $[\![t'(\sigma X.\varphi_1)]\!]\,\rho = [\![f(t'(\varphi_1), X, \sigma)[\sigma X.f(t'(\varphi_1), X, \sigma)/X]]\!]\,\rho = [\![\sigma X.f(t'(\varphi_1), X, \sigma)]\!]\,\rho = [\![t(\sigma X.\varphi_1)]\!]\,\rho$. By Proposition 1 and inductive hypothesis, it follows that $[\![\sigma X.f(t'(\varphi_1), X, \sigma)]\!]\,\rho = [\![\sigma X.t'(\varphi_1)]\!]\,\rho = [\![\sigma X.\varphi_1]\!]\,\rho$.   □

We conclude this section by an estimation of the size $|t(\varphi)|$ (number of operators and variables in $t(\varphi)$). The application of $t(\varphi)$ consists of flattening and unfolding steps performed in a bottom-up manner on the fixed point subformulas of φ. Flattening does not change the size of formulas, since it simply replaces some occurrences of variables by constant boolean operators. A direct implementation of fixed point unfolding would yield, for each $\sigma X.\varphi'$ subformula of φ, a size $|f(t'(\varphi'), X, \sigma)[\sigma X.f(t'(\varphi'), X, \sigma)/X]| \leq |f(t'(\varphi'), X, \sigma)|^2 = |t'(\varphi')|^2$, leading to an overall size $|t(\varphi)| \leq |\varphi|^{2 \cdot |\varphi|}$.

An implementation of unfolding by using factorization of common subformulas would yield, for each $\sigma X.\varphi'$ subformula of φ, a size $|f(t'(\varphi'), X, \sigma)[\sigma X.f(t'(\varphi'), X, \sigma)/X]| = |f(t'(\varphi'), X, \sigma)| + |\sigma X.f(t'(\varphi'), X, \sigma)|$. Note that the second summand above appears only once for each subformula $\sigma X.\varphi'$: since $f(t'(\varphi'), X, \sigma)$ is guarded w.r.t. $\{X\}$, all fixed point subformulas $\sigma X.f(t'(\varphi'), X, \sigma)$ substituted for X in $f(t'(\varphi'), X, \sigma)$ will occur in the scope of modalities and will remain unchanged during later flattening steps. In this way, each fixed point subformula of φ will be duplicated only once (at the moment of its unfolding) and reused in later steps, leading to an overall size $|t(\varphi)| \leq |\varphi|^2$.

The translations to guarded form proposed in [15,23] perform the flattening of a formula $\sigma X.\varphi$ by converting φ in conjunctive normal form (considering modal and fixed point subformulas as literals) before replacing the top-level unguarded occurrences of X in φ with F or T. This yields a worst-case exponential size of the final formula, even if a factorization scheme is applied.

2.3   Simplification of Guarded Mu-Calculus on ALTSs

We show in this section that guarded μ-calculus formulas can be considerably simplified when interpreted on ALTSs $M = (S, A, T, s_0)$, consequently increasing the efficiency of model-checking. For technical reasons, we need to use the negation operator ($\neg$) on state formulas. The negation of a state formula φ, noted $\neg\varphi$, is interpreted in a context ρ as $[\![\neg\varphi]\!] \rho = S \setminus [\![\varphi]\!] \rho$. For the sake of simplicity, we did not use the negation operator in the definition of μ-calculus given in Section 2.1. In the presence of negation, to ensure the well-definedness of the interpretation of fixed point formulas, we must impose the *syntactic monotonicity* condition [15]: in any fixed point formula $\mu X.\varphi$ or $\nu X.\varphi$, all free occurrences of X in φ must be in the scope of an even number of negations. Using *duality* (see below), any syntactically monotonic formula can be converted in *positive form*, i.e., an equivalent formula without negation operators.

The *dual* of a state formula φ w.r.t. a set of propositional variables $\{X_1, ..., X_n\}$ is the negation of φ in which all free occurrences of $X_1, ..., X_n$ are respectively replaced by $\neg X_1, ..., \neg X_n$. However, to facilitate the reasoning by structural induction, we prefer an inductive definition of dual formulas.

Definition 4 (dual formulas). *Let φ be a state formula and let $\mathcal{X} = \{X_1, ..., X_n\}$ be a set of propositional variables. The formula $d(\varphi, \mathcal{X})$ defined inductively below is called the* dual *of φ w.r.t. $\mathcal{X}$.*

Proof. We show only the case $\sigma = \mu$, the other case being similar. Since some occurrences of X in φ have been replaced by F in $f(\varphi, X, \mu)$, it follows by monotonicity that $[\![\mu X. f(\varphi, X, \mu)]\!]\, \rho \subseteq [\![\mu X.\varphi]\!]\, \rho$. To show the converse, let $U \subseteq S$ such that $[\![f(\varphi, X, \mu)]\!]\, \rho[U/X] \subseteq U$. Using Lemma 1, this implies $[\![\varphi]\!]\, \rho[U/X] \subseteq [\![f(\varphi, X, \mu)]\!]\, \rho[U/X] \cup U = U$. This further implies $\{U \subseteq S \mid [\![f(\varphi, X, \mu)]\!]\, \rho[U/X] \subseteq U\} \subseteq \{U \subseteq S \mid [\![\varphi]\!]\, \rho[U/X] \subseteq U\}$, which by interpretation of formulas (Table 1) yields $[\![\mu X.\varphi]\!]\, \rho = \bigcap\{U \subseteq S \mid [\![\varphi]\!]\, \rho[U/X] \subseteq U\} \subseteq \bigcap\{U \subseteq S \mid [\![f(\varphi, X, \mu)]\!]\, \rho[U/X] \subseteq U\} = [\![\mu X. f(\varphi, X, \mu)]\!]\, \rho$. □

The transformation defined below, consisting of two mutually recursive functions t and t', reduces state formulas to guarded form. These functions implement the transformation outlined in the previous example when φ_1 was translated to φ_3: for every fixed point formula $\sigma X.\varphi$, the unguarded occurrences of X are brought to the top-level of φ using $t'(\varphi)$ and then they are eliminated by flattening using $f(t'(\varphi), X, \sigma)$. By applying $t'(\varphi)$, the fixed point subformulas of φ that are not in the scope of a modality are unfolded ($\varphi'[\varphi''/X]$ denotes the syntactic substitution of the free occurrences of X in φ' by φ'').

Definition 3 (translation to guarded μ-calculus). *Let φ be a state formula. The functions t, t' defined inductively below translate φ in guarded form.*

φ	$t(\varphi)$	$t'(\varphi)$
F	F	F
T	T	T
$\varphi_1 \vee \varphi_2$	$t(\varphi_1) \vee t(\varphi_2)$	$t'(\varphi_1) \vee t'(\varphi_2)$
$\varphi_1 \wedge \varphi_2$	$t(\varphi_1) \wedge t(\varphi_2)$	$t'(\varphi_1) \wedge t'(\varphi_2)$
$\langle \alpha \rangle\, \varphi$	$\langle \alpha \rangle\, t(\varphi)$	$\langle \alpha \rangle\, t(\varphi)$
$[\alpha]\, \varphi$	$[\alpha]\, t(\varphi)$	$[\alpha]\, t(\varphi)$
X	X	X
$\sigma X.\varphi$	$\sigma X. f(t'(\varphi), X, \sigma)$	$f(t'(\varphi), X, \sigma)[\sigma X. f(t'(\varphi), X, \sigma)/X]$

The interested reader can easily check that $t(\varphi_1) = \varphi_3$. The syntactic and semantic properties below state that this transformation indeed reduces formulas to guarded form while preserving their interpretation.

Proposition 2. *Let φ be a state formula. Then:*

$$g(t(\varphi), \emptyset) \wedge wg(t'(\varphi), fv(\varphi))$$

where $fv(\varphi)$ is the set of free variables of φ.

Proposition 3. *Let φ be a state formula. Then:*

$$[\![t(\varphi)]\!]\, \rho = [\![t'(\varphi)]\!]\, \rho = [\![\varphi]\!]\, \rho$$

for any propositional context ρ.

Proof. By structural induction on φ. We show only the case $\varphi = \sigma X.\varphi_1$, the other cases being straightforward. By definition of t' and unfolding of fixed points, we have $[\![t'(\sigma X.\varphi_1)]\!]\, \rho = [\![f(t'(\varphi_1), X, \sigma)[\sigma X. f(t'(\varphi_1), X, \sigma)/X]]\!]\, \rho = [\![\sigma X. f(t'(\varphi_1), X, \sigma)]\!]\, \rho = [\![t(\sigma X.\varphi_1)]\!]\, \rho$. By Proposition 1 and inductive hypothesis, it follows that $[\![\sigma X. f(t'(\varphi_1), X, \sigma)]\!]\, \rho = [\![\sigma X. t'(\varphi_1)]\!]\, \rho = [\![\sigma X.\varphi_1]\!]\, \rho$. □

unfolding the fixed point formulas, the above equality becomes $[\![\varphi]\!]\,\rho[A/X] \cap$
$[\![d(\varphi, \{X\})]\!]\,\rho[B/X] = \emptyset$.

Suppose this equality does not hold, and let $s \in [\![\varphi]\!]\,\rho[A/X] \cap [\![d(\varphi, \{X\})]\!]$
$\rho[B/X]$. By applying Lemma 2, and since $g(\varphi, \{X\})$ by hypothesis, this implies
$s \xrightarrow{*} s'$, where $s' \in A \cap B = [\![\varphi]\!]\,\rho[A/X] \cap [\![d(\varphi, \{X\})]\!]\,\rho[B/X]$ and $s' \neq s$. Thus,
from every state $s \in A \cap B$ there is a non empty transition sequence to another
state $s' \in A \cap B$. Since the state set $A \cap B$ is finite, this means there is a cycle
between states in $A \cap B$ (contradiction with M acyclic). □

The practical consequence of Theorem 1 is to allow the simplification of
guarded state formulas interpreted on ALTSs by converting all occurrences of
maximal fixed points into minimal fixed points (or vice-versa, which would lead
to an equivalent simplification). The resulting formulas φ are *alternation-free* [9]
because they do not contain mutually recursive minimal and maximal fixed point
operators, and consequently their model-checking on ALTSs $M = (S, A, T, s_0)$
has a time and space complexity $O(|\varphi| \cdot (|S| + |T|))$ [5].

Together with the translation in guarded form given in Section 2.2, the re-
duction provided by Theorem 1 yields an overall complexity of $O(|\varphi|^2 \cdot (|S| + |T|))$
for the model-checking of arbitrary μ-calculus formulas on ALTSs. Moreover, the
space complexity of model-checking can be improved in this case to $O(|\varphi|^2 \cdot |S|)$,
as shown in the next section.

3   Local Model-Checking on Acyclic LTSs

After applying the translation to guarded form and the simplification defined
in Sections 2.2 and 2.3, we obtain simplified guarded state formulas $\mu X.\varphi$ that
contain only minimal fixed point variables[1]. The local verification of this kind
of formulas on ALTSs could be easily handled by the existing model-checking
algorithms for alternation-free μ-calculus [1,24,17,7]. However, by exploiting the
absence of cycles in the ALTS and the guardedness property of the formulas, we
can devise algorithms with a better space complexity.

We adopt an approach that has been used for model-checking the alternation-
free μ-calculus [1,24]. The approach consists of translating the verification problem to the local resolution of a boolean equation system, which is performed by
on-the-fly exploration of the dependency graph between boolean variables.

3.1   Translation to Boolean Equation Systems

We encode the model-checking problem of a guarded simplified formula on an
ALTS by using boolean equation systems (BESs) [18]. A (simple) BES (see Table 2) is a system of minimal fixed point equations $\{z_i = op_i Z_i\}_{1 \leq i \leq n}$ whose
left hand sides are boolean variables $z_i \in Z$ and whose right-hand sides are
pure disjunctive or conjunctive boolean formulas. Empty disjunctions and conjunctions are equivalent to F and T, respectively. The interpretation of a BES

---

[1] Any formula φ can be converted to the form $\mu X.\varphi$, where X is a "fresh" variable.

w.r.t. a boolean context $\delta : \mathcal{Z} \to \{F, T\}$ is the minimal fixed point of a vectorial functional $\overline{\Psi}_\delta$ defined over $\{F, T\}^n$.

Table 2. Syntax and semantics of BESs

$$\{z_i = op_i Z_i\}_{1 \le i \le n}$$
where $op_i \in \{\vee, \wedge\}$, $Z_i \subseteq \mathcal{Z}$ for all $1 \le i \le n$

$$[\![op_i\{z_1, ..., z_p\}]\!]\delta = \delta(z_1)\ op_i...op_i\ \delta(z_p)$$
$$[\![\{z_i = op_i Z_i\}_{1 \le i \le n}]\!]\delta = \mu\overline{\Psi}_\delta$$
where $\overline{\Psi}_\delta : \{F, T\}^n \to \{F, T\}^n$,
$$\overline{\Psi}_\delta(b_1, ..., b_n) = ([\![op_i Z_i]\!]\ \delta[b_1/z_1, ..., b_n/z_n])_{1 \le i \le n}$$

The function h_1 defined below constructs a BES encoding the model-checking problem of a guarded simplified formula $\mu X.\varphi$ on an ALTS. For each subformula φ' of φ and each $s \in S$, the BES defines a boolean variable $Z_{\varphi',s}$ which is true iff s satisfies φ'. The auxiliary function $h_2(\varphi', s)$ produces the boolean formulas in the right-hand sides of the equations, by introducing extra variables in order to obtain only pure disjunctive or conjunctive formulas.

Definition 5 (translation to BESs). *Let $\mu X.\varphi$ be a closed simplified guarded formula and $M = (S, A, T, s_0)$ be an ALTS. The translation $h_1(\mu X.\varphi, s)$ defined below yields a BES encoding the satisfaction of $\mu X.\varphi$ by a state $s \in S$.*

φ	$h_1(\varphi, s)$	$h_2(\varphi, s)$
F	$\{\}$	$\bigvee \emptyset$
T		$\bigwedge \emptyset$
$\varphi_1 \vee \varphi_2$	$\{Z_{\varphi_1,s} = h_2(\varphi_1, s), Z_{\varphi_2,s} = h_2(\varphi_2, s)\} \cup$	$Z_{\varphi_1,s} \vee Z_{\varphi_2,s}$
$\varphi_1 \wedge \varphi_2$	$h_1(\varphi_1, s) \cup h_1(\varphi_2, s)$	$Z_{\varphi_1,s} \wedge Z_{\varphi_2,s}$
$\langle \alpha \rangle \varphi$	$\{Z_{\varphi,s'} = h_2(\varphi, s') \mid s \xrightarrow{a} s' \wedge a \in [\![\alpha]\!]\} \cup$	$\bigvee\{Z_{\varphi,s'} \mid s \xrightarrow{a} s' \wedge a \in [\![\alpha]\!]\}$
$[\alpha] \varphi$	$h_1(\varphi, s)$	$\bigwedge\{Z_{\varphi,s'} \mid s \xrightarrow{a} s' \wedge a \in [\![\alpha]\!]\}$
X	$\{\}$	$Z_{X,s}$
$\mu X.\varphi$	$\{Z_{X,s} = h_2(\varphi, s)\} \cup h_1(\varphi, s)$	

The size of the resulting BES is linear in the size of the formula $\mu X.\varphi$ and the size of the ALTS: there are at most $|\varphi| \cdot |S|$ boolean variables and $|\varphi| \cdot (|S| + |T|)$ operators in the right-hand sides. The functions h_1, h_2 are very similar to other translations from fixed point formulas to BESs given in [5,1] or [18, chap. 2]. The local model-checking problem of $\mu X.\varphi$ on the initial state of $M = (S, A, T, s_0)$ reduces to the resolution of variable Z_{X,s_0} in the BES $h_1(\mu X.\varphi, s_0)$.

Proposition 5. *Let $M = (S, A, T, s_0)$ be an ALTS and $\mu X.\varphi$ be a closed, simplified guarded formula. Then:*

$$[\![\mu X.\varphi]\!] = \{s \in S \mid ([\![h_1(\mu X.\varphi, s)]\!])_{X,s} = T\}.$$

Note that during the translation given in Definition 5, the transitions $s \xrightarrow{a} s'$ are traversed forwards, which enables to construct the ALTS simultaneously with the BES in a demand-driven way.

3.2   Local Resolution of BESs

For developing our resolution algorithm, we use a representation of BESs as *boolean graphs* [1], which provide a more intuitive way of reasoning about dependencies between boolean variables. To every BES $\{z_i = op_i Z_i\}_{1 \leq i \leq n}$ corresponds a boolean graph $G = (V, E, L)$, where: $V = \{z_1, ..., z_n\}$ is the set of *vertices* (boolean variables), $E = \{(z_i, z_j) \mid 1 \leq i, j \leq n \wedge z_j \in Z_i\}$ is the set of *edges* (dependencies between boolean variables), and $L : V \rightarrow \{\vee, \wedge\}, L(z_i) = op_i$ is the *vertex labeling* (vertices are conjunctive or disjunctive according to the operator in the corresponding equation). The set of successors of a vertex z is noted $E(z)$. We assume that vertices in $E(z)$ are ordered from $(E(z))_0$ to $(E(z))_{|E(z)|-1}$. A boolean graph is represented *implicitly* by the successor function, which associates to each vertex z the set $E(z)$.

Note that the boolean graphs produced from BESs encoding the local model-checking of guarded μ-calculus formulas on ALTSs are acyclic (otherwise there would be either a cycle in the ALTS, or an unguarded occurrence of a propositional variable in the formula).

The DAGSOLVE algorithm that we propose for the local resolution of a BES with acyclic boolean graph is shown in Figure 1. It takes as input a boolean graph $G = (V, E, L)$ represented implicitly and a vertex $x \in V$ denoting a boolean variable. Starting at vertex x, DAGSOLVE recursively performs a depth-first search of G and for each vertex y encountered it computes its truth value $v(y)$. A counter $p(x)$ indicates the next successor of x to be visited. The vertices already visited are stored in a global set $A \subseteq V$ (initially empty). The exploration of the successors of x is stopped as soon as its truth value can be decided (e.g., if $L(x) = \vee$, then $v(x)$ becomes T as soon as a successor $y \in E(x)$ with $v(y) = \mathsf{T}$ has been encountered). Upon termination of the call DAGSOLVE $(x, (V, E, L))$, vertex x is contained in A and its final truth value is given by $v(x)$.

DAGSOLVE is similar in spirit with other local BES resolution algorithms [1, 24,7] based upon exploration of the dependency graph between boolean variables. Like these algorithms, DAGSOLVE has an $O(|V| + |E|)$ time complexity, equivalent to $O(|\varphi| \cdot (|S| + |T|))$ in terms of the state formula and the ALTS. However, by exploiting the absence of cycles in G, DAGSOLVE does not need to keep track of backward dependencies for updating the value of variables, and therefore it does not store the transitions of G in memory. This yields for DAGSOLVE a space complexity $O(|V|)$, equivalent to $O(|\varphi| \cdot |S|)$, instead of $O(|V| + |E|)$ like the algorithms in [1,24,7] when they are executed on acyclic boolean graphs.

3.3   Handling of Unguarded Alternation-Free Mu-Calculus

To verify an alternation-free μ-calculus formula φ on an ALTS $M = (S, A, T, s_0)$, one could first transform φ in simplified guarded form by using the translations

```
A := ∅;
procedure DAGSOLVE (x, (V, E, L)) is
    v(x) := if L(x) = ∨ then F else T endif;
    p(x) := 0; A := A ∪ {x};
    while p(x) < |E(x)| do
        y := (E(x))_{p(x)};
        if y ∉ A then
            DAGSOLVE (y, (V, E, L))
        endif;
        if v(y) ≠ v(x) then
            v(x) := v(y); p(x) := |E(x)|
        else
            p(x) := p(x) + 1
        endif
    end
end
```

Fig. 1. Local resolution of BESS with acyclic boolean graphs

given in Sections 2.2 and 2.3, and then apply the DAGSOLVE model-checking algorithm given in Section 3.2. If φ is already guarded, this procedure would yield a time complexity $O(|\varphi| \cdot (|S| + |T|))$ and a space complexity $O(|\varphi| \cdot |S|)$.

However, if φ is unguarded, this would yield a worst-case time complexity $O(|\varphi|^2 \cdot (|S| + |T|))$ instead of the complexity $O(|\varphi| \cdot (|S| + |T|))$ obtained by using an existing linear-time model-checking algorithm [1,24,7]. Although unguarded formulas are seldom in practice, and the blow-up caused by translation in guarded form is often less than quadratic, the above procedure may be unacceptable in some cases. Therefore, we search to devise a linear-time, memory efficient algorithm for checking unguarded alternation-free formulas on ALTSs.

Unguarded propositional variables occurring in a formula $\mu X.\varphi$ will induce cyclic dependencies in the corresponding BES (i.e., cycles in the boolean graph), even if the LTS $M = (S, A, T, s_0)$ is acyclic. However, these cycles have a rather simple structure: they contain only vertices of the form $Z_{\varphi_1,s}$, $Z_{\varphi_2,s}$, ..., where φ_1, φ_2, ... are subformulas of φ dominated by boolean or fixed point operators, and the state s remains unchanged along the cycle. Vertices belonging to a strongly connected component (SCC) of the boolean graph are reachable from the vertex of interest Z_{X,s_0} only through the root of the SCC, which is always a vertex $Z_{X',s}$ corresponding to a closed subformula $\mu X'.\varphi'$. Moreover, assuming there is no factorization of common subformulas in the initial formula $\mu X.\varphi$, a vertex of a SCC is reachable from the root of the SCC via a single path.

The AFMCSOLVE algorithm that we propose for solving these BESS is shown in Figure 2. We consider here only the case of minimal fixed point BESS, the other case being dual (every alternation-free formula can be checked by combining these two algorithms [1,20]). Besides an implicit boolean graph $G = (V, E, L)$

and a vertex $x \in V$, AFMCSOLVE takes as input a predicate $root : V \to \{F, T\}$ indicating the roots of the SCCs of G.

```
A := ∅;
procedure AFMCSOLVE (x, (V, E, L), root) is
    v(x) := if L(x) = ∨ then F else T endif;
    p(x) := 0; stable(x) := F; A := A ∪ {x}; unstable := F;
    while p(x) < |E(x)| do
        y := (E(x))_{p(x)};
        if y ∉ A then
            AFMCSOLVE (y, (V, E, L), root)
        endif;
        if stable(y) then
            if v(y) ≠ v(x) then
                v(x) := v(y); p(x) := |E(x)|; stable(x) := T
            else
                p(x) := p(x) + 1
            endif
        else
            unstable := T
        endif
    end;
    if ¬stable(x) then
        stable(x) := ¬unstable ∨ root(x);
        if unstable ∧ root(x) then v(x) := F endif
    endif
end
```

Fig. 2. Local resolution of BESs produced from unguarded alternation-free formulas

AFMCSOLVE is similar to DAGSOLVE, except that the value $v(x)$ of some vertices x (which have an outgoing path leading to an "ancestor" vertex currently on the call stack of AFMCSOLVE) cannot be decided upon termination of the call AFMCSOLVE $(x, (V, E, L), root)$. This information is recorded using an additional boolean $stable(x)$, which is set to T in the following situations: (a) $v(x)$ has been decided after exploring a stable successor $y \in E(x)$; (b) $v(x)$ has not been decided after exploring all successors in $E(x)$, but either no unstable successor of x has been encountered, or x is the root of a SCC of G (in this last case, $v(x)$ is set to F, since G denotes a minimal fixed point BES).

After deciding $v(x)$, there is no need to propagate this value to the "descendants" of x already explored, because these vertices will not be reached anymore in the SCC of x. Therefore, AFMCSOLVE does not need to store the transitions of G in memory, achieving a space complexity $O(|V|)$, equivalent to $O(|\varphi| \cdot |S|)$.

4   Conclusion and Future Work

We showed that full modal μ-calculus interpreted on acyclic LTSs has the same expressive power as its alternation-free fragment. We also proposed two local model-checking algorithms: DAGSOLVE, which handles formulas φ with alternation depth $ad(\varphi) \geq 2$ and has time complexity $O(|\varphi|^2 \cdot (|S| + |T|))$ and space complexity $O(|\varphi|^2 \cdot |S|)$; and AFMCSOLVE, which handles alternation-free formulas and has time complexity $O(|\varphi| \cdot (|S| + |T|))$ and space complexity $O(|\varphi| \cdot |S|)$. Both algorithms have been implemented using the generic OPEN/CÆSAR environment [12] for on-the-fly exploration of LTSs, and are integrated within the EVALUATOR 3.5 model-checker [20] of the CADP verification toolbox [10].

These results are currently applied in an industrial project involving the verification and testing of multiprocessor architectures designed by BULL. One of the verification tasks concerns the off-line analysis of large execution traces (about 100,000 events) produced by intensive testing of a hardware cache coherency protocol. Several hundreds correctness properties, derived from the formal specification of the protocol, are checked on the set of traces (grouped in one ALTS). Most properties are expressed as PDL [11] formulas $[R_1] \langle R_2 \rangle$ T, where R_1 and R_2 are complex regular expressions encoding sequences of request and response actions. These formulas are translated in guarded alternation-free μ-calculus, simplified by replacing maximal fixed points with minimal ones, and checked on the ALTS using DAGSOLVE. Compared to standard algorithms for alternation-free μ-calculus, this procedure improves execution time (the number of ALTS traversals is reduced) and memory consumption (ALTS transitions are not stored).

The model-checking approach we proposed can be directly applied to other forms of trace analysis (e.g., run-time monitoring, security log file auditing, etc.) by encoding these problems as model-checking of temporal formulas on single trace ALTSs. Moreover, our simplification of guarded μ-calculus interpreted on ALTSs (equivalence between minimal and maximal fixed points) can be useful as an intermediate optimization step in other model-checkers, by allowing to simplify temporal formulas in a similar manner when verifying ALTSs. For instance, when checking CTL [3] formulas on ALTSs, our simplification makes valid the equality A $[\varphi_1$ U $\varphi_2]$ = ¬E $[¬\varphi_2$ U ¬$(\varphi_2 \vee (\varphi_1 \wedge$ EX T$))]$, which allows to derive all CTL operators from E $[.$U$.]$ and to reduce the model-checking of CTL to the search of finite transition sequences satisfying E $[\varphi_1$ U $\varphi_2]$.

Two directions for future work seem promising. Firstly, one could devise a local model-checking algorithm for guarded μ-calculus that works without backtracking in the ALTS (this is not guaranteed by DAGSOLVE, which uses a depth-first traversal of the boolean graph). When analyzing a trace in real-time during its generation, this algorithm would scan it only once, potentially leading to performance improvements. Secondly, our model-checking procedure could be used for comparing on-the-fly an LTS M_1 with an ALTS M_2 modulo a bisimulation or preorder relation. This problem has various practical applications (search for execution sequences, interactive replay of simulation trees and model-checking diagnostics, etc.) and could be solved by building a guarded characteristic formula [14] of M_1 and verifying it on M_2 using the DAGSOLVE algorithm.

References

1. H. R. Andersen. Model checking and boolean graphs. *Th. Co. Sci.*, 126:3–30, 1994.
2. J. C. Bradfield and C. Stirling. Modal Logics and Mu-Calculi: an Introduction. In *Handbook of Process Algebra*, pp. 293–330, Elsevier, 2001.
3. E. Clarke, O. Grumberg, and D. Peled. *Model Checking*. MIT Press, 2000.
4. R. Cleaveland, M. Klein, and B. Steffen. Faster Model Checking for the Modal Mu-Calculus. In *CAV'92*, LNCS vol. 663, pp. 410–422.
5. R. Cleaveland and B. Steffen. A Linear-Time Model-Checking Algorithm for the Alternation-Free Modal Mu-Calculus. *FM in Syst. Design*, 2:121–147, 1993.
6. F. Dietrich, X. Logean, S. Koppenhoefer, and J-P. Hubaux. Testing Temporal Logic Properties in Distributed Systems. In *IWTCS'98*, pp. 247–262, Kluwer, 1998.
7. X. Du, S. A. Smolka, and R. Cleaveland. Local Model Checking and Protocol Analysis. *Springer STTT Journal*, 2(3):219–241, 1999.
8. M. Ducassé. OPIUM: An Extendable Trace Analyzer for Prolog. *Journal of Logic Programming*, 39(1–3):177–224, 1999.
9. E. A. Emerson and C-L. Lei. Efficient Model Checking in Fragments of the Propositional Mu-Calculus. In *LICS'86*, pp. 267–278, IEEE, 1986.
10. J-C. Fernandez, H. Garavel, A. Kerbrat, R. Mateescu, L. Mounier, and M. Sighireanu. CADP (CÆSAR/ALDEBARAN Development Package): A Protocol Validation and Verification Toolbox. In *CAV'96*, LNCS vol. 1102, pp. 437–440.
11. M. J. Fischer and R. E. Ladner. Propositional Dynamic Logic of Regular Programs. *Journal of Computer and System Sciences*, (18):194–211, 1979.
12. H. Garavel. OPEN/CÆSAR: An Open Software Architecture for Verification, Simulation, and Testing. In *TACAS'98*, LNCS vol. 1384, pp. 68–84. Full version available as INRIA Research Report RR-3352.
13. K. Ilgun, R. A. Kemmerer, and P. A. Porras. State Transition Analysis: A Rule-Based Intrusion Detection Approach. *IEEE Tr. on Soft. Eng.*, 21(3):181–199, 1995.
14. A. Ingolfsdottir and B. Steffen. Characteristic Formulae for Processes with Divergence. *Information and Computation*, 110(1):149–163, June 1994.
15. D. Kozen. Results on the Propositional μ-calculus. *Th. Co. Sci.*, 27:333–354, 1983.
16. K. G. Larsen. Efficient Local Correctness Checking. In *CAV'92*, LNCS vol. 663, pp. 30–43.
17. X. Liu, C. R. Ramakrishnan, and S. A. Smolka. Fully Local and Efficient Evaluation of Alternating Fixed Points. In *TACAS'98*, LNCS vol. 1384, pp. 5–19.
18. A. Mader. *Verification of Modal Properties Using Boolean Equation Systems*. VERSAL 8, Bertz Verlag, Berlin, 1997.
19. Z. Manna and A. Pnueli. *The Temporal Logic of Reactive and Concurrent Systems*, volume I (Specification). Springer Verlag, 1992.
20. R. Mateescu and M. Sighireanu. Efficient On-the-Fly Model-Checking for Regular Alternation-Free Mu-Calculus. To appear in *Science of Comp. Programming*, 2002.
21. P. Stevens and C. Stirling. Practical Model-Checking Using Games. In *TACAS'98*, LNCS vol. 1384, pp. 85–101.
22. C. Stirling. *Modal and Temporal Properties of Processes*. Springer Verlag, 2001.
23. I. Walukiewicz. A Complete Deductive System for the μ-calculus. In *LICS'93*, pp. 136–147. Full version available as DAICS Research Report RS-95-6, 1995.
24. B. Vergauwen and J. Lewi. Efficient Local Correctness Checking for Single and Alternating Boolean Equation Systems. In *ICALP'94*, LNCS vol. 820, pp. 304–315.

The ForSpec Temporal Logic: A New Temporal Property-Specification Language*

Roy Armoni[1], Limor Fix[1], Alon Flaisher[1], Rob Gerth[2], Boris Ginsburg,
Tomer Kanza[1], Avner Landver[1], Sela Mador-Haim[1], Eli Singerman[1],
Andreas Tiemeyer[1], Moshe Y. Vardi**[3], and Yael Zbar[1]

[1] Intel Strategic CAD Labs
[2] Intel Israel Development Center
[3] Rice University

Abstract. In this paper we describe the *ForSpec Temporal Logic* (FTL), the new temporal property-specification logic of *ForSpec*, Intel's new formal specification language. The key features of FTL are as follows: it is a linear temporal logic, based on Pnueli's LTL, it is based on a rich set of logical and arithmetical operations on bit vectors to describe state properties, it enables the user to define temporal connectives over time windows, it enables the user to define regular events, which are regular sequences of Boolean events, and then relate such events via special connectives, it enables the user to express properties about the past, and it includes constructs that enable the user to model multiple clock and reset signals, which is useful in the verification of hardware design.

1 Introduction

One of the most significant recent developments in the area of formal verification is the discovery of algorithmic methods, called *model checking*, for verifying temporal-logic properties of *finite-state* systems. Model-checking tools have enjoyed a substantial and growing use over the last few years, showing ability to discover subtle flaws that result from extremely improbable events. While until recently these tools were viewed as of academic interest only, they are now routinely used in industrial applications [Kur97]. Several model-checking tools are widely used in the semiconductor industry: SMV, a tool from Carnegie Mellon University with many industrial incarnations (e.g., IBM's RuleBase); VIS, a tool developed at the University of California, Berkeley FormalCheck, a tool developed at Bell Labs and marketed by Cadence; and Forecast, a tool developed in Intel and is used for property and equivalence formal verification.

A key issue in the design of a model-checking tool is the choice of the formal specification language used to specify properties, as this language is one of the *primary* interfaces to the tool. [Kur97]. (The other primary interface is the modeling language, which is typically the hardware description language used by the designers). In designing a formal specification language one has to balance several competing needs:

---

* A longer version of this paper can be found at www.cs.rice.edu/~vardi/papers/

** Supported in part by NSF grants CCR-9700061, CCR-9988322, IIS-9908435, IIS-9978135, and EIA-0086264, by BSF grant 9800096, and by a grant from the Intel Corporation.

J.-P. Katoen and P. Stevens (Eds.): TACAS 2002, LNCS 2280, pp. 296–311, 2002.
© Springer-Verlag Berlin Heidelberg 2002

- **Expressiveness:** The language has to be expressive enough to cover most properties likely to be used by verification engineers. This should include not only properties of the unit under verification but also relevant properties of the unit's environment.
- **Usability:** The language should be easy to understand and to use for verification engineers. This rules out expressive languages such as the μ-calculus, [Koz83], where alternation of fixpoints is notoriously difficult to understand. At the same time, it is important that the language has a rigorous formal semantics to ensure correct compilation and optimization and enable formal reasoning.
- **Compositionality:** The language should enable the expression of complex properties from simpler one. This enables maintaining libraries of properties and property templates. Thus, we believe that the language should be closed under *all* of its logical connectives, both Boolean and temporal, enabling property reuse. The language should also enable modular reasoning, since current semiconductor designs are exceedingly complex and are amenable only to modular approaches.
- **Implementability:** The design of the language needs to go hand-in-hand with the design of the model-checking tool. In considering various language features, one should balance their importance against the difficulty of ensuring that the implementation can handle these features.
- **Dynamic Validation:** Once a property is specified, it should be used by both the formal verification capabilities and by the dynamic validation, i.e., simulation, capabilities. Thus, a property must have the same semantics (meaning) in both dynamic and formal validation and should also be efficient for both.

In spite of the importance of the formal specification language, the literature on the topic is typically limited to expressiveness issues (see discussion below). In this paper we describe FTL, the temporal logic underlying *ForSpec*[1], which is Intel's formal specification language. The key features of FTL are as follows:

- FTL is a *linear* temporal logic, based on Pnueli's LTL, [Eme90],
- it is based on a rich set of logical and arithmetical operations on bit vectors to describe state properties (since this feature is orthogonal to the temporal features of the logic, which are the main focus of this paper, it will not be discussed here),
- it enables the user to define temporal connectives over time windows,
- it enables the user to define regular events, which are regular sequences of Boolean events, and then relate such events via special connectives,
- it enables the user to refer to the history of the computation using past connectives, and
- it includes constructs that enable the users to model multiple clocks and reset signals, which is useful in the verification of hardware design.
- it has a rigorous formal semantics for model verification and simulation, and the complexity of model checking and reasoning is well understood.

The design of FTL was started in 1997. FTL 1.0, with its associated tools, was released to Intel users in 2000. FTL 2.0 is currently under design, in collaboration with

---

[1] ForSpec includes also a modeling language. It also includes various linguistic features, such as *parameterized templates*, which faciliates the construction of standard property libraries.

language design teams from Co-Design Automation, Synopsys, and Verisity Design, and is expected to be realesed in 2002[2]. The language described in this paper is close to FTL 2.0, though some syntactical and semantical details may change by the final release. The goal of this paper is not to provide a full documentation of FTL, but rather to describe its major features, as well as explain the rationale for the various design choices. Our hope is that the publication of this paper, concomitant with the release of the language to users, would result in a dialog on the subject of property-specification logic between the research community, language developers, and language users.

2 Expressiveness and Usability

2.1 The Nature of Time

Two possible views regarding the nature of time induce two types of temporal logics. In *linear* temporal logics, time is treated as if each moment in time has a unique possible future. Thus, linear temporal formulae are interpreted over linear sequences, and we regard them as describing the behavior of a single computation of a system. In *branching* temporal logics, each moment in time may split into various possible futures. Accordingly, the structures over which branching temporal formulae are interpreted can be viewed as infinite *computation trees*, each describing the behavior of the possible computations of a nondeterministic system.

In the linear temporal logic LTL [Eme90], formulas are composed from the set of propositional constants using the usual Boolean connectives as well as the temporal operators G ("always"), F ("eventually"), X ("next"), and U ("until"). In the branching temporal logic CTL [Eme90], every temporal operator is preceded by the *universal* path quantifier A or the *existential* path quantifier E. Most incarnations of SMV, (see [BBL98] and [CCGR00]), as well as VIS, use CTL, or extensions of it, as their property specification logic. In contrast, Cadence SMV uses LTL, while FormalCheck uses a set of property templates that collectively has the expressive power of ω-automata (also a linear-time formalism) as its property specification language [Kur98]. Temporal e, a property-specification language used in simulation, is also a linear-time formalism [Mor99]. Our first decision in designing a property-specification logic for the next generation Intel model-checking tool was the choice between the linear- and branching-time approaches.

We chose the linear-time approach after concluding that the branching-time framework suffers from several inherent deficiencies as a framework for property specification logics (for a more thorough discussion of these issues see [Var01]):

- Verification engineers find branching time unintuitive. IBM's experience with Rule-Base has been that "nontrivial CTL equations are hard to understand and prone to error" [SBF+97].
- The branching-time framework was designed for reasoning about *closed* systems. Bran-ching-time modular reasoning is exceedingly hard [Var01].

---

[2] See press release at http://biz.yahoo.com/bw/011105/50371_1.html.

– Combining formal and dynamic validation (i.e., simulation) techniques for branching-time model checking is possible only in a very limited fashion, as dynamic validation is inherently linear.

LTL includes several connectives that handle unbounded time. For example, the formula eventually p asserts that p will hold at some point in the future. There's, however, only one connective in LTL to handle bounded time. To assert that p will hold at time 5, one has to write next next next next next p. Asserting that p will hold between time 10 and time 15, is even more cumbersome. By using *time windows* FTL provides users with bounded-time temporal connectives. (Bounded temporal connectives are typically studied in the context of real-time logics, cf. [AH92]). For example, to express in FTL that p will hold between time 10 and time 15, one simply writes eventually $[10, 15]$ p.

2.2 ω-Regularity

Since the proposal by Pnueli in 1977 to apply LTL to the specification and verification of concurrent programs, the adequacy of LTL has been widely studied. One of the conclusions of this research is that LTL is not expressive enough for the task. The first to complain about the expressive power of LTL was Wolper [Wol83] who observed that LTL cannot express certain ω-regular events (in fact, LTL expresses precisely the star-free ω-regular events [Eme90]).

The weakness in expressiveness is not just a theoretical issue. Even when attempting to verify simple properties, users often need to express relevant properties, which can be rather complex, of the environment of the unit under verification. These properties are the *assumptions* of the Assume-Guarantee paradigm (cf. [Pnu85]). Assume-guarantee reasoning is a key requirement at Intel, due to the high complexity of the designs under verification. Thus, the logic has to be able to express assumptions that are strong enough to imply the assertion under verification. In other words, given models M and E and a property ψ that $E|M \models \psi$ (we use $|$ to denote *parallel composition*), the logic should be able to express a property ψ such that $E \models \varphi$ and $M \models \varphi \rightarrow \psi$. As was shown later [LPZ85], this makes LTL inadequate for *modular* verification, since LTL is not expressive enough to express strong enough assumptions about the environment. It is now recognized that a linear temporal property logic has to be expressive enough to specify all ω-regular properties [Pnu85]. Several extensions to LTL have been proposed with the goal of obtaining full ω-regularity: (a) Vardi and Wolper proposed ETL, the extension of LTL with temporal connectives that correspond to ω-automata [Wol83, VW94]), (b) Banieqbal and Barringer proposed extending LTL with fixpoint operators [BB87], yielding a linear μ-calculus, (cf. [Koz83]), and (c) Sistla, Vardi, and Wolper proposed QPTL, the extension of LTL with quantification over propositional variables [SVW87].

As fixpoint calculi are notoriously difficult for users, we decided against the fixpoint approach. Keeping the goal of implementability in mind, we also decided against a full implementation of ETL and QPTL, as full QPTL has a nonelementary time complexity [SVW87], while implementing full ETL, which explicitly incorporates Büchi automata, requires a complementation construction for Büchi automata, still a topic under active research [Fin01]. Instead, FTL borrows from ETL, as well as PDL [FL79], by extending LTL with regular events[3]. As we show later, this extension provides us with full ω-regularity.

2.3 The Past

There are two reasons to add past connectives to temporal logic. The first argument is that while past temporal connectives do not add any expressive power, the price for eliminating them can be high. Many natural statements in program specification are much easier to express using past connectives. In fact, the best known procedure to eliminate past connectives may cause an exponential blow-up of the considered formulas.

A more important motivation for the restoration of the past is again the use of temporal logic in modular verification. In global verification one uses temporal formulas that refer to locations in the program text. This is absolutely *verboten* in modular verification, since in specifying a module one can refer only to its external behavior. Since we cannot now refer to program location we have instead to refer to the history of the computation, and we can do that very easily with past connectives This lead to the study of extensions of temporal logic with past connectives (cf. [KPV01]). These extensions allow arbitrary mixing of future and past connectives, enabling one to say, for example, "eventually, sometimes in the past, p holds until q holds".

For the same motivation, FTL also includes past connectives. Unlike the aforementioned extensions of LTL with past connectives, the usage of past connectives is circumscribed. We found little practical motivation to allow arbitrary mixing of future and past connectives, and such mixing has a nonnegligible implementation cost[4]. In fact, since the motivation of adding the past is to enable referring to the history of the computation, FTL's past connectives allow only references to such history. Thus, FTL allows references to past values of Boolean expressions and regular sequences of Boolean expressions. FTL does not allow, however, references to past values of temporal formulas. Thus, past connectives in FTL are viewed as Boolean rather than temporal connectives.

2.4 Hardware Features

While the limited mechanisms for automata connectives and quantification over propositional variables are sufficient to guarantee full ω-regularity, we decided to also offer direct support to two specification modes often used by verification engineers at Intel: *clocks* and *resets*. Both clocks and resets are features that are needed to address the fact that modern semiconductor designs consists of interacting parallel modules. As we shall see, while clocks and resets have a simple underlying intuition, explained below, defining their semantics formally is rather nontrivial.

Today's semiconductor design technology is still dominated by synchronous design methodology. In synchronous circuits, clocks signals synchronize the sequential

---

[3] For other extensions of LTL with regular events see [ET97,HT99]. These works propose adding regular events to the until operator. We prefer to have explicit connectives for regular events, in the style of the "box" and "diamond" modalities of PDL.

[4] It requires using two-way alternating automata, rather then one-way alternating automata [KPV01].

logic, providing the designer with a simple operational model. While the asynchronous approach holds the promise of greater speed, designing asynchronous circuits is significantly harder than designing synchronous circuits. Current design methodology attempt to strike a compromise between the two approaches by using multiple clocks. This methodology results in architectures that are globally asynchronous but locally synchronous. The temporal-logic literature mostly ignores the issue of explicitly supporting clocks (clocks, however, are typically studied in the context of modelling languages, see [CLM98]). Liu and Orgun [LO99] proposed a temporal framework with multiple clocks. Their framework, however, supports clocks via a clock calculus, which is separate from the temporal logic. Emerson and Trefler [ET97] proposed an extension of LTL in which temporal connectives can be indexed with multiple independent clocks.

In contrast, the way clocks are being used in FTL is via the *current clock*. Specifically, FTL has the construct **change_on** $c\ \varphi$, which states that the temporal formula φ is to be evaluated with respect to the clock c; that is, the formula φ is to be evaluated in the trace defined by the high phases of the clock c. The key feature of clocks in FTL is that each subformula may advance according to a different clock.

Another aspect of the fact that modern designs consist of interacting parallel modules is the fact that a process running on one module can be reset by a signal coming from another module. Reset control has long been a critical aspect of embedded control design. FTL directly supports reset signals. The formula **accept_on** $a\ \varphi$ states that the property φ should be checked only until the arrival of the reset signal a, at which point the check is considered to have *succeeded*. In contrast, **reject_on** $r\ \varphi$ states that the property φ should be checked only until the arrival of the reset signal r, at which point the check is considered to have *failed*. The key feature of resets in FTL is that each subformula may be reset (positively or negatively) by a different reset signal.

3   Basic Features

Core FTL: Formulae of FTL are built from a set **Prop** of propositional constants. (Actually, FTL provides a rich set of logical and arithmetical operations on bit vectors to describe state properties. All vector expressions, however, are compiled into Boolean expressions over **Prop**, so in this paper we suppress that aspect of the language). FTL is closed under the application of Boolean connectives (we use !, ||, and &&, **implies** , **iff** for negation, disjunction, and conjunction, implication, and equivalence, respectively). FTL also enables us to refer to future and past values of Boolean expressions. For a Boolean expression b, we refer to the value of b in the next phase[5] by **future** (b); this is essentially the "primed" version of b in Lamport's Temporal Logic of Actions. For a Boolean expression b, FTL uses **past** (b, n), where n is a positive integer, to refer to the value of b, n phases in the past. Note that **past** and **future** are Boolean connectives, so, for example, "ack **implies past** $(send, 10)$" is also a Boolean expression. Note also that the **future** connective is more limited than the **past** connective; one cannot write **future** $(b, 2)$. The rationale for that is that **future** is a somewhat nonstandard Boolean connective, since the value of **future** (p) is indeterminate at a given point in time. The

---

[5] Note that the notion of next phase is independent from the notion of the next clock tick, which is discussed later in the paper.

role of future is mostly to define *transitions*, e.g., (!*b*)&& future (*b*) holds at points at which *b* is about to rise. FTL is also closed under the temporal connectives next, wnext, eventually, globally, until and wuntil.

FTL is interpreted over *computations*. A *computation* is a function $\pi : N \to 2^{\mathsf{Prop}}$, which assigns truth values to the elements of Prop at each time instant (natural number). The semantics of FTL's temporal connectives is well known. For example, for a computation π and a point $i \in \omega$, we have that:

- $\pi, i \models p$ for $p \in$ Prop iff $p \in \pi(i)$.
- $\pi, i \models$ future (*b*) iff $\pi, i + 1 \models b$.
- $\pi, i \models$ past (*b*, 1) iff $i > 0$ and $\pi, i - 1 \models b$.
- $\pi, i \models$ past (*b*, *n*) iff $i > 0$ and $\pi, i - 1 \models$ past (*b*, *n* − 1).
  Note that the past operator cannot go "before 0". Thus, $\pi, 0 \not\models$ past (*b*, 1). In other words, the default past value is 0.
- $\pi, i \models \varphi$ until ψ iff for some $j \geq i$, we have $\pi, j \models \psi$ and for all k, $i \leq k < j$, we have $\pi, k \models \varphi$.

We say that a computation π *satisfies* a formula φ, denoted $\pi \models \varphi$, if $\pi, 0 \models \varphi$. We use $models(\varphi)$ to denote the set of computations satisfying φ.

Time windows modify the temporal connectives by specifying intervals in which certain events are expected to occur. The aim is to enable the expression of assertions such as globally (*req* $\to$ next [10] *ack*). The syntax of temporal connectives with intervals is as follows:

1. next [*m*] φ, where $1 \leq m < \infty$
2. eventually [*m*, *n*]φ, globally [*m*, *n*]φ, φ until [*m*, *n*]ψ, and φ wuntil [*m*, *n*]ψ where $0 \leq m \leq n \leq \infty$ (but $m = n = \infty$ is not allowed)

The semantics of temporal connectives with time windows is defined by induction on the window lower bound. For example,

- $\pi, i \models$ next [1] φ if $\pi, i + 1 \models \varphi$
- $\pi, i \models$ next [*m*] φ, for $m > 1$, if $\pi, i + 1 \models$ next [*m* − 1] φ
- $\pi, i \models \varphi$ until [0, *n*] ψ if for some $k, n \geq k \geq 0$, we have that $\pi, i + k \models \psi$ and for all $j, 0 \leq j < k$, we have that $\pi, i + j \models \varphi$.
- $\pi, i \models \varphi$ until [*m*, *n*] ψ if $\pi, i + 1 \models \varphi$ until [*m* − 1, *n* − 1] ψ

Clearly, time windows do not add to the expressive power of FTL, since formulae with time windows can be translated to formulae without windows. Since the lower and upper bounds of these windows are specified using decimal numbers, eliminating time windows may involve an exponential blow-up. (See discussion below of computational complexity.)

The practical implication of this result is that users should be careful with time windows. The formula next [*m*] *p* could force the compiler to introduce *m* BDD variables, so large windows could result in "state explosion".

Regular events: *Regular events* describe regular sequences of *Boolean events*, where Boolean events are simply Boolean expressions in terms of propositional constants. For example, the regular expression (*send*, (!*ack*)*, *send*) (comma denotes concatenation) describes a sequence in which there is no *ack* event between two *send* events.

Thus, the formula **globally** $!(send, (!ack)^*, send)$ forbids the occurrence of such sequences. Regular events are formed from Boolean events (denoted here with a_i, b_i, etc.) using the follwing constructs[6]: (a) ,: concatenation, (b) \: glue ($a_1 \ldots a_m \backslash b_1 \ldots b_n$ is $a_1 \ldots a_m \&\& b_1 \ldots b_n$), (c) ||: union, (d) $a*$: zero or more, (e) $a+$: one or more, and (f) $e\{m, n\}$: between m and n occurrences of e. With each regular event e we associate, in the standard way, a language $L(e)$ of finite words over the Boolean events. (It is important to note that our semantics refers only to $L(e)$ and not to the syntax of e. Thus, adding further regular operators can be accomplished without any need to adapt the semantics. (The ForSpec compiler only requires a translation of regular expression to finite-state automata.) In this respect FTL differs from other property-specification languages, such as Sugar [BBDE$^+$01] or Temporal e [Mor99], where the syntax of regular events is intertwined with the semantics of the logic.) We do not allow regular events whose language contains the empty word (this is checked by the compiler).

We define the semantics of regular events in terms of *tight satisfaction*: $\pi, i \models e$ if for some $j \geq i$ we have $\pi, i, j \models e$. The intuition of tight satisfaction is that the event e holds *between* the points i and j. Formally, $\pi, i, j \models e$ if there is a word $w = b_0 b_1 \ldots b_n \in L(e)$, $n = j - i$ such that $\pi, i + k \models b_k$ for all k, $0 \leq k \leq n$.

We can also use regular events to refer to the past. If e is a regular expression, then **ended** (e) is a Boolean expression saying that the regular event e has just "ended". Formally $\pi, i \models$ **ended** (e) if there is some $j < i$ such that $\pi, j, i \models e$. Note that j need not to unique. For example, **ended** $(true, (true, true)*)$ holds at all even $(0, 2, \ldots)$ time points.

Since we have defined $\pi, i \models e$, we can now combine regular events with all other connectives. Thus, **globally** $!(req, (!ack)^*, ack)$ says that the computation cannot contain a sequence of states that match $(req, (!ack)^*, ack)$ and

$$\text{globally } (p \text{ iff } \textbf{ended } (req, (!ack)^*, ack)$$

says that p holds precisely at the end of sequences of states that match $(req, (!ack)^*, ack)$. FTL has two additional temporal connectives to faciliate assertions about regular events. The formula e **follows_by** φ, where e is a regular event and φ is a formula, asserts that some e sequence is followed by φ. The formula e **triggers** φ, where e is a regular event and φ is a formula, asserts that all e sequence are followed by φ. The **follows_by** and **triggers** connectives are essentially the "diamond" and "box" modalities of PDL [FL79]. Formally:

- $\pi, i \models e$ **follows_by** φ if for some $j \geq i \ \pi, i, j \models e$ and $\pi, j \models \varphi$.
- $\pi, i \models e$ **triggers** φ if for all $j \geq i$ such that $\pi, i, j \models e$ we have $\pi, j \models \varphi$.

For example, the formula

$$\text{globally } ((req, (!ack)^*, ack) \text{ triggers } (true^+, grant, (!rel)^*, rel))$$

asserts that a request followed by an acknowledgement must be followed by a grant followed by a release. Note that **follows_by** and **triggers** are dual to each other.

Lemma 1. $\pi, i \models !(e \text{ follows_by } \varphi)$ *iff* $\pi, i \models e$ **triggers** $(!\varphi)$.

---

[6] FTL 2.0 will include some additional regular constructs.

4 Hardware Features

FTL offers direct support to two specification modes often used by verification engineers at Intel: *clocks* and *resets*. While these features do not add to the expressive power of FTL, expressing them in terms of the other features of the language would be too cumbersome to be useful. While these features have a clear intuitive semantics, capturing it rigorously is quite nontrivial, as we show in the rest of this section. Our semantics, however, is defined in a modular fashion, so users who do not use these advanced features can continue to use the semantics of Section 3. Defining the semantics in a modular fashion was necessary to achieve a proper balance between expressiveness and usabilty, ensuring that users do not need to understand complex semantic aspects in order to use the basic features of the language. (The ForSpec User Guide describes the language at an intuitive level, while the ForSpec Reference Manual provides the formal semantics in a modular fashion.)

Clocks: FTL allows formulae of the form change_on c φ, which asserts that the temporal formula φ is to be evaluated with respect to the clock c; that is, the formula φ is to be evaluated in the trace defined by the high phases of the clock c. Every Boolean expression can serve as a clock. Note that the computation is sampled at the high phases of c rather than at the points where c changes. Focusing on the high phases is simpler and more general. For example, as we saw earlier the high phases of the Boolean expression $(!b)$&& future (b) are the points at which b is about to rise.

As soon as we attempt to formalize further this intuition, we realize that there is a difficulty. How does one guarantee that the clock c actually "ticks", i.e., has high phases? We could have required that all clocks are guaranteed to tick infinitely often, but then this would have to be checked. Since we wanted to give users the ability to use arbitrary Boolean events as clocks, we decided not to require that a clock be guaranteed to tick. Instead, we introduced two operators. The formula change_on c φ asserts that c *does* tick and φ holds with respect to c, while change_if c φ asserts that *if* c ticks *then* φ holds with respect to c. Since the concept of "next tick" is now not always defined, we need to introduce a weak dual wnext to the next connective; next requires the existence of a next tick, while wnext does not (see formal semantics below).

What should be the formal meaning of "holds with respect to c"? Suppose for simplicity that c has infinitely many high phases. It seems intuitive to take the *projection* $\pi[c]$ of a computation π to be the sequence of values $\pi(i_0), \pi(i_1), \pi(i_2), \ldots$ of π at the points $i_0, i_1, i_2, \ldots$ at which c holds. We then can say that π satisfies change_on $c\,\varphi$ if $\pi[c]$ satisfies φ. The implication of such a definition however, would be to make clocks *cumulative*. That is, if change_on $d\,\psi$ is a subformula of φ, then ψ needs to be evaluated with respect to a projection $\pi[c] \ldots [d]$. This went against the intuition of our users, who want to make assertions about clocks *without* losing access to faster clocks. For example, the subformula change_on $d\,\psi$ could be a library property, describing an environment that is not governed by the clock c. (Recall that multiple clocks are needed to capture local synchrony in a globally asynchronous design.) This led to the decision to define the semantics of clocks in a non-cumulative fashion. This is done by defining the semantics as a four-way relation, between computations, points, clocks, and formulae, instead of a three-way relation as before. That is, on the left-hand-side of $\models$ we have a triple π, i, c, where c is a *clock expression* (see below), which is the *context* in which the formula is evaluated.[7] Before we issue any change_on c or change_if c, the default clock expression is true. That is, $\pi, i \models \varphi$ if $\pi, i, \text{true} \models \varphi$.

The semantics of propositional constants is insensitive to clocks:

– $\pi, i, c \models p$ if $\pi, i \models p$.

FTL , however, has a special propositional constant clock that enables users to refer explicitly to clock ticks. To avoid circularity, however, clock expressions are Boolean expressions that do not refer to clock . Given a clock expression c and a Boolean expression d, we denote by $[c \mapsto d]$ the result of substituting c for clock in d. For example if c is !p&& future (p) and d is clock &&q, then $[c \mapsto d]$ is (!p&& future (p))&&q. Note that $[c \mapsto d]$ is a clock expression, since it does not refer to clock . The semantics of clock is defined as follow:

– $\pi, i, c \models$ clock if $\pi, i \models c$.

In this case we say that c ticks at point i of π, or, equivalently, that i is a tick point of c on π. When we refer to tick points $i_1 < \ldots < i_l$ at or after i, we assume that no other point between i and i_l is a tick point.

We start defining the four-way sematics by defining satisfaction of the future and past connectives. Recall that the role of future is to define transition constraints. Consequently, its semantics is insensitive to clocks.

– $\pi, i, c \models$ future (b) if $\pi, i + 1 \models b$.

In contrast, the past operator is extended to allow reference to clocks. For a Boolean expression b, FTL uses past (b, n, d), where n is a positive integer and d is a Boolean expression, to refer to the value of b in the phase of the clock d, n ticks in the past. Formally,

– $\pi, i, c \models$ past $(b, 1, d)$ if $\pi, j, [c \mapsto d] \models b$, where j is the the largest integer less than i such that $\pi, j, [c \mapsto d] \models d$.
– $\pi, i, c \models$ past (b, n, c) if $\pi, j, [c \mapsto d] \models$ past $(b, n - 1, d)$ where j is the the largest integer less than i such that $\pi, j, [c \mapsto d] \models d$.

Note that if there is no $j < i$ such that $\pi, j, [c \mapsto d] \models d$, then $\pi, i, c \not\models$ past (b, n, c).

We continue defining the four-way sematics by defining satisfaction of regular events. Recall that satisfaction of regular events is defined in terms of tight satisfaction: $\pi, i, c \models e$ if for some $j \geq i$ we have $\pi, i, j, c \Vdash e$. Tight satisfaction, which is a five-way relation, is defined as follows: $\pi, i, j, c \Vdash e$ if

– there are $n \geq 0$ tick points $i_1 < \ldots < i_n$ of c after i such that $i = i_0 < i_1$ and $i_n = j$,
    there is a word $B = b_0 b_1 \ldots b_n \in L(e)$ such that $\pi, i_m, c \models b_m$ for $0 \leq m \leq n$.

Note that eveluation of regular events always starts at the present point, just as a Boolean event is aways evaluated at the present point. Once we have defined tight satisfaction with clocks, the semantics of ended is as before: $\pi, i \models$ ended (e) if there is some $j < i$ such that $\pi, j, i \not\models e$.

FTL has a special regular event tick, which is an abbreviation for the regular event $((! \text{clock})^*, \text{clock})$. Thus, $\pi, i, j \not\models$ tick if j is the first tick point of c at or after i.

We can now define the semantics of the temporal connectives. For example:

- $\pi, i, c \models$ next φ if for some $j \geq i + 1$ we have that $\pi, i+1, j, c \models$ tick and $\pi, j, c \models \varphi$.
- $\pi, i, c \models$ wnext φ if for some all $j \geq i + 1$ we have that if $\pi, i+1, j, c \models$ tick, then $\pi, j, c \models \varphi$.
- $\pi, i, c \models \varphi$ until ψ if for some $j \geq i$ we have that $\pi, j \models c$ and $\pi, j, c \models \psi$, and for all k, $i \leq k < j$ such that $\pi, k \models c$, we have $\pi, k, c \models \varphi$. (Note that only tick points of c are taken into consideration here.)
- $\pi, i, c \models e$ triggers φ if for all $l \geq k \geq j \geq i$ such that $\pi, i, j, c \models$ tick, $\pi, j, k, c \not\models e$ and $\pi, k, l, c \models$ tick, we have that $\pi, l, c \models \varphi$. (Note that the evaluation of e starts at the first tick point at or after i, and the evaluation of f starts at the first tick point at or after the end of e.)

We now define the semantics of change_on and change_on :

- $\pi, i, c \models$ change_on $d\ f$ if there exists some $j \geq i$, such that $\pi, i, j, [c \mapsto d] \not\models$ tick and $\pi, j, [c \mapsto d] \models f$.
- $\pi, i, c \models$ change_if $d\ f$ if whenever $j \geq i$ is such that $\pi, i, j, [c \mapsto d] \not\models$ tick, then $\pi, j, [c \mapsto d], a, r \models f$.

Both change_on and change_if force the evaluation of the formula at the nearest tick point, but only change_on requires such a tick point to exist. As one expects, we get duality between next and wnext and between change_on and change_if .

Lemma 2.

- $\pi, i, c \models !(\text{ next } \varphi)$ *iff* $\pi, i, c \models$ wnext $!\varphi$.
- $\pi, i, c \models !(\text{ change\_on } c\ \varphi)$ *iff* $\pi, i, c \models$ change_if $c\ (!\varphi)$.

As an example, the formula change_on $c1$ (globally (change_if $c2\ p$)) asserts that the clock $c1$ ticks and p also holds at the first tick, if any, of $c2$ at or after a tick of $c1$.

Resets: FTL allows formulae of the form accept_on $a\ \varphi$, which asserts that the property φ should be checked only until the arrival of a reset signal a, at which point the check is considered to have *succeeded*, and reject_on $r\ \varphi$, which asserts that the property φ should be checked only until the arrival of a reset signal r, at which point the check is considered to have *failed*. In reset control-design methodology, a local reset signal does not replace a global reset signal. Thus, while our semantics for multiple clocks was non-cumulative, our semantics for resets is cumulative. Another important feature of our semantics is that reset signals are *asynchronous*, that is, they are not required to occur at tick points; rather, they are allowed to occur at any point. To capture *synchronous resets*, the users can write accept_on $(a\&\& \text{ clock}) \varphi$ or reject_on $(r\&\& \text{ clock}) \varphi$. As we shall see, we pay a price for the added expressiveness of asynchronous resets with additional complexity of the semantics, as we have to account for resets between tick points.

As we saw earlier, we capture the semantics of clocks by adding a clock to the context in which formulae are evaluated, resulting in a four-way semantical relation. To capture the semantics of resets, we have to add both the accept signal and the reject signal to the context, resulting in a six-way semantical relation. That is, on the left-hand-side of $\models$ we have a quintuple π, i, c, a, r, where π, i, c are as before, and a and r are *disjoint* Boolean events defining the accept and reject signals, respectively. Before we issue any accept_on a or reject_on r, the default reset signals are both false, respectively. That is, $\pi, i \models \varphi$ if $\pi, i, \text{true}, \text{false}, \text{false} \models \varphi$.

The semantics of accept_on and reject_on is defined by:

- $\pi, i, c, a, r \models$ accept_on $b\, \varphi$ if $\pi, i, c \models a||(b\&\&!r)$ or $\pi, i, c, a||(b\&\&!r), r \models \varphi$
- $\pi, i, c, a, r \models$ reject_on $b\, \varphi$ if $\pi, i, c \not\models r||(b\&\&!a)$ and $\pi, i, c, a, r||(b\&\&!a) \models \varphi$

Note how the cumulative semantics ensures that the accept and reject signals are always disjoint. Also, outer resets have preference over inner ones.

The presence of reset signals requires us to redefine the very basic semantics of propositions and Boolean connectives. An important issue now is the meaning of negation in the reset-control design methodology. Since negation switches success and failure, it should also switch accept and reject signals. We therefore define

- $\pi, i, c, a, r \models p$, for $p \in$ Prop if either $\pi, i, c \models a$ or $\pi, i, c \models p$ and $\pi, i, c \models !r$ (That is, the accept "signal" always makes a proposition true, while the reject "signal" always makes it false. It may seem that we are giving the accept signal a preference over the reject signal, but as the accept and reject signals can never be true simultaneously, their roles are actually symmetric.)
- $\pi, i, c, a, r \models !\varphi$ if $\pi, i, c, r, a \not\models \varphi$.

We now define satisfaction of regular events. Recall again that satisfaction of regular events is defined in terms of tight satisfaction: $\pi, i, c, a, r \models e$ if for some $j \geq i$ we have $\pi, i, j, c, a, r \models\!\!\!\models e$. Tight satisfaction, which is a seven-way relation, is defined as follows: $\pi, i, j, c, a, r \models\!\!\!\models e$ if

- $\pi, k, c \models !a\&\&!r$ for $i \leq k < j$,
- there are precisely $l \geq 0$ tick points $i_1 < \ldots < i_l$ of c such that $i = i_0 < i_1$ and $i_l \leq j$,
- there is a word $B = b_0 b_1 \ldots b_n \in L(e)$, $n \geq l$ such that $\pi, i_m, c \models b_m$ for $0 \leq m < l$, and either
  - $\pi, j, c \models a$ and $i_l = j$, or
  - $\pi, j, c \models a$ and $\pi, i_l, c \models b_l$, or
  - $l = n$, and $i_n = j$, and $\pi, j, c \models b_n$, and $\pi, j, c \models !r$.

Note that in the first case, only the prefix $b_0 b_1 \ldots b_{l-1}$ is checked, in the second case, only the prefix $b_0 b_1 \ldots b_l$ is checked, and in the third case the word B is checked in full.) As we remarked earlier, the complexity of the semantics is the result of the need to account for resets between tick points. In the first two cases, the checking of B is terminated due to an accept signal. We denote this by $\pi, i, j, c, a, r \models\!\!\!\models_a e$.

Let π be a computation, i a point, c a clock expression, and a and r reset expresions. Then $tick(\pi, i, c, a, r)$ is the least j such that $j \geq i$ and $\pi, i, j, c, a, r \models\!\!\!\models$ tick (note that there is at most one such j). Note that $tick(\pi, i, c, a, r)$ need not be defined, since we may have that $\pi, i, j, c, a, r \not\models$ tick for all $j \geq i$. If it is defined, we write $tick(\pi, i, c, a, r) \downarrow$. Note that $\pi, i, j, c, a, r \models$ tick can hold in two (nonexclusive) ways:

- $\pi, j \models c$, in which case we write $tick(\pi, i, c, a, r) \downarrow_c$, or
- $\pi, j, c \models a$, in which case we write $tick(\pi, i, c, a, r) \downarrow_a$.

We write "$j = tick(\pi, i, c, a, r)$" as an abbreviation for "$tick(\pi, i, c, a, r) \downarrow$ and $j = tick(\pi, i, c, a, r)$."

We now illustrate the semantics of temporal connectives by considering the triggers connective:

- $\pi, i, c, a, r \models e$ triggers φ if $j = tick(\pi, i, c, r, a)$ entails that
  - $tick(\pi, i, c, r, a) \downarrow_r$ does not hold and
  - for all $k \geq j$ such that $\pi, j, k, c, r, a \not\models e$ we have that
    * $\pi, j, k, c, r, a \not\models_r e$ does not hold and
      · $l = tick(\pi, k, c, r, a)$ entails that $tick(\pi, k, c, r, a) \downarrow_r$ does not hold
      · $\pi, l, c, a, r \models f$.

Note that the definition is a direct extension of the earlier definition of triggers. The impact of resets is through the various conditions of the definition. The events tick, e, and again tick function as antecedents of an implication, and thus have negative polarity, which explains why the roles of a and r are reversed in the antecedents.

As a sanity check of the not-immediately-obvious semantics of resets we state another duality lemma.

Lemma 3.
$\pi, i, c, a, r \models !(\text{accept\_on } d\,\varphi)$ iff $\pi, i, c, a, r \models$ reject_on $d\,(!\varphi)$.

As an example, the formula change_on c (accept_on a (p until q)) declares c to be a strong clock and a to be an accept signal, relative to which p holds until q holds.

5   Expressiveness and Complexity

The addition of regular events and the new connectives (follows_by and triggers) has both a theoretical motivation and a pragmatic motivation. Regular events were shown to be useful in the context of hardware verification, cf. [BBL98,Mor99]. More fundamentally, as noted earlier, it was observed in [Wol83] that LTL cannot express certain ω-regular events, and it was shown in [LPZ85] that this makes LTL inadequate for modular verification. Let *regular LTL* be the extension of LTL with regular events and the connectives follows_by and triggers. Regular LTL, which is strictly more expressive than LTL, is expressive enough to capture ω-regularity.

Theorem 1. *Let L be an ω-regular set of computations. Then there is a formula φ_L of regular LTL such that $models(\varphi_L) = L$.*

Proof Sketch: Every ω-regular language can be expressed as a finite union of terms of the form $L_1 \cdot L_2$, where L_1 is a regular language (of finite words) and L_2 is a language of infinite words defined by a deterministic Büchi automaton. Thus, we can express L as a disjunction of formulae of the form e follows_by φ, provided we can express languages of deterministic Büchi automata. Such languages can be expressed by disjunctions of formulae of the form e_1&&(e_1 triggers e_2), where both e_1 and e_2 are regular events.

□

A consequence of this theorem is that FTL *fully supports* assume-guarantee reasoning, in the following sense. On one hand, we have that, for all models M and E and for all FTL formulas φ, ψ, if $E \models \varphi$ and $M \models \varphi \rightarrow \psi$ then $E|M \models \psi$. On the other hand, for all models M and E and for every FTL formula ψ such that $E|M \models \psi$, there is an FTL formula φ such that $E \models \varphi$ and $M \models \varphi \rightarrow \psi$. Furthermore, every FTL formula can serve both as an assumption and as an assertion (guarantee), and as assume-guarantee reasoning is performed via model checking, the complexity of such reasoning is the same as that of model checking. (Note, however, that full support of assume-guarantee reasoning is not guaranteed by the mere inclusion of regular events. Sugar adds regular events to CTL, resulting in a mixed linear-branching semantics [BBDE+01], in the style of CTL* [Eme90], which makes it rather difficult to fully support assume-guarantee reasoning [Var01]. In Temporal e, the main focus is on describing finite sequences using regular expressions. It is not clear whether the language has full ω-regularity [Mor99], which is required for full support of assume-guarantee reasoning.)

Reasoning and verification for FTL formulas is carried out via the automata-theoretic approach [Var96]: to check satisfiability of a formula φ, one constructs a nondeterministic Büchi automaton accepting $models(\varphi)$ and check its emptiness, and to model check a formula one constructs a nondeterministic Büchi automaton for the complementary formula, intersects it with the model and check emptiness. Because of the richness of FTL, the construction of the automaton is quite non-trivial, and will be described in full in a future paper. The ForSpec compiler actually generates a symbolic representation of the automaton; the size of this representation is linear in the length of the formula and in the size of the time windows. Since the lower and upper bounds of these windows are specified using decimal numbers, time windows may involve an exponential blow-up, as the formula next $[2^n]$ p is of length $O(n)$. (It was noted in [AH92] that such succinctness cause an exponential increase in the complexity of temporal reasoning.)

Theorem 2. *The satisfiability problem for* FTL *without time windows is PSPACE-complete. The satisfiability problem for* FTL *is EXPSPACE-complete.*

While reasoning in FTL is exponential in terms of the formula size and time windows' size in the worst case, aggressive optimization by the compiler ensures that the worst case almost never arises in practice; the computational bottleneck of model checking is due to the large nummber of design states. (In fact, in spite of the increased expressiveness of the language, the FTL model checker is much more efficient that Intel's 1st-generation model checker.)

The linear-time framework enable us to subject FTL properties to validation by both formal verification (model checking) and dynamic validation (simulation). The semantics of FTL is over *infinite* traces. This semantics induces a 3-valued semantics over *finite* traces, which are produced by simulation engines: "pass", "fail", and "ongoing". A formula φ *passes* (resp., *fails*) a finite trace τ if τ is an *informative prefix* for φ (resp., $\neg\varphi$) [KV01]. If it neither passes not fails, it is "ongoing". For example, eventually !p passes on the finite trace $p, p, p, \overline{p}$ and is ongoing on the trace p, p, p, p. The formula globally p fails on the trace $p, p, p, \overline{p}$. The fact that simulation semantics is induced by the standard semantics means that the language requires only a single compiler, ensuring consistency between formal and dynamic validation.

6 Discussion

This paper describes FTL, the temporal property-specification logic of ForSpec, Intel's formal specification language, which is being used by several formal-verification teams at Intel. FTL is an industrial property-specification language that supports hardware-oriented constructs as well as uniform semantics for formal and dynamic validation, while at the same time it has a well understood expressiveness and computational complexity, and it fully supports modular reasoning. The design effort strove to find an acceptable compromise, with trade-offs clarified by theory, between conflicting demands, such as expressiveness, usabilty, and implementability. Clocks and resets, both important to hardware designers, have a clear intuitive semantics, but formalizing this semantics is nontrivial.

References

[AH92]   R. Alur and T.A. Henzinger. Logics and models of real time: a survey. In J.W. de Bakker, K. Huizing, W.-P. de Roever, and G. Rozenberg, editors, *Real Time: Theory in Practice*, Lecture Notes in Computer Science 600, pages 74–106. Springer-Verlag, 1992.

[BB87]   B. Banieqbal and H. Barringer. Temporal logic with fixed points. In B. Banieqbal, H. Barringer, and A. Pnueli, editors, *Temporal Logic in Specification*, volume 398 of *Lecture Notes in Computer Science*, pages 62–74. Springer-Verlag, 1987.

[BBDE$^+$01] I. Beer, S. Ben-David, C. Eisner, D. Fisman, A. Gringauze, and Y. Rodeh. The temporal logic sugar. In *Proc. Conf. on Computer-Aided Verification (CAV'00)*, volume 2102 of *Lecture Notes in Computer Science*, pages 363–367. Springer-Verlag, 2001.

[BBL98]   I. Beer, S. Ben-David, and A. Landver. On-the-fly model checking of RCTL formulas. In *Computer Aided Verification, Proc. 10th International Conference*, volume 1427 of *Lecture Notes in Computer Science*, pages 184–194. Springer-Verlag, 1998.

[CCGR00]   A. Cimatti, E.M. Clarke, F. Giunchiglia, and M. Roveri. Nusmv: a new symbolic model checker. *It'l J. on Software Tools for Technology Transfer*, 2(4):410–425, 2000.

[CLM98]   R. Cleaveland, G. Luttgen, and M. Mendler. An algebraic theory of multiple clocks. In *Proc. 8th Int'l Conf. on Concurrency Theory (CONCUR'97)*, volume 1243 of *Lecture Notes in Computer Science*, pages 166–180. Springer-Verlag, 1998.

[Eme90]   E.A. Emerson. Temporal and modal logic. In J. Van Leeuwen, editor, *Handbook of Theoretical Computer Science*, volume B, chapter 16, pages 997–1072. Elsevier, MIT press, 1990.

[ET97]   E.A. Emerson and R.J. Trefler. Generalized quantitative temporal reasoning: An automata theoretic. In *Proc. Theory and Practice of Software Development (TAPSOFT)*, volume 1214 of *Lecture Notes in Computer Science*, pages 189–200. Springer-Verlag, 1997.

[Fin01]   B. Finkbeiner. Symbolic refinement checking with nondeterministic BDDs. In
            Tools and algorithms for the construction and analysis of systems, Lecture Notes in
            Computer Science. Springer-Verlag, 2001.

[FL79]   M.J. Fischer and R.E. Ladner. Propositional dynamic logic of regular programs.
            Journal of Computer and Systems Sciences, 18:194–211, 1979.

[HT99]   J.G. Henriksen and P.S. Thiagarajan. Dynamic linear time temporal logic. *Annals
            of Pure and Applied Logic*, 96(1–3):187–207, 1999.

[Koz83]   D. Kozen. Results on the propositional μ-calculus. *Theoretical Computer Science*,
            27:333–354, 1983.

[KPV01]   O. Kupferman, N. Piterman, and M.Y. Vardi. Extended temporal logic revisited.
            In *Proc. 12th International Conference on Concurrency Theory*, volume 2154 of
            Lecture Notes in Computer Science, pages 519–535, August 2001.

[Kur97]   R.P. Kurshan. Formal verification in a commercial setting. In *Proc. Conf. on Design
            Automation (DAC'97)*, volume 34, pages 258–262, 1997.

[Kur98]   R.P. Kurshan. *FormalCheck User's Manual*. Cadence Design, Inc., 1998.

[KV01]   O. Kupferman and M.Y. Vardi. Model checking of safety properties. *Formal methods
            in System Design*, 19(3):291–314, November 2001.

[LO99]   C. Liu and M.A. Orgun. Verification of reactive systems using temporal logics with
            clocks. *Theoretical Computer Science*, 220:377–408, 1999.

[LPZ85]   O. Lichtenstein, A. Pnueli, and L. Zuck. The glory of the past. In *Logics of Programs*,
            volume 193 of *Lecture Notes in Computer Science*, pages 196–218, Brooklyn, June
            1985. Springer-Verlag.

[Mor99]   M.J. Morley. Semantics of temporal *e*. In T. F. Melham and F.G. Moller, editors,
            Banff'99 *Higher Order Workshop (Formal Methods in Computation)*. University of
            Glasgow, Department of Computing Science Technic al Report, 1999.

[Pnu85]   A. Pnueli. In transition from global to modular temporal reasoning about programs.
            In K. Apt, editor, *Logics and Models of Concurrent Systems*, volume F-13 of *NATO
            Advanced Summer Institutes*, pages 123–144. Springer-Verlag, 1985.

[SBF⁺97]   T. Schlipf, T. Buechner, R. Fritz, M. Helms, and J. Koehl. Formal verification made
            easy. *IBM Journal of Research and Development*, 41(4:5), 1997.

[SVW87]   A.P. Sistla, M.Y. Vardi, and P. Wolper. The complementation problem for Büchi au-
            tomata with applications to temporal logic. *Theoretical Computer Science*, 49:217–
            237, 1987.

[Var96]   M.Y. Vardi. An automata-theoretic approach to linear temporal logic. In F. Moller
            and G. Birtwistle, editors, *Logics for Concurrency: Structure versus Automata*, vol-
            ume 1043 of *Lecture Notes in Computer Science*, pages 238–266. Springer-Verlag,
            Berlin, 1996.

[Var01]   M.Y. Vardi. Branching vs. linear time: Final showdown. In *Proc. Tools and Al-
            gorithms for the Construction and Analysis of Systems (TACAS)*, volume 2031 of
            Lecture Notes in Computer Science, pages 1–22. Springer-Verlag, 2001.

[VW94]   M.Y. Vardi and P. Wolper. Reasoning about infinite computations. *Information and
            Computation*, 115(1):1–37, November 1994.

[Wol83]   P. Wolper. Temporal logic can be more expressive. *Information and Control*, 56(1–
            2):72–99, 1983.

Fine-Grain Conjunction Scheduling for Symbolic Reachability Analysis

HoonSang Jin[1]*, Andreas Kuehlmann[2], and Fabio Somenzi[1]**

[1] University of Colorado at Boulder
{Jinh,Fabio}@Colorado.EDU
[2] Cadence Berkeley Labs
kuehl@cadence.com

Abstract. In symbolic model checking, image computation is the process of computing the successors of a set of states. Containing the cost of image computation depends critically on controlling the number of variables that appear in the functions being manipulated; this in turn depends on the order in which the basic operations of image computation—conjunctions and quantifications—are performed. In this paper we propose an approach to this ordering problem—the conjunction scheduling problem—that is especially suited to the case in which the transition relation is specified as the composition of many small relations. (This is the norm in hardware verification.) Our *fine-grain* approach leads to the formulation of conjunction scheduling in terms of minimum max-cut linear arrangement, an NP-complete problem for which efficient heuristics have been developed. The cut whose width is minimized is related to the number of variables active during image computation. We also propose a clustering technique that is geared toward the minimization of the max-cut, and pruning techniques for the transition relation that benefit especially from the fine-grain approach.

1 Introduction

Reachability analysis computes the set of states of a state-transition system that are reachable from a set of initial states. Besides explicit methods [18] for traversing states one by one and SAT-based techniques [1] for deciding distance-bounded reachability between pairs of state sets, symbolic methods [9,5] are the most commonly used approach to this problem. Symbolic methods employ BDDs for two purposes: (1) to collect the set of reachable states for deciding when a fixpoint is reached, and (2) to represent the systems' transition relation. Without loss of generality, we will limit our description to forward state exploration. Because of their symmetry, all methods presented in this paper are equally applicable to backward state traversal.

Each traversal step consists of an image computation that calculates the set of states reachable in one transition from a set of current states. For this purpose, the BDD representing the transition relation is conjoined with the BDD of the current states. This is followed by an existential quantification of the current state variables to eliminate the

---

* Work performed in part while the author was at Cadence Berkeley Labs.
** Work supported in part by SRC contract 2001-TJ-920 and NSF grant CCR-99-71195.

J.-P. Katoen and P. Stevens (Eds.): TACAS 2002, LNCS 2280, pp. 312–326, 2002.
© Springer-Verlag Berlin Heidelberg 2002

origin information, and a renaming step to re-encode the state set in terms of the current-state variables. Except for small systems, the transition relation can seldom be stored as a single BDD. Instead, it is represented in a partitioned manner. The conjunctively partitioned transition relation [4] is the most common form and consists of a set of *conjuncts*. The advantage of the partitioned form is that the image step can be performed step-wise by a series of AND operations between the current-state BDD and the individual conjuncts of the transition relation. This allows the application of early quantification to eliminate variables as soon as they become dead, i.e., they become unreferenced by any of the following conjuncts. This significantly alleviates the computational complexity of the image computation step.

The partitioned implementation of the image computation step poses an optimization problem with two interdependent goals: (1) to find a partitioning of the transition relation that has small BDD representations for the individual conjuncts, and (2) to determine a conjunction and early quantification schedule that minimizes the maximum BDDs size of the intermediate results. This problem is referred to as the *conjunction scheduling problem*; a simplified version of it is NP-complete [14].

Traditional approaches to the conjunction scheduling problem are based on coarse-grain methods [12,17,15,8]. Their motivation comes from the incentive to avoid the large number of intermediate variables that are needed for a finer grain partitioning. Coarse-grain methods start from large conjuncts, typically entire next-state functions, and try to further cluster them with the goal of finding a schedule that can eliminate a maximum number of variables as early as possible. Only if the BDD for a next-state function cannot be built within a given memory limit, cutpoints are applied to partition its clusters [2]. In these methods the insertion of cutpoints is driven by BDD size limits only and does not take into account its effect on the clustering result.

In this paper we propose a different approach to the clustering and scheduling problem. Instead of starting from large clusters that represent significant fractions of the next-state functions, we begin the process with a fine-grain partitioning based on single gates or small fanout-free sub-circuits. The resulting large number of conjuncts is then carefully clustered with the objective to *minimize the maximum number of variables* that are alive during image computation, and to further *eliminate as many variables as possible* by making them local to single conjuncts. This variable elimination process can also be used to remove state variables, which in turn prunes the corresponding registers from the transition relation.

2   Motivation

We motivate the fine-grain approach of this paper by demonstrating the effect of different clusterings on the complexity of the transition relation and quantification schedule. We use a logic circuit example as it best demonstrates our intention; however, the proposed approach is equally applicable to structures that model other systems. Fig. 1(a) shows a sequential circuit with two primary inputs, one primary output, and three registers storing the circuit state. Part (b) gives the corresponding state-transition graph of the circuit with an initial state described by the predicate $I = \neg x_1 \wedge \neg x_2 \wedge \neg x_3$.

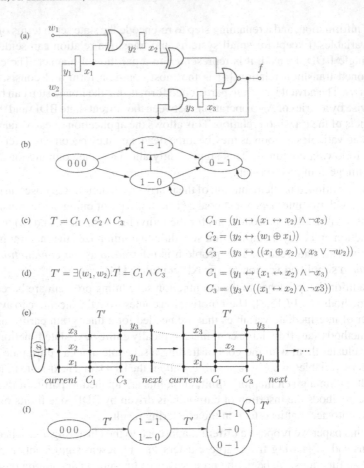

Fig. 1. Example to illustrate the impact of clustering on register pruning: (a) circuit structure, (b) state-transition diagram, (c) original partitioned transition relation, (d) transition relation after one pruning step, (e) quantification schedule used for reachability analysis, (f) state sets visited during breath-first forward traversal

The transition relation T is constructed using one pair of variables for each state holding element. In the example, $\{x_1, x_2, x_3\}$ and $\{y_1, y_2, y_3\}$ denote the *current-state variables* and *next-state variables*, respectively. For the input variables and individual conjuncts of the partitioned transition relation we use $\{w_1, w_2\}$ and $\{C_1, C_2, C_3\}$, respectively. The transition relation T for the given circuit is shown in Fig. 1(c).

Since the primary input variables w_1 and w_2 occur only locally within C_2 and C_3, respectively, T can immediately be pruned by existential quantification resulting in T' (Fig. 1(d)). The elimination of w_1 causes C_2 to become a tautology, which can be removed from T. As a result the current-state variable x_2 is no longer driven by its next-state variable y_2 and becomes unconstrained. This effectively removes the corresponding register from reachability analysis because x_2/y_2 are not involved in the renaming step and are also not part of the BDD recording the set of reachable states. It should be noted that this differs from removing peripheral λ-latches [6] because the register x_2/y_2 feeds other gates. Since the removal is caused by the disappearance of a next-state variable, we will refer to this techniques as *backward register pruning*. In this example, the variable x_2 cannot be further pruned because it occurs in two conjuncts. However, in general pruning can be applied in multiple iterations.

Fig. 1(e) gives the resulting quantification schedule using the pruned transition relation T'. As shown, in the first image computation step x_2 must be constrained by the set of initial states. In the following steps x_2 remains local to T', establishing a relation between C_1 and C_2 only. Note that in this example, only one backward pruning step was applied, thus the transition relation for the first and following image step is identical. However, in general, multiple backward pruning iterations, interleaved with *forward pruning* (as described later), can successively remove more registers. Generally, a transition relation that has been pruned by i forward pruning iterations must not be used before image computation step $i + 1$, otherwise unreachable states could get introduced in the reachability results. For the given example, Fig. 1(f) depicts the individual sets of reached states as they are encountered during breadth-first forward traversal.

A different clustering of the transition relation can further reduce the size of its conjunctive form. Similar to the complete elimination of w_1 and w_2, additional variables can be removed by existential quantification *if they are made local to a single conjunct*. Fig. 2(a) shows the modified circuit example with the additional variable w_3 for partitioning the conjuncts C_1 and C_3 and part (b) gives the updated transition relation. Besides C_1, C_2, and C_3, which express the next-state relations of the registers, it also includes the conjunct C_4, which relates the variable w_3 to its driving function.

This finer grain partitioning provides more freedom to iteratively quantify variables. As shown in Fig. 2(c-e), multiple pruning steps can successively reduce the transition relation until it contains only a single, simple conjunct. First, the existential quantification of w_1 and w_2 eliminates C_2 resulting in T'. In contrast to the clustering applied in the previous case, here x_2 becomes now local to C_4 and can be quantified in the next pruning step resulting in T''. As explained above, T'' cannot be applied for the first image computation since at that point x_2 must be constrained by the initial states. Fig. 2(f) shown the quantification schedule to be used for exact reachability analysis. After the initial application of T' all following steps can use the pruned relation T''.

Similar to backward pruning, *forward register pruning* denotes the removal of registers based on the disappearance of current-state variables. In the given example, forward pruning can be applied to remove register x_1/y_1 since x_1 has disappeared from T'' as a result of the previous pruning step. In other words, the absence of the current-state variable x_1 in T'' makes the actual binding of the next-state variable from the previous image step superfluous. Thus y_1 can be removed from T'' by existential quantification, which in turn eliminates C_1. As a result w_3 becomes local to the only remaining conjunct C_3 and can also be eliminated producing T'''.

Due to the existential quantification of y_1, the use of T''' for forward image computation results in an over-approximation of the set of resulting states. The corresponding effect is demonstrated in the top part of Fig. 2(h). As shown, the application of T''' for the second traversal step produces, among others, the unreachable state $(0, 1, 0)$. Note

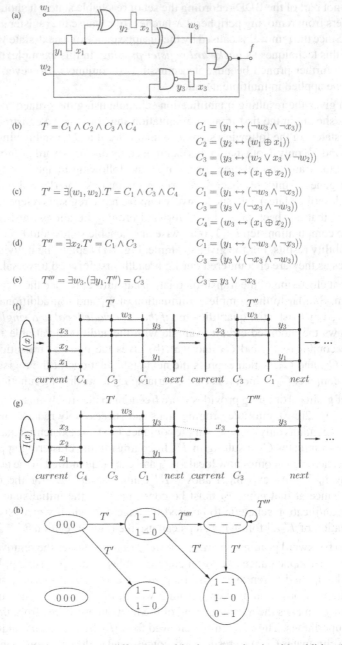

Fig. 2. Example of Fig. 1 using a different partitioning: (a) circuit with additional cut variable w_3, (b) original transition relation, (c-e) transition relation after multiple pruning steps, (f) quantification schedule using T' for the first image step and T'' for all following steps, (g) pruned schedule using T''' for the second and following steps, (h) over-approximated reachability result using pruned schedule (top part) and result after applying one correction step using T''

that the application of a transition relation which has been forward pruned once can only result in an *over-shooting* by at most one transition. In other words, in case of simple forward pruning, the maximum distance of an over-approximated state from a truly reachable state is one. In general, the application of j forward pruning iterations results in a maximum over-shooting distance of j. Therefore, the over-approximated reachability results can be corrected by applying a sequence of j additional image steps using the unpruned transition relation. The bottom part of Fig. 2(h) illustrates this correction for the given example.

In summary, the application of pruning requires that the image computation at step i must not use a transition relation that has been backward pruned more than $i - 1$ times. Furthermore, over-approximated reachability results that are produced by a transition relation derived from j forward pruning iterations, can be corrected by j application of the exact transition relation. In Section 3.4 we describe an algorithm that dynamically prunes the transition relation as the state traversal progresses.

The advantage of the presented approach is that the majority of image computation steps can use the pruned transition relation. Once a fixpoint is reached, the exact set of reachable states is determined from the over-approximation by applying one or more exact steps. Since the computational bottleneck of BDD-based reachability analysis typically occurs in the middle of the traversal, this methods can significantly improve the overall efficiency. Further, the over-approximation is tight, in many practical cases even exact. If a given set of properties can be proven for this tight approximation, the correction step is not needed.

3   Algorithms

3.1   Preliminaries

We model a sequential circuit as a transition structure $K = \langle T, I \rangle$ consisting of a transition relation $T(y, x)$ and an initial predicate $I(x)$. The binary variables $x = \{x_1, \ldots, x_m\}$ are the current state variables, while the binary variables $y = \{y_1, \ldots, y_m\}$ are the next state variables. Given a predicate $P(x)$ describing a set of present states, the set of their successors, $S(y)$, is the *image* of $P(x)$ and is given by

$$S(y) = \exists x \, . \, P(x) \wedge T(y, x) \, . \tag{1}$$

The states of K reachable from the states in I can be computed by successive image computations. Denoting by $\mathsf{EY}\, P(x)$ the predicate obtained by replacing the y variables with the x variables in the image of $P(x)$, the reachable states are given by

$$R(x) = \mu Z(x) \, . \, I(x) \vee \mathsf{EY}\, Z(x) \, , \tag{2}$$

where μ indicates computation of the least fixpoint. We assume that the transition relation is given as the composition of elementary relations. If $w = \{w_1, \ldots, w_n\}$ is a set of binary *internal* variables with $n \geq m$, our assumption amounts to writing:

$$T(y, x) = \exists w \, . \, \bigwedge_{1 \leq i \leq m} (y_i \leftrightarrow w_i) \wedge \bigwedge_{1 \leq i \leq n} T_i(w, x) \, . \tag{3}$$

The variables in w are usually associated with the outputs of the combinational logic gates of the sequential circuit; each T_i is called a *gate relation* because it usually describes the behavior of a logic gate. For instance, if w_i is the output variable of a two-input AND gate with inputs w_j and x_k, then $T_i = w_i \leftrightarrow (w_j \wedge x_k)$. If, on the other hand, w_i is a primary input to the circuit, then $T_i = 1$. Each term of the form $y_i \leftrightarrow w_i$ equates a next state variable to an internal variable. (The output of the gate feeding the i-th memory element.)

When computing (2) for large circuits it is seldom practical to evaluate $T(y, x)$ before computing the images. This is especially true when BDDs [3] are used to represent the relations. Instead, one substitutes (3) into (1) to get

$$S(y) = \exists x \cdot \exists w \cdot P(x) \wedge \bigwedge_{1 \leq i \leq m} (y_i \leftrightarrow w_i) \wedge \bigwedge_{1 \leq i \leq n} T_i(w, x) \ . \tag{4}$$

The main advantage of using (4) stems from the ability to apply *early quantification* while conjoining the terms of the transition relation to the set of states. Indeed,

$$\exists a \cdot g(b) \wedge f(a, b) = g(b) \wedge \exists a \cdot f(a, b) \ , \tag{5}$$

though, in general, existential quantification does not distribute over conjunction. Application of (5) turns an image computation into a series of passes. Each pass replaces two terms with their conjunction and quantifies all variables that appear in only one of the resulting terms.

Early quantification reduces the number of variables that appear in the BDDs obtained as intermediate results during the computation of (4). Its impact depends largely on the order in which the terms are conjoined. The *conjunction scheduling problem* is the problem of determining an order of the terms in (4) that reduces the time and memory requirements of image computation. The evaluation of (2) requires in general repeated image computations. It is usually advantageous to take the conjunctions in (4) that do not involve $P(x)$ only once before reachability analysis is started. After these conjunctions have been taken, image computation amounts to evaluating

$$S(y) = \exists x \cdot \exists w \cdot P(x) \wedge \bigwedge_{1 \leq i \leq k} C_i(y, w, x) \ , \tag{6}$$

where each C_i is a *cluster* obtained by conjoining one or more terms from (4), and quantifying w variables not appearing in any other cluster. During the computation, early quantification is applied according to the following scheme.

$$S(y) = \exists v^1 \cdot (C_1 \wedge \cdots \wedge \exists v^k \cdot (C_k \wedge \exists v^{k+1} \cdot P)) \ , \tag{7}$$

where v^i is the set of variables in $(x \cup w) \setminus \bigcup_{i < j \leq k} v^j$ that do not appear in $C_1, \ldots, C_{i-1}$.

Too many clusters lead to needless recomputation, whereas too few clusters, or ill-assorted clusters, may adversely affect early quantification. The *clustering problem* is the problem of finding a suitable partition of the terms of (4) into clusters that reduces the time and memory requirements of image computation.

Though in principle the scheduling and clustering problems cannot be separated, it is common practice to order the conjuncts before clustering them. Clustering is then restricted to terms that form intervals in the order [17]. (See, however, [14] for a dissenting voice.)

3.2 Conjunction Scheduling via Linear Arrangement

We formulate the conjunction scheduling problem in terms of linear arrangement of a hypergraph.

Definition 1. *A hypergraph $G = (V, H)$ consists of a set of vertices V and a multiset of hyperedges H. Each hyperedge is a subset of V. A linear arrangement of G is a bijection $\alpha : V \rightarrow \{1, \ldots, |V|\}$.*

The maximum cut-width $\Gamma(G, \alpha)$ of hypergraph G under linear arrangement α is the maximum number of hyperedges crossing a section of the graph. Formally,

$$\Gamma(G, \alpha) = \max_{1 \leq i \leq |V|} |\{h \in H : \exists u \in h . \exists v \in h . \alpha(u) \leq i \leq \alpha(v)\}| . \tag{8}$$

The *minimum max-cut problem* asks for a linear arrangement α of hypergraph G that minimizes $\Gamma(G, \alpha)$. This problem is NP-complete [11], but effective heuristic techniques have been developed for it.

Given a set of clusters $C = \{C_i(y, w, x)\}$, let $\sigma(C)$ be the set of variables appearing in the clusters of C. We consider the hypergraph

$$G_C = (C, \{\{C_i : v \in \sigma(\{C_i\})\} : v \in y \cup w \cup x\}) . \tag{9}$$

In G_C each vertex models a cluster, and each hyperedge models a variable. The vertices connected by a hyperedge are the clusters in which the corresponding variable appears. Hyperedges may be repeated because several variables may appear in exactly the same clusters. (This is a slight departure from the standard definition of hypergraphs.)

A linear arrangement α of G_C corresponds to a conjunction schedule for image computation. The maximum cut-width $\Gamma(G_C, \alpha)$ is the maximum number of live variables during image computation. Solving the minimum max-cut problem for G_C is therefore related to finding a good conjunction schedule.

When the transition relation of structure K is given in the form of a logic circuit, the list of clusters C is obtained as follows. Initially, one conjunct is created for each gate in the circuit, and for each next state function as shown in (3). For large circuits, the resulting large number of conjuncts may hinder the computation of a good linear arrangement. Therefore, *fanout-free* regions of the circuit are selectively collapsed.

The same conjunction schedule for a given transition relation is typically used for the computation of the images of several sets of states. In general, the predicates representing these states will depend on different sets of variables. We make the conservative assumption that all current state variables appear in these sets of states. This is achieved by augmenting C with a dummy cluster that depends on all variables in x. The position of this cluster is fixed at the beginning of the linear arrangement. Likewise, a second dummy cluster depending on all next state variables is added to C and its position is fixed at the end of the linear arrangement.

Once the initial list of clusters C is obtained, we invoke CAPO, [7] to obtain a single-row placement of the vertices of G_C. CAPO produces a linear arrangement with a small maximum cut-width, while also trying to reduce the total wire length. The length of a (non-empty) hyperedge is the maximum distance in the arrangement between two vertices belonging to the hyperedge. In the context of image computation, the maximum cut-width translates into the peak number of variables during image computation, while the length of a hyperedge corresponds to the lifetime of a variable. Is is noted in [15] that reducing the average lifetime of variables reduces the sizes of the BDDs and the cost of operating on them. In terms of the *dependency matrix* of the transition relation, a good linear arrangement results in a small *bandwidth*.

It is also possible to use linear arrangement to produce a static variable order for the BDDs (cf. [13]). For that we model a variable as a vertex, and a cluster as a hyperedge connecting all the variables appearing in the cluster. The BDDs of the clusters are ordered according to the arrangement of the vertices before the clustering algorithm of Section 3.3 is applied.

3.3   Clustering

Clustering reduces the number of conjunctions that must be taken during image computation by collapsing groups of clusters. Another important objective is to make the early quantification of variables from the transition relation possible.

The input to clustering is a linearly arranged set of clusters. The output is a reduced set of clusters. Each output cluster is the conjunction of a set of contiguous input clusters. In other words, the clustering process respects the given linear arrangement.

Definition 2. *Given a linear arrangement α of a set of clusters C, a variable v is dead outside positions i and j if v appears in cluster C_k only if $i \leq \alpha(C_k) \leq j$. The number of variables that are dead outside positions i and j is denoted by $D_{i,j}$. The number of variables that are not dead outside positions i and j, and that appear in clusters C_k such that $i \leq \alpha(C_k) \leq j$ is denoted by $V_{i,j}$.*

According to this definition, $D_{i,j}$ is the number of variables that can be quantified if the clusters between positions i and j are merged, while $V_{i,j}$ is an upper bound on the number of variables appearing in the result of the merger after quantification.

Fig. 3 shows a heuristic clustering algorithm. The algorithm iterates until no new clusters are created in one pass. At each pass, it creates a list of candidates. Each candidate is a contiguous set of clusters. The list is ordered in decreasing order of $D_{i,j}$ to favor candidates that allow many variables to be quantified. As a tie-breaker, the upper bound on the number of variables in the resulting cluster is used. This policy favors the creation of small clusters that may be merged in subsequent passes.

The number of candidates considered by the algorithm of Fig. 3 is quadratic in the number of clusters. This may be inefficient. Therefore, the actual implementation limits the maximum number of clusters in a candidate to 200.

Once the list has been sorted, the candidates are examined in turn. If the result of merging all the clusters in the candidate is smaller than a specified threshold, the candidate is accepted and the result of the merger replaces all the clusters in the candidate. All other candidates having clusters in common with the accepted one are rejected.

To limit the cost of this phase, the conjunction of the clusters in a candidate is abandoned as soon as it exceeds the threshold (even though conjoining more clusters may eventually bring the size down again). Furthermore, all candidates that are supersets

```
GREEDYCLUSTERING(C) {
    while (1) {
        Calculate D_{i,j} and V_{i,j} of C;
        nClusteringDone = 0;
        F = ();
        for (i = 0; i < |C|; i++) {
            used[i] = new[i] = false;
            for (j = i + 1; j < |C|; j++)
                Insert quadruple f = (i, j, D_{i,j}, V_{i,j}) into F;
        }
        Sort F in order of decreasing D_{i,j}
            in case of tie, give higher priority to entries with smaller V_{i,j};
        for each f in F {
            if (used[i] || ··· || used[j]) continue ;
            C_{i,j} = C_i ∧ ··· ∧ C_j;
            if (BDDSIZE(C_{i,j}) <TheholdValue) {
                nClusteringDone++;
                for (k = i; k < j; k++) used[k] = true;
                C_j = C_{i,j};
                new[j] = true;
            } else free C_{i,j};
        }
        if (nClusteringDone == 0) break ;
        Remove from C clusters that are marked used and not new;
    }
}
```

Fig. 3. Greedy clustering algorithm

of the set of clusters whose conjunction exceeded the threshold are discarded. These details are omitted from the pseudocode of Fig. 3 to avoid clutter.

3.4 Pruning

During the initial linear arrangement and clustering the assumption is made that all current state variables will appear in the predicate $P(x)$ whose image must be computed. As seen in Section 2, relaxing this assumption may lead to more extensive application of early quantification. We now describe how this process is carried out.

The algorithm of Fig. 4 applies pruning while computing the states reachable from I according to the transition relation described by C.

Theorem 1. *If forward pruning is excluded, then algorithm* REACHABLE *of Fig. 4 correctly computes the states reachable from I according to C.*

Proof. We show by induction that at the i-th iterations of the main loop $R(x)$ describes the states reachable from I in i steps or less. This trivially holds for $i = 0$. For the

```
REACHABLE (C, I) {
    R(x) = P(x) = I(x);
    while (1) {
        PRUNE (C, P);
        S(x) = EY P(x);
        N(x) = S(x) ∧ ¬R(x);
        if (N(x) = 0) return R(x);
        R(x) = R(x) ∨ N(x);
        P(x) = PICK (N(x), S(x));  // choose a small BDD for P such that N ≤ P ≤ S
        existentially quantify from P(x) the variables not in S(x);
    }
}


PRUNE (C, P) {
    X = {xⱼ : yⱼ ∉ σ(C) ∧ xⱼ ∉ σ({P}) ∧ ∃i . xⱼ ∈ σ({Cᵢ}) ∧ xⱼ ∉ σ(C \ {Cᵢ})};
    C = ∃X . C;  // backward pruning
    Y = {yⱼ : xⱼ ∉ σ(C) ∧ ∃i . yⱼ ∈ σ({Cᵢ}) ∧ yⱼ ∉ σ(C \ {Cᵢ})};
    C = ∃Y . C;  // forward pruning
    do {  // intermediate variable quantification
        W = {wⱼ : ∃i . wⱼ ∈ σ({Cᵢ}) ∧ wⱼ ∉ σ(C \ {Cᵢ})};
        C = ∃W . C;
    } while (W ≠ ∅);
}
```

Fig. 4. Reachability analysis algorithm

inductive step, we prove that pruning the transition relation does not change the result of successive image computations. Since pruning consists of existential quantifications, the new transition relation contains the old one. Hence, no state is dropped from $S(x)$.

To see that no states are added, assume that at the start of the i-th iteration, P describes states reachable from I in exactly $i - 1$ steps, and the states reachable in i or more steps can be correctly computed using the current C.

Suppose x_j is pruned at the i-th iteration. Then, it does not appear in P, and it appears in exactly one C_i. Therefore, if the original C were used for image computation, early quantification would apply, and pruning of x_j would occur as part of image computation. Hence, pruning of x_j does not affect S. By simple induction on the number of pruned variables one concludes that backward pruning does not change the result of image computation. (Quantifying w_j obviously does not change the result if w_j appears in exactly one C_i.)

Since y_j does not appear in C if x_j is pruned, then x_j does not appear in $S(x)$. Furthermore, the choice of P for the next iteration preserves this property. Since $P \leq S$, after quantification of the variables not in S from P, the result is still contained in S. Since the variables not in the incoming P are not in the new P either, the pruning at iteration i is valid also at successive iterations.   □

Notice that the quantification of the variables not in S from P is can be avoided at the expense of complicating the proof. Moreover, the *restrict* operator [10] can be used to select P so that no variables not in S appears in P.

It should be noted that the effectiveness of pruning is enhanced by the ability of the clustering algorithm to reduce the number of terms in which a variable appears.

Lemma 1. *Let $T_0, \ldots, T_k$ the sequence of transition relations generated by forward pruning. Specifically, let $T_0 = T$, and $T_{i+1} = \exists Y_i . T_i$, where Y_i is the set of next-state variables quantified because their corresponding current-state variables X_i are not in T_i. (That is, $X_i \cap \sigma(T_i) = \emptyset$ and $Y_i \cap Y_j = \emptyset$ for $0 \leq j < i$.) Let EY_i compute the successors of a set of states using transition relation T_i. Then*

$$\exists X_i . \mathsf{EY}_i \, Z(x) = \mathsf{EY}_{i+1} \, Z(x) .$$

Lemma 2. $R_{i+1}(x) \vee \exists X_i . I(x) = \exists X_i . R_i(x).$

Proof. Expanding both sides, and observing that $I(x) \leq \exists X_i . I(x)$, we get

$$\exists X_i . I(x) \vee \bigvee_{j>0} \mathsf{EY}_{i+1}^j \, I(x) = \exists X_i . I(x) \vee \bigvee_{j>0} \exists X_i . \mathsf{EY}_i^j \, I(x) .$$

The two sides can be shown to be identical by recursive application of Lemma 1. □

Theorem 2. *Let $R^+(x)$ be the result produced by reachability with forward pruning. Then the reachable states are given by*

$$R(x) = \nu Z(x) . R^+(x) \wedge (I(x) \vee \mathsf{EY} \, Z(x)) . \tag{10}$$

Proof. Let $R_i(x)$ be the result of reachability analysis using T_i. We have:

$$R_i(x) = I(x) \vee \mathsf{EY}_i \, R_i(x) ,$$

which, applying (5) and Lemma 2, becomes

$$R_i(x) = I(x) \vee \mathsf{EY}_i \, R_{i+1}(x) . \tag{11}$$

Therefore, we can compute the exact reachable states $R(x) = R_0(x)$ by starting with $R^+(x) = R_k(x)$, and iteratively applying (11). We now observe that $T_i \geq T$ for $0 \leq i \leq k$, and consequently,

$$R_0(x) \leq I(x) \vee \mathsf{EY} \, R_{i+1}(x) \leq R_i(x) .$$

Therefore, $R_0(x) = \nu Z(x) . R^+(x) \wedge (I(x) \vee \mathsf{EY} \, Z(x))$. Convergence is guaranteed in k iterations. □

Theorem 3. *Procedure* REACHABLE *computes the reachable states of $K = \langle T, I \rangle$.*

Proof (sketch). To account for the interleaving of backward and forward pruning, we observe that each transition relation T_i obtained by forward pruning is applied from a set of set of states that is between $I(x)$ and $R_{i-1}(x) \leq R_i(x)$. Hence, if used to convergence, it computes $R_i(x)$. □

4   Experiments

We implemented the proposed method in VIS [2]. Experiments are conducted on 1.7GHz Pentium 4 with 1GB of RAM running Linux. We compare the fine-grain method (denoted by FG) to the IWLS95 [17], Hybrid [16], and MLP [15] methods. In these experiments, we turned on dynamic variable ordering for BDDs and we set the data size limit to 700MB. Figure 5 compares the four methods in the context of reachability analysis. Each experiment was allotted 20,000 seconds.

The experiments show overall improvements in CPU time and memory usage. The proposed method outperforms the IWLS95, Hybrid, and MLP methods in most hard benchmark examples, such as s4863, am2901, prolog, and s3330. In the case of rotate32, which is the 32-bit rotator, all the transition functions contain all the present state variables. It means that there is no good quantification schedule without intermediate variables. The good result for FG witnesses its ability to choose a good set of intermediate variables.

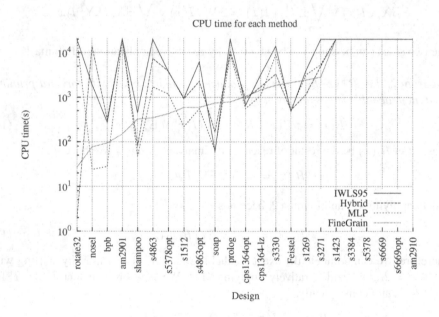

Fig. 5. Performance comparison

Table 1 reports the number of state variables before and after applying pruning. We can prune all the state variables in the case of s4863 and s4863opt; hence, the transition relations can be reduced to the constant 1. This means that the reachability analysis step is trivial. However, the recovery step is hard because it computes the exact reachable states from the set of all states. In Fig. 5, most CPU time of s4863 and s4863opt is consumed by the recovery step.

Table 1. Number of state variables before and after optimization

Design	Before		After	
	Present State	Next State	Present State	Next State
prolog	136	136	114	112
s1269	37	37	36	36
s1423	74	74	72	72
s1512	57	57	46	46
s3271	116	116	115	115
s3330	132	132	113	112
s3384	183	183	120	119
s4863	104	104	0	0
s4863opt	88	88	0	5
s5378	179	179	159	159
s5378opt	121	121	83	83
s6669	239	239	175	164
s6669opt	231	231	167	148

5 Conclusions

We have presented an approach to image computation for symbolic reachability analysis
that exploits the fine-grain structure of the transition relation. In the case of hardware
circuits, such structure is represented by the combinational gates that make up the next-
state functions; the approach, however, is general. The advantage of a fine-grain approach
is the ability to accurately place intermediate variables in the transition relation so as
to promote extensive early quantification. We have presented three techniques that rely
on this feature: A procedure for the computation of the conjunction schedule based on
minimum max-cut linear arrangement; a clustering algorithm, and a variable pruning
algorithm that works in conjunction with the standard symbolic reachability analysis
procedure.

Preliminary experimental results show great promise for the fine-grain approach,
especially in cases when the circuit implementing the transition relations are deep and
have large BDDs. In these cases other image computation procedures tend to place
intermediate variables suboptimally. There is still considerable work to be done to reduce
the overhead of our clustering algorithm.

Acknowledgments. The authors would like to thank Igor Markov of the University of
Michigan for his help in installing and customizing CAPO for the experiments.

References

[1] A. Biere, A. Cimatti, E. Clarke, and Y. Zhu. Symbolic model checking without BDDs. In
*Fifth International Conference on Tools and Algorithms for Construction and Analysis of
Systems (TACAS'99)*, pages 193–207, Amsterdam, The Netherlands, March 1999.

[2] R. K. Brayton et al. VIS: A system for verification and synthesis. In T. Henzinger and
R. Alur, editors, *Eighth Conference on Computer Aided Verification (CAV'96)*, pages 428–
432. Springer-Verlag, Rutgers University, 1996. LNCS 1102.

[3] R. E. Bryant. Graph-based algorithms for Boolean function manipulation. *IEEE Transactions on Computers*, C-35(8):677–691, August 1986.

[4] J. R. Burch, E. M. Clarke, D. E. Long, K. L. McMillan, and D. L. Dill. Symbolic model checking for sequential circuit verification. *IEEE Transactions on Computer-Aided Design*, 13(4):401–424, April 1994.

[5] J. R. Burch, E. M. Clarke, K. L. McMillan, D. L. Dill, and L. J. Hwang. Symbolic model checking: 10^{20} states and beyond. In *Proceedings of the Fifth Annual Symposium on Logic in Computer Science*, pages 428–439, June 1990.

[6] G. Cabodi, P. Camurati, and S. Quer. Improved reachability analysis of large finite state machines. In *Proceedings of the International Conference on Computer-Aided Design*, pages 354–360, Santa Clara, CA, November 1996.

[7] A. E. Caldwell, A. B. Kahng, and I. Markov. Optimal partitioners and end-case placers for standard-cell layout. *IEEE Transactions on Computer-Aided Design*, 19(11):1304–1314, November 2000.

[8] P. P. Chauhan, E. M. Clarke, S. Jha, J. Kukula, T. Shiple, H. Veith, and D. Wang. Non-linear quantification scheduling in image computation. In *Proceedings of the International Conference on Computer-Aided Design*, pages 293–298, San Jose, CA, November 2001.

[9] O. Coudert, C. Berthet, and J. C. Madre. Verification of sequential machines based on symbolic execution. In J. Sifakis, editor, *Automatic Verification Methods for Finite State Systems*, pages 365–373. Springer-Verlag, 1989. LNCS 407.

[10] O. Coudert and J. C. Madre. A unified framework for the formal verification of sequential circuits. In *Proceedings of the IEEE International Conference on Computer Aided Design*, pages 126–129, November 1990.

[11] M. R. Garey, D. S. Johnson, and L. Stockmeyer. Some simplified NP-complete graph problems. *Theoretical Computer Science*, pages 237–267, 1987.

[12] D. Geist and I. Beer. Efficient model checking by automated ordering of transition relation partitions. In D. L. Dill, editor, *Sixth Conference on Computer Aided Verification (CAV'94)*, pages 299–310, Berlin, 1994. Springer-Verlag. LNCS 818.

[13] A. Gupta, Z. Yang, L. Zhang, and S. Malik. Partition-based decision heuristics for image computation using SAT and BDDs. In *Proceedings of the International Conference on Computer-Aided Design*, pages 286–292, San Jose, CA, November 2001.

[14] R. Hojati, S. C. Krishnan, and R. K. Brayton. Early quantification and partitioned transition relations. In *Proceedings of the International Conference on Computer Design*, pages 12–19, Austin, TX, October 1996.

[15] I-H. Moon, G. D. Hachtel, and F. Somenzi. Border-block triangular form and conjunction schedule in image computation. In W. A. Hunt, Jr. and S. D. Johnson, editors, *Formal Methods in Computer Aided Design*, pages 73–90. Springer-Verlag, November 2000. LNCS 1954.

[16] I.-H. Moon, J. H. Kukula, K. Ravi, and F. Somenzi. To split or to conjoin: The question in image computation. In *Proceedings of the Design Automation Conference*, pages 23–28, Los Angeles, CA, June 2000.

[17] R. K. Ranjan, A. Aziz, R. K. Brayton, B. F. Plessier, and C. Pixley. Efficient BDD algorithms for FSM synthesis and verification. Presented at IWLS95, Lake Tahoe, CA., May 1995.

[18] C. H. West and P. Zafiropulo. Automated validation of a communications protocol: The CCITT X.21 recommendation. *IBM Journal of Research and Development*, 22:60–71, 1978.

A Temporal Logic Based Theory of Test Coverage and Generation[*]

Hyoung Seok Hong[1][**], Insup Lee[1], Oleg Sokolsky[1], and Hasan Ural[2]

[1] Department of Computer and Information Science, University of Pennsylvania
[2] School of Information Technology and Engineering, University of Ottawa

Abstract. This paper presents a theory of test coverage and generation from specifications written in EFSMs. We investigate a family of coverage criteria based on the information of control flow and data flow and characterize them in the branching time temporal logic CTL. We discuss the complexity of minimal cost test generation and describe a method for automatic test generation which employs the capability of model checkers to construct counterexamples. Our approach extends the range of applications of model checking from formal verification of finite state systems to test generation from finite state systems.

1 Introduction

Testing has always been an essential activity for validating the correctness of software and hardware systems. Although testing cannot provide an absolute guarantee on correctness as is possible with formal verification, a disciplined use of testing can greatly increase the effectiveness of system validation, especially when performed by suitable tools. In this paper, we study the problem of test coverage and generation from specifications written in extended finite state machines (EFSMs). EFSMs extend finite state machines with variables and operations on them and are widely used as an underlying model of many specification languages such as SDL[2], Estelle[4], and Statecharts[12]. Because an EFSM specification typically allows an infinite number of executions, it is not possible to determine whether an implementation under test conforms to its specification by considering all executions of the specification. In the last two decades, a number of methods and tools have been proposed for test generation from EFSMs (for survey, see [3,8]) and most of them focus on a family of coverage criteria based on the information of control flow (e.g, states and transitions) and data flow (e.g., definitions and uses of variables).

We show that the problem of test generation from EFSMs based on control flow and data flow oriented coverage criteria can be formulated as a model checking problem. Given a system model and a temporal logic formula, model checking

[*] This research was supported in part by NSF CCR-9988409, NSF CCR-0086147, NSF CISE-9703220, ARO DAAD19-01-1-0473, and DARPA ITO MOBIES F33615-00-C-1707.
[**] Partially supported by the Advanced Information Technology Research Center (AITrc) at Korea Advanced Institute of Science and Technology (KAIST).

J.-P. Katoen and P. Stevens (Eds.): TACAS 2002, LNCS 2280, pp. 327–341, 2002.
© Springer-Verlag Berlin Heidelberg 2002

establishes whether the model satisfies the formula. If so, model checkers are capable of supplying a witness that explains the success of the formula. Conversely, if the model fails to satisfy the formula, a counterexample is produced. In our approach, each coverage criterion is associated with a set of temporal logic formulas and the problem of test generation satisfying the criterion is formulated as finding witnesses for every formula in the set with respect to a given EFSM. The capability of model checkers to construct witnesses and counterexamples allows test generation to be automatic.

We illustrate our approach using the temporal logic CTL[7]. First we define the semantics of EFSMs in terms of Kripke structures. We then describe how to express each coverage criterion as a set of formulas in CTL, parameterized with the propositions of a given EFSM. Each formula is defined such that the formula is satisfied by the EFSM if and only if the EFSM has an execution that covers the entity described by the formula such as a specific state, transition, or definition-use association[21]. If the entity can be covered in the EFSM, a witness for the corresponding formula is constructed. A test suite is a set of finite executions of the EFSM such that for every formula, the test suite includes a finite execution which is a witness for the formula. In addition to the coverage criteria that cover states, transitions, and definition-use associations, we also consider more complex ones that are based on the affect relation in program slicing[24] and are applied to protocol conformance testing[22]. They deal with data flow from input variables to output variables through an arbitrary number of definition-use associations between local variables. Hence they cannot be characterized as CTL formulas and we characterize them as least fixpoints of predicate transformers over CTL formulas. Witnesses for such least fixpoints can be constructed in the way similar to CTL formulas.

We then discuss the problem of minimal test generation. Typically, a CTL formula can be represented by several different witnesses. By selecting the right witness for each formula, one can minimize the size of the test suite according to two costs: the number of test sequences in the suite or the total length of test sequences in the suite. We show that these optimization problems are NP-hard and describe a simple heuristic similar to the test generation method in [10], which enables the application of existing CTL model checkers such as SMV[19] to automatic test generation.

Related Work. Widely-used system models in the testing literature include finite state machines (FSMs) and labelled transition systems (LTSs), especially in hardware testing and protocol conformance testing. Testing methods based on such models primarily focus on control flow oriented test generation (for survey, see [3,8,17]). Although these methods are well-suited for hardware circuits and control portions of communication protocols, they are not powerful enough to test complex data-dependent behaviors.

EFSMs extend FSMs with variables to support the succinct specification of data-dependent behaviors. If the state space of an EFSM is finite, one can construct the equivalent FSM by unfolding the values of variables. Thus, EFSM-based testing with finite state space can be reduced in principle to ordinary

FSM-based testing. Of course, this approach suffers from the well-known state explosion problem which makes test generation often impractical. Even when test generation is feasible, this approach is often impractical because of the test explosion problem, i.e., the number of generated tests might be too large to be applied to implementations. A promising alternative is to apply conventional software testing techniques to test generation from EFSMs [22]. In this approach, an EFSM is transformed into a flow graph that models the flow of both control and data in the EFSM and tests are generated from the graph by identifying the flow information. The approach abstracts the values of variables when constructing flow graphs and hence it can be applicable even if the state space is infinite. However, it requires posterior analysis such as symbolic execution or constraint solving to determine the executability of tests and for the selection of variable values which make tests executable.

The approach we advocate here is based on constructing Kripke structures from EFSMs and hence also suffers from state explosion. Our approach, however, enables the use of symbolic model checking[5] that has been shown to be effective for controlling state explosion for certain problem domains. Second, our approach overcomes the test explosion problem by using control and data flow information of EFSMs like the flow-graph approach. Finally, our approach can be seen as complementary to the flow-graph approach. In particular, flow graphs can be constructed from system models whose state space is infinite, whereas our approach has the advantage that only executable tests are generated which obviates the need of posterior analysis. Ideally, one would eventually like to be able to combine these two approaches.

Recently, connection between test generation and model checking has been considered in the testing literature. [11,20] use binary decision diagrams (BDDs) to represent EFSMs and describe symbolic approaches to test generation for state and transition coverage criteria. [14] describes a test generation method by adapting local or on-the-fly model checking algorithms. [23] describes an on-the-fly test generation method which utilizes SPIN[13] to generate the information necessary for test generation. Test generation using the capability of model checkers to construct counterexamples has been applied in several contexts. [1] describes the application of model checking to mutation analysis. [6,9] generate tests by constructing counterexamples for user-specified temporal formulas. No consideration is given to coverage criteria. [10] generates tests from SCR specifications using two model checkers SMV and SPIN for control flow oriented coverage criteria, which are similar to transition coverage criterion. We are not aware of any work that considers the model checking approach to both control flow and data flow oriented coverage criteria.

2   Logic: CTL

Syntax. CTL[7] is a branching time temporal logic widely-used for symbolic model checking. Formulas in CTL are built from atomic propositions, boolean connectives, path quantifiers **A** (for all paths) and **E** (for some path), and modal operators $\mathbf{X}$ (next time), $\mathbf{U}$ (until), $\mathbf{F}$ (eventually), and $\mathbf{G}$ (always). Formally, CTL is the set of state formulas defined as follows:

- Every atomic proposition is a state formula,
- If f and g are state formulas, then $\neg f$, $f \wedge g$ are state formulas,
- If f and g are state formulas, then $\mathbf{X}f$, $f\mathbf{U}g$, and $\mathbf{G}f$ are path formulas,
- If f is a path formula, then $\mathbf{E}f$ is a state formula.

The remaining formulas are defined by: $\mathbf{EF}f \equiv \mathbf{E}[true\mathbf{U}f]$, $\mathbf{AX}f \equiv \neg\mathbf{EX}\neg f$, $\mathbf{A}[f\mathbf{U}g] \equiv \neg\mathbf{E}[\neg g\mathbf{U}\neg f\wedge\neg g] \wedge \neg\mathbf{EG}\neg g$, $\mathbf{AF}f \equiv \neg\mathbf{EG}\neg f$, $\mathbf{AG}f \equiv \neg\mathbf{EF}\neg f$.

Semantics. The semantics of CTL is defined with respect to a *Kripke structure* $M = (Q, Q_0, L, R)$ where Q is a finite set of states; $Q_0 \subseteq Q$ is the set of initial states; $L: Q \rightarrow 2^{AP}$ is the function labeling each state with a set of atomic propositions in AP; and $R \subseteq Q \times Q$ is the transition relation. A sequence q_0, q_1, q_2, ... of states is a *path* if $(q_i, q_{i+1}) \in R$ for all $i \geq 0$. Given a path π and an integer i, $\pi(i)$ denotes the i-th state of π. The satisfaction relation $\models$ is inductively defined as follows:

- $M, q \models p$ if $p \in L(q)$;
- $M, q \models \neg\phi$ if $\neg(q \models \phi)$;
- $M, q \models \phi \wedge \phi'$ if $q \models \phi$ and $q \models \phi'$;
- $M, q \models \mathbf{E}f$ if $\pi \models f$ for some path π such that $\pi(0) = q$;
- $M, \pi \models \mathbf{X}f$ if $\pi(1) \models f$;
- $M, \pi \models f\mathbf{U}g$ if $\pi(i) \models g$ for some $i \geq 0$ and $\pi(j) \models f$ for all $0 \leq j < i$;
- $M, \pi \models \mathbf{G}f$ if $\pi(i) \models f$ for all $i \geq 0$.

We write $M \models f$ if $M, q_0 \models f$ for every initial state $q_0 \in Q_0$.

Witnesses. One of the important features of model checking is the ability to generate witnesses and counterexamples. If a formula $\mathbf{E}f$ is true, we can demonstrate the success of the formula by finding a witness which is a path π such that $\pi \models f$. Likewise, if a formula $\mathbf{A}f$ is false, there is a counterexample π such that $\pi \models \neg f$. We observe that a witness for a formula of the form $\mathbf{E}f$ is also a counterexample for its negation $\neg\mathbf{E}f$. In general, a witness or counterexample is a set of infinite paths. For example, to demonstrate the success of $\mathbf{EG}p_1 \wedge \mathbf{EG}p_2$ or the failure of $\mathbf{AF}\neg p_1 \vee \mathbf{AF}\neg p_2$, we must find two infinite paths π_1 and π_2 such that $\pi_1 \models \mathbf{G}p_1$ and $\pi_2 \models \mathbf{G}p_2$. However, if we consider a subclass of CTL, which we call WCTL, then it is guaranteed that every witness is a finite path. A CTL formula f is a WCTL formula if (i) f is in positive normal form, i.e., every negation in f is applied only to atomic propositions, (ii) f contains only $\mathbf{EX}$ and $\mathbf{EU}$, and (iii) for every subformula of f of the form $f_1 \wedge ... \wedge f_n$, every conjunct f_i except at most one is an atomic proposition. For example, $\mathbf{EF}(p_1 \wedge \mathbf{EF}p_2)$ is a WCTL formula, while $\mathbf{EF}(\mathbf{EF}p_1 \wedge \mathbf{EF}p_2)$ is not.

For a WCTL formula f and a Kripke structure M such that $M \models f$, we define the set of *witnesses* for f with respect to M, denoted by $\mathcal{W}(M, f)$, as follows:

- $W(M, true) = Q$,
- $W(M, p \wedge f) = \{q_0 \mid q_0 \models p\} * W(M, f)$,
- $W(M, f \vee g) = W(M, f)$ or $W(M, f \vee g) = W(M, g)$,
- $W(M, \mathbf{EX}f) = \{q_0q_1 \mid q_1 \models f\} * W(M, f)$,
- $W(M, \mathbf{E}[fUg]) = \{q_0q_1...q_n \mid q_i \models f \text{ for all } 0 \leq i < n \text{ and } q_n \models g\} * W(M, g)$,
- $\mathcal{W}(M, f) = \{\pi \in W(M, f) \mid \pi(0) \in Q_0\}$,

where $\Pi_1 * \Pi_2 = \{\pi \mid \exists i : \pi_i \in \Pi_1, \pi^i \in \Pi_2\}$, π_i denotes the prefix of π ending at $\pi(i)$, and π^i denotes the suffix of π starting from $\pi(i)$. We extend the notion of witnesses to a set of WCTL formulas. A set Π of finite paths is a *witness-set* for a set F of WCTL formulas with respect to M if, for every formula f in F such that $M \models f$, there exists a finite path π in Π that is a witness for f. Note that Π is a witness-set for F with respect to M if and only if it is a witness-set for $\{f \in F \mid M \models f\}$, or equivalently $F \backslash \{f \in F \mid M \not\models f\}$.

3 Model: EFSM

Syntax. An *extended finite state machine* (EFSM) is a tuple $G = (S, S_0, E, V, T)$ where S is a finite set of states; $S_0 \subseteq S$ is the set of initial states; E is a finite set of events; V is a finite set of variables partitioned into three disjoint subsets V_I, V_L, and V_O comprising input, local, and output variables, respectively; T is a finite set of transitions. A transition is a tuple (s, e, g, A, s') where $s, s' \in S$, $e \in E$, g is a predicate on $V_I \cup V_L$ and A is a set of assignments to $V_L \cup V_O$. In this paper, we consider only deterministic EFSMs. An EFSM is *deterministic* if, for every state s and event e, $g_i \wedge g_j = false$ for all $1 \leq i, j \leq n, i \neq j$, where g_1, ..., g_n are the guards of the transitions whose source state is s and event is e. Figure 1 shows a simple coffee vending machine which has $S = \{\text{IDLE}, \text{BUSY}\}$, $S_0 = \{\text{IDLE}\}$, $E = \{insert, coffee, done, display\}$, $V_I = \{x\}$, $V_L = \{m\}$, and $V_O = \{y\}$. We assume x, m, and y are of integer subrange $[0..5]$.

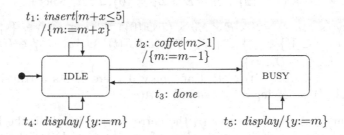

t_1: *insert*$[m+x \leq 5]$
 $/\{m:=m+x\}$

t_2: *coffee*$[m>1]$
 $/\{m:=m-1\}$

IDLE   BUSY

t_3: *done*

t_4: *display*$/\{y:=m\}$ t_5: *display*$/\{y:=m\}$

Fig. 1. An example of EFSMs

Local variables can be defined and used by the EFSM while input variables can only be used and output variables can only be defined. Formally, a variable

v is *defined* at a transition $t = (s, e, g, A, s')$, denoted by d_t^v, if v occurs in the left hand side of an assignment in A, and v is *used* at t, denoted by u_t^v, if v occurs in the guard g or in the right hand side of an assignment in A. For two variables v, v', and a transition t, we say that u_t^v *directly affects* $d_t^{v'}$ at t, denoted by $da_t^{v,v'}$, if v occurs in the guard of t or in the right hand side of the assignment of t whose left hand side is v'. For a transition t, define $DEF(t)$, $USE(t)$, and $DA(t)$ as the sets of definitions, uses, and directly affects occurring at t, respectively. Define $DEF(G)$, $USE(G)$, and $DA(G)$ as $\bigcup_{t \in T} DEF(t)$, $\bigcup_{t \in T} USE(t)$, and $\bigcup_{t \in T} DA(t)$, respectively. Table 1 shows the classification of the variables in Figure 1 as definitions, uses, and directly affects.

Table 1. The definitions, uses, and directly affects in the coffee vending machine

transitions	$DEF(t)$	$USE(t)$	$DA(t)$
t_1	$\{d_{t_1}^m\}$	$\{u_{t_1}^x, u_{t_1}^m\}$	$\{da_{t_1}^{x,m}, da_{t_1}^{m,m}\}$
t_2	$\{d_{t_2}^m\}$	$\{u_{t_2}^m\}$	$\{da_{t_2}^{m,m}\}$
t_3	$\emptyset$	$\emptyset$	$\emptyset$
t_4	$\{d_{t_4}^y\}$	$\{u_{t_4}^m\}$	$\{da_{t_4}^{m,y}\}$
t_5	$\{d_{t_5}^y\}$	$\{u_{t_5}^m\}$	$\{da_{t_5}^{m,y}\}$

Semantics. For a set V of variables, a valuation σ over V is a function mapping variables to their values. The set of valuations over V is denoted by Σ_V. For a set A of assignments, $A(\sigma)$ denotes the valuation defined by $A(\sigma)(v) = value$ if there exists an assignment of the form $v := exp$ in A and $value$ is the value of exp evaluated over σ, and $A(\sigma)(v) = \sigma(v)$ otherwise.

We view EFSMs as Kripke structures to characterize the problems of test coverage and generation in CTL. We call each element in Q of a Kripke Structure a *global state* to distinguish it from a state of EFSMs. Similarly, we call each element in R a *global transition*. The Kripke structure corresponding to an EFSM G is $(S \times E \times \Sigma_V \times (T \cup \{\emptyset\}), S_0 \times E \times \Sigma_V \times \{\emptyset\}, L, R)$ where

- for every $(s, e, \sigma, t) \in S \times E \times \Sigma_V \times (T \cup \{\emptyset\})$, $L((s, e, \sigma, t)) = \{s\} \cup \{e\} \cup \{v = \sigma(v) \mid v \in V\} \cup \{t\} \cup \{d_t^v \mid d_t^v \in DEF(t)\} \cup \{u_t^v \mid u_t^v \in USE(t)\} \cup \{da_t^{v,v'} \mid da_t^{v,v'} \in DA(t)\}$,
- $((s, e, \sigma, t), (s', e', \sigma', t')) \in R$ if and only if there exists a transition $t' = (s, e, g, A, s')$ satisfying $\sigma \models g$ and $\sigma' = A(\sigma)$.

A global state (s, e, σ, t) captures (i) the current state in which the EFSM is, (ii) the event generated, (iii) the values of variables, and (iv) the transition taken. A global transition $((s, e, \sigma, t), (s', e', \sigma', t'))$ represents the execution of its corresponding transition t'.

Test Sequences. Since it is impossible to test infinite executions, we define a *test sequence* of an EFSM as a finite path of its Kripke structure. A *test suite* is a finite set of test sequences. Moreover, we require that the execution of every test sequence end at a specific state, if the state is designated by a tester as the *exit* state of the EFSM. If an initial state of an EFSM is reachable from every state, we oftern require a test sequence end at the initial state because it is convenient to execute another test sequence without resetting an implementation under test into the initial state. In general, a tester may designate an arbitrary state as the exit state and distinguish test sequences ending at that state from others by interpreting the sequences as completed tasks of the EFSM.

4   Test Coverage

This section investigates a family of coverage criteria for EFSMs and character-izes them in terms of witness-sets. For the remainder of the paper, we fix an EFSM G with exit condition *exit*, denoted by $\langle G, exit \rangle$. The condition *exit* is defined as s_e if s_e is the exit state designated by a tester, and *true* otherwise.

4.1   Control Flow Oriented Coverage Criteria

Obviously, the strongest coverage criterion for determining the conformance of an implementation to its EFSM specification is *path coverage* which requires that all paths of the Kripke structure corresponding to the EFSM be traversed. Because there is an infinite number of paths, it is impossible to achieve exhaustive testing and we need to have coverage criteria that select a reasonable and finite number of test sequences. Included are control flow oriented coverage criteria that require that every state or transition be traversed at least once during testing.

State Coverage. A state s of $\langle G, exit \rangle$ is *testable* if there exists a test sequence $q_0...q_n$ such that $q_i \models s$ for some i and $q_n \models exit$. In this case, the test sequence is said to *cover* s. It is easy to see that a test sequence covers s if and only if it is a witness of $\mathbf{EF}(s \wedge \mathbf{EF}exit)$, because the set of witnesses for the formula is $\{q_0...q_n \mid q_i \models s \wedge \mathbf{EF}(exit) \text{ for some } i \text{ and } q_n \models exit\}$.

A test suite Π of $\langle G, exit \rangle$ satisfies *state coverage criterion* if every testable state is covered by a test sequence in Π. We characterize test suites satisfying state coverage criterion as follows. A test suite Π of $\langle G, exit \rangle$ satisfies state coverage criterion if and only if it is a witness-set for

$$\{\mathbf{EF}(s \wedge \mathbf{EF}exit) \mid s \in S\}$$

Note that Π is a witness-set for $\{\mathbf{EF}(s \wedge \mathbf{EF}exit) \mid s \in S\}$ if and only if it is a witness-set for $\{\mathbf{EF}(s \wedge \mathbf{EF}exit) \mid s \in S \text{ and } s \text{ is testable}\}$.

Transition Coverage. A transition t of $\langle G, exit \rangle$ is *testable* if there exits a test sequence $q_0...q_n$ such that $q_i \models t$ for some i and $q_n \models exit$. In this case, the test sequence is said to *cover* t. A test suite Π of $\langle G, exit \rangle$ satisfies *transition coverage criterion* if every testable transition is covered by a test sequence in Π. A test suite Π satisfies transition coverage criterion if and only if it is a witness-set for

$$\{\mathbf{EF}(t \wedge \mathbf{EF}exit) \mid t \in T\}$$

4.2   Data Flow Oriented Coverage Criteria

Data flow oriented coverage criteria establish associations between definitions and uses of variables and require that these associations are examined at least once during testing. We consider two types of associations: definition-use pairs and affect pairs that are central notions in data flow analysis and program slicing, respectively.

Data Flow among Local Variables. For a definition d_t^v and use u_t^v of the same variable v, we say that $(d_t^v, u_{t'}^v)$ is a *definition-use pair* (in short, du-pair) if there exists a test sequence $q_0 \ldots q_n$ such that $q_i \models d_t^v$ and $q_j \models u_{t'}^v$ for some $0 \leq i < j \leq n$, and $q_k \models \neg def(v)$ for all $i < k < j$, where $def(v) = \bigvee_{d_t^v \in DEF(G)} d_t^v$. In addition, if $q_n \models exit$, the du-pair is *testable*. In this case, the test sequence is said to *cover* $(d_t^v, u_{t'}^v)$ and the subpath $q_i \ldots q_j$ is called a *definition-clear path* of $(d_t^v, u_{t'}^v)$. It can be shown that a test sequence covers $(d_t^v, u_{t'}^v)$ if and only if it is a witness of $\mathbf{EF}(d_t^v \wedge \mathbf{EXE}[\neg def(v)\mathbf{U}(u_{t'}^v \wedge \mathbf{EF}exit)])$. Table 2 shows the du-pairs in Figure 1. For example, $(d_{t_1}^m, u_{t_4}^m)$ is a du-pair whereas $(d_{t_1}^m, u_{t_5}^m)$ is not because there is no definition-clear path with respect to m from t_1 to t_5.

Table 2. The du-pairs in the coffee vending machine

variables	du-pairs
m	$(d_{t_1}^m, u_{t_1}^m), (d_{t_1}^m, u_{t_2}^m), (d_{t_1}^m, u_{t_4}^m), (d_{t_2}^m, u_{t_1}^m), (d_{t_2}^m, u_{t_2}^m), (d_{t_2}^m, u_{t_4}^m), (d_{t_2}^m, u_{t_5}^m)$

All-def Coverage. A test suite Π of $\langle G, exit \rangle$ satisfies *all-def coverage criterion* if, for every definition d_t^v, some testable du-pair $(d_t^v, u_{t'}^v)$ is covered by a test sequence in Π. A test suite Π satisfies *all-def coverage criterion* if and only if it is a witness-set for

$$\{ \bigvee_{u_{t'}^v \in USE(G)} \mathbf{EF}(d_t^v \wedge \mathbf{EXE}[\neg def(v)\mathbf{U}u_{t'}^v \wedge \mathbf{EF}exit)]) \mid d_t^v \in DEF(G)\}$$

All-use Coverage. A test suite Π of $\langle G, exit \rangle$ satisfies *all-use coverage criterion* if, for every definition d_t^v, every testable du-pair $(d_t^v, u_{t'}^v)$ is covered by a test sequence in Π. A test suite Π satisfies *all-use coverage criterion* if and only if it is a witness-set for

$$\{\mathbf{EF}(d_t^v \wedge \mathbf{EXE}[\neg def(v)\mathbf{U}(u_{t'}^v \wedge \mathbf{EF}exit)]) \mid d_t^v \in DEF(G), u_{t'}^v \in USE(G)\}$$

Data Flow among Input and Output Variables. For a use u_t^v of variable v and a definition $d_{t'}^{v'}$ of variable v', we say that u_t^v *affects* $d_{t'}^{v'}$ if (i) either $t = t'$ and u_t^v directly affects $d_t^{v'}$, or (ii) there exists a du-pair $(d_t^{v''}, u_{t''}^{v''})$ such that u_t^v directly affects $d_t^{v''}$ and $u_{t''}^{v''}$ affects $d_{t'}^{v'}$. We say that $(u_t^v, d_{t'}^{v'})$ is an *affect-pair* if u_t^v affects $d_{t'}^{v'}$. A *data-flow chain* (in short df-chain) of an affect-pair $(u_t^v, d_{t'}^{v'})$ is a sequence of du-pairs $(d_{t_1}^{v_1}, u_{t_2}^{v_1}) (d_{t_2}^{v_2}, u_{t_3}^{v_2}), \ldots, (d_{t_n}^{v_n}, u_{t_{n+1}}^{v_n})$, $n \geq 0$, such that

- $t_1 = t$ and $u_{t_1}^v$ directly affects $d_{t_1}^{v_1}$, $t_{n+1} = t'$ and $u_{t_{n+1}}^{v_n}$ directly affects $d_{t_{n+1}}^{v'}$, and for every $1 \leq i < n$, $u_{t_{i+1}}^{v_i}$ directly affects $d_{t_{i+1}}^{v_{i+1}}$,
- there exists a test sequence $q_0...q_m$ such that for every $1 \leq i \leq n$, there exists a subpath π_i of $q_0...q_m$ satisfying $last(\pi_i) = first(\pi_{i+1})$ and π_i is a definition-clear path of $(d_{t_i}^{v_i}, u_{t_{i+1}}^{v_i})$.

In addition, if $q_m \models exit$, the affect-pair $(u_t^v, d_{t'}^{v'})$ is *testable*. In this case, the test sequence is said to *cover* $(u_t^v, d_{t'}^{v'})$. Table 3 shows the affect-pairs in Figure 1. For example, from the affect-pair $(u_{t_1}^x, d_{t_4}^y)$, we observe that the use of x at t_1 affects the definition of y at t_4 through a df-chain, say $(d_{t_1}^m, u_{t_4}^m)$.

Table 3. The affect-pairs in the coffee vending machine

variables	affect-pairs
x, m	$(u_{t_1}^x, d_{t_1}^m), (u_{t_1}^x, d_{t_2}^m),$
x, y	$(u_{t_1}^x, d_{t_4}^y), (u_{t_1}^x, d_{t_5}^y),$
m, m	$(u_{t_1}^m, d_{t_1}^m), (u_{t_1}^m, d_{t_2}^m), (u_{t_2}^m, d_{t_1}^m), (u_{t_2}^m, d_{t_2}^m),$
m, y	$(u_{t_1}^m, d_{t_4}^y), (u_{t_1}^m, d_{t_5}^y), (u_{t_2}^m, d_{t_4}^y), (u_{t_2}^m, d_{t_5}^y), (u_{t_4}^m, d_{t_4}^y), (u_{t_5}^m, d_{t_5}^y)$

In contrast to du-pairs, affect-pairs cannot be characterized in terms of WCTL formulas because they require an arbitrary number of du-pairs. Instead, we characterize them using a least fixpoint of an appropriate predicate transformer over WCTL formulas. Note that the computation of fixpoints can be implemented efficiently in symbolic model checking.

For a testable affect-pair $(u_t^v, d_{t'}^{v'})$, we use $Q(u_t^v, d_{t'}^{v'})$ to denote the set of global states q_0 such that $q_0 \models u_t^v$ and there exists a test sequence $q_0 q_1...$ covering the affect-pair. By the definition of affect-pairs, we have the following equation.

$$Q(u_t^v, d_{t'}^{v'}) = (u_t^v \wedge da_t^{v,v'} \wedge \mathbf{EF} exit) \vee$$

$$(u_t^v \wedge \bigvee_{v'' \in DA(t,v)} \mathbf{EXE}[\neg def(v'') \ \mathbf{U} \bigvee_{u_{t''}^{v''} \in USE(G)} Q(u_{t''}^{v''}, d_{t'}^{v'})])$$

where $DA(t, v)$ is the set of variables directly affected by v at t.

We identify every WCTL formula f with the predicate $\{q \mid M, q \models f\}$ in 2^Q. Let $\tau : 2^Q \to 2^Q$ be a predicate transformer defined as follows.

$$\tau(Z) = (u_t^v \wedge da_t^{v,v'} \wedge \mathbf{EF} exit) \vee$$

$$(u_t^v \wedge \bigvee_{v'' \in DA(t,v)} \mathbf{EXE}[\neg def(v'') \ \mathbf{U} \bigvee_{u_{t''}^{v''} \in USE(G)} Z[v''/v, t''/t]])$$

where $Z[v''/v, t''/t']$ is the formula obtained by replacing each occurrence of v and t in Z by v'' and t'', respectively.

Theorem 1 $Q(u_t^v, d_{t'}^{v'})$ *is the least fixpoint of* τ.

PROOF It is easy to see that τ is monotonic.

Let Z_f be $Q(u_t^v, d_{t'}^{v'})$. Suppose that $q_0 \models \tau(Z_f)$, then there exists a path $q_0 q_1 ...$ such that either $q_0 \models (u_t^v \wedge da_t^{v,v'} \wedge \mathbf{EF}\,exit)$, that is, u_t^v directly affects $d_{t'}^{v'}$, or $q_0 \models (u_t^v \wedge \bigvee_{v'' \in DA(t,v)} \mathbf{EXE}[\neg def(v'')\mathbf{U} \bigvee_{u_{t''}^{v''} \in USE(G)} Z_f[v''/v, t''/t]])$, that is, there exists a du-pair $(d_t^{v''}, u_{t''}^{v''})$ such that u_t^v directly affects $d_t^{v''}$ and $u_{t''}^{v''}$ affects $d_{t'}^{v'}$. Hence, $q_0 \models u_t^v$ and $q_0 q_1 ...$ covers $(u_t^v, d_{t'}^{v'})$, that is, $q_0 \models Z_f$. Therefore, we have $\tau(Z_f) \subseteq Z_f$. Similarly, we can show that if $q_0 \models Z_f$, then $q_0 \models \tau(Z_f)$. Consequently, Z_f is a fixpoint of τ.

To prove that Z_f is the least fixpoint of τ, it is sufficient to show that $Z_f = \cup_i \tau^i(false)$, where $\tau^0(Z) = Z$ and $\tau^{i+1}(Z) = \tau(\tau^i(Z))$. It is easy to show by induction on i that for every i, $\tau^i(false) \subseteq Z_f$. Hence, we have the first direction $\cup_i \tau^i(false) \subseteq Z_f$. The other direction, $Z_f \subseteq \cup_i \tau^i(false)$, is shown by induction on the number of du-pairs of the df-chain of $(u_t^v, d_{t'}^{v'})$. Suppose that $q_0 \models Z_f$, then there exists a path $q_0 q_1 ...$ covering $(u_t^v, d_{t'}^{v'})$. Let $j \geq 0$ be the number of du-pairs of in the df-chain of $(u_t^v, d_{t'}^{v'})$. We show by induction on j that for every $j \geq 0$, $q_0 \in \tau^{j+1}(false)$. For the base case, suppose that $j = 0$, that is, u_t^v directly affects $d_{t'}^{v'}$. Then $q_0 \models (u_t^v \wedge da_t^{v,v'} \wedge \mathbf{EF}\,exit)$ and hence $q_0 \in \tau^1(false)$. For the inductive step, suppose that $q_0 \in \tau^{j+1}(false)$ for $j = n$. Let $j = n + 1$ and q_k be the global state in the path $q_0 q_1 ...$ at which the first du-pair in the df-chain ends. Hence, there exist n du-pairs from q_k and we have that $q_k \in \tau^{n+1}(false)$ by the induction hypothesis. Therefore, $q_0 \in (u_t^v \wedge \bigvee_{v'' \in DA(t,v)} \mathbf{EXE}[\neg def(v'') \mathbf{U} \bigvee_{u_{t''}^{v''} \in USE(G)} \tau^{n+1}(false)[v''/v, t''/t]])$ and $q_0 \in \tau^{n+2}(false)$. $\square$

Among the particular affect-pairs of interest to our coverage criteria are those starting with an input variable and ending with an output variable. We say that an affect-pair $(u_t^i, d_{t'}^o)$ is an *io-pair* if i is an input variable and o is an output variable. For example, in Table 3, there are two io-pairs $(u_{t_1}^x, d_{t_4}^y)$ and $(u_{t_1}^x, d_{t_5}^y)$, that is, the use of x at t_1 affects the definition of y at t_4 and t_5. The rationale here is to identify functionality specified by the EFSM in terms of the effects of input variables accepted from its environment on output variables offered to its environment.

All-input Coverage. A test suite Π of $\langle G, exit \rangle$ satisfies *all-input coverage criterion* if, for every use u_t^i of every input variable i, some testable io-pair $(u_t^i, d_{t'}^o)$ is covered by a test sequence in Π. A test suite Π satisfies *all-input coverage criterion* if and only if it is a witness-set for

$$\{ \bigvee_{d_{t'}^o \in DEF(G), o \in V_O} \mathbf{EF}Q(u_t^v, d_{t'}^{v'}) \mid u_t^v \in USE(G), \mid i \in V_I \}$$

All-output Coverage. A test suite Π of $\langle G, exit \rangle$ satisfies *all-output coverage criterion* if, for every use u_t^i of every input variable i, every testable io-pair

$(u_t^i, d_{t'}^o)$ is covered by a test sequence in Π. A test suite Π satisfies *all-output coverage criterion* if and only if it is a witness-set for

$$\{\mathbf{EF}Q(u_t^v, d_{t'}^{v'}) \mid u_t^i \in USE(G), i \in V_I, d_{t'}^o \in DEF(G), o \in V_O\}$$

5 Test Generation

This section defines two optimization problems of minimal cost test generation. They are shown to be NP-hard and a heuristic algorithm is described.

5.1 Complexity

To generate a test suite for a given EFSM and coverage criterion, we construct a Kripke structure M corresponding to the EFSM and a set F of WCTL formulas (or WCTL formulas with a least fixpoint operator). We wish to generate a minimal test suite Π with respect to one of the two costs: (i) the number of test sequences in Π or (ii) the total length of test sequences in Π. After finishing the execution of a test sequence, an implementation under test should be reset into its initial state from which another test sequence can be applied. It is appropriate to use the first cost if the reset operation is expensive, and the second one otherwise.

Let $\mathcal{W}_f$ be the set of witnesses for a formula f in F. First we consider the Minimal Number Test Generation (MNTG) problem which is an optimization problem defined by: given a collection of sets $\mathcal{W}_f$, generate a minimal witness-set Π in the number of witnesses in Π. We show this problem to be NP-hard by considering its corresponding decision problem MNTG': given a collection of $\mathcal{W}_f$ and positive integer k, is there a witness-set Π with $|\Pi| \leq k$? We prove that MNTG' is NP-complete by reducing the Hitting Set problem, which is known to be NP-complete[15], to MNTG'. The Hitting Set problem is defined by: given a collection of subsets C_i of a finite set S and positive integer k, is there a subset $S' \subseteq S$, called *hitting set*, such that $|S'| \leq k$ and S' contains at least one element from each C_i?

Theorem 2 *MNTG' is NP-complete.*

PROOF It is easy to show that MNTG' is in NP. Given an instant of the Hitting Set problem, we construct a Kripke structure (Q, Q_0, L, R) such that $Q = \{q_0\} \cup \{q_c \mid c \in \bigcup C_i\}$, $Q_0 = \{q_0\}$, and $R = \{(q_0, q_c) \mid c \in \bigcup C_i\}$. This reduction is linear in the size of S. For every subset C_i, we construct a set $\mathcal{W}_i$ of witnesses as follows: $q_0 q_c$ is in $\mathcal{W}_i$ if and only if $c \in C_i$. Clearly, there exists a hitting set S' with $|S'| \leq k$ for the collection of C_i if and only if there exists a witness-set $\Pi = \{q_0 q_s \mid s \in S'\}$ with $|\Pi| \leq k$ for the collection of W_i. $\square$

Second we consider the Minimal Length Test Generation (MLTG) problem defined by: given a collection of $\mathcal{W}_f$, generate a minimal witness-set Π in the total length of witnesses in Π. Its corresponding decision problem MLTG' is defined by: given a collection of sets $\mathcal{W}_f$ and positive integer k, is there a witness-set Π such that $\sum_{\pi \in \Pi} |\pi| \leq k$?

Theorem 3 *MLTG' is NP-complete.*

PROOF It is easy to show that MLTG' is in NP. We use the same reduction used as in Theorem 2. Since all paths in Q are of length one, the minimum total-length of the witness-set Π is achieved when Π contains the minimum number of witnesses. Therefore, a solution for the MLTG problem in this case will yield the same witness-set which also is a solution to the MNTG problem. Hence there exists a hitting set S' with $|S'| \leq k$ if and only if there exists a witness-set Π with $\sum_{\pi \in \Pi} |\pi| \leq k$. $\qquad\qquad\Box$

5.2 Heuristic

Because of NP-hardness of the problems, we do not expect optimal solutions to them. Instead we describe a greedy algorithm which can be applied to both MNTG and MLTG problems. Figure 2 shows how the greedy algorithm is applied to state coverage criterion. The algorithm can also be applied to other coverage criteria by changing the set of covered entities to transitions, du-pairs, or io-pairs.

INPUT: a set F of formulas and a Kripke structure M
OUTPUT: a test suite Π satisfying state coverage criterion

```
 1: mark every state in S as uncovered;
 2: Π := ∅;
 3: repeat
 4:     choose a state s ∈ S marked as uncovered;
 5:     model check the negation of f = EF(s ∧ EFexit) in F against M;
 6:     if M ⊨ ¬f
 7:         mark s as untestable;
 8:     else /* M ⊭ ¬f */
 9:         let π be the counterexample for ¬f (equivalently the witness for f);
10:         let Sπ be the set of states covered by π;
11:         mark every state in Sπ as covered;
12:         Π := Π ∪ {π};
13:         for all π' ∈ Π such that Sπ' ⊂ Sπ
14:             Π := Π − {π'};
15: until every state in S is marked as covered or untestable
16: return Π;
```

Fig. 2. A greedy algorithm for state coverage criterion

In the algorithm, we directly employ the capability of model checkers to construct counterexamples because a witness for a WCTL formula or a formula of the form $\mathbf{EF}Q(u_t^v, d_{t'}^{v'})$ is also a counterexample for its negation. Basically we generate a witness for every formula f in F by model checking the negation $\neg f$ and constructing its counterexample. The resulting set of witnesses constitutes a test suite. This naive method would generate a number of redundant witnesses because a witness may cover more than one state at the same time. We remove such redundant witnesses by considering only states which are not already covered by an exiting witness (Line 4) and by removing an existing witness if all the states covered by it are also covered by a new witness (Line 13 and 14).

6   Conclusion and Future Work

We have presented a temporal logic based approach to automatic test generation from specifications written in EFSMs. Our approach considers a family of coverage criteria based on the information of both control flow and data flow. We associate each coverage criterion with a set of CTL formulas and generate a test suite by finding a set of witnesses for each formula in the set. The resulting test suite provides the capability of determining whether an implementation establishes the required flow of control and data prescribed in its EFSM specification. We show that the optimization problems of finding minimal test suites are NP-hard and describe a method for automatic test generation.

Our ultimate goal is to develop an integrated environment for testing reactive systems. Testing reactive systems is a hard multi-faceted problem. We have just touched the surface of the wealth of issues associated with it. Listed below are some possible extensions that we plan to explore.

Nondeterminism. This paper considered only deterministic EFSMs. In the case of non-deterministic EFSMs, there may be more than one possible execution for a given input event sequence. In this situation, a single witness constructed by model checkers is not enough for the input event sequence, since it identifies only one execution among all possible ones. One possible solution to this problem is to treat the witness as prescribing only the input event sequence. An extra step is then necessary to find all executions corresponding to this input event sequence. If we have a model checker that produces multiple (or all) witnesses to a formula, we can express the input event sequence as a formula and give it to the model checker. The resulting set of witnesses constructed by the model checker will contain all possible executions.

Other Coverage Criteria. A number of other coverage criteria based on control and data flow have been proposed in the software testing literature (for example, see [21]). Some of these coverage criteria require that all paths that cover a certain entity be considered as test sequences. For example, all-du-path coverage criterion requires that all definition-clear paths for every definition-use pair be examined. To generate tests for this criterion in our approach, we need to obtain all witnesses to a CTL formula instead of only one.

Other Formalisms. Our characterization of coverage criteria as collections of CTL formulas is language-independent and is applicable with minor modifications to any kind of specification languages based on EFSMs, e.g., SDL, Estelle, and Statecharts. In fact, semantic differences in such languages affect only the way these models are transformed into input to model checkers. However, when we allow a specification language to express concurrent EFSMs, a number of complications arise. First, the construction of a single Kripke structure from several concurrent EFSMs may result in state explosion. Second, the resulting Kripke structure will likely be nondeterministic due to the interleaving of concurrent events. Often, these interleavings are not controllable by testers.

Other Logics. We showed that CTL is not capable of expressing the coverage criteria based on the affect relation and resolved this problem by extending CTL with least fixpoints of specific predicate transformers so that they can be implemented efficiently in symbolic model checking. However, a more elegant way may be to employ a more expressive temporal logic than CTL. We are currently working with a subset of μ-calculus [16]. The presence of explicit fixpoint operators in μ-calculus makes it possible to characterize all coverage criteria considered in this paper in a more uniform way.

References

1. P. Ammann, P. Black, and W. Majurski, "Using Model Checking to Generate Tests from Specifications," in *Proceedings of 2nd IEEE International Conference on Formal Engineering Methods*, pp. 46-54, 1998.
2. F. Belina and D. Hogrefe, "The CCITT-Specification and Description Language SDL," *Computer Networks and ISDN Systems*, Vol. 16, pp. 311-341, 1989.
3. G.v. Bochmann and A. Petrenko, "Protocol Testing: Review of Methods and Relevance for Software Testing," in *Proceedings of the 1994 International Symposium on Software Testing and Analysis*, pp 109-124, 1994.
4. S. Budkowski and P. Dembinski, "An Introduction to Estelle: a Specification Language for Distributed Systems," *Computer Networks and ISDM Systems*, Vol. 14, No. 1, pp. 3-24, 1991.
5. J.R. Burch, E.M. Clarke, K.L. McMillan, D.L. Dill, and J. Hwang, "Symbolic Model Checking: 10^{20} States and Beyond," *Information and Computation*, Vol. 98, No. 2, pp. 142-170, June 1992.
6. J. Callahan, F. Schneider, and S. Easterbrook, "Specification-based Testing Using Model Checking," in *Proceedings of 1996 SPIN Workshop*, also Technical Report NASA-IVV-96-022, West Virginia Univeristy, 1996.
7. E.M. Clarke, E.A. Emerson, and A.P. Sistla, "Automatic Verification of Finite-State Concurrent Systems Using Temporal Logic Specifications," *ACM Transactions on Programming Languages and Systems*, Vol. 8, No. 2, pp. 244-263, Apr. 1986.
8. R. Dssouli, K. Saleh, E. Aboulhamid, A. En-Nouaary, and C. Bourhfir, "Test Development for Communication Protocols: towards Automation," *Computer Networks*, Vol. 31, Issue 7, pp. 1835-1872, June 1999.

9. A. Engels, L. Feijs, and S. Mauw, "Test Generation for Intelligent Networks Using Model Checking," in *Proceedings of TACAS '97*, Lecture Notes in Computer Science, Vol. 1217, pp. 384-398, Springer-Verlag, 1997.

10. A. Gargantini and C. Heitmeyer, "Using Model Checking to Generate Tests from Requirements Specifications," in *Proceedings of the Joint 7th European Software Engineering Conference and 7th ACM SIGSOFT International Symposium on Foundations of Software Engineering*, pp. 6-10, 1999.

11. D. Geist, M. Farkas, A. Landver, Y. Lichtenstein, S. Ur, and Y. Wolfsthal, "Coverage-Directed Test Generation Using Symbolic Techniques," in *Proceedings of Formal Methods in Computer Aided Design*, 1996.

12. D. Harel, "Statecharts: a Visual Formalism for Complex Systems," *Science of Computer Programming*, Vol. 8, pp. 231-274, 1987.

13. G.J. Holzmann, "The Model Checker SPIN," *IEEE Transactions on Software Engineering*, Vol. 23, No. 5, pp. 279-295, May 1997.

14. T. Jeron and P. Morel, "Test Generation Derived From Model Checking," in *Computer Aided Verification '99*, Lecture Notes in Computer Science, Vol. 1633, pp. 108-121, Springer-Verlag, 1999.

15. R.M. Karp, "Reducibility among Combinatorial Problems," in *Complexity of Computer Computations*, R.E. Miller and J.W. Thatcher Eds., Plenum Press, pp. 85-103, 1972.

16. D. Kozen, "Results on the Propositional Mu-Calculus," *Theoretical Computer Science*, Vol. 27, pp. 333-354, 1983.

17. D. Lee and M. Yannakakis, "Principles and Methods of Testing Finite State Machines - A Survey," *Proceedings of the IEEE*, Vol. 84, No. 8, pp. 1090-1123, Aug. 1996.

18. D. Lee and R. Hao, "Test Sequence Selection," in *Formal Techniques for Networked and Distributed Systems*, pp. 269-284, Kluwer Academic Publishers, 2001.

19. K.L. McMillan, *Symbolic Model Checking − an Approach to the State Explosion Problem*, Kluwer Academic Publishers, 1993.

20. D. Moundanos, J.A. Abraham, and Y.V. Hoskote, "Abstraction Techniques for Validation Coverage Analysis and Test Generation," in *IEEE Transactions on Computers*, Vol. 47, No. 1, pp. 2-14, Jan. 1998.

21. S. Rapps and E.J. Weyuker, "Selecting Software Test Data Using Data Flow Information," *IEEE Transactions on Software Engineering*, Vol. 11, No. 4, pp. 367-375, Apr. 1985.

22. H. Ural and B. Yang, "A Test Sequence Generation Method for Protocol Testing," *IEEE Transactions on Communications*, Vol. 39, No. 4, pp. 514-523, Apr. 1991.

23. R. de Vries and J. Tretmans, "On-the-Fly Conformance Testing Using SPIN," *International Journal on Software Tools for Technology Transfer*, Vol. 2, Issue 4, pp. 382-393, 2000.

24. M. Weiser, "Program Slicing," *IEEE Transactions on Software Engineering*, Vol. 10, No. 4, pp. 352-357, Apr. 1984.

Synthesizing Monitors for Safety Properties

Klaus Havelund[1] and Grigore Roşu[2]

[1] Kestrel Technology
[2] Research Institute for Advanced Computer Science
http://ase.arc.nasa.gov/{havelund,grosu}
Automated Software Engineering Group
NASA Ames Research Center
Moffett Field, California, 94035, USA

Abstract. The problem of testing a linear temporal logic (LTL) formula on a finite execution trace of events, generated by an executing program, occurs naturally in runtime analysis of software. An algorithm which takes a past time LTL formula and generates an efficient dynamic programming algorithm is presented. The generated algorithm tests whether the formula is satisfied by a finite trace of events given as input and runs in linear time, its constant depending on the size of the LTL formula. The memory needed is constant, also depending on the size of the formula. Further optimizations of the algorithm are suggested. Past time operators suitable for writing succinct specifications are introduced and shown definitionally equivalent to the standard operators. This work is part of the PathExplorer project, the objective of which it is to construct a flexible framework for monitoring and analyzing program executions.

1 Introduction

The work presented in this paper is part of a project at NASA Ames Research Center, called PathExplorer [10,9,5,8,19], that aims at developing a practical testing environment for NASA software developers. The basic idea of the project is to extract an execution trace of an executing program and then analyze it to detect errors. The errors we are considering at this stage are multi-threading errors such as deadlocks and data races, and non-conformance with linear temporal logic specifications. Only the latter issue is addressed in this paper.

Linear Temporal Logic (LTL) [18,16] is a logic for specifying properties of reactive and concurrent systems. The models of LTL are infinite execution traces, reflecting the behavior of such systems as ideally always being ready to respond to requests, operating systems being a typical example. LTL has been mainly used to specify properties of concurrent and interactive down-scaled models of real systems, so that fully formal correctness proofs could subsequently be carried out, for example using theorem provers or model checkers (see for example [11,6]). However, such formal proof techniques are usually not scalable to real sized systems without a substantial effort to abstract the system more or less manually to a model which can be analyzed. Model checking of programs has

J.-P. Katoen and P. Stevens (Eds.): TACAS 2002, LNCS 2280, pp. 342–356, 2002.

received an increased attention from the formal methods community within the last couple of years, and several systems have emerged that can directly model check source code, such as Java and C [7,21,3,12,2,17]. Stateless model checkers [20] try to avoid the abstraction process by not storing states. Although these systems provide high confidence, they scale less well because most of their internal algorithms are NP-complete or worse.

Testing scales well, and is by far the most used technique in practice to validate software systems. The merge of testing and temporal logic specification is an attempt to achieve the benefits of both approaches, while avoiding some of the pitfalls of adhoc testing and the complexity of full-blown theorem proving and model checking. Of course there is a price to pay in order to obtain a scalable technique: the loss of coverage. The suggested framework can only be used to examine single execution traces, and can therefore not be used to prove a system correct. Our work is based on the belief that software engineers are willing to trade coverage for scalability, so our goal is to provide tools that are completely automatic, implement very efficient algorithms and find *many* errors in programs. A longer term goal is to explore the use of conformance with a formal specification to achieve fault tolerance. The idea is that the failure may trigger a recovery action in the monitored program.

The idea of using LTL in program testing is not new. It has already been pursued in commercial tools such as Temporal Rover (TR) [4], which has motivated us in a major way to start this work. In TR, one states LTL properties as annotations of the program, these being then replaced by appropriate code, that is executed whenever reached[1]. The MaC tool [15] is another example of a runtime monitoring tool that has inspired this work. Here Java bytecode is instrumented to generate events of interest during the execution. Of special interest is the temporal logic used in MaC, which can be classified as a kind of interval logic convenient for expressing monitoring properties in a succinct way. Our main theoretical contribution in this paper is Proposition 1 which shows that the MaC logic, together with 10 others, is equivalent to the standard past time temporal logic. The MaC tool represents a formula as an abstract tree generated by a parser, and repeated evaluations are then done by evaluating the entire tree each time using a general purpose tree traversing evaluation algorithm. What we suggest is to generate a special purpose evaluation program for each formula, that essentially specializes the combination of the general purpose evaluation with the particular parse tree. We further suggest an extra optimization of the generated algorithm, thereby obtaining the most efficient evaluation possible.

Section 2 gives a short description of the PathExplorer architecture, putting the presented work in context. Section 3 discusses various past time logics and shows their equivalences. Section 4 uses an example to present the algorithm for translating a past time formula to code. Section 5 presents a formalization of the algorithm used to generate the code. Section 6 describes our efforts to implement the presented algorithm in PathExplorer for monitoring of Java programs. Section 7 suggests some optimizations and Section 8 concludes the paper.

---

[1] The implementation details of TR are not public.

2   The PathExplorer Architecture

PathExplorer, PAX, is a flexible environment for monitoring and analyzing program executions. A program (or a set of programs) to be monitored, is supposed to be instrumented to emit execution events to an observer, which then examines the events and checks that they satisfy certain user-given constraints. The constraints can be of different kinds and defined in different languages. Each kind of constraint is represented by a rule. Such a rule in principle implements a particular logic or program analysis algorithm. Currently there are rules for checking deadlock potentials, datarace potentials, and for checking temporal logic formulae in different logics. Amongst the latter, several rules have been implemented for checking future time temporal logic, and the work presented in this paper is the basis for a rule for checking past time logic formulae. In general, the user can program new rules and in this way extend PAX in an easy way.

The system is defined in a component-based way, based on a dataflow view, where components are put together using a "pipeline" operator. The dataflow between any two components is a stream of events in simple text format, without any apriori assumptions about the format of the events; the receiving component just ignores events it cannot recognize. This simplifies composition and allows for components to be written in different languages and in particular to define observers of arbitrary systems, programmed in a variety of programming languages. This latter fact is important at NASA since several systems are written in a mixture of C, C++ and Java.

The central component of the PAX system is a so-called *dispatcher*. The dispatcher receives events from the executing program or system and then retransmits the event stream to each of the rules. Each rule is running in its own process with one input pipe, only dealing with events that are relevant to the rule. For this purpose each rule is equipped with an event parser. The dispatcher takes as input a configuration script, which specifies from where to read the program execution events, and then a list of commands - a command for each rule that starts the rule in a process.

The program or system to be observed must be instrumented to emit execution events to the dispatcher. We have currently implemented an automated instrumentation module for Java bytecode using the Java bytecode engineering tool JTrek [14]. Given information about what kind of events to be emitted, this module instruments the bytecode by inserting extra code for emitting events. Typically, for temporal logic monitoring, one specifies what variables to be observed and in particular what predicates over these variables. The code will then be instrumented to emit changes in these predicates, more specifically toggles in atomic propositions corresponding to these predicates. The instrumentation module together with PathExplorer is called Java PathExplorer (JPAX).

3   Finite Trace Linear Temporal Logic

We briefly remind the reader the basic notions of finite trace linear past time temporal logic, and also establish some conventions and introduce some operators that we found particularly useful for runtime monitoring. Syntactically, we allow the following formulae, where A is a set of "atomic propositions":

$$F ::= true \mid false \mid A \mid \neg F \mid F \; op \; F \qquad \text{Propositional operators}$$
$$\circ F \mid \diamond F \mid \square F \mid F \; \mathcal{S}_s \; F \mid F \; \mathcal{S}_w \; F \qquad \text{Standard past time operators}$$
$$\uparrow F \mid \downarrow F \mid [F, F)_s \mid [F, F)_w \qquad \text{Monitoring operators}$$

The propositional binary operators, op, are the standard ones, and $\circ F$ should be read "previously F", $\diamond F$ "eventually in the past F", $\square F$ "always in the past F", $F_1 \; \mathcal{S}_s \; F_2$ "F_1 strong since F_2", $F_1 \; \mathcal{S}_w \; F_2$ "F_1 weak since F_2", $\uparrow F$ "start F", $\downarrow F$ "end F", and $[F_1, F_2)$ "interval F_1, F_2".

We regard a trace as a finite sequence of abstract states. In practice, these states are generated by events emitted by the program that we want to observe. Such events could indicate when variables are changed or when locks are acquired or released. If s is a state and a is an atomic proposition then $a(s)$ is true if and only if a holds in the state s. If $t = s_1 s_2 \ldots s_n$ is a trace then we let t_i denote the trace $s_1 s_2 \ldots s_i$ for each $1 \leq i \leq n$. Then the semantics of these operators is:

$$t \models true \qquad \text{is always true,}$$
$$t \models false \qquad \text{is always false,}$$
$$t \models a \qquad \text{iff } a(s_n) \text{ holds,}$$
$$t \models \neg F \qquad \text{iff it is not the case that } t \models F,$$
$$t \models F_1 \; op \; F_2 \quad \text{iff } t \models F_1 \text{ and/or/implies/iff } t \models F_2, \text{ when } op \text{ is } \wedge/\vee/\rightarrow/\leftrightarrow,$$
$$t \models \circ F \qquad \text{iff } t' \models F, \text{ where } t' = t_{n-1} \text{ if } n > 1 \text{ and } t' = t \text{ if } n = 1,$$
$$t \models \diamond F \qquad \text{iff } t_i \models F \text{ for some } 1 \leq i \leq n,$$
$$t \models \square F \qquad \text{iff } t_i \models F \text{ for all } 1 \leq i \leq n,$$
$$t \models F_1 \; \mathcal{S}_s \; F_2 \text{ iff } t_j \models F_2 \text{ for some } 1 \leq j \leq n \text{ and } t_i \models F_1 \text{ for all } j < i \leq n,$$
$$t \models F_1 \; \mathcal{S}_w \; F_2 \text{ iff } t \models F_1 \; \mathcal{S}_s \; F_2 \text{ or } t \models \square F_1,$$
$$t \models \uparrow F \qquad \text{iff } t \models F \text{ and it is not the case that } t \models \circ F,$$
$$t \models \downarrow F \qquad \text{iff } t \models \circ F \text{ and it is not the case that } t \models F,$$
$$t \models [F_1, F_2)_s \text{ iff } t_j \models F_1 \text{ for some } 1 \leq j \leq n \text{ and } t_i \not\models F_2 \text{ for all } j \leq i \leq n,$$
$$t \models [F_1, F_2)_w \text{ iff } t \models [F_1, F_2)_s \text{ or } t \models \square \neg F_2.$$

Notice the special semantics of the operator "previously " on a trace of one state: $s \models \circ F$ iff $s \models F$. This is consistent with the view that a trace consisting of exactly one state s is considered like a *stationary* infinite trace containing only the state s. We adopted this view because of intuitions related to monitoring. One can start monitoring a process potentially at any moment, so the first state in the trace might be different from the initial state of the monitored process. We think that the "best guess" one can have w.r.t. the past of the monitored program is that it was stationary. Alternatively, one could consider that $\circ F$ is false on a trace of one state for any atomic proposition F, but we find this semantics inconvenient because some atomic propositions may be related, such as, for example, a proposition "gate-up" and a proposition "gate-down".

The non-standard operators $\uparrow$, $\downarrow$, $[-, -)_s$, and $[-, -)_w$ were inspired by work in runtime verification in [15]. We found them often more intuitive and compact than the usual past time operators in specifying runtime requirements. $\uparrow F$ is true if and only if F *starts* to be true in the current state, $\downarrow F$ is true if and only if F *ends* to be true in the current state, and $[F_1, F_2)_s$ is true if and only if F_2 was never true since the last time F_1 was observed to be true, including the state when F_1 was true; the interval operator, like the "since" operator, has both a strong and a weak version. For example, if START and DOWN are predicates on the state of a web server to be monitored, say for the last 24 hours, then $[\text{START}, \text{DOWN})_s$ is a property stating that the server *was* rebooted recently and since then it was not down, while $[\text{START}, \text{DOWN})_w$ says that the server was not unexpectedly down recently, meaning that it was either not down at all recently or it was rebooted and since then it was not down.

What makes past time temporal logic such a good candidate for dynamic programming is its recursive nature: the satisfaction relation for a formula can be calculated along the execution trace looking only one step backwards:

$t \models \diamond F$ iff $t \models F$ or ($n > 1$ and $t_{n-1} \models \diamond F$),
$t \models \square F$ iff $t \models F$ and ($n > 1$ implies $t_{n-1} \models \square F$),
$t \models F_1 \, \mathcal{S}_s \, F_2$ iff $t \models F_2$ or ($n > 1$ and $t \models F_1$ and $t_{n-1} \models F_1 \, \mathcal{S}_s \, F_2$),
$t \models F_1 \, \mathcal{S}_w \, F_2$ iff $t \models F_2$ or ($t \models F_1$ and ($n > 1$ implies $t_{n-1} \models F_1 \, \mathcal{S}_s \, F_2$)),
$t \models [F_1, F_2)_s$ iff $t \not\models F_2$ and ($t \models F_1$ or ($n > 1$ and $t_{n-1} \models [F_1, F_2)_s$)),
$t \models [F_1, F_2)_w$ iff $t \not\models F_2$ and ($t \models F_1$ or ($n > 1$ implies $t_{n-1} \models [F_1, F_2)_w$)).

We call the past time temporal logic presented above *ptLTL*. There is a tendency among logicians to minimize the number of operators in a given logic. For example, it is known that two operators are sufficient in propositional calculus, and two more ("next" and "until") are needed for future time temporal logics. There are also various ways to minimize *ptLTL*. Let $ptLTL{\upharpoonright}_{Ops}$ be the restriction of *ptLTL* to propositional operators plus the operations in *Ops*. Then

Proposition 1. *The 12 logics[2]* $ptLTL{\upharpoonright}_{\{\diamond, \mathcal{S}_s\}}$, $ptLTL{\upharpoonright}_{\{\diamond, \mathcal{S}_w\}}$, $ptLTL{\upharpoonright}_{\{\diamond, [)_s\}}$, *and* $ptLTL{\upharpoonright}_{\{\diamond, [)_w\}}$, $ptLTL{\upharpoonright}_{\{\uparrow, \mathcal{S}_s\}}$, $ptLTL{\upharpoonright}_{\{\uparrow, \mathcal{S}_w\}}$, $ptLTL{\upharpoonright}_{\{\uparrow, [)_s\}}$, $ptLTL{\upharpoonright}_{\{\uparrow, [)_w\}}$, *and* $ptLTL{\upharpoonright}_{\{\downarrow, \mathcal{S}_s\}}$, $ptLTL{\upharpoonright}_{\{\downarrow, \mathcal{S}_w\}}$, $ptLTL{\upharpoonright}_{\{\downarrow, [)_s\}}$, $ptLTL{\upharpoonright}_{\{\downarrow, [)_w\}}$, *are all equivalent.*

Proof. The equivalences follow by the following easy to check properties:

$$\diamond F = true \; \mathcal{S}_s \; F$$
$$\square F = \neg \diamond \neg F$$
$$\frac{}{F_1 \; \mathcal{S}_w \; F_2 = (\square F_1) \vee (F_1 \; \mathcal{S}_s \; F_2)}$$
$$\square F = F \; \mathcal{S}_w \; false$$
$$\diamond F = \neg \square \neg F$$
$$\frac{}{F_1 \; \mathcal{S}_s \; F_2 = (\diamond F_2) \wedge (F_1 \; \mathcal{S}_w \; F_2)}$$
$$\uparrow F = F \wedge \neg \diamond F$$
$$\downarrow F = \neg F \wedge \diamond F$$
$$[F_1, F_2)_s = \neg F_2 \wedge ((\diamond \neg F_2) \; \mathcal{S}_s \; F_1)$$
$$\frac{[F_1, F_2)_w = \neg F_2 \wedge ((\diamond \neg F_2) \; \mathcal{S}_w \; F_1)}{}$$
$$\downarrow F = \uparrow \neg F$$
$$\uparrow F = \downarrow \neg F$$
$$[F_1, F_2)_w = (\square \neg F_2) \vee [F_1, F_2)_s$$
$$\frac{[F_1, F_2)_s = (\diamond F_1) \wedge [F_1, F_2)_w}{}$$
$$\diamond F = (F \rightarrow \neg \uparrow F) \wedge (\neg F \rightarrow \downarrow F)$$
$$F_1 \; \mathcal{S}_s \; F_2 = F_2 \vee [\diamond F_2, \neg F_1)_s$$

---

[2] The first two are known in the literature [16].

For example, the definition of $\odot F$ in terms of $\uparrow F$ and $\downarrow F$ says that in order to find out the value of a formula F in the previous state it suffices to look at the value of the formula in the current state and then, if it is true then look if the formula just started to be true or else look if the formula just ended to be true.

Unlike in theoretical research, in practical monitoring of programs we want to have as many temporal operators as possible available and *not* to automatically translate them into a reduced kernel set. The reason is twofold. On the one hand, the more operators are available, the more succinct and natural the task of writing requirement specifications. On the other hand, as seen later in the paper, additional memory is needed for each temporal operator, so we want to keep the formulae as concise as possible.

4   The Algorithm Illustrated by an Example

In this section we show via an example how to generate dynamic programming code for a concrete *ptLTL*-formula. We think that this example would practically be sufficient for the reader to foresee our general algorithm presented in the next section. Let $\uparrow p \rightarrow [q, \downarrow (r \vee s))_s$ be the *ptLTL*-formula that we want to generate code for. The formula states: "whenever p becomes true, then q has been true in the past, and since then we have not yet seen the end of r or s". The code translation depends on an enumeration of the subformulae of the formula that satisfies the *enumeration invariant*: any formula has an enumeration number smaller than the numbers of all its subformulae. Let $\varphi_0, \varphi_1, ..., \varphi_8$ be such an enumeration:

$$\varphi_0 = \uparrow p \rightarrow [q, \downarrow (r \vee s))_s,$$
$$\varphi_1 = \uparrow p,$$
$$\varphi_2 = p,$$
$$\varphi_3 = [q, \downarrow (r \vee s))_s,$$
$$\varphi_4 = q,$$
$$\varphi_5 = \downarrow (r \vee s),$$
$$\varphi_6 = r \vee s,$$
$$\varphi_7 = r,$$
$$\varphi_8 = s.$$

Note that the formulae have here been enumerated in a post-order fashion. One could have chosen a breadth-first order, or any other enumeration, as long as the enumeration invariant is true.

The input to the generated program will be a finite trace $t = e_1 e_2 ... e_n$ of n events. The generated program will maintain a state via a function *update* : **State** $\times$ *Event* $\rightarrow$ **State**, which updates the state with a given event.

In order to illustrate the dynamic programming aspect of the solution, one can imagine recursively defining a matrix $s[1..n, 0..8]$ of boolean values $\{0, 1\}$, with the meaning that $s[i, j] = 1$ iff $t_i \models \varphi_j$. This would be the standard way of regarding the above satisfaction problem as a dynamic programming problem. An important observation is, however, that, like in many other dynamic programming algorithms, one doesn't have to store all the table $s[1..n, 0..8]$, which would be quite large in practice; in this case, one needs only $s[i, 0..8]$ and $s[i-1, 0..8]$, which we'll write $now[0..8]$ and $pre[0..8]$ from now on, respectively. It is now only a relatively simple exercise to write up the following algorithm for checking the above formula on a finite trace:

```
State state ← {};
bit pre[0..8];
bit now[0..8];
INPUT: trace t = e₁e₂...eₙ;
/* Initialization of state and pre */
state ← update(state, e₁);
pre[8] ← s(state);
pre[7] ← r(state);
pre[6] ← pre[7] or pre[8];
pre[5] ← false;
pre[4] ← q(state);
pre[3] ← pre[4] and not pre[5];
pre[2] ← p(state);
pre[1] ← false;
pre[0] ← not pre[1] or pre[3];
/* Event interpretation loop */
for i = 2 to n do {
    state ← update(state, eᵢ);
    now[8] ← s(state);
    now[7] ← r(state);
    now[6] ← now[7] or now[8];
    now[5] ← not now[6] and pre[6];
    now[4] ← q(state);
    now[3] ← (pre[3] or now[4]) and not now[5];
    now[2] ← p(state);
    now[1] ← now[2] and not pre[2];
    now[0] ← not now[1] or now[3];
    if now[0] = 0 then output(''property violated'');
    pre ← now;
};
```

In the following we explain the generated program.

Declarations. Initially a state is declared. This will be updated as the input event list is processed. Next, the two arrays *pre* and *now* are declared. The *pre* array will contain values of all subformulae in the previous state, while *now* will contain the value of all subformulae in the current state. The trace of events is then input. Such an event list can be read from a file generated from a program execution, or alternatively the events can be input on-the-fly one by one when generated, without storing them in a file first. The latter solution is in fact the one implemented in PAX, where the observer runs in parallel with the executing program.

Initialization. The initialization phase consists of initializing the *state* variable and the *pre* array. The first event e_1 of the event list is used to initialize the *state* variable. The *pre* array is initialized by evaluating all subformulae bottom up, starting with highest formula numbers, and assigning these values to the corresponding elements of the *pre* array; hence, for any $i \in \{0 \ldots 8\}$ $pre[i]$ is assigned the initial value of formula φ_i. The *pre* array is initialized in such a way as to maintain the view that the initial state is supposed stationary before monitoring is started. This in particular means that $\uparrow p$ is false, as well as is $\downarrow (r \lor s)$, since there is no change in state (indices 1 and 5). The interval operator has the obvious initial interpretation: the first argument must be true and the second false for the formula to be true (index 3). Propositions are true if they hold in the initial state (indices 2, 4, 7 and 8), and boolean operators are interpreted the standard way (indices 0, 6).

Event Loop. The main evaluation loop goes through the event trace, starting from the second event. For each such event, the state is updated, followed by assignments to the *now* array in a bottom-up fashion similar to the initialization of the *pre* array: the array elements are assigned values from higher index values to lower index values, corresponding to the values of the corresponding subformulae. Propositional boolean operators are interpreted the standard way (indices 0 and 6). The formula $\uparrow p$ is true if p is true now and not true in the previous state (index 1). Similarly with the formula $\downarrow (r \lor s)$ (index 5). The formula $[q, \downarrow (r \lor s))_s$ is true if either the formula was true in the previous state, or q is true in the current state, and in addition $\downarrow (r \lor s)$ is not true in the current state (index 3). At the end of the loop an error message is issued if $now[0]$, the value of the whole formula, has the value 0 in the current state. Finally, the entire *now* array is copied into *pre*.

Given a fixed *ptLTL* formula, the analysis of this algorithm is straightforward. Its time complexity is $\Theta(n)$ where n is the length of the input trace, the constant being given by the size of the *ptLTL* formula. The memory required is constant, since the length of the two arrays is the size of the *ptLTL* formula. However, one may want to also include the size of the formula, say m, into the analysis; then the time complexity is obviously $O(n \cdot m)$ while the memory required is $2 \cdot (m + 1)$ bits. The authors think that it's hard to find an algorithm running faster than the above in practical situations, though some slight optimizations can be imagined (see Section 7).

5   The Algorithm Formalized

We now formally describe our algorithm that synthesizes a dynamic programming algorithm from a *ptLTL*-formula. It takes as input a formula and generates a program as the one above, containing a "for" loop which traverses the trace of events, while validating or invalidating the formula. To keep the presentation simple, we only show the code for $ptLTL\lceil_{\{\uparrow,\downarrow,[)_s\}}$ formulae. The generated program is printed using the function **output**, which is overloaded to take one or more text parameters which are concatenated in the output.

INPUT: past time LTL formula φ

let $\varphi_0, \varphi_1, ..., \varphi_m$ be the subformulae of φ;

output("**State** *state* $\leftarrow \{\}$;");

output("**bit** *pre*[0..*m*];");

output("**bit** *now*[0..*m*];");

output("INPUT: trace $t = e_1 e_2 ... e_n$;");

output("/* Initialization of *state* and *pre* */");

output("*state* $\leftarrow$ *update*(*state*, e_1);");

for $j = m$ **downto** 0 **do** {

    output("   *pre*[", j, "] $\leftarrow$ ");

    if φ_j is a variable **then** output(φ_j, "(*state*);");

    if φ_j is **true then** output("**true**;");

    if φ_j is **false then** output("**false**;");

    if $\varphi_j = \neg\varphi_{j'}$ **then** output("*not pre*[",j', "];");

    if $\varphi_j = \varphi_{j_1}$ *op* φ_{j_2} **then** output("*pre*[",j_1, "] *op pre*[",j_2, "];");

    if $\varphi_j = [\varphi_{j_1}, \varphi_{j_2}]_s$ **then** output("*pre*[",j_1, "] *and not pre*[", j_2, "];");

    if $\varphi_j = \uparrow \varphi_{j'}$ **then** output("**false**;");

    if $\varphi_j = \downarrow \varphi_{j'}$ **then** output("**false**;");

};

output("/* Event interpretation loop */");

output("**for** $i = 2$ **to** n **do** {");

for $j = m$ **downto** 0 **do** {

    output("   *now*[", j, "] $\leftarrow$ ");

    if φ_j is a variable **then** output(φ_j, "(*state*);");

    if φ_j is **true then** output("**true**;");

    if φ_j is **false then** output("**false**;");

    if $\varphi_j = \neg\varphi_{j'}$ **then** output("*not now*[",j', "];");

    if $\varphi_j = \varphi_{j_1}$ *op* φ_{j_2} **then** output("*now*[",j_1, "] *op now*[", j_2, "];");

    if $\varphi_j = [\varphi_{j_1}, \varphi_{j_2}]_s$ **then**

        output("(*pre*[", j, "] *or now*[",j_1, "]) *and not now*[", j_2, "];");

    if $\varphi_j = \uparrow \varphi_{j'}$ **then**

        output("*now*[", j', "] *and not pre*[", j', "];");

    if $\varphi_j = \downarrow \varphi_{j'}$ **then**

        output("*not now*[", j', "] *and pre*[", j', "];");

};

output("   if $now[0] = 0$ then output(''property violated'');");

output("   *pre* $\leftarrow$ *now*;");

output("}");

where *op* is any propositional connective. Since we have already given a detailed explanation of the example in the previous section, we shall only give a very brief description of the algorithm.

The formula should be first visited top down to assign increasing numbers to subformulae as they are visited. Let $\varphi_0, \varphi_1, ..., \varphi_m$ be the list of all subformulae. Because of the recursive nature of *ptLTL*, this step insures us that the truth value of $t_i \models \varphi_j$ can be completely determined from the truth values of $t_i \models \varphi_{j'}$ for all $j < j' \leq m$ and the truth values of $t_{i-1} \models \varphi_{j'}$ for all $j \leq j' \leq m$.

Before we generate the main loop, we should first generate code for initializing the array $pre[0..m]$, basically giving it the truth values of the subformulae on the initial state, conceptually being an infinite trace with repeated occurrences of the initial state. After that, the generated main event loop will process the events. The loop body will update/calculate the array now and in the end will move it into the array pre to serve as basis for the next iteration. After each iteration i, $now[0]$ tells whether the formula is validated by the trace $e_1 e_2 ... e_i$.

Since the formula enumeration procedure is linear, the algorithm synthesizes a dynamic programming algorithm from an $ptLTL$ formula in linear time with the size of the formula. The boolean operations used above are usually very efficiently implemented on any microprocessor and the arrays of bits pre and now are small enough to be kept in cache. Moreover, the dependencies between instructions in the generated "for" loop are simple to analyze, so a reasonable compiler can easily unfold or/and parallelize it to take advantage of machine's resources. Consequently, the generated code is expected to run very fast. Later we shall illustrate how such an optimization can be part of the translation algorithm.

6   Implementation of Offline and Inline Monitoring

In this section we briefly describe our efforts to implement in PathExplorer the above described algorithm to create monitors for observing the execution of Java programs. We present two approaches that we have pursued. In the first *off-line* approach we create a monitor that runs in parallel with the executing program, potentially on a different computer, receiving events from the running program, and checking on-the-fly that the formulae are satisfied. In this approach the formulae to be checked are given in a separate specification. In the second *inline* approach, formulae are written as comments in the program text, and are then expanded into Java code that is inserted after the comments.

6.1   Offline Monitoring

The code generator for off-line monitoring has been written in Java, using JavaCC [13], an environment for writing parsers and for generating and manipulating abstract syntax trees. The input to the code generator is a specification given in a file separate from the program. The specification for our example looks as follows (the default interpretation of intervals is "strong"):

```
specification Example is
  P = start(p) -> [q,end(r|s));
end
```

Several named formulae can be listed; here we have only included one, named P. The translator reads this specification and generates a single Java class, called Formulae, which contains all the machinery for evaluating all the formulae (in this case one) in the specification. This class must then be compiled and instantiated as part of the monitor. The class contains an evaluate() method which is applied after each state change and which will evaluate all the formulae. The class constructor takes as parameter a reference to the object that represents the state such that any updates to the states by the monitor based on received events can be seen by the `evaluate()` method. The generated `Formulae` class for the above specification looks as follows:

```
class Formulae{
  abstract class Formula{
    protected String name;    protected State state;
    protected boolean[] pre;  protected boolean[] now;

    public Formula(String name,State state){
      this.name = name;  this.state = state;
    }
    public String getName(){return name;}
    public abstract boolean evaluate();
  }
  private List formulae = new ArrayList();
  public void evaluate(){
    Iterator it = formulae.iterator();
    while(it.hasNext()){
      Formula formula = (Formula)it.next();
      if(!formula.evaluate()){
        System.out.println("Property " + formula.getName() + " violated");
  }}}
  class Formula_P extends Formula{
    public boolean evaluate(){
      now[8] = state.holds("s");
      now[7] = state.holds("r");
      now[6] = now[7] || now[8];
      now[5] = !now[6] && pre[6];
      now[4] = state.holds("q");
      now[3] = (pre[3] || now[4]) && !now[5];
      now[2] = state.holds("p");
      now[1] = now[2] && !pre[2];
      now[0] = !now[1] || now[3];
      System.arraycopy(now,0,pre,0,9);
      return now[0];
    }
    public Formula_P(State state){
      super("P",state);
      pre = new boolean[9];  now = new boolean[9];
      pre[8] = state.holds("s");
      pre[7] = state.holds("r");
      pre[6] = pre[7] || pre[8];
      pre[5] = false;
      pre[4] = state.holds("q");
      pre[3] = pre[4] && !pre[5];
      pre[2] = state.holds("p");
      pre[1] = false;
      pre[0] = !pre[1] || pre[3];
    }
  }
  public Formulae(State state){
    formulae.add(new Formula_P(state));
  }
}
```

The class contains an inner abstract[3] class `Formula` and, in the general case, an inner class `Formula_X` extending the `Formula` class for each formula in the specification, where X is the formula's name. In our case there is one such `Formula_P` class. The abstract `Formula` class declares the `pre` and `now` arrays, without giving

---

[3] An abstract class is a class where some methods are abstract, by having no body. Implementations for these methods will be provided in extending subclasses.

them any size, since this is formula specific. An abstract `evaluate` method is also declared. The class `Formula_P` contains the real definition of this `evaluate()` method. The constructor for this class in addition initializes the sizes of `pre` and `now` depending on the size of the formula, and also initializes the `pre` array.

In order to handle the general case where several formulae occur in the specification, and hence many `Formula_X` classes are defined, we need to create instances for all these classes and store them in some data structure where they can be accessed by the outermost `evaluate()` method. The `formulae` list variable is initialized to contain all these instances when the constructor of the `Formulae` class is called. The outermost `evaluate()` method, each time called, goes through this list and calls `evaluate()` on each single formula object.

6.2   Inline Monitoring

The general architecture of PAX was mainly designed for offline monitoring in order to accommodate applications where the source code is not available or where the monitored process is not even a program, but some kind of physical device. However, it is often the case that the source code of an application *is* available and that one is willing to accept extra code for testing purposes. Inline monitoring has actually higher precision because one knows exactly where an event was emitted in the execution of the program. Moreover, one can even throw exceptions when a safety property is violated, like in Temporal Rover [4], so the running program has the possibility to recover from an erroneous execution or to guide its execution in order to avoid undesired behaviors.

In order to provide support for inline monitoring, we developed some simple scripts that replace temporal annotations in Java source code by actual monitoring code, which throws an exception when the formula is violated. In [5] we show an example of expanded code for future time LTL. We have not implemented the script to automatically expand past time LTL formulae yet, but the expanded code would essentially look like the body of the method `evaluate()` above. The "for" loop and the update of the state in the generic algorithm in Section 4 are not needed anymore because the atomic predicates use directly the current state of the program when the expanded code is reached during the execution.

It is inline monitoring that motivated us to optimize the generated code as much as possible. Since the running program and the monitor are a single process now, the time needed to execute the monitoring code can significantly influence the otherwise normal execution of the monitored program.

7   Optimizing the Generated Code

The generated code presented in Section 4 is not optimal. Even though a smart compiler can in principle generate good machine code from it, it is still worth exploring ways to synthesize directly optimized code especially because there are some attributes that are specific to the runtime observer which a compiler cannot take into consideration.

A first observation is that not all the bits in *pre* are needed, but only those which are used at the next iteration, namely 2, 3, and 6. Therefore, only a bit per temporal operator is needed, thereby reducing significantly the memory required by the generated algorithm. Then the body of the generated "for" loop becomes after (blind) substitution (we don't consider the initialization code here):

```
state ← update(state, eᵢ)
now[3] ← r(state) or s(state)
now[2] ← (pre[2] or q(state)) and not (not now[3] and pre[3])
now[1] ← p(state)
if ((not (now[1] and not pre[1]) or now[2]) = 0)
    then output(''property violated'');
```

which can be further optimized by boolean simplifications:

```
state ← update(state, eⱼ)
now[3] ← r(state) or s(state)
now[2] ← (pre[2] or q(state)) and (now[3] or not pre[3])
now[1] ← p(state)
if (now[1] and not pre[1] and not now[2])
    then output(''property violated'');
```

The most expensive part of the code above is clearly the function calls, namely $p(state)$, $q(state)$, $r(state)$, and $s(state)$. Depending upon the runtime requirements, the execution time of these functions may vary significantly. However, since one of the major concerns of monitoring is to affect the normal execution of the monitored program as little as possible, especially in the inline monitoring approach, one would of course want to evaluate the atomic predicates on states only if really needed, or rather to evaluate only those that, probabilistically, add a minimum cost. Since we don't want to count on an optimizing compiler, we prefer to store the boolean formula as some kind of binary decision diagram, more precisely, as a term over the operation _?_ : _, for example, $pre[3] ? pre[2] ? now[3] : q(state) : pre[2] ? 1 : q(state)$ (see [9] for a formal definition). Therefore, one is faced with the following optimum problem:

Given a boolean formula φ using propositions a_1, a_2, ..., a_n of costs c_1, c_2, ..., c_n, respectively, find a (_?_ : _)-expression that optimally implements φ.

We have implemented a procedure in Maude [1], on top of a propositional calculus module, which generates all correct (_?_ : _)-expressions for φ, admittedly a potentially exponential number in the number of distinct atomic propositions in φ, and then chooses the shortest in size, ignoring the costs. Applied on the code above, it yields:

```
state ← update(state, eⱼ)
now[3] ← r(state) ? 1 : s(state)
now[2] ← pre[3] ? pre[2] ? now[3] : q(state) : pre[2] ? 1 : q(state)
now[1] ← p(state)
if (pre[1] ? 0 : now[2] ? 0 : now[1])
    then output(''property violated'');
```

We would like to extend our procedure to take the evaluation costs of predicates into consideration. These costs can either be provided by the user of the system or be calculated automatically by a static analysis of predicates' code, or even be estimated by executing the predicates on a sample of states. However, based on our examples so far, we conjecture at this incipient stage that, given a boolean formula φ in which all the atomic propositions have the same cost, the probabilistically runtime optimal (_?_ : _)-expression implementing φ is *exactly* the one which is smallest in size.

A further optimization would be to generate directly machine code instead of using a compiler. Then the arrays of bits *now* and *pre* can be stored in two registers, which would be all the memory needed. Since all the operations executed are bit operations, the generated code is expected to be very fast. One could even imagine hardware implementations of past time monitors, using the same ideas, in order to enforce safety requirements on physical devices.

8 Conclusion

A synthesis algorithm has been described which generates from a past time temporal logic formula an algorithm which checks that a finite sequence of events satisfies the formula. The algorithm has been implemented in PathExplorer, a runtime verification tool currently being developed. Operators convenient for monitoring were presented and shown equivalent to standard past time temporal operators. It is our intention to investigate how the presented algorithm can be refined to work for logics that can refer to real-time, and data values. Other kinds of runtime verification are also investigated, such as, for example, techniques for detecting error potentials in multi-threaded programs.

References

1. Manuel Clavel, Steven Eker, Patrick Lincoln, and José Meseguer. Principles of Maude. In José Meseguer, editor, *Proceedings, First International Workshop on Rewriting Logic and its Applications*. Elsevier Science, 1996. Volume 4, *Electronic Notes in Theoretical Computer Science*.
2. James Corbett, Matthew B. Dwyer, John Hatcliff, Corina S. Pasareanu, Robby, Shawn Laubach, and Hongjun Zheng. Bandera : Extracting Finite-state Models from Java Source Code. In *Proceedings of the 22nd International Conference on Software Engineering*, Limerick, Ireland, June 2000. ACM Press.
3. Claudio Demartini, Radu Iosif, and Riccardo Sisto. A Deadlock Detection Tool for Concurrent Java Programs. *Software Practice and Experience*, 29(7):577–603, July 1999.
4. Doron Drusinsky. The Temporal Rover and the ATG Rover. In Klaus Havelund, John Penix, and Willem Visser, editors, *SPIN Model Checking and Software Verification*, volume 1885 of *Lecture Notes in Computer Science*, pages 323–330. Springer, 2000.
5. Klaus Havelund, Scott Johnson, and Grigore Roşu. Specification and Error Pattern Based Program Monitoring. In *European Space Agency Workshop on On-Board Autonomy*, Noordwijk, The Netherlands, 2001.

6. Klaus Havelund, Michael Lowry, and John Penix. Formal Analysis of a Space Craft Controller using SPIN. *IEEE Transactions on Software Engineering*, 27(8):749–765, August 2001.

7. Klaus Havelund and Thomas Pressburger. Model Checking Java Programs using Java PathFinder. *International Journal on Software Tools for Technology Transfer*, 2(4):366–381, April 2000. Special issue of STTT containing selected submissions to the 4th SPIN workshop, Paris, France, 1998.

8. Klaus Havelund and Grigore Roşu. Java PathExplorer – A Runtime Verification Tool. In *The 6th International Symposium on Artificial Intelligence, Robotics and Automation in Space: A New Space Odyssey*, Montreal, Canada, June 18 - 21, 2001.

9. Klaus Havelund and Grigore Roşu. Monitoring Java Programs with Java PathExplorer. In Klaus Havelund and Grigore Roşu, editors, *Proceedings of Runtime Verification (RV'01)*, volume 55 of *Electronic Notes in Theoretical Computer Science*. Elsevier Science, 2001.

10. Klaus Havelund and Grigore Roşu. Monitoring Programs using Rewriting. In *Proceedings, International Conference on Automated Software Engineering (ASE'01)*, pages 135–143. Institute of Electrical and Electronics Engineers, 2001. San Diego, California.

11. Klaus Havelund and Natarajan Shankar. Experiments in Theorem Proving and Model Checking for Protocol Verification. In Marie Claude Gaudel and Jim Woodcock, editors, *FME'96: Industrial Benefit and Advances in Formal Methods*, volume 1051 of *Lecture Notes in Computer Science*, pages 662–681. Springer, 1996.

12. Gerard J. Holzmann and Margaret H. Smith. A Practical Method for Verifying Event-Driven Software. In *Proceedings of ICSE'99, International Conference on Software Engineering*, Los Angeles, California, USA, May 1999. IEEE/ACM.

13. JavaCC. Web page. http://www.webgain.com/products/java_cc.

14. JTrek. Web page. http://www.compaq.com/java/download.

15. Insup Lee, Sampath Kannan, Moonjoo Kim, Oleg Sokolsky, and Mahesh Viswanathan. Runtime Assurance Based on Formal Specifications. In *Proceedings of the International Conference on Parallel and Distributed Processing Techniques and Applications*, 1999.

16. Zohar Manna and Amir Pnueli. *The Temporal Logic of Reactive and Concurrent Systems*. Springer, New York, 1992.

17. David Y.W. Park, Ulrich Stern, and David L. Dill. Java Model Checking. In *Proceedings of the First International Workshop on Automated Program Analysis, Testing and Verification, Limerick, Ireland*, June 2000.

18. Amir Pnueli. The Temporal Logic of Programs. In *Proceedings of the 18th IEEE Symposium on Foundations of Computer Science*, pages 46–77, 1977.

19. Grigore Roşu and Klaus Havelund. Synthesizing Dynamic Programming Algorithms from Linear Temporal Logic Formulae. Technical Report TR 01-08, NASA - RIACS, May 2001.

20. Scott D. Stoller. Model-Checking Multi-threaded Distributed Java Programs. In Klaus Havelund, John Penix, and Willem Visser, editors, *SPIN Model Checking and Software Verification*, volume 1885 of *Lecture Notes in Computer Science*, pages 224–244. Springer, 2000.

21. Willem Visser, Klaus Havelund, Guillaume Brat, and SeungJoon Park. Model Checking Programs. In *Proceedings of ASE'2000: The 15th IEEE International Conference on Automated Software Engineering*. IEEE CS Press, September 2000.

Adaptive Model Checking

Alex Groce[1], Doron Peled[2], and Mihalis Yannakakis[3]

[1] Department of Computer Science
Carnegie Mellon University
Pittsburgh, PA, 15213
[2] Department of Electrical and Computer Engineering
University of Texas at Austin
Austin, TX, 78712, USA
[3] Avaya Laboratories
233 Mount Airy Road
Baskin Ridge, NJ 07920, USA

Abstract. We consider the case where inconsistencies are present between a system and its corresponding model, used for automatic verification. Such inconsistencies can be the result of modeling errors or recent modifications of the system. Despite such discrepancies we can still attempt to perform automatic verification. In fact, as we show, we can sometimes exploit the verification results to assist in automatically learning the required updates to the model. In a related previous work, we have suggested the idea of *black box checking*, where verification starts without any model, and the model is obtained while repeated verification attempts are performed. Under the current assumptions, an existing inaccurate (but not completely obsolete) model is used to expedite the updates. We use techniques from black box testing and machine learning. We present an implementation of the proposed methodology called AMC (for Adaptive Model Checking). We discuss some experimental results, comparing various tactics of updating a model while trying to perform model checking.

Keywords: Automatic Verification, Black Box Testing, Learning Algorithms.

1 Introduction

The automatic verification of systems, also called *model checking*, is increasingly gaining popularity as an important tool for enhancing system reliability. A major effort is to find new and more efficient algorithms. One typical assumption is that a detailed model, which correctly reflects the properties of the original system to be checked, is given. The verification is then performed with respect to this model. Because of the possibility of modeling errors, when a counterexample is found, it still needs to be compared against the actual system. If the counterexample does not reflect an actual execution of the system, the model needs to be refined, and the automatic verification is repeated. A similar iterative process

J.-P. Katoen and P. Stevens (Eds.): TACAS 2002, LNCS 2280, pp. 357–370, 2002.

in the framework of abstracted models of systems has been used as a technique for combatting the state space explosion problem [4]. Our technique is substantially different in that rather than using counterexamples to iteratively refine the abstraction used (exposing variables or adding predicates for instance), we use counterexamples to modify incorrect models which are not abstractions of the real system.

Although there are several tools for obtaining automatic translation from various notations to modeling languages, such translations are used only in a small minority of cases, as they are syntax-specific. The modeling process and the refinement of the model are largely manual processes. Most noticeably, they depend on the skills of the person who is performing the modeling, and his experience.

In this paper, we deal with the problem of model checking in the presence of an inaccurate model. We suggest a methodology in which model checking is performed on some preliminary model. Then, if a counterexample is found, it is compared with the actual system. This results in either the conclusion that the system does not satisfy a property, or an automatic refinement of the model. We adapt a learning algorithm [1], to help us with the updating of the model. We employ a testing algorithm [3,10] to help us compare the model with the actual system, through experiments.

Our adaptive model checking approach can be used in several cases.

- When the model includes a modeling error.
- After some previously occurring bug in the system was corrected.
- When a new version of the system is presented.
- When a new feature is added to the system.

We present an implementation of Adaptive Model Checking (AMC) and experimental results. In the limit, this approach is akin to Black Box Checking [9] (BBC), where initially no model is given. The current implementation serves also as a testbed for the black box checking approach, and we present our experimental results.

The black box checking approach [9] is a strategy to verify a system without a model. According to this strategy, illustrated in Figure 1, we alternate between incremental learning of the system, according to Angluin's algorithm [1], and the black box testing of the learned model against the actual system, using the Vasilevskii-Chou (VC) algorithm [3,10].

At any stage we have a model that approximates the actual system. We apply model checking to this model. In our case we use the nested depth-first search algorithm to check for emptiness of the product of the system with a Büchi automaton [6]. We can thus handle general LTL properties, under the assumption that the upper bound on the size of the real system is correct. Because the complexity of learning is dependent on the length of the counterexamples generated, we apply iterative deepening to the nested depth-first search. If we find a counterexample for the checked property, we compare it with the actual system. If it turns out to be a false negative, we feed this example to the learning algorithm, since this is an example of the difference between the model and the system.

This allows us, through the learning algorithm, to improve the accuracy of the model. If we do not find a counterexample (recall that we use an approximation model for model-checking, and not the system directly), we apply the VC algorithm, looking for a discrepancy between the current approximation model and the system. Again, if we find a sequence that distinguishes the behavior of the system from the model, we feed it to the learning algorithm, in order to improve the approximated model.

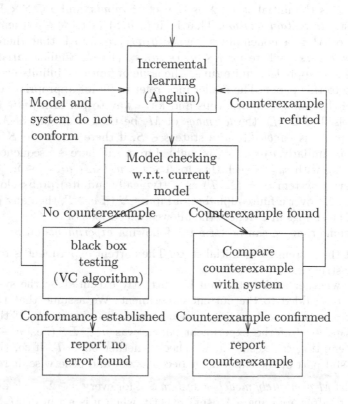

Fig. 1. The black box checking strategy

In this paper, we consider a variant case, in which a model for the tested system is provided, but is inaccurate, due to modeling errors or new updates in the system. Abandoning the model and applying the black box checking approach may not be an efficient strategy due to the inherently high complexity of the black box testing involved. Instead, we attempt to exploit the existing model in order to learn the changes and verify the system. Specifically, we try to diminish the need for the repeated call to the VC algorithm by providing the learning algorithm with initial information taken from the given model. This is in line with our goal of adapting an existing model, as opposed to performing model checking without a model being initially present. We present experimental data that compares the different cases.

2 Preliminaries

A Model and a System

A *model* is a finite automaton $M = \langle S, \iota, \Sigma, \delta \rangle$, where S is the (finite) set of states, $\iota \in S$ is the initial state, Σ is the set of *inputs*, and $\delta \subseteq S \times \Sigma \times S$ is a deterministic *transition relation*. That is, if $(s, a, r), (s, a, r') \in \delta$, then $r = r'$.

A *run* of M is a nonempty sequence $a_1 a_2 \ldots a_n$, such that there exists a sequence $s_0 s_1 \ldots s_n$, where for $i \leq n$, $(s_i, a_i, s_{i+1}) \in \delta$. Similar variants of the definitions also apply to infinite runs. The issue of finite vs. infinite executions is orthogonal to this paper. The reader may refer to [9] for appropriate definitions of a model that allows *infinite* runs and for a way to perform *finite* testing on such models. Let $\mathcal{L}(M)$, the *language* of M, be the set of runs of M. We say that an input a is *enabled* from a state $s \in S$, if there exists $r \in S$, such that $(s, a, r) \in \delta$. Similarly, $a_1 a_2 \ldots a_n$ is enabled from s if there is a sequence of states $s_0, s_2, \ldots, s_n$ with $s_0 = s$ such that for $1 \leq i \leq n$, $(s_{i-1}, a_i, s_i) \in \delta$.

We view a system $\mathcal{S} = (\Sigma, T)$ as a (typically infinite) prefix closed set of strings $T \subseteq \Sigma^*$ over a finite alphabet of inputs Σ (if $v \in T$, then any prefix of v is in T). The strings in T reflect the allowed executions of $\mathcal{S}$.

We assume that we can perform the following *experiments* on $\mathcal{S}$:

- **Reset** the system to its initial state. The current experiment is reset to the empty string ε.
- Check whether an input a can be currently executed by the system. The letter a is added to the current experiment. We assume that the system provides us with information on whether a was executable. If the current *successful part* of the experiment so far was $v \in \Sigma^*$ (i.e., $v \in T$), then by attempting to execute a, we check whether $va \in T$. If so, the current successful part of the experiment becomes va, and otherwise, it remains v.

A model M *accurately models* a system $\mathcal{S}$ if for every $v \in \Sigma^*$, v is a successful experiment (after applying a **Reset**) exactly when v is a run of M. Note that our system generates binary output in accordance with the enabledness of a given input after executing some sequence from the initial state. We can easily generalize the construction and subsequent algorithms to deal with arbitrary output. We deal here with finite state systems, i.e., systems that are accurately modeled by *some* finite state automaton. The *size* of a system is defined to be the number of states of the minimal automaton that accurately models it.

Angluin's Learning Algorithm

Angluin's learning algorithm [1] plays an important role in our adaptive model checking approach. The learning algorithm performs experiments on the system $\mathcal{S}$ and produces a *minimized* finite automaton representing it.

The basic data structure of Angluin's algorithm consists of two finite sets of finite strings V and W over the alphabet Σ, and a table f. The set V is prefix closed (and contains thus in particular the empty string ε). The rows of the table f are the strings in $V \cup V.\Sigma$, while the columns are the strings in W. The set W must also contain the empty string. Let $f(v, w) = 1$ when the sequence of transitions vw is a successful execution of $\mathcal{S}$, and 0 otherwise. The entry $f(v, w)$ can be computed by performing the experiment vw after a **Reset**.

We call the sequences in V the *access* sequences, as they are used to access the different states of the automaton we are learning from its initial state. The sequences in W are called the *separating sequences*, as their goal is to separate between different states of the constructed automaton. Namely, if $v, v' \in V$ lead from the initial state into a different state, than we will find some $w \in W$ such that $\mathcal{S}$ allows either vw or $v'w$ as a successful experiment, but not both.

We define an equivalence relation $\equiv mod(W)$ over strings in Σ^* as follows: $v_1 \equiv v_2 \, mod(W)$ when the two rows, of v_1 and v_2 in the table f are the same. Denote by $[v]$ the equivalence class that includes v. A table f is *closed* if for each $va \in V.\Sigma$ such that $f(v, \varepsilon) \neq 0$ there is some $v' \in V$ such that $va \equiv v' \, mod(W)$. A table is *consistent* if for each $v_1, v_2 \in V$ such that $v_1 \equiv v_2 \, mod(W)$, either $f(v_1, \varepsilon) = f(v_2, \varepsilon) = 0$, or for each $a \in \Sigma$, we have that $v_1 a \equiv v_2 a \, mod(W)$. Notice that if the table is not consistent, then there are $v_1, v_2 \in V$, $a \in \Sigma$ and $w \in W$, such that $v_1 \equiv v_2 \, mod(W)$, and exactly one of $v_1 aw$ and $v_2 aw$ is an execution of $\mathcal{S}$. This means that $f(v_1 a, w) \neq f(v_2 a, w)$. In this case we can add aw to W in order to separate v_1 from v_2.

Given a closed and consistent table f over the sets V and W, we construct a *proposed automaton* $M = \langle S, s_0, \Sigma, \delta \rangle$ as follows:

- The set of states S is $\{[v] | v \in V, f(v, \varepsilon) \neq 0\}$.
- The initial state s_0 is $[\varepsilon]$.
- The transition relation δ is defined as follows: for $v \in V, a \in \Sigma$, the transition from $[v]$ on input a is enabled iff $f(v, a) = 1$ and in this case $\delta([v], a) = [va]$.

The facts that the table f is closed and consistent guarantee that the transition relation is well defined. In particular, the transition relation is independent of which state v of the equivalence class $[v]$ we choose; if v, v' are two equivalent states in V, then for all $a \in \Sigma$ we have that $[va]$ coincides with $[v'a]$ (by consistency) and is equal to $[u]$ for some $u \in V$ (by closure).

There are two basic steps used in the learning algorithms for extending the table f:

$add\_rows(v)$: Add v to V. Update the table by adding a row va for each $a \in \Sigma$ (if not already present), and by setting $f(va, w)$ for each $w \in W$ according to the result of the experiment vaw.

$add\_column(w)$: Add w to W. Update the table f by adding the column w, i.e., set $f(v, w)$ for each $v \in V \cup V.\Sigma$, according the the experiment vw.

The Angluin algorithm is executed in phases. After each phase, a new proposed automaton M is generated. The proposed automaton M may not agree with the system $\mathcal{S}$. We need to compare M and $\mathcal{S}$ (we present later a short description of the VC black box testing algorithm for performing the comparison). If the comparison succeeds, the learning algorithm terminates. If it does not, we obtain a run σ on which M and $\mathcal{S}$ disagree, and add all its prefixes to the set of rows V. We then execute a new phase of the learning algorithm, where more experiments due to the prefixes of σ and the requirement to obtain a closed and consistent table are called for.

```
subroutine ANGLUIN(V, W, f, σ)
      if f, V and W are empty then
            /* starting the algorithm from scratch */
            let V := {ε};  W = {ε};
            add_rows(ε);
      else
            for each v' ∈ prefix(σ) that is not in V do
                  add_rows(v');
      while (V, W, f) is inconsistent or not closed do
            if (V, W, f) is inconsistent then
                  find v₁, v₂ ∈ V,  a ∈ Σ,  w ∈ W,  such that
                        v₁ ≡ v₂ mod(W) and f(v₁a, w) ≠ f(v₂a, w);
                  add_column(aw);
            else /* (V, W, f) is not closed */
                  find v ∈ V,  a ∈ Σ,
                        such that va ∉ [u] for any u ∈ V;
                  add_rows(va);
      end while
      return automaton(V, W, f)
end ANGLUIN
```

Fig. 2. An incremental learning step

The subroutine in Figure 2 is an incremental step of learning. Each call to this subroutine starts with either an empty table f, or with a table that was prepared in the previous step, and a sequence σ that distinguishes the behavior of the proposed automaton (as constructed from the table f) and the actual system. The subroutine ends when the table f is closed and consistent, hence a proposed automaton can be constructed from it.

Let m be the size of an automaton that faithfully represents the system $\mathcal{S}$. Assume that Angluin's algorithm is executed in such a way that each time an automaton that does not faithfully represents the system $\mathcal{S}$ is proposed, a shortest counterexample showing the discrepancy in behavior is presented, without accounting for the time it takes for calculating such a counterexample. This assumption is made in order to decouple the complexity of comparing $\mathcal{S}$ with M from the learning algorithm. Then, the time complexity is $\mathcal{O}(m^4)$.

We do not in practice perform the expensive breadth-first search required to copute the shortest counterexample, but we do apply iterative deepening to the nested depth-first search in order to avoid its preference for very long paths and cycles.

Spanning Trees

A *spanning tree* of an automaton $M = \langle S, \iota, \Sigma, \delta \rangle$ is a graph $G = \langle S, \iota, \Sigma, \Delta \rangle$ generated using the following depth first search algorithm.

explore(ι);
subroutine *explore*(s):
    set *old*(s);
    for each $a \in \Sigma$ do
        if $\exists s' \in S$ such that $(s, a, s') \in \delta$
                and $\neg old(s')$ /* s' was not found yet during the search */
            add (s, a, s') to Δ;
            explore(s');

A spanning tree thus is a subgraph G of M, with no cycles. Let T be the corresponding runs of G. Notice that in Angluin's algorithm, when a proposed automaton M is learned, the set V of access sequences includes the runs of a spanning tree of M.

Separating Sequences

Let $M = \langle S, \iota, \Sigma, \delta \rangle$ be an automaton with a set of states S. Let ds be a function $ds : S \rightarrow 2^{\Sigma^*}$. That is, ds returns, for each state S, a set of words over Σ. We require that if $s, s' \in S$, $s \neq s'$, then there are $w \in ds(s)$ and $w' \in ds(s')$, such that some $\sigma \in prefix(w) \cap prefix(w')$ is enabled from exactly one of s and s'. Thus, σ separates s from s'. We call ds the *separation function* of M (see, [8]).

A simple case of a separation function is a constant function, where for each s, s', $ds(s) = ds(s')$. In this case, we have *separation set*. Note that the set W generated by Angluin's algorithm is a separation set. We denote the (single) set of separating sequences (a *separation set*) for an automaton M by $DS(M)$.

The Hopcroft algorithm [7] provides an efficient $\mathcal{O}(n \log n)$ for providing a set of separating sequences, where n is the number of states.

Black Box Testing

Comparing a model M with a finite state system $\mathcal{S}$ can be performed using the Vasilevskii-Chow [10,3] algorithm. As a preparatory step, we require the following:

- A spanning tree G for M, and its corresponding runs T.
- A separation function ds, such that for each $s \in S$, $|ds(s)| \leq n$, and for each $\sigma \in ds(s)$, $|\sigma| \leq n$.

Let $\Sigma^{\le k}$ be all the strings over Σ with length smaller or equal to k. Further, let m be the number of states of the automaton M. We do the experiments with respect to a conjectured maximal size n of S. That is, our comparison is correct as long as representing S faithfully (using a finite automaton) does not need to have more than n states. The black box testing algorithm prescribes experiments of the form **Reset** $\sigma\,\rho$, performed on S, as follows:

- The sequence σ is taken from $T.\Sigma^{\le n-m+1}$.
- Run σ from the initial state ι of M. If σ is enabled from ι, let s be the state of M that is reached after running σ. Then ρ is taken from the set $ds(s)$.

The complexity of the VC algorithm is $\mathcal{O}(n^2\,m\,|\Sigma|^{n-m+1})$.

3   Adaptive Verification

Our adaptive model checking methodology is a variant of black box check-ing. While the latter starts the automatic verification process without having a model, adaptive model checking assumes some initial model, which may be inaccurate. The observation is that the inaccurate model is still useful for the verification. First, it can be used for performing model checking. Caution must be taken as any counterexample found must still be compared against the actual system; in the case that no counterexample is found, no conclusion about the correctness of the system can be made. In addition, the assumption is that the given model shares some nontrivial common behavior with the actual system. Thus, the current model can be used for obtaining a better model.

The methodology consists of the following steps.

1. Perform model checking on the given model.
2. Provided that an error trace was found, compare the error trace with the actual system. If the trace involves a cycle, the cycle must be repeated a number of times equal to the upper bound given for the real size of the system. If this is an actual execution of the system, report it and stop.
3. Start the learning algorithm. Unlike the black box checking case, we do not begin with $V = W = \{\varepsilon\}$. Instead, we initiate V and W to values obtained from the given model M as described below. We experiment with several ways of doing so.
4. If no error trace was found, we can either decide to complete the verifi-cation attempt (assuming that the model is accurate enough), or perform some black box testing algorithm, e.g., VC, to compare the model with the actual system. A manual attempt to correct or update the model is also possible. Notice that black box testing is a rather expensive step that should be eliminated.

In the black box checking algorithm, we start the learning with an empty table f, and empty sets V and W. This immediately cause the initialization of $V = W = \{\varepsilon\}$ (see Figure 2). As a result, the black box checking algorithm alternates between the incremental learning algorithm and a black box testing

(VC algorithm) of the proposed automaton with the actual system. Applying the VC algorithm may be very expensive. In the adaptive model checking case, we try to guide the learning algorithm using the already existing (albeit inaccurate) model. We assume that the modified system has a nontrivial similarity with the model. This is due to the fact that changes that may have been made to the system were based on the old version of it. We can use the following:

1. A false negative counterexample σ found (i.e., a sequence σ that was considered to be a counterexample, but has turned out not to be an actual execution of the system S). We perform learning experiments with $prefix(\sigma)$, i.e., the set of all prefixes of σ.
2. The runs T of a spanning tree G of the model M as the initial set of access sequences V. We precede the learning algorithm by performing for each $v \in T$ do add_rows(v).
3. A set of separating sequences $DS(M)$ calculated for the states of M as the initial value of the set W. Thus, we precede the learning algorithm by setting f to be empty, and $W = DS(M)$.

Thus, we attempt to speed up the learning, using the existing model information, but with the learning experiments now done on the actual current system S. We experiment later with the choices $1 + 2$ (in this case we set $W = \{\varepsilon\}$), $1 + 3$ (in this case we set $V = \{\varepsilon\}$) and $1 + 2 + 3$.

In order to justify the above choices of the sets V and W for the adaptive model checking case, we will show the following: If the model M accurately models a system S, starting with the aforementioned choices of V and W the above choices allow Angluin's algorithm to learn M accurately, without the assistance of the (time expensive) black box testing (the VC algorithm).

Theorem 1. *Assume that a finite automaton M accurately models a system S. Let G be a spanning tree of M, and T the corresponding runs. If we start Angluin's algorithm with $V = T$ and $W = \{\epsilon\}$, then it terminates learning a minimized finite automaton A with $\mathcal{L}(A) = \mathcal{L}(M)$. Moreover, the learning algorithm will not require the use of the black box testing.*

Sketch of proof. By induction on the length of experiment that is required to distinguish pairs of states of M. As the induction basis, by consistency, we will separate states in V according to whether va can be accessed from the initial state or not, for $v \in V$, $a \in \Sigma$. Then, suppose that the states reached by va and $v'a$ were separated. The table cannot become consistent before we separate va and $v'a$. $\square$

Theorem 2. *Assume that a finite automaton M accurately models a system S. Let $DS(M)$ be a set of separating sequences for M. If we start Angluin's algorithm with $V = \{\varepsilon\}$ and $W = DS(M)$, then it terminates learning a minimized finite automaton A with $\mathcal{L}(A) = \mathcal{L}(M)$. Moreover, the learning algorithm will not require the use of the black box testing.*

Sketch of Proof. Because of the selection of the separation set, each time a new state of M is accessed through an experiment with a string $v \in V$, it will be immediately distinguished from all existing accessed states. Consequently, by the requirement that the table will be closed, the learning algorithm will generate for it a set of immediate successors. Thus, the table f will not be closed before all the states of M are accessed via experiments with strings of V.   □

The above theorems show that the given initial settings do not prevent us from learning correctly any correct finite representation of S (note also that adding arbitrary access and separating sequences does not affect the correctness of the learning algorithm). Of course, when AMC is applied, the assumption is that the system S deviates from the model M. However, if the changes to the system are modest, the proposed initial conditions are designed to speed up the adaptive learning process.

4   An Implementation

Our implementation of AMC is described in this section. We provide some experimental results.

Experimental Results

Our implementation prototype is written is SML (Standard ML of New Jersey) and includes about 5000 lines of code. We have performed several experiments with our AMC prototype. We compared adaptive learning (AMC) and black box checking (BBC). In addition, we compare the behavior of different initial values with which we started the AMC. In particular, we experimented with starting AMC with a spanning tree T of the current model M, a set of distinguishing sequences $DS(M)$, or with both. In each case of AMC, the prefixes of the counterexample that was found during the verification of the given property against the provided, inaccurate, model was also used as part of the initial set of access sequences V.

The examples used in our experimental results are taken from a CCS model of a COMA (Cache Only Memory Architecture) cache coherence protocol [2]. We use the more recent CCS model obtained from the site

ftp.sics.se/pub/fdt/fm/Coma

rather than that in the paper; we also modify the syntax to that of the Concurrency Workbench [5]. We used the Concurrency workbench in order to convert the model into a representation that we can use for our experiment.

The model is of a system with three components: two clients and a single directory. The system $S2$ with 529 states is a set of processes to generate local read and write requests from the client. The system $S3$ with 136 states, allows observation only of which processes have valid copies of the data and which (if any) have write access. (We preserved the names $S2$ and $S3$ from the paper [2]).

Property φ_1 asserts that first the component called 'directory' has a valid copy, then clients 1 and 2 alternate periodically without necessarily invalidating the data that any of the others hold. (The directory is the interface between the two memory units in the cache protocol. COMA models basically have only a cache to handle memory.) Property φ_2 describes a similar property but the traces now concern a cache having exclusivity on an entry (a cache can have a valid copy without exclusivity, which is more involved to obtain). For AMC we have selected properties that do not hold, and tampered with the verified model in order to experiment with finding (false negative) counterexamples and using them for the adaptive learning.

The next table summarizes the experiments done on $S2$. The columns marked BBC correspond to the black box checking, i.e., learning from scratch, while the rightmost column correspond to the three different ways in which the learning algorithm was initialized for the adaptive learning case. The notation $\varphi_1 \gg \varphi_2$ means that the experiment included checking φ_1 first, and then checking φ_2. In the black box checking this means that after a counterexample for φ_1 is found (which is intended to be the case in our experiments), we continue the incremental learning algorithm from the place it has stopped, but now with φ_2 as the property. This possibly causes continuing the incremental learning process for the proposed model automata, and performing the VC algorithm several times. In the adaptive case, it means that we initialize AMC with the information about the previously given model, according to the three choices. The memory and time measurements for these cases are the total memory and time needed for completing the overall checking of φ_1 and φ_2.

In the tables, time is measured in seconds, and memory in megabytes. The experiments were done on a Sun Sparc Ultra Enterprise 3000 with 250Mhz processors and 1.5 gigabytes of RAM.

Property	BBC		$V \neq \{\varepsilon\}$		$W \neq \{\varepsilon\}$		$V, W \neq \{\varepsilon\}$	
	Time	Mem	Time	Mem	Time	Mem	Time	Mem
φ_1	1234	31	423	41	682	32	195	37
φ_2	934	31	424	45	674	42	198	42
$\varphi_1 \gg \varphi_2$	1263	31	454	45	860	44	227	47
$\varphi_2 \gg \varphi_1$	1099	31	453	45	880	40	227	44

The following table includes the *number of states* learned in the various experiments, and the *length of the counterexample*.

Property	BBC		$V \neq \{\varepsilon\}$		$W \neq \{\varepsilon\}$		$V, W \neq \{\varepsilon\}$	
	States	Len	States	Len	States	Len	States	Len
φ_1	258	90	489	211	486	211	489	211
φ_2	174	113	489	539	486	539	489	539
$\varphi_1 \gg \varphi_2$	274	112	489	539	486	539	489	539
$\varphi_2 \gg \varphi_1$	259	160	489	211	486	211	489	211

The next table includes similar time and memory measurement experiments performed with the system $S3$:

Property	BBC		$V \neq \{\varepsilon\}$		$W \neq \{\varepsilon\}$		$V, W \neq \{\varepsilon\}$	
	Time	Mem	Time	Mem	Time	Mem	Time	Mem
φ_1	913	24	14	25	13	24	7	25
φ_2	13917	26	14	25	14	25	7	25
$\varphi_1 \gg \varphi_2$	1187	27	17	25	19	26	10	25
$\varphi_2 \gg \varphi_1$	13873	27	17	26	19	25	10	25

Similarly, the following table includes the number of states and length of counterexample for the experiments with $S3$.

Property	BBC		$V \neq \{\varepsilon\}$		$W \neq \{\varepsilon\}$		$V, W \neq \{\varepsilon\}$	
	States	Len	States	Len	States	Len	States	Len
φ_1	79	25	134	114	135	114	134	114
φ_2	108	118	134	142	135	142	134	142
$\varphi_1 \gg \varphi_2$	81	94	134	142	135	142	134	142
$\varphi_2 \gg \varphi_1$	114	113	134	114	135	114	134	114

In addition, we performed sanity checks. We applied AMC with the three different initializations on $S2$ and $S3$, and checked that we indeed obtained automata with 136 and 529 states, respectively. It should be commented that the deliberate change that was made to the original systems of $S2$ and $S3$ has resulted in no change in the number of states (in the minimal representation) of these systems.

Observing the tables, we see that performing BBC, i.e., learning a model from scratch, was 2.2 to 100 times slower than AMC. In addition, BBC has in some cases learned a model that is less than half of the actual states of the minimal automaton that faithfully represents the system (after the modification), while AMC was able to generate a representation that is less than 50 states short. It turned out that for the smaller system, $S3$, BBC has done a better job in learning a model than for $S2$. This means that it got a model with number of states closer to the actual minimal representation of the system.

We also see that the counterexample for BBC is shorter than that of AMC. This is not surprising, as BBC is 'zooming into' an error by considering incrementally growing automata for representing the system, while AMC is attempting to obtain a close enough representation first.

We comment that the implementation was done using SML, which takes about 20 megabytes for keeping its internal runtime structures. SML performs garbage collection phases during the execution, which slightly affects the running time and memory usage.

Improving the Prototype

Note that there is no guarantee that the adaptive model checking will zoom into a correct model by performing the learning algorithm. After the learning algorithm terminates, it is still possible that discrepancies exist, and to detect them we need to apply the black box testing part and then resume the learning. Of course, it is beneficial to avoid the testing part, in particular for relatively large models, as much as possible. For that, we may enhance the learning part with various heuristics. For example, we start AMC in Section 3 assuming that the actual structure of S would resemble a model M immediately after resetting S. This does not need to be the case. Thus, we may look for behaviors that match or resemble the set of runs T of a spanning tree of the model M from other points in the execution of S. For example, we may augment the learning algorithm by looking forward two or three inputs from every given state, and try to pattern match that behavior with that of set of runs T.

The Vasilevskii-Chow algorithm, used to compare the system with a model, is a bottleneck in our approach. In the limit, when there is no error, the algorithm is exponential in the difference between the conjectured size of the system and its actual size.

We apply the following heuristic improvement. The most wasteful part of the algorithm is manifested when arbitrary sequences of inputs over the input alphabet Σ (of length $n - m + 1$) are required by the algorithm. We generate a smaller set of sequences as follows. Given some information about the inputs, we calculate a partial state and carry the updating of the current state with the generation of the sequence. For example, if we know that some of the inputs correspond to message passing, we may include with each partial state a counter for each message queue. Such a counter will be set to zero in the initial state and will increment or decrement according to the corresponding send and receive events, respectively. Thus, from a current state where a counter that corresponds to some queue is zero, we do not allow an input that corresponds to a receive event.

5 Discussion

Our adaptive model checking approach is applicable for models that are inaccurate (but not completely irrelevant). When a principle change is made, the approach will still work, but the time to update the model may be substantial. In some pathological cases, simple changes can also lead to a substantial update effort. In particular, the following change to a system provides a 'worst case' example: The system functionality is not being changed, except for adding some security code that needs to be input before operating it.

The main problem we have dealt with is the ability to update the model according to the actual system, while performing full LTL model checking. While the changes learned may not fully reflect corresponding changes in the actual system S, the obtained model may still be useful for verification.

We have compared two approaches: one of abandoning the existing model in favor of learning a finite state representation of the system S from scratch (BBC). The other one is using the current model to guide the learning of the potentially modified system (AMC). We argue that there are merits to both approaches. The BBC approach can be useful when there is a short error trace that identifies why the checked property does not work. In this case, it is possible that the BBC approach will discover the error after learning only a short proposed model. The AMC approach is useful when the modification of the system is simple or when it may have a very limited affect on the correctness of the property checked.

References

1. D. Angluin, Learning Regular Sets from Queries and Counterexamples, Information and Computation, 75, 87–106 (1978).
2. G. Birtwistle, F. Moller, Ch. Tofts, The verification of a COMA cache coherence protocol, IEEE Workshop on Formal Methods in Software Practice (FMSP'96).
3. T. S. Chow, Testing software design modeled by finite-state machines, IEEE transactions on software engineering, SE-4, 3, 1978, 178–187.
4. E. Clarke, O. Grumberg, S. Jha, Y. Lu, and H. Veith, Counterexample-guided abstraction refinement, CAV 2000, 154–169.
5. R. Cleaveland, J. Parrow, B. Steffen, The Concurrency Workbench: a semantic-based tool for the verification of concurrent systems, TOPLAS 15(1993), 36–72.
6. Courcoubetis, C., Vardi, M.Y., Wolper, P., Yannakakis, M., Memory efficient algorithms for the verification of temporal properties, Formal Methods in System Design 1(1992), pp. 275–288.
7. J.E. Hopcroft, An n log n algorithm for minimizing the states in finite automata, The theory of Machines and Computation, Academic Press, New York, 189–196, 1971.
8. D. Lee, M. Yannakakis, Principles and methods of testing finite state machines - a survey, Proceedings of the IEEE, 84(8), 1090–1126, 1996.
9. D. Peled, M. Y. Vardi, M. Yannakakis, Black Box Checking, Black Box Checking, FORTE/PSTV 1999, Beijing, China.
10. M. P. Vasilevskii, Failure diagnosis of automata, Kibertetika, no 4, 1973, 98–108.

Parallelisation of the Petri Net Unfolding Algorithm

Keijo Heljanko[1], Victor Khomenko[2], and Maciej Koutny[2]

[1] Laboratory for Theoretical Computer Science,
Helsinki University of Technology
FIN-02015 HUT, Finland
Keijo.Heljanko@hut.fi

[2] Department of Computing Science, University of Newcastle
Newcastle upon Tyne NE1 7RU, U.K.
{Victor.Khomenko, Maciej.Koutny}@ncl.ac.uk

Abstract. In this paper, we first present theoretical results, helping to understand the unfolding algorithm presented in [6,7]. We then propose a modification of this algorithm, which can be efficiently parallelised and admits a more efficient implementation. Our experiments demonstrate that the degree of parallelism is usually quite high and resulting algorithms potentially can achieve significant speedup comparing with the sequential case.

Keywords: Model checking, Petri nets, parallel algorithms, unfolding, causality, concurrency.

1   Introduction

A distinctive characteristic of reactive concurrent systems is that their sets of local states have descriptions which are both short and manageable, and the complexity of their behaviour comes from highly complicated interactions with the external environment rather than from complicated data structures and manipulations thereon. One way of coping with this complexity problem is to use formal methods and, especially, computer aided verification tools implementing model checking ([2,1]) — a technique in which the verification of a system is carried out using a finite representation of its state space. The main drawback of model checking is that it suffers from the state space explosion problem. That is, even a relatively small system specification can (and often does) yield a very large state space. To help in coping with this, a number of techniques have been proposed, which can roughly be classified as aiming at an implicit compact representation of the full state space of a reactive concurrent system, or at an explicit generation of its reduced (though sufficient for a given verification task) representation. Techniques aimed at reduced representation of state spaces are typically based on the independence (commutativity) of some actions, often relying on the partial order view of concurrent computation. Such a view is the basis for algorithms employing McMillan's (finite prefixes of) Petri net unfoldings ([6,

J.-P. Katoen and P. Stevens (Eds.): TACAS 2002, LNCS 2280, pp. 371–385, 2002.

17]), where the entire state space of a system is represented implicitly, using an acyclic net to represent system's actions and local states.

In view of the development of fast model checking algorithms employing unfoldings ([10,11,13]), the problem of efficiently building them is becoming increasingly important. Recently, [5,6,7,15,16] addressed this issue — considerably improving the original McMillan's technique — but we feel that generating net unfoldings deserves further investigation.

The contribution of this paper is twofold. First, we present theoretical results, helping to understand the unfolding algorithm presented in [6,7]. Second, we propose a modification of that algorithm, which can be efficiently parallelised. It does not perform any comparisons of configurations except those needed for checking the cut-off criterion, reducing the total number of times two configuration are compared w.r.t. the *adequate* total order proposed in [6] down to the number of cut-off events in the resulting prefix. This allows to gain certain speedup even in a sequential implementation. Some other optimisations are also mentioned.

Our experiments demonstrate that the degree of parallelism is usually quite high and the resulting algorithms can potentially achieve significant speedup comparing with the sequential case. All proofs can be found in the technical report [12].

2   Basic Notions

In this section, we first present basic definitions concerning Petri nets, and then recall (see also [4,6,7]) notions related to net unfoldings.

Petri nets. A *net* is a triple $N \stackrel{\mathrm{df}}{=} (P, T, F)$ such that P and T are disjoint sets of respectively *places* and *transitions*, and $F \subseteq (P \times T) \cup (T \times P)$ is a *flow relation*. A *marking* of N is a multiset M of places, i.e. $M : P \to \mathbb{N} = \{0, 1, 2, \ldots\}$. As usual, we will denote ${}^{\bullet}z \stackrel{\mathrm{df}}{=} \{y \mid (y, z) \in F\}$ and $z^{\bullet} \stackrel{\mathrm{df}}{=} \{y \mid (z, y) \in F\}$, for all $z \in P \cup T$, and ${}^{\bullet}Z \stackrel{\mathrm{df}}{=} \bigcup_{z \in Z} {}^{\bullet}z$ and $Z^{\bullet} \stackrel{\mathrm{df}}{=} \bigcup_{z \in Z} z^{\bullet}$, for all $Z \subseteq P \cup T$. We will assume that ${}^{\bullet}t \neq \emptyset \neq t^{\bullet}$, for every $t \in T$.

A *net system* is a pair $\Sigma \stackrel{\mathrm{df}}{=} (N, M_0)$ comprising a finite net $N = (P, T, F)$ and an *initial* marking M_0. A transition $t \in T$ is *enabled* at a marking M if for every $p \in {}^{\bullet}t$, $M(p) \geq 1$. Such a transition can be *executed*, leading to a marking $M' \stackrel{\mathrm{df}}{=} M - {}^{\bullet}t + t^{\bullet}$. We denote this by $M[t\rangle M'$. The set of *reachable* markings of Σ is the smallest (w.r.t. set inclusion) set $[M_0\rangle$ containing M_0 and such that if $M \in [M_0\rangle$ and $M[t\rangle M'$ (for some $t \in T$) then $M' \in [M_0\rangle$.

A net system Σ is *safe* if for every reachable marking M, $M(P) \subseteq \{0, 1\}$; and *bounded* if there is $k \in \mathbb{N}$ such that $M(P) \subseteq \{0, \ldots, k\}$, for every reachable marking M.

Branching processes. Two nodes (places or transitions), y and y', of a net $N = (P, T, F)$ are *in conflict*, denoted by $y \# y'$, if there are distinct transitions

$t, t' \in T$ such that ${}^\bullet t \cap {}^\bullet t' \neq \emptyset$ and (t, y) and (t', y') are in the reflexive transitive closure of the flow relation F, denoted by $\preceq$. A node y is in *self-conflict* if $y \# y$.

An *occurrence net* is a net $ON \stackrel{\mathrm{df}}{=} (B, E, G)$ where B is the set of *conditions* (places) and E is the set of *events* (transitions). It is assumed that: ON is acyclic (i.e. $\preceq$ is a partial order); for every $b \in B$, $|{}^\bullet b| \leq 1$; for every $y \in B \cup E$, $\neg(y \# y)$ and there are finitely many y' such that $y' \prec y$, where $\prec$ denotes the irreflexive transitive closure of G. $Min(ON)$ will denote the set of minimal elements of $B \cup E$ with respect to $\preceq$. The relation $\prec$ is the *causality relation*. Two nodes are *concurrent*, denoted y co y', if neither $y \# y'$ nor $y \preceq y'$ nor $y' \preceq y$. We also denote by x co C, where C is a set of pairwise concurrent nodes, the fact that a node x is concurrent to each node from C. Two events e and f are *separated* if there is an event g such that $e \prec g \prec f$.

A *homomorphism* from an occurrence net ON to a net system Σ is a mapping $h : B \cup E \rightarrow P \cup T$ such that: $h(B) \subseteq P$ and $h(E) \subseteq T$; for all $e \in E$, the restriction of h to ${}^\bullet e$ is a bijection between ${}^\bullet e$ and ${}^\bullet h(e)$; the restriction of h to $e^\bullet$ is a bijection between $e^\bullet$ and $h(e)^\bullet$; the restriction of h to $Min(ON)$ is a bijection between $Min(ON)$ and M_0; and for all $e, f \in E$, if ${}^\bullet e = {}^\bullet f$ and $h(e) = h(f)$ then $e = f$. If $h(x) = y$ then we will often refer to x as y-*labelled*.

A *branching process* of Σ ([4]) is a quadruple $\pi \stackrel{\mathrm{df}}{=} (B, E, G, h)$ such that (B, E, G) is an occurrence net and h is a homomorphism from ON to Σ. A branching process $\pi' = (B', E', G', h')$ of Σ is a *prefix* of a branching process $\pi = (B, E, G, h)$, denoted $\pi' \sqsubseteq \pi$, if (B', E', G') is a subnet of (B, E, G) such that: if $e \in E'$ and $(b, e) \in G$ or $(e, b) \in G$ then $b \in B'$; if $b \in B'$ and $(e, b) \in G$ then $e \in E'$; and h' is the restriction of h to $B' \cup E'$. For each Σ there exists a unique (up to isomorphism) maximal (w.r.t. $\sqsubseteq$) branching process, called the *unfolding* of Σ.

An example (based on the one in [7]) of a safe net system and two of its branching processes is shown in Figure 1, where the respective homomorphisms h are shown by placing the names of the nodes of the net system in Figure 1(a) inside the conditions and events of the two branching processes. Note that the branching process in Figure 1(b) is a prefix of that in Figure 1(c).

Sometimes it is convenient to start a branching process with a (virtual) initial event $\perp$, which has the postset $Min(ON)$, empty preset, and no label. We will assume that $h(\perp)^\bullet = M_0$.

Configurations and cuts. A *configuration* of an occurrence net ON is a set of events C such that for all $e, f \in C$, $\neg(e \# f)$ and, for every $e \in C$, $f \prec e$ implies $f \in C$. The configuration $[e] \stackrel{\mathrm{df}}{=} \{f \mid f \preceq e\}$ is called the *local configuration* of $e \in E$. A set of conditions B' such that for all distinct $b, b' \in B'$, b co b', is called a *co-set*. A *cut* is a maximal (w.r.t. set inclusion) co-set. Every marking reachable from $Min(ON)$ is a cut.

Let C be a finite configuration of a branching process π. Then $Cut(C) \stackrel{\mathrm{df}}{=} (Min(ON) \cup C^\bullet) \setminus {}^\bullet C$ is a cut; moreover, the multiset of places $h(Cut(C))$ is a reachable marking of Σ, denoted $Mark(C)$. A marking M of Σ is *represented* in π if the latter contains a finite configuration C such that $M = Mark(C)$.

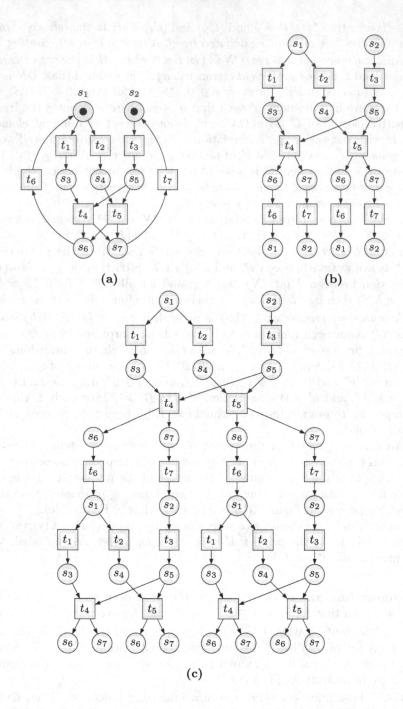

Fig. 1. A net system **(a)** and two of its branching processes **(b,c)**.

Every marking represented in π is reachable, and every reachable marking is represented in the unfolding of Σ.

A branching process π of Σ is *complete* if for every reachable marking M of Σ: (i) M is represented in π; and (ii) for every transition t enabled by M, there is a finite configuration C and an event $e \notin C$ in π such that $M = Mark(C)$, $h(e) = t$, and $C \cup \{e\}$ is a configuration.

ERV unfolding algorithm. Although, in general, the unfolding of a finite bounded net system Σ may be infinite, it is always possible to truncate it and obtain a finite complete prefix, $Pref_\Sigma$. A technique for this, based on choosing an appropriate set E_{cut} of *cut-off* events, beyond which the unfolding is not generated, was proposed in [18]. One can show ([6,9]) that it suffices to designate an event e newly added during the construction of $Pref_\Sigma$ as a cut-off event, if the already built part of a prefix contains a *corresponding* configuration C without cut-off events, such that $Mark(C) = Mark([e])$ and $C \lhd [e]$, where $\lhd$ is an *adequate order*, defined in the following way ([6,7]).

Definition 1. *A strict partial order $\lhd$ on the finite configurations of the unfolding of a net system is an* adequate order *if*

- $\lhd$ *is well-founded,*
- $\lhd$ *refines $\subset$, i.e., $C_1 \subset C_2 \Rightarrow C_1 \lhd C_2$,*
- $\lhd$ *is preserved by finite extensions, i.e., if $C_1 \lhd C_2$ and $Mark(C_1) = Mark(C_2)$ then $C_1 \oplus E \lhd C_2 \oplus I_{C_1}^{C_2}(E)$ for all finite extensions $C_1 \oplus E$ of C_1.*

Here $C \oplus E$ denotes the fact that $C \cup E$ is a configuration and $C \cap E = \emptyset$, and $I_{C_1}^{C_2}$ is a mapping from the finite extensions of C_1 onto the finite extensions of C_2, i.e., it maps $C_1 \oplus E$ onto $C_2 \oplus I_{C_1}^{C_2}(E)$ (see [6,7] for details).

We will also write $e \lhd f$ whenever $[e] \lhd [f]$.

In order to detect cut-off events earlier (and thus decrease the size of the resulting complete prefix), it is advantageous to choose 'dense' (ideally, total) orders, and [6,7] propose such an order $\lhd_{erv}$ for safe net systems; moreover, it is shown there that if a total order is used then the number of non-cut-off events in the resulting prefix will never exceed the number of reachable markings in the original net system (though usually it is much smaller). The $\lhd_{erv}$ order refines the McMillan's partial adequate order $\lhd_m$ ([6,18]), which is defined as $C_1 \lhd_m C_2 \Longleftrightarrow |C_1| < |C_2|$.

It is often assumed that a corresponding configuration of an event e is the local configuration of some event f, which is called a *correspondent* of a cut-off event e.[1]

The unfolding algorithm presented in [5,6,7,15,16] (the *basic* algorithm) is parameterised by an adequate order $\lhd$ and can be formulated as shown in Figure 2. It is assumed that the function call POTEXT(Unf_Σ) finds the set of *possible extensions* of a branching process Unf_Σ (see the definition below).

---

[1] The more general case of non-local corresponding configurations involves performing a reachability analysis each time when checking whether an event is cut-off, which can be quite time consuming ([9]).

input : $\Sigma = (N, M_0)$ — a bounded net system
output : Unf_Σ — a finite and complete prefix of Σ's unfolding

$Unf_\Sigma \leftarrow$ the empty branching process
add instances of the places from M_0 to Unf_Σ
$pe \leftarrow \text{PotExt}(Unf_\Sigma)$
$cut\_off \leftarrow \emptyset$
while $pe \neq \emptyset$ **do**
    choose $e \in pe$ **such that** $e \in \min_{\lhd} pe$
    if $[e] \cap cut\_off = \emptyset$
    then
        add e and new instances of the places from $h(e)^\bullet$ to Unf_Σ
        $pe \leftarrow \text{PotExt}(Unf_\Sigma)$
        if e is a cut-off event of Unf_Σ **then** $cut\_off \leftarrow cut\_off \cup \{e\}$
    else $pe \leftarrow pe \setminus \{e\}$

Fig. 2. The unfolding algorithm presented in [6].

Definition 2. *Let π be a branching process of a net system Σ, and e be one of its events. A possible extension of π is a pair (t, D), where D is a co-set in π and t is a transition of Σ, such that $h(D) = {}^\bullet t$ and π contains no t-labelled event with the preset D. It is a (π, e)-extension if $e^\bullet \cap D \neq \emptyset$, and e and (t, D) are not separated.*

Note that in the algorithm, and further in the paper, we do not distinguish between a possible extension (t, D) and a (virtual) t-labelled event e with the preset D, provided that this does not create an ambiguity. We will also denote by Unf_Σ^S, where $S \subseteq \text{PotExt}(Unf_\Sigma)$, the branching process obtained by adding the events from a set S of possible extensions of Unf_Σ (together with their postsets) to Unf_Σ.

When $\lhd$ is a total order, the algorithm in Figure 2 is deterministic, and thus always yields the same result for a given net system. A surprising fact is that this is also the case for an arbitrary adequate order.

Theorem 1. *If Σ is a bounded net system then the prefixes produced by two arbitrary runs of the algorithm in Figure 2 are isomorphic.*

The above result is also valid in the case when only local corresponding configurations are allowed.

For efficiency reasons, the call to $\text{PotExt}(Unf_\Sigma)$ in the body of the main loop of the algorithm in Figure 2 can be replaced by a call

$$\text{UpdatePotExt}(pe, Unf_\Sigma, e) ,$$

which finds all (π, e)-extensions and inserts such events into pe according to the $\lhd$ order on their local configurations (see [5,6,7,16]).

input : $\Sigma = (N, M_0)$ — a bounded net system
output : Unf_Σ — a finite and complete prefix of Σ's unfolding

$Unf_\Sigma \leftarrow$ the empty branching process
add instances of the places from M_0 to Unf_Σ
$pe \leftarrow$ POTEXT(Unf_Σ)
$cut\_off \leftarrow \emptyset$
while $pe \neq \emptyset$ **do**
   choose $Sl \in$ SLICES(pe)
   if $\exists e \in Sl : [e] \cap cut\_off = \emptyset$
   then
      for all $e \in Sl$ in any order refining $\lhd$ **do**
         if $[e] \cap cut\_off = \emptyset$
         then
            add e and new instances of the places from $h(e)^\bullet$ to Unf_Σ
            if e is a cut-off event of Unf_Σ **then** $cut\_off \leftarrow cut\_off \cup \{e\}$
      $pe \leftarrow$ POTEXT(Unf_Σ)
   else $pe \leftarrow pe \setminus Sl$

Fig. 3. Unfolding algorithm with slices.

Almost all the steps of the unfolding algorithm can be implemented quite efficiently. The only hard part is computing the set of possible extensions carried out on each iteration of the main loop of the algorithm (a decision version of this problem is, in fact, NP-complete, see [8,10]), and in this paper we will focus our attention on its parallelisation.

3   Unfolding with Slices

We now present a general idea behind the parallel unfolding algorithm proposed in this paper. After that we explain how it can be implemented in the case when $\lhd$ refines $\lhd_m$, and discuss further improvements aimed at reducing the amount of performed work.

When looking at the algorithm in Figure 2, one may observe that a possible way of introducing parallelism would be to process several events from pe simultaneously, rather than to insert them one-by-one. This is done in the algorithm in Figure 3 (the *slicing* algorithm), where the main loop of the algorithm has been modified in the following way. A set of events $Sl \in$ SLICES(pe), called a *slice* of the current set of possible extensions, is chosen on each iteration and processed as a whole, without taking any other events out from pe.

It is assumed that for every $Sl \in$ SLICES(pe): (i) Sl is a non-empty subset of pe; and (ii) for every $e \in Sl$, if g is an arbitrary event in the unfolding of Σ such that $f \prec g$ for some $f \in pe$, or $g \in pe \setminus Sl$, then $g \not\lhd e$.   (*)

In particular, if $f \in pe$ and $f \lhd e$ for some $e \in Sl$, then $f \in Sl$. The set $\text{SLICES}(pe)$ is chosen so that it is non-empty whenever pe is non-empty. The algorithm in Figure 2 can be seen as a special case of that based on slices, by setting $\text{SLICES}(pe) \stackrel{\mathrm{df}}{=} \{\{e\} \mid e \in \min_{\lhd} pe\}$.

Note that neither any event in $pe \setminus Sl$ nor any causal descendant of an event in pe can be less w.r.t. $\lhd$ than some event in Sl. Therefore, if $e \in Sl$ is a cut-off event then any of its corresponding configurations is in Unf_{Σ}^{Sl}, where Unf_{Σ} is the already built part of the prefix. This essentially means that the events from Sl can be inserted into the prefix *in any order* consistent with $\lhd$ (the cut-off events in Sl must be identified while doing so). Such a modification of the unfolding algorithm is correct due to the following result.

Lemma 1. *If Σ is a bounded net system then the algorithm in Figure 3 terminates with a prefix which can be produced by some run of the algorithm in Figure 2.*

Although the result given by Lemma 1 is sufficient to prove the correctness of our algorithm, a somewhat stronger result, in fact, holds.

Theorem 2. *Let $Pref'_{\Sigma}$ and $Pref''_{\Sigma}$ be the prefixes of the unfolding of a bounded net system Σ, produced by arbitrary runs of the basic and slicing algorithms respectively. Then $Pref'_{\Sigma}$ and $Pref''_{\Sigma}$ are isomorphic.*

This result, together with Theorem 1, suggests that it is possible to define the 'canonical' prefix, which is always generated by the algorithms in Figures 2 and 3. The theory of such prefixes is developed in [20], where a simpler proof of the correctness of the algorithm in Figure 3 (comparing to the one given in [12]) is provided.

Similarly as for the basic algorithm, the call to POTEXT in the body of the main loop of the slicing algorithm can be replaced by a call

$$\text{UPDATEPOTEXT}(pe, Unf_{\Sigma}, Sl)$$

which finds all events f such that f is an (Unf_{Σ}, e)-extension for some $e \in Sl$. The slicing version of the unfolding algorithm provides a basis for subsequent parallelisation, since now possible extensions are derived not from a single event, but rather from a set of events Sl; it turns out that computing $\text{UPDATEPOTEXT}(pe, Unf_{\Sigma}, Sl)$ can be effectively split into non-overlapping parts and distributed among several processors. Of course, for such scheme to work, we need to ensure that the sets in $\text{SLICES}(pe)$ do satisfy the condition (*) formulated at the beginning of this section.

3.1   The Case of an Adequate Order Refining $\lhd_m$

When $\lhd$ refines $\lhd_m$ (this is the case for $\lhd_{erv}$ and for most other orders proposed in literature), there is a simple scheme for choosing an appropriate set $\text{SLICES}(pe)$, by setting it to contain all non-empty closed w.r.t. $\lhd$ sets of events from pe whose local configurations have the minimal size. Then the condition (*) holds. Indeed, suppose that $e \in Sl \in \text{SLICES}(pe)$ and g be an event in the unfolding of Σ. If $f \prec g$ for some $f \in pe$ then it is the case that $|[g]| > |[e]|$. Hence, since $\lhd$ refines $\lhd_m$, $g \not\lhd e$. Moreover, if $g \in pe \setminus Sl$ then $g \not\lhd e$ as Sl is a closed w.r.t. $\lhd$ set of events from pe.

Notice that in order to achieve better parallelisation, it is advantageous to choose large slices, since this maximizes the number of tasks which can be performed in parallel. Therefore, we can simply choose as a slice the set of *all* events from pe, whose size of the local configuration is minimal (note that this set is closed w.r.t. $\lhd$, and, therefore, is in $\text{SLICES}(pe)$). With this scheme, we may simply consider pe as a sequence $Sl_1, Sl_2, \ldots$ of sets of events such that Sl_i contains the events whose local configurations have the size i (clearly, in each step of the algorithm there is only a finite number of non-empty Sl_i's). Thus inserting an event e into the queue is reduced to adding it into the set $Sl_{|[e]|}$, and choosing a slice in the main loop of the algorithm can be replaced by a call $Front(pe)$, returning the first non-empty set Sl_i in pe. Now all the required operations with the queue can be performed without comparisons of configurations at all.

The resulting algorithm is shown in Figure 4. It uses the strategy of finding cut-offs 'in advance' outlined in [15], i.e., it checks the cut-off criterion as soon as a new possible extension is computed. This guarantees that at the beginning of each iteration of the main loop there are no cut-off events in $Front(pe)$, and thus the restriction that the events from Sl must be processed in an order consistent with $\lhd$ can be safely left out. What is more, this strategy allows one to move the code computing the cut-off criterion into UPDATEPOTEXT — the part of the algorithm which is executed in parallel.

When $\lhd$ is a total adequate order, each time two configurations are compared w.r.t. $\lhd$, one of the events becomes a cut-off event, i.e., the number of the performed comparisons is exactly $|E_{cut}|$ (rather than $O(|E| \log |E|)$ as in former implementations), and the algorithm achieves noticeable speedup even when only one processor is available (see Section 4). One can reduce the number of comparisons even further, using the fact that the local configurations of the events which are already in the prefix are always less than those of newly computed possible extensions. But this would provide almost no speedup, since in this case the sizes of local configurations to be compared always differ, and so the comparisons are fast (we assume that the size of the local configuration is attached to an event).

3.2   Parallelising the Unfolding Algorithm

As it was already mentioned, the events in Sl can be processed in any order. This leads to a possibility of parallelising the unfolding algorithm when $|Sl| > 1$. There are only two kinds of dependencies between the events in Sl. First, the cut-off events must be handled properly; this part of the algorithm was explained in the previous section. Second, the (Unf_Σ, f)-extensions for $f \in Sl$ may have in their presets conditions produced by other events from Sl, inserted into the prefix before f. This can be dealt with by inserting all the events from Sl into Unf_Σ

input : $\Sigma = (N, M_0)$ — a bounded net system
output : Unf_Σ — a finite and complete prefix of Σ's unfolding

$Unf_\Sigma \leftarrow$ the empty branching process
$pe \leftarrow \{\perp\}$
$cut\_off \leftarrow \emptyset$
while $pe \neq \emptyset$ **do**
    $Sl \leftarrow Front(pe)$
    $pe \leftarrow pe \setminus Sl$

    for all $e \in Sl$ **do**
        add e and new instances of the places from $h(e)^\bullet$ to Unf_Σ
    for all $e \in Sl$ **do parallel**
        UPDATEPOTEXT(pe, Unf_Σ, e)
for all $e \in cut\_off$ **do**
    add e and new instances of the places from $h(e)^\bullet$ to Unf_Σ

procedure UPDATEPOTEXT(pe, Unf_Σ, e)
$Ignore \leftarrow$ the set of events added into Unf_Σ after e
$Unf_\Sigma^{[e]} \leftarrow Unf_\Sigma$ with f and $f^\bullet$ removed, for all $f \in Ignore$
for all ($Unf_\Sigma^{[e]}, e$)-extensions g **do**
    if $\exists g' \in Unf_\Sigma \cup pe$ **such that** $Mark([g]) = Mark([g'])$ and $g' \lhd g$
    then $cut\_off \leftarrow cut\_off \cup \{g\}$
    else
        $pe \leftarrow pe \cup \{g\}$
        if $\exists g' \in Unf_\Sigma \cup pe$ **such that** $Mark([g]) = Mark([g'])$ and $g \lhd g'$
        then
            $cut\_off \leftarrow cut\_off \cup \{g'\}$
            $pe \leftarrow pe \setminus \{g'\}$

Fig. 4. A parallel algorithm for unfolding Petri nets.

before the loop for computing possible extensions starts, and ignoring some of the inserted events in UPDATEPOTEXT (see Figure 4).

Since UPDATEPOTEXT is the most time-consuming part of the algorithm, this strategy usually provides quite good parallelisation. In the majority of our experiments, there were less than 200 iterations of the main loop, so the time spent on executing the sequential parts of the algorithm was negligible (this fact was confirmed by profiling the program). The first and the last few iterations usually allowed to execute 5–20 UPDATEPOTEXT's in parallel (which is already enough to provide quite good parallelism for most of the existing shared memory architectures), whereas the middle ones were highly parallel (from several hundreds up to several thousands tasks could potentially be executed in parallel). Thus the scalability of the algorithm is usually very good.

Of course, bad examples do exist, in particular those having 'long and narrow' unfoldings, e.g., the BUF100 net (see Section 4). But such examples are very rare in practice. Intuitively, they have only a small number of different partial order executions of the same length. This means that they have a very small number of conflicts and a low degree of concurrency (as for the BUF100 example, it has no conflicts at all and allows only few transitions to be executed concurrently). Our experiments show that as soon as the initial conflicts are encountered and added into the prefix being built, the number of events in $Front(pe)$ grows very quickly from step to step.

We implemented our algorithm on a shared memory architecture. It should not be hard to implement it on a distributed memory architecture, e.g., on a network of workstations. In that case, each node keeps a local copy of the built part of the prefix and synchronises it with the master node at the beginning of each iteration of the main loop. The master node is responsible for maintaining the queue of possible extensions, checking the cut-off criterion, and for distributing the work between the slaves; the slaves compute possible extensions and send them to the master.

The idea of slicing the queue also may result in developing a more efficient sequential algorithm. Indeed, we now compute possible extensions for all events in a slice and, therefore, can merge common parts of the work. The technical report [12] describes a simple improvement taking advantage of this idea.

4   Experimental Results

We used the sequential unfolding algorithm described in [15,16] as the basis for our parallel implementation and for the comparison (the two implementations share a lot of code, which makes the comparison more fair). In order to experimentally confirm the correctness of the developed parallel implementation, we checked that the produced prefixes are isomorphic to those generated by the sequential version of the algorithm.[2] For this, a special utility for 'sorting' prefixes was developed, so that if two prefixes were isomorphic then after 'sorting' they become equal. It works in the following way:

1. Separate cut-off events, pushing them to the end.
2. Sort non-cut-off events according to $\lhd_{erv}$.
3. Separate post-cut-off conditions, pushing them to the end.
4. Sort non-post-cut-off conditions according to the following ordering: $c' \lessdot c''$ if $e' \lhd_{erv} e''$, or $e' = e''$ and $h(c') \ll h(c'')$, where $\{e'\} = {}^{\bullet}c'$, $\{e''\} = {}^{\bullet}c''$, and $\ll$ is an arbitrary total order on the places of the original net system (e.g., the size-lexicographical ordering on their names).

   Note that e and e' are non-cut-off events, and that the of non-cut-off events of the prefix have already been sorted according to $\lhd_{erv}$ by this step.
5. Sort the presets of the events (including the cut-offs) according to $\lessdot$.
6. Sort the cut-off events according to the following ordering: $e' \lessdot e''$ if ${}^{\bullet}e' \lessdot_{sl} {}^{\bullet}e''$, or ${}^{\bullet}e' = {}^{\bullet}e''$ and $h(e') \ll h(e'')$, where $\lessdot_{sl}$ is the size-lexicographical order,

---

[2] Note that due to Theorem 1, two algorithms using the same adequate order produce isomorphic prefixes (provided that the implementations are correct). See also [20].

built upon $\prec$, and $\ll$ is an arbitrary total order on the set of the transitions of the original net system (e.g., the size-lexicographical ordering on their names).

Note that the conditions which can appear in the presets of the events have already been sorted by this step.

7. Sort post-cut-off conditions according to $\prec$.

Note that all events have already been sorted by this step.

8. Sort the postsets of the events (including the cut-offs) according to the $\prec$ ordering.

Note that all conditions have already been sorted by this step.

This is an enhanced version of the approach described in [15,16], the only difference is that we can no longer assume that the non-cut-off events in prefixes produced by our algorithm are sorted according to $\lhd_{erv}$, and therefore have to explicitly sort them (step 2).

Test cases. The popular set of benchmark examples, collected by J.C. Corbett ([3]), K. McMillan, S. Melzer, and S. Römer was attempted[3] (this set was also used in [5,9,10,11,13,15,16,19]). Also we used the RND(m, n), SPA(n), and SPA(m, n) series described in [15,16]. The experiments were conducted on a workstation with four $Pentium^{TM}$ III/500MHz processors and 512M RAM. The parallel algorithm was implemented using Posix threads.

The results of our experiments are summarised in table 1. The meanings of the columns are as follows (from left to right): the name of the problem; the number of places and transitions in the original net; the number of conditions, events and cut-off events in the built complete prefix; the time spent by the sequential unfolder described in [15,16]; the time spent by the parallel unfolder with different number N of working threads; the average/maximal size of a slice (this characterises the number of independent tasks which may be performed in parallel on each iteration of the main loop). Although, due to the limited number of processors, we could not exploit all the arising parallelism in our experiments, this data shows the potential scalability of the problem.

It is interesting to note that the new algorithm with only one working thread ($N = 1$) works faster than the sequential unfolder described in [15,16]. This is so because it performs much less comparisons of configurations (see Section 3.1) and due to the improvement mentioned at the end of Section 3.2.

One can see that our algorithm does not achieve linear speedup. This was a surprising discovery, since the potential parallelism (the last column in the table) is usually *very high*. Profiling shows that the program spends more than 95% of time in a function which neither acquires locks, nor performs system calls, so that the contention on locks cannot be the reason for such a slowdown. The only rational explanation we could think of is the bus contention: the mentioned function tries to find co-sets forming presets of possible extensions, exploring

---

[3] We chose only those examples from this set whose unfolding time was large enough to be of some interest.

Table 1. Experimental results.

Problem	Net		Unfolding				Time, [s]				
	$\|S\|$	$\|T\|$	$\|B\|$	$\|E\|$	$\|E_{cut}\|$	Seq	N=1	N=2	N=3	N=4	a/m $\|Sl\|$
BUF(100)	200	101	10101	5051	1	31	18	13	13	13	1.94/9
BYZ(1,4)	504	409	42276	14724	752	246	183	110	84	78	184/1536
DME(7)	470	343	9542	2737	49	7	5	2	2	1	42.67/56
DME(8)	537	392	13465	3896	64	16	12	6	5	4	56.35/72
DME(9)	604	441	18316	5337	81	33	26	14	11	10	72.00/90
DME(10)	671	490	24191	7090	100	61	49	28	21	19	89.62/110
DME(11)	738	539	31186	9185	121	105	86	50	39	35	109/132
DPH(6)	57	92	14590	7289	3407	10	7	3	3	2	65.80/135
DPH(7)	66	121	74558	37272	19207	286	211	126	97	90	235/538
ELEV(4)	736	1939	32354	16935	7337	73	42	25	19	17	310/1456
FTP(1)	176	529	178085	89046	35197	2820	1609	975	761	714	1224/3918
FURN(3)	53	99	30820	18563	12207	30	15	9	7	5	132/510
GASNQ(4)	258	465	15928	7965	2876	19	11	6	5	4	145/392
GASNQ(5)	428	841	100527	50265	18751	884	553	334	259	243	716/2000
GASQ(4)	1428	2705	19864	9933	4060	30	18	11	7	6	184/720
KEY(3)	129	133	13941	6968	2911	10	7	4	3	2	62.42/148
KEY(4)	164	174	135914	67954	32049	935	806	485	379	354	466/1311
MMGT(3)	122	172	11575	5841	2529	6	4	2	1	1	138/423
MMGT(4)	158	232	92940	46902	20957	556	339	205	159	150	837/2752
Q(1)	163	194	16123	8417	1188	41	25	15	11	10	103/412
RW(12)	63	313	98378	49177	45069	15	6	3	2	2	316/924
SYNC(3)	106	270	28138	15401	5210	79	62	36	27	24	124/369
RND(5,14)	70	570	802907	185094	156417	546	471	284	225	215	585/1971
RND(5,15)	75	575	842181	195228	163722	665	567	345	274	259	606/1971
RND(5,16)	80	580	886158	206265	171957	787	674	413	329	312	624/2013
RND(5,17)	85	585	987605	229284	191576	942	822	503	404	382	608/2066
RND(5,18)	90	590	1025166	239069	198524	1091	956	584	469	448	614/2114
RND(10,4)	40	540	2344821	252320	237000	216	137	80	61	55	730/2435
RND(10,5)	50	550	2485903	271083	250600	354	236	140	108	101	759/2413
RND(10,6)	60	560	2535070	280560	255010	526	360	216	168	159	751/2345
RND(10,7)	70	570	2537646	285323	254767	724	510	306	242	229	711/2323
RND(10,8)	80	580	2534970	289550	254000	953	681	411	327	312	790/2125
RND(15,2)	30	530	1836868	135307	128358	70	17	9	6	5	695/2046
RND(15,3)	45	545	3750719	271074	255560	270	128	74	56	49	913/2147
RND(15,4)	60	560	3787575	280560	257515	487	277	162	128	117	886/2333
RND(15,5)	75	575	3795090	288075	257515	776	480	286	228	214	826/2488
RND(20,2)	40	540	4744587	256197	245750	176	42	21	14	11	871/2808
RND(20,3)	60	560	5040080	280560	260020	447	203	118	90	82	856/2262
RND(20,4)	80	580	5050100	290580	260020	825	456	271	213	201	873/2535
SPA(7)	167	241	52516	18712	9937	81	48	28	21	19	214/784
SPA(8)	190	385	216772	76181	45774	1005	603	362	280	264	633/2612
SPA(9)	213	657	920270	320582	209449	13512	8066	4854	3750	3537	2268/9469
SPA(2,3)	144	161	15690	5682	2512	8	4	2	2	1	85.68/299
SPA(2,4)	190	385	253219	88944	52826	1412	872	524	406	382	803/3138
SPA(3,2)	144	161	15690	5682	2512	8	4	2	2	1	85.68/299
SPA(3,3)	213	657	1142214	398850	256600	22011	13565	8171	6317	5943	2003/11807

the build part of the prefix. It is a fairly large pointer-linked structure, and the processors have to intensively access the memory in a quite unsystematic way, so that the processors' caches often have to redirect the access to the RAM. Therefore, the processors are forced to contend for the bus, and the program slows down. Since this explanation might seem superficial, we decided to establish that bus contention does reveal itself in practice, and the following experiment was performed. Several processors intensively read random locations in a large array and performed some fake computation with the fetched values. The total number of fetches was fixed and evenly distributed among them. In the absence of bus contention, the time spent by such a program would decrease linearly in the number of used processors, but we observed the degradation of speed similar to that shown by our unfolding algorithm. We hope that future generations of hardware will alleviate this problem, e.g., by increasing the bus frequency or by introducing a separate bus for each processor.

5 Conclusions

Experimental results indicate that the algorithm we proposed in this paper can achieve significant speedups, at least in theory. But this is still not enough for practical size problems, because the number of processors in shared memory multiprocessors is usually quite small. Therefore, generating unfoldings is still a bottleneck for the unfolding based verification of Petri nets. Our future research will aim at developing an effective implementation of this algorithm for the distributed-memory or hybrid architecture. Another promising area is the approach allowing non-local correspondent configurations, proposed in [9]. It sometimes allows to significantly reduce the size of complete prefixes. We plan to investigate if this idea can be efficiently implemented.

Acknowledgements. This research was supported by an ORS Awards Scheme grant ORS/C20/4 and by an EPSRC grant GR/M99293. The financial support of Academy of Finland (Projects 43963, 47754) and Foundation for Technology (Tekniikan Edistämissäätiö) is also gratefully acknowledged.

References

1. E. M. Clarke, E. A. Emerson and A. P. Sistla: Automatic Verification of Finite-state Concurrent Systems Using Temporal Logic Specifications. *ACM TOPLAS* 8 (1986) 244–263.
2. E. M. Clarke, O. Grumberg, and D. Peled: *Model Checking*. MIT Press (1999).
3. J. C. Corbett: *Evaluating Deadlock Detection Methods*. University of Hawaii at Manoa (1994).
4. J. Engelfriet: Branching processes of Petri Nets. *Acta Informatica* 28 (1991) 575–591.
5. J. Esparza and S. Römer: An Unfolding Algorithm for Synchronous Products of Transition Systems. Proc. of *CONCUR'99*, Springer-Verlag, Lecture Notes in Computer Science 1664 (1999) 2–20.

6. J. Esparza, S. Römer and W. Vogler: An Improvement of McMillan's Unfolding Algorithm. Proc. of *TACAS'96*, Margaria T., Steffen B. (Eds.). Springer-Verlag, Lecture Notes in Computer Science 1055 (1996) 87–106.

7. J. Esparza, S. Römer and W. Vogler: An Improvement of McMillan's Unfolding Algorithm. *Formal Methods in System Design* (2001) to appear.

8. J. Esparza and C. Schröter: Reachability Analysis Using Net Unfoldings. Proc. of *Workshop of Concurrency, Specification & Programming 2000 (CS&P'2000)*, H. D. Burkhard, L. Czaja, A. Skowron, and P. Starke, (Eds.). Informatik-Bericht 140, vol. 2. Humboldt-Universitat zu Berlin (2000) 255–270.

9. K. Heljanko: Minimizing Finite Complete Prefixes. Proc. of *Workshop Concurrency, Specification and Programming 1999 (CS&P'99)*, (1999) 83–95.

10. K. Heljanko: Deadlock and Reachability Checking with Finite Complete Prefixes. Technical Report A56, Laboratory for Theoretical Computer Science, Helsinki University of Technology, Espoo, Finland (1999).

11. K. Heljanko: Using Logic Programs with Stable Model Semantics to Solve Deadlock and Reachability Problems for 1-Safe Petri Nets. *Fundamentae Informaticae* 37(3) (1999) 247–268.

12. K. Heljanko, V. Khomenko and M. Koutny: Parallelisation of the Petri Net Unfolding Algorithm. Technical Report CS-TR-733, Department of Computing Science, University of Newcastle (2001).

13. V. Khomenko and M. Koutny: Verification of Bounded Petri Nets Using Integer Programming. Technical Report CS-TR-711, Department of Computing Science, University of Newcastle (2000).

14. V. Khomenko and M. Koutny: LP Deadlock Checking Using Partial Order Dependencies. Proc. of *CONCUR'2000*, Palamidessi C. (Ed.). Springer-Verlag, Lecture Notes in Computer Science 1877 (2000) 410–425.

15. V. Khomenko and M. Koutny: An Efficient Algorithm for Unfolding Petri Nets. Technical Report CS-TR-726, Department of Computing Science, University of Newcastle (2001).

16. V. Khomenko and M. Koutny: Towards An Efficient Algorithm for Unfolding Petri Nets. Proc. of *CONCUR'2001*, Larsen P.G., Nielsen M. (Eds.). Springer-Verlag, Lecture Notes in Computer Science 2154 (2001) 366–380.

17. K. L. McMillan: Using Unfoldings to Avoid State Explosion Problem in the Verification of Asynchronous Circuits. Proc. of *4th CAV*, Springer-Verlag, Lecture Notes in Computer Science 663 (1992) 164–174.

18. K. L. McMillan: *Symbolic Model Checking*. PhD thesis, CMU-CS-92-131 (1992).

19. S. Melzer and S. Römer: Deadlock Checking Using Net Unfoldings. Proc. of *Computer Aided Verification (CAV'97)*, O. Grumberg (Ed.). Springer-Verlag, Lecture Notes in Computer Science 1254 (1997) 352–363.

20. W. Vogler, V. Khomenko, and M. Koutny: Canonical Prefixes of Petri Net Unfoldings. Technical Report CS-TR-741, Department of Computing Science, University of Newcastle (2001).

Black Box Unfolding with Local First Search

Sebastien Bornot, Remi Morin, Peter Niebert, and Sarah Zennou

Laboratoire d'Informatique Fondamentale de Marseille (LIF)
Université de Provence – CMI
39, rue Joliot-Curie / F-13453 Marseille Cedex 13
[bornot,morin,niebert,zennou]@cmi.univ-mrs.fr

Abstract. McMillan's unfolding approach to the reachability problem in 1-safe Petri nets and its later improvements by Esparza-Römer-Vogler have proven in practice as a very effective method to avoid state-explosion. This method computes a *complete finite prefix* of the infinite branching process of a net. On the other hand, the Local First Search approach (LFS) was recently introduced as a new partial order reduction technique which characterizes a restricted subset of configurations that need to be explored to check *local properties*. In this paper we amalgamate the two approaches: We combine the reduction criterion of LFS with the notions of an adequate order and cutoff events essential to the unfolding approach. As a result, our new LFS method computes a reduced transition system without the problem of state duplication (present in the original LFS). Since it works for any transition system with an independence relation, this *black box partial unfolding* remains more general than the unfolding of Petri nets. Experiments show that the combination gives improved reductions compared to the original LFS.

1 Introduction

Model checking as an automatic method for proving simple system properties or finding witness executions of faulty systems suffers from the well known state explosion problem: Typically, the number of states explored by naive algorithms is exponential in the size of the system description, so that often this automatic approach is limited to very small systems. However, the explosion of the number of states is typically due to redundancies in the exploration of the whole global state space and in the interleaving semantics of parallel systems. Both can be circumvented in certain cases, in particular by means of *partial order methods*. There are two prominent approaches:

- *Partial order reduction techniques* (see e.g. [God96,Pel93,Val89]), which try to exploit "diamond" properties to make savings in verification. They are based on a notion of equivalent executions, called Mazurkiewicz traces [DR95], and aim to cut redundant branches (and whole sub state spaces). Partial order reduction techniques have been applied with success notably to deadlock detection and model checking of certain (equivalence robust) linear time temporal properties [Pel93].

J.-P. Katoen and P. Stevens (Eds.): TACAS 2002, LNCS 2280, pp. 386–400, 2002.
© Springer-Verlag Berlin Heidelberg 2002

– *Unfolding based methods* (see e.g. [McM92,ERV96,ER99]): Rather than partially exploring an interleaving transition system, these methods directly construct partial order representations of executions by means of event structures [NPW81] or, equivalently, occurrence nets [Eng91]. Instead of computing successor states, the unfolding approach is based on computing possible event extensions. Using an *adequate order* among events, a *complete finite prefix* of the set of all events is defined and can be computed.

Recently, a new partial order reduction technique has been introduced specifically for the verification of local properties. Such properties depend on a single component of the system so that one should be able to identify equivalent classes of global states and tackle the state explosion while checking their possible reachability. The *Local First Search* approach [NHZL01] gives a combinatorial criterion that shows how to explore a reduced and yet locally complete subset of states in an efficient way. Based on observations linked to the Strahler number of trees [Str52], this new technique characterizes concurrent executions which may be cut off from the exploration while checking *any* local property.

While the first practical experiments indicate a very strong reduction potential for Local First Search in the detection of counter-examples (finding paths leading to local states), the approach of the method to take a part of the past into account when comparing states leads to a costly need to explore certain states more than once (state duplication problem). In practice, this means that the original LFS cannot be used to prove the *absence* of a state, because state copying blows up the explored state space more than the reduction criterion reduces it.

In this paper, we solve the state duplication problem that appears in the original LFS method. Motivated by a strong relationship between Mazurkiewicz traces and event structures [Bed87,NW95], we apply the technique of adequate orders from event structures to trace systems in order to define and construct a *locally complete finite unfolding*.

An essential technical difference between our approach and the classical computation of the complete finite prefix is that the latter uses an event structure as essential data structure whereas the LFS based approach computes on configurations (traces). More precisely, we define a subset of configurations that respect the LFS criterion (which contains all prime configurations). The use of an adequate order [ERV96] gives us an additional *cutoff* criterion that allows us to avoid multiple explorations of the same state.

Moreover, the complicated computation of *possible extensions* for the construction of the complete finite prefix (see [KK01] for an extended discussion) is fully avoided by our approach, at the price of a bigger result (but, as explained in [NHZL01], not necessarily higher computational cost). In addition, it relies solely on abstract characteristics of concurrency within the system, not on a particular representation like Petri nets. In short, it allows *black box unfolding*.

The paper is structured as follows: In Section 2, we introduce the technical framework for the presentation, notably Mazurkiewicz traces, asynchronous transition systems and an unfolding semantics of asynchronous transition systems into trace systems. In Section 3, we formalize the notion of a local property in the context of asynchronous transition systems. In Section 4, we rephrase the main theorem of [NHZL01] in terms of traces and give a summary of its application to the verification of local properties. The main contribution is in Section 5, the development of a *locally complete finite subsystem* and the proof of its completeness for the local reachability problem. In Section 6, we give an actual algorithm for the computation of the locally complete finite subsystem and discuss first experimental results. In Section 7, we conclude and give an outlook for the continuation of this line of research.

2   Basics

In this section, we develop the formal framework for the description of our method.

The description of parallelism in this work is based on Mazurkiewicz trace theory [DR95], of which we recall the notions important to our work. The framework is thus kept as a level of generality so as to apply to a wide variety of system descriptions, not just Petri nets or products of automata. For further motivating examples of this choice, see [NHZL01].

Traces and partial orders. In this paper, we fix a finite alphabet Σ together with an *independence relation* $\| \subseteq \Sigma \times \Sigma$ which is symmetric and irreflexive. Intuitively, this relation represents concurrency between actions occurring on distinct processes in a distributed system. The *trace equivalence* associated to the independence alphabet $(\Sigma, \|)$ is the least congruence $\sim$ over Σ^* such that $ab \sim ba$ for any pair of independent actions $a \| b$. A *trace* $[u]$ is the equivalence class of a word $u \in \Sigma^*$. We denote by $\mathbb{M}(\Sigma, \|)$ the set of all traces w.r.t. $(\Sigma, \|)$. Traces are partially ordered according to the *prefix relation* defined as follows: We put $[u] \preccurlyeq [v]$ whenever there exists a word $z \in \Sigma^*$ such that $u.z \sim v$.

It is a basic observation of Mazurkiewicz trace theory that traces can be viewed as partial orders of events labelled by actions in Σ. We shall here often focus on the number of maximal events in a trace seen as a labelled partial order. For simplification, we can formalize this as follows:

Definition 1. *For a trace* $[w] \in \mathbb{M}(\Sigma, \|)$, *the subset of last actions* $Last([w])$ *consists of all actions that can appear at the end of some sequential view of* $[w]$; *i.e.* $Last([w]) = \{a \in \Sigma \mid \exists v \in \Sigma^*, v.a \in [w]\}$. *Further, the* span $\#_{Last}([w])$ *is the number of last actions of* $[w]$: $\#_{Last}([w]) = |Last([w])|$.

It is clear that $Last([w])$ consists of pairwise independent actions. Now a key notion for our development concerns *prime traces*. The latter admit a single maximal event.

Definition 2. *A trace* $[w]$ *with* $\#_{Last}([w]) = 1$ *is a* prime trace.

In other words, a trace $[w]$ is prime if, and only if, for all words v_1, v_2 and all actions a_1 and a_2, $v_1.a_1 \sim w \sim v_2.a_2$ implies $a_1 = a_2$.

Asynchronous transition systems. A transition system is a triple $T = (S, \rightarrow, s_0)$ with S a set of states, $s_0 \in S$ the initial state, and $\rightarrow \subseteq S \times \Sigma \times S$ a transition relation. In this paper, we require that transition systems are *deterministic*[1], i.e. $\rightarrow$ is a partial function from $S \times \Sigma$ to S. The *language* $L(T)$ of execution sequences of a transition system T is the set of words $w = a_1 a_2 \ldots a_n$ of Σ^* such that there exist states $s_i \in S$, $i = 0, \ldots, n$ such that $s_0 \xrightarrow{a_1} s_1 \xrightarrow{a_1} \ldots \xrightarrow{a_n} s_n$. Due to determinism, for any execution sequence $w = a_1 a_2 \ldots a_n \in L(T)$ there exists a unique state $s \in S$ such that $s_0 \xrightarrow{a_1} s_1 \xrightarrow{a_1} \ldots \xrightarrow{a_n} s_n = s$. We refer to this state as $\sigma(w)$. Of course, there may be several paths leading to the same state, so $\sigma(u) = \sigma(v)$ does not imply $u = v$.

When modelling concurrent machines by transition systems with independence relations, some *diamond properties* frequently appear [Bed87,God96, Shi85]:

Definition 3. *A transition system T is called* asynchronous[2] *w.r.t. the independence alphabet $(\Sigma, \|)$ if for all pairs of independent actions $a \| b$,*

ID: $s \xrightarrow{a} s_1 \xrightarrow{b} s_2$ *implies* $s \xrightarrow{b} s_1' \xrightarrow{a} s_2$ *for some state* s_1' [Independent Diamond]

FD: $s \xrightarrow{a} s_1$ *and* $s \xrightarrow{b} s_1'$ *implies* $s_1 \xrightarrow{b} s_2$ *for some state* s_2 [Forward Diamond]

Axioms ID and FD formalise an intuitive notion of independence: If two independent actions can occur one immediately after the other then they can occur in the opposite order (ID); moreover if two independent actions can occur in a common state, the occurrence of one of them cannot rule out the other one (FD). We remark also that if $u \in L(T)$ and $u \sim u'$ then $u' \in L(T)$ and $\sigma(u) = \sigma(u')$. Therefore we extend the map σ from words in $L(T)$ to the traces in $L(T)/\sim$ as follows: For all $u \in L(T)$, we denote by $\sigma([u])$ the state $\sigma(u)$.

Many examples of independence relations in various modeling frameworks exist: In process algebras, dependency results from communication over shared channels; in Petri nets, transitions sharing places in the presets or postsets may be dependent. In [Pel93], it is pointed out that independence (in use for partial order reduction) need not have concurrency as only source. For instance, two operations "X:=X+1" and "X:=X+2" do also satisfy the diamond properties and can hence be considered independent, although they touch the same variable. In contrast, "X:=X+1" and "X:=X*2" will not satisfy these properties.

Unfoldings. Typically, an asynchronous transition system T is an abstraction for a 1-safe Petri net or a synchronized product of automata; it describes the

---

[1] By introducing new action names, we can transform a non-deterministic system into a deterministic one. Such a transformation doesn't modify the properties (mainly the reachability problem) we are interested in.

[2] This naming in the literature is a potential source of confusion: Asynchronous here refers to the independent progress of the components of a parallel system, not to the communication discipline. In fact, our examples use synchronous communication.

behaviour and the global states (or markings) reached by its components. Although it has usually finitely many states, one aims at avoiding the exploration of all these states or all its execution sequences. For this, we shall construct a *representative part* of its unfolding — which is also called trace system.

Definition 4 (Trace system). *Let $T = (S, \rightarrow, s_0)$ be an asynchronous transition system w.r.t. $(\Sigma, \|)$. Then the* trace system *of T is the transition system $\mathcal{TS}(T)$ whose states are the traces associated to an execution sequence, with the empty trace $[\varepsilon]$ as initial state and such that the transition relation is $\rightarrow = \{([w], a, [w.a]) \mid w.a \in L(T)\}$.*

Thus, we have $[u] \xrightarrow{a} [v]$ in $\mathcal{TS}(T)$ iff $u.a$ is an execution sequence of T and $u.a \sim v$. It follows that $\mathcal{TS}(T)$ is an acyclic (deterministic) transition system which is asynchronous w.r.t. $(\Sigma, \|)$. Furthermore $L(T) = L(\mathcal{TS}(T))$ and the unfolding of $\mathcal{TS}(T)$ is $\mathcal{TS}(T)$ itself. We observe also that the map σ from the traces in $L(T)/\sim$ to the states S induces a homomorphism from $\mathcal{TS}(T)$ to T, since $[u] \xrightarrow{a} [v]$ in $\mathcal{TS}(T)$ implies $\sigma(u) \xrightarrow{a} \sigma(v)$ in T. This map is surjective if T contains no unreachable states. The fact that the original transition system T is a homomorphic image of its trace system justifies the use of the trace system as a semantic model.

In [Bed87], the concurrent executions of an asynchronous transition system are described by a prime event structure. Generalizing the unfolding of 1-safe nets in occurrence nets [NPW81,Eng91], there is a one-to-one correspondence between the set of traces $L(T)/\sim$ and the finite configurations of the associated prime event structure. In this view, $\mathcal{TS}(T)$ appears as an abstract representation of the configuration structure of T. A key observation in [Bed87, chap. 5] is that one can identify the events of the underlying unfolding as the configurations having a single predecessor, that is, the prime traces. For this reason, prime traces are good candidates to check *local properties*, as explained in the next section.

3 Local Properties

In this section, we consider an asynchronous transition system $T = (S, \rightarrow, s_0)$ w.r.t. the independence alphabet $(\Sigma, \|)$.

Definition 5. *We say that $(\Sigma, \|)$ has* parallel degree *m if m is the maximal number of pairwise independent actions in Σ, i.e.*
$$m = \max\{|A| \mid A \subseteq \Sigma \text{ and } a, b \in A, a \neq b \implies a \| b\}.$$

For Petri nets, m corresponds to the maximal number of transitions that can be fired concurrently. In a system of processes, m is an upper bound for the number of sequential components that can work in parallel.

Definition 6 (Local properties). *For a given set $P \subseteq S$ (called* property*), the set of* visible actions *$V_P \subseteq \Sigma$ is the set of all actions $a \in \Sigma$ such that there* *exist* $s_1, s_2 \in S$ *with* $(s_1, a, s_2) \in \rightarrow$ *and either* $s_1 \in P$ *and* $s_2 \notin P$, *or* $s_2 \in P$ *and* $s_1 \notin P$.

A *property* P *has* parallel degree m *if the restricted independence alphabet* $(V_P, \| \cap (V_P \times V_P))$ *has parallel degree* m. *A property is called* local *if it has parallel degree* 1.

The idea of visible actions [Pel93] is that of actions that may affect a property of interest. The naming of local properties is due to the typical case of properties of one process in a network: These are properties that depend only on the local state of the process in question, and this state only changes by transitions involving this process, thus mutually dependent transitions.

Proposition 1. *A property* $P \subseteq S$ *of parallel degree* m *is reachable (i.e. there exists* $[u]$ *such that* $\sigma([u]) \in P$) *if, and only if, there exists an execution sequence* $w = a_1 \ldots a_k$ *leading to a state* $\sigma(w) \in P$ *with* $\#_{Last}([w]) \leqslant m$, *where all last actions in the trace* $[w]$ *are visible actions.*

Proof. Consider an execution sequence $w = a_1 \ldots a_n$ with $s_0 \xrightarrow{a_1} s_1 \xrightarrow{a_2} \ldots \xrightarrow{a_n} s_n$, $s_n \in P$ and moreover $|w|$ *minimal*, i.e. $|w| \leqslant |w'|$ for any other sequence w' leading to a state $s' \in P$. Then each last action of $[w]$ is a *visible* action. Since these actions are pairwise independent, $\#_{Last}([w])$ is at most equal to the parallel degree of P. ∎

In the sequel, we aim at checking whether a given *local* property is reachable in T. Then, Proposition 1 ensures that we need only to explore the *prime* traces $[w]$ of the unfolding $\mathcal{TS}(T)$ and check whether $\sigma([w]) \in P$. Since there are in general infinitely many prime traces, we will need a criterion to explore a finite part of the unfolding, only. In the next section, we describe an efficient strategy to construct prime traces.

4   Local First Search

Since traces are equivalence classes of sequential executions, there are generally several ways to reach the state $\sigma([w])$ of a trace $[w]$. Among all the sequential views $v \in [w]$, the LFS approach tries to minimize the number of last actions seen along v. More formally, the *beam* of a word $v = a_1 \ldots a_k \in \Sigma^*$ is the maximal span $\#_{Last}([u])$ among the traces $[u] = [a_1 \ldots a_j]$ with $j \leqslant k$. Then the *LFS-number* of a trace $[w]$ is the minimal beam of $v \in [w]$. Equivalently, we have:

Definition 7 (LFS-number). *The* LFS-number *of a trace* $[w]$ *is the least number* l *such that there exists a representative* $v = a_1 \ldots a_k \in [w]$ *such that for each* $1 \leqslant j \leqslant k$ *we have* $\#_{Last}([a_1 \ldots a_j]) \leqslant l$.

As explained above, we aim at exploring prime traces. For this, the LFS approach exhibits an upper bound for the LFS-numbers of prime traces. This is based on a combinatorial aspect of the independence alphabet. For any action

$c \in \Sigma$, Σ_c denotes the subset of actions $b \in \Sigma$ which are dependent with c. Then the *communication degree of* $(\Sigma, \|)$ is the maximal parallel degree of the restricted independence alphabet $(\Sigma_c, \| \cap (\Sigma_c \times \Sigma_c))$ when $c \in \Sigma$. In other words:

Definition 8. *The* communication degree *of* $(\Sigma, \|)$ *is the maximal number n of pairwise independent actions which all depend on a common action, i.e.* $n = \max\{|B| \mid B \subseteq \Sigma, \exists c \in \Sigma, (\forall b \in B, \ c \not\| b) \} \ and \ (\forall b, b' \in B, b \neq b' \implies b \| b')\}$.

Obviously the communication degree n is smaller than the parallel degree m of $(\Sigma, \|)$. Actually, in many formalisms for concurrent systems, we observe that n tends to be small compared to m. For instance, many process algebras restrict communication to pairs of *send* and *receive* actions, leading to a communication degree 2. This bound holds for message sequence charts as well. The dependency relations resulting from Petri-nets are bounded by the number of presets and postsets of transitions, which are often very small compared to the size of the entire net.

The main technical result of [NHZL01] can be summarized as follows:

Theorem 1 (LFS-bound). *For all* prime *traces* $[w] \in \mathrm{M}(\Sigma, \|)$, *the LFS-number of $[w]$ is at most* $\lfloor (n-1) \log_n(m) \rfloor + 1$, *where m and n are respectively the parallel degree and the communication degree of* $(\Sigma, \|)$.

We will refer to $\lfloor (n-1) \log_n(m) \rfloor + 1$ as the *LFS-bound* of $(\Sigma, \|)$. Note that for the case of $n = 2$, the LFS-bound simplifies to $\lfloor \log_2(m) \rfloor + 1$ which compares favorably to the naive upper bound m.

Let us discuss the meaning of this theorem concerning the trace system of an asynchronous transition system and how this was exploited in [NHZL01] for the original version of local first search.

The LFS-number yields a partition of the states in the trace system, from 0 (for $[\varepsilon]$) potentially up to m. Then the theorem implies that the prime traces are reachable from the initial state via paths avoiding traces with a span exceeding the LFS-bound, and thus by traces with LFS-number smaller than this bound. On the other hand, *local properties* can be analyzed with attention restricted to prime traces.

The original LFS then exploited these facts via the construction of an extended transition system with states (s, M), where s is a state of the original transition system and $M \subseteq \Sigma$ is the subset of last actions of a trace $[w]$ leading to s. However, the original LFS may have to explore a single state s several times (with different sets of last actions). While the experiments showed that the strategy LFS gives good results if a state searched for exists with a low LFS-number, the construction of the state space up to the LFS-bound typically produced state spaces exceeding the size of the original transition system, i.e. with growing LFS-number the size of the class of states grows quickly and the state doubling phenomenon produces more overhead than can be possibly avoided by the reduction. The aim of this work is to combine notions from LFS with notions known from McMillan unfoldings to overcome this state copying problem.

5 Locally Complete Finite Subsystem of a Trace System

Similar to the *complete finite prefix* of the maximal branching process of a Petri net, we now want to define a subsystem of the trace system with the following properties:

- It should be computable and be no bigger than the state space of the original asynchronous transition system.
- It should be complete in the sense that it preserves reachability of local properties with respect to the unreduced trace system.
- It should not contain traces with LFS-number exceeding the LFS-bound.

The construction is modular and relies on three steps:

- The first step is to define a reduced trace system according to some reduction strategy, that preserves prime traces and thus reachability of local properties. In the present work, we will use the LFS-bound for this purpose but other reductions may work as well. The resulting reduced trace system is typically still infinite.
- The definition of an *adequate order* on the states of the (reduced) trace system that leads the construction of a finite prefix of the reduced trace system (in this particular order).
- The definition of a *cutoff criterion*, which will eliminate states explored "before" according to the adequate order.

In the rest of this paper, we consider a finite asynchronous transition system $T = (S, \rightarrow, s_0)$.

Definition 9. *A (reachable) subsystem of the trace system $\mathcal{TS}(T)$ is a subset of traces $R \subseteq L(T)/\sim$ such that for every trace $[w] \in R$ there exists a (predecessor) trace $[v] \in R$ with $[w] = [v.a]$ for some $a \in \Sigma$.*

In other words, the restriction of the trace system $\mathcal{TS}(T)$ to a subsystem R provides us with a new transition system whose states are reachable from the initial empty trace. Since we want to avoid a complete construction of $\mathcal{TS}(T)$ we will actually build such a subsystem only. However, this subsystem must keep enough information in order to check local properties.

Definition 10. *A subsystem R is* locally complete *if for all local properties P and for all traces $[w] \in L(T)/\sim$ such that $\sigma([w]) \in P$ there exists $[w'] \in R$ such that $\sigma([w']) \in P$.*

Thus, given a locally complete subsystem R, a local property P is reachable in the asynchronous transition system T if, and only if, there is a trace $[w] \in R$ that satisfies P, i.e. $\sigma([w]) \in P$. Therefore, what we need essentially is to build a *finite* and locally complete subsystem of the unfolding $\mathcal{TS}(T)$.

A basic method to stop the construction of traces while exploring a trace system is to fix a set F of "forbidden" traces. Clearly, for any subset $F \subseteq \mathbb{M}(\Sigma, \|)$, there exists a *largest* subsystem R_F that contains no trace of F, i.e.

$R_F \cap F = \emptyset$. This subsystem is called *the subsystem that forbids F*. Note, that conceptually forbidding traces can be done hierarchically, because forbidding $F' \subseteq R_F$ in R_F can be understood to yield the subsystem $R_{F \cup F'}$.

Definition 11. *We call* LFS-excessive *any trace whose LFS-number is greater than the LFS-bound of* $(\Sigma, \|)$. *The* LFS-subsystem *of* $\mathcal{TS}(T)$ *is the subset of all traces that are not LFS-excessive.*

One can easily show that the subsystem R_{LFS} that forbids the set LFS-excessive traces is precisely the *LFS-subsystem* of $\mathcal{TS}(T)$.

Due to Theorem 1, *the LFS-subsystem of* $\mathcal{TS}(T)$ *contains all prime traces*. It is therefore locally complete (Prop. 1). However it is in general still infinite. So we need to forbid some more traces to get a finite subsystem. A key ingredient we borrow from the theory of Petri nets unfoldings is that of an adequate order [ERV96] on traces:

Definition 12 (Adequate order). *A partial order* $\sqsubseteq$ *on the whole set of traces* $\mathbb{M}(\Sigma, \|)$ *is called* adequate *if*

(Ad$_1$) *it is well-founded;*
(Ad$_2$) *it refines the prefix order, i.e.* $[u] \preccurlyeq [v]$ *implies* $[u] \sqsubseteq [v]$;
(Ad$_3$) *it is a right congruence, i.e.* $[u] \sqsubseteq [v]$ *implies* $[u.z] \sqsubseteq [v.z]$ *for any* $z \in \Sigma^\star$.

Noteworthy, the last condition implies that if $[u] \sqsubset [v]$ then $[u.z] \sqsubset [v.z]$ for any word $z \in \Sigma^\star$. We will use some adequate order to specify how traces are explored and which additional traces should be forbidden. We will discuss some examples of adequate orders in the next section.

Definition 13 (Cutoff trace with respect to a subsystem). *Given an adequate order* $\sqsubseteq$ *on traces and a subsystem* R, *we say that a trace* $[v] \in R$ *is a* cutoff trace with respect to R *if there exists a trace* $[u] \in R$ *such that* $[u] \sqsubset [v]$ *and* $\sigma(u) = \sigma(v)$.

Now we can state our main theorem.

Theorem 2. *For all adequate orders, the subsystem* R *that forbids both the LFS-excessive traces and the cutoff traces with respect to the LFS-subsystem, is locally complete and finite.*

Proof. We first show by contradiction that R is locally complete. Let P be a local property of T. Let $[w] \in L(T)/\sim$ be a trace such that $\sigma([w]) \in P$ but for all traces $[w']$ in the subsystem R it holds that $\sigma([w']) \notin P$. Since $\sqsubseteq$ is well-founded (Ad$_1$), we can choose $[w]$ to be $\sqsubseteq$-minimal among the traces $[v]$ with $\sigma([v]) \in P$.

We observe first that $[w]$ is a prime trace. Otherwise we would have $v_1.a_1 \sim w \sim v_2.a_2$ with $a_1 \| a_2$. Since P is local, either a_1 or a_2 is invisible for P and $[v_1]$ or $[v_2]$ satisfies P. Since $\sqsubseteq$ refines the prefix order of traces (Ad$_2$), $[w]$ would not be $\sqsubseteq$-minimal.

Consequently, $[w]$ is a trace of the LFS-subsystem of T (Theorem 1). The reason for it not to make part of the subsystem R must thus rely on an ancestor

$[v]$ of $[w]$ in the LFS-subsystem that is a cutoff trace. So $[w] = [v.v']$. The fact that $[v]$ is a cutoff trace implies the existence of some trace $[u] \sqsubset [v]$ in the LFS-subsystem with $\sigma(u) = \sigma(v)$. Consequently, $[u.v'] \in L(T)/\sim$ and Ad_3 yields $[u.v'] \sqsubset [v.v']$. Since $\sigma(u.v') = \sigma(v.v') = \sigma(w)$, $[u.v']$ satisfies P and $[u.v'] \sqsubset [w]$. This contradicts the assumption that $[w]$ is $\sqsubseteq$-minimal.

We now prove that R is finite. Consider the subsystem R' that consists of all traces $[u]$ with $|u| \leqslant |S|$. Clearly R' is finite. We need just to check that $R \subseteq R'$, by contradiction. Assume $[u] \in R \setminus R'$. For all linear extensions $a_1 \ldots a_k \in [u]$, we have $\sigma(a_1 \ldots a_i) = \sigma(a_1 \ldots a_j)$ for some $1 \leqslant i < j \leqslant k$ because $k > |S|$. Since R forbids cutoff traces, $[u]$ is not reachable in R.   ∎

Corollary 1. *If the adequate order $\sqsubseteq$ is total then $|R| \leqslant |S|$.*

Proof. By contradiction, assume $|R| > |S|$. Then there are two distinct traces $[u], [v] \in R$ such that $\sigma(u) = \sigma(v)$. We may assume $[u] \sqsubset [v]$ because $\sqsubseteq$ is total. Then $[v]$ is a cutoff trace hence $[v] \notin R$.   ∎

6   Algorithmics

In this section, we show how to apply Theorem 2 to obtain a reachability algorithm for local properties.

Theorem 2 relies on an adequate order under which it gives a definition of a locally complete finite subsystem of the trace system, but it does not immediately give an algorithm for computing this subsystem. The crucial step towards an algorithm is the choice of an adequate order with good algorithmic properties. Indeed, so far we did not even require the adequate order to be decidable.

The literature proposes a number of adequate orders that have been used in implementations of McMillan's unfolding method:

1. McMillan's original order was induced by $|w|$, the "number of events" in a trace $[w]$. Let us call this order of $\mathsf{M}(\Sigma, \|)$ the *length order*. Its advantage is its simplicity and low (logarithmic) complexity and that it corresponds closely to breadth first search.
2. Of course, the prefix order itself also is adequate, as is mentioned in some sources. It is however of no practical interest.
3. In [ERV96], an adequate order based on a lexicographic order on the sequences of sets of labels of the Foata normal form of traces was proposed. An important aspect of this order is that it is total. The advantage of a total order is that it results in a subsystem with at most one trace for each state of the unreduced transition system (Corollary 1). This is in contrast to the simpler order of McMillan, which can result in subsystems exponentially larger than the transition system. The price to be paid is that the order based on Foata normal form takes a worst case linear time effort to compute.
4. In [ER99], another *total* adequate order was proposed that – while also having worst case linear complexity – has algorithmic advantages and seems to be faster on average than the one based on the Foata normal form. Since this is the order we currently use, we will introduce it below.

Apart of the complexity of decision and the discrimination (totality), there is another important aspect for the choice of an adequate order: While Theorem 2 uses only the fact that the adequate is well-founded, an algorithm should intuitively construct the subsystem "in that order", i.e. the adequate order should permit to enumerate the traces, otherwise said be of ordinal type ω.

The total orders mentioned above have precisely this property, as they refine the length order and for a given length there is only a finite number of traces. Another interesting property of adequate orders that refine the length order is that they are compatible with *breadth first search*.

A particular adequate order. In order to introduce the adequate order of [ER99], we rely on a concrete representation of independence [Zie87]: Given a finite set of *locations Loc*, a *distributed alphabet* is a family $(\Sigma_l)_{l \in Loc}$ of (finite) local alphabets (which may overlap).

A distributed alphabet $(\Sigma_l)_{l \in Loc}$ induces an independence alphabet $(\Sigma, \|)$, where $\Sigma := \bigcup_{l \in Loc} \Sigma_l$ and $a \| b$ if there does *not* exist $l \in Loc$ such that both $a \in \Sigma_l$ and $b \in \Sigma_l$. Conversely, it is easy to see that for any independence alphabet $(\Sigma, \|)$ there exists a distributed alphabet $(\Sigma_l)_{l \in Loc}$ inducing it[3].

From now on, let $(\Sigma_l)_{l \in Loc}$ be a fixed distributed alphabet and $(\Sigma, \|)$ the induced independence alphabet. Moreover, let $\pi_l : \Sigma^* \to \Sigma_l^*$ denote the *projecting homomorphism* with $\pi_l(a) = a$ for $a \in \Sigma_l$ and $\pi_l(a) = \varepsilon$ for $a \notin \Sigma_l$.

It is a well known fact that for $u, v \in \Sigma^*$ we have $u \sim v$ iff $\pi_l(u) = \pi_l(v)$ for all locations $l \in Loc$ [DR95]. This allows us to call $(\pi_l(w))_{l \in Loc}$ the *distributed representation* of the trace $[w]$. This is a very useful data structure for the manipulation of traces as it allows efficient tests for $\sim$, but also easy (componentwise) concatenation.

Definition 14 (Esparza-Römer order).
Let $\leqslant$ denote a total order on Σ and $Loc = \{1, \ldots, h\}$ be an enumeration of the locations. Let $\leqslant_{lex}$ denote the induced (total) lexicographic order on Σ^* induced by $(\Sigma, \leqslant)$.

For $l \in Loc$ and $u, v \in \Sigma_l^*$, let $u \sqsubset_l v$ iff $|u| < |v|$, or $|u| = |v|$ and $u <_{lex} v$.

The Esparza-Römer order $\sqsubseteq_{ER}$ on traces is defined by $[u] \sqsubseteq_{ER} [v]$ if either $|u| < |v|$, or $|u| = |v|$ and there exists $l \in Loc$ such that $\pi_l(u) \sqsubset_l \pi_l(v)$ and for all l' with $1 \leqslant l' < l$ we have $\pi_{l'}(u) = \pi_{l'}(v)$.

It is easy to verify that $\sqsubseteq_{ER}$ is an adequate order and moreover total. By definition, it refines the length order. For an extended discussion of this order, see [ER99].

An algorithm. Based on a total *adequate order* $\sqsubseteq$ *that refines the length order* as parameter, we give an abstract algorithm for computing the associate locally complete finite subsystem (c.f. Algorithm 1). It computes the non-cutoff traces

---

[3] It is sufficient to take a collection of cliques $(\Sigma_l, \Sigma_l \times \Sigma_l)$ in the graph $(\Sigma, \|)$ such that they cover the graph.

Algorithm 1 Computation of a finite locally complete subsystem

---

Require: $|u| < |v|$ implies $[u] \sqsubseteq [v]$.
  Table $\leftarrow \{(s_0, [\varepsilon])\}$
  Previous_Level $\leftarrow \{(s_0, [\varepsilon])\}$
  while Previous_Level $\neq \emptyset$ **do**
    Current_Level $\leftarrow \emptyset$
    for all $(s, [u]) \in$ Previous_Level **do**
      for all $a \in \Sigma$, $s' \in S$ such that $s \overset{a}{\rightarrow} s'$ **do**
        if $\#_{Last}([u.a]) \leqslant$ LFS-bound **then**
          if $(s', [v]) \in$ Table **then**
            if $[u.a] \sqsubseteq [v]$ **then** {We have $|u.a| = |v|$ and $(s', [v]) \in$ Current_Level}
              Table $\leftarrow$ (Table $\setminus \{(s', [v])\}) \cup \{(s', [u.a])\}$
              Current_Level $\leftarrow$ (Current_Level $\setminus \{(s', [v])\}) \cup \{(s', [u.a])\}$
            end if
          else
            Table $\leftarrow$ Table $\cup \{(s', [u.a])\}$
            Current_Level $\leftarrow$ Current_Level $\cup \{(s', [u.a])\}$
          end if
        end if
      end for
    end for
    Previous_Level $\leftarrow$ Current_Level
  end while
  Return Table

---

level by level (in terms of the number of events) and stores them together with the corresponding state in a set (in practice, in a hash table). Once a level is empty, we stop.

While many algorithmic improvements on the level of detail are possible, we integrate one explicitly into the description of the algorithm: On a given level, we do not explore the traces in the adequate order but in any order. As a consequence, we may have to remove certain states on a given level if we find the same state on the same level with a smaller trace. The advantage is that we only have to test for the adequate order whenever we reach the same state several times, but no (inefficient) enumeration of the traces of one level is required.

First experimental results. Currently, only an early prototype written in Caml exists, which does neither allow insights on the runtime of the procedure, nor the exploration of big examples. However, it allows to measure the size of the state spaces explored and thus it gives hints on the *potential* of the *unfolding LFS* method, also in comparison to the original LFS procedure [NHZL01].

We consider two well known series of examples, that are known to have relative small Petri net unfoldings, the *asynchronous n-token buffer* and the *dining philosophers*. We have not tried to verify any properties on these examples, we only measure the number of states explored with different methods.

Table 1. Experimental results: Number of states with different methods

asynchronous buffers (m)	1	2	3	4	5	6	7	8	12	15	32
no reduction	2	4	8	16	32	64	128	256	4096	32768	2^{32}
original LFS $\#_{Last} \leqslant \lfloor \log_2 m \rfloor + 1$	1	3	8	18	43	100	22	830	24475	165993	–
unfolding LFS $\#_{Last} \leqslant \lfloor \log_2 m \rfloor + 1$	1	3	6	12	24	48	95	192	2829	17006	–
original LFS $\#_{Last} \leqslant 2$	1	3	8	16	30	53	88	138	548	1160	13638
unfolding LFS $\#_{Last} \leqslant 2$	1	3	6	12	23	42	72	116	492	1068	13172
original LFS $\#_{Last} \leqslant 3$	1	3	8	18	43	100	222	484	4850	17406	–
unfolding LFS $\#_{Last} \leqslant 3$	1	3	6	12	24	48	95	184	1865	7359	–

philosophers (m)	1	2	3	4	5	6	7	8	9	10	12
no reduction	2	8	26	80	242	728	2186	6560	19682	59048	531440
original LFS $\#_{Last} \leqslant \lfloor \log_2 m \rfloor + 1$	2	8	37	202	1006	4195	13981	206421	–	–	–
unfolding LFS $\#_{Last} \leqslant \lfloor \log_2 m \rfloor + 1$	2	8	25	79	226	598	1450	5347	13372	31286	142295
original LFS $\#_{Last} \leqslant 2$	2	8	37	129	343	738	1363	2270	3511	5138	9758
unfolding LFS $\#_{Last} \leqslant 2$	2	8	25	67	156	319	582	969	1504	2211	4237
original LFS $\#_{Last} \leqslant 3$	2	8	40	202	1006	4195	13981	38759	–	–	–
unfolding LFS $\#_{Last} \leqslant 3$	2	8	25	79	226	598	1450	3229	6655	12806	39875

The upper parts of the tables expose the number of buffer cells (philosophers respectively), the size of the state space without reduction, then the sizes of state spaces explored with the original LFS procedure of [NHZL01] and for the *unfolding LFS procedure* of this work.

As explained in [NHZL01], the bound $\lfloor \log_2 m \rfloor + 1$ yields a blowup rather than a reduction for the original LFS procedure, as the reduction gains are weaker than the blowup induced by the need to separate states with different sets of maximal events. However, the theoretical bound of $\lfloor \log_2 m \rfloor + 1$ is a sufficient upper bound for a worst case. For our examples, the actual LFS-number of any prime trace is bounded by 2, so that LFS applied with bound 2 is already exhaustive for local properties. Moreover, we have recently established dynamic criteria allowing to determine the absence of any prime trace with an LFS-number exceeding a certain level [LZ02]. For our examples, exploration up to LFS-bound 3 is sufficient to check the absence of local traces with a higher LFS-number.

Hence, we also show the numbers of states explored with bounds 2 and 3 in the lower parts of the tables. With exploration up to these levels, original LFS (with some heuristic improvements explained in [NHZL01]) already gives very good reductions.

The results for unfolding LFS show additional reductions compared to original LFS. As with original LFS, we observe a rapid explosion of the number of states with rising LFS-number. For the examples considered, the theoretical bound of $\lfloor \log_2 m \rfloor + 1$ does give a reduction, but initially not a strong one: Apparently, for a small number of philosphers, a significant fraction of all states have relatively low LFS-numbers.

However, the reduction increases with a growing number of philosophers and thus a growing difference[4] between the LFS-bound and the degree of parallelism (for 12 philosophers, the reduction is already at 75%). Although it is difficult to predict reductions for a big number of philosophers, they can be expected to be stronger and stronger. Indeed, LFS is designed to give reductions for a large number of components.

On the other hand, the reduction using the dynamic LFS-bound (2 and 3, see discussion above) is enormous on the whole. Even for the case 2 (sufficient in this case for the detection of counter-examples) the reduction significantly improves over the already impressing numbers for the original LFS.

Summarizing, we consider the additional reduction a sufficient justification for further exploration of our approach. Of course, further experiments are necessary for a full assessment of the method.

7   Conclusions

In this work, we have conceived a hybrid reduction method combining Local First Search [NHZL01] with important notions from Petri net unfoldings [McM92, ERV96]. This *unfolding LFS* eliminates an essential drawback of the original LFS, the need to explore certain states several times. The result is a method for searching and proving local properties with reductions significantly improving over Local First Search. In contrast to the Petri net unfolding approach, LFS only relies on the dependency relation and is thus *black box*, applicable to any kind of transition system with diamond properties.

On the practical side, there is a lot of work to be done: Apart of improving the complexity of our prototype implementation, heuristic improvements for further cropping of the state space should result in a wider applicability.

An important question concerns potential combination with other partial order reduction methods: Indeed, LFS (original or unfolding based) does eliminate diamonds of big dimensions but not the diamonds of small dimensions (below the LFS-bound), so the reduced systems still expose some potential for further partial order reductions. First steps in this direction are explored in [LZ02].

Acknowledgements. We thank Denis Lugiez for discussions, valuable comments, and human support during the preparation of this work.

References

[Bed87]   M. Bednarczyk, *Categories of asynchronous systems*, Ph.D. thesis, Computer Science, University of Sussex, Brighton, 1987.

[DR95]   V. Diekert and G. Rozenberg (eds.), *The book of traces*, World Scientific, 1995.

---

[4] Note, that the reduction percentage may temporarily increase at jumps in the LFS-bound at powers of 2 in the degree of parallelism, from 7 to 8, for example.

[Eng91]   J. Engelfriet, *Branching processes of Petri nets*, Acta Informatica **28** (1991), no. 6, pp. 575–591.

[ER99]   J. Esparza and S. Römer, *An unfolding algorithm for synchronous products of transition systems*, International Conference on Concurrency Theory (CONCUR), LNCS 1664, 1999, invited paper, pp. 2–20.

[ERV96]   J. Esparza, S. Römer, and W. Vogler, *An improvement of McMillan's unfolding algorithm*, TACAS, LNCS 1055, 1996, pp. 87–106.

[God96]   P. Godefroid, *Partial-order methods for the verification of concurrent systems: an approach to the state-explosion problem*, LNCS 1032, Springer-Verlag, 1996.

[Hol99]   G.J. Holzmann, *The engineering of a model checker: the Gnu i-protocol case study revisited*, Proc. of the 6th Spin Workshop, LNCS, no. 1680, 1999.

[KK01]   V. Khomenko and M. Koutny, *Towards an efficient algorithm for unfolding Petri nets*, International Conference on Concurrency Theory (CONCUR), LNCS 2154, 2001, pp. 366–381.

[LZ02]   D. Lugiez, P. Niebert and S. Zennou, *Dynamic bounds and transition merging for local first search*, SPIN Workshop 2002, LNCS, 2002.

[McM92]   K.L. McMillan, *Using unfoldings to avoid the state explosion problem in the verification of asynchronous circuits*, Computer Aided Verification (CAV), 1992, pp. 164–174.

[NHZL01]   P. Niebert, M. Huhn, S. Zennou, and D. Lugiez, *Local first search – a new paradigm in partial order reductions*, International Conference on Concurrency Theory (CONCUR), LNCS 2154, 2001, pp. 396–410.

[NPW81]   M. Nielsen, G. Plotkin, and G. Winskel, *Petri nets, event structures and domains, part I*, Theoretical Computer Science **13** (1981), no. 1, 85–108.

[NW95]   M. Nielsen and G. Winskel, *Models for concurrency*, Handbook of Logic and the Foundations of Computer Science (S. Abramsky, Dov M. Gabbay, and T.S.E. Maibaum, eds.), vol. IV, Oxford Science Publications, Clarendon Press, 1995.

[Pel93]   D. Peled, *All from one, one for all: On model checking using representatives*, International Conference on Computer Aided Verification (CAV), LNCS, vol. 697, 1993, pp. 409–423.

[Shi85]   M. W. Shields, *Concurrent machines*, The Computer Journal **28** (1985), no. 5, 449–465.

[Str52]   A.N. Strahler, *Hypsometric (area-altitude) analysis of erosonal topology*, Bull. Geol. Soc. of America **63** (1952), 1117–1142.

[Val89]   A. Valmari, *Stubborn sets for reduced state space generation*, 10th International Conference on Application and Theory of Petri Nets, vol. 2, 1989, pp. 1–22.

[Zie87]   Wi. Zielonka, *Notes on finite asynchronous automata*, R.A.I.R.O. – Informatique Théoretique et Applications **21** (1987), 99–135.

Applicability of Fair Simulation

Doron Bustan and Orna Grumberg

Computer Science Department
Technion, Haifa 32000, Israel
{orna,doron2}@cs.technion.ac.il

Abstract. In this paper we compare among four notions of fair simulation: direct [6], delay [7], game [10], and exists [9]. Our comparison refers to three main aspects: The time complexity of constructing the fair simulation, the ability to use it for minimization, and the relationship between the fair simulations and universal branching-time logics.

Based on our comparison we derive several practical implications: We develop an efficient approximated minimization algorithm for the direct/delay simulations. In addition, we suggest a new implementation for the assume-guarantee modular framework presented in [9]. The new implementation, significantly improves the complexity of the framework.

1 Introduction

Temporal logic model checking is a method for verifying finite-state systems with respect to propositional temporal logic specifications. The method is fully automatic and quite efficient in time, but is limited by its high space requirements. Many approaches for overcoming the *state explosion problem* of model checking have been suggested [4]. They are often based on the idea that the model of the verified system can be replaced by a more abstract model, which is smaller in size. The abstract and concrete models are sufficiently similar, so that properties that are verified on the abstract model can be concluded as true for the concrete one. This idea is often formalized by relating models with the *simulation preorder* [14] in which the greater, more abstract model has "more behaviors", and the verified properties are written in a universal branching time logic such as ACTL or ACTL* [9].

In order to avoid unrealistic behaviors introduced to the model by abstraction, it is common to add fairness constraint that distinguish between wanted (fair) and unwanted (unfair) behaviors and to exclude unfair behaviors from consideration. The simulation preorder does not distinguish between fair and unfair behaviors. It is therefore desirable to find an alternative definition that relates only fair behaviors of the two models. This task, however, is not uniquely defined. Indeed, several distinct notions of *fair simulation* have been suggested in the literature [6,7,10,9].

A question that naturally arises is, which notion of fair simulation is preferable. In [10] some of these notions are compared with respect to the complexity of checking for fair simulation. In [7] a different set of notions is compared with

J.-P. Katoen and P. Stevens (Eds.): TACAS 2002, LNCS 2280, pp. 401–414, 2002.

respect to two criteria: The complexity of constructing the preorder, and the ability to minimize a fair model by constructing a quotient model that is language equivalent to the original one.

In this paper we give a wider comparison among four notions of fair simulation: direct [6], delay [7], game [10], and exists [9]. We refer to several criteria, which emphasize the advantages of each of the notions. The results of the comparison are summarized in a table in Figure 1.

Based on our comparison we derive several practical implications. We develop an efficient approximated minimization algorithm for the delay, game and exists simulations. For these preorders, a unique equivalent smallest model does not exist. Therefore, an approximation is appropriate. In addition, we suggest a new implementation for the *assume-guarantee* [8,11,15,16] modular framework, presented in [9]. The new implementation, based on the game simulation rather than the exists simulation, significantly improves the complexity of the framework.

Our comparison refers to three main aspects of fair simulation. The first is the time complexity of constructing the preorder. There, we mainly summarize results of other works (see Figure 1). We see that constructing the direct, delay and game simulations is polynomial in the number of states n and the number of transitions m [7]. In contrast, constructing the exists simulation is PSPACE-complete [12] .

The second aspect that we consider is the ability to use the preorder for minimization. We say that two models are *equivalent* with respect to a preorder if each is smaller by the preorder than the other. The goal of minimization is to find the smallest in size model which is equivalent with respect to the preorder to the original one[1].

We examine for each of the fair simulation preorders the following three issues. Given a model M, 1. Is there a unique smallest in size model that is simulation equivalent to M. 2. Is the quotient model of M, simulation equivalent to M. 3. Is the result of disconnecting little brothers (to be explain in Sect. 3) in M, simulation equivalent to M.

Our examination (see Figure 1) leads to a new minimization algorithm that uses the direct and delay simulations as approximations for the game and exists simulations. The new algorithm obtains a better reduction than the algorithm suggested in [7].

The third aspect is the relationship between the simulation preorders and universal branching-time logics. A basic requirement is that the preorder preserves the specification logic, I.e. if $M_1 \leq M_2$ then, for every formula ϕ in the logic, $M_2 \models \phi$ implies $M_1 \models \phi$. Indeed all four notions of fair simulation satisfy this requirement. A stronger requirement is that the preorder has a *logical characterization* by some logic. This means that $M_1 \leq M_2$ iff for every formula ϕ in the logic, $M_2 \models \phi$ implies $M_1 \models \phi$.

Logical characterization is useful in determining if model M_2 is an abstraction of model M_1, when the logic $\mathcal{L}$ should be preserved. If the preorder $\leq$ is logically

---

[1] Note that this is a stronger criterion than the one used in [7], where only language equivalence is required.

characterized by $\mathcal{L}$ then checking $M_1 \leq M_2$ is a necessary and sufficient condition and will never give false negative result.

Another important relationship between a logic and a preorder is the existence of a *maximal model* $\mathcal{T}_\phi$ for a formula ϕ such that for every model M', $M' \leq \mathcal{T}_\phi$ if and only if $M' \models \phi$. Maximal models are used as tableaux in the framework described in [9] for the *assume-guarantee paradigm*.

In this work we show that there is a maximal model for ACTL formulas also with respect to the game simulation. In addition, we show that other conditions required for a sound implementation of the assume-guarantee paradigm hold for the game simulation.

The results of our comparison are presented in the table in Figure 1. The proofs of the claims that are not cited appear in the next sections. Due to lack of space some proofs are omitted. The rest of the paper is organized as follows:

simulation notion	time complexity of constructing the preorder	minimization			relation to logic	
		unique smallest model	quotient model	little brothers	has logical characterization	maximal model
Direct	$O(m \cdot n)$ [7]	*true*	true	*true*	*false*	*false*
Delay	$O(m \cdot n^3)$ [7]	*false*	true ^{2}	*false*	*false*	*false*
Game	$O(m \cdot n^3)$ [7]	*false*	false [7]	*false*	$\forall AFMC$ [10]	*true*
Exists	PSPACE complete [12]	*false*	*false*	*false*	$ACTL^*$	true [9]

Fig. 1. The properties of the different notions of fair simulation

In Section 2 we define the simulation preorder and the different notions of fair simulation. Section 3 investigates simulation minimization. Section 4 investigates the relationships of fair simulation with logic. In Section 5 we prove that the game simulation can replace the exists simulation in the implementation of the assume-guarantee paradigm. Finally, in Section 6 we discuss some conclusions.

2   Preliminaries

Let AP be a set of atomic propositions. We model systems by a *fair Kripke structure* M over AP, $M = (S, R, S_0, L, F)$, where S is a finite set of states, $S_0 \subseteq S$ is a set of initial states, $R \subseteq S \times S$ is the transition relation, which must be *total*. That is, for every state $s \in S$ there is a state $s' \in S$ such that $(s, s') \in R$ (states which do not satisfy this condition are deleted). $L : S \to 2^{AP}$ is a function that labels each state with the set of atomic propositions true in that state, and $F \subseteq S$ is a set of fair states.

---

^{2} In [7] it is shown that the quotient model is <u>language equivalent</u> to the original model. Here, we show that they are delay equivalent.

Let s be a state in a Kripke structure M. A *trace* in M starting from s is an infinite sequence of states $\rho = s_0 s_1 s_2 \ldots$ such that $s_0 = s$, and for every $i \geq 0$, $(s_i, s_{i+1}) \in R$. The i-th state of trace ρ is denoted ρ^i. In order to capture the infinite behavior of ρ, we define
$\inf(\rho) = \{\, s \mid s = \rho^i$ for infinitely many $i\,\}$.
We say that a trace ρ is *fair* according to the fair set F iff $\inf(\rho) \cap F \neq \emptyset$.

In this work we refer to two branching-time logics ACTL* and ACTL [9]. ACTL* is the universal fragment of the powerful branching-time logic, CTL*. ACTL* consists of the temporal operators **X** (next-time), **U** (until) and **R** (release), as well as the universal path quantifier **A** (for all paths). ACTL is a restricted sublogic of ACTL* in which every temporal operator is immediately preceded by a path quantifier. Due to lack of space we define precisely only ACTL. We define ACTL formulas in negation normal form, namely, negation is applied only to atomic propositions. ACTL is the set of formulas defined as follows:

- if $p \in AP$ then p and $\neg p$ are formulas.
- If ϕ and ψ are formulas, then $\phi \wedge \psi$ and $\phi \vee \psi$ are formulas.
- If ϕ and ψ are formulas, then $\mathbf{AX}\, \phi$, $\mathbf{A}[\phi\, \mathbf{U}\, \psi]$ and $\mathbf{A}[\phi\, \mathbf{R}\, \psi]$ are formulas.

An ACTL formula ϕ is interpreted in a state s, with respect to the fair traces which start at s. The formal definition of the semantics for ACTL can be found in [4]. We say that $M \models \phi$ iff for every initial state $s_0 \in S_0$, $M, s_0 \models \phi$.

2.1   Simulation and Fair Simulation

We start by defining simulation relation over Kripke structures with $F = S$ (Kripke structures with trivial fairness constraints).

Definition 1. *Given two structures M_1 and M_2 over AP, a relation $H \subseteq S_1 \times S_2$ is a simulation relation [14] over $M_1 \times M_2$ iff the following conditions hold:*

1. *For every $s_{01} \in S_{01}$ there exists $s_{02} \in S_{02}$ such that $(s_{01}, s_{02}) \in H$.*
2. *For all $(s_1, s_2) \in H$,*
   a) *$L_1(s_1) = L_2(s_2)$ and*
   b) *$\forall s_1'[(s_1, s_1') \in R_1 \rightarrow \exists s_2'[(s_2, s_2') \in R_2 \wedge (s_1', s_2') \in H]]$.*

M_2 *simulates* M_1 (denoted by $M_1 \leq M_2$) if there exists a simulation relation H over $M_1 \times M_2$. We say that M_1 and M_2 are *simulation equivalent* if $M_1 \leq M_2$ and $M_2 \leq M_1$. Similarly $(s_1, s_2) \in H$ is denoted $s_1 \leq s_2$ and s_1 and s_2 are equivalent if $s_1 \leq s_2$ and $s_2 \leq s_1$ and denoted $s_1 \equiv s_2$.

The relation $\leq$ is a preorder on the set of structures. That is, $\leq$ is reflexive and transitive. In [9,2] it is shown that $M_1 \leq M_2$ iff, for every ACTL* formula ψ (with atomic propositions in AP), $M_2 \models \psi$ implies $M_1 \models \psi$. Thus, simulation relation has logical characterization over structures with trivial fairness constraints.

Next, we define the different notions of fair simulation.

Definition 2. $H \subseteq S_1 \times S_2$ *is a* direct simulation relation *[6]* $(\leq_{di})$ *over* $M_1 \times M_2$ *iff it satisfies the conditions of Def. 1 except that 2a is replaced by:*
$2(a')$ $L_1(s_1) = L_2(s_2)$ *and* $s_1 \in F_1$ *implies* $s_2 \in F_2$.

Definition 3. *[9]* $H \subseteq S_1 \times S_2$ *is an* exists simulation $(\leq_\exists)$ *over* $M_1 \times M_2$ *iff it satisfies the conditions of Def. 1 except that 2b is replaced by:*
$2(b')$ *for every fair trace* ρ_1 *from* s_1 *in* M_1 *there exists a fair trace* ρ_2 *from* s_2 *in* M_2 *such that for all* $i \in I\!N$, $(\rho_1^i, \rho_2^i) \in H$.[3]

The next definitions are based on games. We start with a game that characterizes the simulation over structures with trivial fairness constraints. Given two Kripke structures M_1, M_2, we define a game of two players over M_1, M_2. The players are called the adversary and the protagonist, where the adversary plays on M_1 and the protagonist plays on M_2.

Definition 4. *Given two Kripke structures,* M_1 *and* M_2, *a simulation game consists of a finite or infinite number of rounds. At the beginning, the adversary selects an initial state* s_{01} *in* M_1 *to start from, then the protagonist responds by selecting an initial state* s_{02} *in* M_2 *such that* $L_1(s_{01}) = L_2(s_{02})$. *In each round, assume that the adversary is at* s_1 *and the protagonist is at* s_2. *The adversary then moves to a successor* s_1' *of* s_1 *on* M_1, *after which the protagonist moves to a successor* s_2' *of* s_2 *on* M_2 *such that* $L_1(s_1') = L_2(s_2')$.

If the protagonist does not have a matching state then the protagonist fails. Otherwise, if the protagonist always has a matching successor to move to, then the game proceeds ad infinitum for ω rounds and the protagonist wins. The adversary wins iff the protagonist fails.

Definition 5. *Given two Kripke structures* M_1 *and* M_2, *a strategy* π *of the protagonist is a function* $\pi : (S_1 \times S_2 \to S_2) \cup (S_{01} \times \{\perp\} \to S_{02})$. *The function* π *should satisfy the following: If* $s_2' = \pi(s_1', s_2)$ *then* $(s_2, s_2') \in R_2$.

The protagonist plays according to a strategy π if initially when the adversary selects $s_{0_1} \in S_{0_1}$ the protagonist selects $s_{0_2} = \pi(s_{0_1}, \perp)$ and, for every round i, when the adversary moves to s_1' and the protagonist is in s_2 then the protagonist moves to $s_2' = \pi(s_1', s_2)$. π is a winning strategy for the protagonist if the protagonist wins whenever it plays according to π. We can now present an alternative definition to the simulation preorder. This definition is equivalent to Def. 1 [10].

Definition 6. *Given two Kripke structures,* M_1 *and* M_2, M_2 *simulates* M_1 $(M_1 \leq M_2)$ *iff the protagonist has a winning strategy in a simulation game over* M_1, M_2.

In order to extend the simulation game to fair simulation, we add a winning condition which refers to the infinite properties of the game. We then give two additional definitions of fair simulation, the delay $(\leq_{de})$ and the game $(\leq_g)$ simulations.

---

[3] In such a case we use the notation $(\rho_1, \rho_2) \in H$.

Definition 7. *[7] The protagonist* delay *wins a game over two fair Kripke structures M_1 and M_2 iff the game is played for infinitely many rounds. Moreover, whenever the adversary reaches a fair state then the protagonist reaches a fair state within a finite number of rounds.*

Definition 8. *[10] The protagonist* game *wins a game over two fair Kripke structures M_1 and M_2, iff the game is played for infinitely many rounds. Moreover, if the adversary moves along a fair trace, then the protagonist moves along a fair trace as well.*

We say that π is a delay/game winning strategy for the protagonist if the protagonist delay/game wins whenever it plays according to π.

Definition 9. *[10,7] Given two fair Kripke structures, M_1 and M_2, M_2 delay/game simulates M_1 iff the protagonist has a delay/game winning strategy over M_1, M_2.*

Definitions 2,3,9 are extensions of Def.1 and its equivalent Def. 6. Consequently, on structures with trivial fairness constraints $(F = S)$, all four definitions are equivalent. In [10,7] the following relationships over the fair simulation preorders are shown,
$$M_1 \leq_{di} M_2 \Rightarrow M_1 \leq_{de} M_2 \Rightarrow M_1 \leq_g M_2 \Rightarrow M_1 \leq_\exists M_2$$
Note that the definitions of game/exists simulation are not limited to specific types of fairness constraints. They hold even if M_1 and M_2 each has a different type of fairness constraints. Finally we extend the delay/game simulations for states.

Definition 10. *For all states s_1 and s_2 in a structure M, $s_1 \leq_{de/g} s_2$ if the protagonist has a winning delay/game strategy in a game over $M \times M$ where the adversary starts at s_1 and the protagonist starts at s_2.*

3   Simulation Minimization

For structures with trivial fairness constraints $(F = S)$, two forms of redundancy are considered [3]. These redundancies are handled in [3], by first constructing a quotient structure which results in a structure without equivalent states and then disconnecting *little brothers* eliminating the other redundancy. For structures with trivial fairness constraints, the result of eliminating these redundancies is a unique, smallest in size structure which is simulation equivalent to the original structure [3].

Lemma 1. *For every structure, there exists a unique, smallest in size structure, which is direct simulation equivalent to it.*

The proof of Lemma 1 and the construction of the smallest structure can be obtained in the same manner as in [3]. Unfortunately, performing the same operations for the other notions of fair simulations might result in an inequivalent structure. In this section we investigate minimization with respect to each notion of fair simulation. We start by checking whether the quotient structure is equivalent to the original one. Next we check whether it is safe to disconnect little brothers. We then determine whether there exists a unique smallest in size equivalent structure. Finally we use the results of this section to suggest a new better minimizing algorithm.

Definition 11.

- *The language of s_1 is contained in the language of s_2 ($s_1 \subseteq s_2$) if for every fair trace ρ_1 from s_1 there is a fair trace ρ_2 from s_2 such that $\forall i \geq 0$, $L(\rho_1^i) = L(\rho_2^i)$.*
- *$M_1 \subseteq M_2$ if for every fair trace starting at an initial state $s_{01} \in S_{01}$ there is a fair trace starting at an initial state $s_{02} \in S_{02}$ such that $\forall i \geq 0$, $L_1(\rho_1^i) = L_2(\rho_2^i)$.*
- *M_1 is language equivalent to M_2 if $M_1 \subseteq M_2$ and $M_2 \subseteq M_1$.*

Clearly, all notions of fair simulation imply language containment.

Quotient Structure

In a quotient structure all equivalent states are unified into equivalence classes. The equivalence classes are the states of the quotient structure. There is a transition from one equivalence class to another iff there exists a transition from a state in the former to a state in the latter. An equivalence class is initial if it contains an initial state and is fair if it contains a fair state. For the delay simulation, we presents the following lemma.

Lemma 2. *Let M^Q be the quotient structure of a structure M. Then $M \equiv_{de} M^Q$.*

In [7] it is shown that the quotient structure with respect to game simulation is not equivalent to the original one. We show that for every preorder $\leq_\clubsuit$ that lies between game simulation and language containment, the quotient structure with respect to this preorder may not be equivalent to the original structure.

Lemma 3. *Let $\leq_\clubsuit$ be any preorder such that for every M_1, M_2, $M_1 \leq_g M_2 \Rightarrow M_1 \leq_\clubsuit M_2 \Rightarrow M_1 \subseteq M_2$.*
Then there exists a structure M whose quotient structure with respect to $\leq_\clubsuit$ is not equivalent to M with respect to $\leq_\clubsuit$.

Proof sketch. Consider the structure M_1 in Figure 2. States s_0 and s_2 are equivalent with respect to game simulation. To see that, consider a strategy that instructs the protagonist to move to the same state the adversary moves to. This strategy proves both directions of the game equivalence. Since $M_1 \leq_g M_2 \Rightarrow M_1 \leq_\clubsuit M_2$, s_0 and s_2 are also equivalent with respect to $\leq_\clubsuit$. Since $M_1 <_\clubsuit M_2 \Rightarrow M_1 \subset M_2$, it is sufficient to prove that the result of unifying states s_0 and s_2 is not language equivalent to M_1. To see that, note that the language of M_1 consists of all words in which both a and b occur infinitely often. However, any structure with two states that contains this language, must also contain a word with a suffix of a's only (or b's only). □

Corollary 1. *For exists/game simulation, the quotient structure is not necessarily equivalent to the original structure.*

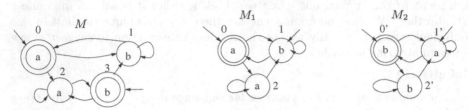

Fig. 2. The structures M_1 and M_2 are equivalent to M with respect to game/exists simulation, and they are both minimal. Note that states 0 and 2 ($0'$ and $2'$) are equivalent but cannot be unified. (double circles denote fair states)

Disconnecting Little Brothers

A state s_2 is a *little brother* of another state s_3 if both states are successors of the same state s_1, $s_2 \le s_3$ and $s_3 \not\le s_2$. Little brothers are disconnected by removing the transition (s_1, s_2) from R.

Lemma 4. *Let $\le_\spadesuit$ be a preorder such that*
$M_1 \le_{de} M_2 \Rightarrow M_1 \le_\spadesuit M_2 \Rightarrow M_1 \subseteq M_2$.
The result of disconnecting little brothers with respect to $\le_\spadesuit$ in a structure M might not be equivalent to M with respect to $\le_\spadesuit$.

Proof sketch. Consider the structure M_1 in Figure 3. State s_2 is a little brother of state s_1 with respect to $\le_\spadesuit$. To see that, note that $s_2 \le_{de} s_1$ and therefore, $s_2 \le_\spadesuit s_1$. Moreover, $s_1 \not\subseteq s_2$, and thus $s_1 \not\le_\spadesuit s_2$.

Since $M_1 \le_\spadesuit M_2 \Rightarrow M_1 \subseteq M_2$, it is sufficient to show that the result of disconnecting s_2 from s_0 is not language equivalent to M_1. But this is true since disconnecting s_2 results in a structure with no fair traces from s_1.   □

Corollary 2. *The result of disconnecting little brothers with respect to delay/ game/exists simulation might not be equivalent to the original structure with respect to delay/game/exists simulation.*

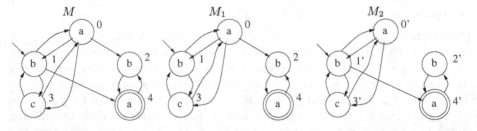

Fig. 3. The structures M_1 and M_2 are equivalent with respect to delay/game/exists simulation to M, and they are both minimal. Note that state 2 ($4'$) is a little brother of 1 ($0'$) but cannot be disconnected.

Unique Smallest in Size Structure

Lemma 5. *Let* $\leq_\spadesuit$ *be a preorder such that*
$M_1 \leq_{de} M_2 \Rightarrow M_1 \leq_\spadesuit M_2 \Rightarrow M_1 \subseteq M_2$.
There is no unique smallest in size structure with respect to $\leq_\spadesuit$.

Consider the structures in Figure 3. Structures M_1 and M_2 are equivalent with respect to $\leq_\spadesuit$ but are not isomorphic. Furthermore, there is no smaller structure that is equivalent to M_1 and M_2.

Corollary 3. *There is no unique smallest in size structure with respect to delay/game/exists simulation.*

An approximate minimization algorithm for delay/game/exists simulation. In [3] two efficient procedures for minimizing with respect to ordinary simulation are presented. In previous sections we have shown that when we consider game/exists simulation these procedures cannot be used. Furthermore, we have shown that there is no equivalent unique smallest in size structure with respect to these simulations. As a result we are suggesting an algorithm that performs some minimization but does not necessarily construct a minimal structure. Our algorithm uses the direct/delay simulations as an approximation of the game/exists simulation. The algorithm is presented in Figure 4. The first step

Given a structure M,

1. Construct a quotient structure M' with respect to delay simulation.
2. Construct M'' by disconnecting little brothers in M' with respect to direct simulation.

Fig. 4. Minimization algorithm for the delay/game/exists simulations.

results in $M' \equiv_{de} M$. The second step results in $M'' \equiv_{di} M'$. Since direct simulation implies delay simulation, $M'' \equiv_{de} M$. M'' is equivalent to M also with respect game/exists simulation. The complexity of the first step is $O(m \cdot n^3)$ [7], and of the second step $O(m \cdot n)$ [3]. Thus the total complexity of the algorithm is $O(m \cdot n^3)$.

4 Relating the Simulation Notions with Logics

In this section we check for each simulation notion whether it has a logical characterization. Then we check whether there exists a maximal structure for ACTL with respect to this notion.

4.1 Logical Characterization

Definition 12. *Logic* $\mathcal{L}$ *characterizes a preorder* $\leq$ *if for all structures* M_1 *and* M_2, $M_1 \leq M_2$ *if and only if for every formula* ϕ *in* $\mathcal{L}$, $M_2 \models \phi$ *implies* $M_1 \models \phi$.

[9] shows that, if $M_1 \leq_\exists M_2$ then the following property holds. $\forall \phi \in$ ACTL*, $M_2 \models \phi$ implies $M_1 \models \phi$. Since all other simulation notions imply the exists simulation, this property holds for all of these notions.

We now investigate which of the fair simulations satisfy the other direction of logical characterization. In [1] it is shown that **CTL*** characterizes the exists bisimulation. The proof that ACTL* characterizes the exists simulation is similar.

Unlike ACTL*, ACTL does not characterize the exists simulation. In [1] two structures M_1 and M_2 are given. It is shown in [1] that for every ϕ in ACTL, $M_2 \models \phi$ implies $M_1 \models \phi$. However, there exists an ACTL* formula φ such that $M_2 \models \varphi$ but $M_1 \not\models \varphi$. Since ACTL* characterizes the exists simulation, $M_1 \not\leq_\exists M_2$.

Unfortunately, the game, direct and delay simulations cannot be characterized by either ACTL* or ACTL. In [10] two structures M_1 and M_2 are given such that $M_1 \leq_\exists M_2$ but $M_1 \not\leq_g M_2$. Since ACTL* characterizes the exists simulation, for every ϕ in ACTL* (and therefore ACTL), $M_2 \models \phi$ implies $M_1 \models \phi$. Therefore, ACTL* (ACTL) does not characterizes the game simulation. Since the direct/delay simulation implies the game simulation, ACTL* (ACTL) does not characterize them as well.

The question that arises is, can the direct/delay/game simulation be characterized by any other logic. [10] shows that the game simulation can be characterized by the Universal Alternating Free μ-Calculus ($\forall$**AFMC**) logic when interpreted over fair structures.

We show that no reasonable logic that describes the fair branching behavior of a structure can characterize the direct/delay simulation. Consider structures M_1 and M_2 in Figure 5. M_1 and M_2 cannot be distinguished by a temporal logic formula. However, $M_1 \not\leq_{de} M_2$ and $M_1 \not\leq_{di} M_2$. Thus both simulation cannot be characterized by any such logic.

$$M_1 \qquad\qquad\qquad\qquad M_2$$

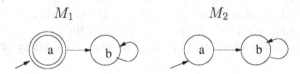

Fig. 5. The direct/delay simulations can not be characterized by temporal logics.

4.2   Maximal Structure

Next, we check for the existence of a maximal structure for a formula with respect to a preorder.

Definition 13. *A structure M_ϕ is maximal for formula ϕ with respect to preorder $\leq$ if for every structure M, $M \models \phi \Leftrightarrow M \leq M_\phi$.*

[9] presents a maximal structure for ACTL formulas with respect to $\leq_\exists$. Here we show that the same structure is maximal with respect to the game simulation. On the other hand we show that the formula $\mathbf{A}[a\,\mathbf{U}\,b]$ has no maximal structure with respect to the direct and delay simulations. This formula is contained in both ACTL and ACTL*.

A maximal structure for ACTL with respect to game simulation. We prove that for every ACTL formula, the tableau of the formula as defined in [9], is the maximal structure for the formula with respect to the game simulation. Before we prove that, we give the main details of the tableau construction. In [9] a different type of fairness constraints called generalized Büchi acceptance condition is used. A *generalized Büchi acceptance* condition is a set $F = \{f_1, f_2, \ldots f_n\}$ of subsets of S. A trace ρ is *fair* according to F iff for every $1 \leq i \leq n$, $\inf(\rho) \cap f_i \neq \emptyset$. Since the game simulation is not limited to a certain type of fairness constraints, we do not have to change anything in its definition.

For the remainder of this section, fix an ACTL formula ψ. Let AP_ψ be the set of atomic propositions in ψ. The tableau associated with ψ is a structure $\mathcal{T}_\psi = (S_T, R_T, S_{0T}, L_T, F_T)$.

We first define the set of *elementary formulas* $el(\psi)$ of ψ. This set consists of the atomic propositions in ψ, subformulas of ψ of the form $\mathbf{AX}\,\phi$, and $\mathbf{AX}\,\mathbf{A}[\phi_1\,\mathbf{U}\,\phi_2]$, $\mathbf{AX}\,\mathbf{A}[\phi_1\,\mathbf{R}\,\phi_2]$, for every $\mathbf{A}[\phi_1\,\mathbf{U}\,\phi_2]$, $\mathbf{A}[\phi_1\,\mathbf{R}\,\phi_2]$ subformulas of ψ.

The set of tableau states is $S_T = \mathcal{P}(el(\psi))^4$. The labeling function is $L_T(s_t) = s_t \cap AP_\psi$. In order to specify the set S_{0T} of initial states and the transition relation R_T, we need an additional function sat that associates with each sub-formula ϕ of ψ a set of states in S_T. Intuitively, $sat(\phi)$ will be the set of states that satisfy ϕ. The set of initial states of the tableau is $S_{0T} = sat(\psi)$. The transition relation is defined so that if $\mathbf{AX}\,\phi$ is included in some state then all its successors should satisfy ϕ.

$$R_T(s_1, s_2) = \bigwedge_{\mathbf{AX}\,\phi \in el(\psi)} (\mathbf{AX}\,\phi) \in s_1 \Rightarrow s_2 \in sat(\phi).$$

The fairness constraint guarantees that *eventuality* properties are fulfilled.

$$F_T = \{\, ((S_T - sat(\mathbf{AX}\,\mathbf{A}[\phi\,\mathbf{U}\,\varphi])) \cup sat(\varphi)) \mid \mathbf{AX}\,\mathbf{A}[\phi\,\mathbf{U}\,\varphi] \in el(\psi) \,\}.$$

The tableau is the maximal structure for game simulation. We now summarize the main steps in the proof that for every Kripke structure M, $M \models \psi$ iff $M \leq_g \mathcal{T}_\psi$. The steps included in Lemma 6 are proved in [9]. The other steps are different from [9] due to the change in the preorder.

Lemma 6. *[9]*

- For all sub-formulas ϕ of ψ and $t \in S_T$, if $t \in sat(\phi)$, then $t \vdash \phi$.
- For every ACTL formula ψ, $\mathcal{T}_\psi \models \psi$.
- if $M \leq_g \mathcal{T}_\psi$, then $M \models \psi$.

---

[4] Some of the states are deleted in order to keep R_T total

Our next step is to prove that $M \models \psi$ implies $M \leq_g \mathcal{T}_\psi$. We show that if $M \models \psi$ then the protagonist has a winning strategy function in a game over $M \times \mathcal{T}_\psi$. We define the strategy function π as follows: $\pi(s_0, \perp) = \{ \phi \mid \phi \in el(\psi), s_0 \models \phi \}$ and $\pi(s', t) = \{ \phi \mid \phi \in el(\psi), s' \models \phi \}$. Thus, whenever the adversary moves to a state s' the protagonist moves to $t' = \pi(s', t)$, such that both s', t' satisfy exactly the same set of elementary formulas of ψ. It can also be shown that s' and t' agree on every subformula of ψ.

Lemma 7. π *is a winning strategy.*

Corollary 4. *For any structure* M, $M \models \psi$ *iff* $M \leq_g \mathcal{T}_\psi$. *Thus,* $\mathcal{T}_\psi$ *is the maximal structure for* ψ *with respect to game simulation.*

A Maximal Structure for Direct/Delay Simulation

We now show that it is impossible to construct a maximal structure for the formula $\phi = \mathbf{A}[a \,\mathbf{U}\, b]$ with respect to the direct/delay simulations. Thus, any logic that contains this formula or an equivalent formula, in particular ACTL and ACTL*, does not have a maximal structure with respect to these simulations. Since the direct simulation implies the delay simulation, it is sufficient to prove this result for the delay simulation. Consider the structures $M_0, M_1, \ldots$ in Figure 6, each of which satisfies $\mathbf{A}[a \,\mathbf{U}\, b]$. The following lemma shows that no finite structure can be greater by the delay simulation than all of these structures.

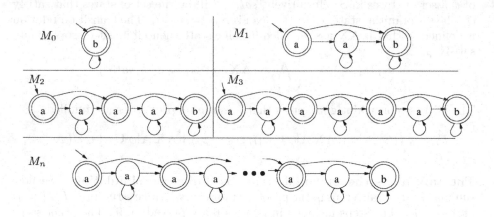

Fig. 6. There is no finite structure M' such that for every n in $I\!N$, M' is greater by direct/delay simulation than M_n, and $M' \models \mathbf{A}[a \,\mathbf{U}\, b]$

Lemma 8. *For every* $n > 0$ *and every structure* M', *if* $M_n \leq_{de} M'$ *and* $M' \models \mathbf{A}[a \,\mathbf{U}\, b]$ *then* $|M'| \geq n$.

5   A New Implementation for the Assume-Guarantee Framework

This section shows that the game simulation can replace the exists simulation in the implementation of the assume-guarantee paradigm [8,11,15,16] as suggested in [9].

[9] suggests a framework that uses the assume-guarantee paradigm for semi-automatic verification. It presents a general method that uses models as assumptions; the models are either generated from a formula as a *tableau*, or are abstract models which are given by the user. The proof of $\psi M \phi$ meaning that, if ψ is true in the environment then $M \models \phi$, is done automatically by verifying that the composition of the tableau for ψ with M satisfies ϕ. The method requires a preorder $\leq$, a composition operator $\|$ and a specification language $\mathcal{L}$. In [9] an implementation for this framework is presented. The implementation uses the $ACTL$ logic as the specification language, the exists simulation preorder and a composition operator. The ability to replace the exists simulation by the game simulation is implied by Lemma 9.

Lemma 9. *1. For every two structures M_1, M_2, if $M_1 \leq_g M_2$ then for every formula ψ in $\mathcal{L}$, $M_2 \models \psi$ implies $M_1 \models \psi$.*
2. For every two structures M_1, M_2, $M_1 \| M_2 \leq_g M_1$.
3. For every three structures M_1, M_2, M_3, $M_1 \leq_g M_2$ implies $M_1 \| M_3 \leq_g M_2 \| M_3$.
4. Let ψ be a formula in $\mathcal{L}$ and $\mathcal{T}_\psi$ be a tableau for ψ, then $\mathcal{T}_\psi$ is the maximal structure with respect to the preorder $\leq_g$.

Complexity. Verifying a formula of the form $\psi M \varphi$ is PSPACE-complete in the size of ψ [13]. However, the real bottleneck of this framework is checking for fair simulation between models, which for the exists simulation is PSPACE complete in the size of the models (typically models are much larger than formulas). Thus replacing the exists simulation by the game simulation reduces this complexity to polynomial and eliminates the bottleneck of the framework. However, the algorithm for game simulation, presented in [7], refers to Kripke structures with regular Büchi constraints, and the implementation presented in [9] refers to Kripke structures with generalized Büchi constraints. In order to apply the algorithm suggested in [7] in the assume-guarantee framework, we need a translation between these types of fairness constraints.

[5] defines a transformation of a Büchi automaton with generalized fairness constraints into a Büchi automaton with regular fairness constraints. The result of the transformation is game equivalent to the original structure, thus can replace it. The translation effects the size of the structure and thus the complexity of the construction of the preorder. The sizes of S and R are multiplied by $|F|$, where $|F|$ is the number of sets in F. Thus the complexity of constructing the preorder is $|F| \cdot |R| \cdot (|S| \cdot |F|)^3 = |R| \cdot |S|^3 \cdot |F|^4$. Note that in the tableau for a formula, $|F|$ is bounded by the size of the formula and the size of the tableau is exponential in the size of the formula, thus, the transformation of the tableau to regular fairness constraints is logarithmic in its size.

6   Conclusion

The main consequence of this work is that there is no notion of fair simulation which has all the desired advantages. However, it is clear that the exists and game simulations have advantages in the relationship with the logics over the delay and direct simulations. On the other hand, the delay and direct simulations are better for minimization. Thus, it is advantageous to refer to the delay and direct simulations as approximations of the game/exists simulations. These approximations enable some minimization with respect to the exists and game simulations. Out of the four notions, we consider the game simulation the best due to its complexity and its applicability for modular verification.

References

1. A. Aziz, V. Singhal, T.R. Shiple, A.L. Sangiovanni-Vincentelli, F. Balarin, and R.K. Brayton. Equivalences for fair kripke structures. In *ICALP*, LNCS 840, pages 364–375, 1994.
2. S. Bensalem, A. Bouajjani, C. Loiseaux, and J. Sifakis. Property preserving simulation. In *Computer-aided Verification*, volume 663 LNCS, pages 260–273, 1981.
3. D. Bustan and O. Grumberg. Simulation based minimization. In *Conference on Automated Deduction*, volume 17, pages 255–270, 2000.
4. E.M. Clarke, O. Grumberg, and D.A. Peled. *Model Checking*. MIT Press, 1999.
5. C. Courcoubetis, M. Vardi, P. Wolper, and M. Yannakakis. Memory efficient algorithms for the verification of temporal properties. In *Proceedings of Computer-Aided Verification*, volume 531 of *LNCS*, pages 233– 242, 1991.
6. D.L. Dill, A.J. Hu, and H. Wong-Toi. Checking for language inclusion using simulation relation. In *Computer-Aided Verification*, LNCS 575, pages 255–265, 1991.
7. K. Etessami, Th. Wilke, and R. Schuller. Fair simulation relations, parity games, and state space reduction for Büchi automata. In *Automata, Languages and Programming, 28th international collquium*, LNCS 2076, pages 694–707, 2001.
8. N. Francez. *The Analysis of Cyclic Programs*. PhD thesis, Weizmann Institute of Science, 1976.
9. O. Grumberg and D.E. Long. Model checking and modular verification. *ACM Trans. on Programming Languages and Systems (TOPLAS)*, 16(3):843–871, 1994.
10. T.A. Henzinger, O. Kupferman, and S. Rajamani. Fair simulation. In *Proc. 8th Conference on Concurrency Theory*, LNCS 1234, 1997.
11. C. B. Jones. Specification and design of (parallel) programs. In *In International Federation for Information Processing (IFIP)*, pages 321–332, 1983.
12. O. Kupferman and M.Y. Vardi. Verification of fair transition systems. In *Computer Aided Verification (CAV'96)*, LNCS 1102, pages 372–382, 1996.
13. O. Kupferman and M.Y. Vardi. Modular model checking. In *Proc. Compositionality Workshop*, LNCS 1536. Springer-Verlag, 1998.
14. R. Milner. An algebraic definition of simulation between programs. In *Proc. of the 2nd International Joint Conferences on Artificial Intelligence (IJCAI)*, pages 481–489, London, UK, 1971.
15. J. Misra and K.M. Chandy. Proofs of networks of processes. *IEEE Transactions on Software Engineering*, 7(7):417–426, 1981.
16. A. Pnueli. In transition for global to modular temporal reasoning about programs. In K. R. Apt, editor, *Logics and Models of Concurrent Systems*, volume 13 of *NATO ASI series F*. sv, 1984.

Simulation as Coarsest Partition Problem

Raffaella Gentilini, Carla Piazza, and Alberto Policriti

Dip. di Matematica e Informatica,
Università di Udine
Via Le Scienze 206, 33100 Udine - Italy.
{gentilini|piazza|policriti}@dimi.uniud.it

Abstract. The problem of determining the coarsest partition stable
with respect to a given binary relation, is known to be equivalent to the
problem of finding the maximal *bisimulation* on a given structure. Such
an equivalence has suggested efficient algorithms for the computation of
the maximal bisimulation relation.

In this paper the *simulation* problem is rewritten in terms of coarsest
stable partition problem allowing a more algebraic understanding of the
simulation equivalence. On this ground, a new algorithm for deciding
simulation is proposed. Such a procedure improves on either space or
time complexity of previous simulation algorithms.

1 Introduction

In this work we deal with the problem of determining the so-called *simulation*
relation on a given (Kripke) labeled structure $G = \langle N, E, \Sigma \rangle$. Such a problem
consists, given G, in getting to the (unique) maximal binary relation $\leq_s$ such
that

1. a node can simulate another one only if they have the same label;
2. if a node m simulates another node n, then any successor of n can be simulated by some successor of m.

On the ground of the above definition the notion of *sim-equivalence* $\equiv_s$ is introduced: $m \equiv_s n$ iff $m \leq_s n$ and $n \leq_s m$. In particular, we are interested in
computing the similarity quotient $G/\equiv_s$.

The notion of simulation is very similar (less demanding, in fact) to the notion
of *bisimulation*: an extremely pervasive idea proposed in many different fields,
such as Modal Logic, Concurrency Theory, Set Theory, Automata Theory, etc.
(cf. [1,15,11,14]). Two nodes m and n are bisimilar ($m \equiv_b n$) iff:

1. they have the same label;
2. any successor of n is bisimilar to some successor of m, and vice-versa.

If the naturalness of the concept of bisimulation explains its large usage—
especially in connection with circular structures—, from a computational point of
view the main reasons for its fortune and for its best solution lie in the possibility
of re-formulating a bisimulation problem in purely (elementary) algebraic terms:

J.-P. Katoen and P. Stevens (Eds.): TACAS 2002, LNCS 2280, pp. 415–430, 2002.

a bisimulation is the coarsest partition finer than an input one and *stable* with respect to the relation E of the graph (a partition is stable with respect to E iff any of its classes is either sent by E entirely within or entirely outside any other of its classes).

Both bisimulation and simulation (as well as other possible relations of the same sort) are used in order to *simplify* the input structure by collapsing all the nodes of the same equivalence class into a single node. As explained in [13] "in many cases, neither trace equivalence nor bisimilarity, but similarity is the appropriate abstraction for computer-aided verification ...". In the case of finite-state systems the similarity quotient $G/\equiv_s$ can be computed in polynomial time, while this is not the case for trace equivalence quotient. In the case of infinite-state systems, finitely represented using hybrid automaton and other formalisms, the similarity quotients can be computed symbolically and in many cases the quotients are finite (see [13]). Since the conditions in the definition of simulation are weaker than the ones in the definition of bisimulation, simulation provides a better space reduction than bisimulation (i.e., $|G/\equiv_s | \leq |G/\equiv_b |$) and it is still adequate for the verification of all the formulae of the branching temporal logic without quantifiers switches (e.g. the formulae of ACTL*, see [16]).

Several polynomial-time algorithms for computing similarity quotients on finite graphs have been proposed: the ones presented in [2], [5], and [6] achieve time complexities of the orders $O(|N|^6|E|)$, $O(|N|^4|E|)$, and $O(|E|^2)$, respectively. A simulation procedure running in $O(|N||E|)$ time was independently discovered in [13] and [3]. All of the algorithms just mentioned ([2], [5], [6], [3], [13]) obtain the similarity quotient as a by-product of the computation of the entire similarity relation on the set of states N. Their space complexity is then limited from below by $O(|N|^2)$.

Recently Bustan and Grumberg in [4] and Cleaveland and Tan in [7] improved the above results.

The procedure by Bustan and Grumberg [4] gives in output the quotient structure with respect to $\equiv_s$ and the simulation relation among the classes of $M = N/_{\equiv_s}$ without computing the entire simulation on N. Hence, its space requirements (often more critical, especially in the field of verification) depends on the size of M and are lower than the ones of the algorithms in [2], [5], [6], [3], and [13]. In more detail, the so-called *Partitioning Algorithm* described in [4] uses only $O(|M|^2 + |N| \log(|M|))$ space whereas its time complexity is rather heavy: it is $O(|M|^4(|E| + |M|^2) + |M|^2|N|(|N| + |M|^2))$.

The procedure in [7] combines the fix-point calculation techniques in [3] and [13] with the bisimulation-minimization algorithm in [17]. A system, G_2, is determined being or not capable of simulating the behavior of G_1, by interleaving the minimization via bisimulation of the two systems with the computation of the set of classes in G_2 able to simulate each class in G_1. The time complexity achieved is $O(|B_1||B_2| + |E_1| \log(|N_1|) + |B_1||E_2| + |\varepsilon_1||B_2|)$, where ε_i and B_i represent the bisimulation reduced relation and states'space of T_i. Compared with the time complexities of [13] and [3], the latter expression have many occurrences of $|N_i|$ and $|E_i|$ replaced with $|B_i|$ and $|\varepsilon_i|$. Indeed, the experimental results in [7] prove that the procedure by Tan and Cleaveland outperform the ones in [13] and [3]. The space complexity of [7] depends on the product of the sizes of the two bisimulation quotients involved. Being bisimulation finer than simulation, such a space requirement may be more demanding than the one in [4].

In our work we start by observing that a simulation equivalence can be seen as a bisimulation in which the condition on the children is weaker than the condition on the parents: in order to have $m \equiv_s n$ is sufficient that a back-and-forth condition involving $\leq_s$ is satisfied. In the case of $\equiv_b$, instead, in order to have $m \equiv_b n$ any child of m (resp. n) must be in the same relation $\equiv_b$ with some of n's (resp. m's) children. This fact is, ultimately, the reason why on the one hand, the computational steps for determining a simulation must compute (successive approximations of) both $\equiv_s$ and $\leq_s$ and, on the other hand, it is not easy to rephrase the notion of simulation in purely algebraic terms as for bisimulation.

Here we show that such a rephrasing is in fact possible and that the simulation problem can be rewritten in terms of a coarsest stable partition problem in which partitions are also equipped with an acyclic relation over their classes. The simulation quotient equipped with the partial order induced on it by $\leq_s$ is shown to correspond to the "coarsest partition-pair" stable w.r.t. a suitable condition. Such a characterization of $\equiv_s$ (as well as of $\leq_s$) gives new insight on to the algebraic properties of the simulation equivalence. Moreover, it underpins the designing of a new space-efficient, and not too costly in time, algorithm for determining M and the simulation among its classes.

The key idea in our approach is that of using, in a sequence of approximation steps determining M, a graph (the $\exists\forall$-structure, similar to the structures used in [8]) whose nodes are equivalence classes and whose edges are capable to convey all the necessary information present in the original structure G. Such information is captured in a very natural way: since in the approximations nodes are in fact classes of nodes, we introduce two kind of edges between classes α and α', corresponding to the case in which either *there is* an edge between an element in α and one in α', or to the case in which *all* nodes in α are sent in α' by E. The stability condition (to be proved) equivalent to the notion of simulation is the following: a class β simulates a class α only if whenever there is an $\exists$-edge between α and γ, then there exists a $\forall$-edge between β and δ simulating γ (cf. Figure 1).

The use of the above structure and the formulation of the simulation problem as a coarsest stable partition problem allows us to define an algorithm computing the simulation relation as follows:

1. [13] can be used on a suitable $\exists\forall$-structure to move from an approximation to the next one, without wasting space (moreover, at any step the partition Σ_i is modified);
2. the algorithm stops when stability is reached.

The space complexity of our algorithm is $O(|M|^2 + |N|\log(|M|))$, exactly the same as [4] with which our algorithm shares the general structure. However, due to the use of [13] as subroutine, our time complexity turns out to be $O(|M|^2|E|)$, much better than $O(|M|^4(|E|+|M|^2)+|M|^2|N|(|N|+|M|^2))$ which is the time complexity of the algorithm in [4].

All the proofs of the claims in this paper can be found in [12] (available on the web).

2   Preliminaries

As far as the notions of *quasi order* and *partial order* are concerned, we refer to [9]. We will use Q^+ to refer to the transitive closure of a relation Q and Q^* to refer to its reflexive and transitive closure.

Definition 1. *A triple $G = \langle N, E, \Sigma \rangle$ is said to be a* labeled graph *if and only if $G^- = \langle N, E \rangle$ is a finite graph and Σ is a partition over N. We say that two nodes $n_1, n_2 \in N$ have the same* label *if they belong to the same class of Σ.*

Given a node $n \in N$ we will use $[n]_\Sigma$ (or $[n]$, if Σ is clear from the context) to denote the class of Σ to which n belongs.

Definition 2. *Let $G = \langle N, E, \Sigma \rangle$ be a labeled graph. A relation $\leq \subseteq N \times N$ is said to be a* simulation *over G if and only if:*
1. $n \leq m \rightarrow [n]_\Sigma = [m]_\Sigma$;
2. $(n \leq m \wedge nEn_1) \rightarrow \exists m_1(mEm_1 \wedge n_1 \leq m_1)$.

In this case we say that m simulates *n. We also say that m and n are* sim-equivalent *($m \equiv_s n$) if there exist two simulations $\leq_1$ and $\leq_2$, such that $n \leq_1 m$ and $m \leq_2 n$.*

A simulation over $G = \langle N, E, \Sigma \rangle$ is said to be *maximal* if it is maximal w.r.t. $\subseteq$.

Proposition 1. *Given a labeled graph $G = \langle N, E, \Sigma \rangle$ there always exists a unique maximal simulation $\leq_s$ over G and $\leq_s$ is a quasi order over N. The relation $\equiv_s$ (sim-equivalence) is an equivalence relation over N.*

Definition 3. *Given a labeled graph $G = \langle N, E, \Sigma \rangle$ the problem of computing the* similarity quotient *of G consists in computing the quotient $N/\equiv_s$, where $\equiv_s$ is the sim-equivalence over G.*

In [4] it has also been proved that there always exists a unique smallest labeled graph that is simulation equivalent to G, i.e. there is a unique way to put a minimum number of edges between the elements of $N/\equiv_s$ in order to obtain a labeled graph similar to G.

3   Simulation as Coarsest Partition Problem

In this section we introduce the *Generalized (Stable) Coarsest Partition Problem* (GCPP) which is the central notion in our approach. We call it *generalized* because we are not only going to deal with partitions to be refined (as in the classical coarsest partition problems [18,17,14]), but with *pairs* constituted of a partition and a relation over the partition. The equivalence of the similarity quotient problem and the GCPP will be proved at the end of this section.

Definition 4. *Let $G = \langle N, E \rangle$ be a finite graph. A partition-pair over G is a pair $\langle \Sigma, P \rangle$ in which Σ is a partition over N, and $P \subseteq \Sigma^2$ is a reflexive and acyclic relation over Σ.*

Given a labeled graph $G = \langle N, E, \Sigma \rangle$ an example of a partition-pair over G is given by the pair $\langle \Sigma, I \rangle$, where I is the identity relation over Σ.

Given two partitions Π and Σ, such that Π is finer than Σ, and a relation P over Σ, we use the notation $P(\Pi)$ to refer to the relation *induced* on Π by P, i.e.:

$$\forall \alpha\beta \in \Pi((\alpha, \beta) \in P(\Pi) \leftrightarrow \exists \alpha'\beta'((\alpha \subseteq \alpha' \land \beta \subseteq \beta' \land (\alpha', \beta') \in P)).$$

Denoting by $\mathcal{P}(G)$ the set of partition-pairs over G, we now introduce the partial order we need in order to be able to define the notion "$\langle \Sigma, P \rangle$ is *coarser* than $\langle \Pi, Q \rangle$".

Definition 5. *Let $\langle \Sigma, P \rangle, \langle \Pi, Q \rangle \in \mathcal{P}(G)$:*

$$\langle \Pi, Q \rangle \sqsubseteq \langle \Sigma, P \rangle \text{ iff } \Pi \text{ is finer than } \Sigma \text{ and } Q \subseteq P(\Pi).$$

The following definition introduces structures that in the algorithm, will suggest us the use of a subroutine based on the simulation algorithm by Henzinger, Henzinger, and Kopke in [13]. The use of such a subroutine guarantees a weak form of stability (see Definition 10) in the intermediate stages and is one of the keys in the improved time performance of our algorithm w.r.t. the one by Bustan and Grumberg [4].

Definition 6. *Let $G = \langle N, E \rangle$ be a graph and Π be a partition of N. The $\exists$-quotient structure over Π is the graph $\Pi_\exists = \langle \Pi, E_\exists \rangle$, where*

$$\alpha E_\exists \beta \quad \text{iff} \quad \exists n \exists m (n \in \alpha \land m \in \beta \land nEm).$$

The $\forall$-quotient structure over Π is the graph $\Pi_\forall = \langle \Pi, E_\forall \rangle$, where

$$\alpha E_\forall \beta \quad \text{iff} \quad \forall n(n \in \alpha \rightarrow \exists m(m \in \beta \land nEm)).$$

The $\exists\forall$-quotient structure over Π is the structure $\Pi_{\exists\forall} = \langle \Pi, E_\exists, E_\forall \rangle$.

Notice that $\alpha E_\forall \beta$ iff $\alpha \subseteq E^{-1}(\beta)$ and $\alpha E_\exists \beta$ iff $\alpha \cap E^{-1}(\beta) \neq \emptyset$. Similar notations (called *relation transformers* and *abstract transition relations*) were introduced in [8] in order to combine Model Checking and Abstract Interpretation.

We introduce here a definition, strongly connected to the definition of the quotient structures, that we will use later in the description of our algorithm (see Section 5).

Definition 7. *Given a graph, $G = \langle N, E \rangle$, and two partitions of N, Σ and Π, with Π finer than Σ, the $\exists\forall$-induced quotient structure over Π is the structure $\Sigma_{\exists\forall}(\Pi) = \langle \Pi, E_\exists^\Sigma(\Pi), E_\forall^\Sigma(\Pi) \rangle$, where:*

$$\alpha E_\exists^\Sigma(\Pi)\beta \text{ iff } \quad \alpha \cap E^{-1}(\beta) \neq \emptyset$$
$$\alpha E_\forall^\Sigma(\Pi)\beta \text{ iff } \quad \alpha E_\exists^\Sigma(\Pi)\beta \quad \land \quad \alpha \subseteq E^{-1}(\beta') \land \quad \beta \subseteq \beta' \in \Sigma$$

with $\alpha, \beta \in \Pi$.

We are now ready to introduce the fundamental notion in the generalized coarsest partition problems, that is the notion of stability of a partition-pair w.r.t. a relation:

Definition 8. *Given a graph $G = \langle N, E \rangle$, we say that a partition-pair $\langle \Sigma, P \rangle$ over G is stable w.r.t. the relation E if and only if*

$$\forall \alpha, \beta, \gamma \in \Sigma((\alpha, \beta) \in P \wedge \alpha E_\exists \gamma \rightarrow \exists \delta \in \Sigma((\gamma, \delta) \in P \wedge \beta E_\forall \delta)). \tag{1}$$

Condition (1) in the previous definition is equivalent to:

$$\forall \alpha, \beta, \gamma \in \Sigma((\alpha, \beta) \in P \wedge \alpha \cap E^{-1}(\gamma) \neq \emptyset \rightarrow \exists \delta \in \Sigma((\gamma, \delta) \in P \wedge \beta \subseteq E^{-1}(\delta))). \tag{2}$$

The stability condition is exactly the condition which holds between the classes of $N/\equiv_s$: if $\alpha, \beta \in N/\equiv_s$ with $\alpha \leq_s \beta$ (i.e. all the elements of α are simulated by all the elements of β), and an element a in α reaches an element c in γ, then all the elements b of β must reach at least one element d which simulates c. Taking, in particular, all the maximal (w.r.t. $\leq_s$) elements d simulating c reached by elements in β, we have that all the elements in β reach a class δ which simulates c and, hence, which simulates γ.

In Figure 1 we give a graphical representation of the notion of stability using both the characterizations (1) and (2).

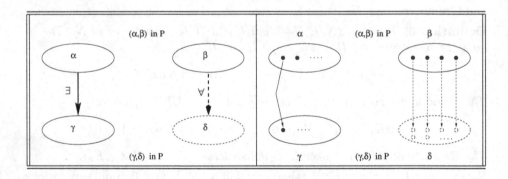

Fig. 1. The Stability Condition.

We will use the notion of stability of a partition-pair w.r.t. a relation in the definition of generalized coarsest partition problem, in the same way in which the notion of stability of a partition w.r.t. a relation is used in the definition of coarsest partition problem.

Definition 9 (Generalized Coarsest Partition Prob. – GCPP). *Let $G = \langle N, E \rangle$ be a graph and $\langle \Sigma, P \rangle$ be a partition-pair over G the generalized coarsest partition problem consists in finding a partition-pair $\langle M, \preceq \rangle$ such that:*
(a) $\langle M, \preceq \rangle \sqsubseteq \langle \Sigma, P^+ \rangle$ and $\langle M, \preceq \rangle$ is stable w.r.t. G;
(b) $\langle M, \preceq \rangle$ is $\sqsubseteq$-maximal satisfying (a).

If $\langle \Pi, Q \rangle$ is a partition-pair which satisfies (a) only, we say that it is a stable refinement of $\langle \Sigma, P \rangle$.

Notice that in the above definition $\langle M, \preceq \rangle$ is a refinement of $\langle \Sigma, P^+ \rangle$, while it can be the case that it is not a refinement of $\langle \Sigma, P \rangle$. In particular this happens always in case $\langle \Sigma, P \rangle$ is not stable while $\langle \Sigma, P^+ \rangle$ is stable. In this case $\langle \Sigma, P^+ \rangle$ itself is a solution of the GCPP. In general, the solution of the GCPP can always be found by a suitable sequence of splits (of classes) and adequate completion of the relation in order to take the newly generated classes into account.

Remark 1. Notice that it is important that $\preceq$ is reflexive (it is reflexive, since $\langle M, \preceq \rangle$ is a partition-pair). This is necessary in order to prove that the maximal solution is unique. Given $G = \langle N, E \rangle$ with $N = \{n_1, n_2\}$ and $E = \{(n_1, n_2)\}$, and $\langle \Sigma, P \rangle$ with $\Sigma = \{N\}$ and $P = \{(N, N)\}$. It holds that both $\langle \Sigma, \emptyset \rangle$ and $\langle \Pi, Q \rangle$ with $\Pi = \{\{n_1\}, \{n_2\}\}$ and $Q = \{(\{n_1\}, \{n_1\}), (\{n_2\}, \{n_2\}), (\{n_2\}, \{n_1\})\}$ are maximal solutions of the partition problem, but the first is not a partition-pair. Similarly, the acyclicity condition is important because otherwise we could coarsen the partition by merging all the classes which form cycles.

We prove that a GCPP has always a unique solution and then we spell out the connection between similarity quotient problems and GCPP's.

Theorem 1. *The GCPP over G and $\langle \Sigma, P \rangle$ has a unique solution $\langle M, \preceq \rangle$ and the relation $\preceq$ is a partial order over M.*

The proof of this theorem is carried out by proving that each generalized coarsest partition problem has a unique solution which can be determined by solving a similarity quotient problem.

Also the opposite direction is true: a similarity quotient problem can be solved using a generalized coarsest partition problem.

Theorem 2. *Let $G = \langle N, E, \Sigma \rangle$ be a labeled graph. Let $\langle M, \preceq \rangle$ be the solution of the GCPP over $G^- = \langle N, E \rangle$ and the partition-pair $\langle \Sigma, I \rangle$, where I is the identity relation over Σ. M is the simulation quotient of G and*

$$\forall n, m \in N \ n \leq_s m \ \text{iff} \ [n]_M \preceq [m]_M.$$

Hence, in order to solve the problem of determining the similarity quotient of a labeled graph $G = \langle N, E, \Sigma \rangle$ we can, equivalently, solve the generalized coarsest partition problem over $\langle N, E \rangle$ and $\langle \Sigma, I \rangle$. If $\langle M, \preceq \rangle$ is the solution of the GCPP (i.e. the maximal refinement of $\langle \Sigma, I \rangle$ stable w.r.t. E), then the relation $\leq_{\langle M, \preceq \rangle}$ defined as

$$\forall n, m \in N (n \leq_{\langle M, \preceq \rangle} m \ \text{iff} \ [n]_M \preceq [m]_M)$$

is the maximal simulation over G, and M is the partition which corresponds to the sim-equivalence $\equiv_s$ (c.f. Definition 2).

4   Computing a Solution to the GCPP

We now introduce an operator σ mapping partition-pairs into partition-pairs, which will turn out to be the engine of our algorithm. The results in this section will allow us to conclude that a procedure which computes σ can be used to solve GCPP's and, hence, to compute similarity quotients: it is only necessary to iterate the computation of σ at most $|M|$ times.

In particular, the operator σ is defined in such a way that it refines the partition-pair $\langle \Sigma, P \rangle$ obtaining a partition-pair $\langle \Pi, Q \rangle$ which is *more stable* than $\langle \Sigma, P \rangle$ and is never finer than the solution of the GCPP over $\langle \Sigma, P \rangle$. In the first condition of σ we impose to split the classes of Σ which do not respect the stability condition w.r.t. themselves: if a class α is such that $\alpha E_\exists \gamma$ and it does not exists a class δ such that $(\gamma, \delta) \in P$ and $\alpha E_\forall \delta$, then the pair (α, α) does not respect the stability condition, hence we must split α. The first condition is used to build Π, and then the second and the third conditions are in σ used to define Q using the Π already obtained. Intuitively, the second and the third conditions allow to obtain Q from P by starting from $P(\Pi)$ and removing the minimum number of pairs which contradict stability.

Definition 10. *Let* $G = \langle N, E \rangle$ *be a graph and* $\langle \Sigma, P \rangle$ *be a partition-pair over* G, *the partition-pair* $\langle \Pi, Q \rangle = \sigma(\langle \Sigma, P \rangle)$ *is defined as:*

(1σ) Π *is the coarsest partition finer than* Σ *such that*

$$(a) \ \forall \alpha \in \Pi \ \forall \gamma \in \Sigma(\alpha E_\exists \gamma \rightarrow \exists \delta \in \Sigma((\gamma, \delta) \in P \wedge \alpha E_\forall \delta));$$

(2σ) Q *is the maximal relation over* Π *such that* $Q \subseteq P(\Pi)$ *and if* $(\alpha, \beta) \in Q$, *then:*

$$(b) \ \forall \gamma \in \Sigma(\alpha E_\forall \gamma \rightarrow \exists \gamma' \in \Sigma((\gamma, \gamma') \in P \wedge \beta E_\exists \gamma')) \quad and$$
$$(c) \ \forall \gamma \in \Pi(\alpha E_\forall \gamma \rightarrow \exists \gamma' \in \Pi((\gamma, \gamma') \in Q \wedge \beta E_\exists \gamma')).$$

By abuse of notation we use $E_\exists$ and $E_\forall$ also when the classes belong to different partitions.

Condition (a) in (1σ) imposes to opportunely split the classes of the partition Σ: these splits are forced by the fact that we are looking for a partition-pair *stable* w.r.t. the relation of the given graph and we know that in each partition-pair $\langle \Sigma, P \rangle$ the second component is reflexive (i.e. $\forall \alpha \in \Sigma(\alpha, \alpha) \in P$). Using condition (b) in (2σ), together with condition (a) in (1σ) and exploiting the fact that P is acyclic, it is possible to prove that Q is acyclic: the acyclicity of P ensures that a cycle could arise only among classes of Π which are all contained in a unique class of Σ, then using condition (a) in (1σ) and (b) in (2σ) we obtain a contradiction. Condition (c) is fundamental, together with condition (a), in order to obtain the result in Theorem 4: if it holds that $\alpha E_\forall \gamma$, then *no matter how we split* α one of the subclasses generated from α has a chance (in the solution of GCPP) to be in relation with at least one of the subclasses generated from β only if $\beta E_\exists \gamma'$ and γ is in relation with γ'. The following results guarantee the correctness of σ and, hence, of our approach.

Theorem 3. *Let* $G = \langle N, E \rangle$ *be a graph and* $\langle \Sigma, P \rangle$ *be a partition-pair over* G. *There always exists a unique partition-pair* $\langle \Pi, Q \rangle$ *which satisfies the conditions in Definition 10, i.e.* σ *is always uniquely defined.*

Now that we have obtained that given a partition-pair $\langle \Sigma, P \rangle$, there exists a unique $\sigma(\langle \Sigma, P \rangle)$, we can link fix-points of the operator σ with solutions of GCPP's.

Lemma 1. *Let $\langle \Sigma, P \rangle$ and $\langle \Pi, Q \rangle$ be two partition-pairs and let $\langle M, \preceq \rangle$ be the solution of the GCPP over the graph G and $\langle \Sigma, P \rangle$. If $\langle M, \preceq \rangle \sqsubseteq \langle \Pi, Q \rangle$, then $\langle M, \preceq \rangle \sqsubseteq \sigma(\langle \Pi, Q \rangle)$*

Theorem 4. *Let $G = \langle N, E \rangle$ be a graph and $\langle \Sigma, P \rangle$ a partition-pair over G with P transitive. Let $\langle M, \preceq \rangle$ be the solution of the GCPP over G and $\langle \Sigma, P \rangle$. If i is such that $\sigma^i(\langle \Sigma, P \rangle) = \langle \Sigma_i, \mathsf{P}_i \rangle$ and $\sigma^{i+1}(\langle \Sigma, P \rangle) = \langle \Sigma_i, \mathsf{P}_{i+1} \rangle$, then $\mathsf{P}_{i+1} = \mathsf{P}_i$ and $\langle \Sigma_i, \mathsf{P}_i \rangle = \langle M, \preceq \rangle$.*

The meaning of this theorem is that if $\langle \Sigma, P \rangle$ is a partition-pair over a graph G such that P is transitive, then there exists an i such that $\sigma^i(\langle \Sigma, P \rangle) = \sigma^{i+1}(\langle \Sigma, P \rangle)$, and $\sigma^i(\langle \Sigma, P \rangle)$ is the solution of the GCPP over G and $\langle \Sigma, P \rangle$. In particular, when we iteratively apply the operator σ until we reach a fix-point, at each iteration we refine the partition and we remove pairs from the relation. What we proved in the above theorem is that it is never the case that there exists an iteration in which we do not refine the partition, but only remove pairs from the relation. In a certain sense this means that the two conditions (b) and (c) we gave in (2σ) to remove pairs are *optimal*. This property gives us the upper bound to the index i which is at most $|\Sigma_i|$, which in the worst case is $O(|N|)$.

Corollary 1. *The solution $\langle M, \preceq \rangle$ of the GCPP over a graph G and a partition-pair $\langle \Sigma, P \rangle$ can be computed using at most $|M|$ times the operator σ.*

Notice that, given a graph G and a partition-pair $\langle \Sigma, P \rangle$, the solution of the GPPC over G and $\langle \Sigma, P \rangle$ corresponds to the solution of the GPPC over G and $\langle \Sigma, P^+ \rangle$.

The characterizations obtained in this section allow us to conclude that if we are able to define a procedure which, given a partition-pair $\langle \Sigma, P \rangle$ computes $\sigma(\langle \Sigma, P \rangle)$, then we can use it to solve GCPP's and hence to compute similarity quotients. In particular we recall that given a similarity quotient problem over a labeled graph $G = \langle N, E, \Sigma \rangle$, in order to solve it it is sufficient solve the GCPP over G and $\langle \Sigma, I \rangle$ (I is trivially transitive).

Moreover, the last corollary ensures that it will be necessary to iterate the procedure which computes σ at most $|M|$ times. This is a first improvement on the time complexity w.r.t. the algorithm presented in [4]: in a certain sense [4] computes an operator which refines the partition-pair less than σ, and hence it is possible that the computation has to be iterated up to $|M|^2$ times.

In the next section we present the procedure which computes σ.

5 The Algorithm

In this section we outline an algorithm which solves the generalized coarsest partition problem we have presented in the previous section. The **Stable Simulation Algorithm** takes as input a graph $G = \langle N, E \rangle$ and a partition-pair $\langle \Sigma, P \rangle$, with P transitive, calls the two functions **Refine** and **Update** until a fix-point is reached, and returns the partition-pair $\langle M, \preceq \rangle$ which is the solution of the GCPP over G and $\langle \Sigma, P \rangle$. In order to solve the GCPP over G and $\langle \Sigma, P \rangle$

with P not transitive, it is sufficient to first compute P^+ and the cost of this operation is $O(\Sigma^3)$ which, hence, does not affect the global cost of our algorithm. The function **Refine** takes as input a partition-pair $\langle \Sigma_i, P_i \rangle$ and returns the partition Σ_{i+1} which is the coarsest that satisfies the condition (a) in (1σ) of Definition 10. The function **Update** takes as input a partition-pair $\langle \Sigma_i, P_i \rangle$ and the refinement Σ_{i+1} and it produces the reflexive and acyclic relation over Σ_{i+1} which is the largest that satisfies conditions (b) and (c) in (2σ) of Definition 10. In particular, at the end of each iteration of the while-loop in the **Stable Simulation Algorithm** we have that $\langle \Sigma_{i+1}, P_{i+1} \rangle = \sigma(\langle \Sigma_i, P_i \rangle)$. It is immediate to

---

Stable Simulation Algorithm$(\langle N, E \rangle, \langle \Sigma, P \rangle)$

> change := $\top$;
> $i := 0$;
> while change do
>> change := $\bot$;
>> $\Sigma_{i+1} := \mathbf{Refine}(\Sigma_i, \mathsf{P}_i, \text{change})$;
>> $\mathsf{P}_{i+1} := \mathbf{Update}(\Sigma_i, \mathsf{P}_i, \Sigma_{i+1})$;
>> $i := i + 1$;

Fig. 2. The **Stable Simulation Algorithm**.

---

see that the **Refine** function works exactly as described in the proof of Theorem 3 (see [12]), and hence it produces the partition which is the first element of $\sigma(\Sigma_i, \mathsf{P}_i)$.

Corollary 2. *If* $\sigma(\langle \Sigma_i, \mathsf{P}_i \rangle) = \langle \Pi, Q \rangle$, *then* $\Pi = \Sigma_{i+1}$.

The deletion of "wrong" pairs is performed by **Update** through two calls to the function **New_HHK**, which is a version of [13] adapted to our purposes here. The function **Update** removes pairs from $\mathsf{P}_i(\Sigma_{i+1}) = \mathsf{Ind}_{i+1}$ in order to obtain the relation P_{i+1} which satisfies condition (2σ) of Definition 10. In particular Ref_{i+1} (obtained after the first call to **New_HHK** only) satisfies the first of the two conditions but not necessarily the second one.

Notice that the space complexity of the calls to **New_HHK** remains limited since they are made on quotient stuctures. This function is based on the use of the two structures $\Sigma_{i\exists\forall}(\Sigma_{i+1})$ (cf. Definition 7) and $\Sigma_{i+1\exists\forall}$ (cf. Definition 6), and on the following equivalent formulation of condition (2σ).

Proposition 2. *Let* $G = \langle N, E \rangle$ *be a graph,* $\langle \Sigma, P \rangle$ *be a partition-pair and* Π *be a partition finer than* Σ. *Q satisfies (2σ) of Definition 10 if and only if Q is the maximal relation over Π such that $Q \subseteq P(\Pi)$ and if $(\alpha, \beta) \in Q$, then:*

$$\forall \gamma \in \Pi(\alpha E_\forall^\Sigma(\Pi)\gamma \to \exists \gamma' \in \Pi((\gamma, \gamma') \in P(\Pi) \wedge \beta E_\exists^\Sigma(\Pi)\gamma')) \wedge$$
$$\forall \gamma \in \Pi(\alpha E_\forall \gamma \to \exists \gamma' \in \Pi((\gamma, \gamma') \in Q \wedge \beta E_\exists \gamma')),$$

where $E_\forall^\Sigma(\Pi)$ and $E_\forall^\Sigma(\Pi)$ are the edges of the $\exists\forall$-induced quotient structure, while $E_\exists$ and $E_\forall$ are the edges of the $\exists\forall$ quotient structure.

$\textbf{Refine}(\varSigma_i, \mathsf{P}_i, \mathsf{change})$

> $\varSigma_{i+1} := \varSigma_i;$
> for each $\beta \in \varSigma_{i+1}$ do $\mathsf{Stable}(\beta) := \emptyset;$
> for each $\alpha \in \varSigma_i$ do $\mathsf{Row}(\alpha) := \{\gamma \mid (\alpha, \gamma) \in \mathsf{P}_i)\};$
> Let Sort be a topological sorting of $\langle \varSigma_i, \mathsf{P}_i \rangle;$
> while $\mathsf{Sort} \neq \emptyset$ do
> > $\alpha := dequeue(\mathsf{Sort});$
> > $A := \emptyset;$
> > $\mathsf{Split}(\alpha) := \{\beta \in \varSigma_{i+1} \mid \beta E_\exists \alpha\};$
> > for each $\beta \in \mathsf{Split}(\alpha), \mathsf{Stable}(\beta) \cap \mathsf{Row}(\alpha) = \emptyset$ do
> > > $\beta_1 := \beta \cap E^{-1}(\alpha);$
> > > $\beta_2 := \beta \setminus \beta_1;$
> > > if $\beta_2 \neq \emptyset$ then $\mathsf{change} := \top;$
> > > $\varSigma_{i+1} := \varSigma_{i+1} \setminus \{\beta\};$
> > > $A := A \cup \{\beta_1, \beta_2\};$
> > > $\mathsf{Stable}(\beta_1) := \mathsf{Stable}(\beta) \cup \{\alpha\};$
> > > $\mathsf{Stable}(\beta_2) := \mathsf{Stable}(\beta);$
> > $\varSigma_{i+1} := \varSigma_{i+1} \cup A;$
> > $\mathsf{Sort} := \mathsf{Sort} \setminus \{\alpha\};$
> return $\varSigma_{i+1}$

Fig. 3. The **Refine** Function.

$\textbf{Update}(\varSigma_i, \mathsf{P}_i, \varSigma_{i+1})$

> $\mathsf{Ind}_{i+1} := \{(\alpha_1, \beta_1) \mid \alpha_1, \beta_1 \in \varSigma_{i+1}, \alpha_1 \subseteq \alpha, \beta_1 \subseteq \beta(\alpha, \beta) \in \mathsf{P}_i\};$
> $\varSigma_{i\exists\forall}(\varSigma_{i+1}) := \langle \varSigma_{i+1}, E_\exists^{\varSigma_i}(\varSigma_{i+1}), E_\forall^{\varSigma_i}(\varSigma_{i+1})\rangle;$
> $\mathsf{Ref}_{i+1} := \textbf{New\_HHK}(\varSigma_{i\exists\forall}(\varSigma_{i+1}), \mathsf{Ind}_{i+1}, \bot);$
> $\varSigma_{(i+1)\exists\forall} := \langle \varSigma_{i+1}, E_\exists, E_\forall\rangle;$
> $\mathsf{P}_{i+1} := \textbf{New\_HHK}(\varSigma_{(i+1)\exists\forall}, \mathsf{Ref}_{i+1}, \top);$
> return P_{i+1}

Fig. 4. The **Update** Function.

In Figure 5 we present the conditions described in Proposition 2 on the $\exists\forall$-induced quotient structure and on the $\exists\forall$-quotient structure. As a consequence of Theorem 4 these conditions are weaker than the stability condition.

The computation performed by Update correspond to determine the largest relation included in P_i and satisfying conditions (2σ), thereby getting us closer to stability. Such a computation is proved correct as a fix-point computation of an operator τ defined as follows:

Definition 11. *Let $D = \langle S, R_1, R_2 \rangle$ be such that $R_2 \subseteq R_1$, and let $K \subseteq S \times S$. We define $\tau_D(K) = K \setminus \{(b, c) \mid \exists a(bR_2a \wedge \forall d(cR_1d \rightarrow (a, d) \notin K))\}$. We use $Fix(\tau_D)(K)$ to denote the greatest fix-point of τ_D smaller than K.*

Corollary 3. *Let $G = \langle N, E \rangle$ be a graph, and $\langle \varSigma, P \rangle$ be a partition-pair. If $\sigma(\langle \varSigma, P \rangle) = \langle \Pi, Q \rangle$, then $Q = Fix(\tau_{\Pi_{\exists\forall}})(\tau_{\varSigma_{\exists\forall}(\Pi)}(P(\Pi)))$.*

Now we complete the connection between the operator τ and the function **New_HHK** presented in Figure 6.

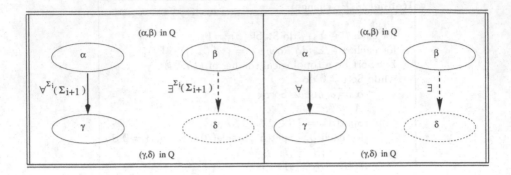

Fig. 5. The conditions in (2σ) on the quotient structures.

New_HHK$(\langle S, R_1, R_2 \rangle, K, U)$

$P := K;$
for each $a \in S$ do
    $sim(a) := \{e \mid (a, e) \in K\};$
    $rem(a) := S \setminus pre_1(sim(a));$
while $\{a \mid rem(a) \neq \emptyset\} \neq \emptyset$ do
    let $a \in \{a \mid rem(a) \neq \emptyset\}$
    for each $b \in pre_2(a), c \in rem(a), c \in sim(b)$ do
        $sim(b) := sim(b) \setminus \{c\};$
        $P := P \setminus \{(b, c)\};$
        if U then for each $c_1 \in pre_1(c)$ do
            if $post_1(c_1) \cap sim(b) = \emptyset$ then $rem(b) := rem(b) \cup \{c_1\};$
    $rem(a) := \emptyset;$
return P

Fig. 6. The **New_HHK** Function.

Lemma 2.

   New_HHK$(D, K, \bot) = \tau_D(K)$ *and* **New_HHK**$(D, K, \top) = Fix(\tau_D)(K).$

Recalling that on the ground of Corollary 3 P_{i+1} can be computed from P_i as fix-point, the correctness of the procedures **Update** and **Refine** is based on:
Theorem 5. $\langle \Sigma_{i+1}, P_{i+1} \rangle = \sigma(\langle \Sigma_i, P_i \rangle).$
As a consequence of Theorem 4 and of Corollary 1, since the **Stable Simulation Algorithm** terminates whenever $\Sigma_{i+1} = \Sigma_i$, we can conclude that it computes the solution $\langle M, \preceq \rangle$ of the GCPP over G and $\langle \Sigma, P \rangle$ performing at most $|M|$ iterations of the while-loop.

    The complexity analysis is based on the following result:
Theorem 6. *Let* $G = \langle N, E \rangle$ *and* $\langle \Sigma, P \rangle$ *be a partition-pair with* P *transitive.* **Stable Simulation Algorithm** *computes the solution* $\langle M, \preceq \rangle$ *of the GCPP over them in time* $O(|M|^2 |E|)$ *and in space* $O(|M|^2 + |N| \log(|M|)).$

6   Related Works

Recently the simulation relation has been algorithmically revisited in [4] and in [7]. Both works exploit a *partition refinement* argument in order to improve on the simulation algorithms in [13] and [3]. Given a labeled graph $G = \langle N, E, \Sigma \rangle$, the latter ([13,3]) can be used to obtain the simulation quotient over N in $O(|N||E|)$ time and $O(|N|^2)$ space. The main aim of the authors of [4] is that of keeping as low as possible the space requirements of their simulation algorithm. Indeed, despite its rather heavy time complexity $(O(|M|^4(|E| + |M|^2) + |M|^2|N|(|N| + |M|^2)))$, the routine in [4] has a space complexity depending only on the size of the simulation quotient, $|M|$, given in output: $O(|M|^2 + |N| \log(|M|))$. As well as in [4], the space parameter is carefully thought of in the algorithm we have presented in this work: our major aim is that of designing a highly space-efficient procedure for deciding simulation equivalence that is not too costly in time. Our **Stable Simulation Algorithm**, as the one in [4], gives in output the simulation quotient together with the simulation partial order over its classes. Moreover it shares with [4] the same structure: each iteration consists of a step of partition's refinement followed by an update of a relation over such a partition. Indeed, the two algorithms have exactly the same space requirements but the procedure presented here has a better time complexity. While the **Partitioning Algorithm** in [4] need $O(|M|^2)$ iterations to get to a fix-point, our **Stable Simulation Algorithms** ends after $O(|M|)$ iterations only (cf. Theorem 6). Intuitively, on the ground of the characterization of the simulation given in Theorem 2, our algorithm updates "deeper" the relation over the partition so that in each refinement step at least one class *must* be split. Moreover, both the refinement and the update steps in the **Stable Simulation Algorithm** are less time-demanding than the corresponding functions in [4]. So, as stated in Theorem 6, the time complexity of our routine is $O(|M|^2|E|)$. Above we show an example in which our algorithm requires few iterations than the one in [4].

Example 1. Parts *a*), *b*) and *c*) of Figure 7 reflect, respectively, the partition-pairs on the depicted labeled graph after: *a*) the initialization phase of the **Stable Simulation Algorithm**; *b*) and *c*) the first and the second call to the subroutine **NewHHK** during the first call to the procedure **Update**. The **Stable Simulation Algorithm** needs only $O(1)$ iterations to get to the simulation quotient of the graph in 7, whereas the procedure in [4] needs $O(N)$ iterations. More in detail using [4], there are $O(N)$ iterations in which the partition never changes while the relation over its classes is successively refined.

The simulation algorithm in [7] also takes advantage of a *partition refinement* argument. However, while the partitions involved in [4] and in the **Stable Simulation Algorithm** are always coarser than the simulation quotient, the ones refined in [7] are always coarser than the bisimulation quotient. Given in input two labeled transition transition systems T_1 and T_2, the algorithm in [7] proceeds simultaneously minimizing via bisimulation the two graphs and determining the set of classes in T_2 able to simulate each class in T_1. The partition over a labeled

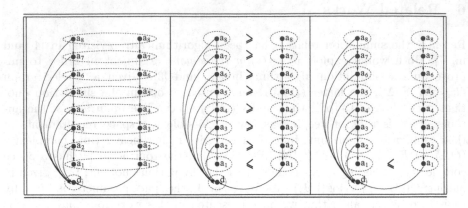

Fig. 7. Example of computation.

graph induced by the bisimulation equivalence is finer than the partition induced by the simulation: hence, a relation over its classes may have higher space requirements. However, the former equivalence can be computed faster than the latter because a "process-the-smallest-half" policy can be used (see [17,14]). Thus the algorithm proposed by Cleaveland and Tan in [7] achieves a time complexity which is today's state-of-the-art: $O(|B_1||B_2|+|E_1|\log(|N_1|)+|B_1||E_2|+|\varepsilon_1||B_2|)$, where ε_i and B_i represent the relation and the states'space of the transition system T_i reduced via bisimulation. Nevertheless, since at least on T_1 the entire bisimulation quotient must be computed, the deeper is the minimizing power of the simulation equivalence with respect to bisimulation, the less space-efficient the algorithm in [7] becomes (with respect to [4] as well as to our routine). For the sake of the argument, a family of examples on which [7] has higher space requirements than [4] as well than our procedure has the following features:

- T_1 is not reducible via bisimulation whereas the simulation equivalence has a deep minimizing power on it;
- T_2 follows T_1 in the simulation preorder over transition systems.

Figure 8 depicts two transition systems with the above features: whatever are the initial states of the two systems, T_2 simulates T_1. All the states belonging to the cycle in T_1 are simulation-equivalent and pairwise not bisimilar. In T_2 there are neither bisimilar nor similar states; hence, [7] require $O(|N|^2)$ space whereas the space requirement of the **Stable Simulation Algorithm** is bounded by $O(|N|\log(|N|))$.

We conclude by observing that, in a minimization framework, choosing the simulation equivalence rather than the bisimulation one is paying only if the simulation's power of reduction strongly overcomes bisimulation's one (because bisimulation is less time demanding than simulation). In other words simulation becomes worthwhile when $|M| << |B|$, i.e. when the routine in [7] and the one proposed here have comparable time complexities.

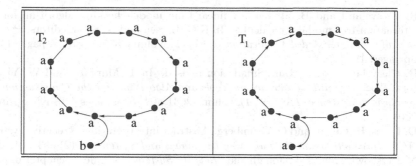

Fig. 8. Space Requirements.

7 Conclusions and Further Work

We think that the circle of ideas presented here can be useful in the study of fast simulation algorithm developed to operate in situations in which strong space constraint are present. Moreover, the use of the ∀∃-structure and the definition of coarsest partition problems on them, seem to be a methodology with some potential in all those situations in which a fix-point in the lattice of equivalence relations is to be computed.

We plain to work on a symbolic implementation of our algorithm which is naturally suggested by the fact that our algorithm always works on sets of nodes (the classes of the partitions).

An attempt to combine negative and positive strategies to solve the coarsest partition problem presented here (as, in the case of bisimulation, has been done in [10]) is under study.

References

1. J. van Benthem. *Modal Correspondence Theory.* PhD thesis, Universiteit van Amsterdam, Instituut voor Logica en Grondslagenonderzoek van Exacte Wetenschappen, 1976.
2. B. Bloom. *Ready Simulation, Bisimulation, and the Semantics of CCS-like Languages.* PhD thesis, Department of Electrical Engineering and Computer Science, Massachusetts Institute of Technology, 1989.
3. Bard Bloom and Robert Paige. Transformational design and implementation of a new efficient solution to the ready simulation problem. *Science of Computer Programming*, 24(3):189–220, 1995.
4. D. Bustan and O. Grumberg. Simulation based minimization. In D.A. McAllester, editor, *Proc. 17th Int'l Conference on Automated Deduction (CADE'00)*, volume 1831 of *LNCS*, pages 255–270. Springer, 2000.
5. R. Cleaveland, J. Parrow, and B. Steffen. The Concurrency Workbench: A Semantics Based Tool for the Verification of Concurrent Systems. *ACM Transactions on Programming Languages and Systems*, 15(1):36–72, 1993.

6. R. Cleaveland and B. Steffen. A linear-time model-checking algorithm for the alternation-free modal mu-calculus. In K.G. Larsen and A. Skou, editors, *Proceedings of Computer Aided Verification (CAV'91)*, volume 575 of *LNCS*, pages 48–58. Springer, 1992.

7. R. Cleaveland and L. Tan. Simulation revised. In T. Margaria and W. Yi, editors, *Proc. 7th Int'l Conference on Tools and Algorithms for the Construction and Analysis of Systems (TACAS'01)*, volume 2031 of *LNCS*, pages 480–495. Springer, 2001.

8. D. Dams, R. Gerth, and O. Grumberg. Abstract interpretation of reactive systems. *ACM Transactions on Programming Languages and Systems*, 19(2):253–291, 1997.

9. N. Dershowitz and J.-P. Jouannaud. *Rewrite Systems*, volume B, chapter 6, pages 244–320. Elsevier/MIT press, 1990.

10. A. Dovier, C. Piazza, and A. Policriti. A fast bisimulation algorithm. In G. Berry, H. Comon, and A. Finkel, editors, *Proceedings of Computer Aided Verification (CAV'01)*, volume 2102 of *LNCS*, pages 79–90. Springer, 2001.

11. M. Forti and F. Honsell. Set theory with free construction principles. *Annali Scuola Normale Superiore di Pisa, Cl. Sc.*, IV(10):493–522, 1983.

12. R. Gentilini, C. Piazza, and A. Policriti. Simulation as coarsest partition problem. RR 04-01, Dep. of Computer Science, University of Udine, Italy, 2001. Available at http://www.dimi.uniud.it/~piazza/simul.ps.gz.

13. M. R. Henzinger, T. A. Henzinger, and P. W. Kopke. Computing simulations on finite and infinite graphs. In *36th Annual Symposium on Foundations of Computer Science (FOCS'95)*, pages 453–462. IEEE Computer Society Press, 1995.

14. J.E. Hopcroft. An $n \log n$ algorithm for minimizing states in a finite automaton. In *Theory of Machines and Computations, Ed. by Zvi Kohavi and Azaria Paz*, pages 189–196. Academic Press, 1971.

15. R. Milner. A calculus of communicating systems. In G. Goos and J. Hartmanis, editors, *Lecture Notes on Computer Science*, volume 92. Springer, 1980.

16. O. Grumberg and D.E. Long. Model checking and modular verification. *ACM Transactions on Programming Languages and systems*, 16(3):843–871, 1994.

17. R. Paige and R. E. Tarjan. Three partition refinement algorithms. *SIAM Journal on Computing*, 16(6):973–989, 1987.

18. R. Paige, R. E. Tarjan, and R. Bonic. A linear time solution to the single function coarsest partition problem. *Theoretical Computer Science*, 40(1):67–84, 1985.

Temporal Debugging for Concurrent Systems

Elsa Gunter[1] and Doron Peled[2]

[1] Department of Computer Science
New Jersey Institute of Technology
Newark, NJ 07102, USA
[2] Dept. of Elect. and Computer Eng.
The University of Texas at Austin
Austin, TX 78712, USA

Abstract. Temporal logic is often used as the specification formalism for the automatic verification of finite state systems. The automatic temporal verification of a system is a procedure that returns a yes/no answer, and in the latter case also provides a counterexample. In this paper we suggest a new application for temporal logic, as a way of assisting the debugging of a concurrent or a sequential program. We employ temporal logic over finite sequences as a constraint formalism that is used to control the way we step through the states of the debugged system. Using such temporal specification and various search strategies, we are able to traverse the executions of the system and obtain important intuitive information about its behaviors. We describe an implementation of these ideas as a debugging tool.

1 Introduction

Temporal logic is a specification formalism that is often used to express properties of software and hardware systems. Model checking techniques allow us to check a finite state description of a system against its temporal specification, and provide a counter example in case the property does not hold.

In this paper we suggest to extend the use of a temporal specification, and use temporal logic for interactively controlling the debugging of systems. We allow specifying temporal properties of *finite sequences*. A debugger is enriched with the ability to progress from one step to another via a finite sequence of states that satisfy a temporal property.

The usual mode of debugging involves stepping through the states of a system (program) by executing one or several transitions (with different granularities, e.g., a transition can involve the the execution of a procedure). Debugging concurrent systems is harder, since there are several cooperating processes that need to be monitored. Stepping through the different transitions can be applied in many different ways. Instead, we allow applying a temporal property that describes a finite sequence of concurrent events that need to be executed from the current state, leaping into the next state.

We interpret linear temporal logic (LTL) on finite sequences. The automatic translation from LTL to finite state automata in [4] is adapted to include the finite case. We describe various search algorithms that can be used for generating appropriate paths and states during a debugging session.

J.-P. Katoen and P. Stevens (Eds.): TACAS 2002, LNCS 2280, pp. 431–444, 2002.

2   Defining LTL on Finite Sequences

One of the most popular specification formalisms for concurrent and reactive systems is Linear Temporal Logic (LTL) [7]. Its syntax is as follows:

$$\varphi ::= (\varphi) \mid \neg\varphi \mid \varphi \vee \varphi \mid \varphi \wedge \varphi \mid \bigcirc \varphi \mid \overline{\bigcirc}\varphi \mid \Box\varphi \mid \Diamond\varphi \mid \varphi\,\mathcal{U}\,\varphi \mid \varphi\,\mathcal{V}\,\varphi \mid p$$

where $p \in \mathcal{P}$, with $\mathcal{P}$ a set of propositional letters. We denote a propositional sequence over $2^{\mathcal{P}}$ by σ, its ith state (where the first state is numbered 0) by $\sigma(i)$, and its suffix starting from the ith state by $\sigma^{(i)}$. Let $|\sigma|$ be the length of the sequence Σ, which is a natural number. The semantic interpretation of LTL is as follows:

- $\sigma \models \bigcirc\varphi$ iff $|\sigma| > 1$ and $\sigma^{(1)} \models \varphi$.
- $\sigma \models \varphi\,\mathcal{U}\,\psi$ iff $\sigma^{(j)} \models \psi$ for some $0 \le j < |\sigma|$ so that for each $0 \le i < j$, $\sigma^{(i)} \models \varphi$.
- $\sigma \models \neg\varphi$ iff it is not the case that $\sigma \models \varphi$.
- $\sigma \models \varphi \vee \psi$ iff either $\sigma \models \varphi$ or $\sigma \models \psi$.
- $\sigma \models p$ iff $|\sigma| > 0$ and $\sigma(0) \models p$.

The rest of the operators can be defined using the above operators. In particular, $\overline{\bigcirc}\varphi = \neg\bigcirc\neg\varphi$, $\varphi \wedge \psi = \neg((\neg\varphi) \vee (\neg\psi))$, $\varphi\,\mathcal{V}\,\psi = \neg((\neg\varphi)\,\mathcal{U}\,(\neg\psi))$, $true = p \vee \neg p$, $false = p \wedge \neg p$, $\Box\varphi = false\,\mathcal{V}\,\varphi$, and $\Diamond\varphi = true\,\mathcal{U}\,\varphi$. The operator $\overline{\bigcirc}$ is a 'weak' version of the $\bigcirc$ operator. Whereas $\bigcirc\varphi$ means that φ holds in the suffix of the sequence starting from the next state, $\overline{\bigcirc}\varphi$ means that *if* the current state is not the last one in the sequence, *then* the suffix starting from the next state satisfies φ.

We distinguish between the operator $\bigcirc$, which we call *strong nexttime*, and $\overline{\bigcirc}$, which we call *weak nexttime*. Notice that

$$(\bigcirc\varphi) \wedge (\overline{\bigcirc}\psi) = \bigcirc(\varphi \wedge \psi), \tag{1}$$

since $\bigcirc\varphi$ already requires that there will be a next state. Another interesting observation is that the formula $\overline{\bigcirc}false$ holds in a state that is in deadlock or termination.

The operators $\mathcal{U}$ and $\mathcal{V}$ can be characterized using a recursive equation, which is useful for understanding the transformation algorithm, presented in the next section. Accordingly, $\varphi\,\mathcal{U}\,\psi = \psi \vee (\varphi \wedge \bigcirc\varphi\,\mathcal{U}\,\psi)$ and $\varphi\,\mathcal{V}\,\psi = \psi \wedge (\varphi \vee \overline{\bigcirc}(\varphi\,\mathcal{V}\,\psi))$.

3   Finite LTL Translation Algorithm

We modify the algorithm presented in [4] for translating an LTL formula φ into an automaton $\mathcal{B} = \langle S, I, \delta, F, D, L \rangle$, where S is a set of *states*, $I \subseteq S$ is a set of *initial states*, $\delta \subseteq S \times S$ is the *transition relation*, $F \subseteq S$ are the *accepting states*, D is a set of *state labels*, and $L : S \to D$ is the *labeling function*. Note that $\mathcal{B}$ is an automaton on finite words, unlike a Büchi automaton, which is usually resulted from translating LTL formulae over infinite sequences, and which recognizes infinite sequences.

As a preparatory step, we bring the formula φ into *negation normal form* as follows. First, we push negation inwards, so that only propositional variables can appear negated. To do that, we use LTL equivalences, such as $\neg\Diamond\psi = \Box\neg\psi$. One problem is that pushing negations into until ($\mathcal{U}$) subformulas can explode the size of the formula. To avoid that, we use the operator *release* ($\mathcal{V}$), which is the dual of the operator *until*. We also remove the eventuality ($\Diamond$) and always ($\Box$) operators using the *until* and *release* operators and the equivalences $\Diamond\psi = true \; \mathcal{U} \; \psi$ and $\Box\psi = false \; \mathcal{V} \; \psi$ as mentioned before.

The algorithm uses the following fields for every generated node of $\mathcal{B}$:

id A unique identifier of the node.

incoming The set of edges that are pointed into the node.

new A set of subformulas of the translated formula, which need to hold from the current node and have not yet been processed.

old A set of subformulas as above, which have been processed.

next A set of subformulas of the translated formula, which have to hold for every successor of the current node.

strong A flag that signals whether the current state must not be the last one in the sequence.

The algorithm starts with a single node, having one incoming edge from a dummy node called *init*. Its field *new* includes the translated formula φ in the above normal form, and the fields *old* and *next* are empty. A list *completed-nodes* is initialized as empty. The algorithm proceeds recursively: for a node x not yet in *completed-nodes*, it moves a subformula η from *new* to *old*. The algorithm then splits the node x into left and right copies while adding subformulas to the fields *new* and *next* according to the following table. The fields *old* and *incoming* retain their previous values in both copies, while the field *strong* can be updated if needed. The algorithm continues recursively with the split copies.

The following split table shows the new values added to the fields *new* and *next* in the left or right copies. The column 'set *strong*' indicates when the current state cannot be the last one in the sequence, namely the formulas in the *next* field are upgraded from weak nexttime to strong nexttime. (There is no need for 'set *strong*' for the right copy, only the left one.) It is sufficient to use the *strong* field rather than keeping two separate fields, for the weak and for the strong nexttime requirements, because of Equation (1).

Formula	left *new*	left *next*	set *strong* left	right *new*	right *next*
$\mu \, \mathcal{U} \, \eta$	$\{\mu\}$	$\{\mu \, \mathcal{U} \, \eta\}$	$\checkmark$	$\{\eta\}$	$\emptyset$
$\mu \, \mathcal{V} \, \eta$	$\{\eta\}$	$\{\mu \, \mathcal{V} \, \eta\}$		$\{\mu, \eta\}$	$\emptyset$
$\mu \vee \eta$	$\{\mu\}$	$\emptyset$		$\{\eta\}$	$\emptyset$
$\mu \wedge \eta$	$\{\mu, \eta\}$	$\emptyset$		–	–
$\bigcirc\mu$	$\emptyset$	μ		–	–
$\bigcirc\mu$	$\emptyset$	μ	$\checkmark$	–	–
$p, \neg p$	$\emptyset$	$\emptyset$		–	–

When there are no more subformulas in the field *new* of the current node x, x is compared against the nodes in the list *completed-nodes*. If there is a node y that agrees with x on the fields *old* and *next*, one adds to the field *incoming* of y the incoming edges of x (hence, one may arrive to the node y from new directions). Otherwise, one adds x to that list and a new node is initiated as follows:

(a) *id* contains a new value,
(b) the *incoming* field contains an edge from x,
(c) the *new* field contains the set of the subformulas in the *next* field of x,
(d) the fields *old* and *next* are empty, and
(e) the field *strong* is initially set to *false*.

After the above algorithm terminates, we can construct the component of the automaton $\mathcal{B}$ for the translated automaton φ as follows. The states S are the nodes in *completed-nodes*. Let $P \subseteq \mathcal{P}$ be the set of propositional letters that appear in the formula φ. The set of labels D are the conjunctions of propositions and negated propositions from P (thus, there are 3^P labels in D, since each proposition may appear, not appear, or appear negated). In the constructed automaton, each node $x \in S$ is *labeled* by the propositions and negated propositions in its field *old*. The initial nodes I are those which have an incoming edge from the dummy node *init*. The transition relation δ includes pairs of nodes (s, s') if s belongs to the field *incoming* of s'. The accepting (final) states satisfy the following:

- For each subformula of φ of the form $\mu \, \mathcal{U} \, \eta$, either the *old* field contains the subformula η, or does not contain $\mu \, \mathcal{U} \, \eta$.
- the *strong* bit is set to *false*.

We may check that there is at least one path from a state in I to a state in F. Otherwise, the automaton does not accept any sequence (and no sequence is accepted by the formula φ).

We denote the system automaton by $\mathcal{A} = \langle X, J, \Delta, E, G \rangle$, where X are the states, $J \subseteq X$ are the initial states, $\Delta \subseteq X \times X$ is the transition relation, $E = 2^P$ are the set of labels, and $G : X \to E$ is the labeling function. Each label $l \in E$ is a subset of the set of propositions $\mathcal{P}$. We can view l as a conjunction, where a proposition $p \in \mathcal{P}$ appears nonnegated if $p \in l$, and negated otherwise. Note that the labels D of $\mathcal{B}$ also allow a proposition not to appear. This allows us to combine several assignments to the propositions into one property automaton state. In the system automaton, this is not necessary, and each system state should induce a truth assignment to all the propositions. For the system automaton there are no accepting states (or we can view it as if all the states in X are accepting).

The set of propositional letters $\mathcal{P}$ available is determined by the variables in the checked program and the set of labeled on nodes in the (automatically generated) flow graphs of its processes. For a process P_i in the program, and a node l in the flow graph for that process, we can have a propositional letter Pi_at_l. In addition, we can have atoms that correspond to comparisons, e.g., for a variable v occurring in the program, and a possible constant value x, we can have propositions representing the comparisons $v = x$, $v < x$, $v > x$, $v \leq x$, and $v \geq x$. In an automaton $\mathcal{A}$ that models the program, each propositional letter obtains the correct truth value in each state. For example, if $p \in \mathcal{P}$ corresponds to $v \leq 3$, then p will belong to (or will hold in) exactly all the states where v is less than or equals 3.

The automata product $\mathcal{B} \times \mathcal{A}$ has the following components:

- The states R are the elements of $S \times X$ where the components have compatible labeling, namely, $\{(s,x)|G(x) \rightarrow L(s)\}$. Note that $G(x) \rightarrow L(s)$ means that the assignment $G(x)$ associated with the system state x satisfies the propositional formula $L(s)$ labeling the property automaton node s.
- The initial states are $(I \times J) \cap R$.
- The transition relation includes the pairs $((s,x),(s',x')) \subseteq R \times R$, where $(s,s') \in \delta$ and $(x,x') \in \Delta$.
- The accepting states of $\mathcal{B} \times \mathcal{A}$ are $(F \times X) \cap R$. That is, a pair in R is accepting, when its $\mathcal{B}$ component is accepting.
- The labeling of any pair $(s,x) \in R$ is that of $G(x)$.

4 The Temporal Debugger

We exploit temporal specification to control stepping through different states of a concurrent system. The basic operation of a debugger is to step between different states of a system in an effective way. While doing so, one can obtain further information about the behavior of the system.

A *temporal step* consists of a finite sequence of states that satisfies some temporal property φ. Given the current global state of the system s, we are searching for a sequence $\xi = s_0 s_1 \ldots s_n$ such that

- $s_0 = s$.
- n is smaller than some limit given (perhaps as a default).
- $\xi \models \varphi$.

The *temporal stack* consists of the different sequences, used in the simulation or debugging obtained so far. It contains several *temporal steps*, each corresponding to some temporal formula that was satisfied. The end state of a temporal step is also the start state of the next step. We search for a temporal step that satisfies a current temporal formula. When such a step is found, it is added to the temporal stack. We can then have several options of how to continue the search, as detailed below.

Searching a path can be done using search on pairs: a state from the joint state space of the system, and a state of the property automaton. Furthermore, each new temporal formula requires a new copy of the search space. Recursion is handled within that space. Thus, when starting the search for formula φ_1, we use one copy of the state space. When seeking a new temporal step for φ_2, we start a fresh copy. If we backtrack on the second step, we backtrack the second search, looking for a new finite sequence that satisfies φ_2. If we remove the last step, going back to the formula φ_1, we remove the second state space information, and backtrack the first state space search. For this reason, we need to keep enough information that will enable us to resume a search after other temporal steps where exercised and backtracked.

The temporal stack contains one path, consisting of the concatenation of the various temporal steps. The last system state component of one temporal step is the first system state component of the next step. For the first step, the first system state is an initial one from the set of initial states J (we may usually assume that there is a unique initial system state). When we start the search for the kth temporal step, we translate the kth temporal property φ_k into a property automaton $\mathcal{B}_k$. We start the search for the kth temporal step with an initial state of $\mathcal{B}_k$ and the last system state on the temporal stack (the last system state of the previous state). We allow the user to observe the sequence of system states that appear on the temporal stack.

The debugging session consists of searching the system through the temporal stack. At each point we may do one of the following (see Figure 1):

- Introduce a new temporal formula and attempt to search for a temporal step from the current state. The new temporal step is added to the search stack. A new automaton for the temporal formula is created, and the product of that automaton with the system automaton with new initial state of the current state is formed. The temporal step is found by finding a path to an accepting state in this product automaton.
- Remove a step. In this case, we are back one step in the stack. We forget about the most recent temporal formula given, and can replace it by a new one in order to continue the search. We also discard the temporal automaton and product automaton generated for that temporal step.
- Backtrack the most recent step. The search process of the latest step resumes from the place it was stopped using the automaton originally created for this temporal step. This is an attempt to find another way of satisfying the last given formula. We either find a new temporal step that replaces the previous one, or report that no such step exists (in this case, we are back one step in the stack and discard the automata created for this step).
- We allow also simple debugger steps, e.g., executing one statement in one process. Such steps can be described as trivial temporal steps (using the nexttime temporal operator).

5   Stepping Modes

A debugger or a simulator allows stepping from one state to another by executing a transition enabled from the current state. Given that there are several enabled transitions, some choice is left to the user. We extend this capability and allow performing 'temporal steps', which are finite sequences of states that satisfy a given temporal formula φ. We are thus confronted with several choices:

1. The size of the step. This can be either a maximal length sequence of states (starting from the current one) that satisfies φ, or a minimal length sequence of states. We may also want to limit the possible number of states in a step, using some user-defined constant value.

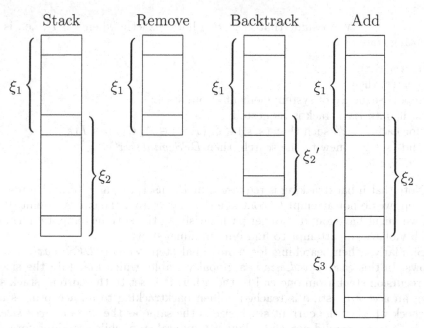

Fig. 1. Temporal stack operations

2. The transfer between different temporal steps. That is, the order in which the system finds the temporal steps. This is greatly affected by the search algorithm that is used.

The *order* between paths is the prefix order '$\sqsubseteq$'. Thus, $\rho \sqsubseteq \sigma$ if there exists ρ' such that $\sigma = \rho.\rho'$. A path generated during the search contains pairs of the form (s, x), where s is a property automaton state and x is a system state. A situation can exist, where there is an infinite sequence of increasingly bigger steps $\sigma_1 \sqsubseteq \sigma_2 \sqsubseteq \ldots$, all of them satisfying the current step formula φ. For example, consider the property $\square p$ and a cyclic path in which all the system states satisfy p. It is possible to identify during a search when such a cycle exists and report it to the user.

Consider now a specification of type $\square p$. A temporal step includes a sequence in which every state satisfies p. We may prefer that such a sequence will be maximal, since a longer sequence gives us more states that satisfy p. Hence more information on how p is preserved (recall that for our finite interpretation of LTL, $\square p$ does not mean an infinite sequence in which every state satisfies p). Similarly, we may prefer that a search based on $\Diamond p$ will result in a minimal sequence that ends with a state that satisfies p. We allow the user to select between searching for a minimal or a maximal search.

Assume for the moment that the search we use is Depth First Search. Searching for a minimal temporal step starting from a pair (s, x), where s is a property automaton state, and x is a system state, is performed by by applying

$DFS\_min(s, x)$. We assume that $accept(s)$ holds exactly when $s \in F$, i.e., is an accepting state of $\mathcal{B}$.

$DFS\_min(s, x)$:
if $accept(s)$ then
    report sequence of system elements from stack;
    wait until Backtrack is requested;
else for each (s', x') such that $(s, s') \in \delta$, $(x, x') \in \Delta$, $G(x) \to L(s)$
    and (s', x') is new to the search, then $DFS\_min(s', x')$;
end DFS_min.

Note that if backtracking is requested by the user, i.e., an alternative temporal step, we do not attempt to continue the search from the current point. If we did, we might have found a longer path satisfying the current temporal formula, which violates the attempt to find only minimal steps.

Similarly, when searching for a maximal step, we use $DFS\_max(s, x)$, as follows. In this case, $saved\_size$ is a global variable, which maintain the size of the recursion stack from one call to the other. It is set to the current stack size when an accepting state is reached. When backtracking to an accepting state, we check whether the current stack size is the same as the one in $saved\_size$. If this is the case, we did not find a longer temporal step while searching forward, and thus the current contents of the stack is a maximal step.

$DFS\_max(s, x)$:
if $accept(s)$ then
    set $saved\_size$ to current size of recursion stack;
for each (s', x') such that $(s, s') \in \delta$, $(x, x') \in \Delta$, $G(x) \to L(s)$
    and (s', x') is new to the search, then $DFS\_max(s', x')$;
if $accept(s)$ and $saved\_size$ equals current stack size then
    report sequence of system elements from stack;
    wait until Backtrack is requested;
end DFS_max;

Notice that we may reach a state in two directions: forward, when entering it, at the beginning of the DFS_min call, and backward, when backtracking from successor states. When we enter an accepting state forward, we set $saved\_size$ to the current size of the search stack. Upon backtracking, we check whether this variable still holds the value of the current size. If this is not the case, we must have found a longer sequence, which contains the current search stack, and satisfies the checked property. Hence the current contents of the search stack is not maximal. Note that when entering an accepting state forward, we do not check the value of $saved\_size$, ignoring possible longer sequences that were generated in different search paths.

Search and Backtracking Options

There are further parameters for the choice of temporal steps, besides the minimality and maximality of the step.

- Allowing or disallowing a different step that ends with the same system state as before. In the former case, we may request an alternative step and reach exactly the same system state, but passes through a different path on the way. The latter case is easily obtained by adding a special flag to each system state that was found during the search.
- Allowing or disallowing the same sequence of system states (recall that we denoted the system as an automaton $\mathcal{A}$) to repeat. Such a repetition can happen, for example, in the following situation. The specification is of the form $(\Diamond p) \vee (\Diamond q)$. Consider a sequence of system states in which $(\neg p) \wedge (\neg q)$ holds until some state in which both p and q start to hold, simultaneously. Such a sequence can be paired up with different property automaton states to generate two different paths. Eliminating the repetition of such a sequence of system states can be obtained by keeping a tree T of nodes that participate in temporal steps reported so far (for a single given temporal step formula). Each node in the tree consists of a system state and a repetition counter (since the same state $x \in X$ can participate in one path as many times as $|S|$, the number of states of the property automaton). Each time a new temporal step is reported, the tree is updated. A new step is reported only if during the search, we deviate at least once from the paths already existing in T. Upon finding a new path, the tree T is updated.
- Allowing *all* possible paths with sequence of system states that satisfy the temporal step formula φ or only a *subset* of them. Typical searches like depth first or breadth first search do not pass through all possible paths that satisfy a given formula φ. If a state (in our case, a pair) participated before in the search, we do not continue the search in that direction. For this reason, the number of paths that can be obtained in this way is limited, and, on the other hand, the search is efficient. There are topological cases where requiring all the paths results in exponentially more paths than obtained with the above mentioned search strategies, see e.g., the case in Figure 2.

The case where similar sequences are generated as a result of repeated backtracking may seem at first to be less useful for debugging. Intuitively, we may give up exhaustiveness for the possibility of stepping through quite different sequences. However, there is a very practical case in which we may have less choice in selecting the kind of search and the effect of backtracking. Specifically, in many cases keeping several states in memory at the same time and comparing different states may be impractical. In this case, we may want to perform memoryless search, as developed for the Verisoft system [5]. In this case, we may perform breadth first search with increasingly higher depth (up to some user defined limit). We keep in the search stack only information that allows us to generate different sequences according to some order, and to regenerate a state. Such information may include the identification of the transitions that were executed from the initial states.

6   An Example

We exemplify the use of our system. Consider Dekker's solution to Dijkstra's mutual exclusion algorithm. The code for the two processes is shown in Figure 3

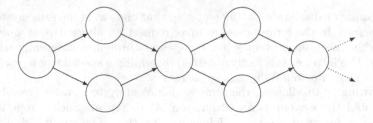

Fig. 2. Exponential number of sequences

and the corresponding flow graphs are shown in Figure 4 (the figures were generated automatically by our system, with the assistance of the DOT program [3]). We show some experiments with the temporal debugger, which allow gaining intuition about the behavior of the algorithm. Note that the critical sections of the processes $P0$ and $P1$ are labeled in Figure 4 by $m8$ and $n8$, respectively.

```
Process P0:                    Process P1:

begin                          begin
  c0:=1;                         c1:=1;
  while true do                  while true do
  begin                          begin
    c0:=0;                         c1:=0;
    while c1=0 do                  while c0=0 do
    begin                          begin
      if turn=1 then                 if turn=0 then
        begin                          begin
          c0:=1;                         c1:=1;
          wait turn=1;                   wait turn=0;
          c0:=0                          c1:=0
        end                            end
    end;                           end;
    critical:=0;                   critical:=1;
    c0:=1;                         c1:=1;
    turn:=1                        turn:=0
  end                            end
end.                           end.
```

Fig. 3. Code for Dekker's Algorithm

At first look at the code, we may be able to identify that the variable *turn* is assigned according to the process that has priority to get to the critical section. The variable ci for $i = 0, 1$ is set to 1 when a process does not attempt to get to the critical section (or does not insist on doing that) and 0 otherwise. The system provides us with automatic translation of the code to a flow graph, and a labeling of the nodes. We use the notation Pi_at_l to denote the predicate that asserts that process Pi is at label l.

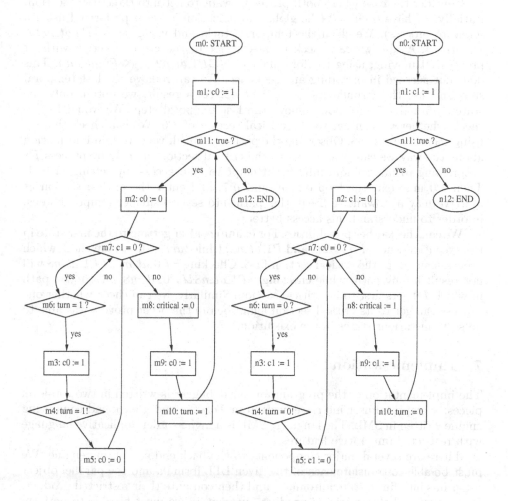

Fig. 4. Dekker's mutual exclusion solution

We can start the debugging with an attempt to understand what happens when process $P0$ attempts to enter and $P1$ does not. We use the formula $\varphi_1 = \Diamond(P0\_at\_m2 \land P1\_at\_n1)$ and search for a shortest temporal step satisfying this. (Our interpretation of at, i.e., that we are at a node, is that the node was the last to be executed in that process.) We check that at this point, $c0 - 0 \land c1 - 1$. We can continue from here by using the formula $\varphi_2 = \Box P1\_at\_n1$, i.e., asserting that process $P1$ does not move. We can use a search that will step through all the states that end a finite sequence satisfying this formula. Alternatively, we may remove the last temporal step and choose $\varphi_2 = (\Box P1\_at\_n1) \land (\Diamond P0\_at\_m8)$

to check whether we can get to the critical section without progressing the $P1$ process.

Consider the case where both processes want to get into the critical section. Initially, we have $turn = 0$ (the global initialization is being performed using a separate process). We clean the temporal stack, and use $\varphi_1 = \Diamond(P0\_at\_m2 \wedge P1\_at\_n2)$. Again, we can check if we can get to the critical section without process $P1$ moving, using the formula $\varphi_2 = (\Box P1\_at\_n2) \wedge (\Diamond P0\_at\_m8)$. This does not succeed in providing any sequence. We can remove the last temporal step and use the formula $\varphi_2 = \Box P1\_at\_n2$. As a result, we obtain only the states $m6$ and $m7$. We now remove the last temporal step. We would like to check whether we can get to the critical section of $P0$. We can check that by using $\varphi_2 = \Diamond P0\_at\_m8$. Observing the paths obtained, we may gain information about the way we can gain access to the critical section, namely by process $P1$ progressing to $n3$, relinquishing its attempt to gain access, by setting $c1 = 1$. Then $P0$ may exit the loop on $m6$ and $m7$, and enter the critical section at $m8$. We may also want to break this path into several smaller temporal steps, in order to understand this access better.

We can check other possibilities. For example, after getting to the first state in the execution where $P0\_at\_m2$ and $P1\_at\_n2$, while $turn = 0$, we can check which process can get to the critical section first. Checking $\neg P0\_at\_m8\,\mathcal{U}\,P1\_at\_n8$ will not result in any path, while checking $\neg P1\_at\_n8\,\mathcal{U}\,P0\_at\_m8$ will show a path in which $P0$ gets first to its critical section. Similarly, we can check whether one process can get to its critical section again before the other process was able to do so from various states in the execution.

7   Implementation

The implementation of the program for our debugger is written in two top-level pieces: a graphical user interface written in Tcl/Tk, and a back end computing engine written in SML. The language SML is a higher-order applicative language with restricted imperative features.

There are several major components to the back end computing engine. We must be able to translate each of the given LTL formula and the parallel object programs into finite state automata, and then compute their restricted product. Having created the restricted product automaton, we must be able to perform a variety of different searches on it.

Because we are likely to need to construct a number of finite state automata in the course of a single debugging session, and each of these automata is likely to be quite large, we take advantage of the higher-order applicative nature of SML to build a generic lazy implementation of these automata. The implementation is parameterized by a type of state information, an initial state, a function for determining when two states should be treated as the same, and a function which, for a given state, computes a list of the states pointed to from the current state.

Initially, to create the desired automata, we create an initial node containing the initial state information and a continuation function which will create the out edges to the next states including a continuation function for each of them to create their out edges. Every time we visit a state node, if its out edges have not yet been constructed, then we apply the continuation to create the adjacent states and we update the node with the new information about its out edges. These details are encapsulated in a abstraction hiding the details of the lazy structure from subsequent search algorithms.

As a result of the lazy nature of the construction of the nodes in the various automata we need, as we explore further and further along possible execution paths in the concurrent system, increasingly more of the state space for the system is constructed, potentially growing until the full automaton has been realized. However, for each of the LTL formulae that we use in taking temporal steps, we only construct as much of the automaton corresponding to the LTL formula and as much of the restricted product automaton as is necessary to find the path, making up the desired temporal step. In the worst case, we could be forced to unfold the full automata, but in general there should be considerable space saving achieved by not expanding all the nodes.

8   Discussion

Temporal logic in conjunction with a search is employed by *model checking* [1,2] techniques. There, we want to check whether all executions (sometimes including infinite ones) starting with a given system state (usually an initial state) satisfy a given property. In our context, we are using temporal specification is a different way, to control the stepping between system states. We are looking for finite sequences of states that satisfy a given temporal specification, and move the current control to the last state of the sequence.

In some sense, our approach is related to the *choppy* temporal logic of Pnueli and Rosner [8]. There, one can use temporal specification over finite sequences and combine them using the *chop* (C) operator. We are effectively stepping through different finite sequences and progressing through the execution. Note that in the temporal semantics of [8], $\varphi_1 C \varphi_2$ holds for a path that concatenates two shorter paths, where the first satisfies φ_1 and the second satisfies φ_2, respectively. In our case, the last state of one temporal step is the first state of the next step. Thus, to obtain the same effect as in the choppy logic, we may want to use φ_1 and $\bigcirc \varphi_2$.

We could have bundled different temporal steps into an equivalent linear temporal property about the entire system. Then we could perform LTL model checking as in SPIN [6]. The property would not look the same in the standard version of temporal logic, since there is no operator that sequentially combines finite temporal assertions. In this case, we either obtain a confirmation for the property, or a single (often lengthy) counterexample that starts from the initial state. In our approach, we examine the behavior of the system in a stepwise manner, and, through the developed tool, were capable of keeping track of the current state, allowing us to zoom quickly into potential programming errors. In fact, we suggest our approach as an extension to LTL based model checkers such as SPIN.

References

1. E. M. Clarke, E. A. Emerson, Design and synthesis of synchronization skeletons using branching time temporal logic. Workshop on Logic of Programs, Yorktown Heights, NY, Lecture Notes in Computer Science 131, Springer-Verlag, 1981, 52–71.
2. E. A. Emerson, E. M. Clarke, Characterizing correctness properties of parallel programs using fixpoints, International Colloquium on Automata, Languages and Programming, Lecture Notes in Computer Science 85, Springer-Verlag, July 1980, 169–181.
3. E.R. Gansner, S.C. North, An open graph visualization system and its applications to software engineering, Software – Practice and Experience, 30(2000), 1203–1233.
4. R. Gerth, D. Peled, M.Y. Vardi, P. Wolper, Simple On-the-fly Automatic Verification of Linear Temporal Logic, *PSTV95, Protocol Specification Testing and Verification*, 3–18, Chapman & Hall, 1995, Warsaw, Poland.
5. P. Godefroid, Model checking for programming languages using Verisoft, POPL 1997, 174–186.
6. G. Holzmann, Design and Validation of Computer Protocol, *Prentice Hall*.
7. A. Pnueli, The temporal logic of programs, 18th IEEE symposium on Foundation of Computer Science, 1977, 46–57.
8. A. Pnueli, R. Rosner, A Choppy Logic, Logic in Computer Science 1986, Cambridge, Massachusetts, 1986, 306–318.

Fate and Free Will in Error Traces[*]

HoonSang Jin[1], Kavita Ravi[2], and Fabio Somenzi[1]

[1] University of Colorado at Boulder
{Jinh,Fabio}@Colorado.EDU
[2] Cadence Design Systems
kravi@cadence.com

Abstract. The ability to generate counterexamples for failing properties is often cited as one of the strengths of model checking. However, it is often difficult to interpret long error traces in which many variables appear. Further, a traditional error trace presents only one possible behavior of the system causing the failure, with no further annotation. Our objective is to "capture more of the error" in an error trace to make debugging easier. We present an enhanced error trace in an alternation of *fated* (forced) and *free* segments. The fated segments show unavoidable progress towards the error while the free segments show choices that, if avoided, may have prevented the error. This segmentation raises the questions of whether the fated segment should indeed be inevitable and whether the free segments are critical in causing the error. Addressing these questions may help the user analyze the error better.

1 Introduction

The algorithmic nature of model checking results in an important debugging capability—the generation of *counterexamples*. A counterexample provides evidence of failure of a *universal* property. Dually, it is possible to provide a witness to an *existential* property. Both counterexamples and witnesses, henceforth referred to as *traces*, are useful in debugging or exploring a design. Counterexamples that are easy to analyze help a developer diagnose problems quickly.

A counterexample may be a finite or infinite trace. The failure that it demonstrates may indicate a flaw in the design being verified, may point to a mistake in modelling its environment, or may be an artifact of the abstraction applied to obtain a simple model. State-of-the-art model checkers provide only one trace. Oftentimes, however, users of model checkers find a single error trace difficult to relate to the exact bug in the design. This may be due to a combination of reasons:

- A trace of a large design often involves tens of state and input variables over tens of cycles. Good presentation in the form of waveforms or diagrams helps manage this complexity, but presentation alone cannot help in the understanding of the problem.
- Counterexamples to invariants are usually guaranteed to be of minimum length. However, for liveness properties, the length of the trace is only heuristically reduced. More importantly, the algorithms that generate the error traces do not attempt to

---

[*] This work was supported in part by SRC contract 2001-TJ-920 and NSF grant CCR-99-71195.

J.-P. Katoen and P. Stevens (Eds.): TACAS 2002, LNCS 2280, pp. 445–459, 2002.

minimize the number of variables appearing along the trace or the changes in these variables (e.g., the number of events). Oftentimes, irrelevant events may occur and distract or mislead the user as to the cause of the failure.

- An error trace provides only one possible path to the failure. The set of all counterexamples is one way to characterize the error completely but producing all counterexamples is computationally hard, hence practically infeasible.
- Often, not all events in the error trace have the same importance, and it is difficult to spot the *crucial events*. In the case of a failing invariant, the last state of the trace is a so-called *bad state*—one in which the invariant does not hold. However, the cause of the failure may have to be looked for several cycles earlier, when an event took place that made the catastrophe inevitable, or at least very likely.

What is most useful in debugging are behaviors of the design most germane to the failure, perhaps a counterexample marked up with important events. Our approach focuses on one such possible property—"inevitability" in the design's behavior towards the failure. We produce an error trace that is annotated with the inevitable segments. Identifying the foregone portions of a counterexample provides a classification of the events in the trace. The user may then analyze the error in terms of whether the foregone portions are correct or whether the remaining events were critically responsible for the error. We explain this in the following example.

Example 1. Consider a circuit for prioritized transfer of requests of two kinds—high priority (HI) and low priority (LO). The transfer is accomplished with two FIFOs, one for each kind of request. Requests arrive one at a time and are sent out in order within each priority. The transfer is controlled by a fast input clock and a slow output clock. A HI request is given priority over a LO request unless the LO request matches the address field of a HI request. In this case, the HI request is not issued until the matching LO request is sent out. Such designs are common in cache interfaces to main memory in processor design. In our implementation of this priority scheme, an unconstrained source of LO requests may cause starvation of the HI requests, as evidenced by the failure of the following CTL property.

$$\text{AG}(\text{match} \rightarrow \text{AF sav} \neq \text{hh}) .$$

In the property, match signals that the address field of a request at the head of the HI FIFO is the same as a LO FIFO request. The value of the head pointer to the HI FIFO (hh) is saved in sav when a match is detected; the variables differ when the HI request is issued. If the matched HI request is eventually issued, the property is satisfied.

An error trace is shown in Fig. 1. Each Column represents a variable of the design. All variables to the left of inaddr are state variables, and those to the right including inaddr are inputs. The error trace consists of a stem from the initial state to a state where a match is detected, and of a cycle back to that state, along which the HI request is not issued. Requests are indicated by validin that signals a valid request, incoming address inaddr, and type of request hl. The head and tail pointers respectively track the emptying and filling of the LO (lt and lh respectively) and HI FIFOs (ht and hh respectively). The first two requests are HI requests (hl=1) for address 0. This is followed by a LO request for the same address. This causes a match (match=1) two input clock periods later, when the slow output clock (sloClk=1) ticks. Along the cycle, the LO FIFO is alternately filled and emptied (notice the values of lt and lh) . Since there is always an entry with address 0 in the LO FIFO, the HI request starves. The vertical bars

```
          Stem---->   Cycle----------------------------------->
Time      0 1 2 3 4   0 1 2 3 4 5 6 7 8 9 10 11 12 13 14 15
sloClk    0     1 0   0     1 0     1 0         1 0          1
match     0         1 1
hh        0           0
ht        0 1 2       2
sav       0           0
lh        0           0         1       2         3
lt        0       1   1 2 3     0         1
inaddr    0           0
hl        1     0     0
validin   1   0 1     1                         0
FFW       f f | f     f f | | f | | | f |   |   |   |   |   |
```

Fig. 1. Counterexample for prioritized requests

and the f label on the last line of Fig. 1 are annotations of the error trace. The annotation at Column i pertains to the transition from Column i to Column $i + 1$. Details will be discussed in Sect. 4. The bars highlight the inevitable segments of the counterexample. The HI FIFO and the LO FIFO receive a request for the same address 0. As long as the LO requests with address 0 continue to enter the LO FIFO (free choices), the rest is inevitable. The annotated segments capture a high level picture of why the error occurred by showing that the LO requests starve the HI requests.

We propose an algorithm to generate an error trace divided into *fated* and *free* segments, so that the eventual demise of a system—as signaled by the failure of a property— can be interpreted as the joint accomplishment of Fate and Free Will. In our approach, Fate can be endowed with varying degrees of power, reflecting the various degrees to which it controls the environment of the system. We argue that this is desirable, and in Sect. 4 we present an approach to determine the extent of Fate's sway.

The paper is organized as follows: Sect. 2 presents the background. Sect. 3 presents the main Fate and Free Will approach and two algorithms that implement it. They are followed by a comparison to related work (Sect. 5) and conclusions.

2   Preliminaries

Let $V = \{v_1, \ldots, v_n\}$ be a set. We designate by V' the set $\{v'_1, \ldots, v'_n\}$ consisting of the primed version of the elements of V. We define an *open system* as a 5-tuple $\langle V, W, I, R, \mathcal{F} \rangle$, where V is the set of (current) state variables, W is the set of input variables, $I(V)$ is the initial predicate, $R(V, W, V')$ is the transition relation, and $\mathcal{F} =$

$\{F_i(V)\}$ is the set of Büchi fairness conditions. The variables in V' are the next state variables. All sets are finite, and all variables range over finite domains. We assume that $R(V, W, V')$ is *deterministic*.

An open system defines a fair labeled transition structure in the usual way, with states Q_Ω corresponding to the valuations of the variables in V, and transition labels corresponding to the valuations of the variables in W. Conversely, a set of states $T \subseteq Q_\Omega$ corresponds to a predicate $T(V)$ or $T(V')$. Predicate $T(V)$ $(T(V'))$ is the characteristic function of T expressed in terms of the current (next) state variables.

The positive (negative) cofactor of predicate $P(V)$ with respect to variable $v \in V$ is denoted by P_v ($P_{\neg v}$) and is obtained by letting $v = 1$ ($v = 0$) in $P(V)$. A *cube* is a predicate that consists of the conjunction of variables and their negations.

By existentially quantifying the input variables from R, one obtains a Kripke structure to which model checking algorithms for various specification mechanisms can be applied [Kur94,CGP99]. We assume that properties are specified in a temporal logic like CTL* [EH86], which conveniently subsumes both CTL [CE81] and LTL [WVS83,LP85]. For ω-regular properties [Kur94], we assume that model checking is reduced to language emptiness check on the composition of the given system and the Büchi automaton for the negation of the property.

In computing the set of states that reach a given target, a symbolic model checker stores the sets of states at a given distance from the target, called *onion rings*. The onion rings are used to produce shortest counterexamples for failing invariants. If forward search from the initial states is used to check an invariant, then a set of rings around the initial states is stored. The shortest path is traced backwards from a bad state t closest to the initial states (from the innermost onion ring). In each step, the predecessors of t are intersected with the onion ring immediately inside the one of t and a state is chosen from the intersection. The process is repeated until an initial state is reached.

An error trace for a liveness property consists of a path leading from an initial state to a fair cycle. The fair cycle consists of paths connecting states from all fairness constraints. Each sub-path is constructed with the help of a set of onion rings around the destination states. Hence, each sub-path is of minimal length, though the overall counterexample may not be minimal. A popular algorithm is described in [CGMZ95], and a comparison of various techniques can be found in [RBS00].

We will use standard future and past tense CTL notation, such as EX, its past-tense dual EY, EU, its past-tense dual ES and EG, with their usual semantics in the rest of this paper.

3   Fate and Free Will in Error Traces

An error trace is composed of *parts*, each of which is made up of *segments*. Dividing an error trace into segments characterized by Fate and Free Will is the main approach in this paper. A counterexample to an invariant consists of one part only: a path from an initial state to a bad state; a counterexample to a liveness property consists of several parts: the stem plus the parts that make up the fair cycle by connecting states satisfying different fairness constraints. In the following we consider dividing one part into *fated* and *free* segments. The method we develop can be applied to each part in turn.

3.1   The Fatal Game

The set of *controlling variables* of an open system $\Omega = \langle V, W, I, R, \mathcal{F} \rangle$, written $\Gamma(\Omega)$, is a subset of W. When Ω is understood, we shall simply write Γ. Informally, Γ consists of the variables that a hostile environment of Ω uses to force the behavior of the system, dictating its *fate*. The remaining variables in W are considered *non-controlling*. They are folded into the system, allowing the system *free-will* in their choice.

Given Ω, Γ, and a target predicate $T(V)$, a two-player concurrent reachability game [EJ91] can be defined as follows. The positions of the game correspond to the states of Ω. The two players are the (hostile) *environment* and the *system*. From position $\tilde{V}$, the environment chooses values for the variables in Γ and simultaneously the system chooses values for variables in $W \setminus \Gamma$. Let $\bar{W}$ be the resulting valuation of W. The new position is computed as the unique $\tilde{V}'$ satisfying $R(\tilde{V}, \bar{W}, \tilde{V}')$. The goal of the environment is to reach a state that satisfies $T(V)$ in spite of the system's opposition.

A (memoryless) strategy for the environment is a function that maps each state of Ω to one valuation of the variables in Γ. Likewise, a strategy for the system is a function that maps each state of Ω to one valuation of the variables in $W \setminus \Gamma$. A position $\tilde{V}$ is a winning position for the environment if there exists an environment strategy such that, for all system strategies, $T(V)$ is eventually satisfied. A position $\tilde{V}$ is a winning strategy for the system if $T(V)$ is never satisfied.

In Sect. 4 we address the automatic identification of variables that may be profitably added to a given (possibly empty) Γ. In the remainder of this section we assume that the controlling variables are given, together with the open system and the (failing) property.

We are interested in showing whether a hostile environment, controlling only variables in Γ, can force the system into a failing run to enhance the information provided by the error trace. Obviously, if Ω is deterministic and $\Gamma = W$, the environment can force the system along any error trace. This is not very interesting as it provides no further illumination on the error when compared to the traditional error trace. Conversely, if $\Gamma = \emptyset$, the environment can force an error only when it becomes inevitable.

The more interesting cases occur when we can use the assumption that the hostile environment can control only some of the input variables, to help explain an error trace. For example, in the case of an asynchronous system under the interleaving model of concurrency, the variables that control the scheduling of the processes are natural candidates for inclusion in Γ. In languages like SMV [McM94], the scheduler variables are easily identified.[1] With languages in which the scheduling must be modeled explicitly, the user can easily identify the relevant variables as Γ. In hardware designs, the system control variables could be a reasonable guess for Γ and the data variables for $W \setminus \Gamma$.

Given an open system Ω, a property φ for which a nonempty set $E(\varphi)$ of error traces exists, and a set of controlling variables $\Gamma(\Omega)$, we can formulate the winning positions of the hostile environment as follows.

Definition 1. *Given a set of states $T(V')$ of Ω, we denote the set of states that the environment can control to T in one step using Γ by*

$$\mathsf{MX}_{\Omega, \Gamma} T = \exists \Gamma . \forall (W \setminus \Gamma) . \exists V' . [R(V, W, V') \wedge T(V')] .$$

---

[1] The scheduler variables have names `<proc>.running` in SMV. They are not input variables, but they can be treated as such.

The dependence on Ω and Γ is usually understood, and hence the subscript to MX *omitted. We similarly define* M SUT *as the set of states that the environment can control to* T *via paths of arbitrary finite length confined in* S. *That is,*

$$M\,S\,U\,T = \mu Z\,.\,T \vee [S \wedge \mathsf{MX}\,Z]\ .$$

M $S\cup T$ computes exactly those states from which a hostile environment has a winning strategy. The i-th iteration of the fixpoint computation corresponding to M $S\,U\,T$ represents the states from which the environment has a winning strategy with i moves.

The operators of Definition 1 are related to the operators of CTL, and indeed are specialized versions of the operators of Alternating-time Temporal Logic [AHK97]. MX differs from EX only in the type and position of quantification of the $W \setminus \Gamma$ variables. The environment and the system are assumed to choose simultaneously the values for the inputs they control. This is reflected in the order in which the input variables are quantified. Since the environment must be able to control the system to some state in T without knowledge of the values of the variables in $W \setminus \Gamma$, the variables in Γ appear in the outermost quantification. On the other hand, the exact state in T to which the system is controlled is immaterial; hence, the next state variables appear in the innermost quantification. MU differs from EU only in the use of MX instead of EX.

The definition of MX T is illustrated in Fig. 2, where a fragment of a system is shown for which $W = \{g, w\}$, $\Gamma = \{g\}$, $T = \{3, 4\}$, and MX $T = \{1, 2\}$. Transitions out of States 0, 3, 4, and 7 are not shown to avoid clutter; they are all to states not in T. The

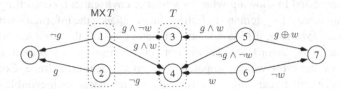

Fig. 2. Illustration of the definition of MX T

environment can force State 2 to State 4 by choosing $g = 0$. Conversely, State 6 cannot be forced to states in T because the system can control State 6 to State 7 by choosing $w = 0$. State 1 can be controlled to a state in T by choosing $g = 1$. (The exact state reached depends on the choice of the system.) However, the environment does not have a choice for the value of g that will work from State 5 regardless of the value of w.

3.2   General Fate and Free Will Algorithm

For a given choice of Γ, the environment may be able to force the system along parts of the error trace, but not the entire trace. For example, in hardware designs where Γ maps to the control variables and $W \setminus \Gamma$ maps to the data variables, a specific data value may be important at some point to trigger the failure, but for the rest, appropriate choices of control variables could force the failure to happen. The choice of the data values can be likened to acts of volition of the system (free will), whereas progress toward the bad states under the control of the environment are akin to the accomplishment of Fate.

In terms of games, the environment may not have a winning strategy from the initial states; the system may have to collaborate at some points along the trace by making the "wrong" choices (mistakes). Consequently, we can formulate the selection of an error trace in terms of a sequence of games between the environment and the system. Each game is an instance of the one described in Section 3.1, generating the fated segments. The sequence of games are interleaved with the (free-will) mistakes of the system. (Henceforth, mistake, free choice and free segment will be used inerchangeably.)

Our objective is to find an error trace $e \in E(\varphi)$ that consists of few, short segments. Such an error trace can be generated by answering the following question.

Question 1. What are the states from which the environment can force the system to T if the system makes exactly i mistakes?

For $i = 0$, these are states computed by the game in Section 3.1. For $i = 1$, these are states from which the system has a winning strategy (the environment has no winning strategy), but with one mistake, the system reaches states from which the environment can force the system to T. For any $i > 0$, these are states from which the system has a winning strategy, and with one mistake reaches states from which the environment can force the system to T with $i - 1$ mistakes of the system. In other words, for any $i > 0$, the system still has a winning strategy for fewer than i mistakes but unavoidably reaches T if it commits i mistakes. An error trace with few segments can be constructed from the initial state that requires the fewest mistakes to reach the target state T.

To compute these states, we first classify states into those from which the system must progress towards the error and states from which the system can avoid reaching the error. We consider a general partition that divides the state space into *layers*, $\{S_i\}$. Each layer S_i has two types of states—boundary states T_i and interior states $S_i \setminus T_i$. From the boundary states, the system can avoid reaching the error and has to make a free choice at these states to move out of the layer. At the interior states, the system can be forced by the environment towards the boundary states of the corresponding layer, and consequently towards the error. With this definition a trace will be annotated by a fated segment (perhaps empty) within each layer, and a free choice at the boundary states (precisely those at which the system can make mistakes).

Our layering scheme starts with the target as the initial set of boundary states and forms concentric layers around the target. The i-th concentric layer contains states that must make i mistakes to reach the target. A trace moving through these layers with decreasing index eventually reaches the target. At the boundary states of each layer, the system can make a free choice into states in the previous layer (closer to the target). The interior states for each boundary is then computed to complete the layer.

Each layer is closed, that is, all states outside of previously computed layers at which the system can be forced to the current boundary are in the current layer. Hence, once a layer is computed, a new set of boundary states is determined. This ensures that fated and free segments alternate in our algorithms.

Consider the state graph in Fig. 3, State 1 is the initial state and State 5 is the target. Suppose $W = \{w\}$ and $\Gamma = \emptyset$ for this graph. The layer set A is an example of the layers defined above. The layers are ordered by increasing index. The index indicates

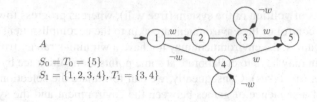

A

$S_0 = T_0 = \{5\}$
$S_1 = \{1, 2, 3, 4\}, T_1 = \{3, 4\}$

Fig. 3. Example showing set of layers A

the number of wrong choices that the system has to make to progress towards T. For instance, State 1 is forced to reach either State 3 or 4 (boundary states T_1), therefore it is in S_1. States 3 and 4 can make a free choice to go to 5.

Fig. 4 implements this approach to computing the layers $\{S_i\}$. Its arguments are the target states T and the states that reach T and are reachable from the initial states, H. A list L is instantiated to store the layers. In each iteration of the loop, the boundary states are computed as T_i in Line 9 and the layer is completed as S_i in Line 5. Since the layers start at T, one of the concentric layers is formed in each iteration. Previously computed states are removed from T_i. The while-loop stops when there are no more states.

```
1    FATEANDFREEWILLLAYERS (T, H) {
2        L := ();
3        i := 0; T_0 = T;
4        while (H ≠ 0) {
5            S_i := M H ∪ T_i;
6            L := CONCATENATE(S_i, L);
7            H := H \ S_i;
8            i := i + 1;
9            T_i := (EX S_i) ∩ H; }
10       return L; }
```

Fig. 4. General Fate and Free Will algorithm

Some observations on the layers computed in Fig. 4 are listed below.

Observation 1. *For each $i, j, S_i \cap S_j = \emptyset$.*

Consider the sequence of onion-rings R around T restricted to the set H. The rings are computed using a backward search with $R_0 = T$. and form a partition of H.

Lemma 1. *For each $i, R_i \subseteq \bigcup \{S_j | j \leq i\}$.*

By the construction of the layers, a trace passing through S_i has to make a free choice out of T_i. Due to Lemma 1, no free choices are possible from S_i to S_j for $j < i - 1$.

Observation 2. *The lower bound on the number of free choices from a state in S_i to T is i.*

Theorem 1. *The algorithm in Fig. 4 terminates.*

Corollary 1. *By Theorem 1 and Observation 1, the set of layers $\{S_i\}$ form a partition of the states in H.*

Theorem 2. *It is possible to construct a trace from a state in S_n to T by making exactly one free choice out of every layer S_i to layer S_{i-1} for $i \leq n$.*

The algorithm in Fig. 4 requires linear (in the number of states) MX and EX steps but is more expensive than generating the traditional trace. MX computations may be more expensive than EX computations when using BDDs (in terms of BDD sizes) due to the difference in quantification of input variables. The Γ variables cannot be quantified before $W \setminus \Gamma$ and the $W \setminus \Gamma$ variables cannot be quantified before V' since existential and universal quantifications do not commute. This may cause several BDD variables to be alive over most of the MX computation, which in turn may cause the BDDs to be very large. The extra computational burden may affect performance of this algorithm.

```
1    COUNTEREXAMPLE (S, T, L, R) { // R is the set of rings around T
2        if (T ∩ S ≠ ∅) return (PICKSTATE(T ∩ S));
3        Lp :=layer Li of least index that intersects S;
4        Q := S ∩ Lp;
5        p := INDEX(Lp); π := ();
6        do {
7            Rq := ring Ri of least index that intersects Q;
8            P := PICKSTATE (Q ∩ Rq);
9            π :=APPEND(π, P);
10           Q := EY(P);
11           if ( p > 0 and Q ∩ Lp−1 ≠ ∅) {
12               Q := Q ∩ Lp−1; // make a free choice out of Lp
13               mark P;
14               p := p − 1; }
15       } while (P ∩ T ≠ ∅)
16       return π; }
```

Fig. 5. Counterexample algorithm based on the General Fate and Free Will algorithm in Fig. 4

Based on Theorem 2, we propose an algorithm to construct a trace between S and T given the sequence of layers L computed by Fig. 4. Fig. 5 shows a trace constructed from the layers in L using the fewest free choices. The algorithm takes the following arguments: S initial states, T target states, L sequence of layers and R rings around

T. (States in ring R_i have a path of length i to T.) The algorithm starts with the initial state in the least layer (closest to T) in Line 3 and builds an error trace in a sequence of alternating fated and free segments down the layers in L.

The while-loop terminates when the trace includes a target state. A free choice is made at the earliest opportunity to progress towards T (Line 12). Each state at which the system makes a free choice is marked to annotate the error presented to the user. The rings around T are used to minimize the length of the trace to T (Lines 7–8).

Theorem 2 ensures the correctness of this algorithm. The cost of generating such a trace is comparable to the cost of the traditional method to generating error traces.

A trace generated by Fig. 5 is explained to the user as follows: For each fated segment, from the source state, the system is bound to reach a target set, one state of which is presented as the destination of the fated segment. Each free choice is a step taken by the system towards the error. It would have been possible at these states to avoid reaching the error.

Theorem 3. *The trace produced by the algorithm in Fig. 5 contains the least free segments (markings).*

While algorithm in Fig. 5 computes a trace with fewest free segments, it does not guarantee a counterexample of minimum length.

3.3 Restricted Algorithm

The algorithms of Fig. 4 and Fig. 5 provide a set of layers and a counterexample annotated with the fated and free segments. The general algorithm has the disadvantage of being expensive to compute. Also, since only one state is represented from the boundary, it may be hard to comprehend the fated segment. However, the layers are too large to present to the user. In this section, we present a restricted Fate and Free Will algorithm that has two important advantages—it is less expensive than the general algorithm and the error trace is more self-contained in the information it provides.

This main restriction is that the computed layers in this algorithm are not complete with respect to H. This is achieved by setting the boundary to one state of the T_i computed in Line 9 of Fig. 4 instead of the entire T_i. This modification is likely to make the MU computation less expensive due to a smaller T_i. Additionally, now the error trace presents a complete picture in the fated segment since the fated segment is exactly to the state presented in the error trace.

The restricted algorithm is described in Fig. 6. The input to the algorithm is a set of initial states, S, a set of target states, T, such that $S \cap T = \emptyset$, and a set H of states such that the paths from S to T are confined within H. We can assume that H consists of states reachable from S, and that can reach T. In fact, we only need to compute the states reachable from S, because backward search from T never touches states that cannot reach T. We assume that H is divided into *onion rings* $\{h_i\}$ according to the distance of a state from S.

The output of the FATEANDFREEWILL algorithm is a counterexample C in the form of a list of segments. The segments are constructed backwards from T. The last segment to T is always fated. Fated and free segments alternate, though the fated segments may be empty. A fated segment computation always follows a free segment computation to

```
1    FATEANDFREEWILL (S, T, (h_0, ... , h_m)){
2        prev := free; p = m;
3        if (T ∩ S ≠ 0) return ((PICKSTATE(T ∩ S)));
4        h_p := ring h_i of least index that intersects T;    // closest to S
5        T := CLOSESTSTATE(T ∩ h_p, S);
6        C := ((T));    // initialize counterexample trace,

7        // find segments from violation to the initial states
8        while (T ∩ S ≠ ∅) {    // done, if current target intersects initial states

9            // alternate fated and free segments
10           if (prev = free) {
11               prev := fated;    // flip the flag
12               H := h_0 ∪ h_1 ∪ ··· ∪ h_p;
13               S_1 := M H U T;    // compute states that can be forced to T
14               if (S_1 = T) continue ;    // failed to find non-trivial fated segment,
                                            // now find the free segment
15               // non-trivial fated segment exists!
16               // compute onion-rings to trace shortest path for fated segment
17               h_p := ring h_i of least index that intersects S_1;    // closest to S
18               R := (ρ_0, ... , ρ_q) := RINGS(S_1, h_p ∩ S_1, T);
                                            // rings of E S_1 S (h_p ∩ S_1) up to T
19           } else {    // set the variables for free segment construction
20               prev := free;    // flip the flag
21               h_p := ring h_i of least index that intersects EX T;
22               R := (h_p ∩ EX T, T);    // rings for free segment
23           }

24           // construct current segment, add it to counterexample
25           σ := BUILDSHORTESTPATH(LAST(R), T, R);
26           C := CONCATENATE((σ), C);

27           T := FIRST(σ);    // destination of next segment
28       }
29       return (C);
30   }
```

Fig. 6. Fate and Free Will algorithm

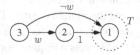

Fig. 7. The rings built during the computation of $M\,H\,U\,T$ do not guarantee shortest paths. State 3 is added to the fixpoint only after two iterations, even though it has a path of length 1 to a state in T. All states are in H. Variable w is controlled by the system

greedily minimize the number of free segments in C. Two consecutive fated segment computations are avoided since the MU computations are closed.

The procedure starts by picking a state in T closest to S in Line 5. The function CLOSESTSTATE tries to pick a state from a set that is closest to a given state in terms of the Hamming distance of the encodings. C is initialized to T. Each iteration of the while-loop computes one segment, either fated or free. The alternation is imposed by the *prev* flag that records whether the current computation is fated or free, and if-else statement (Lines 10–23) performs the other based on the previous value of *prev*. The first segment is set to a fated computation, by setting *prev* initially to *free*.

For a fated computation (Lines 10–18, Lines 25–26), Line 13 computes the states in H that can be forced to the current target T. If the computation was trivial (only states in T result), then the algorithm goes back to the beginning of the while-loop to try free segment computation. Notice that the state sets of the iterations of M $H \cup T$ do not provide a means to trace shortest paths in general. (See Fig. 7.) Hence if the MU computation is non-trivial, onion rings are set up (Lines 17–18) from the state closest to the initial state in the fated set in order to be able to build one short fated segment. For a free segment computation (Lines 19–23, Lines 25–26), the states that can make a free choice into T and the onion rings for this choice are set up in Lines 21–22. The distance from the initial state is guaranteed to decrease since the index p for the onion rings decreases. This is critical for the termination of the algorithm as it ensures that fewer rings are considered every time a free computation is performed.

Lines 25–26 build the actual free or fated segment to be added to the counterexample using the onion rings R. The procedure BUILDSHORTESTPATH traces a minimum-length path from a state in LAST(R) to a state in T using the onion rings R around T as described in Sect. 2. The rings aid in building short segments. Finally, in Line 27, the target T for the next segment is set to the first state in the counterexample constructed thus far.

This algorithm is not guaranteed to produce a counterexample trace of minimum length or least free segments.

Example 2. We have implemented the algorithms in Fig. 6. The counterexample in Fig. 1 for Example 1 is generated using the restricted algorithm in Fig. 6. In this example, Γ is set to `validin` since it is a control input. The counterexample is a liveness property and is generated in parts. Each part is generated with the algorithm in Fig. 6. The first part is the stem that shows a path from the initial state to a state such that there is a match, more precisely to a state that satisfies the formula (`match` $\wedge$ `EG(sav = hh)`). The next part builds a cycle around the state with the match such that the HI request saved in `sav` never gets issued in the cycle.

In the first part, the state in Column 4 is picked as the target. This state indicates a match, with the LO FIFO containing the matched entry. The stem is built backward from the initial state. The HI FIFO gets two requests for address 0 (in Columns 2 and 3, but only one is required) and the LO FIFO gets a request for address 0 causing the match.

In the next part, a cycle is traced through State 4 by setting State 4 as the target T and a successor of State 4 (State 5) as the initial state S. Since the cycle is traced backward, the first fated segment is indicated in Columns 9–15–0. A free choice is made into State 9 with `inaddr = 0` and `hl = 0`. The other fated segments of the cycle (Columns 5–8 and Columns 2–4) are constructed similarly.

The counterexample is read left to right. The free choices allow LO requests to enter the LO FIFO with `inaddr` $= 0$. The fated segments inevitably issue these requests as the `sloClk` ticks. The free choices ensure starvation of the HI request corresponding to the entry in `sav`. This raises the question as whether these free choices are indeed allowed. Avoiding starvation may lie in the answer to this question.

4   The Consequences of Progress

Various choices of controlling variables are possible for a given system. These choices may reflect the control-data dichotomy, or the distinction between external and internal nondeterminism. In this section we discuss an algorithmic criterion for the selection of controlling variables that is based on the notion of *progress* towards the bad states.

Example 3. Consider a system with a master reset input r. Assertion of r causes the system to make a transition to a specified "home" state. Unless the home state is a bad state for the property being verified, r should remain deasserted throughout the error trace, and, unless r is included in Γ, no fated segments can be found.

   In cases like that of Example 3, we would like to automatically detect variables playing a role similar to r, and assign them to Γ. We observe that a trace from some initial states must eventually cross the boundaries between adjacent rings built around the target. If we impose the requirement that at each step some progress be made towards the target, we define a set of transitions that can be used by the error traces. Let $P(V, W, V')$ be the characteristic function of the transitions that leave the current endpoint of the trace and cross the boundary into the next onion ring; let $w \in W$ be an input variable. If $P_w = 0$ or $P_{\neg w} = 0$, the requirement of progress dictates the value of w. We add w to Γ if it is often critical to making progress.
   Extending this principle, if a variable w is such that $\forall w \,.\, P = P_w \wedge P_{\neg w} = 0$, we consider it for inclusion in Γ. If $\forall w \,.\, P = 0$, variable w divides the transitions into disjoint sets. In adding a few such variables to Γ, one hopes that a succinct explanation of the error trace will emerge.

Example 4. Analysis of the progress requirements for the system of Example 1 reveals that sometime input `validin` must have a prescribed value for the system to evolve towards the bad states. In addition, it is always the case that the universal quantification of `validin` from P yields 0. Hence, we choose $\Gamma = \{\texttt{validin}\}$. This choice leads to the counterexample of Fig. 1.

5   Related Work

Not much has been written about the explanation of counterexamples produced by model checkers. The works closest to ours are [dAHM00] and [AHK97], though the points of contact are more in the formulation than in the purpose. Specifically, the game-theoretical formulation we have adopted for the computation of fated segments is related to the approach of [dAHM00]. However, we are interested in explaining counterexamples, as opposed to solving the model checking problem. This leads to a reversal of the roles between environment and system. Another distinguishing aspect is that we may generate multiple fated segments along a trace, and the last of these segments may not reach the target (bad) states. Finally, in our context we can explore scenarios defined by different choices of controlling variables Γ.

The work on vacuity detection [BBER97,KV99] deals with the notion of *interesting witness* to a passing formula. A witness is interesting for φ if it is a witness to all (important) subformulae of φ. Since producing an interesting witness to φ amounts to finding a counterexample for a formula derived from φ, our techniques can be directly applied to the derivation of interesting witnesses that are easier to understand.

6   Experiments

We have implemented the algorithm in Fig. 6 in the model checking tool VIS. The generation of the annotated trace in Fig. 1 took 2.1 seconds on an IBM IntelliStation with a 400 MHz Pentium 2 CPU and 1 GB of RAM running Linux. For comparison, the standard counterexample generation algorithm took 5.7 seconds. We applied this algorithm to two other circuits. The first is a Digital Audio Input/Output Receiver circuit. The property tested failed and the counterexample produced one forced segment of length 31 in 4 seconds as compared to 1.9 seconds in the traditional trace computation. The third example is a buggy implementation of the bakery protocol. The mutual exclusion property failed, producing a counterexample with four fated segments of lengths 13, 6, 4, and 5 respectively. Generating the counterexample took 1.2 seconds, versus 0.1 seconds with the traditional approach.

7   Conclusions

We have discussed the explanation of counterexamples produced by model checkers. The separation into segments and the pinpointing that some sequences are fated while others are free all contribute to explaining the error. We have presented an example with a trace demarcated into fated and free segment to explain our method. The segments help analyze the failure better. We have also presented experimental results for other circuits.

Many extensions and variants of the techniques we have proposed remain to be explored. One direction of interest is the formulation of liveness counterexamples as Büchi games. We are also researching counterexamples for existential properties.

Another area of investigation is to extend an error trace to a bundle of error traces while keeping them readable. We are exploring the idea of extending each state to a set of states represented as a cube in the counterexample. The motivation for this is to reduce the number of relevant variables appearing in the counterexample so it is easier to debug. Towards the same goal is the detection of dependent variables so as to isolate a small basis for variables in the error traces. Also, in case of hierarchical descriptions, we would like to restrict the traces to variables that appear in as few modules as possible.

References

[AHK97] R. Alur, T. A. Henzinger, and O. Kupferman. Alternating-time temporal logic. In *In Proceedings of the IEEE Symposium on the Foundations of Computer Science*, pages 100–109, 1997.

[BBER97] I. Beer, S. Ben-David, C. Eisner, and Y. Rodeh. Efficient detection of vacuity in ACTL formulas. In O. Grumberg, editor, *Ninth Conference on Computer Aided Verification (CAV'97)*, pages 279–290. Springer-Verlag, Berlin, 1997. LNCS 1254.

[CE81] E. M. Clarke and E. A. Emerson. Design and synthesis of synchronization skeletons using branching time temporal logic. In *Proceedings Workshop on Logics of Programs*, pages 52–71, Berlin, 1981. Springer-Verlag. LNCS 131.

[CGMZ95] E. Clarke, O. Grumberg, K. McMillan, and X. Zhao. Efficient generation of counterexamples and witnesses in symbolic model checking. In *Proceedings of the Design Automation Conference*, pages 427–432, San Francisco, CA, June 1995.

[CGP99] E. M. Clarke, O. Grumberg, and D. A. Peled. *Model Checking*. MIT Press, Cambridge, MA, 1999.

[dAHM00] L. de Alfaro, T. A. Henzinger, and F. Y. C. Mang. Detecting errors before reaching them. In E. A. Emerson and A. P. Sistla, editors, *Twelfth Conference on Computer Aided Verification (CAV'00)*, pages 186–201. Springer-Verlag, Berlin, July 2000. LNCS 1855.

[EH86] E. A. Emerson and J. Y. Halpern. 'Sometimes' and 'not never' revisited: On branching time versus linear time temporal logic. *Journal of the Association for Computing Machinery*, 33(1):151–178, 1986.

[EJ91] E. A. Emerson and C. S. Jutla. Tree automata, mu-calculus and determinacy. In *Proc. 32nd IEEE Symposium on Foundations of Computer Science*, pages 368–377, October 1991.

[Kur94] R. P. Kurshan. *Computer-Aided Verification of Coordinating Processes*. Princeton University Press, Princeton, NJ, 1994.

[KV99] O. Kupferman and M. Y. Vardi. Vacuity detection in temporal model checking. In *Correct Hardware Design and Verification Methods (CHARME'99)*, pages 82–96, Berlin, September 1999. Springer-Verlag. LNCS 1703.

[LP85] O. Lichtenstein and A. Pnueli. Checking that finite state concurrent programs satisfy their linear specification. In *Proceedings of the Twelfth Annual ACM Symposium on Principles of Programming Languages*, pages 97–107, New Orleans, January 1985.

[McM94] K. L. McMillan. *Symbolic Model Checking*. Kluwer Academic Publishers, Boston, MA, 1994.

[RBS00] K. Ravi, R. Bloem, and F. Somenzi. A comparative study of symbolic algorithms for the computation of fair cycles. In W. A. Hunt, Jr. and S. D. Johnson, editors, *Formal Methods in Computer Aided Design*, pages 143–160. Springer-Verlag, November 2000. LNCS 1954.

[WVS83] P. Wolper, M. Y. Vardi, and A. P. Sistla. Reasoning about infinite computation paths. In *Proceedings of the 24th IEEE Symposium on Foundations of Computer Science*, pages 185–194, 1983.

TIMES – A Tool for Modelling and Implementation of Embedded Systems

Tobias Amnell, Elena Fersman, Leonid Mokrushin, Paul Pettersson, and
Wang Yi*

Uppsala University, Sweden.
{tobiasa,elenaf,leom,paupet,yi}@docs.uu.se

1 Introduction

TIMES is a modelling and schedulability analysis tool for embedded real-time
systems, developed at Uppsala University in 2001. It is appropriate for systems
that can be described as a set of preemptive or non-preemptive tasks which are
triggered periodically or sporadically by time or external events. It provides a
graphical interface for editing and simulation, and an engine for schedulability
analysis. The main features of TIMES are:

- A graphical editor for timed automata extended with tasks [1], which allows
  the user to model a system and the abstract behaviour of its environment
  In addition the user may specify a set of preemptive or non-preemtive tasks
  with parameters such as (relative) deadline, execution time, priority, etc.
- A simulator, in which the user can validate the dynamic behaviour of the
  system and see how the tasks execute according to the task parameters and
  a given scheduling policy. The simulator shows a graphical representation
  of the generated trace showing the time points when the tasks are released,
  invoked, suspended, resumed, and completed.
- A verifier for schedulability analysis, which is used to check if all reachable
  states of the complete system are schedulable that is, all task instances meet
  their deadlines. A symbolic algorithm has been developed based on the DBM
  techniques and implemented based on the verifier of the UPPAAL tool [2].
- A code generator for automatic synthesis of C-code on LegoOS platform from
  the model. If the automata model is schedulable according to the schedulability analyser the execution of the generated code will meet all the timing
  constraints specified in the model and the tasks.

An screen-shot of the TIMES tool is shown in Fig. 1. In section 3 we describe the
tool and its main functionalities in more details. The modelling language and
the theoretical foundation of TIMES is based on the model of timed automata
with tasks, described in the following section.

---

* Corresponding author: Wang Yi, Department of Information Technology, Uppsala
  University, Box 325, 751 05, Uppsala, Sweden. Email: yi@docs.uu.se

J.-P. Katoen and P. Stevens (Eds.): TACAS 2002, LNCS 2280, pp. 460–464, 2002.

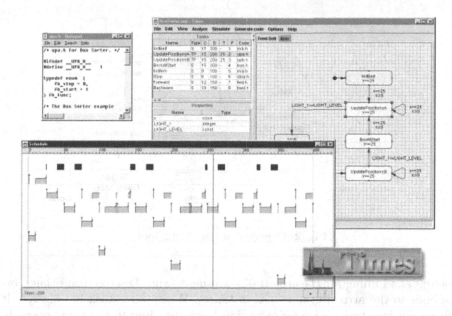

Fig. 1. Screen-shot of the TIMES tool.

2   Input Language

The core of the input language of TIMES is timed automata with real time tasks (TAT), described in details in [1] included in this volume, with one major addition that shared variables between automata and tasks are allowed. Here we give a brief introduction to the model. A TAT is a timed automaton extended with tasks triggered by events. A task is an executable program (written in a programming language e.g. C) characterized by its worst execution time and deadline, and possibly other parameters such as priorities etc. for scheduling. A task may update a set of variables using assignments in the form $x := E$ where x is a variable and E is an expression (computed by the task and the value of E is returned when the task is finished). The variables may also be changed and tested by an automaton. Intuitively an edge leading to a location in the automaton denotes an event triggering the task, and the guard (clock constraints) on the transition specifies the possible arrival times of the event. This allows us to describe concurrency and synchronization, and real time tasks which may be periodic, sporadic, preemptive and (or) non-preemptive, with or without precedence constraints. An automaton is schedulable if there exists a (preemptive or non-preemptive) scheduling strategy such that all possible sequences of events accepted by the automaton are schedulable in the sense that all associated tasks can be computed within their deadlines.

Semantically, an extended timed automaton may perform two types of transitions just as standard timed automata. But the difference is that delay transitions correspond to the execution of running tasks with highest priority (or earliest

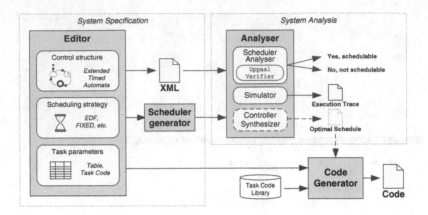

Fig. 2. Overview of the TIMES tool.

deadline) and idling for the other tasks waiting to run. Discrete transitions corresponds to the arrival of new task instances. Whenever a task is triggered, it will be put in a task queue for execution (corresponding to the ready queue in operating systems). Thus there may be a number of processes (released tasks) running logically in parallel during the execution of an automaton.

The scheduling problem of TAT is to verify that all released tasks are guaranteed to always meet their deadlines when executed according to a given scheduling policy. In TIMES the analysis is performed by transforming a TAT system into ordinary timed automata extended with subtraction operations on clocks, and encoding the schedulability problem to a reachability problem as described in [1].

3 Tool Overview

An overview of the TIMES tool is shown in Fig. 2. The tool is divided in three parts: a system specification part, a system analysis part, and a code generator[1].

In the system specification part, the user models a system to be analysed. A system specification in TIMES consists of three parts: the control automata modelled as a network of timed automata extended with tasks [1], a task table with information about the processes triggered (released) when the control automata changes location, and a scheduling policy.

The System Editor tool, shown in Fig. 1, is a an editor for drawing the control automata of the system model. It also provides a table for defining the task parameters. The task parameters currently supported are: (relative) deadline, execution time, period, priority, a reference to the task code, and a field indicating the task behaviour. A task has one of the following three behaviours: "S"

---

[1] The components indicated with dashed lines in Fig. 2 are planed extension not yet included.

for sporadic, "TP" for temporarily periodic, and "P" for periodic. The currently supported scheduling polices are: first-come first-served, fixed priority (i.e. according to the priorities assigned in the task table), rate monotonic, deadline monotonic, and earliest-deadline first. All polices can be either preemptive or non-preemptive.

The output of the System Editor is an XML representation of the control automata. The information from the task table and the scheduling policy, are used by the Scheduler Generator to generate a scheduler automaton that is composed in parallel with the controller automata to ensure that the system behaves according to the scheduling policy and the task parameters. If the scheduling policy is non-preemptive, the scheduler automaton is an ordinary timed automaton. If the scheduling policy is preemptive, the scheduler automaton is modelled as a variant of timed automata in which clock variables may be updated by subtractions. For more information about how to solve scheduling problems of timed automata with tasks using timed automata, see [1].

The parallel composition of the control automata and the scheduler automaton is used as input to the System Analyser that consist of two main components: a Simulator, and a Schedule Analyser. In the Simulator the user may debug the system by exploring the dynamic behaviour of the system model and observe how the tasks execute according to the chosen scheduling policy. Screen-shots of the Simulator are shown in Fig. 1 and 4. As shown, the Simulator displays a diagram with $n + 1$ lines, where n is the number of tasks. On the upper line, it is indicated in blue (or black) when no task is executing. The lower n lines are associated with one task each, and used to show in red (or gray) when the corresponding task is executing. As time progresses the diagram grows to the right (i.e. the time line goes from left to right). Note that at any moment in time either, one or zero tasks are executing, or a switch takes place.

From the System Analyser it is also possible to invoke the Schedule Analyser that performs schedulability analysis of the system. The analysis is performed by rephrasing scheduling to a reachability problem that is solved with an extended version of the verifier of the UPPAAL tool [2]. In case the output of the analysis is negative, the analyser generates a trace of the system that ends in a state in which one of the system task fails to meet its deadline.

The Code Generator of TIMES uses the control automata and the task programs to synthesise executable C-code. Currently the only supported platform is the LegOS operating system. Support for other platforms will be included in future versions.

4   Example: Box Sorter

In this section, we describe how TIMES is applied to the box sorter example of [2]. The system sorts red and black boxes arriving on a belt by kicking the black boxes of the belt. The physical components are the feed belt, a light sensor, and a kick-off arm. The programs controlling the feed belt and the arm are modelled using two timed automata with tasks, as shown in Fig. 3.

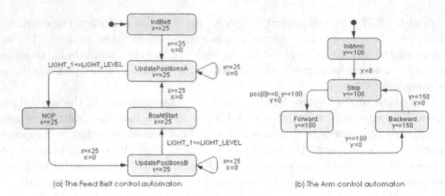

(a) The Feed Belt control automaton   (b) The Arm control automaton

Fig. 3. The two Control Automata of the Box Sorter.

The tasks of the automaton in Fig. 3(a) uses a global array named pos to store the positions of the black boxes on the belt. The automaton in Fig. 3(b) controls the kick-off arm.

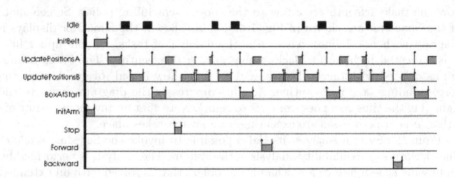

Fig. 4. The Box Sorter Schedule.

Fig. 4 shows an execution trace of the box sorter system, as it appears in the simulator window of the TIMES tool. Note how the simulator indicates that e.g. the second invocation of task UpdatePositionsA is delayed and preempted twice by higher priority tasks.

References

1. Elena Fersman, Paul Pettersson, and Wang Yi. Timed Automata with Asynchronous Processes: Schedulability and Decidability. In *Proc. of the 8th Int. Conference on Tools and Algorithms for the Construction and Analysis of Systems*, 2002.
2. Kim G. Larsen, Paul Pettersson, and Wang Yi. UPPAAL in a Nutshell. *Int. Journal on Software Tools for Technology Transfer*, 1(1–2):134–152, October 1997.

Compositional Verification Using SVL Scripts

Frédéric Lang

INRIA Rhône-Alpes - VASY
655, avenue de l'Europe - F-38330 Montbonnot, France
Frederic.Lang@inria.fr

1 Introduction

User-friendliness of complex software has traditionally been enhanced in two complementary ways: graphical user interfaces and scripting languages. The CADP toolbox[1] [3,5] is a complex software suite integrating numerous verification tools. Since 1995, it has been equipped with EUCALYPTUS, a graphical user interface. However, a dedicated scripting language to automate repetitive verification tasks was still lacking, resulting in ad hoc shell scripts and MAKEFILES used for this purpose. The main problem was that they were usually too verbose and lacked built-in features to support model-based verification. This has motivated the definition and implementation of the scripting language SVL[2] [4].

An SVL script is a sequence of *statements*, which describe verification operations (such as comparison modulo various equivalence relations, deadlock and livelock detection, verification of temporal logic formulas, etc.) performed on *behaviors*. Basic behaviors are either Labeled Transition Systems (LTSs) described in a number of formats, networks of communicating LTSs, LOTOS descriptions, or particular processes in LOTOS descriptions. Behaviors can be combined using operations such as parallel composition, label hiding, label renaming, LTS generation, minimization, and abstraction w.r.t. an interface. SVL has also *meta-operations* implementing higher-order strategies for compositional verification.

To execute SVL scripts, a compiler (7,000 lines) has been developed. As depicted in Figure 1, it translates an SVL script into an executable Bourne shell script, which is run to perform the requested operations by calling either the CADP or the FC2 [1] tools (e.g., ALDÉBARAN, BCG_MIN, or FC2MIN for minimization). SVL is particularly useful in compositional verification, which we illustrate in this paper with two unpublished examples.

2 Basic Compositional Verification

Compositional verification intends to avoid state explosion by using divide-and-conquer techniques. When verifying a network of concurrent processes, it consists in replacing each process by an *abstraction* (e.g., a minimization modulo an appropriate equivalence relation) simpler than the original process but still preserving the properties to be verified on the whole system.

---

[1] CADP web site: "http://www.inrialpes.fr/vasy/cadp".
[2] SVL on-line user-manual: "http://www.inrialpes.fr/vasy/cadp/man/svl.html".

J.-P. Katoen and P. Stevens (Eds.): TACAS 2002, LNCS 2280, pp. 465–469, 2002.

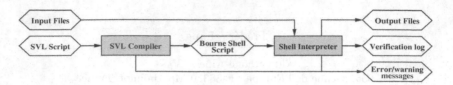

Fig. 1. The SVL tool

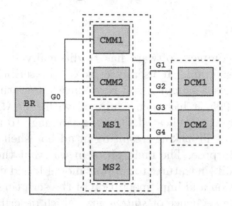

Fig. 2. Architecture of the HAVi Protocol

We illustrate compositional verification with a case study [8] concerning the leader election protocol used in the HAVi standard for home audio/video networks. Figure 2 depicts this protocol modelled in file "HAVi.lotos" as a network of seven concurrent processes (BR, DCM1, etc.) communicating on gates G0 to G4. Due to its complexity, the state space cannot be generated directly, but can be generated compositionally using the following SVL script, which replaces the 85-line MAKEFILE developed by Judi Romijn for the same task:

```
% DEFAULT_LOTOS_FILE="HAVi.lotos"
"HAVi.exp" = leaf strong reduction of                    (* 1 *)
    (BR |[G0, G4]|
      ((DCM1 ||| DCM2)
       |[G1, G2, G3, G4]|
        ((CMM1 |[G0]| CMM2) |[G0, G4]| (MS1 |[G0]| MS2))));
"HAVi.bcg" = strong reduction of "HAVi.exp";             (* 2 *)
```

In step (1), the LTSs of the seven processes are generated and minimized for strong bisimulation (as specified by the "leaf reduction" meta-operation), then composed in parallel to form a network of LTSs named "HAVi.exp". In step (2), the LTS corresponding to "HAVi.exp" is generated, minimized for strong bisimulation, and stored in file "HAVi.bcg" (5, 107 states and 18, 725 transitions). The verification takes 5 minutes on a standard 450 MHz Linux PC.

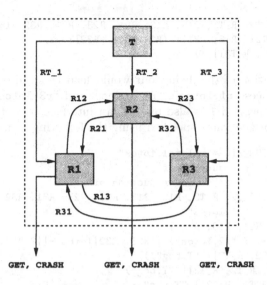

Fig. 3. Architecture of the rel/REL Protocol

3 Refined Compositional Verification

The basic compositional verification approach presented in Section 2 may fail because generating the LTS of each process separately may lead to state explosion, whereas the generation of the whole system of concurrent processes might succeed if processes constrain each other when composed in parallel [6,7]. To overcome this problem, processes may be restricted w.r.t. so-called *interfaces* expressing the behavioral restrictions imposed on each process by synchronization with its neighbor processes.

Technically, an expression written "$B -|[GL]| I$", where I is the interface (an LTS), B the behaviour to restrict, and GL a set of gates named *synchronization set*, denotes the biggest sub-LTS of B of which states and transitions can be reached following observable execution sequences of I, where actions on gates in GL only are considered observable. "$B -|| I$" is a shorthand notation for "$B -|[GL]| I$", where GL is the set of gates occurring in I. Interfaces can be given by the user (in which case their correctness must be checked) or generated automatically. The "?" symbol, possibly placed before the interface (see below), indicates that correctness of the interface w.r.t. the environment must be checked during state space construction.

To illustrate how SVL supports refined compositional verification, we use the reliable atomic multicast protocol [2] example presented in [7][3]. Figure 3 describes a protocol configuration consisting of one transmitter (process T) and three receivers (processes R1, R2, R3). This protocol can be represented by the following LOTOS and SVL like parallel composition expression:

---

[3] SVL supersedes the DES2AUT tool described in [7]; see [4] for a comparison.

```
hide R_T1, R_T2, R_T3, R12, R13, R21, R23, R31, R32   in
((R1 |[R12, R21, R13, R31]| (R2 |[R23, R32]| R3))
 |[R_T1, R_T2, R_T3]| T)
```

Direct generation of this behaviour would lead to state explosion. Instead, user-given interfaces "r1.lotos", "r2.lotos", and "r3.lotos" are used to restrict each receiver, and T is also used as an interface to restrict intermediate compositions. Verification is specified using the following SVL script :

```
% DEFAULT_LOTOS_FILE="rel_rel.lotos"
"T.bcg" = strong reduction of T;                               (* 1 *)
"rel_rel.exp" = leaf strong reduction of                       (* 2 *)
    hide R_T1, R_T2, R_T3, R12, R13, R21, R23, R31, R32   in
  ((((R1 -||? "r1.lotos")
     |[R12, R21, R13, R31]|
     (((R2 -||? "r2.lotos") |[R23, R32]| (R3 -||? "r3.lotos"))
      -|[R_T2, R_T3]| "T.bcg"))
    -|[R_T1, R_T2, R_T3]| "T.bcg")
   |[R_T1, R_T2, R_T3]| "T.bcg");
"rel_rel.bcg" = strong reduction of "rel_rel.exp"              (* 3 *)
```

In step (1), process T of "rel_rel.lotos" is generated and minimized for strong bisimulation. In step (2), for each Ri an LTS is generated using the PRO-JECTOR tool of [7], by taking into account the restrictions specified by the corresponding "ri.lotos" interface. The resulting three LTSs are then minimized for strong bisimulation, composed in parallel (following the restrictions specified by T), and finally minimized for strong bisimulation. This produces an LTS which is composed in parallel with T to form (after hiding internal gates) a network of LTSs named "rel_rel.exp". Note that since R_T1 does not occur in R2 and R3, it obviously does not appear in the synchronization set of the restriction w.r.t. T of the R2 and R3 composition. In step (3), the LTS corresponding to "rel_rel.exp" is generated and minimized for strong bisimulation. During the state space construction, the correctness of interfaces preceded by "?" is checked automatically. The final LTS (150, 911 states and 1, 249, 375 transitions) is obtained in 15 minutes on a 450 MHz Linux PC.

4   Other Forms of Scripted Verification

Besides compositional verification, SVL is also convenient to perform other forms of verification (e.g., those based on bisimulations or temporal formulas) permitted by the CADP tools. For instance, the following script verifies that it is always possible to perform the "S !1" action from any state of the LTS "f.bcg". This is checked by hiding all labels but "S !1", then comparing modulo branching equivalence the resulting LTS to another LTS with a single state and a single looping transition labeled "S !1", contained in file "r.bcg".

```
"d.seq" = branching comparison
    (total hide all but "S !1" in "f.bcg") == "r.bcg";
```

By combining SVL with Bourne shell features, it is also possible to introduce parameterization in verification scenarios. The following script uses a "for" loop to verify eight temporal logic properties (contained in files "prop1.mcl", ..., "prop8.mcl") on the LTS "f.bcg". Lines starting with "%" are meant to be Bourne shell. Other shell control structures ("if...fi", "case...esac", function definitions, etc.) can be used similarly.

```
% for N in 1 2 3 4 5 6 7 8; do
     verify "prop$N.mcl" in "f.bcg";
% done
```

5   Conclusion

Scripting languages will certainly play a growing role in advanced verification tool sets. The SVL scripting language added recently to CADP makes compositional verification simpler than ever by interconnecting many verification tools and file formats transparently. Although very recent, SVL is already used in both academic and industrial projects, e.g., at the University of Twente (The Netherlands) and Ericsson (Sweden). Practical experiments (19 out of the 29 CADP demos have been rewritten in SVL) indicate that SVL leads to more readable, shorter, and safer scripts than equivalent MAKEFILEs and shell scripts.

References

1. A. Bouali, A. Ressouche, V. Roy, and R. de Simone. The Fc2Tools set: a Toolset for the Verification of Concurrent Systems. In *CAV'96*, *LNCS* vol. 1102.
2. S. Bainbridge and L. Mounier. Specification and Verification of a Reliable Multicast Protocol. Technical Report HPL-91-163, HP Labs, Bristol, 1991.
3. J.-C. Fernandez, H. Garavel, A. Kerbrat, R. Mateescu, L. Mounier, and M. Sighireanu. CADP (CÆSAR/ALDEBARAN Development Package): A Protocol Validation and Verification Toolbox. In *CAV'96*, *LNCS* vol. 1102.
4. H. Garavel and F. Lang. SVL: a Scripting Language for Compositional Verification. In *FORTE'01* (Kluwer) and INRIA Research Report RR-4223.
5. H. Garavel, F. Lang, and R. Mateescu. An overview of CADP 2001. INRIA Technical Report RT-0254, 2001.
6. S. Graf and B. Steffen. Compositional Minimization of Finite State Systems. In *CAV'90*, *LNCS* vol. 531.
7. J.-P. Krimm and L. Mounier. Compositional State Space Generation from LOTOS Programs. In *TACAS'97*, *LNCS* vol. 1217.
8. J. Romijn. Model Checking the HAVi Leader Election Protocol. Technical Report SEN-R9915, CWI, Amsterdam, 1999.

STG: A Symbolic Test Generation Tool

Duncan Clarke[1], Thierry Jéron[2], Vlad Rusu[2], and Elena Zinovieva[2]

[1] University of South Carolina,
Columbia, South Carolina, USA
[2] IRISA/INRIA Rennes,
Campus de Beaulieu, Rennes, France
dclarke@cse.sc.edu, {jeron|rusu|lenaz}@irisa.fr

Abstract. We report on a tool we have developed that implements conformance testing techniques to automatically derive symbolic tests cases from formal operational specifications. We demonstrate the application of the techniques and tools on a simple example and present case studies for the CEPS (Common Electronic Purse Specification) and for the file system of the 3GPP (Third Generation Partnership Project) card.

1 Introduction

The work that we present is an attempt to leverage the ideas underlying protocol conformance testing [9] and high-efficiency test generation as embodied in the TGV [6] and TorX [2] tools, to automate the generation of tests for smart-card applications. Most existing test generation tools perform their analysis by enumerating the specification's state space. This leads to two problems: (1) state-space explosion, as the variables in the specification are instantiated with all of their possible values, and (2) tests that are not readily understandable by humans. To avoid these problems we introduce symbolic generation techniques.

2 STG: The Symbolic Test Generation Tool

Based on the theory of symbolic test generation presented in [8] we have created the STG tool that implements the process illustrated in Fig.1. The system at the user level is described in NTIF a high-level, LOTOS-like language developed by the VASY team, INRIA Rhône-Alpes. The STG tool for symbolic test generation uses IOSTS (Input Output Symbolic Transition Systems) [8] as an internal model for reactive systems. To obtain such a model, the system written in NTIF is automatically translated into IOSTS (*cf.* Fig.1 above the dashed box).

Currently the STG tool supports two processes (*cf.* Fig.1), which are briefly described below.

Symbolic test generation. The process of symbolic test generation takes a specification of the system together with a test purpose and produces a symbolic test

J.-P. Katoen and P. Stevens (Eds.): TACAS 2002, LNCS 2280, pp. 470–475, 2002.

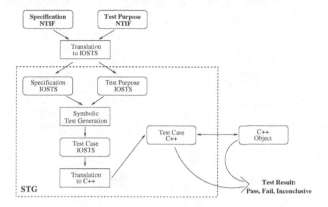

Fig. 1. Symbolic Test Generation Process

case, which is a reactive program covering all the behaviors of the specification that are targeted by the test purpose. A detailed description of symbolic test generation and its properties can be found in [8].

IOSTS to C++. To obtain an executable test, the abstract, symbolic test case obtained after symbolic test generation is translated into a concrete test program capable of interacting with an implementation interface-compatible with the original specification. The test program is then ready to be compiled and linked with the implementation for test execution. The results of a test execution are "Pass", which means no errors were detected and the test purpose was satisfied, "Inconclusive" - no errors were detected but the test purpose was not satisfied, or "Fail" - an error was detected. Here, "error" means a non-conformance between the implementation and the specification. The conformance relation is defined in [9,8]

We illustrate the symbolic test generation process on a simple example.

The specification. Fig.2 presents the IOSTS specification of a coffee machine. As shown in the figure, the IOSTS is made up of control states called *locations* and of transitions between locations that describe either input, output, or internal actions and manipulate symbolic data. A transition can be fired if its *guard* is true, then executes its action and performs assignments that set its variables to new values

The machine starts in the *Begin* location with the initial condition $pPrice > 0$, that is, the price of any beverage dispensed by the machine is strictly positive. Then, the machine moves to the *Idle* location by initializing the *vPaid* variable, which memorizes the amount already paid. Next, the machine expects a coin, denoted by the *Coin?* input action that carries in *mCoinValue* the value of the inserted coin, and the variable *vPaid* is increased by *mCoinValue* and the machine moves to the *Pay* location. If the payment is not enough

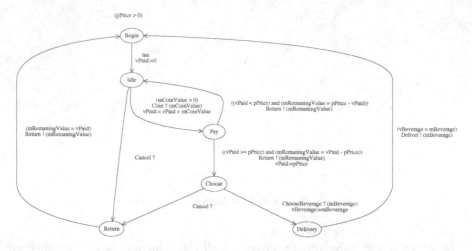

Fig. 2. Example of IOSTS: a Coffee Machine

i.e., *vPaid* < *pPrice*, the machine moves back to the *Idle* location and returns (through the *Return!(mRemaningValue)* output action) the difference between the paid amount and the cost of beverage, *i.e. pPrice − vPaid*. Otherwise, the machine moves to the *Choose* location and returns in *mRemaningValue* the difference between *vPaid* and *pPrice*. In the *Choose* location, the machine waits for the choice of the beverage (tea or coffee), then delivers the beverage, and moves back to the *Begin* location. Note that in locations *Idle* and *Choose*, the *Cancel* button can be pressed, in which case the machine returns the amount already paid and moves back to the initial location.

The test purpose. Fig.3 presents one possible test purpose for the coffee machine, which describes behaviors where the machine delivers coffee and the user does not introduce coins more than once and does not cancel. An accepted behavior is indicated by arrival at location *Accept*. The test purpose rejects behaviors that correspond to delivery of tea to the user, or pressing the *Cancel* button, or inserting more than one coin. Note that rejected behaviors are not necessarily erroneous, they are just behaviors that are not targeted by the test purpose.

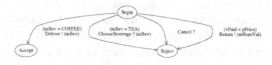

Fig. 3. Test Purpose

The test case. Fig.4 presents the IOSTS test case automatically generated by STG which covers all the behaviors of the specification (*cf.* Fig.2) that are targeted by the test purpose of (*cf.* Fig.3). Note that the test case is limited to the behaviors targeted by the test purpose: it accepts only one payment and does not exercise pressing the cancel button or require delivery of tea (*cf.* Fig.4).

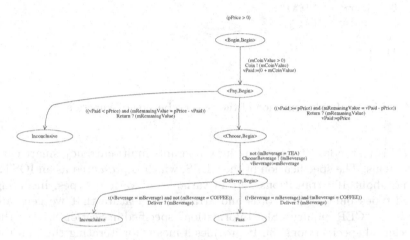

Fig. 4. Test Case

Test case execution. The test case is now ready to be translated to C++ and to be linked and executed on an implementation under test. For example, suppose the implementation has a method as shown in Fig.5, which corresponds to the *ChooseBeverage!* output in the test case (*cf.* Fig.4). The returning value of this function corresponds to the *Deliver?* input. Then, the delivery of tea after the coffee request (*cf.* Fig.5: lines 4, 5) denotes such a non-conformance [9,8], *i.e.* a difference between the implementation and the specification. As a consequence, by execution the test case on such an implementation we get a "Fail" verdict.

STG uses OMEGA [7] to detect unsatisfiable guards for simplifying the test cases, and *dotty* [5], a tool for drawing graphs to view IOSTS in graphical form. Figures 2, 3, 4 were produced by *dotty*.

3 Case Studies

The STG tool was applied for testing simple versions of the CEPS (Common Electronic Purse Specification) [3] and of the file system of the 3GPP (Third Generation Partnership Project) card [1].

```
...
 1. BeverageType ChooseBeverage(BeverageType mBeverage){
 2.   cerr << "ChooseBeverage(";
 3.   if(mBeverage == COFFEE){
 4.    cerr << "TEA)";
 5.    return TEA;
 6.   }
 7.   if(mBeverage == TEA){
 8.    cerr << "TEA)";
 9.    return TEA;
10.   }
11. }
...
```

Fig. 5. Implementation of the "ChooseBeverage" Function

The CEPS is a standard for creating inter-operable multi-currency smart card e-purse systems. The specification of the CEPS, which is presented as an IOSTS model, has about 100 transitions and 40 variables of various types, including structured types built with records and arrays. The feature that we generate tests for is the "CEP Inquiry - Slot Information" specified in Section 8.7.1 of the CEPS technical specifications [3]. It provides a means for iterating through the slots, where each slot corresponds to one currency and its respective balance. The paper [4] presents our results of this experiment.

The 3GPP card is a multi-applications microprocessor smart card. We generate tests for the file system of the card, which is organized as follows: it has one *master* file (a root of the system) which contains *dedicated* (directory files), *application dedicated* (special directory files for the applications), and different kinds of *elementary* files where data are organized either as a sequence of bytes or a set of records. The current specification of the file system for the 3GPP card allows to create files on the card, to search a record in the files, and to get a response from the card after the search is performed. The specification has been written in the NTIF language, and automatically translated into the IOSTS model, which has about 100 transitions, 50 locations, and 30 variables of various types, including structured types built with records and arrays.

Using STG we automatically generate executable test cases for these systems. The test cases are executed on implementations of the systems, including mutants. Various errors in the source code of the mutants were detected.

4   Summary

This paper has presented a tool that automates the derivation of test cases in order to check conformance of an implementation with respect to the behaviors of a specification targeted by test purposes; and determines whether the results of the test execution are correct with respect to the specification. It performs test derivation as a symbolic process, up to and including the generation of test program source code. The reason to use symbolic techniques instead of enumerative is that symbolic test generation produces (1) more general test cases with parameters and variables which need to be instantiated only at the test execution time, and (2) test cases that are more readable by humans.

We have presented a simple example that demonstrates the application of the method and the tool to a software testing problem, and reported case studies for the CEPS and for the file system of the 3GPP card.

References

1. 3GPP. Third Generation Partnership Project (http://www.3gpp.org).
2. A. Belinfante, J. Feenstra, R. de Vries, J. Tretmans, N. Goga, L. Feijs, and S. Mauw. Formal test automation: a simple experiment. In *International Workshop on the Testing of Communication Systems (IWTCS'99)*, pages 179–196, 1999.
3. CEPSCO. Common Electronic Purse Specifications, Technical Specification (http://www.cepsco.org), May 2000.
4. D. Clarke, T. Jéron, V. Rusu, and E. Zinovieva. Automated test and oracle generation for smart-card applications. In *Proceedings of the International Conference on Research in Smart Cards*, volume 2140 of *LNCS*, pages 58–70, Cannes, France, September 2001.
5. E. R. Gansner and S. C. North. An open graph visualization system and its applications to software engineering. *Software: Practice and Experience*, 30(11):1203–1233, September 2000.
6. T. Jéron and P. Morel. Test generation derived from model-checking. In *Computer Aided Verification (CAV '99)*, volume 1633 of *LNCS*, pages 108–122, 1999.
7. W. Kelly, V. Maslov, W. Pugh, E. Rosser, T. Shpiesman, and D. Wonnacott. The Omega library interface guide. Available at http://www.cs.umd.edu/projects/omega.
8. V. Rusu, L. du Bousquet, and T. Jéron. An approach to symbolic test generation. In *International Conference on Integrating Formal Methods*, volume 1945 of *LNCS*, pages 338–357, Dagstuhl, Germany, November 2000. Springer-Verlag.
9. J. Tretmans. A formal approach to conformance testing. In *The 6th International Workshop on Protocol Test Systems*, number C-19 in IFIP Transactions, pages 257–276, 1994.

Real-Time Systems Design with PEP

Christian Stehno

Fachbereich Informatik,
Carl von Ossietzky Universität Oldenburg,
D-26111 Oldenburg, Germany
Christian.Stehno@informatik.uni-oldenburg.de

Abstract. The PEP tool provides an integrated development and verification environment for parallel systems. Beginning with version 2.0 it also offers use of timed systems. This paper describes a sample session for the design and the verification by partial order based techniques of a simple real-time model for a mutual exclusion algorithm.

1 Overview of PEP

The PEP tool is a **P**rogramming **E**nvironment based on **P**etri nets[1]. It supports the development, the simulation and the verification of parallel programs by a variety of tools and techniques through its graphical user interface.

While PEP is mainly an integrated development environment for the parallel programming language B(PN)^2 [3], including a C code generator [11] and allowing programs to be transformed into Petri nets for verification, it also includes a complete Petri net tool providing editors, simulators and a large number of analysis and verification tools. An overview of the capabilities of PEP can be found in Sect. 2, while Sect. 3 describes a sample modelling session and Sect. 4 concludes the paper.

2 Components of the PEP Tool

Development Level. Due to the compactness and simplicity of notations used, this level is frequently used for large systems specification and design. In addition to an editor for B(PN)^2, there are also ones for the Specification and Description Language SDL [7] and for parallel finite automata [9]. The C code generator produces plain C code which supports the parallel execution of B(PN)^2 programs by the means of Unix processes. This code can be extended by a programmer to complete the algorithm written in B(PN)^2 and produce an executable for some target machine.

---

[1] http://parsys.informatik.uni-oldenburg.de/~pep

J.-P. Katoen and P. Stevens (Eds.): TACAS 2002, LNCS 2280, pp. 476–480, 2002.

Net Level. On the net level, the Petri net tool part of PEP is located. This level provides editors and simulators for high and (timed) low level nets, and more. The net editor contains a composition interface for nets supporting system design with Petri nets. All systems designed on the development level can be compiled into a Petri net representing their semantics. Along with this transformation, references are generated between representations providing the ability of PEP to simulate not only the nets but also the higher level systems directly.

Analysis Level. The analysis level includes Petri net specific verification checks and model checking of all models used within PEP. The behaviour of a net can be examined in many ways, ranging from state space analysis to model checking with linear and branching time logics. The next section will focus on those verifiers capable of using timed systems as input.

3 Timed Systems Analysis

3.1 Preliminaries

For the time being, PEP supports timing information within the Petri Box Calculus (PBC, [2,13]), on the low level nets (according to [15]), within all programs that support the finite prefix (which can be built for Time Petri nets, cf. [4,8]), and the INA tool [16]. The net editor supports time only on the editing level, simulation is rudimentary, i.e. only for the display of counterexamples.

We will model a variant of Fischer's protocol (cf. [1]) for two processes. This protocol provides a very simple mutual exclusion algorithm for an arbitrary number of processes, such that only one of them may enter the critical section and then halts, although the protocol may be extended for more than one round. The crucial cause of the correctness of the protocol are time intervals for writing and reading a global variable, making this an interesting timed protocol.

3.2 Modelling the Petri Net

The lack of high level timed models within PEP forces a system designer to start at the net level. As the PBC offers a simple and structured interface to (Time) Petri nets, we use it as the starting point for our example. The PBC provides a basic set of operations for combining nets into more complex ones. Most notably there are sequential (;), parallel (||) and choice operators ([]), synchronous communication mechanisms with optional block encapsulation and some primitive variable and data type facilities, including (finite) integer numbers, stacks and channels.

For the example, the shared variable v is needed. The macro for a variable is D_BOX(v,0,{0..2}), which creates a variable v with type {0,1,2} and initial value 0. Access to this variable is provided by action symbols of the form v_pre_post, changing v from pre to post. This box is put in parallel with two processes, each of which consists of three sequential steps (see Fig. 1, lines 4 and

6). Each step is given by the action symbol to be executed and a time interval (attached to it by an @) defining earliest and latest execution times after enabling. Thus, an interval $[m, n], m \leq n, m, n \in \mathbb{N}$ allows to execute the action after waiting at least m (integral) time steps; after n time steps the action has to occur, if still possible.

In each process the variable is initially checked for value zero, which has to be done immediately (interval [0,0]). After waiting at most one time step, the variable is set to value i for the ith process, which is done in a choice as other processes might have changed the value of v already. In a third step, the variable is checked for a value of i, in which case process i is allowed to enter its critical section[2] after waiting strictly longer than one time unit.

Finally, all components are glued together by the scoping operation over all used symbols, creating the correct links between the processes and the variable.

```
[{v,v_0_0,v_0_1,v_0_2,v_1_0,v_1_1,v_1_2,v_2_0,v_2_1,v_2_2}:
D_BOX(v,0,{0..2})
||
(v_0_0@[0,0]; (v_0_1@[0,1][]v_1_1@[0,1][]v_2_1@[0,1]); {v_1_1,cs}@[2,4])
||
(v_0_0@[0,0]; (v_0_2@[0,1][]v_1_2@[0,1][]v_2_2@[0,1]); {v_2_2,cs}@[2,4])
]
```

Fig. 1. Fischer's protocol for 2 processes in PBC syntax

The program in Fig. 1 can be compiled into the Time Petri net shown in Fig. 2. The transformation is almost a 1:1 correspondence, mapping actions and their accompanying time restrictions onto transitions. Arcs are created depending on the control flow of the program and the communication structure with the global variable. Further action will take place on the net rather than the PBC code.

3.3   Verification

With the latest version of its unfolder, PEP is able to create the finite prefix of a net analogously to [14,6] for Time Petri nets [4,8]. The finite prefix contains the complete information on the behaviour of nets in a compact way using partial order. The PEP model checker and some other analysis tools use the unfolding as input. On the finite prefix for Time Petri nets, these tools can be used for timed nets. For reachability and deadlock problems, the clp tool [12] and mcsmodels [10] are, besides the original PEP deadlock checker, capable of using finite prefices and thus checking Time Petri nets.

By reachability checking, all properties of interest can be verified, notably:

---

[2] Denoted by the extra symbol cs, which does not affect the net.

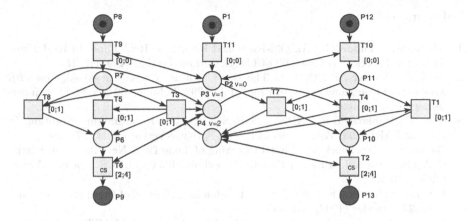

Fig. 2. Fischer's protocol for 2 processes as Time Petri net

- Each process may enter its critical section (P9 or P13 resp.).
- Only one process is in the critical section at a time (¬ P9 ∧ P13).

As checking the second property generates a positive answer, the protocol ensures mutual exclusion. For the first property, the system generates a witnessing firing sequence that might be simulated by the net editor. This holds in general for possible counterexamples and provides an easy way of debugging erroneous code.

Although reachability checking suffices for this example, usually many properties are not expressible that easy and use some kind of temporal logics. To verify them, a set of model checkers is provided by PEP. The PEP model checker uses the CTL fragment defined in [5]. It provides *place assertions* to express properties of the current marking of the net and two temporal operators *"possibly"* for reachability and its dual *"always"*, which may be nested. A second model checker available for Time Petri nets in PEP is the CTL analyser of INA. Both may also check the reachability and mutual exclusion problems stated above, but go far beyond these, and also beyond the scope and space of this paper.

4 Conclusion

We have described a sample session of modelling and verifying a timed system. PEP provides a comprehensive, easy-to-use graphical user interface that supports the entire development process. This includes design, verification, simulation and debugging with a variety of different tools. Although the current implementation offers just a basic approach to timed systems, it alleviates their design by far. Further development will include timed high-level models, e.g. Real-time B(PN)^2, a more complete subset of SDL, or Timed Automata.

Acknowledgements. The author would like to thank Eike Best, Hans Fleischhack and the anonymous referees for their comments on this work.

References

1. Abadi, M., Lamport, L.: An Old-Fashioned Recipe for Real-Time. In Real Time: Theory in Practice. Volume 600 of LNCS. Springer-Verlag (1992) 1–27
2. Best, E., Devillers, R., Hall, J.: The Box Calculus: a New Causal Algebra with Multi-Label Communication. In Proc. of APN'92. Volume 609 of LNCS. Springer-Verlag (1992) 21–69
3. Best, E., Hopkins, R.P.: B(PN)^2– a Basic Petri Net Programming Notation. In Proc. of PARLE'93. Volume 694 of LNCS. Springer-Verlag (1993) 379–390
4. Bieber, B., Fleischhack, H.: Model Checking of Time Petri Nets Based on Partial Order Semantics. In Proc. of Concur'99. Volume 1664 of LNCS. Springer-Verlag (1999) 210–225
5. Esparza, J.: Model Checking Using Net Unfoldings. Science of Computer Programming **23**. Elsevier (1994) 151–195
6. Esparza, J., Römer, S., Vogler, W.: An Improvement of McMillan's Unfolding Algorithm. In Proc. of TACAS'96. Volume 1055 of LNCS. Springer-Verlag (1996) 87–106
7. Fleischhack, H., Grahlmann, B.: A Compositional Petri Net Semantics for SDL. In Proc. of ATPN'98. Volume 1420 of LNCS. Springer-Verlag (1998)
8. Fleischhack, H., Stehno, C.: Computing the Finite Prefix of a Time Petri Net. Submitted paper. 2001
9. Grahlmann, G., Moeller, M., Anhalt, U.: A New Interface for the PEP Tool – Parallel Finite Automata. In Proc. of AWPN'95, AIS **22**. FB10 Universität Oldenburg (1995)
10. Heljanko, K.: Using Logic Programs with Stable Model Semantics to Solve Deadlock and Reachability Problems for 1-Safe Petri Nets. In Proc. of TACAS'99. Volume 1579 of LNCS. Springer-Verlag (1999) 240–254
11. Jaeger, J.: Portable Codegenerierung für eine parallele Programmiersprache. Masters thesis. Universität Hildesheim (1997) *in German*
12. Khomenko, V., Koutny, M.: LP Deadlock Checking Using Partial Order Dependencies. In Proc. of CONCUR'2000. Volume 1877 of LNCS. Springer-Verlag (2000) 410–425
13. Koutny, M.: A Compositional Model of Time Petri Nets. In Proc. of Application and Theory of Petri Nets 2000. Volume 1825 of LNCS. Springer-Verlag (2000) 303–322
14. McMillan, K.: Symbolic model checking: An approach to the state explosion problem. Kluwer Academic Publishers (1993)
15. Merlin, P., Faber, D.: Recoverability of Communication Protocols – Implication of a Theoretical Study. IEEE Transactions on Software Communications **24** (1976) 1036-1043
16. Starke, P.: INA – Integrated Net Analyzer Version 2.2. Humboldt-Universität Berlin (1999)

Author Index

Lecture Notes in Computer Science

For information about Vols. 1–2221
please contact your bookseller or Springer-Verlag